Praise for *The Brotherh*

"*The Brotherhood of the Screaming .* book. Beautifully written by Dennis M. paints a complex picture of the late, great genius, master orator, and seer Terence McKenna, of their lives and adventures together, and of their boots-on-the-ground approach to investigating the mysteries of consciousness that psychedelics reveal. Highly recommended!" —Graham Hancock, author of *Supernatural: Meetings with the Ancient Teachers of Mankind*

"In *The Brotherhood of the Screaming Abyss*, Dennis McKenna has formulated a potent alchemical potion full of wild adventures and remarkable encounters as well as thoughtful contemplations on society, politics, and culture; everyone needs a drink of this awe-inspiring medicine." —Monica Gagliano, PhD, Research Associate Professor of Evolutionary Ecology at Southern Cross University, coeditor of *The Mind of Plants: Narratives of Vegetal Intelligence*, and author of *Thus Spoke the Plant: A Remarkable Journey of Groundbreaking Scientific Discoveries and Personal Encounters with Plants*

"Serving as a valuable resource on the brothers McKenna, *Brotherhood* reminds us of the plant (and planetary) agents that represent seeds of hope in dark times." —Graham St. John, author of *Terence McKenna: The Strange Attractor* (forthcoming from MIT Press)

"I owe my family to Terence McKenna. Jeremy and I met at a party fêting him, and over time, his 'little brother' Dennis has become a trusted colleague. The tales in this book paint a glorious masterpiece: the wondrous relationship between two brothers, their ancestry and progeny, their journeys inward and outward, and their consequential contributions, both scientific and cultural, to the psychedelic ecosystem." —Julie Holland, MD, author of *Good Chemistry: The Science of Connection, From Soul to Psychedelics*

"As profound an experience as it was to read, it is difficult to describe. It is a biography of Terence, an autobiography of Dennis, a series of even increasingly scary adventures, laced with visionary insights obtained by over-the-top amounts of psychedelics, and the implications of all of the above. Terence became a charismatic visionary whose enthralling narratives dominated a generation of psychedelic seekers, while Dennis became a respected ethnopharmacologist, transporting and translating plants' wisdom into the scientific world. And if that wasn't enough, Dennis' reflections about how their collective impact blended and disrupted the prevailing cultural narrative are perhaps the book's greatest takeaway." —James Fadiman, author of *The Psychedelic Explorer's Guide: Safe, Therapeutic, and Sacred Journeys*

"This intimate narrative of two lives intertwined with worlds, communities, and cultural transformation is a gift to those interested in psychedelics. As attention to psychedelics with their medicinal and poisonous powers is ignited by the current frenzy of enthusiasm for biomedicalization and commodification, it is more important than ever that the deep history of contemporary engagement with these materials be told. This beautiful book contributes wonderfully to that." —David E. Presti, Professor of Neurobiology at University of California, Berkeley, and author of *Foundational Concepts in Neuroscience: A Brain-Mind Odyssey* and *Mind Beyond Brain: Buddhism, Science and the Paranormal*

"It's hard to imagine two more influential psychedelic voices than the brothers McKenna, but if, up till now, the late Terence has rather hogged the limelight, Dennis now gets a chance to shine. He presents a rounded and at times uncompromising picture of his elder sibling, but one that is steeped in a brother's enduring love. An essential read for trippers, McKenna fans, psychedelic historians, and anyone wanting to know more about fin-de-siècle American psychedelia from someone who was there, right at the center of the cyclone." —Andy Letcher, PhD, Senior Lecturer and Program Lead for the MA in Engaged Ecology at Schumacher College and author of *Shroom: A Cultural History of the Magic Mushroom*

"Yet another McKenna mix of brilliant insight, insane adventure, and strange interludes. Highly recommended!" —Mark Plotkin, Ethnobotanist and President of the Amazon Conservation Team

"Of the two McKenna brothers, as much as I've benefited by playing with Terence's wild ideas, I've learned more from Dennis' scientifically grounded investigations. The road to deep psychedelic consciousness starts in the ineffable and winds its way towards practical manifestations in the material world. Few grasp this trajectory as well as Dennis, as is lucidly depicted in this insightful personal history. He shows you how it's done." —Ken Jordan, Editorial Director, Lucid News

"What a delightful tale! A memoir of brothers—Terry and Denny—growing up, four years apart, exploring the world and varied states of consciousness, and sharing so much more than most brothers ever do. This book is a mitzvah, a memoir in which Dennis reflects on both his own life and that of the silver-tongued brother who died all too young." —Ethan A. Nadelmann, Founder and Former Executive Director of the Drug Policy Alliance

"Little appreciated in the current renaissance is the place the brothers McKenna played in working out and publishing (as Oss and Oeric) how anyone with a few items from their local hardware store can grow psilocybin mushrooms at home. A very under recognized contribution whose scale of reach has few equals. This book is a clear-eyed treatment of seminal influences that led to that and other contributions." —Carey Turnbull, Vice President, Heffter Research Institute

The Brotherhood of the Screaming Abyss

The Brotherhood of the Screaming Abyss

My Life with Terence McKenna

Dennis McKenna

Foreword by Bruce Damer

SYNERGETIC PRESS
SANTA FE • LONDON

Published by Synergetic Press | 1 Blue Bird Ct. Santa Fe, NM 87508
& 24 Old Gloucester St. London, WCIN 3AL, England

The following are used by permission:

Photograph on the front cover by Hazelle McKenna. Photographs on pages 47, 191,
    204, 235, and 254 by Sara Hartley. Photograph on page 292 by Jeremy Bigwood.
    Photograph on page 402 by Jill Wagner.
Maps on pages 7, 207, and 331 by Mark Odegard.
Frontispiece drawing by Janet Gordon.
Excerpts from *True Hallucinations* by Terence McKenna. Copyright © 1993 by Terence
    McKenna. Reprinted courtesy of HarperCollins Publishers.
Poem by William P. Watson, "Pursuing to Peru the G'nostic Guru," printed by permis-
    sion of the author.
Portions of Chapter 46 are adapted from an essay by the author that appeared in *Aya-
    huasca Reader: Encounters with the Amazon's Sacred Vine*, edited by Luis Eduardo Luna
    and Steven F. White (2000).

Library of Congress Control Number: 2022945336

ISBN 9781957869018 (paperback)
ISBN 9781957869025 (e-book)

Cover design by Synergetic Press
Book design by Brad Greene
Managing Editor: Amanda Müller
Developmental Editor: Noelle Armstrong
Production Editor: Allison Felus

Printed in the United States of America

To our Mother and Father, Hazelle and Joe McKenna,
who loved us through it all.

The past is never dead.
It's not even past.

—William Faulkner

Contents

Part One: Beginnings

Part Two: Into the Abyss

Part Three: Invisible Landscapes

Reality is a hallucination concocted by our brains.

Memory is a fragmented tapestry patched with confabulation.

Within those constraints, I have portrayed the events and people
in this book as accurately as possible.

A few names have been changed to protect the innocent,
or in some cases, the guilty.

Foreword

If geography portends destiny, then this book's cover photo of youthful Denny and Terry McKenna, taken during a visit to the Black Canyon of the Gunnison National Park, gives us a hint of the two brothers' future life paths. A taller, dreamy Terence leans into his brother who has taken the binoculars still slung around Terence's neck and is peering across the abyss. One can imagine their exchange—Terence taking his fill of the scene, waxing poetic, rapping on the reality of the hugest thing they had probably yet seen. Dennis taking it all in, parsing his brother's interpretation, but then grabbing the binoculars to take a look for himself, similarly awestruck but looking for particulars.

Even at such an early age, the differing paths of inquiry and lifestyle were being crystallized: Terence seeking the farthest-out places then returning to tell their tale, while Dennis returned from the same realms with samples to tease apart their catalytic magic. Terence's 20-year storytelling arc from the late '70s to his last public appearance at the 1999 AllChemical Arts gathering in Hawaii served to *valorize* the psychedelic experience for the next generation and ready it for the oncoming digital age. Dennis's dedicated lifetime of work in ethnopharmacology sought to *validate* the action of the plants and bring these practices from their Indigenous roots out into a transformative role for the future of our world.

At the end of the 55th anniversary meeting honoring and extending the groundbreaking 1967 conference entitled Ethnopharmacologic Search for Psychoactive Plants, Dennis asked me, "how did it all go?" Before answering I recalled the time he and I first met in person, on a boat in the San Francisco Bay during an evening cruise for the 2013 MAPS Psychedelic Science Conference. Dennis and I had just completed a two-year remote collaboration that had us researching and communicating about many aspects of his brother's life and legacy. The first edition of this book was written and published during that time, and to celebrate Terence's life I organized two retrospective events, one at Sierra Madre, California, and the other at the Esalen Institute in Big Sur, both places that had great meaning for him.

My own personal time with Terence came during the closing years of the 1990s and was focused on introducing him to the medium of virtual worlds, a form of invisible landscape created by the language of code. Terence was fascinated by this emerging form of cyberspace, the first steps toward a true "metaverse." For a time, we exchanged places, and while Terence explored tryptamine-inspired digital realms walking about in his avatar *Zone Ghost*, I journeyed into my first bemushroomed experience of entheospace. We then met at his house in Hawaii with his son Finn to host a Virtual AllChemical Powwow with his fanbase and compare notes. Terence shared that these new worlds of cyberspace were "not unlike DMT." Happily basking in this experience of tech-novelty, we were unaware that he would undergo his own version of a singularity, passing away just over a year later in April 2000. Five years after that, I committed to help bring him back (digitally) and worked with a group of dedicated souls to rescue his talks from hundreds of cassette tapes and commit his voice to the then emerging podcast medium. It was then that I became more of a scholar of Terence and his work, so when Dennis and I were first introduced, he kindly offered me early drafts of this book to review.

In composing a rendition of Terence's life story for the events I organized in 2012, I not only encountered the full scope and scale of his influence on psychedelic culture, but also uncovered evidence of his suffering later in life around the growing contradictions of his path. These emerged from the challenges of becoming a *speaker for the ineffable*, a sage on the stage committed to a grueling schedule "on the circuit." I, and others close to him at the time, noticed that, in the 1990s, Terence's stories and proposals were spinning ever farther out. His purported date for humanity's cosmic escape (or rescue) in the year of 2012 was particularly outlandish, and I questioned him on it at the time. Perhaps the cage of fame requires the songbird within to sing with ever greater embellishment, and so Terence might have concluded that, to keep his audience returning, he had to rise to that call. Reports surfaced that in that period Terence had largely ceased using the substances he was promoting to an up-and-coming generation. This brought up incongruities that I felt needed to be revealed and worked through during our events. Tension between Terence and his brother had grown, partly due to disagreements around his unbridled yarn-spinning, into a full separation of their paths. As you will read in this book, they were only reunited as brothers in the months leading up to Terence's death. At Esalen in June 2012, as I convened a group of close friends to celebrate Terence's life, we collectively undertook to work through these revelations. We felt that it was time to gently lift some of Terence's more potent spells and provide a cautionary note to those craving contact with the Machine Elves by imbibing 5-7 dried grams in silent darkness. These key truths being understood, we felt that Terence was then freed from the incongruities of his later life and welcomed him back. We loved and accepted him, now perhaps just a bit more fully baked.

Since that moment on the boat in the Bay, Dennis and I have sat together in ceremony in the Sacred Valley in Peru, chewed coca leaf at Machu Picchu, engaged in fireside chats and Zoom sessions, and compared many notes. I've had the pleasure of getting to know Dennis much better than his (then) more famous brother and have found him to be a rare soul with a true, kind, and gentle nature but also an incisive scientific mind. He has grown into an elder looking to the future for all of us through his own unique pair of binoculars. So, finally, to answer Dennis's question "how did it all go?" I can now more completely reply here with, I hope, appropriate sensitivity to the complex interweaving of these two extraordinary lives:

> "It seems to me that the time of Terence's tales of hyperspace was necessary, and your brother filled that role exquisitely. It also ultimately turned out to be challenging for him, but we collectively revealed and healed this. Your path was different and comes to the fore today in the science, in the meetings like this one, and in community building. This is the work of now, and you have provided a magnificent advancement of it."

Thank you, Dennis and Terence! In your brotherhood, through all of its ins and outs, two boys entered the abyss and showed the way for countless others to take their first journeys out along the cliff edge of the psychedelic chasm, returning to share their own tales. Future generations will experience extraordinary states of spirit and mind and reset their own destinies, ever in gratitude to you.

—**Bruce Damer**
Boulder Creek
July 2022

Foreword to the First Edition

When Dennis asked me to write a foreword for this book, I was surprised and delighted. It had never occurred to me that such a book would require any foreword at all. Dennis is a well-respected researcher and thinker, and many of us have read his scientific papers or listened with pleasure to his interdisciplinary lectures, which combine ethnobotany, psychopharmacology, history, and philosophical reflections. But this is not an academic book. It is the long-awaited account of his lifelong relationship with his older brother Terence, the great raconteur of wide-reaching philosophical and eschatological ideas. In other words, what we have here is the privilege of going behind the curtains and peering into the private lives of these two extraordinary brothers, the poet and the scientist, the public figure and the more retiring originator of ideas, one who haunts us from the invisible yet pervasive World Wide Web (his words still fresh and even more relevant twelve years after his death), the other still with us, wise, and with an acute sense of humor. Like his brother, Dennis is a teacher from whom we still have much to learn.

I had the great good luck to meet Terence in my native Colombia at the end of 1971, when we were both still young. It was the beginning of a friendship that lasted until 2000, the year he died. I met Dennis in 1981, though in a sense I knew him well before then, because Terence spoke frequently of his brother, describing him as a genius and the source of some of the ideas that captivated him.

When Terence and I met, I was on vacation, visiting my family in Florencia, then a small frontier town located between the flanks of the Cordillera Oriental, the eastern range of the Andes, and the Amazon rainforest. I recently had finished five years of studies at the Universidad Complutense in Madrid and planned to return to Europe two months later. Earlier the same year, Terence, Dennis, and some friends, while traveling in the Colombian Amazon area, had performed what they called the "experiment at La Chorrera," later described by Terence in his book *True Hallucinations*. Terence was an enthusiastic and effervescent thinker, and I was an eager listener and interlocutor. Terence and his companion at the time, known in this book as "Ev," moved with me to "Villa Gloria," a pompous name for a simple wooden country house that belonged to my parents. Located a few kilometers outside Florencia, with one faucet and no electricity, the place had the advantage of seclusion for work and experimentation. Terence was starting to write what later became *The Invisible Landscape* with his brother Dennis as coauthor, while I was being introduced to the world of Carl Jung, Mircea Eliade, Alfred North Whitehead, James Joyce, and Carlos Castaneda. I had my first *yajé* experience in Villa Gloria, with a potion prepared by Don Apolinar Yacanamijoy, an Ingano shaman I had known since childhood, though at that time I was uninformed about the Indigenous uses of that substance.

Two years later, in 1973, Terence and I were in Berkeley. This was a crucial summer for me in that, thanks in part to him, I discovered a wealth of ethnobotanical studies by the field's great pioneers: Richard Evans Schultes, Gerardo Reichel-Dolmatoff, R. Gordon Wasson, Peter Furst, Johannes Wilbert, Michael Harner, and others whom I had the privilege of meeting at different points later in my life. In the evenings, when we weren't watching the Watergate hearings on an old TV, Terence entertained his spellbound friends with his eloquence, his command of ideas in various disciplines, and his great gifts as a storyteller. His was not a modest enterprise: only "the big picture" would suffice. There was never a dull moment in his company, and I accepted, albeit naively and uncritically, virtually everything he said. I was even expecting the end of times on December 21, 1973, before his revision of the final ingression of novelty in his "Timewave Zero" model to December 21, 2012, a date that coincides with the end of the present era in keeping with the Mayan calendar. The months I spent with Terence in Villa Gloria and Berkeley were perhaps the most interesting of my life. Those extraordinary conversations catapulted me into years of passionate interdisciplinary research that tempered my enthusiasm and gave me a firmer ground from which to work, without ever weakening the admiration I had for him.

In 1980, Terence would once again play a decisive role in the path of my life. I went to visit him and his wife, Kat Harrison, at their home in Sebastopol, California. Terence had been told about Don Emilio Andrade Gómez, an *ayahuasquero* whom he had never met who lived close to Iquitos, Peru. Don Emilio soon became one of my dear friends and mentors. He was the person who introduced me to the concept of plants as teachers, calling ayahuasca one of the *doctores* from whom it is possible to learn. He also opened me to the world of ayahuasca *vegetalista* traditions as practiced by the Mestizo population of the Peruvian Amazon.

Since we met, my working relationship with Dennis has been even closer than my friendship with his brother, since I only saw Terence sporadically during the years when his fame peaked. Dennis and I did fieldwork, traveled, and published together. We've stayed in luxurious hotels at conferences in various countries as well as in humble *posadas* in the Amazon. I have visited him in every city where he and his wife, Sheila, have lived. And, above all, Dennis and I have experienced great adventures of the mind together due to our common interest in psychoactive plants and modified states of consciousness.

In 1985, I invited him to participate in what was the first international and interdisciplinary symposium on ayahuasca, which I organized in Bogotá as part of the forty-fifth International Congress of the Americanists, an academic conference that takes place every two years, alternating between Europe and the Americas. After the event, I flew to Pucallpa, Peru, where Dennis introduced me to the artist Pablo Amaringo, with whom I collaborated for several years. Our book, *Ayahuasca Visions: The Religious Iconography of a Peruvian Shaman*, first published in 1991, explores the complexity and sophistication of the Peruvian Mestizo ayahuasca tradition. In 1988, Pablo and I created the Usko-Ayar Amazonian School of Painting, which was destined to have a lasting influence on the art scene of the Peruvian Amazon. By the time I resigned in 1995, the school had grown to some 300 students, all of whom got their tuition and art materials free of charge. During the last ten years, Dennis has been one of the main lecturers at Wasiwaska Research Center for the Study of Psychointegrator Plants, Visionary Art, and Consciousness, a small educational institution that my wife, Adriana Rosa, and I created in southern Brazil. Dennis always arrives with new ideas and an intellectual curiosity that has grown with time. His presence has become ever more significant in the current transcultural and interdisciplinary global community concerned with the large questions of temporality, reality, and consciousness.

It has been a real treat for me to read *The Brotherhood of the Screaming Abyss*. I had heard Terence and Dennis relate fragments of their stories here and there, but it is not the same as experiencing the continuous chronological narrative presented in these pages. I gained new insights into their background and development. Dennis's narrative is lively, often humorous, and at times brutally frank. He gives his straightforward opinion about people and events, as well as astute observations about political, ethical, and transcendent questions. This book is not only a biographical account, but also a portrait of the counterculture of the 1960s, '70s, and '80s in certain regions of the United States, an era with a marked global impact, avidly scrutinized by segments of today's youth in these times of planetary crisis and renewed interest in modified states of consciousness and alternative worldviews. In reading this book, I have learned a great deal that I did not know about the lives of my two great friends. In addition, I got the chance to relive and reflect on my generation's time in history.

Dennis convinced me to write this foreword by saying that I was there pretty much at the beginning of Terence's career as a bard, and also at the end. In the summer of 1999, Dennis and I decided to spend some days with Terence in Hawaii. His brain tumor had been diagnosed, and he was considering what path to follow while dealing with his emotions. Dennis and I would have liked to pull the plug on all electronic communication and work on Terence's health with the tools to which we have dedicated our lives. Much to our chagrin, Terence continued to work furiously on the preparations for what became the AllChemical Arts Conference dedicated to psychedelics and creativity that took place in September that year in Hawaii. On March 20, 2000, following a conference entitled "Ayahuasca: Amazonian Shamanism, Science, and Spirituality" organized by Ralph Metzner in San Francisco, Dennis and I went to see Terence, who was spending the last weeks of his life in the home of friends in California. He was in a wheelchair, barely able to speak. At some point he said, "I am having hallucinations." Dennis asked, "Do you mean psychedelic hallucinations?" He said, "What are psychedelic hallucinations?" At the end of our visit, I embraced Terence and thanked him for all he had given me. As I was leaving, just a few steps from him, he suddenly said with a faint voice, *"Buena suerte."* I knew I would not see him again. I was back home in Brazil when the phone rang on April 3. It was Dennis. He was crying as he told me that Terence had just passed away. Later, I went outside to contemplate the sky. As Dennis put it, Terence was by then traveling up and down the genetic ladder, becoming his parents and his children at one and the same time. Perhaps he is waiting for us now in the mystery of eternity.

—**Luis Eduardo Luna**
Wasiwaska
Florianópolis, Brazil
August 3, 2012

Preface

A lot of water has passed under the bridge since my book was launched, now ten years ago. Most of the events narrated in it happened even earlier—the book ends in 2000, the year that my brother passed on, with only a few allusions to later events. In many ways it seems quite dated now, a story of an era long past. And yet it has stood the test of time, evoking those long-gone years. The quote from William Faulkner in the front of the book says: "The past is never dead; it isn't even past." How true that is! But my life—and events in the world—have been borne by time's relentless flow since my brother passed on and since my memoir was released. Ten years on, I reflect again on those years past from the perch of the present moment, while also gazing into a murky future, however far along that path I may live to travel. For this reason, I am pleased that my friends at Synergetic Press enthusiastically received my proposal to publish a second edition, and that is what you hold now in your hands. I have resisted the temptation to revise the original manuscript; it remains as it was when completed in the fall of 2012. For this new edition, I have added this preface and a new chapter—a look back into the past, some reflections on the peculiar historical juncture in which we find ourselves, and some speculations on the road ahead. Hopefully it will be a long road, but whatever it may be, I am pleased to be able to share this journey once again with you, my dear readers.

Preface to the First Edition

For those who lived through what is sometimes called the Psychedelic Revolution, Terence McKenna is a legend. Once referred to as "the intellectual's Timothy Leary," Terence attained iconic status as a radical philosopher, futurist, cultural critic, and raconteur. His unorthodox ideas about the evolutionary and cultural impact of psychedelic drugs shocked many and resonated with many others. In 1971, we embarked on an expedition to the Amazon, bent on uncovering the real mystery behind the psychedelic experience. As chronicled in his book *True Hallucinations*, that journey has become the stuff of contemporary myth. Our adventures inspired many of Terence's unorthodox ideas about time and the nature of history, which in turn became fertile ground for certain apocalyptic beliefs about the year 2012.

Terence died in 2000, never to learn if his predictions about the end of the world, in his particular sense, were true. Since then, he has achieved a kind of virtual immortality, his voice and image as near as the click of a mouse. Ghostlike, he haunts the Internet, a talking head on YouTube, the articulate prophet of an end time he didn't live to see. In addition to *True Hallucinations*, Terence authored or coauthored several books, including *Food of the Gods*, *The Archaic Revival*, *The Evolutionary Mind*, and *The Invisible Landscape*, among others. His wide-ranging thoughts and observations remain as fresh and timely as though uttered yesterday. He lives on as the beloved paterfamilias of a younger generation of psychedelic seekers, though most were still in diapers when Terence was at the peak of his career.

As Terence's younger brother and only sibling, I grew up with him in a small town in western Colorado during the 1950s and '60s. Traveling together in the Colombian Amazon in 1971 with a few other kindred spirits, we called our band "the Brotherhood of the Screaming Abyss." Even on the cusp of uncovering the mysteries of existence, my brother and I managed to keep a sense of humor. It helped to be Irish. We didn't know what we were searching for beyond the conviction it was a profound insight, and that it would change us, and everything, forever. We were right on both counts, though not in the ways we imagined.

Terence was twenty-four at the time; I was only twenty. In 1975, we cowrote *The Invisible Landscape*, our first attempt to construct a rational explanation for what had happened to us on that trip. In 1993, Terence recounted our experiences more directly in *True Hallucinations*, but still with important elements elided or omitted. What has since been memorialized in the annals of psychedelia as "the experiment at La Chorrera" was a pivotal moment for both of us. The curious events that overtook us in that primeval rainforest haunted Terence until the end of his life, and surely the same will someday be said of me.

As Terence's brother, I helped him create and develop many of "his" ideas. Our adventures—intellectual and otherwise—spanned the turbulent decades of the late 20th century. Driven by a shared passion for novelty and a yearning for answers to the ultimate questions, we traveled to the ends of the earth and explored the outer limits of the psychedelic experience. The quest that seized both of us at an early age was to discover insights into the astonishing mysteries of time, mind, and the improbable reality of existence.

While our lives were entangled as only the lives of brothers can be, after the events at La Chorrera we later found ourselves on separate paths. Terence became the spokesman for the alien dimensions accessed through psychedelics, a philosopher of the unspeakable, a beloved and sometimes reviled bard of the marvels and occasional terrors waiting in the recesses of human consciousness. By choice and inclination, I stayed in the background, pursuing a scientific career in disciplines that ranged from ethnopharmacology and ethnobotany to neuroscience.

Since Terence's death, we've witnessed the first decade of a new era that by all early indications will be as strange and disturbing, as full of hope and despair, as any period that humanity has yet endured. The closer I've gotten to his predicted end date for the world, however, the more I've been drawn to look back at how our personal world began. I wanted to retrace the journey that took us from childhood to our separate destinies, stopping to revisit the people and ideas that shaped us. Surely our lives were destined to be unique in many ways, as all lives are, and yet I've also realized how much Terence and I were the products of our age and its dreams. My hope is that many others will see their own experiences reflected in those that befell us. This is our story.

PART ONE: BEGINNINGS

The original screaming abyss: Black Canyon, Gunnison River, Colorado.

1 Beginnings

In many respects this book is about time. Its very structure relies on a particular understanding of time borrowed from the view of it that prevails in our culture. From Judeo-Christian perspective, time is a linear arrow with a beginning, middle, and end. For good or ill, and whether "true" or not, this linear conception of time permeates the Western worldview. It certainly influenced the idea of time that Terence and I shared while growing up. In fact, had we lived in a culture that viewed time as cyclical, this tale could have ended very differently, or never been told at all. I'll have a lot more to say about middles and ends later, but right now let's look at beginnings.

I say "beginnings" because any single point of origin for this book is hard to nail down. In the narrowest sense, the project began in the spring of 2011 when, having decided to undertake it, I took steps to make it happen. The story I wanted and needed to tell was summed up by its subtitle: "My Life with Terence McKenna." I knew, of course, that many of those who were familiar with Terence's work had already heard or read about me before. As the brother of a controversial and charismatic cultural icon, a renowned teller of tall tales, I was already the character in a narrative that a man known as the Irish bard of psychedelia had told and retold many times. But that was Terence's account, not mine. There existed another version of those events known only to me.

Having made the decision to share my side of our story, I had to create a way to actualize it. Past experience had taught me that authors are rarely well compensated for their efforts; purely mercenary reasons led me to an alternative approach that would maximize my return. Somehow I needed to find the resources to self-publish the book and to buy the time to complete the task. "Time is money," our father often reminded us, and was he ever right! After consulting with a number of people in the publishing industry, I turned to crowdfunding, a new fundraising strategy best exemplified by the website Kickstarter. And it worked beyond my wildest expectations. I made Kickstarter history by raising more money for a book project than ever before on the site. The window for the fundraising effort closed on June 6, 2011. What I wrote a few days later, condensed below, reflects my dread and elation at realizing the means to undertake my task had just been dropped into my lap:

> Well, here I am. These are the first words I've committed to paper for what is supposed to be my magnum opus, *The Brotherhood of the Screaming Abyss*. After a successful Kickstarter campaign, I now have the funds to cover self-publishing, and (hopefully) to secure the time to write this screed. And time is short! During the Kickstarter appeal, I plumbed the depths of social media, putting myself "out there" in numerous podcasts, websites, and webinars. In doing so I've discovered a vast community of friends I never knew I had. These friends have shown great faith in me, but they also have great expectations: they expect me to deliver!
>
> Right now I am sitting at my kitchen table with that sort of "uh-oh" queasy feeling that one gets when starting a new project that is likely to be all-consuming for months, and even emotionally traumatic at times. So now to work! I will revisit this intro in a few days, after I've started to generate text, and report how things are going.

A few days turned into a few weeks, and then into a couple of months. It was not until early September that various commitments allowed me to begin in earnest. During the summer, I had traveled to California to attend a wedding in the family. In October I was off again, this time to Colorado, where the 97th birthday of a beloved aunt brought me back to many of my boyhood haunts on the Western Slope. What seemed like interruptions at the time were actually part of the process, a chance to reflect on what, and whom, my story was really about.

The longest pause was a trip that August to Iquitos, Peru. Reality had intervened in the form of a three-week intensive course in the jungle for 14 pharmacy students, most from the University of Missouri, Kansas City. To call it a "course in the jungle" is a bit of an exaggeration; much of it took place in and around dirty, noisy, chaotic, vibrant Iquitos, with occasional day trips to the surrounding forest. The kids had a cushy B&B to return to every night, a swimming pool, good food, Wi-Fi, and plenty of bandwidth for the ubiquitous iPhones and iPads. Hardly roughing it. We later spent three days at a camp on the Napo River north of Iquitos. Overall, it was pleasant work, and the compensation for a few lectures too good to pass up.

Iquitos and I go way back. I had first visited the city in 1981 as a graduate student at the University of British Columbia, off to conduct fieldwork for my thesis. But even that visit was a return of sorts, an evocation of my first trip to the Amazon with Terence almost exactly a decade earlier. Terence also joined me for part of that second expedition, which marked yet another crucial point in our lives, closing a chapter that began with our trip to La Chorrera even as it opened another. Though we remained close as time went on, our lives took parallel tracks. For one thing, Terence never again visited South America, while I kept finding reasons to return.

Iquitos, at first glance, looked pretty good to me on that visit in 1981, having just spent a month in Pucallpa, a frontier town to the south, under conditions that even then qualified as primitive. Iquitos, a city on the Amazon—indeed the farthest major port from the Atlantic almost 2,000 miles away—was the epitome of civilization by comparison. The prospect of a cheap hotel room, a cold shower (no hot water then), and a colder beer loomed large on my agenda.

Iquitos has changed in many ways since then, due largely to the influx of ayahuasca tourists. I suppose my research in ethnopharmacology has fed the interest in that psychedelic brew, so I share a small part of the credit for the new Iquitos, or blame, depending on how one sees it. In 1981, Iquitos was charming, a sleepy hamlet of maybe 50,000 souls, not the hammering, noisy city of 400,000 that awaited me in 2011. There were no three-wheeled *moto-carros*—now the bane of Iquitos—back then, and only a few automobiles. Many of the characters of modern botanical legend—Richard Evans Schultes, Timothy Plowman, Alwyn Gentry, Nicole Maxwell, Gunther Schaper, Neil Towers—were familiar with the town, and I've had the good fortune to know some of them. As it had for them, Iquitos played a formative role in the course of my scientific career.

I've lost count of the times I've returned to Iquitos. One reason I keep coming back is my interest in the Mestizo shamanism that flourishes there. Iquitos is both the gateway into the upper Amazon and a center for the many Indigenous peoples who over the decades have been compelled to leave their ancestral lands. As such, the city has become a repository of cultural knowledge, much of it related to plants and their medicinal uses.

Another reason I return is my friendship with Juan Ruiz Macedo, an amazing botanist who knows the region's plant life as well any other. Juan is now the curator of the Herbarium Amazonense at the Universidad Nacional de la Amazonía Peruana. In 1981, he was working under the herbarium's former curator, Franklin Ayala, his mentor and supervisor. My supervisor, Neil Towers, PhD, had written me a letter of introduction that I gave to Ayala, who assigned poor Juan the thankless task of leading a small band of geeky and basically clueless North American tenderfoots into the jungles on the Río Ampiyacu, the "river of poisons." That's another story, as we shall see. When Ayala later retired to work on a massive study of plants in the Peruvian Amazon, Juan assumed the top position admirably, and we have worked together on various projects in recent years.

But over the years, Iquitos has lost much of its charm for me. In 2011, I found the streets torn up all over town for a massive sewage reengineering project, no doubt sorely needed. In addition to the usual crowded sidewalks pocked with (often) gaping holes, construction machinery and concrete blocks were strewn everywhere, making it more crucial than ever to watch your step. But the true scourge remains the *motocarros*, which over the years have solved Iquitos's mass-transit problems at an unfortunate price. Thirty to sixty cents gets you anywhere in the city in about 20 minutes, but on vehicles that are noisy, dirty, and proliferating. I've often thought that, with some international help, Iquitos could be turned into a "green" model for post-petroleum mass transit in developing countries by converting those little carbon generators to electric power. The result would be a cleaner, quieter mass-transit system quite unlike anything else on earth. I have no hope of that happening soon, or ever. Iquitos has been moldering since its glory days during the Amazonian rubber boom a century ago, a burst of wealth extracted from the surrounding jungle, largely on the backs of the region's enslaved native peoples. Under the rubber barons, life in old Iquitos was almost obscenely opulent for the upper crust and brutally hard for everyone else—which may not be so different from the new Iquitos, come to think of it.

The city has a way of wearing me down. And this time, the noise of the *motocarros*, loudspeakers blaring from the electronics stores, the dust, the fumes, the oppressive heat, the sights, smells, and sheer urban madness overwhelmed me more quickly than ever. The same stimuli that initially made Iquitos exciting and exotic soon triggered a certain narrowing of focus, a kind of recoiling into a shell. To be honest, my visit in 2011 was cushy compared to my earlier ones—I had my own apartment. But I felt it more this time. Old age was creeping in.

After the students left for Cuzco and Machu Picchu, I helped the

ethnobotanist Kathleen Harrison move into the apartment next to mine. Kat is my brother's former wife and the mother of their two grown children. We spent a few days working together in the herbarium, and then I left Iquitos, thinking I'd need a very good reason ever to return.

I had planned to head straight to what would have been my first visit to the Burning Man festival in Nevada, but again reality intervened, this time in the form of some nagging health issues. Suffice it to say that it didn't seem like a great idea to spend four days in the desert with no water and primitive toilets. Instead I returned home to Minnesota and threw myself into the project I'd told so many I'd complete. As I write this today, on May 10, 2012, after eight months of work, I've finished a draft. And now that I have, my perspective has changed from "Can I do it?" to "I have done it." Readers who have struggled with similar creative endeavors will recognize the significance of this shift. There is plenty left to do, but the heavy lifting is over. I've been sleeping somewhat better as a result.

But even as I say that, my comfortable writer's life is about to end.

Ironically, I'm about to depart for six weeks in Peru, beginning with a course for a group of pharmacy students in Iquitos. I said I'd need a good reason to return, knowing on some level I'd find a reason, or one would find me. Once again I'll assume the fetal scrunch that modern air travel requires, put myself into a foggy daze, and squeeze through that uncomfortable wormhole to emerge into the odd parallel universe that has figured so crucially in my fate.

So that's one take on where this book began. A far more important point of origin lies much further back—or much, much further, depending on where you start counting. We could begin with the Big Bang and the inflation of the cosmic egg into the universe of stars, galaxies, and planets in which we now find ourselves, even if we have only the vaguest notions of how we got here, and almost no understanding of why, or even if there is a why. But without that primordial event, there would have been no world in which our story, or any other, could be set. I won't go back quite that far, but I do feel obliged to express gratitude to whomever or whatever created this marvelous and improbable universe and thereby provided a stage for all souls to live out their fables and foibles.

Instead of recounting all creation, I'll focus on my brother's and mine. Our family story begins with our ancestors, without whom we would not have existed. And like any other personal narrative, ours can be traced back to embryogenesis. Every human life so far has begun with the mingling of genes between a man and a woman. Given time and a little luck, the resulting embryo develops in the womb into a viable infant that emerges into the world to begin its own unique journey through linear time, leaving its tracks on the continuum in ways that might make a difference in the order of things, or might not. In the near future, it may be possible for humans to incarnate by other means like cloning, but not yet through complete gestation outside a living womb, as envisioned by Aldous Huxley in his novel *Brave New World*. I might hope we'll never achieve this capability, although it seems inevitable. One thing is certain: the entities generated by such a process will be something other than human, or at least not entirely human.

For now, anyway, it remains the case that every human being is the result of a combination of genes shared between a unique man and woman. That means you can't really talk about beginnings without talking about the two individuals whose shared genes initiated the life of that unique individual, their child. That was certainly the case with Terence and me, two separate beings born of the same mother at different points in her life. I'm sure there

were times when both our parents wondered if they had somehow devi-
ated from this universal scenario and given birth to the veritable spawn
of Satan. I suppose sooner or later this thought occurs to everyone who is
blessed with challenging, rebellious offspring who, from the womb, seem
bent on testing a parent's skills (and patience) to the limit. Terence and I
were (and are) most assuredly human—in many respects all too human.
To my parents, now long dead, I can only tender a belated apology for the
trouble we caused them, and ask the reader's indulgence in accepting it on
their behalf. It seems only fair to look back at their lives and families long
before we arrived and disrupted things.

2 Three Sisters

One way or another, directly or indirectly, my ancestors were drawn to Colorado by the promise of wealth from the ground. My mother's people made a living off the fruit that grew on trees; my father's came for the ore to be mined from rock. It's as if Terence and I were later compelled on a quest that somehow synthesized theirs, searching for a modern analog to the philosopher's stone in the molecules of mushrooms and plants. Maybe our journey was the westward trek of our ancestors continued in another dimension.

Looking for hints to our curious fate, I turned to our family's past. As in any family, there are certain types and quirks that seem to recur over generations, conveyed through biology and learning, of course, as well as other mechanisms understood by no one but at least acknowledged by storytellers. I can tell you my brother was not the first willful teenager in the lineage to flee from home, or the first to imagine he'd find what he was looking for in California. He wasn't the first to have a way with words, a love of books, or the terrible misfortune of dying young. His private library was consumed by fire on two different occasions, each time destroying an eloquent statement of who he was. But even that, in a sense, may not have been unprecedented.

If family lore can be trusted, a similar fate befell Teresa Aurelia Balena, born in Salerno, Italy, on August 2, 1886. My maternal grandmother's origins were a mystery, even to her. Teresa's parents died when she was very young, leaving her alone in an orphanage. All clues to her past were lost when the orphanage burned down, taking her documents with it. Whether she was adopted before reaching America, or arrived some other way, is also unclear. She may have been swept up in the "orphan trains" that beginning in 1854 carried some 200,000 orphans and street kids from the big eastern cities westward over the decades, to be handed out in towns along the way. Though portrayed at times as a shameful practice that forced many children into virtual servitude, many others benefited. There's some evidence that

Honey, as she became known, was not among the fortunate ones at first. She ran away from her foster family at 15 or 16, apparently fleeing mistreatment. Her luck changed when she eventually reached Riverside, California, where a kindly woman befriended her and gave her a good home.

Honey was 25 in 1911 when she met Joseph Kemp, a Coloradan who had traveled to Southern California looking for seasonal work in the citrus orchards. Joseph, my grandfather, was 13 years older than Honey and a widower with four kids. The earliest evidence of his verbal flair may have been the fact he returned from his fruit-picking sojourn with a new fiancée. After their marriage in 1912, the couple moved into a house our grandfather already owned in Paonia, a town in the North Fork Valley on the western edge of the Rockies. At the time, my grandfather was a fruit worker in that mile-high, temperate Eden, whose tree crops began gaining renown shortly after European settlers drove out the area's Utes in the 1880s. Well into the mid-20th century, the area's two signature commodities remained cherries and coal. Our mother, Hazelle, or Hadie as she was called, was Honey's first child, born on June 4, 1913. Another daughter, Mayme, was born in 1914, followed by Tress in 1921, and a son, Harold, in 1925. Honey died of a heart attack in 1947, a few years before my birth. I've never heard her described as anything but exceptionally kind and decent, and I regret I never knew her. Her four children, our aunts and uncles, were very much a part of our world growing up. So were the two middle kids from our grandfather's first family—daughter Murrie and son Clare. John and Margie, the youngest and the oldest, were rarely around, as I recall.

All told, our grandfather fathered and raised eight children, four with each of his two wives. By the time I showed up, he was known among his descendants as Dad Kemp. He had been born prematurely in Janesville, Wisconsin, on December 9, 1873, a child so small he fit comfortably into a shoebox lined with cotton. His mother, Nancy Narcissa Luce Kemp, used the warming oven of her kitchen stove as an incubator, which obviously worked. Dad Kemp enjoyed a robust life until his death in 1959 at the age of 86. By then he'd witnessed two world wars, the Korean War, the Great Depression, Prohibition and its repeal, the Dust Bowl, and the launch of new technologies ranging from the automobile and electric light to radio, TV, and Sputnik. He married his first wife, Margaret Lucretia (Lu) Hossak, in 1900. The story was that Lu's mother had murdered Lu's father in his sleep as a result of his constant abuse, which, if so, is perhaps the closest thing in the family closet to an actual scandal. Lu died giving birth to her fourth child, Margie, in 1909.

After returning to Paonia with Honey, his second wife, our grandfather held several jobs, beginning in the local fruit industry. From 1927 until 1932, he served as Paonia's town clerk and later as an accountant at the local power company, a position he held until he lost his sight to glaucoma in his late 50s. His impact on us was profound and lasting. I only knew him in the final decade of his life, but even then he was a character, and many of the quirks of personality that Terence and I shared can ultimately be traced to that man, whether due to genetics or from traits we picked up from being around him. He loved language, loved using it, loved writing it, and that's surely one reason why Terence and I, both avid readers, took an early and lifelong delight in books, language, and all their possibilities. He had a touch of the Irish bard in him, though he wasn't Irish; the Irish side of the family was my father's. I remember my grandpa using a white cane on the rare occasions he went out. More often I encountered him sitting in a rocking chair in front of the tiny potbellied stove in his living room, always ready to reel off a story about his life on the prairies during the pioneer days. He seemed to have an endless stock of stories and was always happy to share them with an attentive and fascinated grandson.

Our grandfather was famous for his colorful phraseology. For instance, he called something new or unusual a "fustilarian fizgig from Zimmerman." A summer downpour was a "frog strangler," and a delicious meal or dish was "larrupin." I have no idea where these phrases originated, but they have persisted in our family to this day. In fact, his fustilarian fizgigs from Zimmerman may have been my first introduction to the notion of something incomprehensible and alien, from another dimension or place. Needless to say, that concept became useful much later when we started dealing with DMT and other psychedelics. The things seen on DMT were and are fustilarian fizgigs from somewhere (even if only in one's consciousness) and the characterization is at least as apt as Terence's later descriptions of these alien entities as "singing elf machines" or "bejeweled hyperdimensional basketballs." I've seen fizgigs defined as a kind of fireworks that fizz as they whirl. Even better. It seems quite apt to describe the objects seen on DMT as fizgigs of the mind.

Our mother, smart and well-read, had surely been influenced by her father's love of books and words as well. She was a small-town girl; indeed, our childhood home was on the same block in Paonia as hers, just a half a block or so up Orchard Avenue. All three Kemp sisters were known for their beauty and could go out with whomever they wanted, though what "going out" meant in those days is probably not what we mean today. Occasionally, Hadie and Mayme, being close in age, competed for suitors. Mayme was exceptionally bright and managed to skip a year in school, allowing both sisters to graduate from Paonia High School together in 1931. After graduation, our mother attended a business college in Grand Junction, about 70 miles west of Paonia. Later Mayme followed her there. Such training was one of few options open to bright young women at the time.

Despite her humble origins, our mother was a remarkable woman who didn't spend her entire life cloistered in Paonia. After completing her courses, she moved to Delta, the county seat 30 miles from Paonia, and took a job in the clerk and recorder's office. She was living in a boardinghouse when she met a handsome fellow tenant named Joe McKenna, who had recently arrived from the Colorado town of Salida to work as a shoe salesman. After a protracted courtship, our parents married on June 10, 1937. Our father was an adventurous sort and fascinated by flying; he managed to get his pilot's license the same year he was married. In 1939, he rented a plane and flew our mother to an Elks convention in Chicago. On the way back, they ran out of gas and had to put down in a cornfield somewhere in Kansas, turning the trip into more of an adventure than they had bargained for. Our parents eventually moved to Oakland, California, where our father sold shoes again for a while. After the United States entered World War II, he enlisted, opted for flight school, and waited to be called up. He found a better if more dangerous job as a steel rigger in the Kaiser shipyards in nearby Richmond, where many of the new cargo vessels known as Liberty ships were being built at a great speed. The young couple's California interlude ended abruptly when the call arrived in 1943. My father's dream of serving as a pilot ended when he was passed over for flight training in favor of higher-priority cadets. After training, he reported for active duty with the rank of tech sergeant and departed for England to serve in the 615th Bombardment Squadron. By August 1944, he was a top gunner and engineer on a B-17 bomber flying over Europe and Germany.

During that period, our mother worked in Oakland as a personal assistant (the term then was "secretary") to Henry J. Kaiser, one of the iconic industrialists of the day, now remembered as the founder of Kaiser Aluminum, Kaiser Steel, the HMO Kaiser Permanente, and the philanthropic Kaiser Family Foundation. How she landed in the office and sometimes, literally, in the lap of Kaiser, I am not certain, but I fantasize that the comely young woman must have caught his eye at a company function staged for the benefit of the shipyard workers. Subsequent discreet enquiries would have revealed her to be fresh out of business school and eminently qualified in all the secretarial arts—typing, dictation, filing—as well as being quite easy on the eyes. Old Henry J. must have made an executive decision that she was just what he needed to give his office a little class, to say nothing of an efficient assistant. I have no idea if there was ever any real hanky-panky between them; I doubt it, but I do remember that Dad used to tease Mom about it. The fact is I think my parents were so much in love and enthralled with each other that there was no room for jealousy. Dad was a very lucky man to have our mother, and he knew it; they were in love right up until the day she died. After surviving his combat missions, our father returned and became an instructor at what I believe was the Army Air Field in Charleston, South Carolina. He mustered out of the service shortly after VE Day, May 8, 1945, when the war in Europe ended. After reuniting out East, my parents embarked on a road trip back to California. My mother's job at Kaiser was waiting and my father expected to work at an insurance company in San Francisco. Their itinerary included a stop in Paonia, where, on the spur of the moment, they decided to stay. They temporarily moved in with Dad Kemp in our mother's childhood home until they could build a house of their own.

From my perspective, staying in Paonia was either the best or the worst decision they ever made. I have often speculated about how differently our lives might have gone had they stuck to their plan and settled in the Bay Area. Upon reflection, I'd say it was probably a lucky turn of events, because it allowed us to grow up where we did. The perspective of age has helped me appreciate what a special place Paonia was then and still is, though in our youth both Terence and I hated it and wanted nothing more than to escape, as eventually we did, each in our own way. Now I might consider expending almost equal effort to live there again, though the practicalities of life make it quite unlikely that will ever happen.

One reason our parents suddenly decided to put down roots was tied to the fact that Mayme and her husband already had. Mayme, a home-body, was more timid and less adventurous than her older sister. After the business-training program in Grand Junction, she returned to Paonia and took a job at the Oliver Coal Company. There she met a young coal miner named Joe Abseck from Somerset, a small town just a few miles up the North Fork of the Gunnison River. Mayme kept an orderly house and an orderly life. During that era, women were supposed to find fulfillment in raising kids and being good homemakers, and most men would have been surprised if not offended to learn that a young housewife might have greater ambitions. Yet my mother and her sisters were all smart women—smart enough, I suspect, to let their men think that as husbands they were in charge.

By the time Mayme married Joe Abseck in 1934, he and Joe McKenna, my father, were fast friends. I suspect they bonded in part over getting to double-date the two prettiest girls in Paonia. Doubtless many of the young men in town were disappointed when Mayme became the first of the Kemp sisters to be taken out of circulation. In 1941, Joe Abseck moved to Ogden, Utah, to work as aircraft inspector at Hill Field, now Hill Air Force Base. Mayme stayed on at the coal company. Their two daughters, identical twins, were born in September that

Joe and Hadie McKenna
during World War II.

year. Mayme and the girls joined Joe in Ogden in 1944. After the war they all returned to Paonia—and stayed there.

The trick was how to make a living in the rather narrow local economy. Joe and George, his younger brother, decided to start an electrical appliance and repair business. When my parents made their fateful stop, the Absecks urged my father to become their partner. The new venture made sense—construction was booming across the country as a wave of enlisted men returned, all looking to forget the war, settle down, build a house, have a family, and live the American Dream. For my parents, the prospect of a "normal" life in a quiet little Colorado town must have won out over the lure of big-city excitement on the coast. My father signed on.

Thus marked the founding of A&M Electric (as in Abseck and McKenna), the name under which the business thrived until it was sold decades later. My father, however, afflicted by perpetual restlessness, was by then long gone. After a few years at A&M, he cashed out and began working for a Denver company, Central Electric Supply, as a sales rep in western Colorado and northern New Mexico. His position at Central Electric, a midsized firm managed by a Jewish family, proved a better fit; he worked there until his retirement in 1972. It was the kind of job you could expect in those days, but not anymore—lifetime employment, modest but livable salary, a good pension. He was on the road every Monday, beyond the reach of the home office, and spent each weekend in Paonia with the love of his life. Mom spoiled him outrageously. There was a chocolate cake waiting for him every Friday, and steak and baked potatoes for dinner every Saturday. It was a point of pride with Dad that he could afford steak once a week, and indeed times were good back then on his $20,000 a year.

The good thing about the new job was that it didn't tie him to a desk. Being in constant motion appealed to our father, though it may have had adverse consequences for the rest of us, given his five-day absence every week. After a few years, he got a small plane and covered his territory by air. This allowed him to be home more. The plane also transformed one of the major stresses of his job, driving the mountain passes under treacherous conditions, to one of the major pleasures of his life, flying the mountain passes under treacherous conditions. He didn't mind that at all; in fact, I believe it was one of the few times when he really felt free. Being a weekend father probably made putting up with his sons more tolerable, at least for him. In later years, as we began pushing back against parental constraints, his absence undoubtedly changed the family dynamic in profound ways. His traveling was probably healthy for our parents' marriage, however, in that it kept them from ever tiring of each other. If "Terry and Denny" had never happened along, it might have been a perfect marriage.

There is little doubt that our presence threw a wrench into their idyllic 1950s fairy tale. Elder relatives have told me that kids were never part of the plan, or at least not part of our father's. Our mother might have had other ideas and "pulled a fast one," as one relative suggested, by getting pregnant with Terence. After that, another fast one was almost inevitable, and four years later that led to me. Whether I was an accident or deliberately foisted on my unsuspecting father, I'm grateful for the outcome.

Until her death in early 2012 at age 97, Aunt Mayme was the beloved matriarch of an enormous and tight-knit brood of grandchildren, great-grandchildren, and great-great-grandchildren, all of whom can be traced back to her and her daughters, Jody and Judy. Both "the twins," as we called them, married local boys and have lived in the area their entire lives. Thanks to them, I am blessed with a loving family of cousins, nieces, and nephews and still feel tied into the ancestral village where it all began. On my rare visits, I am welcomed with love like the proverbial prodigal son, which I suppose I am.

I remember Mayme as a worrier, prone to fret over the littlest things. Snakes terrified her, as did thunderstorms. She'd read somewhere that she'd be safe in a car from lightning because cars were grounded. Accordingly, Mayme would get in her car and wait out storms in the garage. Her daughter Judy's husband, Laddie, once joked that you could go into her refrigerator on any given day and reach for the half-and-half without looking because it had been in exactly the same place for 30 years.

When I was a kid, the twins were a trip, of course. Born in 1941, they were teenagers by the mid-1950s, the early era of rock and roll—Buddy Holly, James Dean, Elvis. That was the strange, surrealistic decade when the country, still benumbed by the trauma of the war, was yearning to redis-cover some semblance of normalcy, either unaware or in denial of the forces that were gathering beneath the surface, ready to burst into what American culture became in the 1960s. But for the moment it was an innocent, if less than fully conscious, time.

It must be exceedingly odd to be an identical twin, in that no one is really identical even if they have exactly the same genes. In the 1950s, that fate had to be even more difficult, because society at the time placed such emphasis on conformity, on fitting in.

That left Judy and Jody not only genetically identical but faced with the expectation that they should be as identical as possible. They wore the same clothes, listened to the same music, dated the same boys—until finally Judy broke the pattern and fell in with Laddie, a James Dean type and perhaps Paonia's first existentialist. He looked and dressed the part of a juvenile delinquent: flattop hairstyle, low-cut jeans, leather jacket, and large-buckled belt. It was all just an act. In reality he was something far more dangerous: a brooding, bookish intellectual, fond of reading Nietzsche and Heidegger, who kept such interests well concealed lest he reveal his true identity to his less brainy peers. Eventually Judy and Laddie married, and Laddie became the superintendent of schools in Delta County. He had radical ideas about education, which is to say he sought to change a local system that in the past had stifled curiosity and the desire to learn. His reforms led to a remarkable crop of well-educated students who actually knew how to think. Unfortunately, all that happened in the 1980s and '90s, long after Terence and I would have had a chance to benefit from the changes. But Laddie was a big influence on us in subtler ways. He was one of the few people in our youth who could actually hold his own with Terence and in fact could beat him in most arguments. I think Terence was a little afraid of him, because he knew Laddie saw right through him. He remains one of the smartest and most perceptive people I've ever known.

Our mother's youngest sister, Tress, was destined to affect our lives as well. Like Mayme, she started at Paonia High a year early; the fact that one of her half-sisters was married to the town's venerated football coach may have helped her pull some strings. After she graduated in 1938, Tress did not attend business college like her sisters. Instead she moved to Delta and spent the summer with Hadie and Joe, my parents. She had earned a scholarship at the University of Colorado, if I recall, but couldn't afford the other expenses. That fall she moved to Glendale, California, and enrolled in junior college while living with her half-brother John—the oldest son of her father's first family—and John's wife. After the school year ended in 1939, she and a classmate, Ray Somers, eloped to Tijuana, where the going price for a wedding ring at the time was 10 cents. Tress and Ray had a "proper" ceremony later that year (and remained married until Ray's death in 1982). They briefly returned to Paonia, where their son, Grant, was born in 1940, followed by their daughter Carolyn in 1944. Kathi, born in June 1947, was the closest in age to Terence.

After the attack on Pearl Harbor, the Somers moved back to Glendale, and Ray got a job building Liberty ships—a profession apparently open to young men as the war effort mounted. I mentioned how our father found such work in the Bay Area, as did one of his brothers. Ray's stint in the Los Angeles shipyards lasted until 1944, when he reported to Fort Ord near Monterey for basic training. He figured he'd soon be on his way to Japan, but the war ended before then. In 1946, he landed his first teaching job, in Glendale, at a salary of $2,400 a year. Tress also got her teaching certificate, and the family moved north to Mountain View, California, where they both taught school until they retired in the late 1960s. Terence lived for a time with the Somers during his teens, with rather unhappy results—an episode I'll revisit later.

Despite her West Coast life, Tress's ties to Colorado remained strong. In 1952, the couple bought a spread in the Crystal River Valley, just across

McClure Pass from Paonia, and operated it as a dude ranch during the summers. They continued teaching in California in the off-season, except for a winter in the mid-1950s when they stayed at the ranch so the kids could experience a cold and snowy Colorado winter with no electricity and only a wood stove for heat.

Chair Mountain Ranch—"the ranch" to us—figured large in our childhood. Dad was an avid fisherman, and the Crystal River was known for its excellent trout fishing. Mom and Tress were close, so we ended up spending almost every summer weekend at the ranch. Mom, Terry, and I would leave on Thursday night or early Friday morning, braving the treacherous ride over McClure Pass in our Chevy coupe. It was a scary drive back then, switchbacks and gravel all the way, except when the road turned to mud in the rain. Dad would come off his weekly travels on Fridays and meet us there, and we'd have the most idyllic weekends. Dad got his fishing in, and we'd hang out with our three cousins. During the dude ranch years, there were horses to ride by day and campfires at night, complete with roasted marshmallows, stories, and games of charades. Our cousin Grant was good on a guitar and seemed to know all the old folk songs. I was especially fond of "Wreck on the Highway," a tune made popular by the country star Roy Acuff in the early 1940s. "There was whiskey and blood all together," one verse began, "mixed with glass they lay; death played her hand in destruction, but I didn't hear nobody pray." The images were just grisly and graphic enough to appeal to me as a seven-year-old. But as a good Catholic boy at the time, I wasn't deaf to its stark warning about what happened to those who drank too much, drove too fast, and didn't pray. Although not usually characterized as such, that song was the first I'd ever heard about the dangers of drug abuse—in this case alcohol—and I took it to heart. A decade later, I had a similar reaction to the lyrics of "Heroin," the famous song by Velvet Underground. I have never tried heroin in my life, and have never wanted to. Hearing that song as a teenager probably helped me avoid getting tied up with one of the more harmful and dangerous recreational drugs. On the other hand, I got very involved with the psychedelics and cannabis, perhaps encouraged by the seductive lyrics of songs like "Lucy in the Sky with Diamonds," "Mr. Tambourine Man," "White Rabbit," and so on. The moralists have leveled much criticism at rock lyrics that extol drugs, and I suppose they have a point. But for me, "Heroin," at least, was a distinct disincentive and probably prevented me from going down a path that is better left untraveled.

Not all the songs my cousin Grant played were so grim, of course, and those summer nights beside the fire, like so many other moments at Chair Mountain Ranch, are boyhood memories I cherish.

3 Roots and Wars

Left to right: grandmother Molly McKenna, Terence, father Joe McKenna, Dennis with Skelly, and grandfather Joseph McKenna.

Writing about our father's family is problematic, partly because I know so little about them. Writing about our father himself is even harder, given that he was always a bit of a cipher and remains so to this day. More to the point, it's hard to discuss a person who had so much influence on us and yet with whom we were so frequently in conflict. In a fragmentary memoir, his younger brother Austin remembers Dad as an Irish storyteller who saw the humor in everything and could confabulate with the best of them. His wild accounts were usually well worn, if never told the same way twice. Mom would often call him out. "Oh, Joe," she'd say, "you're exaggerating; it didn't happen like that at all." And he'd look hurt and pretend to protest, but with a twinkle in his eye. He was bullshitting, and he knew it, and he knew you knew it, but the tale was so good it didn't matter. Terence inherited his father's talent, or flaw, for never letting facts get in the way of a good story. That partly explains why, in looking back, I haven't always been sure where the yarn spinning ends and the family history begins.

I do know my father was born high—almost two miles high, in Leadville, Colorado, on September 23, 1915. He had an older sister, Amelia, and two younger brothers, Ed and Austin, the youngest, now nearing 90 and the only sibling still alive. Their parents, Joseph and Mary (who went by Molly) were both Irish Catholics. Over the years, both my Uncle Austin and Aunt Amelia described their family as tight-knit and affectionate; they clearly treasured their childhood memories and praised their parents for filling their household with a sense of security and love. I have the impression my paternal grandparents had permissive ideas about child-rearing compared to the norms of their day. When my father was eight or nine, the family moved 60 miles south and a few thousand feet downhill, to Salida. My grandfather worked in a Crews-Beggs department store, one of several such branches in southern Colorado at the time. His brother, Patrick, also lived in Salida with his wife. Their sister, Mary, moved to Aspen and raised three children.

Having met her once when I was very young, I remember little except my amazement that a person could be so old. My great-grandfather was one John McKenna, a miner, who may also have used the surname McKinney or McKenney at times. He apparently married a woman who ran a boardinghouse; they definitely had a son—Joseph, my grandfather. The couple eventually separated and John returned to Ireland, where rumor had it he remarried. His former partner, her name now lost, remarried as well; she then may have been widowed and married again. The actual kinship ties between my grandfather and his siblings, known and unknown, are thus unclear.

According to one account, our great-grandfather had a brother, Patrick, who was one of the first prospectors in Leadville and Aspen back when the silver boom began in 1879. The two McKennas supposedly filed claims for sites around Aspen, according to my Uncle Austin, who had seen documents to that effect, but whatever they made was "lost to drink and poker," or so their ancient sister once recalled. Dad used to say that his great-uncle had once been offered the central city blocks of Aspen in exchange for a map to his grubstake mine on the flanks of Aspen Mountain. It's nice to think the family came that close to owning a chunk of what is now some of the most valuable real estate on the planet, but then again, our father's stories had a reputation for being notoriously inaccurate.

I'm not sure how our paternal grandparents met. Our father's mother, Molly, was second-generation Irish; her ancestors had moved to America during Ireland's great potato famine, around 1850. She was born in Denver, one of four siblings resulting from the marriage of Fred Hazeltine, a Pennsylvania mining engineer, and the former Sarah Quinn. At some point, Molly moved back to Pennsylvania to care for her mother's disabled sister. There she met a second aunt, Lizzie Quinn, a Roman Catholic nun who went by the name of Sister Mary Amelia, who thought her bright young niece deserved a high school education. Thanks to her aunt, Molly found herself in Kansas living at an academy run by the Sisters of Charity of Leavenworth, a Catholic order founded in 1858 by the members of a convent in Nashville.

Molly's stay there would be the middle chapter in the family's three-generation involvement with that organization. Our dad's sister Amelia was named after the aunt who had done so much to help her mother. A bookish child, Amelia was considered the intellectual of the family. Eventually, she too became a nun with the Sisters of Charity. It was a natural progression. Career opportunities for brainy, ambitious women were limited then, and joining a convent that administered both schools and hospitals was a way to escape the era's conventional expectations. Our Aunt Amelia, known as Sister Rose Carmel, took full advantage of her opportunities at the convent, and her family connections to it, and remained in the order for the rest of her life. She eventually earned the equivalent of a PhD in chemistry, taught for years in Leavenworth, and later became a pastoral counselor in several of the hospitals administered by the order, in Denver; Santa Monica, California; and Helena, Montana. Aunt Amelia and Terence had similar personalities and much in common, which is probably why they never got along (or, more precisely, why Terence never got along with *her*). Both were brilliant, headstrong, and rebellious. Amelia might have been a nun, but she was anything but meek and mild. She was a rabble-rouser and a trouble-maker, questioning many tenets of dogma and accepted practices that were intended to keep nuns in their place. In later years, Amelia developed strong opinions regarding the exclusion of women from the priesthood, and was even heard to voice certain unflattering observations about the pope, much to the chagrin of her more timid colleagues. As a teacher she was terrifying; many of her students relate stories of how they lived in fear of her wrath, but many of these same students recalled her tough love with affection and respect. She loved her students, but she brooked no bullshit and expected them to meet her high expectations.

She brought the same approach to her dealings with Terence and managed to infuriate him regularly. Terence was always a smooth talker and a skilled bullshitter; there was an unspoken assumption in our family that Terence was smarter than any of us, including me. This, combined with his gift of gab, enabled him to make many provocative statements that went unchallenged. Terence loved nothing more than to shock people, a trait that later served him well as a public figure. The shock-resistant Amelia would have none of it. She was every bit as smart as Terence; she was as well or better read; and she was unflappable, and that drove Terence nuts. Though she lived her adult life as a nun, she read widely and was actually one of the most open-minded people I have ever known. There was nothing that she could not or would not discuss. It was quite remarkable, really. Terence resented this, or claimed to; he didn't like to be challenged, and he was so smooth that he could pull the wool over most anyone's eyes. Amelia saw through all this and managed to get under his skin on a regular basis.

Though Terence would never admit it, I think eventually he came to respect Amelia as a worthy sparring partner. There is no doubt of Amelia's affection for Terence. She was there for him at every important twist of his life, including the terrible summer of 1999, my brother's last, a good part of which Amelia and I spent with him in Hawaii. Our beloved aunt, Sister Rose, the "old battle-ax" in Terence's words, outlived him by three years. She died at age 90 in 2003 at her convent, surrounded by family and friends. There was more of Amelia in Terence than he would ever admit. She cut a wide swath, and, like Terence, there will never be another like her.

I have different recollections of our father's brothers, Ed and Austin. I remember Ed chiefly because he had a large family of eight kids. As a young man, he attended various colleges in Colorado and then went to engineering school in Oakland, where he lived near Lake Merritt in the same apartment building as my parents. Following school, he left to work on the construction of the Alaska Highway during the War. He'd been barred from the military, classified as 4-F because of a heart leakage. The Al-Can project, as Canadians called it, was considered essential for national defense, and so he served that way. He utterly ignored the advice of his doctors to take it easy in light of his heart condition; he loved hunting and fishing, played hard, worked at hard jobs like laying track, and drank like a fish. After the war, he ended up with a high-pressure job in Seattle as a sales manager for a belt and pulley company. According to a new coinage at the time, he was a Type-A personality. He was very strict with his kids and always seemed to be simmering with barely suppressed anger. Or so I gathered on the few occasions when we spent any time with him or his family. Accordingly, I made no effort to get to know him, preferring to stay out of his way.

As for Austin—Uncle Aut, as I call him—I became better acquainted with my father's youngest brother later in life. Like his sister Amelia, Aut was smart and had a rebellious streak, but as a man he had more choices when it came to escaping the constraints of convention. Before the war, he started art school in San Francisco and became the bohemian of the family. He lived in a boardinghouse in Pacific Heights and earned his keep by helping the landlady with cooking and cleaning. Some of his roommates were fellow artists, others led different lives, but most were characters of one kind or another. Among his colorful housemates were at least two gay couples, his first encounter with gays—a real education for a small-town boy, and a step toward developing an unusual sense of tolerance that defines him to this day.

For a short while there, around the start of the war, all three brothers lived in the Bay Area. Aut's brief memoirs suggest they regularly got together on weekends and did their share of partying. Our parents and uncles were not prudes. Dinners and ballroom dancing were favorite pastimes during the swing era with its famous big band leaders and singers, from Tommy Dorsey and Guy Lombardo to Frank Sinatra and Ella Fitzgerald. The McKennas clearly enjoyed their drinking, but they weren't lushes. Had they been young adults 30 years later, I'm sure they would have been passing joints, dropping acid, and going to see the Grateful Dead and Jefferson Airplane just as we did.

Once the war began, Aut's boardinghouse days came to an end. He moved to Berkeley and, like our father, worked for a while in the Kaiser shipyards. Having registered for duty shortly after Pearl Harbor, he was biding his time. Through a lucky break, he got a job at a mine back home, not far from Salida. It was another "essential" defense-related job, mining fluorspar, a mineral used in steel manufacturing. Meanwhile, he waited to be called; like most everyone else in those days, he wanted to serve.

Eventually inducted at Fort Logan in Denver, he endured basic training in Missouri, which nearly killed him, he admitted, and got assigned to a topographic battalion in West Virginia. He caught another break when it came to light that he was an excellent skier, a sport he'd pursued as a kid. The army was then forming a mountain battalion modeled after the Finnish ski units that helped to slow a Soviet invasion of Finland launched in

1939. Aut was able to leverage his knowledge of skiing and cartography into a transfer to the Tenth Mountain Division, which became famous for its exploits in defeating the German troops in the Apennines of northern Italy in 1945. His wartime experiences had an enormous impact on his life. Over the decades, he kept in touch with his buddies from that era and treasured their friendship. For a person like me who has never been in war, it's almost impossible to understand how important those experiences were for him.

All this happened well before Terence and I were born, at a time when settling down to have a family was the last thing on the minds of these young men. The war abruptly severed them from the past and profoundly altered their futures, to the point where what they began afterward were virtually second lives. Things were never the same again.

Aut returned and married his first wife, Mary Lou, in 1948. They settled in Denver, where Aut ran the graphics department at a local ad agency—a stressful job, like his brother Ed's. On our rare visits he seemed grumpy and short-tempered, at least to my eight-year-old sensibilities. He probably would have been quite happy teaching art in a small college, but the pressures of earning enough to support his three adopted children and achieve the postwar American Dream led him to pursue what was perhaps a less satisfying career in management at various companies.

Mary Lou died of cancer in 1976. Eleven years later Aut remarried and retired to Hawaii, beginning what might be called his third life. Following Terence's move to Hawaii in the early 1990s, I traveled there fairly often to see him, trips that grew more frequent after Terence learned of his illness in 1999. I've continued to visit Hawaii at least once a year to teach courses, often visiting Aut, whom I know much better now than I did as a boy. He's a great guy, one of the most open-minded and mellow people I know. Aut has forged a new identity as a local artist of some renown in Kona. He's a beloved figure in the local arts scene, where he's known as Mac. He and his wife Fran are, to me, exemplars of what it means to be elderly, vibrant, and engaged, both locally and, through the Internet and television, with the rest of the world. They are living proof that misery and loss of cognitive functions aren't inevitable with age. The rest of us should be so lucky.

I've talked about our mother and her family, and our father's family as well; let me try to address the enigmatic figure of our father, Joe. According to Aut, our dad grew up reading adventure novels and longing for a glamorous life. Again, as with his storytelling, I detect shades of the father in his sons. He missed out on a lot of active life as a boy, being rather sickly. When he was 11 or 12, he contracted a severe case of rheumatic fever following an episode of strep throat. In the mid-1920s, there were no antibiotics, and his prolonged illness kept him out of school and bedridden for months at a stretch. Although he eventually recovered and led a normal life, the residual damage to his heart caught up with him in his early 60s when surgeons replaced his leaky heart valve with a pig's.

His long childhood convalescence may have been a blessing in disguise. For one thing, it left him more bookish than many of his peers. Though our father never had the benefit of a college education, he had a lifelong passion for reading. During his illness he discovered the novels of Zane Grey, which he loved. He also devoured a lot of early science fiction, a genre that, thanks to him, had a huge impact on Terence and me. His favorites included the works of Edgar Rice Burroughs, especially the Tarzan and Barsoom books, the latter set amid a doomed civilization on Mars, and the early Tom Swift novels, a series created by Edward Stratemeyer in 1910. In my preteens, I became similarly enamored of a second series that began in 1954 and featured Tom Swift Jr., the elder Swift's brilliant son. The closest analog to Tom Swift Jr. in pop culture today may be Tony Stark, the hero of the popular Iron Man movies starring Robert Downey Jr. Stark is smart, technically savvy, rebellious, handsome, and sexy, with oodles of money and plenty of cool toys, not to mention babes. The Swift series put less emphasis on girls, but their heroes represented the same fantasy ideal for our father and me that Stark surely does for young males today.

After consuming all those pulp adventure novels, it's little wonder that our father, his health restored, left Salida shortly after high school in 1933 to seek his fortune. That quest took him to Delta, where, as mentioned, he sold shoes and fell for an older woman, two years older—my mother, Hadie Kemp. He was 22 when they married in 1937. Seven years later, he'd find himself in a B-17 flying missions aimed at crippling the Nazis' industrial base.

Our father never talked much about his experiences during the war. His reticence stemmed from the fact that his combat experiences were traumatic, as they were for many soldiers; the horrors of war would shadow my father for the rest of his life. No wonder he was reluctant to discuss events that must have seemed best forgotten. During the 1950s, he developed vitiligo, a skin disease he described as an "allergy to sunlight." He always wore large hats and long-sleeved shirts to minimize his exposure to the sun, which for an outdoorsman was a major inconvenience. His skin became mottled with large white patches amid normally pigmented skin, and sunlight would exacerbate this condition. Vitiligo struck me as mysterious at the time, but a minute's research on the Internet reveals a wealth of information about this autoimmune disorder. Its exact mechanisms remain unclear, but some say that stress and trauma may be triggering factors. He may have had a genetic predisposition to the condition that his wartime ordeal activated. As the decade wore on, his symptoms gradually faded.

What didn't fade, however, was his new determination to seek normalcy at any cost. After the war, he seemed to retreat from his former devil-may-care persona. He still loved adventure novels, but he wanted only to settle down and live quietly. In this respect he was not alone. The craving for stability was common among his generation, and especially among those who had fought in the war. The goal was not to stand out too much.

On the cultural level this found expression in *The Man in the Gray Flannel Suit*, the 1955 novel by Sloan Wilson that later became a movie. The story chronicles the postwar experiences of Tom Rath and his wife Betsy as they struggle to find happiness in a material world bereft of spiritual meaning. I don't know if our father was familiar with either version, let alone whether the story spoke to him. I rather doubt it, though I'm pretty sure our mother read the book. I do know my father's war experiences deeply influenced him and, in turn, his relationships with Terence and me. He viewed himself as an average guy, and that's what he wanted to be—just one of the herd. This rather unappealing archetype was held up to Terence and me as an ideal throughout the 1960s and sparked many an argument. The last thing we wanted to be was average or normal. In fact, the counterculture was a reaction against that ideal. Like others in our generation, we were busy rebelling against the conformity that had stifled creativity after the war. We wanted to celebrate our individuality. We wanted to be unique, creative, one of a kind. Average was boring. Boring was death.

But average is a statistical fiction; there is no such thing. The irony is that there was nothing average about our father. He was unique in so many ways—ways that directly influenced who his sons grew up to be. For reasons that remain unclear to me, he chose not to take advantage of the GI Bill, the 1944 law that guaranteed college tuition for veterans. Being a few years older than the average returning soldier, he may have felt that he'd seen and survived too much to resume student life (which never particularly appealed to him). Nevertheless, he continued to learn.

A pilot, a woodsman, a lifelong reader, an avid follower of popular science and science fiction, he was an interesting person and yet a person determined to hide his light under the cloak of normalcy, almost as though he was afraid his friends might discover he wasn't the good conformist they thought he was. This self-deprecating attitude, this denial even to himself of his uniqueness, drove Terence and me up the wall. We had many fierce arguments about it, arguments that only hardened positions on both sides, reinforcing our determination never to be average guys and never, ever, to be like our father.

I now have more perspective on how history, largely in the form of war, left its mark on all of us. My parents came of age in an era dominated by World War II, and the looming specter of global conflict, followed by its horrific reality, had a lasting impact on how their lives unfolded. But after Pearl Harbor and Hitler's invasions of Poland and France, it was clearly a just war, a "good" war their generation had to fight. If you were able-bodied, you enlisted; it was the right thing to do. You rearranged your plans and made the sacrifices that most everyone else was making in order to save what amounted to human civilization. The young had little choice but to put their private dreams on hold until this horrific bit of geopolitical business had been dealt with. That imperative limited the options that were available to my parents and their contemporaries, even as it shaped their enduring attitudes and worldviews.

I sometimes wonder if, in our father's situation, I would have had the courage to enlist. I suppose I would have; peer pressure alone would have made it tough to do otherwise. There was an antiwar movement during World War II but it was small, and our parents surely had nothing to do with it. The prevailing view was that the war had to be fought, a view I share.

My generation was also deeply affected by war, but in very different ways. Our war, in Vietnam, was shot through with moral ambiguity, a war this country had no clear need or justification to fight. It seemed to be a grim game played with the lives of young Americans (not to mention untold numbers of Vietnamese) who were asked (and ordered, via the draft) to serve a cause whose rationale was murky indeed, lost in the obfuscations and double-talk of warmongering generals, breast-beating super-patriots, and mealy-mouthed politicians. With time, a moral imperative to the war did emerge, and the imperative was: Don't go. Resist. Tell the government and the politicians to take their war and shove it. And that's what a lot of us did.

Certainly that's what Terence and I did. Like many of our peers, we'd had our minds blown with LSD and had bought into the hippie-dippie, peace-and-love counterculture paradigm. Naturally, this trend shocked and appalled many in our parents' generation, as did the disrespect for authority that resistance to the war necessitated. In my opinion, the Vietnam War and the widespread use of LSD were the two events that contributed most to the ideological and cultural divisions that ripped apart the country in the 1960s. Those wounds remain open even today, a time when any form of healing, of tolerance for diverse moral and ethical perspectives, seems more remote than ever. Fortunately, Terence and I did not have to confront the full force of those conflicts at home. Yes, our parents looked harshly on hippies and the counterculture; they hated and feared LSD and other such drugs, along with the demagogues like Timothy Leary who promoted them. But they also knew the war was an unwarranted and unnecessary travesty. They didn't encourage us to protest in the streets (we did anyway), but they did strive to keep us in school so we'd qualify for student deferments.

Like many others, my brother and I could avoid the war by graduating from high school and getting into college. That we succeeded can be traced back to the early emphasis our parents placed on books and reading. When they were kids, higher education was still hard to come by; it was seen as a privilege, the key to a better life and career that not everyone could hope to achieve. Though our father decided not to attend college, both our parents were determined that we would. I'm eternally grateful that they passed on a love of learning to us. We didn't have the sense to realize it at the time, let alone to appreciate how hard they worked to keep us in school while our less fortunate peers were tapped for sacrifice to the god of war. Now, of course, I do appreciate it—now that it's too late to thank them.

4
Terry and Denny

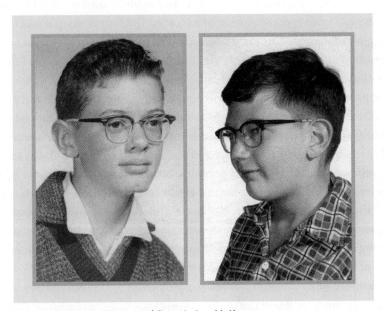

Terence Kemp McKenna and Dennis Jon McKenna

Terence Kemp McKenna emerged from his mother's womb on November 16, 1946. It was the end of a difficult pregnancy. My twin cousins assure me that my brother was a challenge from an early age and quickly earned the appellation "Terrible Terry." Many infants and toddlers try the patience of their parents, but Terence, a "temperamental" child in modern parlance, apparently pushed ours to the limit. Fortunately, Mom had her sisters to help her through these trying episodes. Their support throughout our childhood was surely a major reason she remained as sane as she did. In fact, our mother was wise and compassionate and if anything too tolerant. I know we hurt her, profoundly and deeply, many times, and many times in the four decades since her death I have wanted to apologize. I have to believe she knew we loved her despite it all. I suppose this lament is no different from that of any mother's son. How many of us really honor and appreciate our mothers the way we should? Yet they always forgive us. In my heart, I believe our mother knew we loved her and has forgiven us.

Some time after Terry was born, the little family moved out of our mother's childhood home to an upstairs apartment in a house near the Bross Hotel (then as now Paonia's only hotel). They had just settled into their newly built home at Fourth and Orchard when I arrived, on a cold December day in 1950, a week before Christmas. I have no idea if I was planned or not, but whatever the case, when I joined the family my parents were delighted. Compared to Terry, I was a model of mellowness, or what some would call a "placid" baby. Though I'm still evenly tempered, certain critics, notably my wife, tell me I'm not as laid back as I like to pretend. Whatever. Compared to Terry, raising me was easy for my parents—at least early on.

Terence was a month past his fourth birthday when I showed up. Until then, he'd been the master of his universe, getting all the attention he craved. Like most any child, he perceived my arrival as a threat to his hegemony, which it was, and for years his primary agenda would be to neutralize this threat by any means. Had I been the elder sibling when he burst into my sweet scene in all his mewling, puking, disgusting glory, I'm sure I would have done the same. I daresay this was probably normal sibling behavior, at least in American society in the 1950s. The difference was that Terry, being smart and creative, took brotherly terrorism to some rather interesting places. I see this as a very good reason not to have more than one child, or, if you do, to time them closer together or much farther apart. Four years strike me as exactly the wrong spacing.

There's another factor that complicates my attempt at an early psychological portrait of Terence. At some point shortly before I was born, when Terence was three or four, there was an incident that drove a wedge between him and our father, changing their relationship forever. Indeed, the moment may have negatively affected Terence's relationships until the end of his life. According to what Terence told me decades later, he and a friend were playing in a sandbox. Being curious, and being boys, they began playing with each other's genitals, and, somehow, handling each other's shit. From a modern perspective, this behavior would be considered totally within the bounds of normality for kids that age, and most parents today would laugh it off. But when our dad encountered the scene he apparently freaked out. All his repressed fears about homosexuality, and sexuality in general, instilled in him as a Catholic child, bubbled up in a blind rage, and he spanked Terence rather badly for this transgression. In a way, he was exorcising his own demons from these forbidden realms; the outburst might have been directed at his son, but I am sure it rose out of his own fears.

Terence could not have understood that. All he knew was that his dad had suddenly turned on him in a vicious and painful way and beaten the living daylights out of him. His response, understandably, was one of rage and resentment. He couldn't really show his extreme anger without risk of another beating, but the resentment soaked in, and lingered forever.

"That was it," Terence said when he told me the story. "That was it between us." He slammed an emotional door on our father that was never to be reopened, or so I believe. In that one instant, he resolved to protect himself at any cost, to never show vulnerability, and to put his own (perceived) self-interests front and center at all times. It would seem that, in his own mind, his mistreatment justified his extreme hostility over the years toward our parents, especially our father, and also toward me. As Terence matured he got better at relationships, but they were never easy for him. He told me this story with great vehemence and as if it had happened yesterday. I am left wondering if this experience had resulted in a loss of some essential willingness to trust in others. The story explained my experience of an emotional firewall that I often encountered at the core our relationship and what I could perceive of his relationships with others. As for me, he eventually discovered that I wasn't just a younger, weaker brother to torture. He did express his love for me, but only after years of abuse.

I don't remember when Terry instituted his reign of terror against me, but it must have been when I was about four or five. Terry was a very creative tormentor. He employed both physical techniques and, even deadlier, a variety of psychological techniques to good effect. For physical torture, tickling was his method of choice. It was a good choice—I was very ticklish, probably in part because I became oversensitized to it during our torture sessions. But it worked for Terry because it didn't leave marks, and superficially it didn't seem "that bad" because it made me laugh. But the laughter was not voluntary or enjoyable.

Terry was bigger than me, obviously. His favorite method was to hold me down on the floor, placing a knee on my chest and using both hands to pin my arms, then using his sharp chin to poke and prod me. This became known as the "chin-ee" method. Other techniques were applied as well, but it was the chin-ee that I hated the most. It was all good-natured fun—for Terry. I don't think he intended to hurt me, at least not with his tickling, but the impulse was hard to resist because I so reliably reacted in a satisfying way. On other occasions the torture was more overt and I ended up bawling a lot. Perhaps nothing about this was abnormal—siblings compete, a primate pecking order must be established, this is just what humans do. Like most big brothers, I suspect, Terry both hated and loved the little squirmy worm that I was. It was fine for him to torture me—he considered it a perquisite of being the big brother—but if anyone else threatened me, he was there to protect me.

If the physical teasing I endured was mundane and run-of-the-mill, the psychological teasing reached another level. Terry consistently tried to create a climate of fear based on unpredictability. His mischief had to be done under the radar, of course, without drawing my parents' attention. My reality was one of whispered innuendoes and muttered threats about what would happen the instant they turned their backs: dire consequences awaited me if I failed to toe the line. What was the line? Well, it was nothing less than total subjugation. Often, Terry would thrust his face into mine and rasp, in a low whisper, while staring at me with a hypnotic gaze, "Never oppose my will. Never, ever oppose my will!" I hated this and didn't react submissively. On the occasions when I dared to express actual defiance, however, his responses got physical, and more often than not I'd end up crying.

I was not always the innocent victim, of course, though I got very skilled at playing one. Like many little brothers before me, I developed offensive countermeasures as well as defenses. My offensives had to be stealthy. I cultivated the art of timing. I became skilled at selecting, or creating, situations in which it appeared that Terry had done something to me but hadn't really (or in which I was complicit), and I'd make sure our parents noticed. While presenting a picture of angelic innocence to them, I'd telegraph Terry, via a smirk, that this was sweet revenge. Blame and sometimes punishment would then follow, all the more resented by him because it was unjustified. I knew that sooner or later there would be retribution, but I didn't care. Knowing that I'd managed to stick it to him for a change was extremely satisfying.

What was driving Terry? By the time I showed up, his encounter with our father was in the past, but I'm sure it still stung. In what must have been a strategy for survival, he had hardened his emotional armor and adopted the "me-first" attitude that persisted well into his adult life. I don't think he ever harbored the hatred for our mother that he did for our father. Part of it was that he had learned to trust her as someone who would protect him from Dad—which she did many, many times. She was kind and nurturing and perhaps just a little afraid of her husband. Over the years, she often refrained from telling him about the horrible things "the boys" had been up to in his absence, perhaps fearing he'd overreact in some regrettable way that could not easily be undone. To be fair, our father physically punished us only on the rarest of occasions that even today some parents might view as deserving such a response. Those instances tended to occur on Friday nights after Dad returned from a hard week on the road, only to find we'd been busy in his absence driving our mother crazy. That's when the belt would come off and we'd get a thrashing. I must also add that never once did I see our father lay a hand on our mother in anger. In our family, that was a line that was never crossed.

Having reread what I've written above, I have to ask myself—are these things I should share with the world? Do others really need to know the intimate details of our early lives? If I am to tell an honest tale, the answer is yes. We grew up in small-town *Leave It to Beaver, Father Knows Best* America. But there was a darkness hidden beneath that portrayal of middle-class life, as many others who grew up in that era are surely aware. Certain unconscious emotions erupted all the more violently when, in the 1960s, the layer of "niceness" was ripped away to reveal the wounds still festering underneath.

So yeah, a lot about that era was ugly and unacknowledged at the time, in our family and perhaps in most families. Each had its dark secrets, and ours were not particularly that horrible by comparison. Just so I don't give the wrong impression, let me stress that much—much—about our life together was very good indeed, even if as kids we didn't always realize it. I know our parents loved us. They did the best they could in raising two difficult and recalcitrant boys. It took decades, but Terence eventually overcame much of his animosity toward our father. He certainly found a kind of love for our mother, which I saw most vividly in the kindness and solicitude he showed her when years later she developed cancer. As we grew up and overcame our sibling rivalries, we developed a mutual sense of affection and respect, and I'm grateful for that. Later, our closeness allowed us to experience some of the strangest adventures two brothers have ever shared. Had we not grown up in the twisted climate of the 1950s, so rife with angst and neuroticism, we might never have forged the strong bonds that became the Brotherhood of the Screaming Abyss.

* * *

What are your earliest childhood memories? How far back can you cast your mind? Recollecting childhood can be a tricky exercise because the earliest memories are prelinguistic; there is no cognitive framework within which they can be placed. Mine are mostly gestalt impressions: my father's rough, stubbly cheek when he kissed me, contrasted with my mother's smooth skin when she held me to her breast (though I'm pretty sure I was never actually breastfed—it just wasn't what "modern" mothers did in those days, and Mom wanted to be modern). The eyes, the breath, the smell of various adults; the icy sting on my face on a crisp, cold morning, or the warm caress of sunshine on a summer afternoon. These vague recollections are entirely sensual and without context. It's been said that we can't recall anything earlier than about the age of three or four. Others dispute this and assert that one can have memories from a time as early as two—mostly visual snapshots without narrative or structure. Based on my own vague memories, I'd have to go with the latter hypothesis. A recent Harvard study suggests that recalling childhood memories can make one more helpful and charitable, increasing "prosocial" behavior tied to recollections of a time when things were morally clear and pure. Based on my own experiences, I take that with a grain of salt. I have no doubt that childhood memories can stick with one throughout life. If they are good memories, they have a positive influence; if they are bad—memories of trauma, for example—they can be quite profound and even limiting. In my familial universe, Terence's memories of the sandbox incident would be Exhibit A.

Among the most curious of my earliest remembrances are those that may not be real. I mentioned that our parents left their apartment and moved into their new home shortly before my birth. And yet I have a vague memory of Terence pushing me down those apartment stairs. It's certainly a traumatic memory, but did it really happen? I have no idea. Maybe it happened to someone else and I falsely remember the experience as mine. Or perhaps I dreamt it. I have a similar recollection of my mother leaving me in her Chevy with the motor running outside her father's house when I was three or even younger. Though I do believe she actually did this—foolishly, in that era before car seats and seat belts—my apparent memory of the event may actually have been a dream. I "remember" the car rolling slowly down the street a short way until it halted against a curb, my mother by then standing beside it in hysterics. But I'm not sure that part actually happened. To this day I sometimes dream I'm driving in a car, then look down to see there's no steering wheel, or the steering wheel has come loose in my hands. The issue? Probably losing control, my wife would say. My "memory" of being trapped in the runaway Chevy was perhaps just an early instance of grappling with that in my sleep.

My earliest reliable memories date from when I was four. By then, Terence was often at school for much of the day, giving me a welcome respite from his tortures. That comfort with solitude has persisted throughout my life. I enjoy being alone with nothing but the whisper of my thoughts. And besides, back then I wasn't alone. I had a whole gaggle of imaginary friends, some of them as real to me as my actual friends, of which I then had few. (With no kindergarten in Paonia, my socializing didn't really begin until first grade.) I preferred hanging out with my imaginary friends because they were always there and more interesting. Some were even animals—how cool is that? We'd cross the street to the city park or, more accurately, I'd go to the park and "manifest" them, as if they were always there, waiting to play. And play we did! I created all sorts of adventures to share with them, performing all the roles and voices. As a child I had a very active dream life. In fact I'm not sure I ever really slept in the conventional sense. Or maybe I was in a constant state of high REM sleep, always dreaming. My imaginary friends were also available in my dreams, where our little dramas often continued. It was tremendously entertaining and fun, but one sad day I dismissed them, just bade them good-bye. It was all very formal. "OK, I'm moving on, you're not going to see me again," I informed them, and they were quite dismayed. But it had to be done. Time to move on. I could not have been more than eight.

Though manifesting various identities or personalities may be a disorder in adults, I agree with those who view such behavior as normal in young children. A child's personality, or what eventually becomes his or her personality, condenses and coalesces out of a multitude. When it fails to do that, then you have pathology. Reflecting on this, I have to wonder about the similarities between the consciousness of a child and the consciousness of an Indigenous person. To a child, these imaginary entities are real, as real as anything in the so-called real world. It must be much the same for an Indigenous person who inhabits a world of spirits, of human and non-human entities, where the distinctions between dreams and reality are not so clear. I do not mean to imply that an Indigenous person is childish, but rather that Indigenous people and children may share some traits in their mentation. What I'm speaking of is not an age-dependent characteristic; rather it's related to a state of preliteracy. I think that as our brains develop, and particularly as we develop literacy, the brain becomes more compart-mentalized. We develop a point of view, an ego, a sense of self, but we also sacrifice a lot to acquire those things. We give up a lot for our left-brain dom-inance. I think we sense that loss; that's why we like to step out of it once in a while, using psychedelics or other altered states. Psychedelics make you childlike; they can reconnect you with that primal, preliterate, precognitive state. How can this not be a good thing? More people should try it. We take ourselves, most of the time, much too seriously!

5
Happy Day Rides

Denny with Skelly.

For the last two decades, my family and I have lived in Marine on St. Croix, a town in eastern Minnesota just across the St. Croix River from Wisconsin. Last year, as every year, a good crowd turned out to celebrate the Fourth of July. The festivities started the night before with a spectacular fireworks display over the river, then resumed in the morning with a parade down Judd Street, Marine's main drag. The parade was, as usual, a motley assemblage; pretty much anyone could take part, though it helped to have some kind of message or theme. The big news in July 2011 was the political stalemate that had led Minnesota's state government to shut down a few days earlier. The winning float featured a gaggle of marchers carrying blank banners—their way of mocking a state that couldn't even pay for ink. As always, the show was silly, hokey, drenched in small-town Midwestern charm, and quite moving in a nostalgic way. It's a yearly reminder that though the pace of change in the world is ever accelerating, certain aspects of small-town life remain frozen in a timeless eternity of iconic Americana.

My memories of childhood in Colorado include the treasured recollections of events that could have been plucked from the same summer-dazed grab bag as the Fourth of July in Marine. As a kid in Paonia, the Fourth was second only to Christmas on my personal liturgical calendar. It was also Cherry Day, a series of events celebrating the luscious Bing cherries that were picked, in a good year, from the fruit orchards that covered the surrounding mesas. Back then, the local economy, such as it was, relied on two things: coal mining and fruit cultivation (apples, peaches, plums, apricots, and those sweet and succulent Bings, ranging in color from dark ruby to midnight black). The mining persists and has actually been more active in recent years, with the growing market for the area's high-quality coal reserves. But due to climate change and the uncertain harvests, the fruit industry has devolved into a gentleman's hobby. Even back then, a late spring freeze regularly wiped out the cherry crop, which meant the town had to get its cherries from Fruita, near Grand Junction, about 70 miles to the west. True to its name, Fruita always seemed to have a good harvest by the Fourth, a fact that many of Paonia's farmers probably resented. There in the vaunted home of the best cherries in western Colorado, it was never clear before the end of May if the festivities in their honor could count on local supplies to meet demand.

Though the cherries were good enough to tempt me and many other kids into diarrhea-inducing excess, they were not the highlight of my Fourth of July. What I most eagerly awaited was the appearance of the traveling carnival. Happy Day Rides was a dusty, ragamuffin caravan of carneys that would show up one day unannounced (at least, unannounced to me) a week or so before the Fourth. Their arrival served as a midpoint in the bucolic three-month ecstasy that was summer in Paonia. Here was proof that, yes, Cherry Day would happen, cherries or no cherries, and that the summer would spin itself out like every summer before it. Their two-week stay was an enchanted time, at least in the lives of young boys, inevitably followed by a touch of sadness. Their departure meant the end of another glorious, school-free, sun-drenched summer was not that far away.

I was blessed among my peers to live across the street from Paonia Park, where, in one corner, Happy Day Rides would set up shop. I'd get up one June morning and there they'd be, having quietly straggled into town during the night. They didn't look like much: just two or three semitrailers and a few flatbed trailers and smaller trucks. They had no large animals, no lions or tigers or elephants, probably because it was too expensive to keep such a menagerie fed and cared for on the road. None of this mattered. I was most interested in the rides, which the carneys would spend the next few days unpacking and assembling like a scuffed-up, adult-scale erector set. As these marvels took shape—the roller coaster, the Ferris wheel, the Tubs of Fun, the electric train, and, in later years, the Octopus and the Loop-O-Planes—I tracked the progress in minute detail, utterly engaged. Major fun was a few days out, and I was on it, monitoring the situation from morning till night.

In retrospect, it's a wonder the carneys didn't chase me off more than they did, which wasn't often. According to conventional wisdom, these people were apt to be thieves, sleazeballs, and bums. And yes, our parents warned us about the dangers of hanging out with them, of being abducted and forced into labor (or worse). But Happy Day Rides wasn't just any sleazy carnival— it was *our* sleazy carnival, a "clean," family-oriented operation that the town mostly welcomed. Whether their good reputation was deserved or not, I had no idea. What mattered to me were their fantastic machines, which created much happiness until they were broken down and carried off as quickly and quietly as they arrived, leaving a new faint grief over the approach of fall. Beyond that, there was Christmas to look forward to, and the autumn distraction of Halloween, but in the distorted time scale of boyhood consciousness, those events seemed as distant as the next glaciation.

I may have had a touch of Asperger's syndrome or perhaps even high-functioning autism as a child. I hazard this self-diagnosis because I loved to rock, and often did so, back and forth in my chair, quite happily for hours. I remember the big rocking chair in the living room of my aunt and uncle's ranch on the Crystal River, the place where we spent so many weekends. The chair was old and had a long back-and-forth arc to it and a very satisfying creak. As soon as we arrived on a Friday night, I'd head for the chair and start to rock and pretty much stay there for the duration, only stopping for meals or when my folks insisted I go outside and play in the beautiful forests and pastures. I enjoyed all that, but I was always happy to return. Unlike the present era, where the slightest behavioral anomaly is viewed as pathological, my rocking was seen as a little quirky but not really harmful, and anyway, "He'll grow out it." And I did.

One lifelong characteristic that my rocking did reveal was a fondness for novel experience and stimulation. From an early age I was a junkie for proprioceptive novelty; I loved the feelings of floating and flying, of centrifugal acceleration and g-forces, of distorted body image and queasy stomach butterflies. The carnival rides, especially the Octopus and the Tubs of Fun, delivered these sensations more reliably and intensely than I could induce in my chair, or on the swing set in the park, or in the occasional weightless episodes that Dad liked to indulge in when he took me up for a spin in his Piper Tri-Pacer. These were all cool and fun, but nothing delivered like the carnival rides! The rides were the ultimate cheap thrill (actually not so cheap to an eight-year-old, but I had saved my allowance).

Looking back, I have to believe that much of my later interest in drugs originated from my early love for "funny feelings" accessed through the carnival and other DIY methods of altering consciousness. In his book *The Natural Mind*, Andrew Weil writes that it is almost universal for children of a certain age to spin themselves into a falling-down state of dizziness (I tried that, too) because they enjoy the unfamiliar feeling engendered by the disorientation and loss of balance. Indeed, Weil argues that the human brain and nervous system are hardwired to seek out novel perceptions, distorted body images, visionary episodes, and other forms of ecstatic experience, and this inbuilt proclivity explains much of our fondness for substances that can trigger these altered states. Much of this activity is motivated by a curiosity akin to a scientist's—the individual is posting data points in the unmapped territory of possible sensation. Some people go in for extreme sports like bungee jumping or skydiving for similar reasons; others pursue novel sensations through drugs, and, of course, there are those who enjoy combining pharmacologically induced alterations with their favorite risky sports, though not me. In fact, when it came to really risky behaviors like downhill skiing, rock climbing, or auto racing, I was a bit of a wimp. I was overcautious about engaging in behaviors that were likely to get my bones broken or my ass killed, and this may be one reason I eventually came to favor drug-induced novelty over extreme sports.

This cautious streak probably stood me in good stead when it came to drugs, because as a rule I paid attention to those key variables of "set and setting" that Leary and the rest were always harping about. It made sense that one should explore altered states in a relatively safe environment. Not all my friends approached pharmacology with such common sense, and some lived to regret it; others never had that luxury, because they didn't live. I daresay I learned a thing or two from the wondrous contraptions that showed up each summer with Happy Day Rides. My carnival experiences were formative for me and gave me an early fondness for funny feelings that has persisted throughout my life.

6 The Nobody People

The campaign of brotherly terror that Terence waged on me from age four or five continued for many years. It was during the nights, of course, that it reached its zenith. We shared a bedroom and had separate beds. According to Terence, he would sometimes quietly slip out of his bed, tiptoe across to mine, and stand above my sleeping form, hands raised in the tickle-attack mode, ready to pounce. And in this position he'd stand for hours, savoring the psychological meltdown he'd trigger if he acted. But he never did. It was satisfying enough just knowing that he could. Looking back, I doubt he really did this. I think his story was just another way to maintain the climate of fear.

A major element in that were the frightening stories he used to whisper as we cowered under the covers, long after lights-out. A scary TV show, a ghost story, or just some confabulation from his fertile and twisted mind would serve as fodder for these nightly horrors. Once we watched a TV adaptation of H.H. Munro's short story "Sredni Vashtar," presumably from a 1961 series, *Great Ghost Tales*, which first aired when I was 10. It's a nasty little horror story about a young boy who keeps a polecat-ferret in a shed and worships the animal as a vicious, vengeful god, a secret he keeps at first from his overbearing guardian, to her ultimate misfortune. For months, Terry was able to strike the most abject fear into me by simply uttering the story's title.

But by far the most terrifying theme of Terry's nocturnal campaign, revisited night after night, was the Nobody People, aka the No-Body People. In the language of 19th-century ghost stories, the entities would be known as wraiths. Terence gave them a name and turned them loose in my already overactive and hypersuggestible imagination.

The Nobody People lived in shadows; in fact, they *were* shadows, or they existed on some gloomy threshold between the insubstantial and the real. You could see them, or sense them, at night, lurking in the shadows of the closet, or under the bed, or in the hollow of the bathtub. Rarely, you could sense them during the day, in the corners of dimly lit rooms, in basements or cellars, in the crawl spaces under the house. But primarily they were creatures of the dark and the night. You were not likely to run into a Nobody Person outside on a bright, sunny day. No, they were denizens of a shadow world; they liked to hang out in graveyards (especially in open graves), and gloomy glens, and caves.

Not that I was into hanging around such places, not on your life! I didn't have to. The Nobody People were especially fond of the shadowy parts of our bedroom. It was Nobody People Central, our bedroom. You knew they were there, Terry said, because sometimes you'd walk into the dark room and something would flit by, maybe brush you gently in passing, and then melt into the shadows again. I bought it; I agreed that this could happen, and had happened, though of course it never did. For one thing, due to my constant, fully deployed Nobody People antennae, the idea that I would ever, under any circumstances, for any reason, walk into a darkened room without turning the light on was simply preposterous. I would be sure to snake my hand around the doorjamb and hit the light switch *before* entering a room. Terry knew of this practice and threatened to be hiding on the other side of the threshold one day where he could seize my hand and scare the living bejeezus out of me. But he never did. I guess he was too busy carrying out the rest of his terrorist agenda and just never got around to this one.

As far as I remember, the Nobody People never actually did anything bad, or did very much at all. I guess they were frightening because of the idea that we are at all times surrounded by unseen, barely sensed entities living among us, conducting their dreary affairs in a shadowy parallel world (though the term "living" is probably a misnomer, because they were understood to be, possibly, the remnants of the dead, or at least not living in the sense that we were living). They would have had very little power to frighten me if I had not been a willing participant-observer. I believed in them just enough that I could convince myself, in that delicate twilight between waking and actual sleep, that I could see them materializing out of the shadows, stately processions of them wafting across the room and merging with the shadows on the other side. It's a testament to the power of suggestion. Plant the seed of an idea in someone's mind, repeat it often enough, and pretty soon they begin to believe it even though, rationally, it makes no sense. It also helps if the victim's reasoning faculties and cognitive categories are still rather fluid and not yet fully formed, which was likely when I was between five and eight, the period when the Nobody People were most active.

Which moves me to ponder another aspect of this. Why do people like to be frightened? You have only to look at a list of recent blockbusters or scan the late-night TV schedule for proof that people love having the daylights scared out of them! It's a multibillion-dollar industry. And it wouldn't work without a voluntary and deliberate suspension of disbelief, to some extent. One has to agree to buy into the premise. Certainly I pretended not to enjoy Terence's psychological tortures, but I suspect a part of me did enjoy them. I was titillated; there was a kind of thrill in being frightened, and it was not entirely unpleasant. To titillate now means to stimulate or excite, especially in a sexual way, but its archaic meaning was to touch lightly, or tickle. Aha! As I've noted, Terence refined the practice of tickling me into a dark art. Though I hated it, I was ambivalent. Sometimes I almost liked being tickled mercilessly, just as I sometimes liked being frightened to death.

The Nobody People were my first encounters with the idea that one can coexist with an unseen world of spirits or other entities. Certainly this perspective is integral to the shamanic worldview, and it is encountered in altered states triggered by the Amazonian brew known as ayahuasca, among other shamanic substances. The ayahuasca landscape is a virtual battleground populated with malevolent spirits but also with allies, plant teachers, animal spirit guides, ancestral spirits, and other morally ambiguous entities. The shaman's task is essentially one of extradimensional diplomacy, that is, to identify and forge alliances with the beneficial entities while guarding against those that don't necessarily have one's best interests in mind. When I eventually accessed such realms with ayahuasca, the idea of a morally ambiguous dimension in which one rubbed up against ghostly entities (sometimes literally) was already familiar. I had been introduced to it long before by the Nobody People. One can access those dimensions through pharmacological triggers other than ayahuasca. In fact, the nightshades, which include belladonna, the genus *Datura*, and the South American "tree daturas," are even more reliable. A full dose of datura will put you right into that twilight world where wraiths and ghosts lurk, where you can see and talk to them (though they rarely respond). I believe that accidental or deliberate encounters with the shadowy datura spaces are the basis for the belief, in many cultures, in a land of the dead or of ghosts. When encountered, these dimensions and entities certainly *seem* real enough, at least as real as ordinary waking consciousness. With practice, you can work magic in these realms that can have real impact in the ordinary reality of waking consciousness. Certainly, if you can contrive to get some of the substance into your intended victim, they can be manipulated or influenced in ways they might otherwise resist, because datura induces confusion and delirium; it undermines a person's will and, conveniently enough, wipes out memories of what has happened. *Datura*, nightshade consciousness, is the ultimate power trip. It is the basis of witchcraft in European traditions and of *brujeria*, or black magic, in South America. It is not to be trifled with.

7 The Collector

Terence in the Amazon, 1971.

According to some relatives, Terence's early mischief was not confined to the family. He had a reputation for being hard on his peers, and some parents devised strategies to protect their offspring from his excesses. I suspect, however, that many of those kids experienced a certain thrill when Terence's attention swung their way, unnerving though it could be. From an early age he was front and center, the producer, director, and star of his own movie; everyone else was supporting cast. A lot of people wanted to be in his movie. A lot of people still do. And when I was a child, nobody wanted in more than I did.

Viewing their eldest child as the "smart one," our parents made every effort to encourage Terence's intellectual development and to participate in his numerous hobbies. It took them about a decade to realize that I was also smart, though not in the same way. Was their reluctance to see that earlier an unconscious expression of their guilt over foisting a pesky little brother on Terry, or was it just the natural fate of a younger child? Terence was indeed a smart and curious boy, interested in many things. He also had a way of sucking the air out of a situation that could leave me gasping. Perhaps the firstborn is destined to get all the attention, the new clothes, the privileges, while a younger sib has to make do. Anyway, that's how it seemed in our family. In many of our shared activities, Terence led and I followed, at least when he allowed it, and I didn't really mind that. The four-year age difference made whatever Terence was into that much cooler than my own pursuits, so I obviously wanted to tag along and get involved.

Collecting was a big thing for him, as it was for many other kids back then who aspired to be scientists of a sort. The scientific interest in collections—of rocks, plants, animals, insects—now seems like a quaint relic of the Victorian era. But the life sciences have been impoverished by the decline in collecting. Today, it's possible to get so deeply immersed in genetics and molecular biology that one never fully appreciates biodiversity from the organismic level. A student can now get a degree in biology without ever having taken a course in ecology or organismic biology, which is really a shame. Something essential is lost when you only look at biology through the lens of molecular biology.

Terry spent much of his childhood happily collecting stuff—shells, rocks, fossils, and other curiosities—and over time he built some impressive collections. Our father built him a homemade rock polisher, one of many things Dad did over those years to try to connect with his geeky, brilliant son. The reading and learning that went along with the collecting actually helped to foster Terence's interest in science and nature—and mine as well. I was never happier than on those occasions when Terence would allow me to tag along on his collecting forays. Among the best times I remember were our occasional trips to the 'dobes, an arid region near town that once had been submerged beneath an inland sea. My mother would pack a picnic lunch and we'd head out to the badlands for a few hours of searching for sharks' teeth. The tiny, shiny, prehistoric remains were everywhere. You could sift through the soil and come up with several hundred in the course of an afternoon. We accumulated jars and jars of the darned things, learning about biology, geology, evolution, and the notion of "deep time" in the process.

Another favorite weekend outing for us was to visit the north rim of the Black Canyon National Monument, located near the town of Crawford, about an hour's drive south of Paonia. It's one of the most spectacular geo-logical formations on the continent. Though much smaller than the Grand Canyon, which is broad but relatively shallow, the Black Canyon is a narrow gorge slashed out of the rock over at least two million years of relentless erosion by the fast-flowing river. The gorge is one of the most extreme ver-tical environments I've ever seen, with depths that approach 3,000 feet. The Black Canyon was my first encounter with the concept of an abyss. A family story relates that when we visited the canyon on one occasion shortly after I began to talk, my mother picked me up so I could look over the railing. My comment at the time was "Big hole." Indeed, it was.

At age 11 or 12, Terence began collecting insects and built up a fine but-terfly and moth collection, including a few exotic specimens he purchased. His tarantulas, blue morpho butterflies, and gigantic horned stag beetles arrived via the mail-order catalogs he found listed in the back of *Science News*, a thin weekly bulletin we subscribed to for years. Terence's ento-mological interests proved more lasting than his other collection-related pursuits, and as a young adult he continued to seek out butterflies on his global ramblings. Though his passion was very real, he found the persona of the collector to be a good cover when traveling in tropical countries. As he noted, "When you show up in a village with a butterfly net, it's immediately obvious to even the youngest child why you are there; and it's non-threatening, it's friendly. You are immediately tagged as a harmless eccentric." Terence would know, having spent months exploring the outer islands of Indonesia under that guise in 1970, on the run from Interpol for smuggling hashish. Later, the same cover worked pretty well on our travels in Colombia when our real quest was for exotic hallucinogens.

Collecting for Terence was both a passion and a useful skill. His ability to write those tiny, tiny labels used in mounting specimens landed him a work-study job as an entomology technician at the California Academy of Sciences during his undergraduate years at Berkeley. Later, after returning to Berkeley from South America in 1972, he made good money mounting butterflies for a Japanese purveyor of exotic specimens. The best part about it was that he could do it totally stoned, and while holding his customary afternoon salons with the friends who dropped by his loft apartment to smoke hash and hang and rave. I fondly remember some of those sessions myself, with the late afternoon sun illuminating the dancing dust motes. That loft was the site of many a fine conversation accompanied by multiple bowls of excellent hash.

Decades later, after Terence had passed on, his lifelong interest in collecting came up in a touching and beautiful way. Many of the collections that Terence made in Indonesia and Colombia were never mounted. They remained stored in small triangular envelopes folded from paper squares, a common method of handling specimens in the field. The envelopes had been sealed with a few mothballs in large cracker tins and other containers, then packed in a trunk, and hence were perfectly preserved for decades while Terence was busy elsewhere.

After he died, his daughter Klea, then only 19, inherited them, and she turned out to be the perfect recipient. An excellent photographer with a highly refined aesthetic, Klea, the younger of Terence's two children, eventually used her artistic skills and vision to transform the collection into a beautiful tribute to her father. She didn't mount the specimens in the conventional way. Instead, she created a work in which each butterfly was photographed together with its envelope. Terence had snipped those little wrappers out of foreign newspapers, hotel stationery, notebook pages, or any other handy piece of paper. Once a specimen had been caught, he wrote the date and location on the envelope in his tiny, meticulous script. Klea's display of these images amounted to a chronicle of Terence's travels through the Indonesian archipelago and the jungles of Colombia. It also evoked a moment in cultural history. The newspaper clippings revealed fragments of articles and headlines about Kent State, Nixon, Vietnam; others were faded pieces of full-color magazine ads, hotel receipts, and Chinese newsprint. Together they formed a snapshot of a moment in time, juxtaposed and reinforced by the ephemerality of the specimens they held, still as vibrant and bright as the day they were collected.

Klea's gallery installation in San Francisco in 2008 was entitled *The Butterfly Hunter,* and she later released the project as a limited edition artist book (see www.kleamckenna.com). She took care to ensure her quiet tribute wasn't about Terence per se. She didn't want to capitalize on his fame but rather present him in a pristine light as simply the butterfly hunter, someone who existed before she did, someone who became her father. His early passion would not be how the world came to know him. Many of those who saw the exhibition were not aware that it was about a celebrated figure. Her simple, elegant presentation was of a man who collected butterflies, and this man was her father. What else needs to be said?

* * *

Although Terence's passion for insect collecting lasted well into adulthood, none of his boyhood hobbies could match amateur rocketry for sheer excitement. When he got interested in this incendiary pastime, at age 11 or 12, our father was an enthusiastic partner. What is it about guys? They just like to blow things up—the noisier, more dangerous, and spectacular the better. Model rocketry, which was just then catching on, definitely called for adult supervision, and Dad devoted many a weekend to helping Terry build and launch the solid-fuel rockets that arrived as mail-order kits. These usually consisted of a reinforced cardboard tube, a wooden nose cone, balsa wood fins, five or six solid-fuel cartridges, some fuse cord, and (in the deluxe models) a paper parachute tied to a plastic monkey that was supposed to safely eject at the apogee of the flight. That part usually failed, and when it did work, the monkey-naut ended up getting lost in the bush somewhere. But some of those kits performed pretty well; on a good day, when there was no wind, those rockets could rise a couple thousand feet.

I'm pleased to report this is still an active hobby for a lot of youngsters. Even the venerable company we came to rely on for our kits, Estes Industries, is still in business, but their newer vehicles look a lot more impressive than the ones we launched. It's nice to know that in this age when parents feel compelled to overprotect their kids and never let them do anything remotely dangerous (or fun), it's still an option for young boys and girls to get into serious mischief through the reckless deployment of model rockets.

With our father keeping an eye on things, we were actually quite safety conscious. We did most of our launching at the Paonia airport where he kept his plane, about four miles outside of town. The airstrip was on a narrow mesa the size and shape of a large aircraft carrier, surrounded for miles by sage and scrub, making it the perfect site. We dug a bunker in the earth of the hillside and reinforced it with scrap plywood and sheet metal we found in the airport hangers. The next step was to set up the rocket on its pad, attach some fuse cord to the fuel cartridge, and string it back to our makeshift barrier. Ensconced behind it, we'd light the long fuse with a match and recite the mandatory "ten-nine-eight" incantation down to liftoff. How many laws we violated on these outings I have no idea, and it didn't really matter. It was rather rare for a plane to land at the airport back then, so we were never reported as a hazard to aviation. Once you're under the spell of high explosives and glimpse the potential for some really spectacular launches, you want them to be better, higher, faster, and more dangerous. What you want, in fact, is a liquid-fueled rocket. Liquid fuels like methanol and other even more volatile substances can propel a rocket 5,000 feet straight up in a flash. But liquid-fueled rockets are also inherently more dangerous; the "burn" is hard to control, and if there is an undetected leak or weakness in the rocket wall, it can easily rupture. Liquid-fuel rockets are basically small bombs, which is why our father drew the line there, forbidding us to work with them.

Having never seen a line he didn't want to cross, Terence decided that's exactly what we'd do. We began a secret R&D program, pursued only on weekdays when our father was on the road. Terence somehow got plans for building a tiny liquid-fueled rocket out of a CO_2 cartridge like the kind used in pellet guns, about four inches long and less than an inch in diameter. I've forgotten what the actual fuel was, but it was probably methanol. We built a customized launch pad for this diabolical device using angle iron and conduit piping. The rocket sat at the base, loosely cradled between three conduits that provided flight guidance, or at least pointed the thing in the general direction of the sky.

Our invention took its only flight one balmy midsummer evening. Our mother had left for her bridge club, leaving us to our own devices for a few hours. We waited until it was sufficiently dark before we lugged the pad and the diminutive rocket to the football field cross the street. By then we were using a battery-operated gizmo that lit the rocket with a spark just under the exhaust nozzle—very cool. Once we'd mounted our vehicle on the pad, we conducted the obligatory countdown and triggered the ignition. Immediately a tremendous sonic boom reverberated across the valley! The rocket broke the sound barrier before it even cleared the pad, and disappeared faster than the eye could track, never to be seen again.

But we had more immediate concerns. We were utterly convinced that the sonic boom had shattered every window within a five-mile radius. We grabbed the launch pad and hightailed it back to the house, where we stashed the evidence in the patio storage room and hid ourselves in the bedroom, expecting the police to show up at any minute. But they never did. When our mother came home, we asked her as innocently as we could if she'd heard a loud noise earlier in the evening, which she hadn't, and there were no shattered windows reported the next day. The boom we heard in our boyhood imagination was perhaps not as loud as it had seemed. Then again, maybe we were just lucky and no one had been paying attention. After that episode, we halted our rocket experiments—that one was hard to top—and moved on to other things. We'd scared ourselves into discontinuing the secret program, never quite sure if we'd parked that damn thing in low earth orbit or not.

8 Flying, Fishing, and Hunting

Denny and his father beside the Piper Cub, in 1956.

Our father enjoyed sharing his passion for flying with us, but by the time Dad got his own plane, Terence had reached early adolescence and the tensions between them were well advanced. Whereas I flew a lot with Dad as a teenager, Terence remained mostly outside that bond. I learned to fly and land the plane pretty well, but I never got my license. The idea of sitting in a classroom studying engine mechanics and navigation never appealed to me. What's more, though for many years I fantasized about being a professional pilot, I had severe myopia from birth and wore thick glasses, so there was little chance I'd ever achieve that childhood dream—one of many. My visual limitations led me to put a pilot's life on the shelf, and there it stayed.

Flying was ecstasy for our father, and we shared that feeling when we flew together. Dad never felt freer or more alive than in the air, high above the cares and tribulations of the world. When I was starting to experiment with psychedelics as a teenager, I tried to explain my interest in altered states by comparing it to flying—it was a thrill, it was a rush, it was ecstasy! He couldn't really see it. To him, everything about "drugs" was bad, and it was impossible to have a rational conversation about the topic. In that, he was like many in his generation. Their drugs of choice, alcohol and tobacco, were so accepted as not to be considered drugs. My father once told me that the effects of alcohol were due to its effect on the muscles! The idea that it affected the brain was an alien concept to him. As for all the other substances that were referred to then (and now) as drugs in a catchall sense, he clearly knew those did affect the brain, and that had to be a bad thing.

Dad not only greatly enjoyed flying, he was an excellent pilot known for his skill at flying in the Colorado Rockies. It was a skill worthy of recognition; flying in the high mountains is tricky and dangerous, given the changeable weather, unpredictable winds, and other hazards. Dad was often called out by the local Civil Air Patrol to search for some plane that had gone down in the mountains. Most of these crashes were caused by ignorance, bad judgment, or inexperience on the part of pilots my father called "flatland furriners" with no business flying in that rugged terrain. In most cases he was right. He flew for years in the mountains, under some pretty harrowing conditions, and never had any problems. He had good judgment and knew when not to push it.

My father spent years sharing a Piper Cub with the other members of a local flying club before he got his Tri-Pacer. I mentioned how he used his plane to cover his vast sales territory, which he enjoyed. The plane also gave him more time with us in Paonia, which on balance was probably a good thing, though it increased the opportunities for conflict. Wings certainly gave us options that weren't available to other families, like weekend trips. We could take off for the Grand Canyon, Mesa Verde, Carlsbad Caverns, or Arches National Monument and be back home in time for school on Monday morning. It was great fun, and I think it broadened our perspective beyond that of most of our peers. In the summer of 1962, when I was 11 and Terry was 15, my father borrowed a somewhat bigger plane, a Piper Comanche, and took us on a two-week trip to the Seattle World's Fair, an amazing experience for both of us. The theme of the fair, Century 21, was a paean to the utopian, Jetsons-style future that supposedly lay just a few short decades ahead. For two geeky boys who were already steeped in science fiction and popular science, to tour that world was a thrill.

My most memorable flying experiences took place closer to home. My father had a friend who had a ranch farther up the Crystal River valley from the one owned by my aunt and uncle. He also owned a small plane and had built a rough dirt airstrip on his land beside some of the river's best fishing spots. My father had permission to fly in and catch a few fish whenever he wanted. It became a regular thing for the two of us to get up early in the morning, fly over, and return in time for breakfast with a mess of fresh trout to fill out the menu.

This was an incredibly cool thing to do, but also tricky! Getting in and out of that airstrip required every bit of Dad's skill as a pilot, due to the updrafts and downdrafts he had to contend with. Once you came over the ridge on the way in, you had to drop like a stone in order to lose enough altitude to make a run at the strip, and you only got one chance. He had to put the plane into what felt like a suicide dive, only pulling up at the last minute to make a perfect landing. Flying out was similar. When taking off in the thin mountain air, the danger was that we wouldn't have the lift to clear the ridge. As soon as we left the ground, Dad had to put the plane into a steep climb and risk stalling in order to avoid the downdrafts from the winds that were howling over the ridge. If we didn't make the altitude on the first try, there was no going back; we'd end up as a crumbled piece of tinfoil on the unforgiving rocks below. I didn't realize at the time that we were taking a significant risk every time we made that trip. Dad must have known, but I did not. I never worried for a minute about the danger. My dad, my amazing father, the legendary mountain pilot, was at the controls, and there was simply no way we were going down. It couldn't happen, and it didn't. He was that good. I was that naive. Looking back on these experiences, I think we both must have been a little nuts to have attempted them.

If you were a kid growing up in western Colorado in the 1950s and '60s, "huntin' and fishin'" were just things you did. They were pretty much in your blood. Except when they weren't, which was the case with me. Our father was an excellent fly-fisherman. I tried to learn to fly-fish, but I was lousy at it. I could never get the hang of casting the fly into the right ripple in the stream where the fish were lurking, let alone to know, as he did, they'd be there. On the rare occasions when I did catch something, I'd have to kill it, usually by beating its head against the nearest rock. I didn't like killing fish; it was the most distasteful part of the whole exercise. I got pretty good at cleaning them, but I didn't care for that either, especially the part where I had to remove the fish shit from their intestinal tract, located just below the spinal column. Yuck! So I never really made the cut as a fisherman, much to our father's disappointment, I'm sure. Later, our outings got better once he abandoned any expectation that I'd actually fish. Instead he'd fish and I'd go off somewhere, smoke a little weed, and hunt mushrooms. By then I'd developed a passion for hunting mushrooms, and I had a pretty good eye. I was always looking for the Holy Grail in the form of *Amanita muscaria*, but they were rare. I did find plenty of delicious edibles, though, and enjoyed many a feast.

I was only a little more successful at hunting than fishing. I had a .410 shotgun inherited from my great-grandfather, a beautiful gun that fired a single shell, handcrafted for his wife when he was stationed at a military post in South Africa. Or so went the family legend, which may or may not have been true. Dad had a bigger gun, a 12-gauge double-barrel. Shooting ducks and pheasants wasn't that hard, and I regularly brought them down. But as with the fish, you then had to clean them, a messy business neither of us liked; we were always trying to give away our kill to friends. I'm sorry to admit it, but the pleasure for us was in the hunt. Hunting elk and deer was a more serious business, not least because we used high-powered rifles, and you could get yourself seriously killed if you weren't careful. Shotguns could be just as dangerous, of course, but they lacked the aura of lethality that rifles had. Also, hunting large animals was more associated with the whole manhood thing. It was a shamanic activity, a rite of passage. Somewhere in all manly men (and manly men we were, or at least wanted to be), there is a Paleolithic warrior lusting to take spear in hand and head out on the ice sheet in search of saber-toothed cats. We were living out that primal quest, reconnecting with our hunter-shaman selves, albeit with better technology. That included the car ride we'd take every fall to stage our reenactment at Lee Sperry's ranch on West Muddy Creek.

Lee was a real cowboy, a cattleman who operated an enormous ranch with several thousand head. Every hunting season, he opened the place to tourist hunters from Texas, mostly, but also my father and his friends. For two weeks we lived there in a caveman's paradise, surrounded by a testosterone-drenched, stinking, grizzled bunch that drank hard liquor and communicated in grunts. In reality, of course, these folks (with the exception of Lee, who was as tough as he looked) were soft tenderfoots—accountants and salesmen, teachers and grocers, mostly sedentary and well padded. But for two weeks we were the fucking Clan of the Cave Bear. I recall it as a fantastic experience, though much of it I disliked. I was afraid of the horses we had to ride; I didn't enjoy getting up in the cold at four in the morning, breaking the ice in the watering trough in the early dawn; I didn't want to spend all day on the trail getting my ass rubbed raw, freezing most of the time, then getting sunburned and eaten by bugs, before dragging back, dog-tired, at day's end. It was terrible. It was wonderful! These were some of the richest experiences I ever shared with my dad. I never complained or whined, because real men don't whine, and I wanted more than anything to be accepted as part of the clan.

Dad and his friends were looking to bag elk. Hunting for deer was beneath them; deer were for tourists and wimps (and children, like me). Elk were big and dangerous, a fitting prey for manly men, and besides, you got a lot more meat when you brought one down. And bringing one down was a big deal. For one thing, it meant that the hunt was probably over for the day, because you had to gut and haul the animal, sometimes in pieces, back to the curing house at the ranch. Elk are huge animals that easily weigh 500 pounds. It took several men to hoist one up in a tree using a block and tackle slung over a limb. The next step was to slit the animal's throat and let the blood drain, then cut open the body and remove the viscera. After cutting the skin at certain places, we'd peel it back to reveal the muscles and tendons. To call this "dressing" the animal struck me as odd, because what we were actually doing was undressing it. After that, the smaller carcasses could be loaded on a packhorse and carted back to the ranch. The bigger ones had to be cut in half and loaded on two horses—a grisly, bloody, smelly mess.

Back at the curing house, we'd hoist the dead creature on hooks, and there it would hang for up to two weeks. What was known as "curing" really amounted to rotting, but it did seem to tenderize the meat and improve its flavor. Uncured meat had a gamey taste that made it less appealing. Frankly, it always tasted pretty gamey to me, but I learned to like it at least enough to eat it. Once cured, the carcass went to Chapman's Storage Lockers, where it was cut into pieces with band saws and other tools and stored. That was our meat for the winter. At home, we had elk steaks every Saturday night for the next six months whether we wanted them or not, and believe me, at the end of six months you didn't want them. What I would have done by then for a nice beef burger or a piece of fried chicken! Sometimes I'd complain that the meat was tough, and my father would respond with a standard retort: "It's a lot tougher when there isn't any!" Hard to argue with that.

I took part in the annual hunt for a few years, until I was 12 or 13. Terence had gone through the same initiation, but the two of us never had a chance to partake in that rite together. By the time I was old enough to go, Terence had lost interest or had already left for California, where he spent his last two years of high school.

The truth is I was no better at hunting than I was at fishing, so I never ended up killing anything. Or almost never. Which was fine by me. Despite the discomforts, I enjoyed riding horses all day through the aspen forests of the high country. At that time of the year, the aspens were putting on their brightest colors, blinding yellows and oranges in great swaths as far as the eye could see. The air was crisp and tangy, just cold enough so you could see your breath; the sky was a robin's-egg blue, as blue as it gets. The West Muddy was a beautiful place to be that time of year. Bagging an elk or deer, fulfilling the mission to actually kill something, seemed like an afterthought.

Eventually, on what must have been my third or fourth trip, I did succeed in killing my first and only deer, a nice-looking four-point buck. I was with Dad when I spotted it in a little glen down the ridge, standing in a cluster of aspen trees 60 or 70 yards away. Dad spotted it at the same time. He instructed me to get off the horse quietly, crouch down, and take my time aiming. By the time I had, the thing had disappeared before my eyes, as if it had melted back into the trees. But I went ahead and took aim at the spot where it had been a moment before. I squeezed off a shot, more or less blindly. And as blind luck would have it, the deer had not moved; my aim was true. It was a clean shot to the neck, and the thing flopped down.

Leading our horses, we walked slowly down the ridge to where the animal lay, still breathing but obviously near death. Dad unsheathed his hunting knife, walked up, and slit its throat to end its suffering. I felt no joy at witnessing this, no sense of triumph, no sense of pride. At that moment, I didn't feel anything like a manly man. I felt like a murderer. I had killed something beautiful and wild and free. But I could not show this emotion to my Dad or to the other men who by then were approaching. I bit my lip to keep from crying, pulled myself together, and began the grim task of skinning the creature I had slain.

That was the last time I went hunting with our father on the West

Muddy. I had undergone the rite of passage. I was now officially a member of the clan, a manly man among manly men. And that was enough. I have to admit I felt a touch of pride, though not for a killing a deer—I felt only nauseated and weak-kneed about that. No, the pride was in knowing that I had made my father proud. Together we had shown his peers, now my peers, that I wasn't just some geeky weirdo four-eyed gawky kid. I could be a brute with the best of them. In that weird, twisted, uniquely male world where killing something is seen as a good thing, I had risen to the occasion. The values of the clan were again affirmed.

9 Goodbye to All That

Terence and Dennis dressed for church, 1959.

So this was the picture of our family life at the end of the 1950s, pulled from memory like a faded snapshot from those innocent years. For me, it evokes the breathless moment of eerie calm that settles over the landscape before a summer thunderstorm: nothing is happening, yet the air is charged with anticipation. There was a foreboding intuition that the old order, the old certainties, would soon be swept away. Despite an apparent calm, social forces beyond anyone's control were massing on the horizon, ready to rip the idyllic Norman Rockwell fantasy to shreds. Indeed, everything we thought we knew, everything we thought we were, would soon be transfigured by the winds of change.

Like most Americans, my brother and I had little sense of what forms this change would take. But the signs were there, discernible at least to a few astute observers. With respect to psychedelics and their impacts—both on us personally and on the wider culture—there were only hints. Although the effects of LSD had been known since the Swiss chemist Albert Hofmann accidentally exposed himself to the drug in 1943, five years after he'd discovered it at Sandoz, it remained a curiosity, the plaything of a few psychologists, writers, artists, and covert researchers at the CIA. In 1953, William Burroughs, the literary icon of the Beat generation, had wandered the Putumayo region of the upper Amazon looking for ayahuasca; his correspondence with the poet Allen Ginsberg on the topic became a book, *The Yage Letters*, a decade later. That journey prefigured our own quixotic quest to the area in the early 1970s. Though Burroughs was often out front when it came to drugs, ayahuasca was already old news by the time he went looking for it, at least to Richard Evans Schultes, the Harvard ethnobotanist who had been documenting the region's plants and their pharmacological properties since 1941. Aldous Huxley's classic 1954 essay on his experience with mescaline, *The Doors of Perception*, stirred interest and criticism, though largely at first among philosophers and theologians. Timothy Leary's fateful encounter with magic mushrooms at a resort in Cuernavaca, Mexico, in August 1960 radically altered the direction of his life, but his name was not widely known until the scandal that led to his dismissal from Harvard in 1963.

In the McKenna household and surely many others, there was one outstanding exception to this blackout: R. Gordon Wasson's report on his rediscovery of the long-suppressed tradition of shamanic mushroom use among the Mazatecs of Mexico, published in *Life* magazine on May 13, 1957. With its millions of subscribers, *Life* was the epitome of the era's glossy photo magazine—and the unlikely portal through which awareness of the magic mushrooms and the strange realms they rendered accessible filtered into mass consciousness. It was a rather stealthy debut; there was no pejorative spin to the story, no cautionary warnings about the dangers of drug abuse, the risk of insanity, leaping out of buildings, or chromosome damage. All that came later and in any event was mostly aimed at psilocybin's more potent, scarier cousin, LSD—itself the subject of a *Life* cover story in March 1966. No, the 1957 piece was presented as a gee-whiz travelogue in the best *National Geographic* style. The intrepid explorers were on a fearless quest to be "the first white men in recorded history to eat the divine mushrooms." A New York banker turned ethnobotanist accompanied by a society photographer friend, Wasson summed up their first ritual succinctly: "We chewed and swallowed these acrid mushrooms, saw visions, and emerged from the experience awestruck." A day later, Wasson introduced his wife and daughter to the remarkable fungi, with the same results. Along with Allan Richardson's photos, the article was accompanied by stunning watercolor paintings by the mycologist Roger Heim of the seven types of psychoactive mushrooms that were then known. (Today the count is close to 200.) Most readers probably overlooked the article, but the magazine's wide circulation ensured an audience amounting to hundreds of thousands.

Among those intrigued was Albert Hofmann, who soon afterward isolated the psychoactive molecule in the fungi—psilocybin. Directly or indirectly, Wasson's account jettisoned Leary out of a mainstream academic career and into a new role of bringing psychedelics to the masses. Terence and I were influenced as well, though I must admit the article was of more interest to him than to me; I was only six. Terence was 10 and curious about everything—and because he was curious, I was curious, without really knowing what the piece was about. I do remember him trailing our mother as she did her housework, waving the magazine, demanding to know more. But of course she had nothing to add. Terence's curiosity would linger, even if at the time he had no intimation of how important psychedelics, and especially mushrooms, would become for us in events still years away.

10 The Big Picture

Television, glorious television, found its way into our home around 1958. In many ways, its appearance marked the true end of the innocent era I've described, an era when local preoccupations were paramount. Like so many western towns, Paonia had its initial emblazoned on a nearby hill. If you looked out past the end of Main Street, there it was, an affirmation of local identity tied somehow to the high school football team. As the only point high enough to receive the signal from stations in Grand Junction and Montrose, that hill, known as the P, was destined to have a role in plugging us into the Global Village. So were Joe and George Abseck of A&M Electric. For better or worse, they took the initiative to set up and maintain the booster station atop the P that captured the broadcasts.

The picture was black and white, of course, and its quality was dismal, grainy and full of static. I know we got CBS and some other programs, but it would be a while before all the major networks reached us in full. Nevertheless, TV opened a window onto the wider culture, formerly accessible only through radio. We could watch *The Ed Sullivan Show*, *The Twilight Zone*, *Gunsmoke*, *Have Gun–Will Travel*, *Rawhide*, and *Sea Hunt*. Another favorite, *The Outer Limits*, arrived later. I remember the first televised presidential debate in the fall of 1960, when John F. Kennedy, the shining knight, vanquished Richard Nixon, with his five o'clock shadow and threatening frown. Three years later, we'd watch the somber pageantry of Kennedy's funeral cortege: the coffin on the caisson and the prancing black horse in the dreary November gloom, the whole country in mourning, stunned, wondering what the hell had gone wrong with America.

The Kennedy era began on a note of optimism. There was a feeling of welcome change in the air as the staid Eisenhower administration came to a close and a vibrant young president and his stylish wife moved into the White House with their two young children. The Cold War still loomed, as it had throughout the 1950s, and so did the threat of a spreading proxy war in Southeast Asia. But the general feeling was that the nation had entered an era of prosperity, innovation, and scientific advance.

Those years were marked by events and tensions that would shape American life for decades. In January 1961, Ike bid farewell with a famous speech that warned the country about the dangers posed by a growing military-industrial complex. A few days later, Kennedy gave his famous "Ask not" inaugural address, encouraging Americans to look beyond self-interest to what they could do for their country. Making good on a campaign promise, he started the Peace Corps in March. Just before he took office, the country had severed diplomatic ties with Castro's Cuba. The new president's first major blunder occurred in April at the Bay of Pigs, a failed Cuban invasion mounted by anti-Castro exiles with American help. In November, Kennedy made a second profound mistake, sending thousands of "advisors" to Vietnam. By year's end American helicopters were providing support for South Vietnamese troops. Declared or not, the Vietnam War, and the number of Americans fighting and dying there, would grow for years.

That wasn't the only action in 1961 with a long, lingering effect on the national psyche. A treaty known as the Single Convention on Narcotic Drugs was signed in March, codifying into international law a number of bad ideas that have plagued drug regulation ever since. In May, the civil rights movement entered a critical phase when the Freedom Riders, challenging racial segregation on a bus trip through the South, were assaulted by mobs in Alabama and later jailed in the Mississippi State Penitentiary, despite Supreme Court actions that should have protected them. In October, the Soviets detonated a 58-megaton hydrogen bomb in the Arctic Ocean—still the largest explosive device ever triggered. The United States continued to expand its arsenal of intercontinental ballistic missiles with the first test launch of a Minuteman I. Meanwhile, the country deployed numerous shorter-range missiles in Italy and Turkey, putting Moscow within range of a nuclear strike.

The Beatles began the string of appearances at Liverpool's Cavern Club that led to their global renown. The Rolling Stones formed a year later. On April 12, 1961, Soviet cosmonaut Yuri Gagarin became the first human to orbit the Earth, with Alan Shepard making the first American space flight—a short suborbital one—within a matter of weeks.

The space race had begun with the launch of the Soviet satellite Sputnik 1 in October 1957, but now it suddenly dominated the popular consciousness. If the Red Menace had pulled ahead at first, apparently endangering our cherished way of life, John Glenn's orbital mission in early 1962 made it feel like a dead heat. Satellite communications began, and one of two Mariner probes successfully sent back data from its flyby of Venus. Kennedy's agenda for his New Frontier would find its most potent symbol in his plan to land men on the moon. "We choose to go to the moon in this decade and do the other things," he declared in Houston in September 1962, "not because they are easy, but because they are hard." Within a month, the Cuban missile crisis became the world's first nuclear showdown, a confrontation averted when the Soviet leader Nikita Khrushchev agreed to remove those weapons, backing down from Kennedy's ultimatum.

For my family, these and other events amounted to the background murmur of our daily lives. At the time, neither Terence nor I paid much attention to the news. Our concerns were still personal and local. Though the arrival of television had a huge impact on us, by then we were already bookish geeks, firmly ensconced in the Gutenberg era and under no real threat of TV taking us over. Television was entertainment, distracting fluff. For us, real learning and knowledge would always come from books. The major exceptions to our disregard for current events were the space missions and the tense weeks of the missile crisis. By the time of Gagarin's historic flight, Terence and I were already steeped in the lore and excitement of space exploration, thanks to our father's interest in space and aviation, and to the pulp science fiction magazines he'd leave around the house for us to read, along with the occasional issue of *Popular Science* and *Scientific American*. He was a great believer in technology; like many in his generation, he envisioned a scientific utopia on the near horizon, powered by atomic energy and replete with space stations, robots, and flying cars. Computers and their transformative effects on society weren't yet on the radar for most, and wouldn't be for at least a decade. But thanks to science fiction, we lived in eager anticipation of such marvelous advances. In our imaginations, we were already well beyond the solar system, having long since left behind such mundane scenarios as orbital space stations and voyages to the moon. We were enthralled by the idea that mankind's unknown destiny lay far beyond this planet. Years before *Star Trek* mass-marketed our mix of optimism and yearning, we were certain that humans were bound to explore the trackless reaches of outer space and that we'd be among those who would go.

No wonder amateur rocketry was one of Terence's main pursuits as a boy. Though I participated in those exploits with him, amateur astronomy was my major preoccupation. I dreamed of someday becoming an astrophysicist and spent many a crystal clear winter night freezing my keister off in the city park, trying to adjust my Edmunds Scientific 4½-inch reflector telescope to the celestial coordinates needed to capture some nebula or galactic cluster. I never did really get the hang of that, but I managed to find, by lucky accident, an abundance of marvelous celestial objects. Cold or not, I was hooked. I still am, though now I do most of my sky surfing with an iPhone app. These days, you don't have to search; you just hook your telescope up to your laptop, dump in the coordinates, and it finds the object for you. Where's the fun in that?

I loved reading popular expositions of the latest cosmological ideas, like those written by George Gamow and Fred Hoyle, vocal proponents of, respectively, the Big Bang and steady-state theories. I always leaned toward Gamow, a Russian-born émigré, partly because he was a professor of astrophysics at the University of Colorado at Boulder, and I nurtured an ambition of one day studying under him. Another reason was that the steady-state theory seemed rather boring to me; I liked the idea that the universe began with a really, really big bang. I was quite serious about my studies. Besides reading the popular science literature on astronomy, space exploration, and related topics, I also delved into the technical side in the obsessive way I had of getting into things. Terence gave me a subscription to *Sky & Telescope* one year for my birthday, and I cherished it, reading every issue from cover to cover even though I understood only about half of it. One summer I resolved not only to read but to copy everything in the *Encyclopaedia Britannica* related to astronomy, cosmology, and astrophysics. Every afternoon I'd show up at the Paonia Public Library, notebook in hand, select a volume of the *Britannica*, and retire, monk-like, to a carrel in the upstairs reading room. I was quite content to spend those summer days transcribing various essays while my peers were playing outside. It didn't seem to harm me; in fact it was good training for future scholarly endeavors that required a lot of focus. But after that one intense summer, I realized the task was hopeless and pointless, and I gave it up.

From the beginning, Terence and I were both Big Picture people. We weren't sweating the details; we wanted the answers to the ultimate questions. This inclination partly explains our early interest in metaphysics and philosophy. We were dissatisfied with the pat and shallow answers proffered by our Catholic faith and with the priests who, with a few exceptions, responded angrily, or disingenuously, to our insistent questions. It became clear to us early on that Catholic dogma was pretty much a fairy story concocted to satisfy the incurious masses, and we were buying none of it. That skepticism became a motivation to look beyond the boundaries of our religious faith, as eventually we did.

On the practical level, though, the space race brought it all home, literally, into our living rooms through the new medium of television. Suddenly, the notion of space exploration was no longer confined to the pages of pulp sci-fi magazines or geek publications like *Popular Science*—the geek label itself, as currently understood, was another spin-off of 1950s sci-fi first used by the writer Robert Heinlein, though the term's popularity still lay decades ahead. Space exploration was real, it was happening, and you could watch it on TV. And you could do it with no less a luminary than CBS newscaster Walter Cronkite to narrate the adventure. Like Edward R. Murrow and Howard K. Smith, Cronkite belonged to a generation of old-school journalists who started out in print and radio and led the transition to television. Theirs was a respectable profession then; journalists were trusted to give us the straight story, and no one in the 1960s and '70s was more trusted than the fatherly Cronkite. He didn't soft-pedal the truth. The Kennedy assassination, the civil rights movement, the Vietnam War, Watergate—Cronkite calmly explained them, articulating the real-time history of a confusing and rapidly changing world.

But what captivated me was Cronkite's coverage of the space launches: first the timid suborbital flights of the Mercury astronauts, then the Gemini missions, followed by the climactic Apollo voyages—the trip around the moon and then the momentous landing of *Apollo 11* in July 1969. "Uncle Walter" was our witness through all of it, and never more so than during those early morning vigils in my living room when, in his company, I waited through yet another endless delay in the countdown due to some technical glitch or quirk in the weather. He always had a trove of technical details to share, his droning recitations of statistics and flight specs making the interminable holds tolerable, even interesting, for a bored and sleep-deprived youngster up at a brutally early hour. On those occasions I bonded to Walter, wanted if possible to *be* him someday. I often pictured myself as the fearless purveyor of truth, bravely resisting a jostling, angry crowd as I reported on the political unrest in some foreign hot spot. A lot of my peers have similar recollections of Cronkite, surely linked to our collective experience of monitoring those early launches. We believed in Cronkite then, like we believed in a lot of things that, with time, have grown to seem much less certain.

"And that's the way it is," he'd famously say after his evening newscast, and we had no reason to doubt him.

The early days of the space race were on my mind in July 2011 as I followed the successful launch and landing of the orbiter *Atlantis*. With that—the 135th and last flight of the space shuttle—another phase in the brief history of space exploration came to an end. The shuttle era had begun with the launch of the orbiter *Columbia* 30 years earlier, on April 12, 1981. That date was the 20th anniversary of Yuri Gagarin's flight in 1961, the first time a human had ever traveled beyond the planet's atmosphere. However short, Gagarin's journey was a feat of evolutionary significance. Though rarely discussed in such terms, it was the first time since life had left the oceans for land billions of years ago that DNA-bearing organisms had penetrated a new and alien environment. Many attempts to leave the sea had surely occurred and failed, but only one had to succeed for life to gain a permanent terrestrial foothold. The same may be true of our first halting steps into space.

Gagarin's flight is more often remembered for its geopolitical importance. The evil Russkies were about to beat us in space, it seemed, and at the technology game in general. In schools and on the launch pads, we had to respond posthaste if we wanted to save our cherished way of life from the Red Menace. The Soviet success pressed Kennedy to make his clarion call: America would put a man on the moon by the end of the decade. And so it came to pass. For a couple of decades, much of humanity dared to believe our future did lie amid the stars. That aspiration seems charmingly naive and innocent now, in this age of ever-diminishing global resources, looming environmental catastrophe, and flagging belief in our own capabilities, reflected in our diminished imagination about what the future can be.

With the end of the shuttle program, NASA seems to epitomize this uncertainty; indeed, some would say that it lost its guiding vision (and justification for existence) when the Apollo program ended in 1972. In this, the space agency is not unlike the rest of America. As a people and a country, America has lost its way; the future is no longer viewed as an uncharted vista, beckoning us with its promise of exploration and discovery, but as a prospect of dread, as something to be feared and delayed as long as possible. In the current political and social climate, denial of the future has become pervasive. Many political and cultural leaders now seek to return to some delusional golden age that never existed, some Reagan-era fantasy where it is again Morning in America. It is not going to happen, and it never has happened. America veered off course decades ago, though only now are we beginning to see the consequences of our lack of vision. The future is not only coming, it's already here. And I am concerned that we are facing it not as a challenge but as a threat.

Although Kennedy's challenge to America was inspiring and certainly stimulated much technological change, I can't shake a feeling it was fundamentally flawed. I believe it reflected a failure to understand the impact of imagination on the unfolding of history. Kennedy's vision appealed to a kind of chest-beating patriotic fervor about America and its greatness, but what were its practical benefits? We did go to the moon and back, repeating the trick several times. We also collected a lot of rocks and learned a lot about our technological limits. But beyond that, what did we gain? Certainly not the extraterrestrial foothold that many intuit to be the next step in human destiny.

In fact, we achieved nothing even close to that until three decades later, when the first piece of the International Space Station was launched in 1998. The ISS has garnered much less attention than the Apollo program. The space station may not be as inspiring or as sexy as the lunar program, but it is potentially far more significant. I have often wondered how different the 21st century might have been if Kennedy had given careful thought to the real goals of space exploration. What if he had called for a permanent manned space station instead of a lunar program whose consequences were pretty much limited to proving that, yes, 'Merica could do it? If Kennedy had made such an orbital base the country's goal, we now might be mining asteroids for the bulk of our water and minerals, generating all of the world's energy from solar-powered satellites, and maintaining bases on the moon, possibly on Mars, and even in orbit around the outer planets. Instead he chose machismo over substance, threw down a technological gauntlet to the Russians, and pushed the Cold War to further heights of hostility.

Hindsight, of course, is always sharper than foresight. But our lack of clarity in understanding the significance of space exploration, not only for humanity but for earthly life, represents one of those bifurcations in the time stream that will have serious consequences for the survival of our species and the larger biosphere. My fear is that we've reached that fork and taken the wrong branch. As a result, the future before us is not one of colonizing the solar system and eventually spreading earthly life throughout the galaxy. Instead, what we confront is an era of dwindling resources, ever more repressive political systems, the rising hegemony of know-nothing fundamentalism, and the accelerating contamination of our planet as we lurch toward a tipping point that could destabilize the homeostatic feedback mechanisms that have kept Earth hospitable to life for the last 3.9 billion years. Ironically, we face the prospect of drowning in our own waste even as many deny that what is piling up around us is waste.

I'm quite sure that the actions we take—or fail to take—over the next decade will be critical for the continued existence of earthly life. I also believe that in 50 years we'll look back and realize we made the wrong choices. We will have also failed to construct an escape hatch. I doubt this will mean an abrupt end to life here, although it could. But instead of remaining an island of life for millions of years, Earth will remain livable for at most a few centuries. We could still avert that fate if we woke up, but the chances of that look rather dismal. My fear is that it is too late to change course.

Fifty years of manned spaceflight is a tiny slice of time when we're considering evolutionary processes that have played out over eons. Whether we'll ever raft our species and other life forms beyond the planetary surface remains to be seen. Though our tentative efforts to date may not prevail, perhaps others will. As a Big Picture person, I find some consolation in the belief that our world is not the only place where this grand experiment is underway. Life surely permeates the cosmos, and though our pathetic steps may fall short, others elsewhere will someday succeed. Still, it's a cold comfort here on earth, particularly for those with children.

11 First Loves: 1962

In the fall of 1961, at age 10, I started fifth grade at Paonia Junior High School, leaving behind Paonia Elementary and its undemanding teachers. Some of them were the archetypal sweet old ladies, others were kind of scary, and a few were slightly nuts. I had a lasting tie to my first school through Mrs. Mordica, a beloved first-grade teacher who lived alone in a tiny house across the street from ours. Years after I had moved away, I would stop by and say hello to her on my holiday visits. By then I must have looked pretty scary myself with my thick beard and long hair. That didn't matter to Mrs. Mordica, who I always felt could see past appearance and judge us by our souls. One year I returned and learned that she'd passed on. I can hardly imagine all she must have witnessed in her life, and the knowledge that died with her.

In fifth grade I met a new set of teachers, but the old pattern held: some were good and some were not. I was still deeply into the Catholic religion at the time, but over the years ahead I'd learn there were different kinds of priests as well.

I was what some called a "good doggon," meaning a faithful Catholic who regularly goes to mass and confession. My father was a good doggon, too. Though not a Catholic at first, my mother eventually joined the church and always had the mindset. She even taught catechism; I was in her class. I was also an altar boy. Living a block or so from the church, I was regularly tapped to serve early morning mass on weekdays. I hated being rousted out of bed at 6:30 to get ready, especially on icy winter mornings. The only other people there were the two old women who maintained the sacristy, setting out the priest's vestments, the communion wafers, the ciborium, and the wine in preparation for mass. They seemed incredibly ancient to me, wrinkled and bent over, invariably wearing scarves, like the peasant women from Eastern Europe I'd seen pictured in the *Book of Knowledge*. I regarded them as just part of the furnishings, like the statues or the crucifix over the altar.

It was a small parish and the priests didn't have a lot to do, so at times I'd hang out with them on summer afternoons. Some were interesting, others forbidding. Some were probably also alcoholics, though that's a guess. The first priest I remember, Father McGrath, was by far the scariest. He was an Irishman who lived in the rectory with his elderly mother. Lacking any sense of humor, he had a rather dour outlook on life, and on little boys in particular. To him almost everything was a mortal sin, but especially masturbation and impure thoughts, as he often told me so in a rumbling, gravelly brogue like the voice of doom. "It is a *moooortal* sin, Dennis!" It never occurred to me that I might just discontinue the practice. Instead I learned to live with the guilt. I was relieved when Father McGrath got shipped off. I was still a horrible person, but at least he wasn't around to remind me of it. His replacement, Father Hickey, was also an Irishman, but a basically nice guy who didn't seem to think less of me when I confessed my various thought crimes. I had to wonder what he missed.

The Cuban missile crisis occurred at the height of my involvement with the priests and the church. The conflict began in mid-October 1962 when an American spy plane spotted new bases in Cuba being built for an arsenal of Soviet nuclear missiles. The Soviets must have felt justified in parking their weapons so near the American mainland after the United States had placed similar ones in Europe within striking distance of Moscow. The two-week confrontation pitted Kennedy, the young, untested president, against Nikita Khrushchev, the wily, experienced geopolitical strategist; it ended when both leaders agreed to a secret deal brokered by United Nations Secretary-General U Thant. In return for the Soviets dismantling their systems in Cuba, the Americans lifted their naval blockade, vowed not to invade Cuba, and secretly agreed to deactivate their missiles in Italy and Turkey.

During the 1950s, we'd grown used to living in the shadow of nuclear holocaust. Its apparent inevitability created an anxiety that permeated the culture, much as the threat of terrorism does today. Many families built bomb shelters in the backyard (though we never went that far) even as the nation became numb to the notion that the world teetered, perpetually, on the nuclear brink. The missile crisis made us realize, however, that mutually assured destruction could actually happen; pushed to the wall, our leaders might just be crazy enough to blow up the world. In my belief that the end could not be averted, I calmly prepared to die. I had accumulated quite a few sins and wanted to get my account cleared before I departed. Fortunately, the priest at the time was Father Hickey. When I showed up at the rectory and asked for confession he was happy to provide it, but he also tried to comfort me, saying that he didn't believe the two leaders would come to nuclear blows, and that if it came to that God himself would intervene to stop it. What else could he say? Then again, for all anyone knows, maybe God did.

Later came Father Dan, who at first seemed pretty cool. He actually had a degree in engineering and had worked on construction projects before becoming a priest. He was a big, bearish guy, and the altar boys loved him. It turned out he also loved the altar boys—a little too much. He took us on trips to explore the ghost towns around Telluride and swim in the hot springs at Ouray, where he gave us piggyback rides in the pool. He was known to ask inappropriate questions, prying for salacious details when we'd confess our struggles with the usual prepubescent temptations. Word of that got out among the young people, including some girls, and we came to realize that Father Dan was a little bit twisted.

My own encounter with him in this regard happened when I confided in him about my ticklishness. I wanted to overcome it because, as I've mentioned, Terence often used tickling to torture me. Father Dan suggested he could help. He took me down into the rectory basement and made me disrobe. Then he started touching me all over, assuring me that I could cure my ticklishness if I learned to relax. It wasn't much of a molestation; it was more like a massage. He didn't touch my genitals, but he saw enough to tell me that, yes, I was indeed circumcised. Was I traumatized by this treatment? Actually, I wasn't. I was so clueless about sexual matters that it never even occurred to me that I was being molested, though of course I was. And I trusted him completely. I was well into my 20s when, after hearing of reports of a sexual abuse scandal involving the church, I thought, So *that's* what was going on!

What is it about priests and pedophilia? Church officials would like to blame the trend on a few bad apples, but I think it's much more common than they'll ever admit. The idiotic celibacy rule undoubtedly contributes to the problem. Being a priest must be a very lonely job. They are expected to counsel people about their most intimate matters, including sexual matters, and yet with rare exceptions they have no experience with sex, relationships, family life, or any of that. I think it twists their personalities in many cases, but not all. I've known and learned from priests who never laid a hand on me—decent sorts like Father Hickey, and a few good conversationalists with sharp Jesuit minds. As always it comes down to the individual.

Nevertheless, I no longer have any use for the Catholic Church. It is corrupt through and through, as far as I can see, particularly regarding the abuse issue and the cover-ups associated with it. It makes me sick every time I see the pope making some pronouncement on sexuality, gays, abortion, birth control, priestly marriage, or "proper" moral conduct. To have a claim to moral authority, you have to be moral. As a nest of pedophiles, the church long ago sacrificed any legitimate claim to that. The sooner it collapses under the weight of its own rot, the better.

Partly because of these early influences and partly thanks to Terence, who despised Catholicism even more than I do, I've lost respect for virtually all organized religions. While they may have addressed the spiritual needs of people at some point in history, they are now largely political institutions that use their false authority and threats of eternal damnation to bludgeon people into conformity and silence. Who needs them?

Given the four-year gap between our births, Terence and I were never students together in the same school. In a town where the primary and secondary school systems were divided into four-year terms, I started junior high in 1961 just as Terence, then 14, moved on to high school. Being very much in Terence's shadow, I probably benefited from this separation, which gave me a chance to stand on my own among my peers. I'm not sure what would have happened otherwise. Terence might have been protective of me, his little brother, or he might have piled on with older kids to make my life harder. I certainly would have been viewed as "Terry McKenna's brother," but since no other student in PJHS had been in Terence's class, I had no reputation to defend. The teachers were a different story. With his exceptional intelligence and aggressiveness, Terence had been on their radar, and some surely had developed a dislike for him. Then again, others could see there was something special about him, despite how obnoxious he could be at times.

Quieter and more easygoing, I must have been a pleasant surprise to the teachers who had survived Terence. Though I was shy and well behaved, a kid who kept his light under a hat, some teachers discerned that I too was intelligent—and that I often judged myself in comparison to my more flamboyant brother. They encouraged me to be myself and not imitate Terence, and even today I remain grateful for their efforts to help me find my own path. One of them was Mrs. Campbell, from whom I took courses in both fifth and sixth grade. Mrs. Campbell and her husband, Cal, a science teacher, were really my first academic mentors. Mrs. Campbell had also taught Terence and may well have become fed up with him. Or so Terence believed, having often come home to report, "Mrs. Campbell despises me." She was kind to me, however, and we had a couple of heart-to-heart discussions whose drift was that I stop trying to be like Terence. This was easier said than done at a time when I still worshipped my big brother. I do think she helped me develop enough self-esteem to realize I was as smart as Terence, but different.

Fifth grade was also the year I became aware of my own sexuality, or rather, that such feelings could be directed toward other people. Until then, my erotic activities were solitary and sometimes aided by the "men's magazines" that my father occasionally brought home from his trips and hid (not very well) in his suitcase. At the time, my nascent sexual identity was ambiguous. I was definitely attracted to the opposite sex, but like many males I went through a phase where I wasn't sure whether I was drawn to my own gender or not. In fact, it took a few years and some "close encounters" before I understood that I was straight. Why even discuss this? Well, for one thing, I believe it's normal for boys to wonder about, and come to terms with, their sexual identities. Most Americans now accept that being homosexual is no cause for shame. Fifty years ago, however, it was still regarded as a deep, dark, scandalous secret to be concealed at all costs. I agree with most current informed opinion on child development that, with possible rare exceptions, one is born homosexual, or heterosexual, and that the main determinants are genetic. Homosexuality is an ingrained biological trait, not a choice, unlike what certain fundamentalist moralists would have us believe. That said, it is not unusual for the young to dabble in homosexual urges or even activity in that period before sexual identity has solidified.

I mention this in light of what may have been my first "love," though if so it was distinctly platonic. In a roundabout way, I can thank Mrs. Campbell for my encounter with Gerard as well. She was somehow related to a family from Chile who spent that year living with her. I'm not sure which if either of Gerard's parents was actually Chilean, let alone what led them to Paonia; I do know he was their only child. As fellow fifth graders we had some classes together, and I soon became completely obsessed. Gerard was the most exotic creature I'd ever seen. It was his foreignness that fascinated me—a boy from a faraway land, better educated, more polite, and more mature than my uncouth peers. He dressed well and spoke well. He had a very pale complexion and dark lashes. He might have grown up to be gay for all I know, but I saw no hint of this and would not have known what to look for anyway. He was to my mind the very paradigm of sophistication, and I aspired to be like him, if possible, since I could not actually be him. Though my attraction wasn't overtly sexual, at some subliminal level I suppose it was, even if such emotions never penetrated my conscious awareness. In fact, for much of his stay we had no relationship; I was much too shy. We eventually developed a tentative friendship, though I never let on how completely smitten I was. By the end of the school year, he and his parents were gone. We kept in touch for a while, our letters growing more infrequent until our correspondence faded away.

With the arrival of fall and the start of sixth grade, Gerard was all but forgotten in favor of other crushes, this time on those wonderful, exotic, and scary creatures—girls! Not that I had much luck or confidence with them. My next obsession was Liz, a lovely blonde. Her family had recently moved to Paonia and ended up in my grandfather's house, joining a series of tenants who had rented the place since his death a few years earlier. That she lived just a half block away only intensified my longing. I had a job at the time delivering the *Daily Sentinel*, published in Grand Junction and trucked up to Paonia every night. Dropping the paper at Liz's house was the highlight of my route. There was always the chance I'd see her hanging out on the porch swing. And when I did see her, in all her lissome, long-legged loveliness, it would keep me charged up for days. I could literally think of nothing else and lived in a perpetual state of unrequited longing. Besides being attracted, I was also terrified and had no idea how to convey what I felt. I invested great effort in pretending to be indifferent, fearing I'd say or do some foolish thing that would blow my cover. I don't know whether she was ever aware of how I felt. This was the first time I was head over heels in love, an intense state bordering on pathology. Though erotic obsession is by no means normal, it is a state that most of us long for. Indeed, I feel sorry for those who have never been overwhelmed by such desire, even though it is a kind of exquisite torture, especially if those emotions are not returned.

After the school year ended, Liz and her family moved away, leaving me heartbroken for about a week. It didn't take long before I found another girl to obsess over. My third debilitating crush also remained a secret, though a secret I kept less well. Rosalie, the daughter of a local coal miner, was a pretty brunette. She also happened to be Catholic, so I got the double charge of seeing her in school and in church. I'm sure she was a nice Catholic girl, which didn't stop me from routinely entertaining sexual fantasies about her while I was supposedly praying. I was no less terrified of Rosalie than of my earlier crushes, and I was too shy to say much beyond a few murmured pleasantries. To say more might have revealed what I was really thinking and wanting, or so I feared. But I couldn't forever keep those feelings to myself. I decided to write her an anonymous letter, which I did—and immediately regretted sending the moment I dropped it in the mail. I was mortified. Then I realized in my nervousness I'd forgotten to put a stamp on it. I'd been saved! I allowed myself to believe the letter never reached her. Thinking back on life in our small town, I now guess it probably did reach her, and that poor Rosalie was either too appalled or too kind to let on that it arrived. Or maybe she really didn't know who had sent it.

It's strange to think back on these ancient episodes of puppy love and the anxiety and guilt and longing and fear they caused in me. Being in love, at least at that age—on the cusp of puberty—was a kind of mental illness that rendered me dysfunctional for months. Outwardly I was fine. I did my homework, went to school, and behaved more or less normally. But in truth I was like a zombie, just going through the motions. My real life, my inner life, was preoccupied with the bittersweet contemplation of my beloved—bittersweet because the object of my desires knew nothing, and could know nothing, about feelings I was afraid to express. Later, of course, I'd have relationships that were more mature in that they led to actual connection and communication, even consummation, but they too could bring anxiety and frustration. I suppose all this is completely within the range of normality, and that almost everyone has similar experiences as they grow up. Not that crossing the threshold into adulthood makes it any easier. If anything, love only becomes more complicated and problematic. Being "in love" is an altered state, as much as or more than any state induced by a psychoactive drug. With its radical and prolonged shifts in hormone balances and neurotransmitter fluxes, reflected in behavioral and cognitive responses, the neurophysiology of love is a rich area for exploration, as neuroscience is discovering.

In a simpler sense, it's strange to think back upon those young, lovely girls and realize they're now nearing old age, as I am. What have they felt and experienced over the past decades, what grief and joy? It's hard to imagine. I hope that life has been kind to them. I wish all of them well, and thank them for what they meant to me, even if they never knew it.

12 The California Crusade

While I was discovering the joys and frustrations of unrequited love in the sixth grade, Terence was in 10th grade and already plotting his breakout. At some point the year before, he'd resolved to get out of stifling, conservative Paonia and finish high school in California while living with Aunt Tress and Uncle Ray. Since then, he'd spared no effort to convince our parents to let him go. Most people with such an agenda would have tried to be extra nice, to use charm and persuasion to bring their parents around to seeing the merits of the idea. This was not Terence's style. Instead, he amped up his usual steady drumbeat of obnoxious behavior, and why not? That had always worked before.

He single-mindedly pursued this campaign throughout his sophomore year. There was a new math teacher at the school whom I'll call RJ. RJ was an unconventional soul, or what was known as a beatnik back then, before the invention of hippies. He was a smart person, a bachelor, kind of pudgy, straight, harmless, perhaps lonely and insecure. But he'd read a lot of books and had many funny ideas—meaning liberal ideas. He did not fit into the red meat, gung-ho, sports-obsessed culture of Paonia High School any more than Terence did, and they immediately recognized each other as kindred spirits. Despite RJ's basic decency, our parents, especially my father, were quite suspicious of Terence's friendship with him. I don't know what his concern was beyond not wanting Terence to be exposed to his unconventional ideas. It was the non-intellectual's distrust of the egghead. RJ was also the art teacher, and he worked with Terence on various projects, like an eight-by-four-foot mural in the style of Jackson Pollock—"Looks like somebody spilled a bunch of paint and then rolled in it," grumbled our father— that Terence insisted on hanging in our bedroom.

Our parents' disapproval was a red flag for Terence, who spent as much time as possible with RJ as a convenient way of irritating them. The other prong in his offensive, the one that probably broke them, began when he started pursuing the daughter of the local librarian. She was a nice girl about two years older than Terence, but because of the age difference she might as well have been the Whore of Babylon as far as our father was concerned. He became convinced that Terence was going to "knock her up." This possibility was seen as the worst possible outcome, and it had to be thwarted. I doubt my brother and his friend ever had sex, as later events seemed to confirm, but I suspect Terence wanted our dad to think that they were. Today, more liberal parents might address such a situation by discussing condoms or birth control with their son. In our Catholic, sexually repressed family 50 years ago, the mere idea of birth control was a heresy that could not be raised in rational conversation. In those days, if you got a girl pregnant, you married her, and that effectively ended your life.

In the spring of 1963, in the middle of this campaign, Dad suffered his first and only heart attack. I suspect today it might be viewed as a mild one, but any heart attack then was considered serious, a brush with death. Dad spent a lot of time recuperating in bed, a common mode of treatment at the time. He also gave up the unfiltered Camels he'd been smoking since the war, which did not help his mood. You'd think if your father had just suffered a heart attack, perhaps caused in good measure by the stress of dealing with you, his recalcitrant son, you might ease up a little and cut the guy some slack. Yet, as I recall, Terence raised the pressure even higher. Finally our parents relented; Terence got their permission to go. In the end, I think, my mother was worried that if he stuck around, there was a good chance he'd upset my father enough to trigger another heart attack. Once again Terence got his way, as he always did, by pressing so hard they finally caved in.

That's how, in the fall of 1963, Terry ended up attending Awalt High School in Mountain View, California, with our cousin Kathi. (The school was renamed Mountain View High in the early 1980s.) He soon befriended a coterie of strange and interesting people, some of whom went on to play a role in both our lives. He also encountered an abundance of unconventional and even dangerous ideas. Meanwhile, Terence's departure meant enormous change for me at home. His habit of tormenting me had already diminished by then, partly because he'd found other interests and partly because I'd grown big enough to pose the risk I'd retaliate. Nevertheless, I was delighted to be suddenly free of all torture and to have my own room to boot! At the same time I was sad to see him go because he always had enough stuff going on to keep things interesting.

A seventh grader, I'd been left to my own devices, which included astronomy, cosmology, and astrophysics. I'd eventually abandon my ambitions in those fields as I grew to realize I couldn't cut the math, though looking back I think I could have succeeded if I'd stuck with it. What seemed then to be an insurmountable barrier was an early factor in directing my aspirations toward biology. I was also into classical music. I was a snob about pop music at the time. It took a year or so of Terence's influence on visits back from the West Coast to make me appreciate the virtues of rock and roll and folk music. My hero was the classical guitarist Andrés Segovia. At one point my parents let me take the bus alone to visit a friend whose family had moved to Phoenix the year before. Segovia was giving a concert at Arizona State University, and seeing him in person was a highlight of my young life. I wanted to be either the world's next best classical guitar player or a conductor like Leonard Bernstein. As director of the New York Philharmonic, Bernstein hosted a series of television specials, called the Young People's Concerts, that I loved. I was all over those broadcasts as much as any space shot.

Though life was better at home, my relationships at school were deteriorating. I never had a lot of friends in junior high; I suppose I was too weird for many of my peers, or too nerdy as we'd say now. I was a bookish fellow with eclectic interests that few of my fellow students shared. And that was fine with me. I had plenty to keep me occupied and didn't feel the need of a large social group. I had a few close friends who either tolerated my eccentricities or were eccentric as well.

But for a while that year, a certain group of boys took it upon themselves to single me out for bullying. Most I considered meatheads. The exception was Richard, one of my closest friends, so his involvement was all the more hurtful and confusing. Like the others, he was a year ahead of me. He sometimes tried to defend me or persuade the others to leave me alone, but just as often he joined in the taunting, which developed into a daily occurrence and quickly became intolerable. Richard may have been insecure about his status—although why was a mystery to me, as he was admired as an athlete and was attractive to girls. In any case, I think he felt compelled to participate in the bullying as a way to demonstrate solidarity with his peers, and for that I don't blame him. Seventh grade seems to be a critical time in childhood when acceptance by the group becomes particularly important, and if acceptance requires one to display loyalty to the "gang" by ostracizing another, so be it.

This went on for weeks. It was my custom to walk the few blocks home for lunch, returning to school half an hour before the noon break ended. And there they'd be, waiting. I hardly remember what if anything the harassment was about beyond snide remarks about my sexuality, allusions that I was "queer" even though I clearly wasn't, snatching my glasses, hitting, poking, pulling on my clothes, silly things like that. Without really knowing what I was doing, except that the harassment had to be stopped, I did bring it all to an abrupt end one day. A kid named Sheldon often led the proceedings. My tormentors usually greeted me when I returned, forming a kind of gauntlet I'd have to run up the front steps into the building. While they seldom pursued me beyond that point, this time Sheldon blocked my path, standing on the top steps in front of the double doors with their large plate glass windows. Though I was cornered, by then I'd had enough. I gave Sheldon a push, a rather gentle push, actually, but he lost his balance and staggered back. I saw the cracks appear in the glass around a Sheldon-shaped impression as the heavy glass shattered and he fell through. There was a moment of stunned silence. Imagine the tableau: Sheldon on his back amid a pile of shattered glass, me standing over him shaking with rage, the others paralyzed at the foot of the stairs, appalled at what had happened. The freeze-frame lasted only a second; time started to flow again as I turned toward them and screamed, "Just leave me alone, all I want is to be left alone!" Or something lame like that.

Before we knew it we were all sitting in the office of the school principal. Mr. Etherton was a cool guy, actually, well liked and rather easygoing. Though he had known about the bullying for some time, he'd made no effort to intervene. This was his chance. Things were quickly sorted out, blame was laid (on all of us, including me), and justice dispensed: all parties had to avoid each other, and all had to chip in to repair the window. The first condition worked; the harassment ended. As for the second, I was never asked to help pay for the window, nor were my tormentors, as far as I know.

Ironically, some of these older guys became my best friends in high school. By then the hippie meme had arrived, and suddenly I was cool, having gotten my hands on some cannabis and turned them on. Strong friendships were forged on our mutual interest in novel and prohibited intoxicants. While a few of those bonds have persisted to this day, over the years some of us drifted apart, and some have passed away. As for my nemesis, Sheldon, he wasn't part of that group, but we left each other alone. He wanted to be a lawyer, if I recall. I don't know if he achieved his ambitions, but I think he would have made a great prosecutor.

I can't conclude my remembrance of seventh grade without mentioning Madeline. She was a special friend of a quite different order than the other girls I longed for and lusted over at that age. Though she was perhaps more beautiful than they were, and certainly smarter, our relationship remained platonic, except for one abortive effort during my first summer back from the University of Colorado in Boulder. We both realized then that an amorous relationship was not to be our fate, though at times I've regretted that. In many ways we were soul mates. What we shared was a love of books and ideas, and that gave us plenty to talk about, even as it separated us from most of our peers. We were "extra-environmental," a term coined by the media theorist Marshall McLuhan to describe someone who is in a culture but not of it, like an anthropologist living with some exotic tribe. Both introverts, we came to see ourselves as kindred spirits trapped in a milieu of meatheads, jocks, and mean girls. We weren't part of the cool cliques and didn't care; we took pride in our extra-environmental status and cultivated a bemused detachment from the games that shaped the social dynamics among our peers. Sexual attraction didn't come into it, and I really don't know why.

But I thank my lucky stars for Madeline. Our friendship made school life almost tolerable. She belonged to the little band of rebels that coalesced around me in high school, whose main preoccupation was the exploration of altered states of consciousness accessed through various pharmacological portals. The two of us remained close throughout high school and beyond, until we lost touch in the 1970s. I know she moved away; I may have heard that she'd married a teacher, or perhaps had become a teacher herself. I haven't seen her in many years, but she lives on, fondly, in memory.

The biggest trauma that school year occurred far from school. Kennedy's assassination on November 22, 1963, exploded onto the global stage, throwing the country into a paroxysm of shock and horror. Though Terence was in California, both he and I were similarly affected, as a letter to me revealed. How could this vibrant, handsome president who symbolized hope and progress for so many, including us, be gunned down by a madman with a cheap mail-order rifle? It was too much. Such a thing could not happen in a sane and rational world, only in a world under the sway of dark and sinister forces. Or at least that's how we felt. America's age of innocence was over, and in many ways, so was ours.

Along with the rest of the country, we did little in the following days except stare at the television as the grim spectacle unfolded: Oswald, the alleged assassin, shot as he was led from his cell in Dallas; Kennedy's body lying in state in the Capitol rotunda as the silent crowds shuffled past; the funeral cortege, the riderless horse, the burial at Arlington National Cemetery; all the futile pomp and effort to bind the wound where a country's heart had been ripped out. It's been said that the idealism of a generation died with Kennedy, but the America that shaped our idealism may have died as well. As I look back, it appears increasingly certain that none of what was lost then will ever be recovered—not our hope, our optimism, or our direction. Though the country's fortunes have since gone through many apparent ups and downs, in retrospect that half-century looks more like a steady devolution, an unraveling, as we spiral inevitably toward some unknown outcome. A country cannot foresee its fate in world history, of course, but it's gotten harder for me to envision ours with a happy ending.

Many people have remarked that they sense time is somehow accelerating, or that more and more events are being crammed into less and less time. That was certainly how it felt as the dark days of late 1963 gave way to a new year. The rhythm of current events seemed to be picking up, and so did the pace of personal events. The latter may have been an illusion, or just a matter of being older with more to do, but nonetheless over the next few years our own lives felt as if they were moving ever faster.

In January 1964, President Lyndon Johnson used his first State of the Union address to announce his War on Poverty. In February, the Beatles arrived for their inaugural US tour and dominated pop radio with a string of hits. Spring brought the first Rolling Stones album, the first student protests against the Vietnam War, and the first draft card burnings. In July, Johnson signed the Civil Rights Act of 1964, outlawing segregation, and Barry Goldwater, the Republican presidential nominee, famously stated, "Extremism in the defense of liberty is no vice." In August, Congress passed the Tonkin Gulf Resolution, which allowed the president to wage war in Southeast Asia without having that war actually declared. By year's end, American troops in South Vietnam numbered 23,300. Johnson beat Goldwater in the November elections, Martin Luther King Jr. won the Nobel Peace Prize, and comedian Lenny Bruce was sentenced to four months in the workhouse for using offensive language at a New York club.

A wider debate over what could and could not be said in public had erupted that fall at the University of California, Berkeley. Known as the Free Speech Movement, or FSM, it began in September when UC officials decided to enforce a long-ignored rule against leafleting and recruiting for various off-campus political concerns on university property. Civil rights and the war were two such concerns, but the ban curtailed conservative activities as well. A series of rallies ensued, including a massive sit-in that led to the arrest of hundreds. Terence, then a high school senior, closely followed those events in Berkeley, which later had a profound if indirect affect on him—and on me as well.

In what might be termed "drug news" of the day, in 1964 Congress recognized bourbon whiskey (our father's drug of choice, though he never acknowledged it was a drug) as "a distinctive product of the United States." The Catholic church condemned the female contraceptive pill. The novelist Ken Kesey embarked on the decade's strangest book tour, aboard a painted bus with his fellow Merry Pranksters, a trip later recounted by Tom Wolfe in *The Electric Kool-Aid Acid Test*. Timothy Leary, Ralph Metzner, and Richard Alpert published *The Psychedelic Experience*, a tripper's guide loosely based on *The Tibetan Book of the Dead*. Bob Dylan turned the Beatles on to cannabis.

By then, drugs were just beginning to seep into our personal sphere. At Awalt High in Mountain View, Terence had met some of the friends who figured so importantly during his Berkeley years and beyond, who may have introduced him to marijuana as Bob had the Fab Four. But drugs had not become a major preoccupation for either of us. My involvement with drugs at the time was nil, and my interest even less. We were shown "drug education" films in school assemblies like *Reefer Madness*, which even then were three decades out of date. While that film is now viewed largely as a spoof, we were expected to take it seriously, and we did. The scare tactic worked. I couldn't imagine any reason why I would ever smoke that evil weed, ever. Not that it was an option; as far as I knew, there was no marijuana to be had within a hundred miles, although there were probably a few beatniks and bohemians in Aspen who were smoking it. In my universe, marijuana did not exist.

In the spring of 1964, my guess is Terence was far more concerned with sex than drugs. Getting laid, I think, was one of life's milestones he was determined to put behind him. Predictably, there was a scandal, the details of which remain sketchy to me. According to my aunt, a sixth-grade teacher at the time, one of Terence's female classmates was a former student of hers.

That young woman's mother, who I'll call Mrs. Z, apparently had a taste for inexperienced teenagers, and it didn't take long before Terence got on her radar. There were a number of parties and encounters that spring, according to my aunt. She and my uncle frowned on this, perhaps having prior knowledge of the woman's proclivities. At any rate they forbade Terence to see her, but of course he ignored them and continued going over to her house. The deed must have occurred at one of these clandestine meetings because, as my aunt later related, Terence came home one night in an agitated state, perhaps intoxicated, and took several showers in a row. This suggests to me that perhaps the union had been consummated, and the emotional impact was more than he'd bargained for.

A huge fight ensued. According to my aunt, my brother's defiant act was the last straw in a series of conflicts with his temporary guardians. Since the school year was all but over, they announced they'd had enough: Terence would not be welcomed back in the fall for his senior year. My aunt and uncle drove him home to Paonia when they returned for their summer stay at Chair Mountain Ranch. Terence was quite agitated the entire trip; harsh and hurtful words were exchanged by both sides. As if that wasn't bad enough, Mrs. Z, the seductress, also drove to Paonia to "rescue" Terence, possibly by taking him to California or absconding with him elsewhere. I don't know how all this finally ended, except that Terence never did return to Awalt High. In fact, there must have been a concerted effort to protect me from this melodrama, because I was barely cognizant of it then and only learned about it when I interviewed my aunt for this book. I did know, however, that the episode, whatever it was, created a rift between Terence and my aunt and uncle that was never resolved. Terence deleted them from his universe. His reaction was much like that toward our father after Terence was caught doing something naughty in the sandbox and was beaten at age three or four. Before and after the falling out with Tress and Ray, forgiveness was not apparent in Terence's nature.

It is a pity, really, because it meant he slammed the door on an entire segment of our family—including the cousins we'd grown up with during those long summers on the ranch. My aunt and uncle made several attempts to reestablish ties with Terence, but their efforts were rebuffed. In fact, the next time he had contact with our aunt was in the spring of 2000, only days before he passed on. In those final, heart-wrenching days, he was paralyzed, unable to speak. I was with him at the time. In what may have been a misguided attempt to bring some healing, I called my aunt and held the phone to Terence's ear. I don't know what was said, or if it comforted Terence or not. I hope it did. In this awkward situation I was trying, clumsily perhaps, to heal a rift that should have been healed decades earlier, and this wasn't the first time I'd made such an effort. In my role as Little Brother, I often found myself reluctantly trying to clean up messes resulting from Terence's conflicts with our parents. From what I could tell, once you got on his shit list, you stayed there; there was no going back. This dynamic was a constant throughout Terence's life and, in my opinion, negatively affected his relationships with many people, including our parents and many of his lovers and friends.

As I have said, Terence seemed not to have an empathetic bone in his body, and yet that capacity was there somewhere. Although he seemed to have cut himself off emotionally from our parents, I later realized he still loved them. I saw that in the spring of 1964 when we learned our mother had breast cancer. Treatments were crude in those days, as they are still, and such a diagnosis was tantamount to a death sentence. The doctors performed a mastectomy and started radiation treatments. We were told there was a 50-50 chance the cancer would go into remission. If so, and if the cancer did not recur for at least five years, that would be interpreted to mean she was cancer free. When we got this news, five years seemed like an eternity, an abstraction that paled beside the shock of realizing our mom might die within months. I was "lucky," if you can call it that; I was still at home to give her daily support and comfort (though whether I rose to that challenge as I should have I can't recall). For Terence, in California, the impact of the news was less immediate, but his reaction surprised me. He undertook to send our mother a postcard every day until he returned that summer. The cards said nothing of importance; they were general expressions of encouragement and love. But when they began to arrive every day, it was very moving, and I think it helped our mother immensely just to know her eldest son cared enough to write. It helped her to realize that this headstrong, rebellious teenager who had done so much to hurt her over the years still loved her and chose to express it in this way. I was impressed as well.

The summer following the Mrs. Z affair was tense around our house. In letting Terence attend school in California, our parents had trusted him to act responsibly, a trust he had breached. They would have been justified in telling Terence he'd now have to finish high school in Paonia, but they didn't do that. Terence continued to press for some other outcome. Common sense might have led him to be a little conciliatory, but he remained confrontational. Finally our father relented, again, and persuaded his old war buddy Truman to "take Terence on" for his last year of high school. Truman and his wife, Iris, lived in Lancaster, California, a community near Edwards Air Force Base about 70 miles north of Los Angeles. Truman had been a pilot in the war and still had close connections to the military, working in some capacity on the nearby base, if I recall. My father might have thought that a few months with a military man might be good for Terence. In fact, if the goal was to reform Terence or "make a man out of him," so to speak, perhaps it was already too late for that.

Terence spent his senior year at Antelope Valley High in Lancaster, a school whose graduates included the musicians Frank Zappa and Don Van Vliet, better known as Captain Beefheart. His tenure there had its moments, but it wasn't as bad as the year before at Awalt, at least from our parents' perspective. By then Terence had rejected all adult authority, including the kind that came from family members or family friends like Truman and Iris. They were all impossibly lame and irrelevant in Terence's view. It was Terence against the world; adults and authority figures were the enemy. J. D. Salinger's *The Catcher in the Rye* and Ayn Rand's manifestos influenced Terence's thinking heavily at the time. They validated, for him, his anti-authoritarian stance as well as his belief that it was perfectly OK to be totally selfish. In this respect, he wasn't the first headstrong 17-year-old to feel this way. In the zeitgeist of the day, rejection of authority, particularly parental authority, was what you did.

13 The Experimental College: 1965

I've already admitted that when Terence first left Paonia I was happy to see him go. I enjoyed my new status as an only child, feeling it might lead to more attention from our parents. But it wasn't long before I started to miss my brother, the first sign of how our relationship would change. Over the next few years, Terence ceased to be the resident tormentor-in-chief; instead he became my absent mentor. And I was less the little brother to be alternately ignored and harassed than a colleague and intellectual equal.

In California, he met others every bit as out there as he was, an interesting bunch who presented new opportunities for mischief and outrage but also for intellectual stimulation and growth. I had a chance to meet some of them on their summer visits, and a few became important influences for me as well. Terence and I discussed many of his newfound "funny ideas" in our occasional correspondence and on his visits. Some of our common interests existed before he'd left, others we explored together after he'd been exposed to them and passed them on. By then he'd realized, to his surprise, that I had my own intellectual chops. I grew to look forward to his returns, knowing we'd engage in hours of engrossing conversation on topics utterly foreign to almost all my peers. There was a certain smug satisfaction in knowing that we "knew stuff" no one else knew we knew.

When Terence arrived at the University of California, Berkeley, for the fall semester in 1965, he was still in full rebellion against those "authoritarian oppressors" who embodied everything he condemned. While he often lumped our parents in that group, he was happy to let them pay for his college education—an ethical dissonance that infuriated him when reminded of it, as my father made a point of doing on Terence's Christmas visit. I recall those confrontations as quite uncomfortable. Terence would accuse my parents of being fascists, a word that was often brandished thoughtlessly in those days, and in their case, unjustifiably. Our father never supported the war in Vietnam and was never fooled by government doublespeak. Given that he'd risked his life to fight real fascism in World War II, my brother's accusation struck me as offensive and unnecessary but not surprising. Terence was always and ever the master of the provocative statement, as those familiar with his work are well aware. He frequently said outrageous things just to get a response. Whether there was any truth to his claims hardly mattered.

But thanks to our parents' tolerance, and our father's checkbook, which remained open despite the insults and invective, Terence's wish to begin his academic career at Berkeley had come true. As far he was concerned, he'd reached the Promised Land. Berkeley—or "Berzerkeley" as it was sometimes called in those heady times—had a longstanding reputation as a hotbed of radical ideas and social change. During the 1950s, the University of California made its employees take an anticommunist loyalty oath, leading to charges of McCarthyism. Not only was Berkeley the epicenter of the protest movement and the burgeoning counterculture, both of which Terence threw himself into, but also this time, for the first time, he'd escaped all adult supervision. Many of his high school friends from Mountain View and Lancaster were fellow students at Berkeley; others migrated there just to be where the action was. The transition thus did little to disrupt his previous circle, which soon encompassed a broader set of intelligent, interesting, wild-eyed characters. The staid conventions of the 1950s were under full assault, and we all wanted to help bring down the old order and usher in the new—though we had little idea what the new would look like.

The pressing issues of the day were Vietnam and civil rights. In early March 1965, some 3,500 Marines had been sent to defend the American airbase in Da Nang, becoming the first combat forces to arrive in Vietnam. On March 7, Alabama state troopers violently blocked a peaceful crowd of 600 as it left Selma on foot for Montgomery, a turning point in the civil rights movement remembered as Bloody Sunday. Two weeks later, Martin Luther King Jr. tried again, leading another march that reached its destination. In September, a reporter for the *San Francisco Examiner*, in a story on life in the Haight-Ashbury district, became one of the first to use the term "hippie" in print.

Writing in *The Nation*, Hunter S. Thompson examined Berkeley's "nonstudent left," that is, the growing numbers who were part of the local scene but not officially taking classes. In the wake of the Free Speech Movement, California had passed a law that was supposed to keep outsiders from disrupting university affairs, but the forces of change were everywhere. Draft card burnings and Vietnam protests continued to grow in Berkeley and beyond, and many of the bands that generated the sounds of the psychedelic 1960s had just been formed: The Grateful Dead, Jefferson Airplane, Velvet Underground, The Doors, Pink Floyd. By year's end, Ken Kesey and company had begun staging the first LSD-driven "Acid Tests" in the Bay Area. Timothy Leary's prominence culminated in a bust for marijuana possession in December as he tried to reenter the country from Mexico.

The Free Speech Movement is worth a closer look, in light of its impact on Terence. As described earlier, the FSM coalesced in the fall of 1964 after university officials tried to curtail certain forms of political activity on campus. In the first protest, a crowd surrounded a police car outside the administration building, Sproul Hall, and trapped it there for more than a day. The protesters, led by students Mario Savio, Bettina Aptheker, and others, insisted the school was infringing on their right to political expression and assembly. Some were also demanding academic reforms at an institution less committed to educating students, they said, than producing parts for a social machine shaped more and more by corporate interests. Events went critical in December when 2,000 students occupied Sproul Hall after officials said they intended to punish four FSM organizers for their part in the disturbance two months earlier. Some time after midnight, Alameda County Deputy District Attorney Edwin Meese III (later California governor Ronald Reagan's chief of staff, and later yet President Reagan's attorney general) ordered the mass arrests of "the 800" as they were known, though the actual count was slightly less. A strike ensued, halting campus activity for a couple of days. In fact, the FSM's demands were quite reasonable, and in early 1965 the university agreed to most of them, lifting the rules against political activity on campus.

By the time Terence began classes, the FSM had all but ended, its immediate goals mostly realized. Campus activists had turned to reorganizing student government, forming a teaching assistants' union and investigating the ties between academia, corporations, and the military that had become an issue the year before. Many had turned their efforts against the Vietnam War. The historical and cultural fallout from the FSM would linger for decades. The movement remains a kind of model for student protest that is still emulated on campuses today. And the steps of Sproul Hall are still a site for political harangues, a street theater stage for every social movement from the far left to the far right and everything in between. It's democracy in action, the way it's supposed to work. A speech is now given every year in memory of Mario Savio, the most visible FSM leader, who died in 1996. His speeches in 1964 were crucial to defining the movement's goals and galvanizing support for them among students and the faculty. The role of Twitter and Facebook during the Arab Spring, the Occupy Wall Street movement, and other events in 2011 suggest the power of social media as a tool for democratic reform—but only as a tool. As for the retreat of many other causes largely into cyberspace, I doubt that's to their benefit. The resulting lack of visibility removes them from the radar and affords the so-called mainstream media a perfect excuse to minimize and marginalize their coverage.

Mainstream attention can have a downside as well, of course. Long after most of the FSM's issues were resolved on campus, the inevitable backlash helped Ronald Reagan get elected as California's governor in 1966, on his promise to "clean up the mess in Berkeley." Clark Kerr, president of the UC system, was forced from office in 1967 for allegedly being too soft on the protesters. A similar impact rippled out through the larger culture. While the ideals extolled by the Free Speech Movement continued to spread, so did a reaction against the widespread flouting of conventional mores that appeared to accompany them. The sexual and psychedelic revolutions, along with the strange music and exotic fashions that the young had adopted, all provoked a hostile response from the more rigid members of society, who convinced themselves that the very foundations of civilization were under threat.

The FSM marked the historical genesis of what we now call the culture wars, the split between the country's social conservatives and its liberals. The lines in the sand have been drawn for decades, and indeed have deepened into trenches from which activists on both sides lob their rhetorical salvos. Freedom of speech is alive and well in this country, thanks partly to the FSM; unfortunately, the spread of free speech doesn't appear to be accompanied by a concomitant increase in thoughtful listening (or thought of any kind), with the result that political discourse has largely degenerated into a screaming match between ideologues.

That historical shockwave, and the polarization it triggered, were relatively new when Terence arrived in Berkeley, fired up with rebellion, aflame with new ideas, and surrounded by peculiar yet fascinating friends. As I said, he'd been reading Ayn Rand, who ironically is now emblematic of a certain brand of right-wing intellectualism inspired by her me-first-and-everyone-else-be-damned philosophy. Indeed, as a college freshman Terence was very much caught up in the exercise of his own freedoms. I dare say he was also influenced by whatever drugs he'd gotten his hands on by then. (There were rumors of some kind of scandal involving either morning glory seeds or nutmeg during his senior year in Lancaster, but I was never told the details.) In Berkeley, pot and LSD were easily had, Leary was urging the young to turn on, and there was a great deal of ferment and curiosity about psychedelics, fed by the Acid Tests and other "happenings," not to mention the live accompaniment provided by San Francisco's trippy bands.

Terence was spared a probable fate of being enlisted into some cause or movement by sheer good luck. Of the 27,000 students at UC Berkeley at the time, he was one of 150 incoming freshmen admitted that year into the new Experimental College Program. Though plans for the program began before the Free Speech Movement, many later mistook it for a response, given its intent to personalize the learning experience at a huge school where students, especially new ones, could easily feel alone and alienated.

Founded by Joseph Tussman, the chairman of the philosophy department, the experimental college operated as a kind of university within the university. The approach was modeled on a similar experiment established in the 1920s by Alexander Meiklejohn, a thinker and free-speech advocate at the University of Wisconsin–Madison, where Tussman had been a student. Tussman's program focused on big questions and the periods of historical crisis that had catalyzed fundamental shifts in worldviews going back to ancient Greece. Students and faculty gathered not in a classroom building but on the edge of campus, in a house. No grades were given; evaluations were based on intense dialogues with faculty members and fellow students and extensive, eclectic reading lists that participants were encouraged to develop on their own.

Academically, this was the best thing that could have happened to Terence; he was ripe for something like this. The program also introduced him to others who were similarly brilliant and passionate in the way that only 19-year-olds can be. Some of the friendships formed in that crucible lasted for years and figured significantly in his later adventures. Recalling how Terence discussed the experience, I can see that Tussman was a significant mentor for him. My brother immensely respected the man, who, as his intellectual match in every way, challenged him to think critically and question his assumptions. Tussman did exactly what any smart philosophy professor trained in Socratic dialogue would do: he dared Terence to think for himself. Did the fact that the man looked exactly like our father (or so Terence believed) have anything to do with it? It's hard to say, but I suspect so. On some level, Terence may have found in Tussman his intellectual father, one who respected him as a person and yet couldn't be bamboozled. (That's not to say our real father was stupid, but that after a while he just gave up.) The two-year Tussman cycle was an extremely good maturation experience for my brother. Terence eventually graduated with a self-designed major in shamanic studies from the Natural Resources department, but in many ways the experimental college was the pinnacle of his academic life. It's significant that Tussman's program only lasted for a couple of cycles, ending in 1969. The program continued to enrich both our lives for another reason: it was there that Terence discovered his talents as a bibliophile and a collector of rare books. Both of us had cherished and collected books from an early age, and Terry's love of reading stimulated my desire to read. As a result, I had pretty much mastered the art well before first grade. I thank Terence, and my own good luck, for that. Reading is the skill most integral to an active life of the mind. I am only happy that I've been able to pass on that love to my daughter, a bookworm and an aspiring writer. Reading and loving to read is an inoculation against ignorance, which is on the rise again, I think, partly because people tend to read much less now.

In the pressure cooker of the Tussman program—just because it was unstructured and ungraded didn't mean there weren't demands—Terence encountered a vast diversity of ideas, from classical philosophy and Eastern religion to media theory. There he first studied Mircea Eliade, Edmund Husserl and the phenomenologists, and deepened his appreciation for the works of Carl Jung, who in turn led him fatefully to the *I Ching*. He discovered the Western esoteric traditions and explored alchemy and black magic. He began to accumulate a serious book collection, spurred on by Tussman's encouragement to explore every avenue of interest, and by his own curiosity and passion. And he shared these discoveries with me. Once our geographical separation had brought us closer and fostered a new mutual respect, we corresponded fairly regularly. With Terence in the thick of Berkeley's intellectual and social ferment, I acutely felt my isolation. Getting a letter from him was like a castaway finding a message in a bottle, a reassurance that beyond the stultifying confines of Paonia there indeed existed an exciting world of ideas. I longed to escape as he had years before. Our extended discussions over his Christmas visits, along with the books he'd bring with him, provided plenty for me to chew on during his absences.

In the fall of 1967, after completing his stint in the experimental college, Terence took off on his first world tour. Before leaving, he packed up his entire library (by then well over a thousand volumes) and shipped it to me for safekeeping. I was extraordinarily proud that he'd entrusted me to look after his books and that he knew I'd appreciate them. Has ever an older brother given a younger brother a more meaningful gift? I can't think of one. During that year, my junior year, which turned out to be my last in Paonia, I made every effort to devour as many of those books as I could. I made a fair dent, but I didn't read them all.

Terence had a reputation for having a fantastic library, and it was. Or rather, both were. He assembled two major libraries during his lifetime, and he had bad luck with both of them. After he returned from his first global sojourn in the spring of 1968, that initial collection was shipped back to the Bay Area and stored in the family home of Terence's best friend from the Tussman program, Michael. The books remained there in the Berkeley Hills until the summer of 1970, when Terence was traveling again in Asia. It was a particularly dry summer and wildfires swept the area, destroying many expensive homes, including that of Michael's parents. Terence's books were carried off as so much ash on the hot winds.

It took him 30 years to reproduce that wonder. His second library is the one that has become part of the Terence McKenna legend. Following his death in 2000, his books and papers were given to the Esalen Institute in Big Sur. After considerable struggle I managed to ship them back from the Big Island of Hawaii where Terence had been living before he passed on. Esalen's curators temporarily stored the collection in an old building in downtown Monterey, awaiting the construction of a proper place for it on the Esalen campus. The century-old structure turned out to be a tinderbox. In early February 2007, a fire broke out in a sandwich shop on a lower floor, consuming a number of businesses and Terence's books, which were stowed above. Yet again, a priceless trove had been reduced to ashes in a matter of minutes. The volumes included rare first editions of alchemical texts that existed nowhere else. It seemed almost like a curse, the curse of the Terence McKenna library! It was a terrible, terrible tragedy—for Terence's legacy, for Esalen, for our family, and for esoteric bibliophiles everywhere.

I was devastated when I heard the news. It was not only the loss of the library, which was bad enough, but it was also, for me, a final, forced letting go of Terence. So much of him was embodied in his library. I felt that as long as it existed, even if it was not within our family, his spirit lived on. Now that spirit was gone forever, finally, irrevocably, utterly, destroyed and expunged from the earth. It was a shocking and painful thing.

14 Cannabis: 1966

The fall of 1965 marked a transition for me as well. As a freshman at Paonia High School, I was once again sharing the halls with the older guys who had harassed me in eighth grade, but they left me alone. My friendship with Richard had survived despite his half-hearted alliance back then with my former tormentors. It wasn't until the spring that I actually started hanging out with those guys, some of whom were destined to become my partners in mischief well into the future. Madeline remained my closest friend, both of us too bookish and nerdy to fit in the other cliques, which worked out well. We didn't want to be part of those circles any more than they wanted us.

While Terence was starting his first semester at Berkeley constructing his intellectual foundations, I was stuck there in Paonia, a stranger in a strange land—an introverted "extra-environmental" in my sweet and dearly loathed hometown. Paonia was, and is, a nice little community. It never had more than 1,500 residents, and most lived on the outlying mesas. At times I've toyed with the idea of moving back, only to realize the dream was impractical. During high school, my attitude was less sentimental. I hated the place and wanted nothing more than to escape. I was insanely jealous of Terence for pulling that off, and I thought I deserved no less. Many of my friends felt the same, though not everyone made it out. Our nicknames for Paonia—"Peyote" or sometimes "Pissonya"—expressed our contempt. Tolkien's popular *Lord of the Rings* trilogy provided us with another epithet: Mordor, as in the accursed land of shadows and home to evil sorcerer Sauron. A slight exaggeration, perhaps, but we were teenagers and felt our angst palpably.

Like it or not, Paonia was where I'd remain for the time being, and I still had many significant experiences there, being 15 and eager for novelty and mischief. I also had Terence egging me on from a distance, always ready to lead me into the Next Big Thing.

That school year marked the true start of my pharmacological education, which has been ongoing ever since. The scare movies I'd seen in junior high were supposed to convince us that smoking marijuana even once would lead to addiction, madness, and promiscuity (we wished!). Like any narcotic, that propaganda worked only so long and then began breaking down. As for the morality tales about big-city degenerates getting hooked on heroin, those were simply irrelevant. In fact, I had no interest in "drugs" in junior high, but that had begun to change. Timothy Leary was active on the national stage, and that spring I read *The Doors of Perception*. Continuing its campaign either to corrupt or educate America's youth, *Life* had published its famous LSD cover story on March 25, 1966, entitled "The Exploding Threat of the Mind Drug That Got Out of Control." You had to hand it to *Life*, even if its editors were motivated by nothing but the most craven sensationalism. While their LSD feature was more alarmist than their landmark article on magic mushrooms in 1957, it probably led millions of otherwise wholesome young Americans down the primrose path to psychedelic perdition. It certainly got *my* attention.

By that summer I was quite aware of cannabis and psychedelics. Thanks to Terence and my own inherent curiosity, I was interested in giving pot and LSD a try, if either could have been had in Paonia. Like most small-town kids, my first real drug trip would be courtesy of that dreary nerve poison, alcohol. I was hanging out with those new friends who were all a year ahead of me in school. We didn't do much on the weekends except cruise Grand Avenue, all three blocks of it, just slowly driving from one end of it to the other, hoping to attract the attention of girls (not that there were any we could see). We varied the routine by taking off for the city park, often in the company of a guitar or two. We were part of a procession of similarly bored teenagers, in our town and towns across the country, without much else to do.

Despite being underage, we occasionally scored some 3.2 beer, the only kind sold in town. The watery stuff made me a little woozy but had little effect beyond that. So when my friend Tom got his hands on two pints of blackberry brandy just in time for the Fourth of July dance at the high school, we knew we were in for a good time. Tom was older and more sophisticated than I was. I looked up to him. He was good-looking, played a mean guitar, owned a really cool 1948 Plymouth coupe, and knew how to charm girls, or at least I thought he did; he certainly gave the impression of being wise in the ways of love. As we drove to the dance in Tom's black coupe, our blackberry brandy in the glove compartment, I was up for anything, but the night didn't go as planned.

I drank three-quarters of one bottle within the first hour, sitting in Tom's car. I was feeling pretty good, brave and dashing, and had completely lost my usual shyness as I headed for the gym, hoping to pick up a girl, or at least talk to one. I don't remember exactly what transpired, or what I said or did, but later I learned I'd been pretty obnoxious; in fact, I had acted like a complete jerk. After thoroughly insulting several girls, I was asked to leave. And I did, or rather, Tom steered me to the car, where we drank more, and then he drove me home despite my vehement objections. I sat in my bedroom for a while, furious at him for spoiling my fun, and then decided to return to the dance and set out reeling down the street. I arrived to find Tom was nowhere to be seen. My condition soon attracted the notice of the local cop, who took me home in the patrol car. Somewhat sobered and intimidated, I made it to my room and fell into a fitful sleep. The next day the cop dropped by and talked to my father, who wasn't too upset. He'd probably done similar things as a teenager. Such was the coming of age for many a small-town boy back in the day.

I took my first puff of cannabis about five days after that misadventure. Terence had come home for a few weeks after his first year at Berkeley, along with his new cute girlfriend, who I'll call Elaine. Terence was smitten with her, and it was easy to see why. Elaine was a pretty girl, from upstate New York, if I recall. The fact that she was Jewish may have added to her attraction for Terence. He might have hoped our Catholic parents would be shocked at this liaison, but if so they didn't let on. Anyway, the two arrived with a lid of what was probably terrible weed and a couple of capsules of acid. Terence solemnly informed me that each contained "a thousand mikes"—1,000 micrograms, an enormous dose. If so, the LSD must have been very pure, because the two large gelatin caps appeared to be empty. I just got to look at them once, and I don't know if they took them on their visit.

The cannabis was a different story. Terence kept it in a little bottle in a silken Chinese pouch, together with a tiny pipe. One lazy afternoon they invited me to stroll across the street to the park, where we spread out one of Mom's patchwork quilts beneath a big tree, unpacked some soft drinks and sandwiches, and proceeded to toke up, right there in plain sight. Terence and Elaine didn't seem too concerned when I wondered aloud about smoking the "stuff" in public. In fact there were few people in the park that day and nobody was paying attention. Terence said no one would know what we were doing anyway, and he was apparently right. We shared a pipe or two. Nothing happened. I didn't feel a thing, though the "grass" tasted good going down. But I really didn't know what I was supposed to feel, and the result was disappointing.

It took perhaps three more sessions there under the trees before I finally got it. When I finally did learn what it was to be stoned—and I think it is a learned state—suddenly everything seemed hilarious. When I closed my eyes and lay back in the sunshine, a flurry of geometric patterns flooded my closed lids; when I opened them and examined the blanket, the texture of the weave was revealed in almost microscopic detail, and I could have scrutinized it for hours. The abstract patterns on one of the stitched-together swatches appeared like writing in an alien language. Thought became fluid, spontaneous. Peculiar ideas, those patterns behind the eyes, sensual and emotional impressions flowed together in a cascading rush of images, memories, puns, snatches of remembered songs, faces of friends—and all of it happening in a circus-like atmosphere of joyousness and hilarity. I thought I must be making a spectacle of myself and actually came to my senses for a moment. But nothing was happening; we were simply three people sitting quietly on a blanket in the park.

This was great! The cannabis high was so much better than the alcohol-fueled debacle of a few days before. I couldn't believe how crude alcohol intoxication was in comparison. I could handle this. And it was so much more interesting. There was actual content to this experience, interesting ideas and thought fragments, and these in turn sparked scintillating conversation. I immediately understood—this was my drug.

Following my initiation, Terence returned to Berkeley for his second year in the Tussman program. I don't remember much about that fall except that I missed my brother and the glamorous life he was living out on the coast. I chafed at the idea of being imprisoned in town. What's more, I had no dope, no cannabis to salve my angst, and no one to really talk to except Madeline, Richard, and the new friends I'd grown closer to over the summer. I welcomed their company, but I couldn't share ideas with them in the way I could with Terence.

What my friends and I did share was the goal of scoring some weed, which rumor had we could find in Aspen if we asked the right people. Aspen was already notorious as a place for beatniks and weirdos, a bohemian enclave and a playground of the decadent rich. The only person I knew in Aspen who might be able to help was a guy from Paonia who had moved to Aspen to work in construction. We took a trip there one weekend in Tom's coupe and found him living in a boardinghouse along with a number of other dirty, longhaired people—actual hippies! I was delighted to encounter such kindred spirits just down the road. The feeling was not mutual. They didn't want to be bothered by some snot-nosed kids from home, let alone supply them with drugs. We returned empty-handed and had only weak beer to console us.

Over the summer, drugs had emerged as a bone of contention between Terence and our parents, especially our father. Along with the radical political views, the hirsute appearance, the strange clothing—in other words, the appurtenances of the hippie persona that Terence was adopting—drug use was beyond the pale. All drugs were "garbage" in our father's view, the worst possible thing one could be into; there was simply no way the topic could be rationally discussed.

We both found this attitude rather puzzling; after all, Mom and Dad were not prudes. They enjoyed drinking and had lived rather wildly as young adults in California before and during the war. But in our father's mind, alcohol was not a drug—its effects were on the muscles, in his thinking, and not the brain. He viewed drinking as essentially benign, a thing one did recreationally to relax in social situations. All drugs, on the other hand, he equated to heroin—all were addictive, destructive, and evil. Part of his attitude toward drugs resulted from an experience he had during the war (so he said). On a bombing mission over Germany, one of his crewmates had been badly injured by flak shrapnel, but when his buddies broke open the medical kit to give him a shot for his terrible pain, they found that, as Dad said, "Some hophead had stolen the morphine."

After an incident like that, one could see why he didn't have much sympathy for drug addicts, but that was irrelevant; we weren't talking about addictive drugs. To him it didn't matter. There was no difference between cannabis, LSD, or heroin; all were intrinsically bad. Like many others, he made the mistake of seeing evil as a moral quality imbued in the substances, not a product of how they were used. All of this, of course, was more grist for the ongoing contentious conversations between Terence and our father. Terence was in rebellion against everything our parents' generation stood for, and drugs were a hot-button issue, another excuse for screaming matches.

Terence didn't come home for Christmas in 1966. He remained in

Berkeley, where my mother and I visited him around the new year. He was living in a kind of scholar's retreat, a tiny loft in a broken-down Victorian house on Tunnel Road. It was a great place, a kind of aerie surrounded by a walled garden, far from the chaotic scene closer to the university. By then Terence was well into the Tussman program and had accumulated the core of his first library, the one destroyed by fire in 1970. He was reading extensively in many esoteric subjects including alchemy, Eastern philosophy, and black magic as well as Jung, Eliade, shamanism, drug literature, and—a new discovery—Marshall McLuhan. McLuhan was getting a lot of press at the time, not all of it conducive to being regarded as a serious thinker. As Terence later put it, McLuhan wanted to cultivate a new sophistication about the media, only to see the media parody him to death. Terence and I delved more deeply into McLuhan's work than most did. I believe he had some rather amazing insights that have stood the test of time. Terence's eclectic reading was totally in keeping with Tussman's insistence that his students explore whatever piqued their interest. This came quite naturally to Terence.

For some reason—inexplicably, given the edgy relations between Terence and our father—I was permitted to go to California and stay with my brother right after Christmas. Mom joined us about a week later. Elaine had gone home for the holidays, so Terence stayed at her apartment while my mother and I shared his. But for a glorious week before that, I stayed with Terence, bedding down on a mattress on the floor. I didn't mind that at all. We were by then full coconspirators, and I relished any chance to hang with him and soak up the rich ideas we exchanged as the long hours of gloomy twilight dissolved into the evenings and the shadows settled into the corners of our little refuge.

Terence had by this time discovered something else that made those evenings together especially pleasurable: hashish! It was my first introduction to hashish, and it was much stronger and far more interesting than the weak cannabis he had brought out the previous summer. We smoked it in a metal water pipe with a tiny bowl and a curved stem, the kind that you could buy in Chinatown (and still can). We passed many an hour in stoned conversations about everything under the sun, passing the pipe and savoring each other's company. We had always been kindred spirits, it seemed, but until then we hadn't really understood that. I cherish the memories of those hours to this day, though time has left only fragments, not a full recollection.

I do remember one important event, however, and that was when

Terence persuaded Mom to try smoking hashish. She had been more open-minded about the drug issue than our father, though she had kept very quiet during the arguments of the previous summer. But the topic was in the air, especially there in the Bay Area with the hippie scene in full flower. A couple of years earlier, I'd overheard my mother and two of her friends talking about LSD. It was a drug, she had read, that could teach you about yourself; you might learn you were capable of murder, or that you had unsuspected knowledge and insights. That comment struck me as odd at the time, but it spoke to the fact that my mother was at least a bit open to the idea that these substances were not entirely bad. So I was surprised, but not too surprised, when Terence gave her the pitch. He made the point that cannabis was really not so bad and indeed there were things you could learn from it. She agreed to try it, and he loaded the pipe and we shared it with her. The results weren't definitive. Mom was so wracked with guilt, and so afraid of how furious Dad would be if he ever found out she'd actually gotten stoned with her sons, she couldn't really let herself go and enjoy the experience. She didn't say much about it afterward except that she had noticed an intensification of colors. And that was about it. It's a pity, really. Had we all been able to sit down and get stoned together, it could have done much to heal the strains in our family. But it was not fated to happen, and as a result the tensions over the issue continued for years to come.

15 The Tutor

I returned from Berkeley determined to secure some cannabis and to continue with my own quiet revolution, in solidarity with my brother. Fired up by our discussions, I became the Tussman program's extension school of one, reading Jung, McLuhan, and Eliade and biding my time. I also got to know one of the new teachers, who was all of 24, cute in a plain way, and fresh out of college. Fay, as I'll call her, had a head on her shoulders and was starved for conversation and company— especially male company. A divorced single mother with a child of four or five, she wasn't exactly welcomed by the ladies auxiliary. The town was narrow-minded in the way only small towns can be, and Fay was an outsider and not allowed to forget it. That made her easy prey for an extra-environmental like me, a young man who felt like an outsider even though he'd been living there all his life.

Actually, it soon became unclear who was preying on whom. Fay and I started hanging out; I'd stop by her house and we'd have long conversations. Nothing untoward happened on those visits, but I think we both wanted it to. We did discuss cannabis, which Fay, though hardly a hippie chick, had smoked a couple times and liked in college. So we hatched a small conspiracy, which involved convincing Terence to mail Fay a lid of weed. Brilliant! The plan worked. Our newly arrived supply of precious weed was probably quite inferior by contemporary standards, but we had it.

We didn't just smoke up; this called for a special occasion. As luck would have it, my father was set to attend his company's annual sales meeting in Denver, a three- or four-day affair that my mother, joining him, turned into a short holiday in the big city. They ended up leaving me on my own for nearly one whole glorious week. I was 16, after all. Besides, by then Terence and I had terrorized every babysitter in the valley, making it unlikely anyone would have signed up to mind me. So a window of opportunity quickly opened for Fay and me to have our special evening. Most readers must know by now where this is headed. I was, of course, a virgin, a status I was determined to change. Fay seemed quite willing to cooperate, though we didn't speak of the matter until that night. I picked her up in my parents' Chevy and brought her back to the house, not wanting anyone to see her car parked outside. I had already prepped the house, closing all the curtains and turning off most of the lights. We toked up and drank a little; we got very stoned and hilarious. The next thing we knew we were groping each other, and a minute later we were on the little bed in my room. I was nervous and didn't know what I was doing. Fay could see this and was kind, and eventually we completed a fairly inept coupling. It's said that is something you never forget, and I guess that's true. We hung out for a while and finished up the pipe, she gathered up her things, and I took her home. I made a quick detour to the bridge to smash the wine bottle on the rocks below and crept back home in the quiet night.

No security breach, no drama.

We never repeated that experience. I think we were both a little appalled at our recklessness. I continued to visit her once in a while, but we began to worry that people would talk, and our conversations became less frequent. At the end of the semester she moved on. Recently, others have informed me that I was not her only conquest. If those other accounts are true, Fay may have arrived with an agenda to sample the pleasures of the local randy but virginal males; there was nothing particularly special about me. So much for my self-flattering belief that Fay liked me for my intellect! I wish her well, wherever she is. She may have had bad judgment, but she was a good spirit, and I shall always be grateful to her for introducing me to the pleasures of sex, awkward and halting though the occasion was. It's gotten both harder and easier, somehow, as life has progressed.

One good thing was, I now had a new supply of cannabis, lovely cannabis! I started smoking it on a regular basis, getting completely baked on ridiculously small amounts. Looking back, I think much of my reaction could be traced to the placebo effect, but placebo or not it was wonderful. Being stoned was the only time I felt normal. I loved nothing more than to sit in my room, have a toke or two, and ruminate. The experiences were similar to those first times on the blanket in the park—strange, fragmentary thought processes leading into interesting, often hilarious byways. The cannabis high is like a state of enhanced bemusement. Every thought is interesting and everything before the open eyes or behind the closed eyelids is endlessly fascinating. There are audial hallucinations, evocations of deep aural spaces, often accompanied by complex hypnagogic tapestries. Music becomes a transformative experience. I noticed in those early days there was a distinct figure/ground phenomenon, where things in the background became the object of attention, while the foreground was not perceived or was relegated to background. I noticed this particularly when reading while stoned. The words would not only resonate in my head, but the spaces between and around the letters became somehow more important than the letters. This happened to the point where it began to interfere with reading. Then, gradually, the problem would fix itself and I could again read smoothly. I'm not sure what was going on, but I think that when one first starts smoking, there's a period of entrainment or adaptation to the state. Once one is entrained, being stoned becomes a lot like being normal. It feels like a normal state of mind; one is comfortable there, but something is lost on the intensity scale. The early experiences were practically psychedelic in their intensity, whereas later I didn't get close to that when I smoked.

But it took a while to reach that point. For now, I had cannabis, and I was extremely sensitive to it. I loved how I could be completely toasted and yet have a perfectly normal conversation with my parents. They hadn't a clue. At first, I guarded my tiny stash jealously. I didn't want to run out, and Terence had sternly admonished me—"You must speak of this to no one!"—in the same tone he used to say, "Never oppose my will!" I got that. After all our talks about black magic and alchemy (Terence had confided that he'd actually taped shut certain grimoires of black magic he had, not trusting himself to open those books), I was down with the idea of secrecy. Cannabis and certain other drugs were really black arts, or at least forbidden knowledge. But the secrecy didn't last. I wanted to share the discovery with my close friends, and as spring faded into summer I started turning them on, starting with Richard, then proceeding through the rest of our stoner band. By the end of June all six of us were regularly crowding into my bedroom and getting loaded.

I smoked whenever I could. I enjoyed smoking with my friends, but some of my best experiences were when I smoked alone, rambling around the sagebrush-covered hills outside of town. And now I had access to a car! I could go out to the 'dobes or the gravel pit or sometimes Bethlehem Cemetery and toke up. I'd get totally, utterly wasted on these solitary wanderings. I'd spend that time ruminating, looking at things like bugs, plants, trees, rocks, whatever—ruminating and creating a narrative.

Bethlehem Cemetery was especially inviting, a small, pretty spot nestled in a little bowl on the drive up to Pitkin Mesa. There was never anyone there, and it was peaceful and shady on a summer's afternoon. I'd get totally loaded and wander around looking at the headstones, speculating about the lives of the names there. Once I found a gravestone bearing the names of a husband and wife, the husband having died a year to the day after her. It was clear to me that he had died of a broken heart. This little vignette, like the others I imagined, seemed enormously romantic and poignant to me. I suppose it was a passionate time of life. I felt things strongly, and the cannabis only made them more intense. On a recent visit to Paonia, I drove up to the cemetery around dusk on a beautiful fall evening. It was just as peaceful and lovely as I remembered it, as though the world had passed it by for the last four-and-a-half decades. It was a timeless little glade, a sanctuary in the midst of an impermanent world, and most reassuring. I did not smoke this time; I had no cannabis with me. It was not necessary. As I wandered along the paths gazing at the old headstones, the memories and the contact high were more than enough.

Once loaded in one of my various countryside haunts, there was the small matter of driving back into town. The main challenge for me was the time-dilation effect. Everything. Was. Really. Slowed. Down. But at least I wasn't tempted to break any speed limits on the way home. In fact I would creep into town at about 10 miles an hour. Nobody ever stopped me or even seemed to notice, probably because in town nobody drove much faster than that anyway.

I wrote less over those months. I had kept a journal the previous summer and written quite a lot. I had discovered Taoism at the time and was fascinated by it, by the idea of living in harmony with nature, so gracefully that one's imprint on the earth was as light as a feather. Taoism seemed to me at the time to be one of the few religions that made sense. It is actually more a philosophy than a religion, and that was appealing. No faith or dogma, just learning to live in harmony—what's not to like about that? Much of my journal writing over the previous summer had been devoted to exploring the character and actions of the ideal man, in Taoist terms, which I aspired to become. I tried to start that up again, but my efforts were half-hearted. Ironically, not writing about the man in Tao was probably a more Taoist thing to do than to write about it. You don't write about the Tao; you live it, or try to live it. But when I was stoned, thoughts came too quickly, they were too interesting, they could not be pinned to the page! Yeah, yeah, I know. Pot makes you lazy. There is something to that. So my literary productivity over the summer suffered. But that was OK. I was too immersed in the richness of rumination to worry about writing it down.

16 A Psychedelic Education

Now that I've conveyed a picture of my teenage self lost in thought, I want to take a wider look at what Terence and I were actually thinking about. As must be clear by now, we lived largely in our heads. Ideas and concepts were what most excited us, and being bookish was a point of pride. We fancied ourselves scholars with more depth than our friends, let alone the "meatheads" we had to suffer on a daily basis. Though we were certainly immersed in the memes then permeating mass culture, our serious interests also colored our worldview. Indeed, both scholarly and popular ideas figured in our efforts to understand our early psyche-delic experiences. Together they formed the conceptual toolkit, however inadequate or incomplete, we later took with us on our South American quest. As such, our influences played a crucial role in what happened to us at La Chorrera.

Our psychedelic education began with cosmology and astronomy, both of which were more my pursuits than Terence's. I mentioned my early dream of studying astrophysics under George Gamow, an originator of the Big Bang theory. I played at observational astronomy without being very good at it; what really excited me was reading about cosmology. I devoured books by Gamow and his scientific rival, the English astronomer Fred Hoyle, along with anything else in the field I could get my hands on. I loved how those ideas freed my imagination. Cosmology deals with the really big ques-tions: How did the universe originate? How did the solar system and the planets form? What will happen to the universe in the distant future? For a 12- or 13-year-old just beginning to realize the tenets of his faith were wear-ing a little thin, the thought there might be scientific answers to questions about humanity's ultimate fate had great appeal. What faith I had I put in science, no longer wasting it on God or the church.

Every culture has its own creation myth, its own cosmology. And in some respects every cosmology is true, even if I might flatter myself in assuming mine is somehow truer because it is scientific. But it seems to me that no culture, including scientific culture, has cornered the market on definitive answers when it comes to the ultimate questions. Science may couch its models in the language of mathematics and observational astronomy, while other cultures use poetry and sacrificial propitiations to defend theirs. But in the end, no one knows, at least not yet. The current flux in the state of scientific cosmology attests to this, as we watch physicists and astronomers argue over string theory and multiverses and the cosmic inflation hypothesis.

Many of the postulates of modern cosmology lie beyond, or at least at the outer fringes of, what can be verified through observation. As a result, aesthetics—as reflected by the "elegance" of the mathematical models—has become as important as observation in assessing the validity of a cosmological theory. There is the assumption, sometimes explicit and sometimes not, that the universe is rationally constructed, that it has an inherent quality of beauty, and that any mathematical model that does not exemplify an underlying, unifying simplicity is to be considered dubious if not invalid on such criteria alone.

This is really nothing more than an article of faith, and it is one of the few instances where science is faith-based, at least in its insistence that the universe can be understood, that it "makes sense." It is not entirely a faith-based position, in that we can invoke the history of science to support the proposition that, so far, science has been able to make sense, in a limited way, of much of what it has scrutinized. (The psychedelic experience may prove to be an exception.) Based on past experience, one may hope that science will eventually produce a valid cosmological model that encompasses all we currently know—at least until new knowledge requires that the model be discarded or radically revised.

In the meantime, we are free to speculate and to watch the cosmologists battle it out via their conferences and writings. Terence and I found our vicarious participation in that process to be great fun. Thinking about cosmology forces one to stretch his or her imagination around some pretty wild ideas. Parallel universes, other dimensions, space-time dilation, black holes, and time travel are alien concepts to most people, but they are bread and butter for amateur cosmologists, among others. In pondering such ideas, one is led inevitably to gaze up at the stars and wonder what other entities are gazing back, perhaps pondering the same things.

Another major early influence was science fiction, and for that I credit my father. Along with the "men's magazines" we weren't supposed to see but did, he occasionally brought home issues of *Fate,* with its focus on the paranormal, and sci-fi pulp mags like *Analog* or *Fantasy and Science Fiction.* His reading was another way he wasn't "average" despite insisting that he was—and, more irksome, insisting we should be as well. I doubt his peers were reading this stuff, but Terence and I were all over it. I still enjoy science fiction, and much of what is written today is far superior to what we read as kids. Science fiction is good for the mind. It keeps one open to possibilities and, more than any other fictional genre, helps one to anticipate and prepare for the future. In fact, science fiction creates the future by articulating a vision of what we as a culture imagine for ourselves. The world we live in today is, in part, a sci-fi vision of the future from the 1950s made real. We now have, and take for granted, pocket phones, global telecommunications, personal computers, genetic engineering, bioterrorism, and environmental collapse; sci-fi writers anticipated them all. They also foresaw much that hasn't been realized, and failed to foresee much that has. The lesson, if any, is that reality will always be stranger, richer, and more complex than fiction.

In the early 1960s, the sci-fi authors we loved were the old-school giants: Isaac Asimov, Theodore Sturgeon, Robert Heinlein, Ray Bradbury, James Blish, and especially Arthur C. Clarke. Jules Verne was an early favorite, as was H. G. Wells, whose novel *The Time Machine* had a big impact on me in my preteen years. The notion of time travel fascinated me then (and does now) and fed a preoccupation with the future and the nature of time that Terence and I shared. But it was Clarke who had the greatest impact on our thinking, thanks largely to his novels *Childhood's End* (1953) and *The City and the Stars* (1956). Those two early books strike me as more inspired than much of his later work, even *2001: A Space Odyssey* (1968), although that comes close.

The City and the Stars begins in Diaspar, a super-technological city a billion years in Earth's future whose inhabitants maintain their longevity through what Clarke termed the Eternity Circuits, an early anticipation of nanotechnology. Only a fraction of the populace is incarnate at a given time; the rest are stored as solid-state templates in the Central Computer. (Clarke's notion of uploaded consciousness is yet another of his glimpses of the eventually possible, though in this case not one in the foreseeable future.) The novel takes the form of a hero's journey, a classic shamanic tale. Its main figure, Alvin, is a "Unique" who, unlike his fellow inhabitants, has an irresistible compulsion to leave Diaspar, though no one has ventured out for more than a hundred million years. *The City and the Stars* is actually a revision of Clarke's first novel, *Against the Fall of Night* (1948). The result is an incredible work—ahead of its time then and ahead of ours now.

Childhood's End, a "first contact" story, is another classic. It begins in what for Clarke was still the near future. Just as the Soviets and Americans near the furious end of their race to launch the first space probe, mile-wide starships appear, poised over every major city in the world. And there they remain, or seem to, asserting their presence but otherwise hardly communicating. Decades pass; eventually the population becomes so accustomed to the vessels they are all but ignored. It is then that the visitors send an emissary to the surface, a figure whose shocking appearance activates a number of archetypes long buried in the human psyche. Several movies have addressed the first-contact theme, including *Close Encounters of the Third Kind* (1977) and *Independence Day* (1996). All of them, even a classic like the 1951 version of *The Day the Earth Stood Still*, are rather lame compared to *Childhood's End*, and it puzzles me that no one has brought the book to the screen. Its themes are even timelier today than when it was published many decades ago.

Terence and I were also drawn to H. P. Lovecraft, an early 20th-century writer who captivated many of our peers. Lovecraft's work is not exactly science fiction but rather belongs, in my view, to a subgenre, science fiction horror. His work is suffused with various horrors originating beyond the stars, from the depths of the oceans, or in the remote past. These things are nonhuman, alien, eldritch—Lovecraft's favored word for the uncanny or strange—that may lie undisturbed for millennia, known only to a few cognoscenti. Inevitably, these horrors erupt into the comfortable, familiar world, usually due to some character's foolish curiosity and inability to resist meddling in matters best left to rest. For us, these themes were far more compelling than those of Edgar Allan Poe, for example. Poe and others tended to write about "ghosties and ghoulies," a more pedestrian brand of horror with origins in the repressed dark side of the Judeo-Christian mindset. Lovecraft went beyond that, hinting at horrors far more ancient than civilization, humanity, or even earth itself. A recurring theme is that scientific curiosity, our pursuit of forbidden knowledge, and our reckless flirtation with malevolent cosmic forces carry the potential to undermine the very foundations of reality.

For whatever reason, we loved these ideas, or at least we loved scaring ourselves with the notion that just beyond the veil of the mundane world were multiple realities that could manifest themselves at any time. Lovecraft made his tales all the more effective by not overdescribing his malevolent entities, leaving the details to the reader's imagination. I suspect the movie *Alien* (1979) was influenced by Lovecraft; the creature is certainly an unspeakable horror from "somewhere else" in the universe (we never do learn where) and "alien" to everything human. One never gets a complete view of it until the climactic moment when Ripley blasts him (her? it?) out the airlock. Until then, one sees fleeting glimpses that evoke our nightmares of things insectile, spidery, reptilian, octopoid, crab-like, slimy, shiny, machine-like, shark-like—but never a full picture. The viewer must fill in the details, to far more terrifying effect.

Another writer we admired was Philip K. Dick, although we didn't read him until the late 1960s. If Lovecraft was the master of transdimensional horror, Dick might be called the master of the "paranoid" genre of science fiction. His fiction often centers on themes of alternate realities, or on characters that discover they are victims of massive political conspiracies, or that their reality is an illusion or a drug-induced hallucination. More than any other sci-fi author at the time, Dick, who died in 1982 at age 53, explored plot devices related to psychoactive drugs and altered states. Amphetamine was his drug of choice, and much of his early fiction was apparently written under its influence. Dick published *The Three Stigmata of Palmer Eldritch*— there's the Lovecraftian influence again—in 1965. Though *Rolling Stone* declared it the "classic LSD novel of all time," according to Wikipedia, Dick evidently wrote it before any personal encounters with the drug. Set in the 21st century at a time when the solar system has been widely colonized, people use a hallucinogen called CAN-D to enter a dreamlike state that allows them to project their shared experiences onto actual props, or "layouts," rendering their fantasies all the more real.

Dick's novels are permeated with themes related to the nature of reality, the fragility of personal identity, drug use, and mental illness. In fact, some of Dick's later novels—especially *VALIS*, *The Divine Invasion*, and *The Transmigration of Timothy Archer*—are centered on characters confronted with continuum-disrupting events that teeter on the thin edge between psychotic breakdown and mystical revelation. These tales bear uncanny similarities to our own experiences at La Chorrera to the extent that they seemed like a validation when they came to our attention in the mid-1970s. Dick was heavily influenced by the ideas of Carl Jung, as were we. Much of Dick's work has been translated into movies, with varying degrees of success. *Blade*

Runner (1982), arguably one of the best science fiction films of all time, was based on his short story "Do Androids Dream of Electric Sheep?" Others include *Total Recall* (1990), *Minority Report* (2002), *A Scanner Darkly* (2006), and *The Adjustment Bureau* (2011). I suspect that many of the filmmakers who are inspired by his work grew up, as we did, in the same milieu as Dick. In fact, certain shared influences—Clarke, Dick, Lovecraft, and others— have become such pervasive elements of contemporary culture because they are echoes of our generation's adolescent experiences, including psychedelic experiences.

If science fiction books influenced our worldview, so did mass market movies and television. While there may have been something unique in how we interpreted all that, our exposure was not unique. Millions shared the experience of watching *The Twilight Zone*, for example, or any number of popular films.

One movie that influenced me was *Charly* (1968), adapted from the 1966 novel *Flowers for Algernon* by Daniel Keyes. As many know, it's the story of a mentally disabled man who undergoes an experimental treatment that dramatically increases his IQ. The movie chronicles the mental, emotional, and social problems he endures as his relationships with family and friends change, only to see his new capabilities slowly fade. This idea of being radically transformed into a superhuman had great appeal for me, probably because I was shy and identified with someone who suddenly found himself attractive to a woman he had secretly loved. The film must have struck some deep chord in my subconscious, because its themes emerged years later during our experiment at La Chorrera, as did aspects of *Planet of the Apes* (1968) and the novels I mentioned by Arthur C. Clarke. Though I'd read those books years earlier, their tropes were still in the archives of my memory, ready to be activated by the right trigger.

Of all of the movies that figured in the zeitgeist back then, none had a more profound impact than Stanley Kubrick's *2001: A Space Odyssey* (1968). Kubrick and Clarke had written the screenplay while the latter was writing his novel of the same name. Their collaboration is still quite possibly the greatest sci-fi film ever made. The film is about humanity's ultimate encounter with a superior yet benevolent alien intelligence that has long been guiding the species' destiny. With its themes of evolutionary transformation, alien contact, and a greater fate awaiting us among the stars, *2001* defined the aspirations of our generation. Though it didn't directly deal with psychedelics, the "light show" at the climax, as David Bowman's module is sucked into the hyperspatial portal, is close enough to the DMT "light show" that many of us assumed the film sequence had been modeled after it. Dimethyltryptamine, a powerful psychedelic, was rare and hard to get at the time and thus all the more mysterious and fascinating. Like Bowman's hyperspatial plunge into the monolith/portal, DMT brings with it a sense of rapid acceleration, of diving headlong into an overwhelmingly bizarre abyss, freighted with portentousness and hints of insect-like metamorphosis.

Kubrick's *2001* was literally about pushing the envelope, including the biggest, the one that limits human experience to the here and now. The film spoke strongly to our generation because we were involved in pushing all kinds of envelopes, testing the limits of conventional morality, politics, academics, and, ultimately, conscious experience. And psychedelics provided the tools. Many of us thought then, and still do, that the consumption of psychedelics, either accidental or deliberate, may have spurred on cognitive evolution, the explosive increase in the size and complexity of the hominid brain between two million and 100,000 years ago. This idea fit the intuition of many psychedelic enthusiasts that these substances were not only transformative for the individual but for the species as a whole.

No wonder we were so ready to interpret *2001* as a hopeful manifesto for our transcendent future. Now more than a decade past the actual 2001, we remember that year not as we had hoped to—as the moment when humanity joined the galactic community—but for the tragic events of 9/11. That trauma has left deep scars on the nation, if not much of the world, and has apparently precipitated a long descent into a very dark age indeed.

Among the things that Terence turned me onto, along with lot of edgy ideas and controlled substances, were folk music and rock and roll. I mentioned that in my preteen years I was a musical snob and dreamed of being a classical guitarist or a conductor. My indifference to pop music began to change when Terence came home for Christmas after his first semester at Berkeley with the latest album by the Beatles, *Rubber Soul*. The following summer he arrived with Bob Dylan's *Bringing It All Back Home* and *Highway 61 Revisited*, both also from 1965. With his cryptic lyrics, gravelly voice, and message of impending change, Dylan especially seemed to speak to the yearnings of our generation. I was soon drawn to others like Peter, Paul and Mary, Joan Baez, and Woody Guthrie. On the rock side, in addition to the Beatles, were the Rolling Stones, the Grateful Dead, and some other psychedelic bands. As all good music should, theirs expressed the mood of the times. My parents didn't get that, as suggested by my father's nickname for Dylan: "Gravel Gertie." He'd grown up listening to Frank Sinatra's silken voice and couldn't appreciate how Dylan's could be considered music. As a result he never actually listened to Dylan's message, which I suspect he didn't want to hear. We appreciated Dylan partly because we understood something about his ties to black music, especially the blues, where a gruff voice was a mark of authenticity. But that my parents didn't embrace such music made it better. We didn't want to identify with anything that was theirs, and we knew this music was ours.

By then I'd begun giving up on my musical ambitions. Besides pop and classical, I loved jazz, and in high school I half-heartedly played the double bass. I fantasized about being one of those cool improvisational jazz guys who played with the likes of Dave Brubeck and John Coltrane, but I had no talent whatsoever. The band director, Mr. Den Beste, was a bit of a stuffed shirt but also a gifted educator. When even he couldn't make a good musician out of me, perhaps I realized my efforts to master the instrument would be in vain. He once used my bass to illustrate the principle of sympathetic resonance. If one plucks an A note, for example, another string tuned to A will also begin to vibrate. And if one then damps off the original string, the sympathetic string continues to resonate. His vivid illustration was an interesting bit of physics trivia at the time, but later became very important at La Chorrera, which is why I mention it here.

While I didn't have much musical talent, I knew others who did. A few of my close friends were pretty good guitar players, thanks in part to growing up with music-loving fathers and brothers. As I noted, their guitars became a big part of our hanging out. Renditions of Dylan were a favorite; nothing could beat hearing my friend Gary angrily rap out "Masters of War" or "A Hard Rain's A-Gonna Fall" in his own rough voice. Those songs reflected our anxieties and our determination never to give in, to fight what we saw as the corruptness of our parents' generation, whose legacy to the world was the specter of nuclear annihilation. Popular music, rock music, became a passion, even an obsession, for many people my age. My wife, for example, is practically a music scholar. She knows the artists, often the specific albums, of almost all popular music from the mid-1950s on. Though I've always enjoyed music, it was not destined to play such an important role in my life. I don't have music constantly playing in the background, because that affects my concentration. Come to think of it, Terence was not very musically inclined either. He enjoyed listening to music, of course, but he never played in a band or took up any instrument. While sitting around, he rarely took the initiative to put on an album, though if someone else did, he was usually happy to listen. I think maybe we were too verbal, too language-oriented, to appreciate music thoroughly. Music can distract from the inner conversation one is always having, and maybe that interfered with our inner dialogue. Music, too, is distinctly a function of the right brain, and we were both left-brain dominant.

Nevertheless, pop music, like pop culture in general, profoundly influenced us, as it did so many others. Though Terence and I were never to be "average" in our father's idealized sense of the word, we were both versions of Everyman, on a personal journey to adulthood through a rapidly changing cultural landscape. Our experiences resonate with those of so many of our contemporaries because they took the same pilgrimage, albeit starting out from different places. Many of our contemporaries have become important figures in the arts, politics, science, and academics, putting them in a position to shape the zeitgeist. Is it any wonder that it sometimes seems as if we're living in a mass hallucination? In fact we are, and it's one we have constructed.

17 Mapping Inner Space: Carl Jung

The works of C. G. Jung played a crucial role in our developing thought—or escalating delusion, as some might have uncharitably described it. Terence encountered Jung shortly after moving to California and soon shared the experience with me. Before the 1960s, Jung's ideas were considered radical; the reigning paradigm of human consciousness could be traced to Freud, Jung's mentor and eventual rival. By the mid-1960s, however, Jung's ideas were gaining credibility. About the time we were exploring Jung, so were many psychologists, as the deficiencies of the Freudian model of mind were becoming more apparent.

Though it's long been held that Jung never used psychedelics, he was aware of them, or at least aware of the American physician Silas Weir Mitchell's experiments with mescaline. Jung's *Liber Novus*, a work long suppressed by his heirs, suggests that Jung may have been more directly involved with psychedelics than previously thought. Published in 2009, *The Red Book*, as it is known, was a journal that Jung began in 1914 shortly after breaking with Freud and then worked on for more than a decade. The iconography of *The Red Book*, which Jung wrote and illustrated by hand, is certainly psychedelic, though overt allusions to plants or mushrooms are absent. For Jung as well as Freud, dreams were the portals to the unconscious. It's reasonable to suppose that had Jung's career peaked a few decades later, he would have probably used LSD or some other substance as an exploratory tool. Indeed, he may have done so in secret, fearing he'd be discredited for venturing beyond accepted practice if word of that got out.

But whether Jung used psychedelics or relied on his own remarkable talent for deep introspection, he was undeniably a pioneer in exploring the unconscious realm. Many of the areas that he investigated early in his career—alchemy, the *I Ching*, archetypes, synchronicity, and personality integration—found new resonance in the 1960s, not only among psychologists but also among those who today we call "psychonauts." For them, Jung's worked provided a framework for understanding psychedelic experiences. States that before could only be accessed through dreams, meditation, or certain other spiritual disciplines could now be attained through drugs. That did not make the territory any less fascinating, confusing, or terrifying. Like R. E. Schultes in his trailblazing studies of psychedelic plants, Jung explored the terra incognita of the unconscious and returned with some of the earliest reliable maps.

For Terence and me, discovering Jung was a revelation. We were aware of psychedelics by then, of course, and deeply interested in what qualified as a cultural phenomenon. If cosmology was the lens through which we learned to view the universe at large, Jungian psychology became our cosmology for the universe within. Buried in every person's neural tissue was a dimension at least as vast and fascinating as that of the stars and galaxies. We knew the cosmic frontier would, for now, remain beyond our reach; humanity had to contemplate and construct its models of that from afar. The universe of the unconscious was different, being right there for exploration, and psychedelics were the chemical starships for bearing us inward. It wasn't for nothing that the psychedelic experience was called a "trip." With such drugs suddenly available, many of our generation opted to take the journey.

Jungian thought forms a fertile environment for any student of the mind, or anyone wanting to make sense of their psychedelic experiences. For Terence and me, there were certain key Jungian concepts that proved indispensable in grappling with what we eventually encountered at La Chorrera. Jung was one of the few Western scholars who had looked at Eastern spiritual traditions for their insights on the nature of mind and consciousness.

Consider the *I Ching*, the ancient Chinese oracle based on 64 hexagrams that became the basis for Terence's Timewave Zero theory. Jung's understanding of the *I Ching* was tied to his idea of synchronicity, the occurrence of two events that are somehow related but not in terms of cause and effect. He also referred to this notion as an "acausal connecting principle" or "meaningful parallelism." Synchronicity is not just random coincidence; rather, it is a phenomenon that expresses both in the mind and in the outer world, in a way that reveals a meaningful but not causal tie between these expressions. The concept provides a rationale for the apparent effectiveness of oracles and other divinatory systems, like the Tarot and astrology. The hexagram patterns derived from the *I Ching* in response to a question are meaningful (usually) because they resonate with something that preexists in the mind, below conscious awareness. The *I Ching* clarifies that relationship and triggers an "aha" moment. Or one's horoscope is meaningful, not because the stars and planets control human destiny but because the archetypal processes they symbolically reflect correspond to subjective interpretations of character. In this respect, the notion of synchronicity is quite profound in that it asserts a correspondence between the mind and the external world—the so-called real world. The Hermetic philosophers said it well: as above, so below.

This mirroring of inner consciousness and the outer world still poses a conundrum for neuroscience and most Western philosophy. Why, and how, do external events meaningfully relate to inner, psychic events? It's as if consciousness, or mind, forms the primary ground of being, while the physical world is secondary—a construct created by the mind. Any Eastern spiritual tradition or philosophy will tell you this is the case. Western thought, with its emphasis on materialism, is uncomfortable with that notion. I'm not aware of any finding in current neuroscience that resolves this question, at least not yet. But we do know enough about brain function to say with fair confidence that, to some extent, the world we call "reality" is a construct of our brains. The brain assembles a coherent story (more or less) by combining sensory experience with memories, associations, interpretations, and intuitions, then presenting the result as the movie, or perhaps more accurately the hallucination, we inhabit. If psychedelics teach us anything, it's how fragile this constructed reality is and how profoundly it can be distorted.

Jung's idea of synchronicity compels us to think about the correspondences between the inner and outer world, and to ponder our experience of time. The other major elements of his model are his ideas about archetypes and the collective unconscious. For Jung, it is as if the mind is a real place, a realm populated by archetypes that reside in some lower psychic stratum all humans share. This is the collective unconscious. In such a view, the idea that each of us is a separate individual is an illusion. We are like an archipelago rising from the sea—on the surface we appear to be separate islands, but underneath we are all connected by a common substrate. This is the best conceptualization I have found of the collective unconscious. Oddly enough, it comes not from Jung but from Arthur C. Clarke in *Childhood's End*. I would like to think that Clarke had read some Jung in his day. Archetypes swim in the surrounding psychic ocean—symbolic constructs shared by all humanity as a result of our common genetics, physiology, evolution, and brain architecture. Jung's archetypes are closely akin to Platonic ideals in that they are never apprehended directly; we see, in effect, the shadows they cast. But because archetypes are shared elements of the collective unconscious, they are expressed in every culture, albeit tarted up with historic and mythic trappings that may be unique to each. Whatever the superficial differences in expression, there are universal archetypes at play just below. The figures of the wise old man, the wise old woman, the demon, the trickster, the hero, the child—all are common archetypes expressed in different but recognizable forms.

And not all archetypes are people. The world tree is an archetype, for instance, as is the mountain, the lake, the abyss, the dragon, and so forth. Almost every symbolic construct derives its meaning from its archetypal roots. One archetype of great interest to Jung was the mandala. A mandala is a four-part, usually circular but sometimes quadrangular design that Jung equated to the archetype of the individuated self. Mandalas are universal in human cultures—examples are the equilateral cross, Buddhist thangkas, Tibetan sand paintings, Sioux dreamcatchers, and Celtic knots. In Jungian psychology, individuation is the therapeutic goal, the outcome of balancing and integrating the four primary qualities of personality (intuition, sensation, emotion, cognition) with one's male and female aspects (the anima and animus) and the elements of the unconscious (the shadow). The individuated person is a fully realized person, aware of both the personal and the collective aspects of the self. Individuation is pursued, though rarely achieved, through a lifetime of discipline and self-actualization.

In this regard, two other Jungian concepts exerted undue influence on Terence and me, or at least figured prominently in our experiences at La Chorrera. One was Jung's speculation that flying saucers were contemporary expressions of the mandala form and its inner meaning. Steeped as we were in science fiction, cosmology, and psychedelics, Terence and I were quite taken by this theory, which Jung presented in *Flying Saucers: A Modern Myth of Things Seen in the Skies*, first published in German in 1958. A 1959 English translation was later included in volume 10 of Jung's *Collected Works: Civilization in Transition* (1964). Jung argued that flying saucers weren't from outer space, but inner space. He proposed that UFOs, those circular, mandalic symbols of wholeness, were shared hallucinations generated by an increasingly desperate collective unconscious seeking our attention in a world on the brink of nuclear catastrophe. Jung didn't dismiss these sightings; he felt they carried an important message—humanity needed to wake up and get its act together in order to avoid destroying the planet.

Interestingly, and oddly, many people, myself among them, have gotten a similar message from their experiences with "plant teachers" like ayahuasca. Whether this has always been the lesson of such substances or a more recent phenomenon is unclear—in fact, that would make an interesting study. But I digress. As to whether flying saucers might be actual objects, Jung didn't really say. By artfully dodging the question, he seemed to hold out the remote possibility that maybe, just maybe, they were physically real. (I wonder what Jung would have made of crop circles had he been around to see them.) In leaving the door ajar, he implicitly acknowledged the connection between mind and matter, and the primacy of mind. He may have thought that under some circumstances flying saucers could physically manifest. They were not extraterrestrial ships, but something material that the mind created.

Needless to say, this notion held great fascination for us. It suggested that it might be possible to build such an object, perhaps by transforming one's body into something like a UFO. And there were plenty of hints about how this might be done in both Western and Eastern traditions. In esoteric Christianity, the idea of the "resurrection body," the physically transformed body after resurrection, was something almost like a cyborg UFO; indeed, in some depictions it is portrayed as circular. Many other esoteric traditions allude to something similar. Though they differ in the particulars, they share the notion that a lifetime of spiritual discipline, usually including physical practices such as yoga, can result not only in an enlightened mind but a transformed body. In the East, this concept is variously represented in Taoism, Sufism, Hermeticism, and certain schools of Buddhism. Many shamanic traditions have developed similar concepts—shamanic initiation entails the novice being torn asunder and reassembled, often with magical objects such as crystals or darts incorporated into the new, more powerful body.

These upgrades function as technology; they are the basis of the shaman's new powers. In all these traditions, we find hints, even explicit instructions, regarding such biophysical technology, a set of techniques that can transform the body into something transcendent, immortal, and endowed with superhuman abilities. These concepts were extremely numinous for Terence and me, and very much in play at La Chorrera. Someone stumbling on an account of our "experiment" there could be excused for thinking we were completely delusional, and we may have been. But we shared that delusion with a long line of spiritual masters.

Alchemy was the other one of Jung's preoccupations that captivated us. The alchemist is generally regarded as a medieval precursor to the modern chemist, a figure engaged in the ultimately futile business of smelting, purifying, or otherwise turning various substances into gold. In fact, many early alchemists subjected all sorts of matter—plants, metals, minerals, even feces and bodily fluids—to a bewildering variety of bizarre manipulations. Over time, they mastered many chemical transformations and learned a great deal about matter, almost accidentally laying the foundations of modern chemistry in the process. But as Jung portrayed alchemy, it had very little to do with chemistry. Rather, it was yet another technique for spiritual transformation and achieving individuation. The alchemists often used a set of allegorical symbols and iconography drawn from their nascent grasp of chemistry, concepts like firing, hardening, purification, condensation, and distillation. But Jung insisted that the significance of these procedures was primarily symbolic. The chemical transmutations effected in the alembic were reflections of psychic processes, transformations taking place in the spirit, or soul, of the alchemist. But here again, some of their writings hinted at techniques for physical perfection, not unlike those texts associated with concepts akin to the resurrection body. In other words, the pursuits of physical and spiritual refinement were alloyed.

Jung asserts that alchemy had nothing to do with transmuting lead into gold; that notion was almost a deliberate obfuscation of what was really going on. The bigger prize was the "philosopher's stone." The philosopher's stone was not simply a lump of alchemical gold. It was a technological artifact of some sort. In fact, the substance in question was the ultimate technological artifact, because it could "do" anything that could be imagined. In this, the stone has much in common with other imagined super-technologies such as flying saucers, starships, time machines, crystal balls, magic mirrors, and so on. All are conceived as artifacts, invented (or conjured) by humans that can do things we normally regard as impossible. Only in an era familiar with nanotechnology, artificial intelligence, genetic engineering, and quantum technologies can we now contemplate actually building devices whose power approaches that attributed to the philosopher's stone.

Does the enduring allure of concepts like the resurrection body and the philosopher's stone suggest they might be more than just delusions? Terence would say they were anticipations of future events, a potent shock wave resonating back through history, beckoning us, luring us, toward their inevitable invention or discovery. (The question of whether one "invents" or "discovers" something like a philosopher's stone is one we'll leave unexamined for now.) Perhaps someday we will produce our own. The fact that we now live in an age where we might actually diagram such a thing says something profound, and perhaps disturbing, about human imagination—and hubris.

This discussion of alchemy requires a further comment. At La Chorrera, Terence and I thought we could build the philosopher's stone (the flying saucer, the time machine, the eschaton, insert your preference here) out of our own bodies, literally singing it into existence through a superconducting fusion of our own DNA with that of a mushroom. In the sober light of today, four decades later, this seems like an utterly crazy notion; but considered in the context of alchemy and other esoteric traditions, the notion is completely in line, though expressed in modern terms. Crazy we may have been, but again, if so, we were in the company of many great visionaries and spiritual masters throughout history.

Alchemists, or many of them, used an essentially empirical approach to pursue their art. Perhaps not fully aware of what they were doing, they mixed and melded matter, then observed the results, interpreting what they saw as reflections of inner, psychological processes. But given that their raw materials—the prima materia—were often derived from plants and animals, could they have accidentally (or deliberately, once trial and error had yielded some result) succeeded in isolating or concentrating psychedelic substances? And having ingested their handiwork, wouldn't they have interpreted the effect as a complete success? Even now, with all our sophistication about chemistry and pharmacology, who cannot be impressed with Albert Hofmann's "accidental" discovery of LSD, or the marvelous molecules invented by Alexander "Sasha" Shulgin? In a sense, their finds, or creations, exemplify the union of spirit and matter that the alchemists sought. By that measure at least, they might be called the alchemists of their day.

The tryptamine-based psychedelics are widespread in plant and animal life, as a result of the tryptamine molecule's close relationship to tryptophan, which is universally distributed in organisms. Tryptamines are alkaloids and thus relatively easy to isolate using simple chemical techniques that would have been available to the early alchemists—just look at any issue of *The Entheogen Review* (now defunct but available online) or visit the Erowid library (erowid.org) to find the methods devised by their modern counterparts! Given the array of materials and manipulations used by alchemists in the past, it strikes me as plausible that a few may have stumbled onto these substances. We have no proof, of course, though there are many bizarre depictions of animals and plants in alchemical iconography. Even these are mere hints, not explicit depictions.

Alchemy was an esoteric practice, after all. Its practitioners were not interested in divulging their secrets and often went to great lengths to obfuscate them. I am no expert on such illustration, but the closest example I have seen to an explicit visual reference to psychedelics is a remarkable woodcut in Johann Daniel Mylius's *Philosophia Reformata*, a text from 1622. The four women depicted represent the four stages of the alchemical transformation process; the patterns of the folds of their dresses appear to be a taxonomically accurate representation of *Psilocybe semilanceata*, known as liberty caps among mushroom enthusiasts. This species is tiny, potent, and common in pastures throughout Europe and the British Isles, and there's no reason to think it hasn't grown there for centuries.

Perhaps some people understood the mushroom's properties and used such imagery as a way of alluding to their secret knowledge. (One of my students astutely noted that the women's headdresses might represent the seed capsules of the opium poppy, another possibility.) Granted, one must be aware of the tendency to see what one wants to see in ancient iconography—a tendency that appears to be particularly strong among those with a special interest in mushrooms, as the author Andy Letcher points out in *Shroom: A Cultural History of the Magic Mushroom*. Nevertheless, the resemblance is remarkable, and readers may draw their own conclusions.

Before leaving Jung, it's worth noting that he considered his work to be scientific. He made a point of insisting that his theories were objectively drawn, based on scientific observation. Indeed, Jungian psychology began as an effort to provide an interpretative structure for what he and others had learned by observing themselves as well as their patients. As he argued, the West devalues inner experience; only what is external, material, and outside the self can qualify as real. But in Eastern thought the opposite is true. The real world in Hinduism, for example, is the inner world; the external world, the material world, is *maya*, illusion. To illustrate the reality of the universe within, Jung noted how often our actions in the external world stem from interior motivations and ideas. This is an important point, particularly when interpreting inner states, including psychedelic states, which are easily dismissed as not real. Jung would vehemently disagree with such appraisals. As he pointed out, inner experiences are often more profound and significant than external events in terms of their influence on human activities and institutions.

18 The Ladders of Ecstasy: Mircea Eliade

Terence and I found another important virtual mentor in the writer and philosopher Mircea Eliade. Born in Romania in 1907, Eliade attended the University of Bucharest and spent several years studying in Kolkata, India. His early work included journalism, novels, and essays, some of which were later criticized for espousing anti-Semitic and extreme right-wing views. After Romania became a Communist country in 1945, Eliade lived for a time in Paris before moving to the United States. From 1964 until his death in 1986, he was a professor of the history of religions at the University of Chicago.

Eliade's vast output ranged from fantasy fiction to scholarly works to what might be called armchair anthropology. Neither Terence nor I made much of a dent in all that; the books that stood out for us were *Shamanism: Archaic Techniques of Ecstasy* (1964) and *Yoga: Immortality and Freedom* (1958). We also were familiar with *The Myth of the Eternal Return: Cosmos and History* (1954) and *The Sacred and the Profane: The Nature of Religion* (1959). We weren't aware of his early, unsavory political opinions, let alone the debate over how those may have influenced his later work. Indeed, much of that critique had yet to be articulated. We were aware that many of his ideas fit in well with those of Jung, whose works we managed to explore more extensively.

Jung and Eliade met in 1950, at the Eranos Conference, a yearly lecture series in Switzerland, and the two subsequently collaborated as colleagues and friends. By the time Terence and I discovered Eliade's writings, we were both steeped in the ideas of transcendence and self-transformation, and his thoughts on yoga and shamanism complemented our interests. Originally published in French, and as early as the 1930s in the case of his yoga studies, these works were (and still are) important scholarly contributions, although they are now a bit dated. For example, Eliade asserted, without evidence, that a shamanic tradition that relied on "narcotics" (meaning "psychedelics," a term not yet coined) was a "degenerate" tradition born of an earlier, more pristine practice that had become corrupted. Our own experiences with psychedelics obviously led us to disagree.

Since then, research on what is now known to be the worldwide phenomenon of shamanism has further discredited his assertion. Though certainly not all shamans use psychoactive substances, those who do use them cannot be regarded as "degenerate." The antiquity and prevalence of these substances would indicate that they are the sine qua non of shamanic practice, at least in the New World. That might be true of Old World shamanism as well, though the knowledge may have been lost much earlier there. This would account for the greater use of psychedelic, or hallucinogenic, plants in the New World compared to the Old, a topic about which Schultes and others have written. One could actually argue that shamanic traditions that do not use psychedelics are "degenerate," representing, as they may, the loss of earlier knowledge—namely, the identity of the shamanic plants and the methods of their preparation. But here we should be careful not to commit the error Eliade made when he dismissed "narcotic" shamanic traditions. We may speculate that some traditions lost this knowledge, as suggested by, for example, soma, a drink of unknown composition mentioned in certain Indian texts and elsewhere. But concrete evidence is hard to come by.

Eliade's writings on yoga and shamanism as techniques of spiritual and perhaps physical transformation added to what we'd learned from Jung, supplying us with specific details from different traditions—the ethnographic backstory. We were also drawn to what Eliade saw as the archaic distinction between the "sacred" and the "profane," as applied to both space (places) and time (events). Many spiritual traditions postulate separate or parallel worlds. There is the mundane, ordinary world we inhabit while alive, which Eliade termed the "profane" realm. Adjacent to this world are other "sacred" realms that are normally unseen and inaccessible to ordinary people, but which are reachable by shamans and other spiritual practitioners. These sacred realms may be the dwelling place of souls awaiting incarnation, or where souls go following death—for example, "heaven" in the Christian mythos. In many cultures, the world is understood to have a three-layered structure. The middle layer is the material world, which lies below a celestial realm inhabited by gods and advanced beings, and above an underworld inhabited by demons or other malevolent entities. While this lower realm may be infernal, it is nonetheless viewed as sacred in its separation from the world of everyday life.

In many cosmologies, these realms are linked by an axis mundi, which is often depicted as a world tree. The concept is also portrayed at times as a mushroom in Siberian shamanic traditions that use the fly agaric (*Amanita muscaria*), or as the ladder-like ayahuasca vine familiar to shamans in the Amazon basin. In all such traditions, the shaman can access the upper and lower realms, either by using a psychoactive substance to induce an altered state or relying on other "techniques of ecstasy," as Eliade describes them. In the ecstatic condition, the shaman might ascend the axis mundi to propitiate the gods or entities in the upper realm, or descend to the lower realm, often to do battle with malevolent entities, retrieve the souls of the sick, or otherwise intervene on behalf of individuals or the tribal community. The key concept here is that both upper and lower realms are intimately linked with the mundane human realm and can be accessed by people with the right training (shamans) and the right tools (often drugs). I might add that these realms, which amount to other dimensions, are just as "real" as the material world, but the term would be useless in this context.

Just as there is sacred space, so there is sacred time—another idea that influenced our thinking. Sacred time is a time out of time, the time of ritual. Sacred time and sacred space are closely linked, because rituals performed in sacred spaces, as they are in most traditions, similarly sacralize time. In an archetypal sense, sacred space is not simply a consecrated or special place; rather, ritual transforms an ordinary place into the actual cosmic center, a place outside profane space. Similarly, when a culture engages in a rebirth ceremony or reenacts its creation myth, it doesn't simply emulate events that took place at the beginning of time; these rituals return their participants to that moment when the cosmos was born. The event is literal, not metaphorical. A sacred ritual accomplishes what Eliade calls a "revalorization" of the sacred space-time of the cosmos in which the culture dwells. It is literally a renewal, a rebirth, the beginning of a new cycle of birth, evolution, and death. Sacred time is cyclical, not linear, and cultures that dwell in sacred time do not live in historical time, or indeed in mundane geography. They inhabit ahistorical time, in a place that is at the center of space and yet also removed from it. The cosmos is constantly being born, evolving, and dying, a cycle of "eternal return" that is the antithesis of our Western concept of historical time.

The distinctions between sacred and profane have profoundly influenced the Western worldview, especially as seen through the lens of the Judeo-Christian tradition. The realm where God dwells is a sacred cosmos, a place and time outside of history and location. It is, in fact, the place that we inhabited before the fall, the human expulsion from Eden. That moment can be understood as the fall into history. We ate the forbidden fruit of knowledge and came to understand our own mortality, our own death.

Such knowledge is not possible in cyclical time; it depends critically on linear time, which by definition has a beginning, a middle, and an end. Linear time is a prison in which humanity is entrapped; salvation consists of an escape from history, a return to an eternal, timeless moment, an eternity spent in blissful contemplation of the Godhead. We are like a starship poised on the threshold of a black hole's event horizon; at that exact point in space-time one is neither in this continuum nor out of it, but rather exists in an eternal moment in which time is literally stopped. Death is indefinitely postponed, as is birth, or any other kind of change. It's a pretty boring place, but not really, because for it to be boring, time must pass, and it does not. I find it extremely strange that black holes, or that region near to black holes known as the event horizon, are actually physical manifestations of this "mythical" concept of a sacred, timeless, space-less point. Perhaps the old cosmological myths were closer to the truth than we might think.

This notion, of an escape from history being the equivalent of salvation, is the whole story of Christianity in a nutshell. Adam and Eve ate the fruit of the tree of knowledge and fell into history, into mortality. Christ, the shamanic psychopomp, had to separate himself from the father and descend into history. He had to take on death itself. In dying, he died for all of humanity, and in being reborn he defeated death for all of humanity. Our lives still unfold in history, in linear time, of course, but at the end, if we die in a state of grace, we can return to that sacred space-time point that is, literally, the instant of creation and that is, literally, the center of the universe (because at the moment of creation the universe is a point, as our cosmological physicists insist).

Thanks to Christ's descent from heaven to defeat death, the Christian is liberated from the prison of history, because the collective curse, the original sin that was cast upon humanity and led to expulsion from the Garden of Eden, has been absolved by Christ's death. In the Roman Catholic tradition, the sacrament of confession gives a person the chance to do on a small, individual scale what Christ did for all humanity: descend into history and return to the beginning, to a pristine, renewed, reborn state in which all the baggage of our history (our sins) is washed away and forgotten. Inevitably, however, we repeat the primal mistake that Adam and Eve made and descend again into memory and historical time.

* * *

It's a pretty profound myth, actually. It is "true" in that metaphysical sense in which all myths are true. And it has greatly impacted the way that we in the West view history and the "profane," everyday world in which we live out history, personal and otherwise. Christianity encourages, nay demands, that in order to achieve salvation, good Christians should keep their sights set firmly on eternity, on the hoped-for moment of eternal bliss that is beyond death, beyond time. In exchange, we are expected to devalue and even reject the physical world in which we inhabit a body and experience all the suffering and pleasure that bodies can experience. We are told that we should not indulge in too much sex, too much eating, too many pleasures of the flesh, because to do so will make us forget that eternal bodiless state of bliss that we long for. We are encouraged to devalue this world, even disrespect it, because it is historical and must end someday. In fact, the sooner it ends the better, in the Christian worldview, because that will mark the return of Christ to Earth, the Final Days, and the crossing of the threshold into the post-historical eternity, the eschaton, the end of the world.

As a myth, this is all very well. Who doesn't long for an escape from history, for immortality and eternal bliss? The problem with the Christian mythos, among other belief systems, is that it can lead to a denial of biology, and a rejection of all that is good about being a living organism. After all, despite its terrible problems, the world is a marvelous place, and being alive is a marvelous state. For two thousand years, the church has foisted what amounts to a Ponzi scheme on the frightened masses, bidding them to forego satisfaction now in exchange for a greater fulfillment after death. If, that is, they've toed the line as defined by the church and what Terence called its "beastly little priestlies." Locating the purpose of life somewhere beyond it is a dangerous form of thought, especially in an age when some not only want to end history but also could attain the technology to do so. It's also irresponsible to indulge such conceits on a planet whose seven billion human inhabitants are depleting most of its resources and poisoning what remains.

And yet such thinking seems justified to many political leaders, some of whom, being fundamentalist zealots themselves, see no reason to preserve nature or maintain global stability. Freedom of religious belief is a constitutional right, and people are free to believe in whatever delusions they want. But when it comes to forging national policies based on those delusions (for instance, the denial of climate change), then thinking citizens must stand up and denounce such ignorance. The sad thing is there are fewer and fewer thinking citizens, or so it appears. A frightened populace just wants to be told what to think and do, and the ideologues are more than happy to oblige them. One result is a trend in the public sphere toward the glorification of a willful shallow-mindedness. In the private sphere, that often manifests itself as a conscious refusal to acknowledge the mind's unconscious depths.

One antidote to both that refusal and to irrational religiosity might be psychedelics. There's reason to believe these substances played a role in the origin of religion—not a particular religion, but the religious impulse itself, the experience of the transcendent. That's why these substances are considered dangerous and their usage so often suppressed. For the religious powers that be, psychedelics are dangerous, not because of any toxicity or physiological threat but because they so often demonstrate the superfluity of faith. To have faith is to believe in something despite the absence of evidence. All religions demand faith from their followers; unquestioning, irrational belief is the tool by which hierarchical religions control their adherents.

No wonder psychedelics are threatening to an authoritarian religious hierarchy. You don't need faith to benefit from a psychedelic experience, let alone a priest or even a shaman to interpret it. What you need is courage— courage to drink the brew, eat the mushroom, or whatever it is, and then to pay attention, and make of it what you will. Suddenly, the tools for direct contact with the transcendent other (whether you call it God or something else) is taken from the hands of an anointed elite and given to the individual seeker. The psychedelic experience is nothing if not intensely personal. Many will be quite willing to interpret it for you, of course; psychedelic spirituality is hardly immune to "guruism." This is not the fault of psychedelics but of the human impulse to seize upon anything numinous and use it to gain power. That's what the early church fathers did with the original, numinous experiences that form the historical precedents of Christianity (and which may well have been psychedelically triggered). Certain demagogues are doing the same today when they frighten their followers into embracing agendas that threaten not only their individual interests but that all of earthly life.

Many will discover that the take-home lesson from their brush with the numinous is a celebration, not a rejection, of biology. Psychedelics are *drugs*; they do what they do because *we are made of drugs*. You can't get more biological than that! Psychedelic experiences are usually not about visiting some transcendent realm of angels and demons (though that does happen); more often than not, they are about experiencing the here and now in a very intense way. Be here now, this timeless moment: these phrases are so much associated with psychedelic experiences they've become clichés. But they well describe what profound psychedelic experiences are like: an immersion in the moment and a sense of "oceanic boundlessness," a sense of being one with nature, connected to all of nature and all other beings.

It's quite unlikely one would return from that experience compelled to reject nature and biology, much less one's own body. Rather, the outcome is an enhanced reverence for nature and our place in that scheme, a feeling that as part of it, we must love it, and learn to nurture it. The psychedelic revelation is the exact opposite of the fundamentalist, apocalyptic view that we should long for release from this "vale of tears" and ascend into some anticipated post-historical eternity, which our religious authorities tell us is waiting for us following death. What psychedelics teach us is that we are already in paradise, as manifested in earthly life. Having learned that lesson, we then must assume the responsibility of protecting nature, the only paradise we are certain we'll ever know.

While the worldview that Terence and I shared certainly owed much to Jung and Eliade, there were of course other influences. During a period of intense interest in philosophy, I read most of Plato's dialogues, some of Aristotle, a good deal of St. Augustine, and a smattering of Locke, Descartes, Kant, and other dead white men. I briefly aspired to study classics at Trinity College in Dublin, but after struggling to learn Greek in my first semester at the University of Colorado in Boulder, I gave that up. In any case, by then I'd already begun to find science and anthropology more interesting.

During his first year in the experimental college, Terence discovered phenomenology through the works of Edmund Husserl, Martin Heidegger, and Maurice Merleau-Ponty—then brought their ideas home to me. I found them exotic and challenging but quite compatible with Jung's assertion that inner experiences should not be dismissed as "unreal" simply because they were immaterial. Anything consciously experienced was "real" in the sense that it could be experienced, even if it had no connection to anything beyond the subjective realm. Like Jung, these thinkers were attempting to bring objectivity to the study of those aspects of consciousness that are usually regarded as subjective, such as dreams, emotions, and intuitions.

Phenomenology is the study of "lived experience" and is rooted in the concept of "intentionality," sometimes called "aboutness." Consciousness is always consciousness *of* something. Intentionality represents an alternative to the representational theory of consciousness, which holds that no thing can be experienced directly—only the representation of that thing in the mind can be experienced. Phenomenology turns this thought on its head and asserts that there is nothing *but* direct experience; whatever is presented to the mind is the grist of experience. Husserl argued that consciousness is not "in" the mind but rather is "of " the intentional object. Consciousness amounts to what is experienced, whether that is a solid, material object or a figment of the imagination. The phenomenological method relies on the description of phenomena as they are given to consciousness in their immediacy, without making judgments about whether they are subjective or not.

The preceding paragraph is a simplistic synopsis of some difficult concepts I don't pretend to completely understand. I won't clumsily attempt to explicate them at greater length; the present description is clumsy enough. The point is that, together with Jung and Eliade, phenomenology was an appealing perspective from which to approach the "phenomena" experienced in psychedelic states. Those experiences may seem implausible, indeed impossible, but that doesn't matter—anything that can be experienced is real and should be approached on its own terms.

So much for the artists and thinkers that led us to the upper Amazon and helped prepare us for the strange events we encountered there. Awakened as kids to the mysteries of the cosmos, we convinced ourselves as teenagers that we might possibly solve them; a few years later we found ourselves in the Colombian jungle believing we actually had. Upon our return, Terence and I began exploring a new set of thinkers and concepts as we struggled to make sense of our experiences. One important influence would be the work of the mathematician and philosopher Alfred North Whitehead. His concept of how "novelty" enters and transfigures nature would play a role in shaping our journey's most prominent artifact: Terence's Timewave Zero theory. Terence's effort to chart the structure of time would lead him to predict a series of dates for the end of time, including one famously slated for the winter solstice in 2012. Our thinking would eventually diverge on certain issues, the timewave among them, but those developments lay beyond La Chorrera, as we shall see.

19
Summer of Love: 1967

In late June 1967 I managed to escape Paonia for three glorious weeks with Terence in California. My partner in this scheme was my friend Tom, he of the Plymouth coupe, who seemed more mature than the others in our band and subject to fewer constraints at home. Our parents should have had their heads examined for letting us go, but for some reason they did. We arrived in Berkeley in early July.

By then Terence had moved into the so-called Telegraph House, a huge, three-story communal place on Telegraph Avenue just a few blocks down from the commercial section. The house was the epicenter of an eclectic scene of wild-eyed freaks, dealers, travelers, and other characters in the Bay Area looking for fun, sex, drugs, and whatever else was to be had. Crashing in an open room, Tom and I were up for all that and more.

Terence fit right into this scene. His room had become a sort of informal salon where people would show up to get loaded and stay to hear him rant. And he always had something to rant about. Unlike most people, who get high and grow quiet, cannabis never affected Terence that way; it only made him more articulate, more talkative, and more able to weave his enrapturing narratives. He often had a receptive audience of very stoned listeners hardly able to speak or move while he regaled them. He was in his element, and he loved it. That may have been when Terence first realized he had the gift of gab, in spades. People just loved to hear him talk; he could keep a group seated on the floor in his bedroom spellbound for hours. It didn't really matter what he said—it was the way he said it. Much later in his life when Terence started to address larger groups in more structured venues, he found the old magic still worked, a talent he eventually leveraged into his public career.

Terence was still seeing his girlfriend Elaine at the time, but she must have gone home for the summer. Many of his other friends stopped by, a few of whom I'd later get to know quite well. Some were former high school classmates who, like Terence, were in Berkeley going to the university or just hanging out. Others he knew from the Tussman program. Michael, for instance, was a Berkeley boy; his parents' home was the one that later burned down, taking Terence's first library with it. Michael certainly didn't fit the profile of the down-and-dirty hippie. With his neatly trimmed beard he looked like an Elizabethan scholar and had the eloquence and learning to match. He eventually moved to New York City and became a successful dealer and curator of Asian art. Another friend, Rick, had been a brilliant classmate of Terence's during his year in Mountain View. Rick eventually moved to England and became a successful dealer of rare scientific books. At the time, Terence admired him for teaching an advanced course in steroid chemistry at Stanford while apparently still a high-school junior.

A third participant was "Vanessa," a lovely, brown-eyed girl from New York. A fellow student at the experimental college, she shared Terence's intensity and passion for ideas. I've adopted the pseudonym Terence gave her in *True Hallucinations* both to honor her role in our band of adventurers and to protect her identity, which she'd probably appreciate as a respected psychotherapist. Vanessa was (and still is) a key member of the Brotherhood of the Screaming Abyss. The Telegraph House is also where I first met Erik, an aspiring poet and writer who had been Terence's best buddy during his senior year in Lancaster, and Lisa, who later became my first serious girlfriend. In 1967, however, neither of us suspected that might happen, let alone that Lisa and Erik would eventually marry. Like Michael, they remained close to Terence until the end of his life.

At the time, Lisa was the girlfriend of the remarkable John Parker, a guy who had an enormous influence on both Terence and me. He'd been another quirky, brilliant, junior-year classmate of Terence's in Mountain View. I'd met John the previous summer when he'd spent a few days in Paonia visiting Terence. I was shy and didn't talk to him much at the time, but later he became one of my most important mentors. John did not affect the beard and long hair that was fashionable at the time. He had a diminutive physique and a perpetual twinkle in his eye; his sexuality was ambiguous, a puzzle. He brought to mind what people might cruelly mean when they refer to a gay person as a "fairy," though he somehow embodied the more literal meaning of the term. John's father, a researcher at the NASA facility in Mountain View, was known, if I recall, for his work on the fire-retardant paint used in certain spacecraft—a modern alchemist if there ever was one. I only met him once, years later, in 1984, when I was in California searching for jobs after completing my PhD. Though he struck me as an odd but harmless fellow in our brief interview, Lisa had a harsher view of him. According to her, if John was a tad eccentric, even a bit mad, his father was partly why.

Whether John got all or some of his funny ideas from his father, he was a fascinating and peculiar figure in his own right. He knew about and practiced black magic, or so he claimed. He was sophisticated about drugs, having tried many kinds, including some I'd never heard of. He knew botany and medicinal plants, chemistry, psychopharmacology, alchemy, yoga, and shamanism. He had very unconventional ideas about drug actions, space and time, other dimensions, aliens, and UFOs. John deserves credit for planting the seeds of many key concepts in my mind over several years of intense correspondence. Many of the ideas we discussed in those letters figured in the conceptual raft that Terence and I constructed before our journey to La Chorrera. All that occurred later, most notably in the fall of 1969 during my first semester at the University of Colorado at Boulder when John spent several weeks visiting me. The extraordinary discussions we had then over many a hashish-stoked evening were the culmination of our long correspondence. Though John did not accompany us to South America, we may never have gone without him; his spirit was with us all the way.

If Tom and I had any agenda in Berkeley that summer, it was fairly loose. We wanted if possible to get laid, and there seemed a good chance that would happen, what with free love in the air and all. Or so it seemed to a randy 16-year-old. But it never happened. We also wanted to take LSD and secure a supply of cannabis and other interesting substances to bring back to our friends. At all that we succeeded.

At some point in our visit, Terence urged us to cross the bay and check out the scene in Haight-Ashbury. He probably just wanted to get us out of his hair for a few days, but he wanted us to investigate the Diggers. The San Francisco Diggers had taken their name and philosophy from a mid-17th-century group in England first known as the True Levellers for their radical egalitarian beliefs, which involved common ownership of property and respect for nature. They became known as the Diggers for their habit of working together in their communal fields. Their hippie counterparts, based in the Haight, gave that ethos an urban spin, opening stores that gave away their stocks and providing free medical care, food, transport, and housing. They also organized free concerts and political street theater, such as the Death of Money parade. They envisioned a society free of money, private property, and all forms of buying and selling.

In many ways, the Diggers tried to actualize the best ideals of hippiedom. Like most utopian communities, however, they found it difficult to make reality fit with the ideal. Inevitably, they seem to founder on the recalcitrance of human nature. For every idealist who is ready to pitch in and work for the common good, there is an opportunist who wants something for nothing, or, worse, to grab power and bend it to his or her own ends. The Diggers were a kind of cult—not a religious but a political cult—and eventually they suffered the fate of all cults. But at the time, the Diggers were happening in the Haight, and it was a beautiful idea.

Tom and I couldn't really connect; we may have been guilty of wanting something for nothing. Certainly we had very little money and we needed a place to stay, food, all those necessities, and we had little to contribute. After a few days we decided it wasn't working for us, and we returned to Berkeley.

Even then you could discern the seeds of destruction in the hippie movement, most notably in the Haight. Trying to run an egalitarian community in a dense city is a challenge under the best of circumstances. And every community that aspires to be spontaneous, to thrive without leaders or hierarchies, must confront the vacuum it creates for the power-crazed. Another factor that contributed to the short life of the hippie movement, at least in the Haight, was that so many of the people who had been drawn there were already damaged in some way. They made the pilgrimage in search of something, though many knew not what. Once they arrived, they were likely to become exposed to drugs and other experiences that they had no tools to deal with, and no clue. Those people quickly became dysfunctional and a liability to the rest of the community. Not everyone suffered this fate, of course. In fact, most people who were motivated enough to make the pilgrimage to California that summer probably benefited from their experience.

Back in Berkeley, we were able to realize our goal of finding some acid. At the time there was little or no quality control on what was available. The LSD of today is pharmaceutical grade compared with what was on the street then. There was no problem locating it; just about every other person you encountered on the "Ave." had something to sell. We bought a couple of tabs of what looked like aspirin, and were aspirin, but with a tiny dot of some purple substance added in the center. This was the famous, legendary LSD, a couple hundred "mikes"—or micrograms— according to the hirsute stranger who had sold it to us, and who vouched for its purity and potency. We had no way to know, but it was the Summer of Love, man, surely no one would sell us bad stuff! In this case, we were lucky. The dealer was as good as his word, as we found out a few days later.

We did not go off half-cocked. We had read *The Psychedelic Experience*, the LSD user's guide, and took it all very seriously. I wrote a long, rambling letter to my friend Gary back in Paonia ruminating on the death-rebirth experience, about how one must be prepared to face death and lose the fear of it if one is to be reborn. It was a long, soul-searching screed, but at least it showed I wasn't taking the event lightly.

On the appointed day we made our way up to Tilden Park, a lovely spot in the hills above Berkeley, and found a secluded glen where we wouldn't be disturbed. We dropped the acid and waited. I think we were expecting an inner journey filled with visions and cosmic insights. What we got was more like a regression to a primate state. All the trappings of civilization fell away, all our intellectual pretensions and expectations. We found ourselves in the prehistoric, preliterate, precognitive condition of ape-men. This included howling like monkeys, swinging from branches, beating hollow logs with sticks, and generally carrying on like wild men. It was a blast! The LSD seemed very friendly, and we became quite attuned to the surrounding nature; colors were intensified, and trees and plants and insects were all revealed in microscopic detail. It was a warm, sunny day, and we loved the feel of the sun on bare skin, loved the sensuality of moving, stretching, walking, and running. Having a body, being in a body, seemed like a wonderful thing. There was not a whiff of anxiety or fear. Our antics alternated with periods of rest when we'd sit in the shade, smoke a little cannabis, and rap. I don't even remember what we discussed, but what we discovered were the first lessons of the first time with this gentle, wise teacher. And we discovered that she was feminine and had a name: Alice D.

We came back off the mountain literally feeling reborn. It was a wonderful first-time experience, and we were grateful to the anonymous dealer, grateful to my brother for hosting us, just grateful to the universe for being alive. We got what we had come for, having crossed the threshold over to those who were "experienced." We certainly hadn't gone mad or suffered harm. In fact, we felt better than ever.

The reality check came quickly, and from an unexpected direction, thanks to that long letter I'd sent Gary back in Paonia a few days earlier. Acting in the foolish way that teenagers sometimes do, I didn't address it to Gary, which would have been logical. Instead I addressed it, in a stilted way that made it seem more important, to "G. Edward," a name Gary had used in a previous correspondence—and which turned out to be the way a long-dead uncle had written the name they shared. The local postmaster, seeing the letter, duly delivered it not to Gary but to his aged aunt. Such are the risks of small-town life, where everybody knows everybody. This good soul opened the letter and was, of course, appalled at my rant about love and death, rebirth and transformation. She lost no time in sharing her concern with Gary's parents, who were even more alarmed; they apparently interpreted the letter as alluding to suicide. That was the furthest thing from my mind when I wrote it, but now I see how it could have been a red flag for them, taken out of context. They were already suspicious of me and took a dim view of my friendship with their son; this only confirmed their worst fears.

Gary's parents contacted my parents, and the leash tightened. Tom and I were ordered to return to Paonia, and we did. My father and I predictably had a huge fight over the debacle. He was enraged and fearful, I think, that my preoccupations were more than a little unhealthy, if not indicative of a serious psychological problem. I tried to explain that the letter meant to be metaphorical, its discussion abstract. I was not about to commit suicide; in fact the LSD experience had left me cherishing life more than ever. But our father didn't want to hear about that. Terence earned his share of opprobrium over the matter as well, for having allowed his little brother to stumble into harm's way.

20 The Secret Encountered

The incident I've just described created a cloud of tension. I was starting my junior year, but most of my friends were seniors looking forward to graduation and escape. Communication with my father had reached a nadir. He was gone most of the week, so my mother was left to deal with a kid who was getting big and hairy. Though inside I felt like a gentle flower child seeking only to "groove" and avoid conflict, I apparently had trouble conveying that as I towered over my fragile, birdlike mom.

Following our return from California, it had emerged that the scourge was not limited to Tom and me. Besides Gary, my friends Richard, Madeline, and Phil had been implicated in my letter as well. While our little group had peripheral members, the six of us formed its core. As ostracized rebels we certainly didn't fit the profile of our peers, who were too preoccupied with football and other wholesome things like sex and drinking to be interested in something as horrible as "drugs." Among our group of bad apples, I was the baddest of the bad, because I had brought this "garbage" from California and corrupted my friends. Richard was the friend I'd known the longest. That fall, his parents and mine had a tense meeting that went nowhere, mostly because my father could not discuss the matter without storming out of the room. To their credit, Richard's parents seemed much more reasonable. Looking back, I'm a little puzzled as to why the hammer didn't come down harder. Not much could have been done; we were in the throes of teenage rebellion, and I think our parents were intimidated. The parents of others in our group really didn't seem to care, or perhaps had given up trying. The so-called generation gap seemed to have widened everywhere, and similar scenarios were surely playing out across the country.

Despite our hasty retreat back to Paonia, Tom and I had accomplished our objective of securing more cannabis—a couple of lids, much better than that first batch but still terrible, I'd guess, by today's standards. We also scored half an ounce of hash, a few hits of acid, something we were told was mescaline but probably wasn't, and—the Holy Grail—half a gram of DMT. I'd bought a small metal opium pipe in Chinatown similar to the one Terence used for smoking hash. As far as our pharmacological adventures went, we were set.

A few of us began finding excuses to take trips up Hubbard Creek, a nearby area accessible by a degraded but passable road. We passed these off as "fishing expeditions," which in a sense they were, but not in any stream—we were bound for the ocean of mind. We dropped acid on one of these occasions, and our trips were similar to what Tom and I had experienced in Berkeley.

But DMT proved even more fascinating. In some ways, DMT is what this book is all about. Terence and I were destined to become preoccupied with this substance; it's what led us years later to the Amazon in search of the Secret. We didn't know what the Secret was, exactly, all we knew for sure was that there was a Secret, and that DMT was somehow the key. It beckoned to us like the glittering jewel of a singularity, a beacon on the threshold of unimaginable dimensions at the edge of space and time. More than 40 years later, it's still a mystery, and it still beckons, though in a different sense. I think it's safe to say that had it not been for DMT, our lives would have turned out quite differently. They would certainly have been more boring.

I had first heard of DMT the previous summer, sitting on the blanket in the city park enjoying cannabis for the first time. Terence spoke of it in hushed tones. He called it "the ultimate metaphysical reality pill," though it wasn't a pill, of course, it was something you smoked. He didn't have any with him, but I was captivated by this description and wanted to try it. Terence insisted that DMT was too much to handle without a lot more experience; I needed more exposure to "mild" hallucinogens before I was ready. As he was my mentor in all things psychedelic, I took his admonitions to heart. In any case, DMT was never easy to come by. It was rare and had a well-deserved reputation for being the ultimate psychedelic. People referred to DMT as "the businessman's trip" because of its short duration; you could smoke it on your lunch break and then return to work. That didn't explain why a businessman would want to return, much less remain a businessman after gazing into the DMT abyss.

But Terence had worked the network, and by the time we got to Berkeley that summer he'd secured several grams of DMT. It was a waxy, orange-colored paste with a foul smell, like ozone, kind of like shit. Terence color-fully described the smell as that "of beryllium welding in interstellar space," and a mere whiff of it seemed to hint at the cosmic dimensions it could open. Pure DMT is a white to off-white crystalline powder and is almost odorless. The stuff on the streets back then was the product of sloppy syntheses, bathtub batches cooked up by crazed chemists who couldn't be bothered to clean up their product. It didn't matter. It delivered. During one of our long conversations in Terence's room in Berkeley, the subject of the philosopher's stone came up, and he remarked, "I know what the philosopher's stone is; it's sitting in that jar right there on the bookshelf." At least to us, this substance was mysterious, magical, and not to be taken lightly.

My first taste of DMT wasn't in Berkeley. Rather, I heeded Terence's advice to get my psychedelic feet wet first before taking the plunge. I brought some home with me, and on one of our visits to Hubbard Creek we "bioassayed" it for the first time. It was everything he had promised, and more. On the second toke, I struggled to hold in the foul-tasting smoke as I watched reality dissolve before my eyes into a billion scintillating fractal jewels, all transforming and squirming before my eyes like iridescent jellyfish while a buzzing, burbling, ripping sound like cellophane being torn to shreds echoed through my aural space; there was a feeling of literally tearing loose, accelerating, falling forward, faster and faster into a twisting, writhing tube or tunnel lined with glistening jewels, a supersonic roller coaster careening through the intestines of God. The term "trip" is a cliché for the psychedelic experience, but in the case of DMT it was very apt. There was definitely a feeling of movement and of crossing a threshold of some kind, of briefly poking one's head into a parallel dimension where the most astonishing things imaginable were going on, all in a frenetic, circuslike atmosphere of hilarious ecstasy. It's almost as if this dimension is always there, just a toke away, and these things, these entities, are bouncing around and cheering, "So happy to see you, so happy to meet you, meatworm, welcome to our world, won't you join the fun?" It was the ultimate carnival ride: climb aboard and away we'll go! Richard described it as being set adrift on a jeweled raft on an ocean of electricity. I thought this was another beautiful description, just as accurate but different. As my explorations continued, that became an axiom. All the trips were different: different on different occasions, but also different for different people. And yet all had similarities.

The problem with DMT and part of its challenge is that the experience is inherently ineffable, it cannot be described in ordinary language, it is translinguistic. You come down, slam back into your body, out of breath, suffused with ecstasy, babbling, sobbing. And yet we are linguistic creatures, and there is a nearly irresistible impulse to try to describe it. This begins almost immediately following the trip, as if verbalization were a protective reflex. DMT is more than the mind can handle; it's overwhelming in its raw nakedness; we feel compelled to try to stuff it back into some kind of linguistic box, and yet to do so is to diminish it. All of the descriptions, even Terence's, as elegant as they are, fall short of the actual experience. This is part of the mystery of DMT. It is a phenomenon that can be repeatedly experienced, and yet it is as astonishing the hundredth time as it was the first, and something that strange is worthy of our attention. Certainly we thought so then, we thought so at La Chorrera, and I still think so.

Nevertheless, I feel compelled to qualify what I've just declared, in light of more recent experiences. While going through an old trunk, I stumbled across a journal from that year, 1967. Amid a mishmash of teenage musings, bad poetry, and expressions of longing for this or that girl, I came upon my account of that first experience with DMT, which if nothing else illustrates how transformative it was:

> Only fragmented and elusive shards of the universe that I visited remain within the grasp of my memory. That is in part what is so baffling about the entire experience: I know that it was the most bizarre thing that ever happened to me, that the reality that I encountered is so totally divorced from normal reality that when my mind re-integrated itself into space-time, it was completely incapable of comprehending, hence of remembering, what it had been through. What is left are only two-dimensional metaphors and shallow dialectical pictures. Even these slip from my consciousness as I attempt, through the use of the inadequate tool of language, to derive some coherence from the half-recollected visions. These were of a bizarre and otherworldly beauty, so alien and yet so beautiful. The human mind cannot endure that much beauty, and that *kind* of beauty, without losing its conception of what reality is.
>
> I have tried, unsuccessfully, to analyze this other reality and fit it into some kind of linguistic description; what I have here set down is the closest I have been able to come. It is extremely unsatisfactory, incomplete, perhaps nonsensical. During the time that I was out, I was unable to speak. My vocal apparatus, had it wanted to, would have been able to form the sound of a habitual expression; but my

mind, or the part of it that normally forms articulate thoughts to be embodied in speech, could not function. Though I could not myself speak, I heard, felt, saw, listened to, perhaps communicated with, a sound that was not a sound, a voice that was more than a voice. *I encountered other creatures whose environment was this alien universe that I had broken through to.* I became aware of, perhaps entered into communication with, actual distinct and separate consciousnesses, members of a race of beings that live in that place, wherever that place may be. These beings appeared to be made of part thought, part linguistic expression, part abstract concept made concrete, part energy. I can say no more as to the nature of these beings except that they do exist.

One thing that is clear is that the experience is a total redirection of karmic goals. I know that after this I am going to strive to be a better person; I am going to try to express the beautiful and concentrate less on the hideous. I am going to see more of [my friend] Dea and try to learn some lessons from her, because I believe that she is good. I am going to try to do good.

And here's an additional passage written some weeks later:

Once again, tomorrow at the rising of the sun, I will do dimethyltryptamine. I have done it too often in recent days, but I regret none of the times; I have profited by each one. I look forward to tomorrow. It will be my last journey for a while to that universe, this time with a girl I could love. Its beauty defies comprehension, but the beauty that it produced and I experienced has made me a better person. As long as one can experience and express (and to experience is to express) the beautiful, then he is saved from madness, he is saved from damnation. I have tried to look at life more positively, I have tried to be more aware of beauty; I have enjoyed the world more and hated myself less.

That I was an insufferable romantic at 16 is certainly clear, but at least I was leaning in the right direction. That experience was therapeutic in many ways. It certainly marked a transition in my life, a pivotal turning point toward the rainforest and beyond. After this (apparent) evidence of the existence of a parallel universe inhabited by nonhuman, intelligent entities, it was a little hard to go back to the routines of daily life.

When I began writing this book in the summer of 2011, it had been more than 15 years since I'd inhaled a hit of DMT. In fact, that occasion, in a hotel room in Rio de Janeiro, involved not DMT per se but its close analog, 5-methoxy-DMT. Some have said that substance is even more bizarre and transformative than DMT, if that's possible. Since then, I've had other encounters with DMT but always in the orally activated form found in ayahuasca. There are definite similarities between DMT and ayahuasca, but those familiar with both states will confirm that they are not identical.

In any case, when a chance arose recently to try some highly purified DMT, I did so, feeling that a return to that "place" was integral to my research. I smoked the DMT on the same evening I'd taken a strong dose of ayahuasca. That experience had ended hours earlier, but I must have still been in a state of extreme MAO inhibition, because it only took one deep breath to plunge me into the abyss of a full-on DMT flash. It was not what I had expected, or remembered. All the elements were there: the frozen feeling bubbling up and permeating my body like quantum foam fizzing up to engulf the fragmenting mind, the feeling of acceleration, my dissolving self urging me to let go, to surrender, as I was sucked into the visionary maelstrom. But there were no entities there this time, no joyous shouts of "hooray" by welcoming, self-transforming, elfin Fabergé eggs as Terence described them to the delight of so many. It was like visiting a brightly lit but abandoned amusement park; the music is playing and all the rides whirl and gyrate and glitter, but there is no one there, no laughter of happy children to add joy and merriment. It was startling to me, and a little sad, how cold and sterile it seemed.

The experience was no less amazing than it used to be, perhaps, but far more austere. Reality is a hallucination generated by the brain to help us make sense of our being; it is made of fragments of memory, associations, ideas, people you remember, dreams you've had, things you've read and seen, all of which is somehow blended and extruded into something resembling a coherent conscious narrative, the hallucination that we call "experience." Dimethyltryptamine rips back that curtain to show the raw data before it has been processed and massaged. There is no comforting fiction of coherent consciousness; one confronts the mindless hammering of frenzied neurochemistry.

Is this the difference between the DMT dimension visited by a lusty, romantic kid of 16 and the jaded man of 61? I honestly can't say. I don't feel that all joy and meaning has fled from my life. I still take ayahuasca regularly and am grateful for the lessons she imparts. But I may never again visit that amusement park of the mind. It is a place for romantics, a place you take your girl on a first date, and I am romantic no longer.

21 The Stoners' Revenge

With the summer of love fading into a fall of discontent and our rebel band growing more alienated from our parents and peers, Terence left to travel the world with his girlfriend. After finishing the Tussman program, he'd decided to drop out of school, which outwardly at least upset our parents. On a deeper level, however, our father's response was probably more complicated. To begin with, he'd paid a lot to support Terence and gotten little gratitude for the sacrifice. He also considered Berkeley to be the epicenter of the degeneracy that was sweeping the younger generation, which it was. Despite the inevitable lecture about Terence needing to complete his education, I think Dad felt some relief when Terence departed with Elaine on the first of his global jaunts.

Terence had worked all summer mounting butterfly specimens at the California Academy of Sciences and had saved enough money to hit the hippie trail, as many others were, bound for India, Nepal, and Jerusalem in search of adventure, good hash, and spiritual fulfillment. Terence, burning with revolutionary fervor and wild ideas, had a book he intended to write before he returned. The work was destined to be the kind of polemical screed a guy writes when he's 20, knows everything, and has bones to pick with everyone; it remains unpublished.

Elaine and Terence were still tight when they set off. After a few months in Europe, they ended up in Jerusalem as planned, but something must have happened along the way, because they soon parted. Elaine joined a kibbutz and remained in Israel. Terence, bereft, continued his wanderings through North Africa to Mombasa, Kenya, where he caught a tramp freighter bound for Seychelles, a tiny archipelago in the Indian Ocean a thousand miles east. He rented a place on Silhouette Island a dozen miles off the main island of Mahé. Terence had done his homework before leaving and had identified Seychelles, then a British colony about to become a commonwealth republic, as just about the closest thing to paradise left on the planet. The plan had been to live there in tropical bliss with Elaine while he wrote his book. He arrived with a broken heart and a supply of cannabis seeds he'd brought with him from California, which he immediately planted in the garden behind his tiny house. His plan was to lay off smoking until his book was done. By then the cannabis would be ready to harvest and he'd reap the rewards born of his patience and discipline. With the seeds in the ground, he started to write.

Back home, life went on as routinely as life can be when one is a restless and rebellious teenager, alienated, brooding, and caught up in the spirit of generational revolution. My closest friends all felt it as well, perhaps even more acutely than other kids because of our isolation as social outcasts. As the town's first hippies, we were regarded with suspicion. It didn't really matter to us; it only reinforced our sense of being special, cut from a different and better cloth than that of our classmates. We had each other, our music, and our dope, and we hung out together as much as we could. We were the only stoners in town; all the others were "alkies," and that only added to our smug sense of superiority. While they were busy getting shit-faced in the gravel pit most weekends, we pursued what we viewed as a better way.

During the week, our little band would often head for my house, haul guitars and albums and pipes and snacks out of the car and sequester ourselves in my bedroom, toke up, and spend hours hanging, talking, playing guitars, and listening to music. We'd have amazing conversations, thanks to the fluid thought processes triggered by the cannabis, and we always seemed to end up with at least one key concept or insight. I don't remember whether my mother was there during these sessions and simply too intimidated to object, or whether we arranged them to coincide with her absences. It wasn't a particularly terrible thing to do; in fact it was a lot less risky and destructive than a lot of teenage behavior at the time.

One group of jocks included kids from some of the "best" families in town. They disdained us as dirty hippies. It was the typical polarity between hippies and rednecks that was playing out in small towns across America. They were infamous in the town as "wild kids," much more publicly obnoxious and confrontational than we were. Their main weekend recreation was to go out somewhere in their fancy cars for bouts of binge drinking. One weekend they all got plastered and drove a convertible down the twisty road between Somerset and Paonia at 120 miles per hour until the car skidded down an embankment and landed, miraculously, right side up in the Gunnison River. The car was totaled but no one was hurt. I daresay getting wasted in my bedroom was much safer. Our belief was that no one knew of our proclivities or newly adopted vices, but some of our peers were on to us as we soon discovered. During that fall, a new variable entered my life in the form of a new friend. Dea grew up on the Western Slope, but she had been living with a dealer in the Haight, a pretty tough guy, I gathered, who was also involved with a motorcycle gang. It was Tom who first encountered her, I don't know where. It turned out she was a "recovering nymphomaniac" in her words; she'd returned from the crazy scene in San Francisco to try to get her life back together. Dea, a brown-eyed, long-haired, slender girl a couple of years older than I was, wore knee-high leather boots, beads, bangles, and enticingly sheer blouses. I was immediately smitten with her, but I told myself that if I treated her well, our platonic ties would naturally evolve toward physical affection.

That never happened, but I still enjoyed hanging out with her. She had a van we'd take on day trips to Hayes Creek Falls or other sites along the Crystal River. We'd sit in the back of the van and get thoroughly baked and then go climbing on the cliffs above the waterfall, giving me a chance to admire her slender grace. We kissed occasionally, and she seemed to enjoy it, but she refused to go beyond that, insisting her past behavior had been a moral failing she had to overcome. Instead, Dea became a kind of muse for me. I wrote poetry and haiku about her; I dreamed of her. She disappeared suddenly from my scene after a series of unfortunate events. For one thing, my father hated her, hippie that she was, and the fact she was older made her a threat to me in his eyes. After we drifted apart, she went back to her former lover in San Francisco, or so I was told. I never heard from her again. She was a fragile figure in many ways, destined, I feared, to break in the course of life. I hope I was wrong.

It wasn't too long into the fall semester of my junior year that our tiny stoner band met its inevitable and humiliating end. I mentioned that we often gathered in my bedroom after school. I'd break out the hash and we'd pass the pipe and have a good time getting quietly baked. My first inkling that security had been breached was when a classmate who lived across the street asked me one day, in a snarky way, "Can I have a drag off'n that there opium pipe a yers, McKinney?" Believe it or not, that's how people talked in Paonia in those days. I barely knew the guy, and his question wasn't welcomed. He and his pals must have been eavesdropping underneath my bedroom window. Though I never knew for sure, I assumed he was the one who informed on our sweet scene and brought us down, an event that branded me as a figure just short of the Antichrist and brought our psychonautic adventures to a temporary end.

On the morning of the day it happened, I had gotten up early and driven to the airport outside of town to meet Dea. Our plan was to smoke DMT together while parked at the end of the runway and watch the sunrise. This we did, without incident. It was just the start of another ordinary school day except that we had gotten together to breach the cosmic portals for a few minutes before the 8:30 bell. Afterward, I said good-bye to her and arrived in class still shimmering from my teleportation and probably reeking of DMT. The day passed uneventfully until the fourth period, when I was in my advanced English class, taught by a teacher, and a good one, we cruelly called "Large Marge." The thing is, she really wasn't large at all. She was a good friend of my mother's, which didn't make what happened any easier. Most of my partners in crime were there as well, though they were seniors and I was a junior. It was the last class of the afternoon.

About midway through it, Large Marge singled out the six of us in our group and sent us to the office. When we got there, the school principal told us to get our collective asses downtown to the city hall, just a couple of blocks away, where all of our parents were waiting. Thank God my father was traveling that week and only my mother was there.

Most of the other rebels weren't so lucky. The jig was up. The sheriff and his deputy took turns lecturing us on what a terrible thing it was for us to be doing, making sure that I was singled out as mastermind and ringleader. I was defiant. I tried to argue with them about the merits of cannabis versus alcohol, but they were not there to be persuaded, they were there to shut us down, hard, which they did.

The parental reactions ranged from extreme anger to stunned incomprehension. Gary's parents were especially furious. They'd never liked me, and here was incontrovertible proof that I had led their precious son astray. He was forbidden on the spot to ever see or associate with me again, a ban that actually held up through most of the year. After that session, all my friends sheepishly filed out, accompanied by their parents. I was not let off so lightly. They kept me behind and gave me a stern lecture, calling me lucky not to be headed for jail. I was sobered and subdued by that time. I realized that they were right. They said that they knew I had supplied the drugs, and that I had the drugs, and that what I needed to do was to go with them back to my house and give them my stash; if I did that, they would overlook this offense, for now. They pressed me on where I had obtained the dope, suggesting that a certain figure from town then living in Aspen had been my source, which I denied, because he hadn't.

We went back to the house, and I pulled out a dresser drawer behind which I had sequestered a lovely, silk-lined box I'd purchased with my pipe in Chinatown that summer. The box held my cannabis, the hash, several tabs of acid and mescaline, and the DMT. They took it all. The search wasn't too thorough; they didn't even check behind the dresser drawer to make sure they had gotten everything, and in fact they hadn't. They'd missed the bottles of brucine and yohimbine (both reputed aphrodisiacs) that I'd ordered from Sigma (anyone could in those days) as well as a bottle of adrenaline. I had an "experiment" underway, an effort to produce adrenochrome, a purported hallucinogen, by irradiating a solution of adrenaline with ultraviolet light. A black light I'd bought to put a glow on my psychedelic posters now illuminated a flask of adrenaline on the shelf above my bed. Perhaps distracted by the wild posters themselves, they didn't even notice that purple solution. After they left I flushed it down the toilet, which was probably just as well.

The following months were tense for our tattered band. We weren't hailed as fearless warriors of the new psychedelic revolution, not by a long shot. We were more isolated than ever, shunned as the school's untouchables for the rest of the year. We were defiant, of course, and for the most part we stuck together more tightly than ever. It wasn't long after the bust that some of us started smoking pipes and cigarettes. It became our custom to spend our lunch hours sitting on the hood and fenders of Tom's Plymouth, parked in the lot across the street in plain sight of school, and enjoy a good long smoke.

This drove the principal crazy, but we weren't on school property and tobacco wasn't restricted in those days. Our smoking was both perfectly legal and a defiant political statement. It's ironic, really. Pipe smoking became a habit that I've only been able to give up in the last couple of years. Of the various drugs I've taken over the years, pipe smoking was probably the most harmful and also one of the most pleasurable. Such is life. Tobacco was not particularly addictive for me; it was easy to quit when I finally made the decision to do so. The fact is, I enjoyed it, and that is why I had persisted in using it.

The principal disliked us, and the feeling was mutual. I recall a coincidence that has stayed with me for being so odd. I was in the library one day under earphones listening to "Ballad of a Thin Man," Bob Dylan's portrait of the clueless square, on the school's cassette recorder. By then its refrain had already become the hip world's view of the straight world reduced to a few words: "Because something is happening here/But you don't know what it is/Do you, Mister Jones?" In the last verse, the thin man walks into a room, eyes in his pocket and "nose on the ground," as the balladeer concludes, "There ought to be a law/Against you comin' around/You should be made/To wear earphones."

And that's what happened. Just as the song neared this point, the principal stepped into the library, walked toward me, and picked up an extra set of earphones just in time to hear Dylan's last verse for himself. The timing was perfect. It was too perfect! I looked up at him and smiled. Not a word passed between us. He took off the earphones and left.

A defining event that school year turned out to be my encounters with a new English teacher. Mack Faith had actually been teaching junior and senior English for a year, but as a sophomore I had not been in his classes. Mack was a recent graduate of the education program at Western State College in Gunnison. He turned out to be a fellow subversive and befriended our alienated group. He and his wife Diana made a charming couple but, like so many faculty who came and went from the local high school over the years, they never quite fit in.

New faculty members were not always welcomed with open arms by their peers. Most teachers had been hired because they could coach a sport, not for their classroom skills. Mack, an intellectual, was different; he loved to teach and was damn good at it. He and his wife were what would be called "liberal" today, often with a sneering tone. They believed in a lot of subversive things like racial equality and social justice.

The town's xenophobic warning systems marked them immediately as radicals, subversives, effete intellectuals, and "not like us." They were outcasts, and so was our little group of protohippies; naturally we were drawn to each other. They welcomed us into their home on many occasions, where we would do pretty much what we did when we got together on our own, sans the dope. Mack wasn't a hippie, or at least didn't look like one, and he never got loaded with us. We respected his decision, knowing he respected ours and never pressed him or brought dope to his house. He became a friend and a mentor to us for most of that year. I think he was still close enough to us in age that he could empathize with many of our concerns. We were all preoccupied with civil rights and the Vietnam War, strongly in favor of the former and vehemently opposed to the latter. The conversations we had with them in the living room of their tiny rented house served to heighten and focus our political consciousness.

Besides teaching English, Mack was the drama and debate coach. Being nerdy, nonathletic types who fancied ourselves intellectuals, we were drawn to those activities, and he encouraged us. The meatheads and jocks were not particularly interested in such things, so it was a chance for us to shine. Our debate and drama practices became rich opportunities to hang out together and share time with this wonderful man. He seemed to believe that maybe we actually had things worth doing, worth saying, worth thinking. We presented George Orwell's *Nineteen Eighty-Four* as that year's junior-senior class play. I had the leading role of Winston Smith, while my buddy Phil played O'Brien, Smith's betrayer and ultimately his inquisitor. The story provocatively highlighted the hypocrisy of the times, and we flung ourselves into it with enthusiasm.

Later that spring, we put together a one-act adaptation of George Bernard Shaw's *Arms and the Man* and entered it into the state drama competition in Denver. This proved to be the stoners' revenge. When we performed the play we were loaded—on cannabis, mostly, though some of us may have been on stronger stuff. We totally swept the board: best actor, best play, best adaptation, best everything. Mack was pleased; the rest of us were stunned and ecstatic. We were a Podunk high school from the Western Slope going up against the best drama departments in Colorado, and we had totally triumphed. I think the faculty and a lot of others at the school didn't know what to say. We were supposed to be the degenerate dirty rotten hippies and we'd brought glory and recognition to our school. We were congratulated—grudgingly—by the principal during a school assembly at the end of the semester. Knowing what he really thought of us, I'm sure that stuck in his craw.

I remember Mack with fondness. He was my first real mentor-teacher. I have been blessed to have others since then, but Mack was the first. He believed in me, in us, when no one else did. I will always love him for that. Not only was he a mentor, he taught me, by example, the importance of that role. I have been a teacher myself now for over a decade, and I try to be a mentor and encourage my students to believe in themselves, to think for themselves, and to not let anyone stop them from doing what they need to do. Some of them have taken that to heart, and I have been proud to see them go forth to pursue careers and life paths that are way beyond anything I could ever accomplish. It's satisfying to know you have made a difference to a bright mind.

22 My Datura Misadventure

Following the bust, our oppressors underestimated our ingenuity and commitment to continuing our explorations. Soon thereafter, my fellow adventurer Richard and I were severely poisoned, thanks to my lack of botanical expertise at the time. According to the mainstream media, a craze had been sweeping the country: young people were flocking to their local garden supply shops to buy morning glory seeds, which had been reported to contain LSD-like compounds. In fact, this is true of certain species. There's evidence that some species of *Ipomoea* and *Rivea* were used as ritual intoxicants by the Aztecs and other Mesoamerican groups, and were known in the Nahuatl language as *ololiuqui*, meaning "round thing" in reference to the seeds. I had known about that for some time, and had tried *Ipomoea* seeds a few months earlier. The dose must have been either too small or insufficiently digested, because I never got anywhere besides a mild nausea after bolting down 300 or so seeds of the Heavenly Blue variety.

But, being the intrepid and reckless psychonaut that I was, I was ready to give it another go. After all, there were very few other options after the bust, and I thought I knew more than I did. (I have since compensated for that in my old age by realizing that I know very little about anything.) There was an odd fellow living in Paonia at the time, a harmless gentleman who worked in the local haberdashery. He was also floridly gay, so naturally he was ostracized, vilified, mocked in the ways that were accepted and yet so needlessly cruel in those days. He lived by himself in a tiny one-room building behind the clothing store, and the yard of this humble dwelling was a weedy lot. Among the weeds growing there was a beautiful, robust plant that had a strong odor and put out enormous white flowers. Fancying that I was a far better botanist than was the case, I determined it to be a moonflower plant, a morning glory species now known as *Ipomoea alba*, which indeed does have enormous, lovely white flowers. And so I thought that its seeds might be a good source of the lysergic acid alkaloids reported in related species. Richard, Phil, and I decided it was worthy of a LAB, that is, a large animal bioassay. So we waited until after dark one night, snuck into George's yard, collected several of the unripe, juicy, spiky seedpods, and went off somewhere to bolt them down.

Those with a modicum of botanical expertise have by now recognized my dangerous mistake. The plant we collected is sometimes referred to as moonflower and does have large white flowers. It is more often called jimsonweed, however, a name applied to several species of *Datura*, a toxic member of the deadly nightshade family. What we'd gotten our hands on was *Datura metel*, which is highly psychoactive but not psychedelic. It contains the toxic tropane alkaloids atropine, hyoscyamine, scopolamine, and related minor alkaloids. They are potent anticholinergics, meaning that they block the action of the neurotransmitter acetylcholine. At high doses they can be fatal, but at the lower doses we (thankfully) had ingested, it induces a state of profound delirium and confusion. One usually has little recall of the experience, because it also wipes out short-term memory.

In my lectures these days, I tell my students that *Datura* is a true hallucinogen but not a psychedelic, whereas psychedelics like psilocybin are true psychedelics but not hallucinogens. I make the distinction on pharmacological and phenomenological grounds. True psychedelics are serotonin or 5-HT_{2A} agonists (serotonin is also called 5-hydroxytryptamine, commonly abbreviated to 5-HT). This means that they activate a particular population of 5-HT receptors in the brain, namely, the 5-HT_{2A} receptor subtypes. True psychedelics like LSD, DMT, psilocybin, and mescaline all have in common that they are 5-HT_{2A} agonists. They induce profound visual distortions and hypnagogic images behind the eyelids but rarely induce true hallucinations, which psychologists define as seeing something that is not there but that one is unable to tell is not there. On psychedelics, one may see things that are not there but generally knows these things are not "real."

The tropane alkaloids from *Datura* and other nightshades act quite differently. They are antagonists—that is, they block the action of the neurotransmitter acetylcholine at a subtype of receptors called muscarinic acetylcholine receptors. And the experience they elicit is quite different than the typical psychedelic experience. They don't cause pretty patterns behind the eyelids, nor do they induce the feelings of ecstasy and oceanic boundlessness that is a typical aspect of the mystical, transcendent states that make psychedelics so interesting. But they do induce true hallucinations, meaning that one sees things that appear to be real but aren't. And there is no way to tell, at least not in the resulting state of delirium and confusion.

The dose we'd taken was more than enough to manifest the full spectrum of tropane alkaloid poisoning for the next 36 hours. We suddenly got a crash course in datura consciousness, although I was trying to fit it into the context of a bad acid trip, based on my assumption that we'd eaten morning glory seeds. I had only taken acid once or twice previously, so as far as I knew, this was the "bad trip" that the supposed experts were trying to scare everyone with. A few weeks later I found a picture of the very plant that grew in the haberdasher's garden, and it was *Datura metel*. Then it all made sense. What we'd survived was not an atypical acid trip, but a textbook example of acute tropane intoxication. The experience was horrific in many respects, and my recollections are fragmentary, given that the drug itself partially blocks short-term memory. From what little I do recall, I can say that the seeds began to act very quickly after we'd eaten them, and things got weird.

After the three of us had collected the seeds, we returned to my home and reclined in my room. Phil, who had to drive home, had decided not to ingest, but Richard and I had done so. It took about 20 minutes for an overwhelming effect to manifest, and by the time I got up to see Richard and Phil out the door, the effects were already out of control. Mom was sleeping, and in my confusion I lost my way and stumbled into her bedroom. She was appalled; she could see something was wrong but couldn't tell what. She became very alarmed, almost hysterical. I thought she was going insane, but just the opposite was true. I brushed past her, muttering something like "It'll be OK," and barricaded myself in my room. I was panicked but I just wanted to sit down and try to get my center.

An effect of the tropane alkaloids is that they induce mydriasis, that is, they markedly dilate the eyes. As a result, you can't focus on anything; your vision is blurry, and if you look at mottled surfaces, anything with texture, they'll appear to be moving or squirming. The tropane-impaired vision, accompanied by tropane-impaired cognitive and interpretive functions, construct a hallucinatory representation of reality that may or may not correspond to consensus reality. Which explains why I saw *bugs*! In my delirious and visually impaired state, every surface in the room appeared to be swarming with insects. I was quite distraught. Finally the situation reached a crescendo when somehow, kind of out of nowhere, emerged what I saw as the Chief Bug, or the seed source of all these bugs. I have no idea what the actual object was; I think it may have been a piece of charred paper or something like that. But I determined that the Chief Bug must be expelled, and so with great fear and loathing I caught the evil thing up and burst out of the room, ran to the trash can in the alley behind the house, and disposed of it. Then I ran back to my room and barricaded myself in again.

This is what I remember happening. I think it happened, but maybe it is a complete fabrication or false memory. All this time, while the drama with the bugs was unfolding in my bedroom, people would appear to me, wraith-like, at the foot of the bed. They were mostly my friends, or at least I thought they were. I would plead for help, crying out help me, help me! And they would just look pitying, and slowly fade away. These prolonged apparitions are completely typical of the tropane experience. Certain *Datura* species and the closely related *Brugmansia* species are used extensively in witchcraft in South America. (The *Brugmansia* species were formerly classified as belonging to the *Datura* genus and are sometimes called "tree daturas.") The plants are widely used for *brujería* both in European witchcraft and in Indigenous practices. This is partly a result of the fact that they are power plants; that is, they can be used to render a person helpless as a result of the confusion and disorientation they can produce. Their ability to evoke an unseen world populated by disembodied or wraithlike spirits may form the basis for such belief systems in both the Western and Indigenous traditions.

After I had succeeded in expelling the Chief Bug from my room, things settled down a bit. The experience was far from over but at least my panic had subsided. I eventually fell into a troubled and dream-wracked sleep, although sleep is a misnomer because the state of datura intoxication is much like being in a dream, or more accurately, a nightmare. Sometime the next morning the effects were diminished enough that I could emerge from my room and talk to my mother. We had a more or less coherent conversation about what had happened. My vision had improved; I was no longer hallucinating bugs, but wraiths were still showing up at the peripheries of vision, and this persisted for hours.

Later that day, we went over to Richard's house and talked to his mother. Richard's experience had also been long and horrific. Like me, he was far from recovered; our symptoms persisted even 18 hours after ingestion. While we were sitting at the kitchen table in Richard's house, the air suddenly filled with a brown fog, and large pieces of hash began to materialize out of the air! Only Richard and I could see it, of course, but despite our best efforts it was not possible to lay our hands on any and smoke it! This was the first manifestation of what came to be known as the Good Shit. It also figured prominently in the aftermath of the experiment at La Chorrera some four years in the future, when I conjured hash out of the air with my guitar while performing with my band, the Good Shit. Of course I had neither guitar nor band, nor Good Shit for that matter, but during my delusions at the time I believed I had both.

The misadventure marked the end of our explorations for a while. My father was furious when he returned and heard about it. By then, I think, he was ready to wash his hands of me. He asked me if I'd learned my lesson, if I'd ever do that again. I said yes, I would, because I saw it as important to confront one's fears. (Remember, I thought I'd survived a bad acid trip.) After that answer, he said that I had to be demented, and perhaps I was.

Within a few weeks, reports of our datura encounter had spread through our circle, inexplicably compelling a couple of girls to try it themselves. After collecting seeds from the haberdasher's plant, they bolted them down at the local pool hall and caused a minor scandal when they took off their clothes and ran into the street. Though I was not present, I was, naturally enough, blamed for it as the pied piper who had led these innocents astray.

Shortly after that, the bush with the big white flowers disappeared. I believe the local sheriff decided it had to be eradicated, and he was probably right. I've noted this already, but it's worth repeating: datura should not be taken lightly. In fact, I don't recommend it under any circumstances. The *Brugmansia* species, the tree daturas, are extensively used in South American shamanism, and the leaves are occasionally used as an admixture in ayahuasca. I've had ayahuasca laced with *toé* (the traditional name for *Brugmansia*) and it doesn't enhance the experience. One can often tell the additive is present in the ayahuasca brew because the tropanes cause a "dry mouth" effect, inducing a persistent, severe thirst, which is part of their anticholinergic effect. If you should ingest ayahuasca that induces this effect, there is a good chance it contains *toé* as an admixture, and *that*, in turn, is a good sign that you are dealing with a *brujo*, a witch, a person of dubious character.

23 Escape from Mordor: 1968

Following the drama festival, the final semester of my junior year rapidly drew to a close. Most of my close friends graduated that spring and began scattering to their various destinies. Richard went off to Aspen and found a cooking job, a move that defined his later career as a highly regarded chef. Tom, who had worked off and on as a carpenter throughout high school, headed for Denver to help out his brother's construction company. Gary had recently met and become engaged to his first wife. Shortly after graduation, the couple resettled in Boulder where Gary began his studies at the University of Colorado. Of the original group, only Madeline, Phil, and I were still stuck in Paonia.

The prospect of returning to school after we'd been ostracized seemed quite bleak. Since Terence had been allowed to complete his final two years of high school in California, it seemed only fair that I should be allowed to go somewhere else for my last year. Determined to escape, I hatched a plan I began to implement shortly after the semester ended.

Crossing the mountain to the Crystal River Valley, I got a summer job as a dishwasher at the Redstone Inn, just up the road from my aunt and uncle's ranch. The inn had been built by John Cleveland Osgood, a coal baron who created a mining and steelmaking empire in the area in the late 19th century. Osgood and his second wife, a Swedish countess, had lived in a lavish Tudor-style mansion half a mile up a private road from his inn. That 42-room house was officially known as Cleveholm Manor, but we called it the Redstone Castle. Osgood, one of the top industrialists of his day, designed Redstone as a company town complete with a theater, library, bathhouse, clubhouse, and school. In addition to 84 chalet-style cottages built to house the married miners and their families, there was the inn, which originally served as lodging for single miners. The Redstone became a high-end inn in 1925 after Osgood lost the mine in a bitter stock dispute, and with minor interruptions (and through many owners), it has operated as a resort ever since.

Kids from Paonia and other nearby towns often got summer jobs in resort towns such as Aspen, Glenwood Springs, and Redstone. The winter ski season was busier, but there was enough summer tourist traffic to make it relatively easy to find work. I was soon ensconced in a dormer room in the Redstone Inn with the other summer slaves. As long as I showed up to wash dishes for the dinner shift each evening, I was free to ramble the surrounding hills. Though my stay was short and uneventful, it was a novel situation for being the first time I'd lived on my own.

I somehow obtained a tab of acid and took it alone one beautiful moonlit night. I felt it was important that I should take it alone, and at night—partly, I think, because I wanted to confront the fears triggered by my misadventure with datura. My third LSD trip went off without a hitch. It was a beautiful experience. I spent half of it wandering the nearby forests and trails and half alone in my room. The highlight was when I looked in the mirror. This is not something you want to do on LSD unless you're prepared! I spent a long time looking into my own eyes, studying my visage. After a few minutes of staring, I met my totem animal: a lion! I was quite surprised but it was unmistakable. Ever since that night I have known and identified with the lion as my shamanic spirit guide. One could do worse.

My three-week stint there ended when I moved on to the Aspen–Snowmass area and its developing hippie scene. It was not exactly the Haight, but it would do. There were drugs to be had, hippie chicks about, and loads of possibilities. Being just that much farther from Paonia was a definite plus, and so was having Richard there as a friend. I quickly secured another dishwashing gig, this time at Cyrano's Restaurant in Snowmass Village, a fancy shrimp and steak house in the center of the Snowmass Mall. The job included accommodations in the half-empty Pokolodi Lodge. This turned out to be a sweet deal. I had a job, I had lodging—little more than a hotel room, but it would serve—and I had most of my meals provided by the restaurant. If you're young and itinerant and don't care about making more than just enough to get by, I highly recommend dishwashing as a profession. There's a need for this skill almost everywhere, and it's a good way to secure employment as soon as you arrive in a new place. It worked for me in Redstone and Snowmass, and at various other times in the years ahead. I was set for a great summer. In fact, it was destined to be one king-hell *crazy* summer, to borrow a phrase from an Aspen local, Hunter S. Thompson.

By this time, Tom, the carpenter, had relocated in Denver and connected with some of the area's recreational psychopharmacologists, an eclectic mix of very smart, occasionally quite dysfunctional people. But they had access to good drugs, and wheels, so my little outpost in Snowmass became a weekend party destination. Practically every weekend one or more of the Denver crowd would show up, ready for some serious bioassays. There was a lovely little lake near the lodge, a short walk away. There was rarely anyone up there, so it became our own private retreat, a place we'd go to trip on the psychedelic of the week, hunt mushrooms, and just hang out.

Into this scene came Terence, fresh from his yearlong ramble through Asia and the layover in Seychelles where he'd written his book. He had the manuscript with him, ready to pitch it to publishers in New York. As I mentioned, his idea had been to plant his cannabis seeds and write until both the book and his crop had reached a finished state. According to a story Terence would later tell, when that day came he got totally baked and realized what he'd written was terrible. He panicked, knowing he had to rewrite the entire thing, which he did, smoking day and night, extending his stay on Silhouette Island an extra month while he bulled it through. He thought the result was much better; at least he would not be embarrassed to show it around. Though I never saw the pre-cannabis version, when I did finally get a chance to read the manuscript I found it interesting but flawed, and Terence would have been the first to agree. Its interesting title suggested a McLuhanesque influence: *Crypto-Rap: Meta-Electrical Speculations on Culture.* It was the kind of book that an intense, angry young intellectual, fueled by psychedelics and radical politics, would write in the waning years of the 1960s. There was plenty of good material in there, but it wasn't going to cause a stir among publishers, as he later discovered. The manuscript still exists. It might be of interest today for historical reasons more than as a work of cultural analysis. That said, it surely holds clues to the evolution of Terence's thought process and may yet find its way into the light.

Terence's stopover in Snowmass was brief but rich. He had arrived back from Asia on the West Coast and was on his way to New York to sell the book and perhaps to pursue a new love interest. I know nothing about her beyond that she lived out East and was one of the magnets drawing him to New York. During his travels in Asia, Terence had done a bit of hash smuggling, which in those days was relatively easy. Before the war on drugs started, a lot of itinerants were able to finance their nomadic lifestyles by sending a few ounces, or a few kilos, of Nepali temple balls or Afghani Red to the hash-starved folks back home. Since he'd be passing through Colorado, he'd decided to direct one of his shipments to Paonia, addressing it to himself at our post office box so he could pick it up.

Needing a respite from Snowmass, we decided to spend a few days in Paonia. Dad flew over in his plane and brought us home. Terence was agitated and insisted on checking the mail every day. He said this was his biggest shipment yet. When it finally arrived, we knew it immediately, because the entire post office was redolent with the aroma of fine Nepali hash. Terence had had the bright idea to conceal the hash in the swollen stomach of one of those "happy Buddha" statuettes. The only problem was, the shippers had done a shoddy job of gluing the thing together, and it had broken open in transit, scattering large balls of hash throughout the packing material.

Terence handled this with aplomb. When he stepped to the window to pick up the package, the postmaster asked if it contained perfume or something. Without missing a beat, Terence replied, "Incense." Our friendly local postmaster might have been a little skeptical at this explanation, but if so he didn't let on. We accepted the package, which was elaborately sewn with a muslin covering, and hightailed it out of there. The good news was that we now had an abundance of hash, including a small personal stash that made my remaining year of high school quite tolerable.

Shortly after that, Terence took off for New York, where he hoped to sell some Tibetan thangkas he'd purchased in Kathmandu—"smelly, moth-eaten things," our father called them—each worth several thousand dollars. Terence got a good price for them in New York among the Asian art dealers. His love interest apparently hadn't panned out, and he only stayed there a few weeks. But his pockets were stuffed again. Everyone who could, it seemed, was hitting the hippie trail in India, Thailand, and Nepal. Terence wasted no time getting back on the road. Having discovered a taste for the nomadic lifestyle and a way to fund it, he was prepared to travel for the rest of his life. I wouldn't see him again for almost two years, just months before our mother's death and our subsequent trip to Colombia. We corresponded, though at a leisurely pace that those who have grown up with e-mail can scarcely imagine. The richness and depth of our exchanges more than made up for their infrequency. Though we didn't really think of it in such terms at the time, we were hatching our plans to actualize the eschaton.

August was fading; already an early autumn chill could be felt in the clear mountain mornings. Terence had left for the East Coast, book and thangkas in tow, and I entered phase three in my plan to evade a return to Paonia for my senior year. Over the summer at Snowmass, I'd become pretty good friends with my boss at the restaurant, whose name was Joe. Joe wasn't that much older than I was, but he qualified as a kind of mentor. He understood why I dreaded going back to Mordor, so he offered to sponsor me, which meant he'd become, if not my guardian, at least a responsible adult willing to look after me. With his support assured, I approached the principal at Aspen High School, who proved to be open-minded about the experiment. It helped that I'd be turning 18 in a few months, making me a legal adult. If Joe was willing to look after me by providing menial employment and a roof to stay under, the principal agreed to let me enroll.

I sprang the surprise on my parents when they arrived to drive me home. Both were unhappy about it, especially my mother, who was probably upset at the thought of losing a second son after Terence had prematurely flown the coop for California. Given that precedent, I insisted that I ought to be allowed to finish school somewhere else, somewhere less narrow-minded. Mom was already quite concerned about her sons, given our interest in psychedelics. She couldn't imagine our explorations in that alien world could lead to anything good. I remember one tearful conversation Terence and I had with her that summer. "You both have fine minds," she said. "I am just so worried that you will lose them to a bunch of drugs." We tried to reassure her that our interest was serious, and that our investigations might one day lead us to become great scientists. Ironically, her words were prophetic, though she wouldn't live to see our departure for La Chorrera and the psychological upset that awaited us there. Nor did she live to see that we were right as well. Indeed, Terence and I would continue to explore our youthful fascinations, if along different paths. I might not have achieved greatness as a scientist, but I have earned a modest reputation investigating the very substances she so feared. It saddens me that our passions were never more than a source of constant worry for her.

On that day in Aspen when I told them I was staying, my father could see I was determined. By arranging to be enrolled, employed, and sponsored by an adult, I had outmaneuvered him, leaving him without much to say. By then he was probably so disgusted with me he might have been happy to let me go, but Mom wasn't ready for the nest to be so abruptly vacated. After intense discussion, we worked out a compromise. I would not complete my senior year at Aspen High, that hotbed of dope and liberal ideas, nor would I return to classes in Paonia. Instead, my mother and I would rent an apartment in Grand Junction and I'd finish my studies there. We would stay at the apartment during the week while my father was on the road and return to Paonia for the weekends. In many ways this arrangement worked out well. For one thing, the sheer size of Grand Junction High School, with its more than 3,000 students, improved my prospects of meeting compatible friends. The school also offered many academic opportunities that weren't available in Paonia, with its student body of 250. As the year wore on, this became the justification my parents often gave their friends when asked why I was attending a different school: I was a brilliant kid, they said, and I deserved some of the advantages that Terence had enjoyed. I heartily agreed. Though I returned to Paonia many times that year, and many times since, I would never again be its prisoner.

I want to pause the narrative there, in 1968, and take a moment to acknowledge how my feelings about Paonia have changed over the decades. I last visited my hometown in the fall of 2011 as a pilgrim doing research for this book. I wanted to reflect on family roots, on the ties that bind a life to a place and time. I flew into Aspen and poked around there for a day, looking for the old haunts where I'd lived in summers past, but everything had changed. Like buildings in the film *Dark City*, those in Aspen had morphed and remorphed over the decades, some torn down, others thrown up, others renovated, many in that pseudo-Tyrolean style that tends to plague ski towns. While Aspen remains a theme park for the über-wealthy, a plastic cocoon of tasteful but corporatized shops and restaurants and galleries, the rest of western Colorado is a different story. Like most everywhere else, circumstances have gotten harder there: foreclosures, unemployment, no healthcare, crumbling infrastructure, a sense of America collapsing into a sort of stunned Third Worldism as the country realizes its day in the sun is over.

And yet, for all that, life was good on that warm and clear October afternoon, with the aspens in full color in the high country, the hills dripping with molten yellows and oranges, aflame with the dying foliage giving up its soul in a carotenoid riot. The sky was brilliant blue with wispy clouds aloft and a lot of lenticular cloud formations—a good sign! I drove out of Aspen and headed for Snowmass Village, still more a bubble than Aspen will ever be, a planned community from the start. I knew Cyrano's, the restaurant, had been gone for decades, but I spent an hour wandering the mall, which was eerily empty in the off-season; I felt I'd stepped into an old computer game like Myst. I stopped where I was pretty sure the restaurant had been, but the surroundings were all different. As for the little lake a short walk from the lodge where I'd stayed in 1968, perhaps that had been an artificial reservoir. I'm not sure, but a later search for it via Google Earth after my trip led me to think it might be gone as well.

Returning to the highway, Colorado 133, I passed through Carbondale with its lovely, redone main drag, lots of cobblestone, little shops, street sculpture, and even a medical cannabis dispensary—a hopeful development. Why shouldn't this simple and good medicine be available at your local apothecary, as it once was? There's far too much handwringing about things like this that could be so simply solved. I took the back way into Redstone, inching through town, watching out for the kids, until I reached the Redstone Inn, as imposing and quaintly out-of-date as ever with its towers and dormers, wraparound balconies and gingerbread banisters. In the plaza formed by its U-shaped driveway was a chromed metal sculpture of a falconer, complete with falcon, seated on a chair. It was a cool sculpture, but I couldn't decide if it fit there or not. Any change from the past as I remembered it introduced a kind of cognitive dissonance. I ate in the inn that evening, but I stayed at Chair Mountain Ranch, always a bittersweet experience. It's hard to be at a place that figured in so many family memories without feeling eight years old again. And yet there, too, much had changed. The lodge's outward appearance was much as I recalled it, but the old cabins were gone, replaced by a row of very nice two-bedroom cabins across from the new fishing pond—"new" meaning not there when I was a boy. The current proprietors are nice folks, but of course they can't understand how, for me, the ranch is like a family heirloom that's been sold off to someone with no connections to its past.

The next day I drove to Delta with my cousin Judy to visit my beloved Aunt Mayme on her 97th birthday. Medicaid paid for her to live in a nursing home in return for the lien on her house, this being the brutal way we provide for the extremely old; finally, you lose everything, they take it all. But it's a good place, clean and bright, and she was well cared for by the attentive staff. Though she could no longer see or hear well, and was out of it most of the time, behind her rheumy eyes her lively spirit and sense of humor were still there, I felt, but just not getting out. I thought she had a flash of recognition at the sight of me, but that may have been wishful thinking. Still and all, it was a somewhat depressing and sobering encounter, her grim plight a reminder of what lies in store for many of us, that is, to live for years beyond the joy of being alive.

I made a mental note to remember to secure myself that tincture of hemlock so it's there when the time comes. I'd rather exit in style, under my own volition, or so I say now. We'll see.

We stayed an hour, sharing a little ice cream until lunch arrived and then quietly slipped out. Though I knew I might not see her again, somehow my sense of loss was not as great as it had been in the past. So much of her was already gone. She died several months later.

The rest of the day was considerably more upbeat. Judy and I stopped by the new Paonia Public Library, a beautiful facility paid for by donations from the community, including the purchase of $50 bricks, which afforded me the treat of standing in the lobby and reviewing the names etched on them, each one evoking old memories, faces, teachers, families. My civically engaged cousin is on the library board and is the curator of the North Fork Historical Society Museum, which we visited next. The place was full of artifacts left by the people who settled and built Paonia, some of them pictured in ancient, faded photos; I couldn't imagine what was masked by the dour expressions on those long-dead faces. There was too much to process—old cameras, musical instruments, bygone baby clothes and adult fashions, an entire high school classroom complete with antique desks, an office, a child's bedroom, an old-fashioned kitchen. I spotted a few familiar items, including my grandfather's old Remington typewriter, an uncle's letter sweater, and the doll furniture and a toy kitchen set that once belonged to Judy and her twin sister. I even recognized the embroidered sentiment that hung in Aunt Mayme's kitchen for decades: "Old friendships are like flowers in memory's scented garden." The flowers are faded now, their scent reminiscent of the inside of my mother's purse when I was a boy, a vague amalgam of cheap lavender cologne and makeup.

Then Judy brought out the real treasures, stored in an old filing cabinet: nearly pristine copies of the *Eyrie*, the Paonia High School yearbook for 1968 and '69. Here were the photos of my former classmates, old friends and enemies, girls I'd pined for with their crazy upswept hairdos—innocent young women, now aging like me. A few of my former schoolmates had departed the world by then, including my friend Tom, who died in 2011. The faces in those portraits had yet to be etched with the lines of character, of adversity confronted and overcome, or not. I was a junior that year, looking serious and not too much a doofus in my horn-rimmed glasses. What a shock it was to turn the page and see my long-lost, long-lusted-for Rosalie—my God, that girl was beautiful! It was strange how just the name of someone I hadn't thought of in years could activate long-dormant neural traces, bringing back a person's laugh or another's goofiness. That all of these people had grown up and lived their lives in some universe worlds apart from my own was almost impossible to get my head around.

That evening I had dinner with an old friend from those days. A few years ago, he returned to the family fruit ranch to care for his aging father, who had since passed on. His father had sold off his arable land and the former apple orchard was bulldozed to make way for grapes—Paonia has quite a reputation these days for its local wines. Without good cropland, my friend was stuck. The estate had yet to be settled, and his siblings hadn't decided on a plan for making the homestead viable in the interim. He had considered building a greenhouse and growing medical cannabis, but the others vetoed the idea, and his parents slowly stopped spinning in their graves.

He looked good, as handsome as he was in high school, the lines in his face only adding to his character. He remained a committed Luddite, utterly convinced that we'll wake up someday and find our smart machines have become our masters. He had no use for e-mail or the Internet, which makes it hard for us to keep in touch, but we manage. I gently broke it to him that the takeover happened years ago and that he may as well get with the program, but he wasn't buying it.

We had a fine meal that night at the Flying Fork, a relatively new restaurant in town. Paonia might have felt like a prison I had to break out of as a kid, but sharing the company of an old friend from those days, I was keenly aware how attached I remained to the land where I'd grown up.

24 The Church Lawn Bunch

By the time my senior year had started in the fall of 1968, Mom and I had moved into a modest apartment in Grand Junction, the lower floor of a duplex with a lovely glassed-in porch. It was perfect for two people and a short walk from my new school. The nine months Mom and I spent there were some of the best of our lives. It was a chance for us to bond again, to get to know each other and heal some of the wounds that my bid for independence had inflicted. I was still a crazy, scary teenager, but when Mom and I were together without Dad in the picture, we got along quite well. I was smoking hash every night in my bedroom, and I think Mom knew that, but she was OK with it, or at least she didn't make a scene about it. Looking back, I am grateful that we had that time together. Neither of us could know, of course, that she had little more than two years to live.

I loved going to a "big city" high school, which it wasn't, really, but it was the biggest institution I'd ever attended. It didn't take me long to find my cohort. There were already a good number of aspiring hippies, stoners, rebels, and alienated intellectuals, and I gravitated to them naturally. The stigmatized group at that school was known as the church lawn bunch, because we passed our lunch hours smoking on the lawn of the First Congregational United Church of Christ across the street. I soon met characters that would shape my experience there and beyond, as many of us were headed for the University of Colorado in Boulder after graduation.

Among the most peculiar was a guy I'll call Craze. In fact, Craze was one of the oddest people I've ever known. Like me, he was a new student that year, having recently arrived in town. He was also the son of a single mother, again like me, or so it appeared to others. Craze was a soft-spoken, very blond, birdlike fellow who parted his hair in the middle. He had a refined aesthetic sense, effeminate mannerisms, and a quavering voice. He may have been into acid, or even on it most of the time, but frankly it was hard to tell. It wasn't easy having a rational conversation with him under the best of circumstances. After graduation Craze moved to Boulder, where during my freshman year our lives became more entangled than I could have wished, mainly because we were both attracted to the same woman.

And what a woman she was! I met Peggy shortly after I started school, and she was to make me both miserable and ecstatic for nearly a decade. Peggy was possibly the prettiest girl I had ever seen. A Nordic blonde, then 17, she had long hair so fair it was almost white, pale translucent skin that was flawlessly smooth, long legs, deep blue eyes, perfect breasts, and a face lovely and entrancing to gaze upon. Peggy was so preternaturally gorgeous her beauty crossed over from the erotic into the angelic, and it almost seemed sacrilegious to picture her indulging in an act as base as sex. I longed to be her lover in part because I thought she was so pure. She needed someone like me—no, she needed *me*—to protect her from the depredations of the other barbarians who only wanted to bring this angel to the ground.

In reality, of course, there was plenty of lust in my feelings, but I was in denial about it. Peggy actually had a gentle personality as attractive as her appearance. And she was kind to me on those rare occasions when I overcame my shyness enough to stammer out a bit of small talk. We developed a tentative friendship over that year. When both of us ended up in Boulder, my obsession continued, as it would off and on for years, evolving through various phases of agony and exhilaration.

At first there seemed little chance of pursuing a deeper relationship with her. She wasn't a druggie or part of the church lawn crowd; she was too ethereal and "nice" for any of that. Another inconvenience was that my new friend Craze shared my obsession and thus posed a threat. That Peggy would show any interest in a guy who was orders of magnitude weirder than I was made no sense. Nor did my jealousy. Peggy was no more involved with Craze than she was with me. But Peggy, being nice, was nice to everybody. She wasn't really in the circuit of dating and relationships at the time, as far as I was aware.

Peggy and Craze are the two figures I remember most from those days, but there were others. Clint, for instance, was an athlete and intellectual, an exemplar of those young men we all knew in school, the high achievers who the rest of us slackers were encouraged to emulate. But Clint was a great guy. He saw through all that and had a balanced perspective on life, and he liked to smoke hash, which is how he fell in with me. He was looked up to and widely admired, but he wasn't full of himself. He ended up going to

Stanford after graduation and lived in Berkeley for a while, so we stayed in touch long after we'd left Grand Junction behind.

Dirk was another memorable figure. He had a nice car, good looks, and a halo of golden hair. He was one of those rare people who shouldn't take psychedelics, ever, because they are too delicately balanced. He may have had a genetic predisposition to psychosis or mania. After one too many acid trips, he fell into a long-term psychosis that spring—some kind of schizophreniform dissociative state—and suffered the interventions of the mental health establishment. He was institutionalized for months. When I next saw him in Boulder he seemed fully recovered, but then started taking acid again and within a few weeks had to be hospitalized. I lost track of him after that. He was a beautiful soul. I hope he recovered and went on to live an interesting life, as I have a feeling he did.

While most of my close friends were committed stoners, they weren't disengaged from school activities. Clint, for instance, was active in band and sports and won a state wrestling championship that year. Others were in the debate and drama societies, which is where I ended up. My experience in Paonia under Mack's tutelage had given me a taste for drama, and I seemed to have a talent for it. I was delighted when I found that my new school had an active drama program, and I found myself in the leading role in the senior class play, Agatha Christie's *Witness for the Prosecution*. I played the Queen's Consul, Sir Wilfred Robarts, opposite a guy named Rory as the solicitor, Mayhew, and we were both well cast. Rory was totally straight, another high achiever and a nice guy. And yet I found him boring precisely because, unlike Clint, he seemed to lack a dark side, which is to say, a complete personality. Academically, we were all high achievers. The idea that smoking dope means one will have poor grades is simply a lie. I smoked dope several times a week, along with my friends, and we had no problem keeping up with our work. One effect it did have, though, was that it made much of school seem pointless—just mere busy work to keep us off the streets as much as anything.

In our last semester, however, I persuaded our teachers to try out a Tussman-style program like the one that led Terence into so many obscure byways of Western and Eastern thought, helping him learn to think in the process. By then my friends and I had already completed our graduation requirements, so the faculty let a small group of us spend the spring reading and discussing various works, all toward the supposed end of writing a massive paper. Because I had suggested the idea (and been blessed to have

Terence's library at my disposal while he was traveling), I heavily influenced the reading list. We spent our final semester sampling Jung, Eliade, and McLuhan, leavened by the occasional piece by Aldous Huxley or William Burroughs, and a little black magic thrown in. It was actually a very productive way to use our time, and I learned quite a bit. Clint and I were the only ones who actually wrote a final paper, but it didn't really matter. The others got exposed to a lot of heretical ideas they would not have otherwise have known, which was my point.

Despite my misadventure with datura the previous year, I had another encounter with the nightshades that spring, courtesy of John Parker. John, you'll recall, was a scholar and keeper of esoteric knowledge, from alchemy and black magic to herbal lore and altered states. He was also one of the most influential of my early mentors, and we'd been corresponding since we'd gotten to know each other in Berkeley in the summer of 1967. Among the topics we'd been exchanging thoughts on that spring were witches' flying unguents. These were topical concoctions that usually contained extracts of belladonna or henbane, sometimes with very toxic plants like monkshood (*Aconitum spp.*) or even hashish and opium. Such ointments were allegedly the secret to how witches could fly to their rituals on a broomstick. They didn't actually fly; they used the broom as an applicator, to apply the unguent to their labia where these substances could be readily absorbed. The resulting state of delirium and disorientation produced by the tropane alkaloids, combined with the cardiac arrhythmias induced by the monkshood, would induce a feeling of rising and falling, and rushing headlong through the air—hence flying. The participation in the eldritch and orgiastic rites of the witches' Sabbath was, under this model, a pure confabulation, as the witches fell into a dreamlike stupor.

John had stumbled across a formulation he attempted to duplicate, though for the baby's fat and bat's blood in the original formula he substituted lanolin. When he sent me a sample, my friends and I were just crazy enough to give it a shot. We set out one moonlit night into the high desert of the Uncompahgre Plateau just out of town. The plateau's name is a Ute word meaning "dirty water." The area has many gulches and arroyos, rocks, and caves, and lots of solitude. Carlos Castaneda's first book, *The Teachings of Don Juan*, had come out a few months earlier and we'd all read it, priming us for some serious shamanic action.

There were four of us, if I recall. We reached a place that had the right feel, with a low overhang of rock to shelter us, and proceeded to strip down and smear the god-awful green slime all over our bodies. Then we sat down to wait. An hour passed. Nothing. Another hour. Still nothing. Finally we decided that we needed to dance or something to facilitate the absorption, so we jumped around chanting and hooting—four gangly teenagers covered in green goo, comporting themselves under the desert moon like demented apes. Fortunately, we had chosen our secluded spot well. Had any of our classmates come upon us we would have had some serious explaining to do. After perhaps another hour we realized the unguent had failed to produce the desired effects. I guess it needed the baby fat and bat's blood, but that was a bit too authentic even for John. Reluctantly, we wiped off the goo as best we could and packed it in.

The rest of the semester passed uneventfully. Like high school seniors everywhere, my peers and I were burnt out. We lost no time in scattering to whatever destinies were in store for us: summer jobs, further schooling, military service, or exile to Canada; the Vietnam War was at its peak. I was more than ready to leave home and get on to the next big thing, whatever that would be. Accepted at CU, I knew I'd see many of my new friends in Boulder at summer's end, but by late May all I wanted was freedom. I had a job lined up for the summer in Aspen, working on the grounds maintenance crew at the Aspen Music School. This was a step up compared to my lowly status as a dishwasher at Cyrano's the previous summer. Skipping the graduation ceremony, I left Grand Junction the day after classes ended, my diploma eventually reaching me by mail. Aspen and unknown adventures beckoned.

25 Busted Again: 1969

My mother and I returned to Paonia, but my stay was brief. My father had a '59 Chevy Impala with enormous fins, a beater he'd been keeping at the airport in Montrose so he could fly in and cover his territory without having to rent a car. He generously gave it to me for the summer and flew me over to Montrose to pick it up. The wheels were a kind of graduation present and just what I needed. I packed up the Chevy with a few basic necessities and headed to Aspen to start my job.

I found a tiny apartment in a condo-like building on a side street in a residential part of town. Every day, my fellow workers and I would catch a bus that took us a few miles up Castle Creek to the campus. There we'd do whatever chores we were assigned—mowing, trimming shrubs, sweeping out the practice rooms, and generally tidying up. It was easy enough to slip into one of those rooms on a break and blast a joint. Supervision was minimal and the work was good exercise. There were a lot of pretty music students around, though as a lowly maintenance grunt I was too timid to try to befriend them.

Into this scene came Lisa. I've already mentioned how I first met Lisa, or at least saw her, on my visit to Berkeley in 1967. Two years later, there she was in Aspen, seeking a place to study Pure Land Buddhism, inspired by *The Secrets of Chinese Meditation*, a book by Charles Luk. Lisa had a friend in town I'll call Erin, a willowy blonde who had fallen in with my friend Richard. Encouraged by Erin, Lisa and I got together and soon were sharing my apartment. According to Lisa (I remember none of this), the landlord was spying on us and we were promptly evicted. We moved to a studio apartment in the back of a house, a distinct step up as it had a private entrance and a primitive kitchen. We lived there for much of that summer until events brought our short idyll to an end.

Our intimacy was a breakthrough for me, a chance to continue my sexual education, and Lisa proved a gentle and wise instructor. I had not had any

171

sexual encounters (or no successful ones, and not for lack of trying) since my furtive episode with Fay two years earlier. Lisa was an angel of mercy who came into my life just when I needed to be rescued. She was very delicate; she had many allergies and was prone to getting sick, but she had a good soul. Wise in the ways of herbs and astrology, she was a good guitar player and singer, a good cook, a good lover. She taught me many things, but I was too inexperienced to give back in kind. I've since apologized for being so inept; I had thought she must have taken pity on me to put up with such awkwardness. I was pleased to hear she'd never felt that way and that the mutual passion we felt made up for my lack of experience.

Nevertheless, I didn't return her affection in the way she might have wanted. The crucial reason was that I was still hung up on Peggy and still clinging to hopes we'd get together in Boulder that fall. During those years, it was a pattern of my erotic life that I spent much of it longing for someone out of reach, someone I couldn't have for one reason or another, to the neglect of the person I was actually with. It wasn't fair to that person, or to myself, because it kept me from fully committing to the relationship. And so it was with Lisa. Ultimately, however, that wouldn't be what pulled us apart.

During that summer, Terence, then rambling through India, had been sending back hashish shipments from Mumbai (still known then as Bombay). Aspen, he thought, was the perfect out-of-the-way spot for these shipments to arrive, and a friend of his, Brett, was there to receive them. For Terence, this was a ramped-up version of what he'd been doing the previous summer when we picked up the smashed Buddha statue at the post office. At least then he'd made an effort to conceal the goods, however inadequately. At some point, however, he seemed to have thrown caution to the wind and started sending his shipments barely concealed in locked tin boxes. That seemed rather reckless to me, and my misgivings proved correct.

Several packages arrived without incident, picked up at any number of rented PO boxes up and down the valley. Most of the product was then taken to Denver and turned over to Tom, who had plenty of hash-starved customers ready to purchase whatever he had for sale. Brett, impatient and a little greedy, was quite happy to sell ounces locally, and in fact out the door of his cottage. I knew because he was living in the same cluster of cottages as Lisa and I. I thought he should show some restraint, but he didn't listen; soon, half the hippies in town were beating a path to his door. His place quickly became widely known as the go-to source for the best hash to hit Aspen in months, maybe ever. As it turned out, his actions didn't make much difference. When the end arrived, it came from a completely unexpected direction.

Most people with counterculture ties back then remember where they were on Woodstock weekend, August 16–17, 1969. I certainly do, but the famous music festival was not the reason why. I spent that weekend in the county jail in Glenwood Springs, awaiting transfer to a federal detention facility in Denver, where my companions and I were to be arraigned on hashish smuggling charges the following Monday. It went down like this: I worked at the Aspen Music School until the end of July and then began getting ready to move to Boulder for the start of classes. Brett had temporarily moved in with Lisa and me, a cramped but tolerable situation, given that we'd only be sharing the space for a couple of weeks. But Lisa wanted nothing to do with a smuggling conspiracy. Deciding to bail early, we arrived in Boulder in the first week of August and found an apartment. Luckily, she stayed there when I headed back to Aspen to finish packing up.

In the course of moving out, we'd stored some dishes and linens at a house in Glenwood Springs, about 45 miles north of Aspen. On the day I left Aspen, I wanted to pick up those boxes before continuing over McClure Pass for a brief visit in Paonia. It was a sunny Thursday, August 14, when I pulled out in the old Chevy. As best I can recall, Erin and Richard had plans to spend the weekend at the house in Glenwood, and Brett decided to drive his own car over to see them.

He also wanted to check the post offices in Snowmass and Basalt, because one of Terence's shipments had been delayed. Two packages had already come through but not the third, so he was concerned there might be a glitch. We drove separately to the post office in Basalt, and I waited in my car while he went inside to check. When he emerged carrying a large muslin-wrapped package and a big smile, I realized the Good Shit had arrived. We continued on to the house in Glenwood in our separate cars.

In the parking area in front of the house, Brett locked his car but didn't bring anything in. I remember Erin being there, but not Richard. I went down to the basement to get my boxes, and when I came up Brett was looking worriedly out through the drawn curtains of the living-room window. There were two or three cars visible from the house with two men sitting in each. Not a welcome sight: it looked like the place was staked out. Brett decided to leave and take the package back to Aspen or try to ditch it somewhere, but by then it was too late. Both cars converged on his, blocking his exit, while four men emerged from the car, guns ready, and forced Brett out of the car. He stood there, helpless, arms outstretched, while two of the men came up to the house and called us out. I'm sure we all looked shocked and confused and more than a little scruffy as we emerged. Before long we were in handcuffs being booked at the county jail.

We were sequestered in separate cells and left to chill for a couple of hours, pondering our grim fates. I was despairing and traumatized. I wasn't a "bad kid," let alone a criminal, despite that little session back in Paonia two years earlier. I was just a hippie who liked to smoke a little hash and groove on psychedelics. Now here I was in the slammer. But this was worse. This was serious shit. This was a federal bust of an international smuggling ring.

By the time I was collected from my cell and ushered into an interrogation room, I'd had plenty of time to reflect on the error of my ways and to conjure up some dreary scenarios of where I was headed as a result. Agent Grissom, as I'll call him, a narcotics enforcement officer with US Customs, was tall, elegant, and soft-spoken; his colleague was short and squat, had a fat face, and looked like he was a bit too fond of those jelly donuts that cops are supposed to like. In this case, it was the fat jolly one who played the good cop. He was friendly enough as he explained to me that this was not about whether I liked to smoke grass or not; this was a felony conspiracy to import a dangerous drug, and they expected me to tell them everything I knew. Meanwhile, Grissom, playing the bad cop, kept his silence and just looked at me with pity and loathing, as if to say, "You poor sap, you are so fucked." Well, I was fucked. I don't recall any recitation of my rights, or anyone advising me that I didn't have to talk to these guys. But I resisted. I insisted that I wasn't part of the conspiracy, that I was just a friend of the others, and that I had no part in the smuggling operation. I had not received shipments nor had I sold any hash or facilitated any sales.

In fact this was true, but circumstantially it didn't look good. After all, I had been hanging out with the others all summer. Brett was even staying in our apartment, and Lord knows I was quite happy to smoke the abundant hash. But was there direct evidence linking me to the conspiracy? Not really, and association with criminals does not necessarily make one a criminal. But I didn't know that at the time.

In fact it became clear that they had no background information on the case. Richard got picked up later, but the authorities didn't know Brett had been living in my apartment; they didn't know about Lisa, who had already moved to Boulder. For them, the case began with the package they'd tracked to the Basalt post office. They produced my wallet, which they'd taken earlier, and started going through the paper scraps in it, scribbled grocery lists and phone numbers and so forth. One of those was the smoking gun: Terence's address in Bombay! They jumped on that, and pressed me: had Terence originated the shipment? He was the one, wasn't he? If you confirm this for us, they said, if you rat on your brother and your buddies, we'll make sure you get released when you're arraigned in federal court on Monday. It was obvious that Terence was on the other end of the Bombay to Aspen pipeline. Who else could it be? I broke down completely, and in tears I confessed: "Yes, it's all true!"

Looking back on this, I am still ashamed. What kind of a worm rats out his own brother? I did it then, I didn't see any alternative, and I'm not proud of it. What can I say? I was 18. I was scared out of my wits. And the cops were playing me like a fiddle. I got no Miranda warning, so I when I was interrogated I was under the impression I really had no rights. The cops did their best to reinforce that belief, to make me think they were ready to lock me up for good right then and there. Had I known of my rights, I'd like to think I would have resisted and, as in the movies, thrown it back in their faces: "You'll never make me talk, you dirty coppers." It's a little different when you're a terrified kid.

Terence's address in my wallet was the damning evidence, and I think it would have been even if I'd said nothing. Under the circumstances, I may well have confessed even if I had been read my rights. Then again, had I been able to talk to an attorney, I would have learned that the case against me was weak. The fact that I had driven to Glenwood in my own car and happened to be at the house when the bust went down was not sufficient evidence to charge me. And a good attorney would have told me that. The cops were able to assure me that I'd be released after my arraignment because they knew very well they lacked the evidence to hold me, and they would not have held me even if I'd said nothing. But they didn't divulge that. They played on my fear and ignorance of the law to make me spill.

I spent the next two nights in the holding cell at the county jail. My parents knew I was supposed to come to Paonia that weekend, but I hadn't been allowed to contact them, and actually I didn't want them to know. Foolishly, I thought I could somehow conceal this from them. Knowing I'd be released on Monday, I wrote them a letter, sent from jail, assuring them all was well and that I'd be there in a couple of days. It was a total lie of course, but I thought it would buy time, which it did, a little. On Saturday, we were transported in shackles to the holding pen at the Federal Building in Denver to await our arraignment. Or I should say I was transported. I didn't see the others until the hearing. Those 24 hours in the holding pen were a real education for me. People were being held on all sorts of charges, ranging from drugs to armed robbery. Some were old hands, career criminals who had been in and out of jail for much of their lives. They were a much more cynical bunch. Others were scared kids like me, in there on pot charges.

The next morning, Monday, I was led to the hearing room. My associates were already there. As we sat waiting, I could not look them in the eyes. I was consumed with guilt and shame at my supposed betrayal, about which they knew nothing. But I also saw a path to redeem myself, at least partially. The hearing opened, and I was called up first. Agent Grissom and his buddy were as good as their word, or so I thought. The judge said, "As to the case of Dennis McKenna, no charges will be filed as there is insufficient evidence to charge him." I was enormously relieved, unaware that I would have heard those words even if I'd said nothing. Afterward, I was allowed to leave, but not until I'd watched my friends being shepherded back to their cells.

In retrospect, I have to marvel at how limited the police work was. The tools for investigation and surveillance were relatively primitive back then, before GPS and the Internet. They had no idea where we lived in Aspen, or even who we were when they made the bust. They apparently knew that a shipment was coming in, addressed to unknown persons, and they had staked out the post office, waiting for someone to claim the package. That's where they picked up the trail. As a result, they were unaware that another one had been picked up without incident at a different post office a few days earlier. That package was still sitting in the closet at the apartment back in Aspen, waiting for Tom to collect it and sell it in Denver as earlier arranged.

My task was clear: I somehow had to get the package in Aspen and hide it in a safe place, then show Tom its location so he could retrieve it later. I'd just been sprung; I was loose on the streets of Denver with no car and very little money. Then I had an idea. I called up a guy named Brandon I'd met a few months earlier. Brandon had a sleek sports car and a sleek girlfriend, both of which I admired. I phoned him up and explained the situation. I offered to give him some of the Good Shit if he'd drive me back to Aspen to get the stuff and then take me somewhere to hide it. He agreed—in fact, he said it would be fun.

Brandon and his girlfriend picked me up a few blocks from the Federal Building, and we headed west over the mountains. When we arrived in Aspen, I told them to park a few blocks from my former cottage and wait while I checked out the place, wary of a trap. It was late and the place was quiet. I'd sequestered a key near the entrance so I didn't have to break in, but I still feared I'd be arrested in some crazy scene as cops burst out of the bathroom. But I had to do it. This was my chance to help my friends, an obligation I felt most acutely since I had betrayed them, or so I thought.

No one was there. The hash, in its metal box, was still in the closet. I returned to the car, and we drove back and collected the package and took it up to the secluded lake outside of Snowmass where I'd hung out the summer before. We found a spot that looked like it would be easy to locate again, dug a hole, and buried the package—that is, after I'd cut my driver his chunk. With the deed complete, we started back over the mountains. It was a clear, moonlit night. There was no Eisenhower Tunnel back then; to get to Denver from the Western Slope you had to cross the Continental Divide via Loveland Pass, about 12,000 feet at the summit—a spectacular place, but terribly cold at night, even in August. We had almost made it to the summit when we saw lights flashing behind us. My heart jumped. It was three in the morning and we were the only ones on the road. This had to be it! I was sure the cops had followed us all the way to Aspen and back, ever since they'd turned me loose after the hearing. We sat petrified, hunkered down in the car, as the cop approached the driver's side, the typical picture of a state trooper: helmet, wraparound shades (yes, shades) glinting in the moonlight, revolver in his holster, the whole bit.

"Some problem, officer?" Brandon said.

"Did you know you have a taillight out on the left side? Better have that looked at when you get back to Denver."

"Yes, officer, why thanks, officer, no, I didn't know," Brandon said, "I'll take care of it right away."

He bid us a good night, and without even a warning ticket we drove on. I had practically fainted and was literally shaking. I was grateful that Brandon did not affect a hippie style. No long hair or wild clothes, he looked quite respectable, like a clean-cut preppie college student. I don't know if that made a difference, but whether it was that or sheer dumb luck, we had ducked a potentially disastrous outcome.

Brandon let me off in Boulder at about six in the morning. I was completely exhausted. I went to our new apartment and woke Lisa.

She already knew from Tom what had happened but was still frantic for the details. I related the whole sorry tale, from the bust in Glenwood to our mad run to Aspen and back. But I was not done. I still had to return to Snowmass with Tom so I could show him where the stuff was stashed. For Lisa, who had wanted no part of these dealings from the start, this was the last straw. She decided to leave Boulder and return that same day to Berkeley. I agreed, though I knew it meant the end of our relationship.

Indeed, I would not see her again for years.

After getting in touch with Tom, he and I decided to catch a plane back to Aspen. Our friends were still in jail waiting to be released on bail. To get the process rolling presumably meant retrieving and selling some of the hash. As we took off from Stapleton Airport sitting in the back of a chartered six-seater, Tom pulled out a tiny cellophane bag with a few crumbs of hash in it and waved it before me. I was appalled at his recklessness, but he just laughed.

Flying to Aspen took about an hour. We rented a car and headed for the lake above Snowmass where I'd buried the stash some hours earlier. We walked in on foot. There was no sign of any disturbance or ambush. I pointed out the location to Tom, and we got back to the car and drove to Glenwood. The idea was that he'd return for the package later and take it to Denver, and I assume that's what he did.

I found my car in the parking lot, keys still in it, outside the house where we'd been caught. My parents had gotten the letter I'd sent from jail at about the same time they were reading an article in the *Daily Sentinel* about the bust. Needless to say, the conflicting accounts had created some confusion and distress. They had heard that we'd been taken to the courthouse in Denver, but not that I'd been released. Based on that, Mom and Dad had immediately driven to Denver to bail me out. By then I had already made my clandestine trip to Aspen and back, returned to Aspen with Tom on the plane, and found my way to the scene of the bust a few days earlier to get my car.

When we finally did connect, my mother was sick with worry and my father was both worried and furious. I couldn't blame him. I told them I'd be driving back to Paonia that evening, which I did. I was completely thrashed and almost fell asleep at the wheel several times, but finally I made it to the empty house. My parents, meanwhile, were driving back from Denver.

When they arrived the next morning I'd had at least a few hours sleep. The scene was tense. My father was out of his mind with anger, and appropriately so. There was nothing I could say in my defense, so I said as little as possible. I explained what had gone down, including Terence's connection to the mess. He was off in India somewhere; a Bombay address at least a couple of months old was the last one we had, and we weren't sure he knew yet what had happened. It speaks amazingly well of our father that, despite his fury at the two of us and his hatred of drugs and anything to do with them, he still saw it as his duty to protect his son.

In doing so, he probably committed a felony himself. He sent two cables to Terence's last known address: "Interpol is looking for you, get out now!" A pretty unambiguous message. Meanwhile, the others had been released and had sent Terence a more cryptic message: "Colorado Fuel and Iron gone down." That was their code name for the operation, Colorado Fuel and Iron, named after the company founded by John C. Osgood, the builder of the Redstone Inn. In either case, the message was clear. Something had gone seriously wrong, and Terence needed to hightail it out of wherever he was.

He got both messages and immediately dropped off the radar. No one heard from him for several weeks; we had no idea where he was. It wasn't until the end of September that a postcard finally arrived, dated three weeks previously, postmarked Benares, and signed by one HCE, a reference to a character in Joyce's *Finnegans Wake*. This would become his nom de guerre over the next year as he moved clandestinely from country to country, hiding out. Postcards from HCE showed up irregularly, tracking his travels in southern India, then Thailand, then ever more remote locations in the Indonesian archipelago as he made his way to the outer islands in search of butterflies and anonymity, tracking back to Taipei, several months in Tokyo teaching English, finally ending up in Vancouver in the fall of 1970 where I was able to visit him. It was a life on the run. It might have even seemed romantic at the time, but the uncertainty of ever being able to return was worrisome.

The legal consequences from this episode have long since been settled, and Terence's involvement in it has been public knowledge for decades. He discussed the bust in *True Hallucinations* and elsewhere; it is even mentioned in his obituary in the *New York Times*. I haven't told the story here to depict Terence and myself as romantic outlaw renegades but rather as a cautionary tale. Like many 18-year-olds, I made some foolish choices, especially under pressure. Whatever my beliefs about one's right to experience certain altered states, the bust was a searing reminder that the law is the law. And to break the law is to invite anguish not only into one's own life but into other lives as well.

Following the bust and its aftermath, the waning days of August were fraught with tension. I had no cred left with my father, and for good reason. Both Terence and I had disappointed our parents. Our father was either a fool or far more enlightened than I could understand at the time, and I now believe it was the latter. He didn't approve of us or of what we'd done. But according to his moral compass, you stood by your kids no matter what they did. He never disowned us, and he never cut off financial support for me, though it was perhaps really our mother he was trying to protect. We had hurt her deeply. She had been in delicate health for years, and now with all these new stresses I think Dad was concerned that she was at risk for some serious illness. As it turned out, we had no idea how serious.

As the time neared for me to start classes, my father determined that my mother would take me to Boulder and help me get settled. To provide moral support, Mom's good friend Marge, the English teacher from whose class I'd been summoned by the sheriff two years before, accompanied us. Marge was wise in ways I hadn't realized. She was there for Mom, but she also realized I wasn't a bad kid, just a little misguided, or perhaps a lot misguided. Nonetheless, her presence helped me as well.

I had to find a place to live. Mom wanted me to live in the dorm at least for the first semester, but I was adamantly opposed. I didn't want to face the restrictions that would entail, especially the restrictions on being able to smoke dope whenever I wanted. Plus, I was an introvert and repelled by the kind of social interaction that dorm life entailed.

So I pushed back. I found another place, a tiny apartment in a three-story hippie house filled with a motley assortment of freaks and with a landlord who didn't much care what you did as long as you paid the rent on time. It was just what I was looking for! It was Mom's worst nightmare for the same reasons. But I insisted and tried to convince her it would be OK, and actually Marge came to my defense. So it was that I found myself in Number 7, 1507 Pine.

Shortly after my mother returned to Paonia she fell and broke her ankle. Here was yet another challenge, as if the worry we'd caused her wasn't enough. She had always been fragile, and probably at her age, 56, she may have been developing some osteoporosis. This injury further exacerbated the arthritis that she was suffering. Although we didn't realize it at the time, the arthritis and the ankle injury were harbingers of a much more serious illness she'd face some months later.

I settled into my studies in the warm autumn of 1969, happy to have the bust behind me, happy to be in Boulder living on my own. I wasn't sure what courses to take; like many freshmen I had no idea what I wanted to specialize in. I knew I wanted to pursue something related to psychedelics, but I was uncertain whether it would be neuroscience, chemistry, anthropology, or botany. I had a vague idea that I wanted to be an ethnobotanist, but there was nothing in the curriculum that matched that, so I started taking classes in basic botany—plant taxonomy, mostly—and anthropology.

One of my classes was an introductory ethnography course taught by Omer Stewart, an authority on the Native American Church and later the author of *Peyote Religion: A History* (1987). As I've noted, Carlos Castaneda's *The Teachings of Don Juan* had come out the previous year and had an enormous impact on me. Since then, much if not all of Castaneda's work has been discredited as confabulation, but that first book may have had some basis in truth. At the time I had no reason to doubt it, nor did I want to doubt it. In fact, I credit it, along with Eliade's work, in fostering my interest in psychedelic shamanism. It provided a context for the use of psychedelics that I couldn't find anywhere else at the time, certainly not from Timothy Leary or the other mass-market gurus. The revelation for me was that psychedelics were nothing new; rather, they were part of a shamanic tradition stretching way back, possibly to the Paleolithic or even earlier. If one wanted to understand psychedelics and how to use them, consult the peoples who had been using them for thousands of years. This made sense to me and still does.

Part of the reason that psychedelics were so disruptive to society (or were perceived to be) when they burst on the scene in the 1960s was that we had no context for them. They were not part of the Western religious tradition (although they may once have been, that connection has long since been suppressed), and their role in witchcraft and alchemy was esoteric knowledge—that is, largely forbidden knowledge. So psychedelics were fascinating to many of my generation, but there was no map, no guidance on their usage that could be adapted to the contemporary societal context. This partly explains why many people got into unfortunate situations with them. It was not widely understood at the time that proper "set" and "setting" were essential to safely using psychedelics for purposes of spiritual discovery and the exploration of consciousness. In fact, this is largely what shamanism is—a set of procedures, practices, and beliefs that provide a structure or context for understanding and controlling the experiences, within limits. Without that context, one is left to random experimentation without any framework for interpreting the results. In that respect, I think Castaneda's first book did a service for a generation of psychedelic novices. It made us aware that at least there was a context and a tradition, even if the one he described, through the character of Don Juan Matus, a supposed Yaqui sorcerer, was largely the product of the author's fertile imagination.

While taking Stewart's class I visited his office to discuss *The Teachings*, which he had read carefully. He assured me the book almost had to be a fabrication; there was nothing in Yaqui traditions that even hinted at the practices it described. Either Don Juan was an idiosyncratic figure whose belief system bore no relationship to Yaqui culture or he and his practices had been constructed out of whole cloth. Stewart's critique was a wake-up call. I had learned early on a valuable lesson about accepting, without corroborating evidence, the assertions of self-styled gurus, shamans, and other supposedly wise teachers. It's good to keep an open mind. There is much we don't know, as one should never forget. But it's just as crucial never to sacrifice the capacity for critical thinking and skepticism. Stewart's lesson is one that many who fall prey to cults of one sort or another (and I include most of the major world religions here) would do well to heed.

The value of skepticism was reinforced in a second course I took that fall, on the comparative anthropology of religion. To discover the variety of what passed for religious or spiritual practice was eye-opening. One person's abomination or blasphemy could easily be another's sincere belief. I remember reading *When Prophecy Fails* by Leon Festinger, Henry Riecken, and Stanley Schachter, first published in 1956. It's the study of a Midwestern UFO cult that claimed to be channeling messages from aliens. Newly recruited members were told they'd be picked up on a specific date and saved from the imminent end of the world. The members quit their jobs, gave up their possessions, and gathered together, waiting to be saved. When the appointed date came and went, they grew even more convinced that the revelations were valid. It wasn't until two later predictions also failed that members became disillusioned and the cult fell apart. The case is an interesting commentary on the folly of human belief systems, including most millenarian cults. The dynamic of the true believer is much too prevalent in today's mass consciousness and in political and religious discourse: My mind is made up, don't confuse me with facts!

All this amounts to a cautionary tale for those anticipating the end of history as predicted by Terence and others for the winter solstice in 2012—or on any other such date. No prophecy of major global catastrophe or the end of history has ever come true. Terrible events can and do happen in both human and natural history, but prophets cannot predict them. And yet it is virtually certain that some believers will find a way to rationalize the fact of a prophecy proven wrong. From a sociological perspective, it will be interesting to observe what happens in the days before and after the latest in a long line of such predictions. I don't expect the world to end, of course, but it wouldn't surprise me if there were major social disruptions resulting from mass hysteria.

Much of my education during that first semester in Boulder did not occur in the classroom. It happened when my friend and mentor John Parker came out from California and spent several weeks with me in my apartment. John and I had been carrying on regular correspondence for a couple of years. His eclectic interests—in drugs, magic, shamanism, biology, chemistry, alchemy—likewise fascinated me. Our hashish-fueled conversations lasting well into the wee hours were a supreme pleasure. During those weeks together, we explored many of the ideas that Terence and I would later call upon to force open the portal to hyperspace at La Chorrera.

26 Girl with a Gun: 1970

John eventually returned to Berkeley, and I finished my first semester in Boulder. The end of that semester corresponded to the end of the 1960s, though that troubled decade's social ferment continued undiminished. The Vietnam War dragged on; Nixon's illegal invasion of Cambodia in late April 1970 sparked campus protests across the country, leading to the Kent State shootings on May 4. At CU, a large portion of the student body took to the streets, and I was among them. I had turned 19 the previous December just weeks after the draft lottery went into effect. Though I had a student deferment, the lottery saved me from any risk of being drafted because I had a very high number. Nevertheless, I was as outraged as many of my contemporaries, and our protests shut down the university for the rest of the semester. All final exams were canceled, most of the faculty supported the protests, and students were awarded whatever grades they had before the protests started, so I got off easy. There was no real assessment of my performance after my first year, and many of my peers were in the same position.

I may have come quite close to dying during one of those protests. I was standing in a large group one day that had blocked off University Avenue, between downtown Boulder and the campus on "the Hill." The cops had cordoned off the street below and were directing traffic away from the crowd, which numbered maybe a thousand kids. Suddenly a car broke through the barricades and raced toward us, as if its driver was bent on mowing us down. But suddenly it stopped, screeching to a halt very near to where I stood. The woman in the car had the windows rolled up and the doors locked. She was obviously in some sort of distress, though it was hard to tell if she was angry or scared, let alone why she'd driven into the crowd in the first place. I started to reach for the handle of her car door, I don't know why. I didn't want to haul her out of the car; I had some idea of inviting her to get out and join the protest. Then I saw the gun she was cradling in her arm, her white-knuckled grip on the handle, and I froze. If I'd made any further threatening move, I think I would have been shot dead. Instead I had that "whoa" moment, put my hands up, and backed slowly away. By this time everyone nearby had noticed the gun. The crowd got quiet and moved away, opening a space around the car. The driver put the car in gear and slowly drove back down the hill in the direction she had come from. It was a sobering moment for everyone—one of those bifurcations in the time stream that could have gone very differently.

But I spent most of my days that school year over books, not in the streets. After John left, I continued my academic studies while the two of us pursued our esoteric explorations via letters. Most of my spare time was somewhat hermit-like; I spent long hours at home smoking hashish while reading and studying various obscure tomes in the company of the coal black cat, Ahriman, that Lisa and I had adopted over the summer and brought with us to Boulder. I also got to know my neighbors across the hall, Hans and Nancy, the hippie couple living in Number 6. Hans, whose parents were Dutch, had grown up in Boulder; Nancy, his new wife, was the daughter of a wealthy Denver family. Hans was a good carpenter and made his living that way. We became close friends over those two semesters at 1507 Pine and have remained so ever since.

Into the spring of 1970, Terence remained off the radar, still hiding out in the obscure backwaters of Southeast Asia. My parents would occasionally get postcards from HCE as he slowly worked his way to the outer islands of the Indonesian archipelago in search of butterflies and anonymity. Our correspondence lapsed for a while; there was no place to send a letter because it was impossible to know where HCE would turn up next. After a few months of such rambling, faced with evaporating finances, he ended up teaching in Tokyo in one of the English mills that were ready sources of temporary employment for itinerant travelers. I welcomed this development because it was an opportunity to renew our regular correspondence.

My longed-for love, Peggy, had started school in Boulder in the fall but left for New Mexico in the spring. This disappointed me because it meant there was no chance to get better acquainted, despite a few pleasant moments spent together early in that school year. She was invariably nice to me but my passions were not reciprocated. I clung to the hope that I'd have another chance to get together with her when she returned after the semester, but reality intruded when she did. I discovered she'd met someone else, only to have that relationship fall apart, leaving her sobered and saddened. I was furious and heartbroken, though I knew I had no real justification for such feelings. A mere casual friend, I had no claim on her. And yet, if only she had stayed, we might have developed something together. Or so I told myself. It was a complete delusion, of course. But the heart does not listen to logic or reason. It is a creature of pure emotion; it knows only what it wants, and it knows only pain when it doesn't get what it wants.

I did my best to present a facade of sympathy to her. She was not in a happy place either. She knew she had screwed up badly, had made some bad decisions, and wanted to move beyond feelings that were surely quite similar to mine in the wake of her ill-considered relationship. I did my best to be kind, though in reality I was seething with jealousy. I wanted nothing more than to track down the monster who had despoiled my perfect, pure, virginal angel and tear him limb from limb. I also knew that had the tables been turned I would have done the same thing.

The denouement of that very depressing spring came when my father arrived to take me back to Paonia for the summer. My mother had been feeling increasingly poorly all winter, ever since she'd broken her ankle the previous September. She'd suffered from arthritis for years, and that accident had made it worse. She had gone to the Penrose Cancer Center in Colorado Springs, one of the premier oncology centers in the country at that time, not because she thought she had cancer but because severe arthritis often accompanies cancer, and she thought they might have new treatments that would help her. It didn't take long for these trained oncologists to uncover the much grimmer truth: she had metastatic bone cancer and probably had only months to live. Cancer, not arthritis, was the cause of her severe joint pain and fragile bones. Now it was clear.

She had undoubtedly broken her ankle because even then her bones were losing their strength. Our family physician had misdiagnosed her problem because he lacked the training or had misinterpreted the signs. Years later, in my own reading on the topic, I found that bone cancer was the most common sequela of breast cancer, which my mother had survived five years previously. In fact, just prior to her ankle fracture she had passed the five-year threshold that was thought to signify that she was cancer-free. Though I don't blame her doctor for missing the diagnosis, catching the cancer nine months earlier might have bettered her chances. As it was, it was too late. Mom did not live to see the end of the year.

We did not realize then, at the end of May, that there was no realistic hope for a cure. Dad was utterly shattered but also completely determined to make sure Mom got the benefit of whatever modern medicine could bring to bear on this terrible disease, costs be damned. Dad was fighting to save the love of his life. I was there with him, fighting to save my mother, so long neglected, so wounded by her children. There was no question of staying in Boulder or finding work elsewhere that summer. I needed and wanted to be at home.

What followed was an endless series of trips to Colorado Springs where Mom was given chemotherapy and radiation treatments. That's what was available in those days, and it's dismaying how little progress there has been in 42 years. The radical, debilitating treatments that were applied then are not that different from those used today. They cause severe fatigue, make your hair fall out, and destroy your immune system. The treatments are torture for the person getting them and cause great distress for the loved ones who must watch someone they love suffer so much. Bone cancer itself is extremely painful. Mom never complained. She never said she was in pain, though she must have been. She had severe nausea from the chemotherapy, and I wanted to get her some cannabis to help control the nausea. It was just beginning to be recognized that cannabis could help control chemo-induced nausea and pain. For once, Dad was actually open to the idea that it might help. He was ready to try anything. It was my mother who nixed the idea, mostly I think because she didn't want to offend him. I felt a lot of guilt over what had happened. I understood I hadn't caused her cancer, but I did feel that the stress I'd caused her during the hashish caper might have compromised her immune system and made it harder to fight off the cancer. This wasn't rational; she'd undoubtedly had cancer for months before she broke her ankle. Nevertheless I still felt that had I been a better son and caused her less worry things might have turned out differently.

So Ahriman and I returned to Paonia and prepared to settle in for what was sure to be a glum summer. By this time, my friend Craze had relocated to Boulder and needed temporary quarters, so I sublet him my apartment after a promise he'd vacate it when I returned for school.

I'd been in Paonia for about a month when my friend Tom, who had been working construction for his brother in Denver, also showed up. His brother's contract had ended, meaning no job, so Tom decided to see what work he could find around Paonia. I was delighted by this news. We got along well and he had ready access to good drugs thanks to the contacts he'd made selling hash. I had few other friends left in town, but it seemed the summer might not be as slow as I had feared.

Tom also had a new girlfriend. By the time I met Deborah, she was a teenage runaway. She'd been living with her folks in California near a penitentiary where her father worked as a guard. Like a lot of young people back then, she was in active rebellion against her parents, who were strict fundamentalists. She'd been visiting a cousin in Denver when Tom and a friend had picked them up at an amusement park. The girls were looking for fun and excitement, and Tom and his companion were happy to provide it. It was the perfect concatenation of desire and opportunity. Deborah didn't want to return to her repressive parents; Tom was interested basically in casual sex. She was willing. So Deborah went on the lam and lit out for the Western Slope with her new lover. Tom couldn't show up at his parents' home with a runaway girl in tow, so they established a remote camp on Hubbard Creek, a few miles past the spot where we'd conducted our psychedelic fishing trips in the fall of 1967. I first met Deborah when she and Tom made a trip into town and dropped by to smoke a bowl. My mother, I believe, was in Colorado Springs for the first of her radiation treatments, and my father may have been in Delta or Grand Junction playing golf with his friends, as he did most weekends. Deborah was a hippie chick—small and slender, almost scrawny, with long strawberry-blonde hair and blonde eyelashes, and the reddish complexion and freckles typical of redheads. She was not stunningly beautiful; she was merely pretty, and clearly vulnerable. My first impression was that there wasn't a thought in her head. She was on the run, and Tom was only too happy to contribute to her delinquency. I could fault Tom for being an opportunist, but in a way it was a mutual exploitation. When we met that first time I found her attractive, but she was Tom's lady and I wasn't about to infringe.

That changed a few weeks later. I was making periodic trips to Colorado Springs to be with my mother during her treatments, which weren't helping. My father and I, however, weren't ready to admit what was grimly obvious. I was in denial; I didn't want to think about it. We were fortunate, however, in that one of my father's best friends, a fellow salesman for Central Electric, lived in Colorado Springs and had offered to let my mother stay in his home. This was an excellent and kindly gesture, given how debilitated and fatigued my mother was much of the time. Making frequent trips back and forth to Paonia would have been extremely hard on her.

Around mid-August, I returned from one of my stays in Colorado Springs and made the trek up Hubbard Creek to see Tom and Deborah. Upon arriving, I quickly realized the bloom was off the rose. Deborah's prolonged stay in the wilderness had taken its toll. She looked even scrawnier than when I'd met her, as if she wasn't eating well, and was covered with scabs, bruises, and bug bites. Tom, working on various jobs, had grown accustomed to leaving her alone, sometimes for days at a time. As a runaway, she had little recourse but to put up with it. For his part, Tom was growing tired of her. He grumbled to me that she had nothing to say and she didn't know how to cook. Having someone to cook for him was important, something he expected in a woman, but Deborah was "lecherously lazy" as he put it. In his view, women existed to provide sex, to cook, and to keep house, not necessarily in that order. There was no equality in his relationship with Deborah, let alone love or tenderness. For Tom, it was a relationship of convenience that had grown inconvenient.

Deborah could sense this and the situation was tense; she was trapped. I felt bad for her in her obvious distress. My attitudes toward women were perhaps not that much more refined than Tom's at the time, but I could empathize with someone's pain. I felt Deborah's plight and, yes, a strong sexual attraction to her. That was not blunted when I rose from my sleeping bag early the next morning and spied her bathing, naked, in the stream a few yards away. I averted my eyes but couldn't help an occasional glance. I said nothing to her about this, much less to Tom, but in a brief glance when my eyes had met hers, I knew I had to "rescue" her.

The opportunity came about a week later. Tom had gone to Grand Junction on a job for a few days, leaving Deborah alone at the camp with barely enough food, and a gun. I knew this was my chance. I started up to Hubbard Creek one moonless night. It was hard to find the trail in the dark, and I hadn't brought a flashlight. I went crashing through the forest, making a lot of noise. Finally I saw the glimmer of a campfire. Then I saw Deborah, standing in the clearing, terrified and holding the gun. "Don't shoot!" I shouted. "It's me!" She lowered the gun as I stepped into the firelight. She was immensely relieved, though not as relieved as I was. It was the second time in the past year that I'd nearly gotten shot.

She was no doubt happy to have any company, but especially happy to have mine. We sat by the fire and smoked some weed, and then some cigarettes, and talked awhile. I expressed my desire and attraction for her. I told her I abhorred the way Tom was treating her and that I intended to help her. One thing led to another, as these things will, and we soon were in her sleeping bag with our clothes off making love. Thus began an attachment between us that would last for years. Whatever Deborah's faults—and she had her share, as I would learn—she enjoyed sex. Her childlike enthusiasm and seemingly uncomplicated emotions were just what I needed at that moment in my life. Afterward, I promised to get her out of there. She could go to Boulder, I said, and stay with the friend who was living in my apartment. I'd be arriving in about ten days to start the new semester. The next day I took her to Delta and gave her the bus fare to Boulder. I also contacted Craze and let him know what was coming his way. I trusted him enough to believe he'd look after her.

I expected an unpleasant confrontation with Tom when he found out I'd stolen his girlfriend. In fact, I was worried that he would beat the hell out of me, which he easily could have done. But instead he was relieved. He'd gotten tired of her and was wondering whether to send her back to California or perhaps even abandon her, he said, although I doubt the latter would have happened; Tom might have been a Neanderthal but he wasn't a monster. In any event, it seemed I'd neatly solved his problem.

The situation got a lot more complicated when I showed up in Boulder. It turned out Craze had immediately pounced on Deborah, and she'd given in. I guess you could say her boundaries were loosely defined. Then again, what are you going to do when you are a desirable and naive waif dependent on the kindness of strangers? Their brief fling quickly ended. All Craze had to do was to be his usual weird self and that put Deborah off. By the time I arrived, she'd taken refuge next door with Hans and Nancy.

I wasn't angry with her but I was furious with Craze, and not only because he had moved in on my new girlfriend. He also refused to give up my apartment! But another unit had just opened up, and better yet it was bigger. Deborah and I were soon installed in Number 9. Craze remained in Number 7, but he appeared to have been neutralized.

PART TWO: INTO THE ABYSS

27 The Brotherhood Forms

The semester I spent with Deborah, the fall of 1970, was one of the happiest times of my life. Even though my mother was dying, even though there were auguries of the peculiar events that would overtake us a few months later, it was a wonderful, emotionally rich time. Even now I look back on it with fondness, despite the pain I'd experience as a consequence of loving Deborah over the next seven years. But that lay in the future. At the time, our little apartment was a blissful refuge. Deborah was not emotionally complex. She really loved me, in a simple way, and I loved her back. I enjoyed introducing her to books and ideas. She was not an intellectual, had never really been exposed to any intellectual stimulation, though I discovered she was far from stupid. I treated her well, and I felt a responsibility to protect her, to keep her safe—and to keep her runaway status hidden.

Since then I have wondered about the ethics of what I did. I was motivated by compassion and love for her and, yes, probably some possessiveness. I was good to her, and she was good to me. For both of us, perhaps, our relationship was a sexual awakening. Deborah loved sex in a way that I have rarely encountered, and I was only too happy to oblige. She was "always up for it," she told me, and we enthusiastically practiced, as often as we could manage. At that age, one seems to have endless time and energy for sex; how much that has diminished as I have aged is a bit depressing, but I suppose that is the natural order of things.

Besides making love, Deborah and I really enjoyed tripping together. There was some good mescaline around (which was probably really MDA), and what on the street was called "woodrose acid" though I don't know if it was actually extracted from Hawaiian baby woodrose or if this was marketing hype. Whatever it was, it was excellent, and we took it a few times. And real Hawaiian baby woodrose seeds were also available through floral shops in Hawaii. We didn't know the proper dosage, and one sunny Saturday we each took about 25 seeds and headed up Boulder Canyon toward Nederland for what proved to be another psychedelic misadventure.

Hawaiian baby woodrose, *Argyreia nervosa*, contains lysergic acid derivatives, some of which have vasoconstrictive effects not unlike the toxic ergot alkaloids. The prudent dose is actually 6 to 10 seeds, and no more than 12, so we'd taken about twice that. We were soon having cardiovascular symptoms—difficulties breathing and what felt like a racing pulse. On top of that we were fully loaded, and the physical effects were making me paranoid as well as fearful. We walked into town and went into a bar, where we tried calling Hans to pick us up, but he was out. People were giving us funny looks, or so we thought. I was fairly sure we were maintaining our cool, but it was impossible to know. Worried that someone would call the cops, we headed for the highway and caught a ride as soon as we put our thumbs out. The nice folks shared a joint with us in their car, and we made it safely home.

I'd later try Hawaiian woodrose seeds on several occasions, at more reasonable doses. Doses of eight to ten ground seeds produced a smooth, long-lasting, psychedelic high, not unlike about 100 mikes of acid. At that dose nausea is mild and transient, and there are no cardiovascular effects. Surprisingly, there's no record that the seeds were ever used traditionally as a psychedelic. There are 11 species of *Argyreia* native to India, presumably all similarly high in alkaloids, but there is no record of their shamanic or recreational use in India's cultures. In light of its effects, this particular psychedelic appears to be somewhat problematic, which probably explains why it has not become popular. The seeds can be legally obtained, but there are safer and more satisfying natural psychedelics out there.

While Deborah and I were enjoying our domestic bliss, I continued to take courses in anthropology as well as botany and plant physiology. Terence, still on the run in Asia, had wrapped up his butterfly hunting in Indonesia and was in Tokyo teaching English. We were corresponding more and had begun planning our trip to South America in search of the Secret. What the Secret was, however, we weren't yet fully sure; the outlines of our quest emerged gradually. We knew it had something to do with DMT. The mystery of DMT became the siren song beckoning us to the Amazon. As I've described, the DMT experience is overwhelming and yet ephemeral, lasting only 10 to 15 minutes when smoked. We thought that if we could somehow remain in that "place" a little longer, we'd better understand what was going on. If we could find an orally active form of DMT that might be absorbed and eliminated more slowly, perhaps the high could be extended.

The role of certain DMT-containing admixture plants in giving aya-huasca its psychedelic kick was just beginning to be understood, thanks to papers by Ara DerMarderosian and others (1968) as well as Homer Pinkley (1969). Then we stumbled on a 1969 paper by the ethnobotanist R. E. Schultes in the *Harvard Botanical Museum Leaflets* entitled "*Virola* as an Orally Administered Hallucinogen," an account of his work in the lower Colombian Amazonas among the Bora and Witoto tribes. Both peoples used a most interesting preparation known among the Witoto as *oo-koo-hé*. It was prepared from the sap of various species of the genus *Virola*, which belong to the nutmeg family. Reports on the composition of this sap in the phytochem-ical literature revealed that many species contained high levels of DMT and the related compound, 5-Methoxy-DMT; both were known to be powerful hallucinogens. The sap was used as a snuff by several other tribes in the Amazon, but the oral preparations were restricted to the few tribes whose ancestral home was in the Colombian Putumayo region, near the mission town of La Chorrera, on a tributary of the Putumayo, the Río Igara Paraná. According to Schultes, the effects manifested rapidly and were strong and bizarre. *Oo-koo-hé* had to be the Secret!

There were intimations in the paper that the Witoto used the substance to see and speak with the "little people." Could these be the same cartoon-ish elves that we had encountered smoking synthetic DMT? This was our most solid lead yet; we determined we had to go to La Chorrera and find *oo-koo-hé*. That exotic preparation took on the aspect of the Holy Grail, the coveted aspiration that any obsessive quest needs to justify the effort and sacrifice.

That fall, a harbinger of what awaited me at La Chorrera arrived in a few puffs of acrid smoke. I had a small amount of DMT I broke out one night, asking Deborah to handle and light the pipe, which is how we did it, one at a time, so the person getting high didn't have to deal with the pipe, which is quite difficult when you're deep in the state. After I'd prepared the pipe, Deborah held it to my lips, and I took three or four enormous breaths in quick succession. With that my mind exploded with the force of the pri-mordial Big Bang! This was the strongest DMT experience I'd ever had; I was literally smeared over the entire span of cosmic space-time. I felt like the edges of my mind had expanded to the boundaries of the universe—in fact, there was no difference, the universe and I were one. I had smoked in our apartment but I had to get outside; I could not contain the energy. I leapt to my feet and raced downstairs into the cool autumn night. I must have presented quite a spectacle as I twirled around on the front lawn, gazing up at the starry heavens and howling with ecstasy! I had to be told about that part; I was unaware of doing so at the time. I was exalted, babbling, weeping, still fully in the grips of cosmic oneness. Gradually the effect faded, and I pulled myself together and climbed the stairs. But fragmented memories of the experience lingered with me for days as I struggled to make sense of what had happened.

By this time, late September, Terence and I had made plans to meet in Vancouver. Terence was sick of Tokyo, sick of the high-density urban environment, and more than sick of teaching English. He'd saved enough to pay for a ticket back to North America. Still an international fugitive, he had luckily met a fellow traveler in Tokyo who was able to furnish him with a false Australian passport. This document allowed him to return to Canada relatively free of scrutiny, though he didn't yet dare use it to try penetrating the belly of the beast itself. Canada was close enough. The fact that a love interest of Terence's, Dhyanna, had planned to be in Vancouver about that time was an added incentive for him. They had last seen each other months earlier in Bali, before Terence set out on his last expedition into the outer Indonesian archipelago.

I arrived at the Vancouver airport about a day after Terence had flown in from Tokyo. His bogus passport worked quite well, but things didn't go quite so smoothly for me. The Canadian customs officers were kind, but not disposed to let me in. They assumed I was trying to avoid the draft like so many of my contemporaries. I had very little money and no real connections in Vancouver. They weren't buying my story that I was there to meet my brother and kept asking, "Why can't he come to the States to see you? Is he a draft dodger, too?" I couldn't exactly tell them he was an international drug smuggler wanted on four continents. Instead I stammered out some story about how he had fled the country to avoid the draft and had found his way to Tokyo because he needed to earn some money—which was at least partly true.

I had the Vancouver phone number of the friend of the helpful Australian who had arranged the false passport for Terence. By prearrangement we had agreed that Terence would go to this person's house and await my call so we could hook up somewhere once I'd cleared the border. The customs officials made repeated calls to the number, but no one there seemed to know of any traveler arriving from Tokyo. Terence was nowhere to be found. About the time they were getting ready to put me on a plane back to the States, someone called and said that, yes, apparently someone had arrived from Tokyo as there was a suitcase in the front hall with a Tokyo tag on it. Apparently that was good enough; the officials agreed to let me enter for a few days. Like most Canadians during the Vietnam War, they were probably sympathetic at heart to draft dodgers. I don't know if they ever really bought my story, but it didn't matter.

Terence by this time had secured lodging in one of the sleaziest hotels in Vancouver's Gastown District, where I finally tracked him down. Today Gastown is a very chichi area of nightclubs and fancy restaurants; back then it was where you went if you were an alcoholic living on welfare, a heroin addict, or otherwise down on your luck. Terence didn't have a lot of money, but I think his standards had seriously eroded during his months of travel in the jungle backwaters. Our room stank of vomit, and the floor seethed with thousands of cockroaches. Waves of them would vanish back into the nooks and corners with a dry clicking sound when the lights were turned on. I didn't relish the prospect of staying in such a place, but Terence seemed unperturbed. Besides, we had some hash and we both agreed—with hash we could put up with anything. It was our first face-to-face meeting since we had said good-bye in Snowmass in the waning summer of 1968. We had a lot of catching up to do. In the interim, I had graduated from high school and relocated to Aspen, the bust had gone down, Mom had gotten cancer, and we were caught up in plans for our trip to South America. The small amount of hash we had was quickly consumed, and we needed more. We walked from Gastown across the Burrard Bridge into Kitsilano, a beachfront community that was the nearest thing to an open-air drug market I've ever seen. Every few houses, someone was sitting on the stoop hawking hash-ish, cannabis, and a smorgasbord of psychedelics, calling out like carnival barkers as we strolled by. It didn't take long to renew our supply, and we returned to the hotel.

The guy who had arranged Terence's false passport had connections into a whole scene in Vancouver, a communal household inhabited by a colorful bunch of freaks. None of these people appeared to have jobs. They were creative types, and their chief activities seemed to be making art, making music, and partying. The pubs in Gastown made the latter easy. By law, no food was served, but a glass of beer cost 20 cents, so for two or three bucks you could drink all night and get thoroughly hammered, which we did.

After a few nights of that I was ready to leave. The customs people had made it clear that I should only stay a few days, and my time was growing short. Besides, I missed my Deborah, who was alone back in Boulder, and I had to get back for my classes. Dhyanna had surfaced about the same time, and Terence, clearly in a lustful frenzy, could hardly wait to get her alone and tear her clothes off. From the looks of her, I didn't blame him.

In any case, our plans had been set. I had brought many of the key references on *oo-koo-hé* and other hallucinogens we might encounter, including psilocybin mushrooms and *Banisteriopsis caapi*, the vine used in ayahuasca. These went into an accordion file of reprints we intended to take on our journey. After poring over the documents, our mission became clear that La Chorrera was indeed to be our destination, *oo-koo-hé* our goal. I mentioned earlier how the author William Burroughs had made virtually the same journey in 1953 in search of ayahuasca, or *yagé* as it is known in the Putumayo. Burroughs had coined it "the final fix." We admired Burrough's work and saw his account of that trip in *The Yage Letters* as both a call to adventure and an augury of our own success. If a junkie could travel to the Amazon to find *yagé* and survive to tell the tale, surely we could do no worse. Failure was not a part of what we understood to be our destiny. It was in that filthy Vancouver hotel room that we first coined the name of our visionary band, known thereafter as the Brotherhood of the Screaming Abyss.

28 Our Mother's Death

Over the weeks of early autumn, our mother's condition steadily deteriorated. All her chemotherapy and radiation treatments had led her inevitably to that depressing threshold when the doctors say, "There's nothing more we can do." We all knew that was coming, even our father, who hadn't wanted to admit that the end was near.

The message arrived on a gray and drizzly day in late October, delivered to my door by a fellow CU student from Paonia. I didn't have a telephone at the time, so her parents asked her to pass on the word that my mother was sinking fast. It was time to get to St. Mary's Hospital in Grand Junction. I'd been expecting something like this, but it is one thing to expect and another to hear. I remember staring out the rain-streaked window. "Everything is dying," I said to Deborah. "Mother will be dead soon." There was little she could say to comfort me as I gathered my things and left for the airport.

By the time I landed in Grand Junction, where my father met me, it was late evening, around nine or ten. We went directly to the hospital and were ushered to Mother's bedside. The lights had been turned down. In the shadows I could barely make out her tiny form huddled under the covers. I was appalled to see how shrunken she had become since I had said good-bye to her in Paonia before returning to Boulder. There is nothing pretty or uplifting or in any way inspiring about a death from cancer; it ravages the body and eventually renders the victim into a hollow husk. This it had done to Mom, my beautiful mother, the prettiest girl in all of Paonia. When I approached the bed, she opened her eyes. She had been sleeping or dozing, it wasn't clear which. She could not speak; she was too far into an opiate fog to do that. I covered her withered, shrunken hands and kissed her gently on the brow, whispered something meaningless to let her know I was there. I don't know if she was even conscious enough to know I was there. She made a whimpering sound but no words came out. I was crying. I tried through my tears to tell her that I loved her, and that I was sorry for all the ways I had hurt her.

She managed to say something like "humph" or "oomph." I don't know what it meant. It sounded to my ears, and in my grief, like a rejection of what I had expressed to her. It was too late now, too late to fix those wrongs. I was overcome by grief and guilt. I begged for her forgiveness, but all that came back was "humph" or "oomph." I broke down, all efforts to hold back the tears were abandoned, and I had to be led out of the room. That was the last time I saw her. By this time it was late. I was tired from the trip, and Dad took me back to the hotel room that he had rented a few blocks from the hospital. He suggested I try to get some sleep. He was going back to the hospital to be with Mom and would come and get me in a few hours. I could not fall asleep. Images from childhood, images of Mom and the times we had shared kept appearing behind my closed eyelids. Finally I must have fallen into a troubled sleep, for the next thing I knew Dad was shaking me awake, saying, "Mother's gone." And so she was, and so she has been, gone for more than 40 years. The day dawned. It was October 25, 1970.

It was bad enough for us to endure the tragedy of Mom's death at the young age of 57, but our grieving was complicated by another drama. While Mom was on her deathbed, Terence was keeping vigil, in close touch via telephone from Victoria, British Columbia, where he had relocated after my visit a few weeks earlier. He was prepared to risk crossing the border on his false passport in order to reach her bedside, and by the time Mom passed he'd already begun the first leg of his trip and was airborne somewhere between Vancouver and Los Angeles. Dad feared the law was tracking Terence and would pounce on him the moment he got off the plane in Grand Junction. Now that Mom had passed, there was no point for him to complete the journey. We needed to get word to him to abort the trip and return to Canada.

Back then, before the cell phone era, this was a considerable challenge. What followed was a series of frantic long-distance calls, first to the airline in Vancouver, who confirmed that he had boarded the plane and would have a layover in L.A. before he flew on to Salt Lake City and then Grand Junction. If possible we needed to get word to him on one of his stops and tell him to turn around. We succeeded in contacting the airline literally as the plane was pushing back from the gate in L.A. Our message was clear: "Do not let him leave on that plane!" Remarkably, they complied, directing the plane back to the gate and letting Terence disembark. Even more remarkably, they didn't ask many questions. In those days, security was almost laughably lax. Today, not only would the airline have refused to divulge any information about a passenger, but the mere fact that we were inquiring would have focused attention on Terence, blowing his cover and turning things very ugly indeed.

In retrospect, I think my father's paranoia about Terence getting caught was overblown. In the overall scheme of things, he was small potatoes. Yes, he was a fugitive, yes, Interpol probably had him listed somewhere, but I doubt they had the time or resources, or even the interest, to follow him that closely. The whole drama that played out just after our mother passed may have been more about taking our father's mind off that fact than about warning Terence. Still, I have to credit Dad—even in his hour of deepest grief he still cared enough about Terence, despite their differences, to take extraordinary steps to protect him.

The four or five days following Mom's death were a blur. We packed up and checked out of the hotel and headed back to Paonia. "Some doors you never want to open again," my father said as we left the hotel room. It was true; this was the end of a long and sad chapter in our lives. At least Mom was no longer suffering. It was a cold comfort.

The funeral was held at the Catholic church in Paonia. Relatives came from near and far for the funeral, including my Aunt Amelia, my father's sister, who drove from Denver, where she was a pastoral counselor at St. Joseph's Hospital. Many in the community loved my mother, and her funeral was well attended. She had done much for the town's elderly and sick, checking on shut-ins and widows, simply because it was the right thing to do. Now her friends and those to whom she had been kind came to pay their respects. Only Terence was missing. It was a time of great sadness and grieving for me. I was depressed and felt helpless at the loss. I was 19, a little more than a month shy of my 20th birthday, but I didn't feel like a young adult. I felt like a child who had lost his mother, which is what I was. I was utterly bereft.

After Mom had been lowered into her final resting place, I returned to Boulder, driven back by Amelia and her companion, a nun who had accompanied her to Paonia. More drama! I was petrified that they would stop and come up to the apartment and discover Deborah there. Until then I'd kept Deborah's presence in my life a secret. On the way back, I placed an urgent phone call to Hans and Nancy in their apartment downstairs from ours, asking them to keep Deborah in their place until I arrived, which they did. In the end, Amelia let me off in front of the house and didn't come upstairs. I have to wonder if perhaps she knew what was going on and didn't want to make a scene. We were all exhausted from the stressful days just past and tired from the trip over the mountains, so she may have just wanted to get home.

I remember little about the remainder of the semester. I was depressed and sad, and Deborah's simple and undemanding affection did little to lift my spirits. Terence was still in Victoria, and our plans to go to South America remained on track. His recent love interest had by then moved on, but he'd been joined by his friend Vanessa, a fellow student in the Tussman program whom I mentioned earlier, and "Dave," a "gay meditator" from upstate New York, as Terence characterizes him in *True Hallucinations*. Dave had been living on the margins in Berkeley when Terence met him one day while both were hitchhiking. He arrived in Victoria with a newly minted degree in anthropology from Syracuse University. The three of them had rented a clapboard house in a quiet neighborhood and had settled in to plan the expedition. They had shared a mescaline trip a couple of weeks after our mother died that Terence described as "full of elf-chatter." Swept by intimations of the adventure ahead, Dave and Vanessa were almost as much in thrall to the notion of our quest as we were. The brotherhood now numbered four.

It was a time of rapid change for all of us. With Mother gone, I felt I had no reason to remain in school. Terence and I had been discussing the ideas that were behind our quest for well over a year. John Parker's visit to Boulder the previous fall had only fanned the flames of curiosity. If ever there was going to be a time to set out in search of the Secret, it seemed, that time was now. Somehow, we convinced our father that it would be OK for me to go off with Terence to the Colombian jungle on what we presented as a butterfly- and plant-collecting expedition. Even today I have no idea why he let me go, given that Terence had proven such a loose cannon, but for some reason he did. My father also agreed to continue sending me the small stipend I'd been getting while in school; this would be mailed to me monthly in care of the American Embassy in Bogotá. He was either incredibly trusting and open-minded or so depressed by Mom's death that he no longer cared what I did. In some ways, I think he was also a little jealous. As a youth my father, craving adventure, had been too sickly to act on his dreams. Then the war started, and his combat experiences had afforded him more adventure than he'd ever bargained for. After that he became much more cautious in life, but perhaps his regret over missed opportunities and a certain nostalgia for how things might have been still tugged at him. I think he understood on some level that this was my chance; I was due for my rite of passage, and this was going to be it. I was grateful to be setting off on this adventure with his blessing.

There was still the matter of what to do with Deborah. We were still very much in love. I did not want our relationship to end, but clearly she couldn't come with me. She was still a runaway, and our situation was very shaky. We had discussed this several times over that autumn, and finally I convinced her that she should return home and get back in school. For her to remain on the lam, loose on the streets of even a place as civilized as Boulder, was not a viable option. She had been lucky to meet someone who had taken her in and protected her. There was no guarantee that whomever she met next would treat her as well. I swore that I loved her, that I would wait for her to finish school and that we would get back together, but for now, going home was the best thing for her and for me.

I sincerely meant it all. I did love her. But I also felt I had no choice but to pursue the adventure that beckoned. Finally, with some help, I persuaded Deborah to call her older brother. Without disclosing much, she told him where she was and that she wanted to return. Her brother agreed to drive out and get her. When he and his wife finally arrived, the meeting proved unexpectedly pleasant. They were decent folks. Her brother was simply grateful to have his little sister back, and happy to see she'd been well cared for rather than exploited or forced into prostitution. They gave no hints of being angry with me. They could see, for one thing, that our affection for each other was real.

And I did care about her. I was sure we'd get back together once she had finished school. As it turned out, that did not come to pass, and in the years that followed I paid a steep price for loving Deborah. When we finally bade farewell on that snowy day in December, my heart was bleeding.

Christmas that year was a cheerless affair. Dad and I were both still grieving over Mom's death, and the last place we wanted to be at Christmas was in Paonia. We ended up going to spend the holiday with Tru and Iris, Dad's old war buddy and his wife, in Lancaster, California—the couple who had taken Terence in for his last year of high school. They suggested that I take the bus to Disneyland for an overnight trip. I immediately agreed, but Disneyland was the last thing on my mind. I saw it as an opportunity to go visit Deborah, by then resettled in her hometown. I managed to time the bus trip just right to spend a few hours with her and make it back on schedule so no one in Lancaster was the wiser about where I'd actually been.

The trip gave me a chance to meet Deborah's parents, which was necessary if I was serious about my commitment to her. Like her brother, they too were surprisingly friendly, almost more so than Deborah herself. She wasn't unfriendly exactly, but I think she'd had time to reflect on her adventures and was sobered by them. The cracks in our relationship were already forming, which I sensed but didn't want to admit to myself. As things turned out, I would have been far better off had I realized that and moved on. But the Secret lay ahead, and I didn't spend much time mulling over the uneasiness I felt after the two of us parted.

29 A Narrow Passage: 1971

John Brown, Puerto Leguizamo, 1971.

Shortly after the new year dawned, I returned to Boulder and stayed with Hans and Nancy for a few days. They had plans to visit Lexington, Kentucky, so I went along for the ride, saving myself a few bucks on airfare. By then Terence and the others were already waiting for me in Bogotá. My journey began in earnest when I said good-bye to my friends at the airport in Lexington and boarded a plane for Miami.

In Miami, I caught a connecting flight on Aeropesca Colombia, a cheap if not exactly safe airline that was later pulled from the skies. "Fish Air" lived up to its name by shuttling fish between Barranquilla, Colombia, and Florida. On return flights, Aeropesca offered passage to a few, like me, who were poor or desperate enough to risk it. The ticket to Barranquilla and on to Bogotá cost 60 dollars. The plane was a four-engine prop job, a Viscount

745D. There were no amenities—the seats were made of aluminum, cushions not included, and the interior smelled of rotten fish. Filthy water sloshed back and forth over the floor, and I don't have to tell you no pretzels were offered. I think we cruised about a thousand feet above the Caribbean most of the way; at least the moonlit waves beneath me looked awfully close.

After disembarking in Bogotá after that hellish and freezing flight, I took a cab to the little pension in the city where I was to rendezvous with my companions. It wasn't hard to tell which room was theirs; the smell of cannabis in the corridor gave me a pretty good clue. Colombia had just legalized possession of small amounts of weed for "personal consumption," their conception of which turned out to be quite liberal. It was OK to possess nearly a kilo, and Terence and company had already stocked up on potent Santa Marta Gold, anticipating it might be hard to come by in the Lower Amazonas. We might not have brought the right equipment or enough medicines or food, but we made damn sure we had plenty of dope.

At this point, the brotherhood consisted of Terence, Vanessa, Dave, and me. A day or so after my arrival, we were joined by a fifth, the young woman known in *True Hallucinations* as "Ev." She and her boyfriend, Solo, had met my brother and the others on their side trip to San Augustín, a hippie destination known for its pre-Colombian ruins and sculptures. Ev and Solo belonged to a radical sect of fruitarians and dressed in white robes and white rubber boots. They eschewed any food of animal origin, and any of vegetable origin for that matter, except fruits that could be harvested without impact on the plant. Even at that, they insisted on using a wooden knife for slicing, never a metal one, lest the blade destroy the fruit's etheric body. This seemed a bit over the line to me in terms of hippie-dippie foolishness. To be fair, Terence had convinced the rest of us to dress for the jungle in white linen, his outfit of choice while hunting butterflies in outer Indonesia, but compared to Ev and Solo we were hidebound rationalists. Their oddities went far beyond their eccentric dietary practices, as we later discovered. In San Augustín, Ev and Solo were in the process of breaking up. After they had, Ev drifted back to Bogotá and fell in with us.

Terence and Vanessa had been on-again, off-again lovers over the previous few years, but they weren't together at the time. When it became clear that Ev was available, Terence implemented a quick seduction (in the same room where the rest of us were sleeping, or trying to) and thus she became the fifth member of the brotherhood, the only one who spoke much Spanish. Vanessa had no problem with the reconfiguration as far as I could tell. I wasn't too happy to see our group expanding beyond manageable proportions, but who was I to object? I was the youngest and in some sense the one most along for the ride. Besides, I could see that having someone along who could speak the language would be an asset. Ev seemed pleasant enough, so why not?

Bogotá in January is cold and wet. Though the city is in the tropics, its high elevation gives it, as Burroughs famously noted, "a damp chill that gets inside you like the inner cold of junk sickness." Fortunately, we were only there a few days. The hostel we'd been staying in was unheated and literally a fleabag; we had all collected our share of bites and welcomed the chance to move to Ev's apartment after her liaison began with Terence. We were there only a couple of nights and then departed for Florencia, the capital city of Colombia's department of Caquetá.

There we encountered a rather unpleasant surprise. When Dave, our anthropologist, had met Solo in San Augustín, he'd been much impressed with the guy's purported knowledge of the forest. Dave later cabled him, inviting him to join us in Florencia for our expedition down the Río Putumayo, and Solo, it seemed, had accepted. This was problematic. That Terence and Ev had coupled up was news to Solo; he thought his former partner had gone to Peru. Nevertheless, he insisted he ought to accompany us, arguing that he was a man of the forest and that we wouldn't find *oo-koo-hé* without him. Finally Terence gave in. There was an unspoken tension between them from the start, but for a while at least an uneasy truce reigned. Solo was a screwball. He believed he'd been at various times the reincarnation of Hitler, Christ, and Lucifer, and that various famous personages inhabited the animals that traveled with him—his kitten, his monkey, and his dog. These creatures were vegetarians like Solo and hence appeared twisted and unhealthy, like Solo, whose teeth were rotting and who looked quite undernourished. Solo communicated with entities he called the Beings of Light, and even the most trivial decision could not be made without consulting with them. Their decrees were expected to be obeyed not only by Solo but by everyone else in our party. It was pretty clear that this situation would become untenable in the very near future.

But for now the brotherhood was six, and after a short stay we moved on to Puerto Leguizamo, the jumping-off point for boats heading down the Putumayo toward Leticia and points east. The grim river town turned out to be singularly lacking in amenities or any kind of charm. Burroughs observed that the "place looks like it was left over from a receding flood" when he passed through in 1953, and apparently little had changed since then.

Puerto Leguizamo is memorable in this tale for two things. One was an American who had lived there for many years, John Brown, a black man and the son of a slave. He was 93, he said, but he must have been older, and he had seen it all. He had left the United States in 1885, never to return. He'd traveled the Caribbean, eventually joining the merchant marine, visiting ports around the world before reaching Iquitos, Peru, in about 1910. The Amazonian rubber boom and the atrocities inflicted on the Indigenous people in the quest for "white gold" were then in full swing. As demand for latex grew in the outside world, native people were forced into slave labor, driven to collect the substance from the forest, among other tasks, under the whips and guns of ruthless foremen. Thousands were raped, tortured, and murdered in a campaign of mass terror that decimated the area's tribes.

John Brown found work with a company run by the notorious rubber baron Julio César Arana. Some implicated Brown in atrocities that were committed in Arana's name, but according to an early account of that era written by Walter Hardenburg in 1913, Brown may have helped to expose

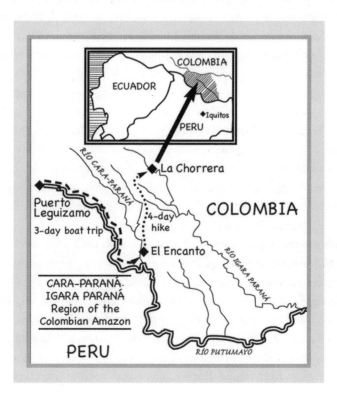

those misdeeds. He cooperated with a Royal High Commission investigation organized by the Irish statesman and human rights crusader Roger Casement, who as British consul in Rio de Janeiro had traveled to Peru to document the violence.

Brown visited La Chorrera for the first time in 1915. He told us about his experience there with ayahuasca, which he called *yagé*. Shortly after he'd taken it alone in the forest, a little man stepped out onto the trail in front of him and said, "I am *yagé*. If you come into the forest with me I will teach you everything there is to know." Brown said he declined the invitation, but I had to wonder. In any case, though stooped with age he cut a most impressive figure. We were awed and intimidated. This man had witnessed and participated in so much of the turmoil that had marked the decades near the turn of the 20th century. Under his ancient gaze, we felt like children, which we were—the oldest among us was 24.

Puerto Leguizamo is also memorable as the site of our first encounter with *Psilocybe cubensis*, the psilocybin-containing mushroom that within a few weeks would replace *oo-koo-hé* as the central focus on our quest. During our stop in Florencia, Terence had found and consumed a single large specimen, but the rest of us weren't so lucky. We had better luck in the pastures around Puerto Leguizamo. Though it hadn't rained for some days, we found enough specimens to allow everyone to give it a try. Since we had nothing better to do, we collected a few of the beautiful carpophores and repaired to our casita at the primitive hostel where we were staying. Except for Terence's low-dose bioassay in Florencia, none of us had ever taken mushrooms before. We identified them from the references we had brought. Back in Berkeley and Boulder, psilocybin and "magic mushrooms" were the stuff of legend but impossible to acquire through our networks. Magic mushrooms are now widely cultivated and relatively easy to find; many people are familiar with their effects. That was not the case when we took them at Puerto Leguizamo. We didn't know what to expect.

We were pleasantly surprised. Psilocybin seemed a lot less "serious" than LSD, whose trip seemed more weighted with personal psychology and psychoanalytical baggage. Psilocybin had its own personality—an elfin, mischievous character. It stimulated laughter and plastered silly grins on our faces. With eyes open, colors were enhanced and there was an almost tactile, silken quality to the air. Closing my eyes resulted in seemingly effortless evocations of the most beautiful, coruscating visions, rich in violet and blue overtones, hard-edged, three-dimensional, and yet somehow organic and sensuous. Along with the visual effects were effects on cognition and language. Puns came easily; our conversation was threaded with merriment and cleverness, all spilling out spontaneously, with no apparent effort. At times it seemed that the mushrooms opened up a direct pipeline to the Logos itself, the bedrock of meaning that underlies all language, indeed, all of human cognition and understanding. At times you could almost see it, like an effervescent foam of meaning bubbling up through the interface between understanding and apprehension, a mercurial lubricant between what Henry Munn, writing in 1973, termed "the contact of the intention of articulation with the matter of experience."

Yes, mushrooms made us laugh and we couldn't stop smiling, but at a more profound level they seemed to enable us to gaze into the fabric of reality itself. They were easy on the body, no nausea or stomach cramps. And they were fun! The experience was nonthreatening in every way. We had found the perfect recreational psychedelic. We had thought we had come in search of bigger fish than this, a misconception of which we would soon be disabused. But for now the mushrooms would do. They would definitely do!

It was only a couple of days after this experience that we finally secured passage on the next leg of our journey. The *Fabiolita* was a barge that plied the Putumayo, hawking tinned meats and fluorescent *gaseosas*, or soft drinks, to the tiny villages dotted up and down the river between Puerto Leguizamo and Leticia. For a few pesos, we were invited to make ourselves comfortable on top of the cases of gaseosas that were stacked up in the center of the flat-bottomed barge and covered with a tarp. The crew furnished no spare tarps to protect us from the blazing Amazonian sun, but fortunately we'd brought our own and were able to set up a makeshift shade cloth.

We departed Puerto Leguizamo on a Saturday, February 6, 1971. One day before our departure, *Apollo 14* had landed on the moon after its launch on January 31. This was only the third Apollo mission to reach the lunar surface. The previous mission, *Apollo 13*, had been aborted following an oxygen tank explosion in the service module on the outbound leg and barely made it back. *Apollo 14* had relatively few problems and hence attracted less attention; a jaded public was already getting bored with the space program despite being perhaps humanity's greatest adventure. *Apollo 14* is mostly remembered for the two golf balls that Alan Shepard hit with a makeshift club he'd brought with him. It was also the mission on which astronaut Edgar Mitchell had his famous *savikalpa samadhi* experience, or mystic glimpse beyond the self into the true nature of things. Mitchell subsequently became interested in consciousness research, paranormal phenomena such as ESP, and went on to become a founder of the Institute of Noetic Sciences (IONS). To the distress of NASA, he also became a public advocate for UFO investigations, insisting the evidence for the extraterrestrial origin of UFOs was very strong despite efforts by a few covert figures inside the US government to cover it up. I'd like to think Mitchell was tapping into some of the same strange vibes that had begun transmitting to us. He may have damaged his reputation, but I admire his honesty.

Whatever the public response, we were acutely aware of the mission through scattered news reports as we made our way into the Colombian Amazonas. We felt an affinity for the astronauts on their journey into the unknown. Drifting downriver, we too were impelled by the call of a mystery we felt to be no less worthy of pursuit. The weather was clear during most of our journey. Occasional afternoon showers yielded to spectacular sunsets, and by the time the moon appeared in all its fullness the skies were crystal clear. One night, gazing up at the full moon, knowing our fellow humans were gazing down on us, we noticed something odd. There appeared to be a black mark, or a large shadow, on the moon. What was it? We speculated that it might be the residue of a science experiment. Perhaps the astronauts were dispersing carbon black over the lunar surface to measure albedo or some such thing. Our conjecture was absurd, though we did learn later that one of the mission's objectives had been to crash the *Saturn IVB* booster into the moon and measure the resulting seismic activity. But that impact could not possibly have been observable from Earth, especially without a telescope. Whatever its source, the smudge was there, at least on one night. We all saw it. It was never mentioned, let alone explained, as far as we knew. I chalk it up to the ingression of one more peculiarity into the "real world" during our adventure. The farther we penetrated into the jungle, the more permeable became the boundary between ordinary reality and that of dreams.

Our destination after leaving Puerto Leguizamo was the mission of San Rafael at the mouth of the Río Cara Paraná. We were looking for "Dr. Alfredo Guzman," as Terence called this figure in *True Hallucinations*. Guzman was a Colombian anthropologist working with the Witoto, together with his English wife and fellow anthropologist, "Annelise." It was Guzman who had originally informed Schultes about the orally active *oo-koo-hé* preparation, so we figured he might give us some leads. From San Rafael, it was only a short trip via canoe to the village of El Encanto, the embarkation point for the trail to La Chorrera. The trail had been cleared in the early 20th century to transport harvested rubber from La Chorrera to San Rafael for transport downriver on barges; tens of thousands had given their lives to build it. We had chosen the overland route because the alternative, to continue down the Putumayo to the next tributary, the Río Igara Paraná, and then take that to La Chorrera hundreds of kilometers upstream, would have added several weeks to our journey. Cutting across to the Igara Paraná, which roughly paralleled the Cara Paraná, would reduce our travel time to four days.

We didn't encounter Guzman and his wife at San Rafael, but the padre assured us we would surely find them at El Encanto, where he'd recently moved to be closer to the Witotos. We lost no time in continuing on to El Encanto, a village whose name meant "the enchantment" or "the haunted," evoking what felt like another synchronicity between the real world and our inner ideations.

There was no way to notify Guzman of our impending arrival, and he seemed unhappily surprised when we showed up. His wife, however, was more open to our company. Living among the Witotos meant her status had to be commensurate with the village's other women. As custom dictated, she'd been living communally with them while Guzman dwelt in his own hut. The arrangement seemed quite exploitative to us, and hardly egalitarian, but who were we to judge? As for our colorful band, I can imagine Guzman's dismay when we showed up in our white linens, long hair, beards, bells, and beads, accompanied by Solo's menagerie of sickly dogs, cats, monkeys, and birds. We could have stepped into his scene directly off the streets of Haight-Ashbury. Nevertheless, he pointed us toward an empty hut where we could hang our hammocks before moving on, which he obviously hoped would be sooner rather than later.

Sensing the tension, we told him what we had come for and assured him we'd be pressing on to La Chorrera as soon as possible. Guzman was not forthcoming when we enquired about *oo-koo-hé*. He seemed quite surprised that we even knew this word, and bluntly stated that to go to La Chorrera and start asking around about *oo-koo-hé* would be an inexcusable breach of protocol. It was a secret, he said, known only to the most powerful shamans and not supposed to be known to the rest of the tribe, let alone to a bunch of freaks from California. We did not press the matter.

Guzman's agitation clearly went beyond his annoyance at us for disrupting his fieldwork. He seemed edgy and hypervigilant, clearly in some kind of state. His habit of chewing copious amounts of coca had apparently triggered something like an amphetamine psychosis that had rendered him extremely paranoid. He carried his machete with him at all times and would wander about, cutting swaths through the grass and muttering things like, "The snakes, the snakes are everywhere, waiting to strike! You must never let down your guard," and on and on, his eyes burning with the intensity of an Old Testament prophet. There were no snakes, at least none that we could see. The man was clearly troubled, possibly worse. It was also clear that his shy and chubby wife was aware of the situation and concerned, possibly terrified, but we weren't about to intervene in their strained relationship. We made plans to move on as quickly as we could, which meant rounding up porters to carry our stuff. It's not as if we needed more motivation to move on, but we got it anyway when a large palm tree next to our hut "spontaneously" caught fire in the middle of our second night there. Whether Guzman had put someone up to that or others resented our presence, we took it as another sign our short welcome had worn thin.

Fortunately, we quickly found a couple of Witoto lads of about 17 to help us. They were short and stocky and went about barefoot, which is actually the best way to go in the Amazon if you have the thick layer of callouses on your feet that these kids had. They were taciturn and spoke almost no Spanish. Being tenderfoot gringos, we were equipped with state-of-the-art backpacks, all nylon, padded straps, with aluminum frames that rested on the hips, really very nice. Our Witoto bearers rejected them. They took their machetes into the forest and returned ten minutes later with some leaves, strips of bark, and fibers from a liana and quickly fashioned them into loosely woven baskets with shoulder straps. They dumped our high-tech packs into these baskets, and the trek began. Theirs was actually the superior technology. I tried on one of the baskets, and it was as comfortable as my North Face version. Like tourists everywhere, we had seriously overpacked. We tried to consolidate our gear into two large packs that the bearers could carry, along with three smaller packs that we could trade off among us. The rest we stuffed into a trunk we'd brought—I don't know what we were thinking—and asked Guzman to store it for us until we returned. He reluctantly agreed, no doubt just to get us out of there.

After a day of preparations we started down the trail, or *troche*, in the early dawn mist. We'd been told the journey would take four days, with crude shelters spaced about a day's walk apart. Our goal was to reach the shelters in time to make camp before darkness fell. We must have presented quite a spectacle as we departed the village, disappearing down the trail in our white linens and robes, Terence leading the way with his butterfly net fully deployed and our bemused porters bringing up the rear. They soon got well ahead of us when we stopped to rest. It was the morning of February 18, 1971.

Looking back, I marvel that we even survived the ensuing trek, which was hellish. Every morning we rose before dawn, made coffee, shared a large spliff, and set out. Much of the Amazon is very flat, but in this area there were many small rivers and shallow ravines, most of which were bridged by crude log bridges. These consisted of nothing more than a large tree felled over the gap, covered with moss and slippery as could be, like much of the trail. We were slipping and sliding through slick mud for much of the way, down one ravine, up to the next ridge, then down again in a monotonous pattern.

I've always feared heights, and every time we came to a bridge I was terrified I'd slip off into the ravine below—not a great distance but enough to do serious damage. My eyes became fixed on the ground to avoid tripping on roots or slipping. We smoked constantly, partly because Terence did so as a rule and saw no reason not to on the trail. The cannabis may have helped us put up with the conditions, but I also think it exhausted us, or compounded our exhaustion. The jungle was not particularly hot during those long afternoons; the canopy overhead protected us from the bright sun, and it was often misty and gloomy under the immense trees. During our frequent rests, I sometimes took off my shirt and hung it on a branch to air it out. It would soon be covered with a dense mass of stingless bees apparently attracted to the sweat. During those breaks, the vast silence of the forest, broken by the occasional bird or insect trill, pressed in on us from all sides. The place felt haunted by its history. I thought of the Huitoto people who had met a horrible fate there, the cruelties they had endured in pushing that trail through thick forest.

It was the second day, I recall, when things finally came to a head between Terence and Solo. The tension between them had been palpable and growing ever since we had departed from Puerto Leguizamo. Solo said little, but his eyes blazed with a glittering fury. He clearly hated Terence for stealing his girlfriend, as he saw it. Solo was growing nuttier by the day. He was also in extreme pain from his rotting teeth and multiple abscesses. He needed to get back to civilization and have them treated. What's more, there was only room for one alpha male in this particular troupe of monkeys, and it wasn't going to be him. Inevitably there was a confrontation. An embarrassing standoff on the trail took place, eventually defused when Vanessa intervened. We continued our slog down the trail in sullen silence. Later, Solo declared that he had decided (perhaps after consulting the Beings of Light) to return to El Encanto and head back upriver. We all mumbled he was probably right in view of his medical situation. The face-saving out enabled him to depart somewhat gracefully. We stopped for the night, and by dawn he'd slipped away.

We passed two more exhausting days on the trail. The women had stopped cooking—there was no way to make a fire with the damp wood. We were reduced to tins of sardines and smoked meat. Our energies were flagging but it didn't matter. As though hypnotized, we pressed on. We were young and in decent shape but not particularly athletic or trained for a wilderness ordeal. Somehow we managed. On the afternoon of the fourth day, right on schedule, we transitioned from the deep gloom of the primary jungle into sparser secondary forest and then emerged into a rough clearing. We could see the mission buildings situated on the far side. A rainbow had accompanied us for the last few kilometers of our journey, and it seemed an appropriate and encouraging omen. We had traversed the narrow passage to La Chorrera.

30 On the Edge of the Abyss

In some respects, everything in life before we arrived at La Chorrera was a prelude to the events that engulfed us there, and everything afterward has been a reflection of them. Terence chronicled the events in *True Hallucinations*. Though his account may seem unlikely and bizarre, I believe it is largely accurate, even if interpretations vary as to what it all meant. I can't vouch for every detail, if only because I was lost in hyperspace for much of the time, or overwhelmed by psychosis, again depending on interpretation. Anyone with an interest in the "facts" of our story, if the word even applies, should regard Terence's narrative as required reading.

As for my narrative, I'm faced with three tasks in the next few chapters. The first is to tell the story of what happened over those weeks. Second, I want to describe my experience while I was away in hyperspace or, if you prefer, disengaged from consensus reality—this is a part of the story only I can tell. My third task is to step back and attempt a more analytical deconstruction, beginning with the first of many philosophical questions: What the hell was going on?

Mission La Chorrera consisted of a small church with a wooden bell tower, the padre's residence, a police outpost near the dock on the river, and a cluster of buildings that included classrooms and a few other simple structures. At the end of our trek, we were exhausted and grateful for the chance to hang our hammocks and recover in an empty hut. After a few days, however, the teachers who usually lived there arrived with the bush pilot on his monthly mail drop, so we relocated. The padre, a Capuchin priest by the name of Father José Maria (another coincidence in that he had the same initials as our father, Joe McKenna), let us stay temporarily near the mission in a hut on stilts we quickly dubbed the "knoll house." A number of Witoto families had recently arrived to pick up their children from the mission school at the end of its academic year. In a few days, the padre told us, the families would depart and there would be numerous empty dwellings

215

to choose from. We had our eyes on another raised hut set off in the forest, but until that opened we were quite happy where we were.

The knoll house stood on a rise perhaps 200 yards away from the mission but still in the pasture, a large area cleared from the forest to accommodate a herd of humped zebu cattle. The riverbank was about 100 yards from the knoll. The impressive geological formation that gave the place its name was called the *chorro*, the Spanish word for a stream or gush. It was something like a waterfall but shallower, the remnant of a primordial volcanic event that had ruptured the underlying bedrock, forming a circular chasm. The Igara Paraná formed a roaring cataract at this point, and below that a small lake. This formation marked the end of the navigable portion of the river, so La Chorrera was the end of the line in more ways than one.

The combination of pastures, cattle, and frequent warm rains had created an ideal habitat for *Psilocybe cubensis*, the same mushroom species we'd encountered earlier in Florencia and Puerto Leguizamo. These mushrooms are known to be pantropical; they occur in both hemispheres, in any place with a warm climate where cattle are raised. In fact, they can be considered symbionts of the cattle, whose dung provides a rich substrate for them. *Psilocybe cubensis*, then classified as *Stropharia cubensis*, are the most widespread and common of the tropical psilocybin mushrooms. We found them growing everywhere in the pastures around the knoll house and beyond. There were big, beautiful clusters of carpophores sprouting out of nearly every cowpat, quite impossible to ignore. We must have arrived at the peak of the season; earlier in our trip we'd only spotted a few specimens. Needless to say, we were delighted at this unexpected good fortune.

By then, Terence and Ev had canoed to a Witoto village upriver and returned with the plant materials for home-brewing some ayahuasca. We still believed the object of our quest, the real mystery, to be *oo-koo-hé*. But mindful of Guzman's cautions, we made discreet inquiries about that while otherwise amusing ourselves with the mushrooms. The specimens were succulent and quite delicious, their slight bitterness easy to overlook in light of our scant food supplies. We'd brought rice, beans, and tinned meats, wrongly assuming we'd be able to purchase other foods along the way. We could buy fruit, eggs, and yuca, or manioc root, from the locals, and condensed milk and noodles from the tiny *tienda* at the mission, but our diet was spare and boring. We found that a few mushrooms added to boiled rice or an omelet provided just the thing to perk up an evening's meal—and the best thing was that the after-dinner entertainment was built in. We had not yet understood that the mushrooms were the real Secret. We regarded them much too casually as mere recreation. As a result we found it very easy to eat them daily, either as part of the meal or as a mid-afternoon snack, with no immediate adverse effects. They were an excellent complement to the cannabis, which we smoked constantly, along with the occasional hit derived from shavings taken from our fresh supply of *Banisteriopsis caapi*, the vine added to ayahuasca as a source of MAO-inhibiting compounds. We found that smoking the bark while on mushrooms synergized the closed-eye hallucinations in a most pleasant and intriguing way. We dubbed this serendipitous discovery "vegetable television."

It didn't take too many days of such behavior for events to evolve in some fairly peculiar directions. As anyone with experience will tell you, the mushrooms stimulate conversation, and they give one "funny ideas" that seem to be quite novel, even hilarious. Being constantly on a low dose of mushrooms gave new verbal agility to an already very verbal bunch. Our conversations, full of non sequiturs and amusing puns, flowed freely, much as they had during our first trips at Puerto Leguizamo. The difference was that we more or less remained in this noetic space all the time. It was as if our group of five had been joined by an extremely erudite, clever, and delightful guest who had come for dinner and decided to stay.

Although we were enthralled by this verbal levity, our exchanges eventually took on a more serious character. Terence recounted the story of a DMT trip he'd shared with an English girl on the rooftops of Kathmandu a year earlier when all hell had broken loose. They ended up locked in an erotic embrace that transcended normal lovemaking; their bodies, seeming to fuse, began exuding a violet, effervescent fluid that evoked a transformation akin to insect metamorphosis. His improbable tale didn't seem all that far-fetched in the bemushroomed ambience of our little hut.

Another idea came up, one tied to a 1968 article by the anthropologist Michael Harner in *Natural History* magazine. According to Harner, the Shuar people of Ecuador (also known as the Jivaro) regarded the ayahuasca dimension as the real world and many regularly drank the brew as a way of accessing it. Curiously, upon entering that world they were often greeted by the "sound of rushing water" in their heads. The better practitioners knew this to be the realm where their magical abilities could be manifested. One such skill was the ability to regurgitate a "brilliant substance" containing "magical darts" that could be used either to cure illness or to induce it.

As I'd later learn, the concept of a magical substance produced from the body was an element of ayahuasca shamanism throughout the upper Amazon. In the Mestizo ayahuasca tradition, this material was referred to as "phlegm," a substance in which *virotes*—the magical darts—are suspended. This amounted to a kind of psychic technology that, like all technology, could be used for both good and evil purposes, depending on the practitioner. A more obscure legend had it that these magical fluids could be vomited and smeared into a kind of screen akin to a scrying mirror or crystal ball. Master practitioners could gaze into the film and envision the future, see distant places, spot game, and diagnose illnesses, among other feats.

The point was that this shamanic phlegm and the "violet psychofluid" that Terence and his consort exuded in Katmandu seemed similar. In the alchemical and magical traditions, these objects can be solid like crystal balls, but they can also take liquid form, as in water or mercury. The unifying concept was that these things were actually a blend of both matter and mind. They were substances, to be sure, but ones in which the future and distant places could be seen, in which anything imaginable, even language itself, literally became visible.

Someone unfamiliar with such chatter would have regarded these ideas as extremely odd if not plain crazy. But as I've described, Terence and I were already steeped in an exotic conceptual stew comprising alchemy, Jungian psychology, ceremonial magic, shamanism, yoga, and science fiction. To some degree that was also true of our companions. Besides, our analytical categories were pretty loose to begin with; we were anything but rigorous reductionists, even if we might have kidded ourselves that we were scientists.

So to us, these ideas weren't that strange. Could the body really produce a substance that was a fusion of matter and mind, and that contained metalinguistic idea-complexes that can only be comprehended in a state of profound tryptamine intoxication? We had no problem with that. In fact, in our state, that concept made perfect sense. And whatever powers the mushrooms may have given us in the service of great conversation, reductionist rigor and skepticism weren't among them.

On the contrary, the mushrooms encouraged the wildest intellectual fantasies, as if egging us on to ever more outlandish scenarios. We heatedly discussed the parallels between alchemical fluids and crystals and shamanic phlegm. We also explored the role played by sound in evoking these phenomena. Anyone who has smoked DMT can testify that sounds heard inside the head are a prominent part of the experience. Sometimes the sounds are like ripping cellophane, sometimes they are more like electrical sounds—buzzing, popping, and humming noises. Not uncommonly, similar sounds are often heard on high doses of mushrooms. As Terence noted, DMT seems to trigger glossolalia and other forms of spontaneous vocalization. Once the interior sound is perceived, there is an impulse to imitate it with the voice, to sing along with it. The sound doesn't lend itself well to imitation, but if one tries, the voice eventually seems to lock onto the inner buzz, which then pours out of one's mouth in a long, powerful ululation that is quite alarming and unlike any sound one would ordinarily utter. And making the sound is cathartic. It triggers an almost orgasmic ecstasy, and it greatly stimulates the closed-eyelids visual phenomena. There is a precedent for this in the traditions of ayahuasca shamanism as well. The *icaros*, the healing songs sung by *ayahuasqueros*, are used to evoke the inner visions and thereby direct the inner journey. There is apparently a tight link between the *icaros* and the inner visions, and the manifestation of these fluid psycho-substances.

Our conversations revolved around these heady ideas night after night as we communed with our new companion. And by then we did have a sense of being in the presence of an "other," an entity of some kind that was fully participating in the conversation, though in a nonverbal or perhaps metalinguistic way. We came to think of this other as "the Teacher," though it was unclear whether that meant the mushrooms themselves or if the mushrooms provided a channel for communicating with some unidentified entity.

Whatever it was, the Teacher was full of interesting suggestions about how our investigations should proceed. We began to think pure Logos had taken physical form, that is, manifested itself as a substance composed of mind, of language, of meaning itself, yet all somehow grounded in a biological substrate. We used the term "translinguistic matter" to describe this mysterious substance, and we speculated that somehow it was produced in the peculiar state created by ingesting tryptamines. We figured this matter was psilocybin or DMT that had been "rotated" through the fourth dimension so that its "trip" was on the outside of the molecule. The more we kicked around these concepts, the more excited we became.

Now the reader may wonder what we meant by fourth-dimensionally "rotated" psilocybin, or a trip being on the "outside" of a tryptamine molecule. These are strange ideas indeed. An analogy might help me explain them. Consider a piece of sheet music made up of printed notes on a page. The notes are an abstract way of denoting sounds of a particular pitch and duration, played in a particular sequence. The sheet music is a representation of the music, in effect a schematic diagram of the music but not music per se. The music manifests itself when the notes are played in a process unfolding through time—the fourth dimension.

We can extend this notion to the idea of a molecule like psilocybin or DMT being four-dimensional. The inert molecule, in a bottle on a shelf, is something like the 3-D score of the molecule's 4-D potential. Only when that mundane crystalline substance is combined with a complex mammalian nervous system does the pharmacokinetic symphony—the trip—unfold. The body in this analogy is the instrument that plays the trip, by metabolizing the molecule.

On our seventh night at La Chorrera, the idea of my body being an instrument became all too real after I took 19 mushrooms, my largest dose yet. As Terence put it, I suddenly stiffened and "gave forth, for a few seconds, a very machine-like, loud, dry buzz" accompanied by what I felt to be an intense welling of energy. In many ways, this was the moment when the weirdness leapt to another level. According to Terence, after my outburst he proceeded to tell his Kathmandu tale as a way to "calm us all." The subsequent talk of psychofluids and so forth may have been calming to some, but not to me. The next morning, February 28, marked the start of my furious writing as I tried to capture the knowledge I'd apparently been chosen to transcribe.

In retrospect, I see how our conceits embodied a paradox of the psychedelic experience. As noted above, on one level we understood that a molecule doesn't "contain" the trip. Rather, the trip is an interaction between a living organism and a molecule's pharmacological properties. These properties may be inherent to the drug, but the trip itself is not. That explains why a drug manifests differently in different organisms, even differently in the same organism at different times.

We got that, sort of. But in our delusion, if that's what it was, we also embraced a conflicting view: we believed an intelligent entity resided in the drug, or at least somehow communicated to us through it. Even as we theorized about the 4-D expression of the drug—that the trip could somehow be expressed on its exterior by rotation through the fourth dimension—we were assuming on another level that a being of some sort was directing the trip.

We weren't the first or the last to make that "mistake." After all, this is very close to shamanistic views of the psychedelic experience, in which the drug speaks through a skilled practitioner. Though psychedelics have been widespread for decades, people still have a natural tendency to describe their experiences as though the trip were in the drug: "The LSD gave me wonderful visions," they might say, or "Ayahuasca showed me," or "The mushrooms told me." I'm keenly aware how seductive this assumption is and how easily I slip into it myself, if only as a figure of speech. And yet as a scientist I must say no. These substances did none of those things. The human mind-brain created these experiences. At La Chorrera, the psilocybin somehow triggered metabolic processes that caused a part of our brains to be experienced not as part of the self, but as the "other"—a separate, intelligent entity that seemed to be downloading a great many peculiar ideas into our consciousness.

That's the reductionist perspective. Is it true? I honestly can't say, even today. It either is true, or the alternative is true, that there actually are entities in "hyperspace" that can communicate with us via something akin to telepathy when the human brain is affected by large amounts of tryptamine. That's a hypothesis worthy of testing, if such an experiment could ever be devised.

But at La Chorrera, we couldn't be bothered with such nuances. Believing the mushroom, or the Teacher, to be urging us on, we conjured up our theory about what was happening and then resolved to test it. Our "experiment" was not to prove if the Teacher existed. We took that for granted. We wanted to see if what the Teacher was teaching us would really deliver.

I should clarify that by "we" I don't mean our entire party. Life in the shadow of the little mission had taken some interesting turns. Vanessa and Dave had moved out of the knoll house to a hut nearer the river. Meanwhile, on March 2, Terence, Ev, and I had moved farther away, down the trail to the forest hut, which by then had opened. The split, while friendly, suggested a philosophic divide. Some of us wanted to run with the ideas we were entertaining, and some did not. I should add that the ideas "we" were entertaining were largely mine, as the next chapter will reveal. Dave and Vanessa were clinging to the reductionist view for all they were worth; the weirdness around us could all be explained, they said, in familiar, psychological terms. The rest of us were suiting up for a plunge into another dimension.

We decided our experiment would occur on the evening of March 4. Terence spent much of March 3 gathering dried roots and sticks from the area around our new hut. On the appointed morning, he used that to build a large fire and boil up some ayahuasca from the plants he'd brought back from the Witoto village. I had it on the Teacher's authority that the beta-carbolines in ayahuasca, present as harmine, might be the special seasoning we needed to make the recipe work, a key component in whatever it was we were concocting. Years later, in his account, Terence would question whether his brew had really been strong enough to "provoke an unambiguous intoxication." His theory was that the MAO-inhibiting effect of harmine might have potentiated the psilocybin we still had in our systems from the large doses of mushrooms we'd already taken. It's worth noting that we hadn't ingested any mushrooms for a couple of days preceding the experiment. Whatever the reason, the abyss had opened, and we were going in.

31

The Experiment at La Chorrera

Whether the ideas that seized us over those days were telepathically transmitted by the mushroom, or by a mantis-like entity on the bridge of a starship in geosynchronous orbit above the Amazon (which we considered), or created within our own minds, I'll never know. I do know that our lively discussions led us to speculate about how the phenomenon might be assessed. I should clarify that. By then, the Teacher had suggested the outlines of an experiment to me.

Or I believed so anyway, in my state of hypermania. Wildly stimulated by the concepts at play, I felt I was downloading explicit instructions from the Teacher, the mushroom, or whatever it was, about our next steps. The goal wasn't simply to test the hypothesis but to fabricate an actual object within the alchemical crucible of my body. This thing would be a fusion of mind and matter created by the fourth-dimensional rotation of the metabolizing psilocybin and its exteriorization, or "freezing," into a physical object. Such an object would be the ultimate artifact. It would be the philosopher's stone, or the UFO space-time machine, or the resurrection body—all these things being conceptualizations of the same thing. The Teacher was downloading the blueprints for building a hyperdimensional vehicle out of the 4-D transformation of my own DNA interlaced with the DNA of a mushroom. But not just blueprints alone. I was also getting step-by-step instructions on how to build this transcendental object.

The basic idea revolved around our discussions about the violet psychofluid, the magical phlegm, and the scrying goo, for lack of a better term. Alchemical symbolism furnished the conceptual framework within which these notions made a kind of sense. The creation of the philosopher's stone, in alchemical parlance, involves a multistep chemical reaction. The metaphors of chemistry are applied to transformative operations on the psyche and spirit of the alchemist. The process is not unlike a chemical synthesis that results in a final product; Jung would say that final product is the individuated self. We were postulating something more literal and much stranger.

Among the many stages in the alchemical synthesis, one essential step is called the "fixing" of the mercury. In this case, mercury symbolizes an inherently volatile, highly reactive substance: mind itself. The volatile substance created in the alchemist's alembic is literally "mercurial," thus making quicksilver a particularly apt analog for mind. The fixing of the mercury is the penultimate step in the alchemical reaction, the step in which the mercury is trapped, in some way tamed in a process that is analogous to crystallization. The completed stone would be my own mind, rendered visible and trapped within a 3-D container, like a Bose-Einstein condensate confined in a magnetic bottle.

To put that another way, what the Teacher had transmitted was a set of procedures for creating, and then fixing, the mercury of my own consciousness, fused with the four-dimensionally transformed psilocybin-DNA complex of a living mushroom.

"What?" the reader may ask. "What does that mean?" I might ask the same question now, but at the time it was perfectly clear.

Bear with me here as I introduce another concept. As the "experiment" became clear to me, I understood that the sounds that could be heard on DMT or on mushrooms at high doses were caused by the "electron spin resonance" of the tryptamines metabolizing in the nervous system. Electron spin resonance (ESR), sometimes called electron paramagnetic resonance, is a phenomenon displayed by certain substances that have one or more unpaired electrons. To study the behavior of unpaired electrons, researchers apply an external magnetic field to the electrons and then measure the changes in their "spin quantum numbers" and "magnetic moment." This technique, known as ESR spectroscopy, resembles the more widely used nuclear magnetic resonance spectroscopy, in which the spin states of atomic nuclei, rather than electrons, are measured. The ESR "signal" is generated by measuring the difference between the low- and high-energy electrons when microwaves of varying frequencies are applied in a magnetic field of constant strength. The signal can provide information about the energetics of the spin states of the unpaired electrons. The signal's output is the microwave frequency that generates the "splitting" of the spin states. It is not an audio signal but it can be expressed as an audio signal, as can any electromagnetic signal if it is channeled through an audio generator.

What I have written above is pretty much all I know about ESR. I didn't understand the physics or the math behind ESR then and I don't understand it now. Nevertheless, the Teacher plainly presented this information as the basis of the "experiment" I was to devise. The ESR signal, it said, would be generated by a molecular complex formed between the DNA in the membranes of my neurons and the metabolizing psilocybin and harmine intercalating—that is, inserting itself—between the base pairs of my neuronal DNA. And here's where the ayahuasca figures into the recipe—as my source of harmine.

Four decades on, we now know that the receptors for psilocybin in the neuronal membranes are proteins, a serotonin receptor classified as a 5-HT_{2A} subtype. In 1971, however, almost nothing was known about the molecular nature of neurotransmitter receptors. Some people even speculated that transmitters might be short sequences of ribonucleic acids localized in the membrane (Smythies 1969). At the time, we believed the newly formed harmine–psilocybin–DNA complex would generate an audible ESR signal. What's more, the Teacher explained that by listening for the audible ESR signal on a high dose of mushrooms, one could imitate this sound and thereby cancel out these harmonic frequencies, bringing about a chemical reaction that would cause the complex to drop into a stable, superconducting state.

Meanwhile, the harmine that had melded with my DNA would amplify its ESR signal and generate a stable standing waveform—essentially a hologram. And the hologram would begin to broadcast the information stored in the DNA, making that data both comprehensible to thought and open to manipulation by thought. If the experiment worked, one of us in the near vicinity would be turned into a DNA radio transmitting the collective knowledge of all earthly life, all the time.

Got that? One thing was certain. I was making creative use of the lesson in sympathetic resonance my high school band director had shown me on the strings of my stand-up bass. Here is an excerpt from the (now barely legible) notes I scribbled madly just hours before the experiment:

The Opus can now be summarized briefly:
1. The mushroom must be heard.
2. The *yagé* must be charged with the over-tonal ESR of the tryptamine via an amplified sound.
3. The [illegible] ESR resonance of the tryptamines in the mushroom

will be cancelled, and it will drop into [a] superconducting state: the physical matter of the mushroom will be obliterated.

4. The superconductively charged psilocybin will pick up the ESR harmonic of the *yagé* complex: This energy will be instantly and completely absorbed by the 4-D tryptamine template. It will be transferred into the mushroom as a sound and condensed onto the tryptamines as a bonded complex of superconductive harmine–tryptamine–DNA.

5. The result will be a material object of fourth-dimensional superconductive matter, that receives and sends messages transmitted by thought, that stores and retrieves information in DNA holographic storage, and that depends on superconductive harmine as a transducer energy source, and superconductive RNA as a temporal matrix.

It is now possible to reconstruct the physical-chemical idea metaphor that we have evolved in the process of understanding this phenomenon, i.e., the fourth-dimensional rotation of matter. . . . It can be explained thus: The tryptamine complex that occurs in the mushroom acts as an antenna for picking up and amplifying the harmonic ESR tones of all tryptophan-derived compounds of all living organisms within its range; since the tryptamine undergoing metabolism is superconductive, this means that its range of reception is theoretically infinite, and the antenna does, to some extent, pick up a signal whose ultimate origin is the totality of living creatures; but since the tryptamine metabolism is carried on within the brain (or mushroom) at a very low voltage level, the antenna behaves as though it were limited, even though it is superconductive. It seems clear therefore that the signal, which in this mushroom and in this ecologically dense area can be discerned so clearly, originates in the ESR resonation of the *yagé* plant, though perhaps all of the biosphere is picked up and broadcast amplified via the *yagé* superconductive transducer. This understanding will clarify precisely what will occur at the moment of 4-D warp. Ingesting the *yagé* harmine will speed up the process of metabolization enough to amplify its ESR tone to an audible level; this ESR tone will harmonically cancel out the ESR tone of the tryptamines within the mushroom, causing it to lose its electric field and snap into a superconducting configuration. The *yagé* ESR will have keyed the mushroom tryptamines into a superconducting antenna; it is then ready to have the tryptamine–harmine–DNA–RNA compound being metabolized within the body condensed onto its charged template matrix. A microsecond after the mushroom tryptamine has been superconductivity charged, its amplified ESR wave will then cancel out the ESR signals of the tryptamines and beta-carbolines metabolizing in the body, as well as the genetic material. This will cause these compounds to drop into superconducting configuration and bond together, at the exact same time that they bond to the waiting mushroom template. This transfer of superconductive compounds charged within the body to a superconductive template prepared within the mushroom will not occur in 3-D space; no actual physical transfer will be visible, as the organically processed superconductive material will bond itself to the mushroom template through the fourth dimension. The result will be the work of works, that wonder which cannot be told: 4 dimensions captured and delineated in 3-D space. The Stone will be all things, but the elements which, superconductively charged, bind together in the fourth dimension to form it are among the most common natural products, and the function and place of each in the Stone can be understood. The Stone is a solid-state hyper-dimensional circuit that is quadripartite in structure: 1. Tryptamines, first charged in the mushroom to act as a grid-template on which the rest of the circuit is condensed. In the final Stone the tryptamines act as a superconductive antenna to pick up on all cosmic energy in space and time. 2. The superconductively charged harmine complex within the Stone itself will act as its transmitter and energy source. It is interesting to note that the same energy that sustains the antenna circuits in superconductivity will sustain the whole of the device: that energy will be the totality of cosmic energy turned upon itself through the fourth dimension. 3. The third component of the Stone is the DNA bonded to and resonating through the harmine. It will constitute the 4-D holographic memory of the device, and will contain and explicate the genetic history of all species. It will be the collective memory of the device, and all times and places and conceivable forms will be accessible within its matrix. 4. The fourth part of the circuit will be the RNA, which will also be superconductively charged. Through its function of self-replication turned through the fourth dimension, the RNA will be able to act as a 4-D, waveform holographic image, and give physical form instantly to any idea. It will perform the same function it has always had in an organism, the process of replication through time. But this time, replication will be subject to the whim of consciousness. Of course a molecule which breaks itself apart and produces two duplicates of itself has to be functionally without electrical fields and hence is of course superconducting.

Does any of that make sense? It clearly isn't a carefully defined protocol for a scientific experiment. The words may sound like scientific jargon but they are nonsense. It's more of an incantation than anything else, a recitation of charged words and phrases intended to evoke a certain state of mind. Nevertheless, this was the information that was downloaded to me by the Teacher, a recipe for constructing a hyperdimensional artifact that would bind four dimensions into three and thereby end history. An object made of mushrooms, bark, and my own DNA, welded together using the sound of my voice. The Teacher was blunt: "If you do this procedure, it will happen." Build it and they will come—more precisely, build it and you will hold all of space-time in your hands in the form of the stone. The philosopher's stone—singing to a mushroom while completely ripped on high doses of psilocybin boosted with harmine from the ayahuasca—will make manifest the most miraculous object imaginable. Mind and matter will fuse into a hyperdimensional object that is the ultimate artifact at the end of time, whose very creation brings an end to time, leading humanity to a state in which all places and all times are instantly accessible at the speed of thought. It's crazy stuff. It reads like the ravings of an unhinged mind, and perhaps that's what it was. There's more:

There comes a time . . . that time has come. History will end in a few hours. The day itself has ordained the command to humankind: March Fourth. March Forth, humanity, to greet a new dawn, as you slid and swam and crawled and walked down the spiral chains of evolutionary metamorphosis to your final awakening. For this is the day when you will sleep no more: you have been blinded by the black veil of unconsciousness . . . for the last time. Why I and my companions have been selected to understand and trigger the gestalt wave of understanding that will be the hyperspatial zeitgeist is becoming more clear to me each moment, though I know I won't understand our mission fully until the work is complete. We will be instructed in the use of the Stone by some infinitely wise, infinitely adept fellow member of the hyperspatial community; of that I feel sure. It will be the taking of the keys to galactarian citizenship. I speculate that we will be the first five human beings to be instructed in its use. Our mission will be to selectively disseminate it to the rest of humanity, but slowly and in such a way as to ease the cultural shock. It is also somehow appropriate that at least some segment of the species has an intimation of the implications and possibilities of this, the last cultural artifact. To many it was given to feel the stirrings of change, but to a few only was complete understanding granted in the final hours before the accomplishment: surely so that the last words ever spoken in language in the final hours of history can be a chronicle of the defeat of the oldest tyrant: Time. And so now, against all the probabilities of chance and circumstance, my companions and I have been given the peculiar privilege of knowing when history will end. It would be a strange position to find oneself in, if being in that position did not bring with it a full understanding of just what forces brought one there. Fortunately, as the phenomenon is an acceleration of understanding, one gains clearer insight into the forces that have bent space and time, and thought and culture back upon themselves to focus them at this point. Now I can look back upon my life spread before the scanner of memory and understand all those moments that have foreshadowed this one. It is easy to look beyond personal history to all of the events of history, and discern therein the prefiguration of this last moment. As a phenomenon, it has always existed and will continue, as it is a moving edge of phenomenal understanding that was generated with the first atom and has gathered momentum in a constant acceleration ever since. What we are moving toward in 3 dimensions is the passing of the wave of understanding into the fourth dimension, the realm of the atemporal. As it happens, it will make the transition through one of us. But there will be no change in the cosmic order, or even a blip on the cosmic circuits, for the phenomenon has gathered constant momentum from the beginning, and will flow through and beyond the fourth dimension with the same smoothness it entered, until finally it has moved through all beings and all dimensions. Its job will then be complete, when, in a billion eternities, it has constellated full understanding throughout creation.

There is rich material here for the student of pathology. I'm acutely aware of that as I read those words penned so long ago in an Amazonian hut by a much younger Dennis who was utterly convinced he was about to collapse, or at least transcend, the space-time continuum. The ravings of a madman, I'll grant that. And yet, there is also poetry here, and beauty, and a longing for redemption. What I expressed is not that different from the vision articulated by the most compassionate and beautiful of the world's religions: the universe will not achieve perfection until all beings have achieved enlightenment. Isn't that what I'm saying? No doubt there is messianic delusion here; indeed, in passages a bit further on in that text I discuss my role as cosmic Antichrist. But there is also a deep wish for healing, not only of myself but of the universe. Our mother had been dead less than six months. I have to believe that much of what happened to us at La Chorrera was linked to that tragic event. So overwhelmed were we by the sense of loss, and of guilt, we were ready to tear space and time apart in order to reverse that cosmic injustice.

On the evening of March 4, Dave and Vanessa joined us for dinner at the forest retreat, but they wanted no part in our looming adventure. The sudden approach of a violent thunderstorm brought us all outside to stare agog at a massive, flickering cloud. Then the wind and rain hit, and Vanessa slipped on the wet ladder as she hurried back into our raised hut, hurting her ankle. After the storm passed and Dave and Vanessa had departed, Terence, Ev, and I completed the experiment's final preparations, as dictated earlier by the Teacher. We knew our success was assured, thanks to the strange signs we were given as the moment neared—from the intense lightning to the apparent breach of physical law, including the eerie steadiness of a tilted candle's flame, our only light. These phenomena (or so we told ourselves) were caused by the shockwave of the continuum-destabilizing events, now just hours ahead, as it rippled back into the past like a kind of temporal echo. We were approaching the singularity. We *knew* we were going to succeed because, just a few hours ahead, we already had.

By then, we'd taken the ayahuasca off the fire and set it aside, along with some bark shavings from the *Banisteriopsis* vine we'd used to make it. We planned to drink a small cup of the brew when we ate the mushrooms and, if necessary, smoke the bark to activate and synergize the psilocybin. Earlier we'd gone to the pasture and located a beautiful specimen of *Psilocybe cubensis* and carried it back, intact and metabolizing on its cow-pie substrate. We had also collected several perfect specimens we'd eat to initiate the experiment. Though we hadn't taken any for a couple of days, the mushroom "ESR" signal had been more or less audible to me ever since our last major session when I'd created the loud buzzing sound for the first time.

On the floor of the hut we drew a circle marked with the four cardinal points and placed drawings of *I Ching* hexagrams at each one, to define and purify the sacred space where the work was to occur. Inside the circle, we placed the mushroom we'd chosen as our receiving template, along with the ayahuasca and the bark shavings. We suspended the chrysalis of a blue morpho butterfly near the circle so the metabolizing tryptamine from that source would be present. Why that of all things? We were attempting a kind of metamorphosis, so clearly we needed a chrysalis close by. Kneeling together in the circle, each of us drank a small cup of the bitter brew, still slightly warm from its preparation. I munched two mushrooms. We climbed into our hammocks to wait.

By then we were fully in the grip of the archetypal forces we'd activated. We were no longer in profane time or profane space; we were at the primordial moment, the first (and the last) moment of creation. We had moved ourselves to the center of the cosmos, that singularity point at which, as the Hermetic philosophers put it, "What is here is everywhere; what is not here is nowhere." We were not in control any longer, if we ever had been. We were acting out our roles in an archetypal drama.

Though we were motionless, cocooned in hammocks in a hut in the Amazon, it felt as though we were approaching the edge of an event horizon. We could clearly perceive time dilating as we neared the moment of "hypercarbolation," our term for the act of sonically triggering the 4-D transformation of the blended psilocybin and beta-carboline. Time was slowing down, becoming viscous as molasses as we fought against the temporal gale howling down from the future. "A series of discrete energy levels must be broken through in order to bond this thing," I said. "It is part mythology, part psychology, part applied physics. Who knows? We will make three attempts before we break out of the experimental mode."

Who knew, indeed? We were following a script, but no longer a script we'd written. I ate one more mushroom and settled back into my hammock, wrapped in my poncho-like ruana. It didn't take long before the mushroom's energy began coursing through my body. I could hear the internal ESR tone getting stronger in my head; it had been easy to evoke, never far from perception for the last several days. I was ready to make the first attempt to charge the mushroom template.

I'll let Terence take it from there:

> Dennis then sat up in his hammock. I put out the candle, and he sounded his first howl of hyper-carbolation. It was mechanical and loud, like a bull roarer, and it ended with a convulsive spasm that traveled throughout his body and landed him out of his hammock and onto the floor.
>
> We lit the candle again only long enough to determine that everyone wanted to continue, and we agreed that Dennis's next attempt should be made from a sitting position on the floor of the hut. This was done. Again a long, whirring yodel ensued, strange and unexpectedly mechanical each time it sounded.
>
> I suggested a break before the third attempt, but Dennis was quite agitated and eager to "bring it through," as he put it. We settled in for the third yell, and when it came it was like the others but lasted much longer and became much louder. Like an electric siren wailing over the still, jungle night, it went on and on, and when it finally died away, that too was like the dying away of a siren. Then, in the absolute darkness of our Amazon hut, there was silence, the silence of the transition from one world to another, the silence of the Ginnunga gap, that pivotal, yawning hesitation between one world age and the next of Norse mythology.
>
> In that gap came the sound of the cock crowing at the mission. Three times his call came, clear but from afar, seeming to confirm us as actors on a stage, part of a dramatic contrivance. Dennis had said that if the experiment were successful the mushroom would be obliterated. The low temperature phenomena would explode the cellular material and what would be left would be a standing wave, a violet ring of light the size of the mushroom cap. That would be the holding mode of the lens, or the philosopher's stone, or whatever it was. Then someone would take command of it—whose DNA it was, they would be it. It would be as if one had given birth to one's own soul, one's own DNA exteriorized as a kind of living fluid

made of language. It would be a mind that could be seen and held in one's hand. Indestructible. It would be a miniature universe, a monad, a part of space and time that magically has all of space and time condensed in it, including one's own mind, a map of the cosmos so real that that it somehow is the cosmos, that was the rabbit he hoped to pull out of his hat that morning. (*True Hallucinations*, pp. 108–109)

This didn't happen, of course. Nor did a new universe emerge from the Ginnungagap, the "mighty gap" or abyss or void from which the universe emerged according to Norse legend. The mushroom did not explode in a cloud of ice crystals as its DNA radically cooled, leaving a softly glowing, lens-shaped hologram humming a few inches above the floor of the hut. That did not happen because it *could* not happen. Such an event would have violated the laws of physics. That didn't bother us in the least—we were convinced we were about to overturn the constraints of conventional physics. Besides, we'd been getting feedback from the future; we knew that we were going to succeed because we already had! Yet what I had confidently predicted didn't occur. What did? Terence again:

Dennis leaned toward the still whole mushroom standing in the raised experiment area.

"Look!"

As I followed his gaze, he raised his arm and across the fully expanded cap of the mushroom fell the shadow of his ruana. Clearly, but only for a moment, as the shadow bisected the glowing mushroom cap, I saw not a mature mushroom but a planet, the earth, lustrous and alive, blue and tan and dazzling white.

"It is our world." Dennis's voice was full of unfathomable emotions. I could only nod. I did not understand, but I saw it clearly, although my vision was only a thing of the moment.

"We have succeeded." Dennis proclaimed. (*True Hallucinations*, p. 109)

Succeeded at what? Not what I had predicted. But clearly something had happened. For one thing, I think we'd painted ourselves into a metaphysical corner. What I had predicted would happen, could not happen—*but we already knew that something would happen, because it already had!* I realize this statement suggests a misunderstanding of the nature of time, because how can something that was still in the future have already happened? Nevertheless, this is what we understood.

After the experiment, Terence was confused. I, on the other hand, thought I had the situation well in hand. As dawn neared, we left Ev in the hut and walked out to the pasture in silence, each lost in our own thoughts. I said something to Terence like, "Don't be alarmed; a lot of archetypal things are going to start happening now." And they did. That might have been the last coherent statement I would utter for the next two weeks.

By then I'd begun to disengage from reality, a condition that progressively worsened throughout the day. The reader may quip that we'd been thoroughly disengaged for quite some time—which might have been true—but even what grip I still had was slipping fast. As we stood in the pasture, Terence staring at me quizzically, I said, "You're wondering if we succeeded?" What unfolded over the next few minutes was an episode of apparent telepathy. I could "hear" in my head what Terence was thinking. I was answering his questions before he articulated them, though with or without telepathy they were easy enough to anticipate. All of them were ways of asking, "What the hell just happened?"

But there was more to it than that. I felt I'd manifested a kind of internalized entity, an intelligence now inside me that had access to a cosmic database. I could hear and speak to this oracular presence. I could ask it questions—and get answers. As I explained to Terence, the oracle could be queried by prefacing the question with the name "Dennis." For instance, "Dennis, what is the name of this plant?" And the oracle would instantly respond with a scientific name. Terence soon learned the oracle could also be addressed as "McKenna." Something very peculiar was going on. Whatever it was, we were both under the thrall of the same delusion.

Shortly thereafter I lost my glasses, or rather I hurled them into the jungle, along with my clothes, in one of my bouts of ecstasy. My blurred vision for the next few weeks surely played into my estrangement from reality. When I tried to share our wondrous discovery with the others, they were underwhelmed. Vanessa, our resident skeptic, asked some mathematical questions of the oracle and it was flummoxed, or it gave answers we couldn't verify. Nevertheless, Terence and I were utterly convinced we had succeeded. We were sure that a wave of gnosis was sweeping the world with the advancing dawn line; people were waking up to find themselves, as Terence put it, "pushing off into a telepathic ocean whose name was that of its discoverer: Dennis McKenna."

32 Waiting for the Stone

A canoe at La Chorrera.

The events at La Chorrera entered a new phase on our walk that morning in the pasture as we tried to sort out what had happened the night before. A full account of the following days would consist of three intertwined narratives. The first is the version told by Terence in *True Hallucinations*, written from the view of a participant in a delusion who nevertheless remained oriented in time and place. The second is the one our companions might have told, had they chosen to, as observers who hadn't been caught up in our bizarre ideations. The third narrative is what I alone experienced, fragmented though it is.

My story began with a tremendous journey outward. To the extent that there existed a precedent for what happened to me, I relate it to my DMT trip in Boulder months earlier when I felt my mind had been blown literally to the edges of the universe. Standing on the lawn that autumn night, I became one with everything; the boundaries of my self were those of the universe. And so it was as I progressively disengaged from reality over the first day after our experiment at La Chorrera. Once again I was smeared across the totality of space and time. Was I reliving that earlier experience, or having one like it? The question makes no sense. There is only one experience like that, and it is always the same one. It takes place in a moment that is all moments and a place that is all places.

At any rate, I was back in that place, at that moment. And my reintegration started there as well. I began to "collapse," or perhaps "recondense" is a better term, on what seemed roughly to be a 24-hour cycle, and with each cycle I got that much closer to reintegrating my psychic structure. By the second day I had shrunk to the size of the galactic mega-cluster, and by the third day to that of the local galactic cluster. I continued to condense at that rate down to the size of the galaxy, the solar system, the earth and all its life, the hominid species alone, my ancestral line, and then my family. The final distinction was between my brother and myself. Throughout this ordeal, I hadn't been sure if we were separate entities or not. Once we had separated and I was "myself" again, it wasn't the old self I had left. Like an ancient mariner returning home after a voyage of many years, I was changed forever. I was still resonating with the memories of those experiences, not fully reintegrated by a long shot but I was grateful to be back in a body, back in a reality that conformed to my expectations—more or less, and most of the time.

But that took a couple of weeks. While I was lost on my shamanic journey, spiraling in closer and closer, Terence was engaged in his own reintegration, in a way that was complementary to mine. I was cruising through multiple spatial dimensions, whereas Terence was anchored in time; he was, in fact, the beacon I was following home. As we understood it, at the moment of hypercarbolation in our hut on March 4, we momentarily became one; then we split apart again, in a way that was analogous to the separation of a positive photographic plate from its negative image. We became temporal mirror images of each other. One of us, Terence, was moving forward in time, while I was moving backward in time, from the future. When both of us reached the point where past and future met, we would become fully ourselves again, except that by then we'd have fully integrated the experience of the other.

To our companions, what was going on must have presented itself as a classic example of folie à deux, a delusion or psychosis shared by my brother and me. None of us had the vocabulary to describe it at the time. It was only years later that we learned that such phenomena are well documented in the psychiatric literature. What happened to us was certainly a shared altered state, but to reduce it to a mere instance of shared psychosis doesn't really do it justice. I say that even as I know I may still be expressing a compulsion to treat it as something other than that, something more.

But as far as Vanessa and Dave were concerned, the lens of psychiatric illness was the one they reflexively adopted to explain our strange behavior. Because we were acting crazy, we *were* crazy, and the best solution, as they saw it, was to get us out of that jungle backwater as quickly as possible and into the nearest psychiatric facility. Considering where we were, that option was problematic. I'm grateful that circumstances did not permit it, but I am equally grateful to Terence for resisting the pressure to leave La Chorrera. He insisted that whatever was happening to us be allowed to unfold in its own time and on its own terms. It was clear to him, at least, that I was slowly getting better, and that there was no need for intervention beyond making sure that I didn't wander off or hurt myself. Against her better judgment, perhaps, Vanessa accepted Terence's argument and agreed to a course of watchful waiting. Had my return been interrupted, I doubt that I would have ever "recovered" completely (if that's even the appropriate word). Under the classic model of shamanic initiation, I'd been torn asunder, but I was able to stitch myself back together. There is no telling how things might have gone had the process been aborted.

Over the next few days, we came to assume our alchemical quest had basically succeeded, but that some of our assumptions had been incorrect. The stone we sought to construct, the transcendental object, the lens, had not materialized in a flash. Would that it had! That would have settled the matter. Instead, our success apparently presented itself as a gift for telepathy and access to a vast database not unlike the akashic records, the mystical library of all human and cosmic knowledge spoken of by the Theosophists. True, our efforts to validate that knowledge had been problematic, but our connection seemed intact. Our shared line to the

Teacher was still open, and we were kept informed, in real time, of what was going down.

We likened this at the time to "how the boar ate the cabbage," our grandfather's phrase for any account that could be trusted as authentic. The Teacher was quite ready to lay down how the boar ate the cabbage. It also insisted we'd gotten everything right, but our time frame was off. The stone had been created, but because it was by its very nature atemporal, it was tricky to predict just when it would manifest. Part of our task became trying to nail down that moment of "concrescence," that moment when the "ampersand," as we called it then, or the "eschaton" as we dubbed it later—in any case, the last event—would arrive.

Indeed, Terence's effort to predict when and where the stone would appear marked the start of his obsessive ruminations on the nature of time, and the clues to that riddle he believed he'd glimpsed in the *I Ching*. In his account, Terence remembers the period of my "shamanic ramble" as the most intense time he'd ever gone through. For the next nine days he "neither slept nor needed sleep." He scanned the environment constantly, hoping to catch the stone in the act of concrescence. Willing himself into a state of hypervigilance, he also watched me constantly—probably a good thing because I had a tendency to wander away from the hut.

Every day we'd go to the pasture, where Terence would demand that I produce the stone. I couldn't do that, of course, but I predicted it was getting closer and closer. He claims that one reason he made this daily demand of me was to keep me focused on condensing myself as well, which is probably true. I now realize his intense preoccupation with time was as much an integrative process for him as my cosmic homecoming was for me. Both were desperate attempts to get reoriented over the next two weeks; both were more or less successful. This process continued well beyond our departure from La Chorrera. Indeed, in some respects, for me it is still ongoing.

Over the next 10 days, there also transpired a series of anomalous events, which Terence describes in detail. Some were tied to the odd skills I'd apparently developed, like my ability to pluck episodes out of his head though I had no prior knowledge of them. One example involved Terence's story about his frenzied coupling in the marinade of psychofluid on that rooftop in Katmandu. Somehow I was able to reenact the conversation he'd had with his English friend in the confusion afterward, when she pointed out that Terence had somehow ended up wearing her "knickers," that is, her panties—an embarrassing detail he'd elected to withhold from us until I repeated the entire dialogue verbatim, lifted from his thoughts.

On another occasion, I connected with a kind of cosmic telephone exchange that enabled me to ring up anybody I wanted, alive or dead, anywhere in time. One of them was my dead mother, who I reached while she was listening to a radio broadcast of the World Series in 1953. She didn't believe it was me on the line because my nearly three-year-old self was sleeping in the crib beside her! Other such events seemed to penetrate into the "real world," though at the time that notion seemed very loose indeed. We were living in a situation where the mind was creating reality, or at least modulating reality at a time when it seemed bizarrely susceptible to the force of our imaginations. None of this surprised us. That's what happens when you seize control of the machinery that generates reality. Reality becomes whatever you want it to be.

What we wanted, it seemed, were unexpected electrical phenomena and rainbows without rain, among other quirks of nature. I'd fallen into the habit of addressing Terence as "ama," the Witoto word for brother. During one of our walks in the pasture, I led him to a large tree, bent down, and pulled the grass back to reveal the weathered letters "A M A" carved into its base—and surely carved years earlier from the looks of them. How had I known that word was there? Why *was* it there? I do not know.

Once, when I got tired of Terence demanding that I produce the stone, I produced instead a tiny silver key. We had been talking about that key, or one just like it, which opened an inlaid wooden box with a secret compartment that had once belonged to our grandfather. Terence was keenly aware of the key's special importance in our childhood as one of our earliest "alchemical analogues of the philosopher's stone." It was he who challenged me to produce the key as a way to prove my new skills, so I did, placing it in his hand. He was shocked. We had assumed the key had long since disappeared, along with the box, and to this day I have no idea how I conjured it, or at the very least one just like it. Interestingly, while rummaging through some stored family boxes recently, untouched for decades, I stumbled on this box, but not the key. Presumably it has disappeared back down whatever wormhole had coughed it up that day in the pasture.

While Terence and I were immersed in our folie à deux, our shared reality or whatever it was, our companions were puzzled if not alarmed. Terence and I were communicating telepathically. What was going on was certainly strange, but we understood each other, or so we believed, and these events made sense to us, especially once we understood they were taking place in a surreal universe created by the Irish author James Joyce. That realization gave a context to the zany things going on; it was a pun-filled farce cooked up by James and Nora Joyce, who happened to inhabit the body of a large rooster and a small hen living near the river hut. We were in on the joke; Vanessa, Dave, and even Ev to a certain extent were not.

Four decades later, I still find it hard to put a label on what was going on. In retrospect, the best explanation is perhaps that we somehow underwent a shared shamanic experience that superficially resembled schizophrenia. The following excerpt is from "A Preliminary Report on an Experiment at La Chorrera," a previously unpublished account we collaborated on, with Terence narrating, in the months after our return from La Chorrera, as we struggled to make sense of what had happened. It gives some sense of how we were interpreting those events at the time. Note that we trace our initial break from reality to the earliest hours of February 28, when I first heard and imitated the harmonic ESR tone after eating 19 mushrooms:

> The most difficult of the aspects of our work at La Chorrera to write about must certainly be the psychological. Here is an area where we are called on to exercise objectivity in discussing personalistic contents and situations. Several themes have suggested themselves as being major motifs of an archetypal nature that our experience caused us to experience . . . the major theme is that of death and resurrection. Silverman has noted two types of schizophrenia under the heading "reactive"; these he calls "essential" and "paranoid," and his descriptions of these two types correspond exactly to the varieties of unusual ideation that were the major confirmation of our success on the submolecular level that we received following our experiences of February 28. From that date on, the normal configurations of both my own and my brother's personalities started a migration toward these two forms of reactive schizophrenia. Dennis evinced enormous mental powers and irritability during the six days following the twenty-eighth; during this time period my own psychology was marked by prolonged states of deep active imagination and "delusions of grandeur."
>
> In the early morning hours of March 5, shortly after the completion of the macroexperiment, the development of both our symptoms took a quantum jump upward. In the space of hardly more than an

hour, my brother entered a progressively more detached and cosmic state of essential schizophrenia; this development, coupled with his assurances that this was the proof of the measure of our success, was causing in me a growing certitude that we had succeeded and that this success meant nothing less than the cessation of all natural limitations in the very near future. For the next thirty-seven days, especially the next fourteen days, my brother's ideation consisted, among other themes but as a dominant theme, of the idea of a shamanic journey of return, from the ends of space and time, to the earth, with the collected energy configuration of everything condensed into a kind of lens or saucer, a true *lapis philosophorum*. He projected, and I, experiencing an intense state of reactive paranoid schizophrenia, accepted, the role of God, or father, big brother, or Christ, or, and especially, moral judgment. He in turn manifested an understanding of the principles and methods of science and information control that was truly miraculous.

He saw himself at times as a giant computer in a starship making a long journey home under the control of his brother, garbed in the dual role of the cosmic shaman and the Adamic Christ.

From the sixth until the twentieth, neither of us slept, and Dennis raved continuously, in telepathic rapport with anyone he wished, in command of enormous technical erudition and of a strange and rapidly evolving hyperspatial cosmogony. He visualized, following a Manichean perception, the solar system as a huge light pump wherein the light of souls was pumped from planet to planet until it finally leaves the solar system altogether and is transmitted to the home lens at the galactic center. Some of his discoveries included that the Saturnian moon Titan is composed of hashish which resonates with the living mycelium of psilocybin culture, that tryptamine fish swim in the harmine seas of Neptune, and, most important, that Jupiter is the reflected image of Earth in hyperspace, is teeming with bizarre life forms, and is somehow an essential key to unraveling the racial fate. Late twentieth century history was seen by Dennis as a frantic effort to build an object which he called "the lens" to allow life to escape to Jupiter on the heels of an impending geomagnetic reversal. Slowly, as the shamanic voyager neared his home, his place in space, his stitch in time, the symptoms faded in each of us. However, the continuing process of understanding triggered by our experiment did not cease. Rather, it continued to exponentially accelerate with the passage of each twenty-four-hour cycle, leading us out of the fantastic ideation of the early days following the experiment—we now understand this ideation as the shape of things to come—and into the understanding that has led us to the ideological model of the eschaton. This model allows us to trace the logic of the eschaton's operation from the molecular levels where our superconductive bond was forged to the macrophenomenon of the particular nature of an individual given historical period, for all phenomena are at root constellated by a wave form which is a reflection of its constituent parts—energy grams identical to those in DNA.

During the model two-part reactive schizophrenia which my brother and I experienced as a result of our experiment at La Chorrera, my brother, manifesting all of the amorphous and dissociated symptoms of reactive process schizophrenia, was clearly assimilated to the archetype of Chaos while I, manifesting the symptoms of paranoid schizophrenia and the complementary archetypes, was assimilated to the King, Hero, and Healer—all expressed in the idea of the shaman-alchemist, who is both poet and redeemer. The body of ideas associated with these concerns, shamanism, poetics, heroics, and alchemy, were in constant circulation between my brother and I. The most relevant idea complex relative to the time cycles and emotional states which I experienced seemed to be that of the Christos, the archetypal shaman redeemer whose intervention into history at the end of time triggers the Apocalypse and the Millennium.

If we correctly understand our accomplishment at La Chorrera, then we did in fact take upon ourselves the eschatological task supposedly reserved for the Son of Man who will come at the end of time to judge the living and the dead, that is to say that by being the instrument by which the wave form of understanding passes out of three dimensions and into the fourth we were able to fulfill the literal expectations of the Apocalypse that sets Christianity apart. For once the hyper-carbolation of the genetic matrix begins, that is, once the molecule begins to form in hyperspace, it is only a matter of time before the mind, as Lapis, becomes visible and independent of the physical body. This is the resurrection body that was such a puzzle to the early Fathers of the Church. We cannot yet settle this ancient controversy, but if we correctly understand the operation of the molecule we have assembled then it would seem that the answer as to the form of the resurrection body is that it is the same in appearance as our present body but with the optional ability to appear as a sphere or rotundum, as the spherical conception of the culmination of the alchemical opus was called. This idea is similar to the Egyptian conception of the soul or "ka" as a mobile lens-shaped object. Jung believes all of these spherical images to be reducible to the self, and further suggests that the form of the so-called flying saucer is a similar phenomenon. It is these two themes, the collective end of time and the resurrection of the body that seem to have been responsible for the nearness to the Christian worldview that was reflected in the psychological contents with which we had to deal as a result of our own "ending of time" through the experiment at La Chorrera.

During that period just after our experiment, I spent most of my time wandering in my own private world; my contact with anyone else's was tangential and occasional. That's a crucial difference between what Terence thought I was experiencing and what I really was experiencing. My thoughts and deeds in what I understood to be hyperspace were far more real to me than external events, even the anomalous ones I participated in and may have caused. But however real those internal processes seemed, they are hard to reconstruct, partly because they lack sequential structure, a chronology that would lend my fragmented memories some coherence.

That Terence retained a chronological sense of the interlude in question is another clue to our different experiences. There were times when my rants or just my wild gaze, absent my glasses, brought him "brief stabs of despair," he writes. He'd been reminded again how far away was the place from which I had to return. Nevertheless, he clung to his position that I was steadily getting better and just needed some time.

33 The Bell Tower and a UFO

While we were reintegrating ourselves, life continued to unfold in the real world shared by Vanessa, Dave, and Ev. Though Ev had observed the experiment and would witness some bizarre events after it, she hadn't been so powerfully affected. As someone I'd describe as half in and half out of our reality, she became a kind of emissary between the camps. Several factors were slowly nudging us toward the merger of our shamanic time frame with theirs. Put more plainly, we were under growing pressure to accept the consensus view that we ought to engineer our exit from La Chorrera sooner rather than later. Vanessa's injured ankle, twisted on the log ladder into our hut, was still swollen and painful; it was hard to imagine her retracing the long hike in. Meanwhile, our supplies were running low. The decisive factor arose suddenly, however, and began with me.

By the morning of March 10 my reintegration had progressed well; I could carry on a conversation and was almost rational in my responses—deceptively so. Terence wrongly assumed he could briefly leave me alone at the hut while he and Ev slipped away for a little Lepidoptera hunting, a field trip they extended for a little lovemaking in the semiprivacy along the trail. Leaving me untended proved to be a mistake. No sooner had they left than I bolted from the hut and headed for the mission's main square, where I created a huge racket by vigorously ringing the church bell, a ritual usually reserved for calling the faithful to Sunday mass. Terence heard the bell and came running, though by then the damage was done. As for me, all I remember is my desire to leave the hut and go among the people, overwhelmed by a messianic impulse to heal. I had discovered the power and I was eager to use it.

Until then, we'd pretty much kept to ourselves. We had little contact with the mission personnel or the area's few Witotos. There had been rumors that one of us was a little bit off, but my spectacular performance at the bell tower turned that to fact, and our isolation abruptly ended. Whatever my

244

reasons, my actions were a serious breach of protocol, and the resulting stir wrested my care out of Terence's hands. Vanessa, already insistent that we get out of there, now had the backing of the padre and the police. Moreover, as she learned, a plane just happened to be on the way. The others quickly decided that Dave would leave on the plane, return to San Rafael to collect our stored supplies, and make his way back up the Putumayo and eventually to Bogotá. No sooner had Dave collected his gear than the plane landed on the water, he got onboard, and the plane took off, vanishing into the clouds.

With Dave's departure, our badly strained brotherhood was now four: Terence, Ev, Vanessa, and me. The others moved me from the forest house into the river house, close to the police station where I could be monitored. Vanessa and Ev took over my care, leaving Terence alone in the other hut. A day later, word reached us that the bush pilot had agreed to return in a few days for the rest of us, a plan Terence had little choice but to accept. None of us knew exactly when the plane would arrive. We were told to have our gear packed and be ready to leave on a moment's notice.

The forces we'd unleashed—whether in our heads, in the external world, or both—remained at play. Many of the oddest and least explicable events involving apparent eruptions of the paranormal occurred in the period between Dave's departure and our extraction five days later. It was shortly after Dave had left that I manifested the silver key. Terence had been freed from the need to keep his sleepless watch over me, but that didn't mean he slept. He passed his insomniac nights beneath the starry canopy, haunting the pasture and trails near the *chorro*, lost in reveries of time and space with the great wheel of the galactic mandala reeling above as though in reflection of the cosmic cycles unfolding in his waking dream. There is a fervent and beautiful vividness to his account of the sweeping thoughts and visions he had in the company of "the deeper something that shared my mind." A reader can't help but feel those hours he spent alone may have been among the most fateful of his life.

Shortly before sunset one evening, Ev noticed a thunderhead suddenly develop on the southeastern horizon, roiling upward into the shape of an enormous mushroom cloud towering over the Amazonian plain. As Terence and Ev were witnessing this, Ev reminded Terence of my quip about the nuclear mushroom cloud being a biophysical pun on the transformative power of *Psilocybe cubensis*. The mushroom at the end of history was of fungal not thermonuclear origin, I maintained, an actual mushroom that would lead our species beyond history. As they stood and watched that churning mass assume its immense form, a bright shaft of light emerged out of the cloud's base and fell on the landscape below. It could not have been the sun because that was setting to the west and they were gazing toward the southeastern horizon. Over the new few days, oddly turbulent clouds, shimmering patches of refracted light, and other atmospheric anomalies persisted in the southeastern sky. The Teacher, still very much in our midst, informed Terence to keep watching. His vigilance continued through yet another sleepless night, this one spent beside the lake. It ended on the morning of March 14 with an encounter that, in his words, "marked for me the culmination of our work at La Chorerra." Here's how he describes it in *True Hallucinations*:

> In the gray of a false dawn, the wave of internal imagery faded away. I rose from where I had been sitting for hours and stretched. The sky was clear, but it was still very early and stars were still shining dimly in the west. In the southeast, the direction toward which my attention had been focused, the sky was clear except for a line of fog or ground mist lying parallel to the horizon only a few feet above the tree tops on the other side of the river, perhaps a half mile away As I stretched and stood up on the flat stone where I had been sitting, I noticed that the line of fog seemed to have grown darker, and now seemed to be churning or rolling in place. I watched very carefully as the rolling line of darkening mist split into two parts and each of these smaller clouds also divided apart. It took only a minute or so for these changes to be executed, and I was now looking at four lens-shaped clouds of the same size lying in a row slightly above the horizon, only a half mile or so away. A wave of excitement swept through me followed by a wave of definite fear. I was glued to the spot, unable to move, as in a dream.
>
> As I watched, the clouds recoalesced in the same way that they had divided apart, taking another few minutes. The symmetry of this dividing and rejoining, and the fact that the smaller clouds were all the same size, lent the performance an eerie air, as if nature herself were suddenly the tool of some unseen organizing agency. As the clouds recoalesced, they seemed to grow even darker and more opaque. As they all became one, the cloud seemed to swirl inward like a tornado or waterspout, and it flashed into my mind

that perhaps it was a waterspout—something I still have never seen. I heard a high-pitched, ululating whine come drifting over the jungle tree tops, obviously from the direction of the thing I was watching.

The siren sound was rapidly gaining pitch, and in fact, everything seemed to be speeding up. The moving cloud was definitely growing larger rapidly, moving straight toward the place where I was. I felt my legs turn to water and sat down, shaking terribly. For the first time, I truly believed in all that had happened to us, and I knew that the flying concrescence was now about to take me. Its details seemed to solidify as it approached. Then it passed directly overhead at an altitude of about two hundred feet, banked steeply upward, and was lost from sight over the edge of the slope behind me.

In the last moment before it was lost, I completely threw open my senses to it and I saw it very clearly. It was a saucer-shaped machine rotating slowly, with unobtrusive, soft, blue and orange lights. As it passed over me I could see symmetrical indentations on the underside. It was making the whee, whee, whee sound of science fiction flying saucers.

My emotions were all in a jumble. At first I was terrified, but the moment I knew that whatever was in the sky was not going to take me, I felt disappointment. I was amazed and I was trying to remember what I had seen as clearly as possible. Was it real in the naive sense in which that question is asked of UFOs and tables and chairs? No one saw this thing as far as I know. I alone was its observer. I believe that had there been other observers, they would have seen essentially what I have reported, but as for "real," who can say? I saw this go from being a bit of cloud to being a rivet-studded aircraft of some kind. Was it more true to itself as cloud or aircraft? Was it a hallucination? Against my testimony can be put my admitted lack of sleep and our involvement with psychedelic plants. Yet curiously this last point can be interpreted in my favor. I am familiar through direct experience with every known class of hallucinogen. What I saw that morning did not fall into any of the categories of hallucinated imagery I am familiar with.

Yet also against my testimony is the inevitable incongruous detail that seems to render the whole incident absurd. It is that as the saucer passed overhead, I saw it clearly enough to judge that it was identical with the UFO, with three half-spheres on its underside, that appears in an infamous photo by George Adamski widely assumed to be a hoax. I had not closely followed the matter, but I accepted the expert opinion that what Adamski had photographed was a rigged up end-cap of a Hoover vacuum cleaner. But I saw this same object in the sky above La Chorrera. Was it a fact picked up as a boyhood UFO enthusiast? Something as easily picked out of my mind as other memories seem to have been? My stereotyped, but already debunked, notion of a UFO suddenly appears in the sky. By appearing in a form that casts doubt on itself, it achieves a more complete cognitive dissonance than if its seeming alienness were completely convincing.

It was, if you ask me—and there is no one else really that one can ask—either a holographic mirage of a technical perfection impossible on earth today or it was the manifestation of something that which in that instance chose to begin as mist and end as machine, but which could have appeared in any form, a manifestation of a humorous something's omniscient control over the world of form and matter. (*True Hallucinations*, pp. 157–59)

A day later, on March 15, with the UFO incident and Terence's account of it still echoing in our memories, a flying object distinctly of this dimension appeared on the horizon. A moment later the bush pilot's floatplane settled on the water and taxied to the dock. It took only a few minutes to toss aboard our gear, which we'd reduced to our notebooks, plant presses, the butterfly net, and specimens, leaving much of the rest behind. Moments later we had cleared the treetops, and the humped cattle in the verdant pasture at La Chorrera disappeared into the mists. The pilot dropped us off in Leticia, a port town on the Amazon in the far southeastern corner of Colombia, near the borders of Brazil and Peru. We checked into a cheap hotel and enjoyed our first hot showers and restaurant food since we'd left Florencia some 45 days earlier. After a couple of days there, we headed for Bogotá.

To all outward appearances, I was much improved. I knew where I was, more or less, and could carry on a conversation, more or less, at least according to Terence. From my own sketchy recollections, I'd say I was far from fully well. I could put on a brave face and maintain decorum in public, but I hadn't yet entirely left the world of fantasy, puns, and wild ideas. Then again, I was definitely on the mend. Whatever had happened to me, whether a protracted biochemical imbalance or a loss of my way in a trackless shamanic wilderness, I was slowly returning.

The Bogotá interlude passed quietly. We spent much of our time in Ev's apartment, where I mostly stayed in bed, often engaged in conversation with a large, skull-shaped stain on the ceiling. Words in conversations would set me off into poetry and puns. I was still in a dream state most of the time, awake or not, but the bizarre ideations and voices were slowly fading.

Terence mentions that on March 20 we all celebrated at one of Bogotá's finer restaurants, and that the others agreed I was "totally back." They weren't aware that, in my mind, I was in telepathic communications with all the waiters, and that our dishes were being wafted to the table by telekinesis. Rather than alarm them, I kept that to myself. But except for a few episodes like that, I was doing all right. I didn't want to talk about triggering the alchemical transmutation of my own DNA and the end of history. I was happy my private voyage had been allowed to play itself out, but I was just as happy to be a human being again, rooted in space and time. I was acutely aware of how close I had come to losing it completely and I was grateful for my good fortune, my guardian angels, and my brother, Terence, who though he may have driven me mad also brought me back, back from the screaming abyss. I am certain to this day that without him I would have remained lost forever.

While I may have been recovering, Terence was not. He often sat cross-legged on the floor near me, reading from what was perhaps the *I Ching*, writing in his tiny script, making his calculations and graphs. As I lay enveloped in my own reveries, I didn't pay close attention to what he was doing there, bent over his notebook like a half-mad Talmudic scholar.

"I was caught up in an obsessive immersion, almost an enforced meditation, on the nature of time," he writes. "My attention was entirely claimed by my efforts to build a new model of what time really is." This marked the start of his effort to commit his timewave concept to paper. He began with a 40-day cycle as the crucial wheel in his temporal engine. Only later did he swap that out for a 64-day cycle tied to the *I Ching*, drawn by the correlation between its 64 hexagrams and the 64 codons that form the basis of the genetic language of DNA. (I'll look at this development later.) That initial "crude, self-referential, and idiosyncratic" work in Bogotá would evolve greatly over the years until the timewave eventually achieved a certain formality and elegance, worthy to behold. Whether his model represents the structure of time at all levels and everywhere, I have my doubts.

Nevertheless, as Terence concludes: "It was only my faith that it could be made coherent and rational to others that kept me at it for those several years, transforming the original intuition into a set of formal propositions."

I'd say that Terence's activity had as much to do with his reintegration as it did with constructing a formal theory of time. As I was condensing through level after level of space, Terence was attempting to build an instrument for temporal navigation. His device would establish, first, our place in time, and then track our movement toward a future moment at which the spiral of time would condense to an infinitesimal point, just as space would collapse to a point that would be its own singularity.

I'll save my critique of the timewave as a scientific theory for another chapter. Whatever its value in that regard, constructing and calibrating the timewave was, for Terence, an alchemical exercise—that is, an ongoing act of individuation in the Jungian sense. Ultimately, it was clear he'd been trying to map his own odyssey through time as much as define time's hidden structure. As all theories of everything must be, his was only partially successful, and so the pursuit of his individuation remained a work in progress, never completed, even at the time of his death. But individuation is almost by definition a life's work, an important task that perhaps in the end few of us ever finish.

After a few more days in Bogotá, we were all in a dissipative state, exhausted from our adventures. We still had no word on the whereabouts of Dave and our supplies. Vanessa saw little point in sticking around and flew home to New York, and then I decided to return to Boulder. I felt well enough to travel, and I wanted to get my feet back on the ground in a familiar place. I also desperately needed new glasses. The replacement pair I'd picked up in Bogotá weren't much good.

I had no idea when I left Colombia that I'd never see Dave again. He remained in South America for the next 35 years. I don't know much about the later life of a man who shared that formative moment so early on in mine. If our trip was any measure, he was a guy whose basic goodness led him to get too caught up in the obsessions of others, namely ours. Then again, that pretty much defines what it is to be young, adventurous, and open to experience. We briefly reconnected by phone and e-mail in 2007 when he returned to visit his aging parents in upstate New York. Shortly before his scheduled departure for his home in Bolivia, he learned he had a virulent form of melanoma. He postponed his return for treatment but it was for naught, and a few months later he was gone.

On March 29, I arrived in Boulder. I'd been gone around 60 days but it felt like centuries had passed. A few days later I left for Paonia to see my father. It was an uncomfortable meeting. He knew something had happened to precipitate our abrupt exit from La Chorrera and my premature return to the States (I had planned to stay until early summer). But we'd supplied no details beyond that I'd gotten "sick" and had to be flown out. I haltingly tried to narrate the events of the trip while omitting the most salient parts. He could certainly sense that there was more to the story, but he didn't probe too deeply, for which I was grateful. By then he may have reached a point where he knew better than to question us too closely. He just assumed we were both mad and probably criminals, and the less he knew the better. I'm quite sure he was still grieving over our mother's death and likely in a deep depression.

Terence and Ev remained in Bogotá for a few days after my departure. They took a brief trip to Florencia to get outside the city and relax, but something was drawing Terence back to Berkeley. He remained preoccupied with the theory of time he'd begun roughing out in feverish notes, more convinced than ever that we had stumbled onto something of vast and unimaginable import for humanity and the planet. In his view, we'd been right all along, and that our only failure had been in our efforts to identify the time and place of the stone's concrescence. But his model of time would fix that. He was obsessed. He needed validation from his friends and intellectual peers.

So Terence, still presumably a wanted man, took a risk and returned to Berkeley with Ev, entering the country on the false passport he'd gotten in Japan. He had no problems clearing the border. Apparently Interpol and the US government had better things to do than to track a minor hash smuggler for a crime committed two years earlier. They reached Berkeley on April 13, and at Terence's insistence I flew out to join them.

Terence and Ev stayed with friends for a couple of days, then Ev departed to visit her parents in Southern California. On the day she left, Terence and I met with a handful of our closest friends, all of them eager to hear our story. Terence remained in a state of persistent cognitive ecstasy, still obsessed with cycles, already beginning to plot his early timewave graphs, utterly convinced that we'd succeeded at whatever it was we'd meant to do. The task was to convince our peers, despite the lack of evidence that anything had happened as far as they could see. Terence's tale left them politely, and not so politely, skeptical. Their basic response was, "You drove your brother crazy, and you followed him over the edge." It's a testament to his powers of persuasion that he was able to seed the tiniest kernel of doubt in their surety we'd lost it. But overall, in their opinion Terence had gone around the bend and I wasn't far behind. Without Ev there to back us up, it certainly looked like a case of folie à deux triggered by too many drugs and too little intellectual rigor.

This wasn't what Terence wanted to hear. I don't know what he expected. His friends certainly didn't fall all over themselves and say, "My God, man, you've done it, you've triggered the millennium, and you and Dennis are the immortalized superconducting progenitors of a transformed species!" It was a lot to ask anyone to believe, and they were anything but a credulous bunch.

For my part, I kept quiet. I didn't dispute what Terence was saying but I was still confused, still sorting things out. And my credibility was pretty much shot. I wasn't sure what had happened. In any case, I'd had enough, at least for a while.

A few days after that meeting, I traveled down the coast to visit Deborah and celebrate her birthday. I hadn't seen her for about four months, and I missed her, but it was a less than a joyful reunion. She was cold and distant, our lovemaking furtive under the circumstances and her heart no longer in it. She had rediscovered her fundamentalist Christian roots since her return and was feeling quite guilty about our liaison. I didn't know it then, but I wouldn't see her again for five years. During that time she would lacerate my heart in so many ways the recollection still pains me.

After a brief return to Berkeley, I departed for Colorado. I'd lost a semester of school by going to Colombia. I suppose it was a measure of my disillusion that I regarded the trip that way—as a loss. I'd yet to realize that my education there went far beyond what I ever would have learned had I spent those months in Boulder. I wanted to get back into summer school, get my teeth into some studies, do some ordinary, tangible things. I had not abandoned or renounced our discoveries. I was still caught up in them, though not as much as Terence. One thing I was clear about: I was going to change my major from anthropology and religious studies to biology and biochemistry.

After La Chorrera, Terence was ready to renounce science. He asserted that our experience had shown science to be bankrupt; science could never explain what had happened to us and we should reject it—an attitude he held for the rest of his life. I was not so sure. I granted that our experiences had certainly stretched the boundaries of the known and that there was no ready scientific explanation of the events that had gone down at La Chorrera. But, I pointed out, we were not scientists. We may have been magicians, shamans, alchemists, or madmen, but we weren't scientists. Not at the time. We had no real scientific training, and we didn't know how to think like scientists. Had we understood the scientific method, we might not have stumbled into a cognitive wilderness where we lost our way.

I knew scientific thought had its limits, but before we could reject science, the most powerful set of intellectual tools ever developed by the human mind, we first had to learn how to *do* science. Then, if we still wanted to reject it, we could do so as scientists, with full knowledge of what it we were rejecting. We had to become scientists, or at least I had to become one. So I set about changing my academic trajectory and started studying both science and the philosophy of science.

That decision was a pivotal diversion in our continued intellectual development. I've spent my life since then studying and practicing science. As I result, I'm now acutely aware of how powerful science is—and how extremely limited. There are many things in heaven and earth that are beyond the ken of science, things that may remain so forever. Anyone who has taken psychedelics seriously or had other transcendent experiences is likely to share that conclusion.

At the same time, science remains the most effective method for asking questions of nature and getting back answers that can be tested and validated. Everything we know about the biological aspects of consciousness, everything we know about how psychedelics do what they do at the molecular level, is the product of hard-won scientific investigation. What science has not yet done—and may never be able to do—is span the gap between what science has revealed about the physicochemical foundations of consciousness and our subjective experiences of truth, beauty, dreams, memories, love and emotions, and, yes, even hyperspatial dimensions, self-transforming machine-elves and all the rest of the shamanic menagerie. Building that bridge is to my mind the great challenge of the 21st century. I have little doubt that science will play a critical role in unraveling these mysteries, if they are to be unraveled at all.

34 Reflections on La Chorrera

The *chorro* at La Chorrera.

The months leading up to our descent into the abyss, followed by the months we spent stumbling out, defined a crucial period in our lives. The two brothers who found themselves in Berkeley in April 1971 were not the same people who shoved off from Puerto Leguizamo in early February, so fired up with dreams and delusions. Now that I have finished my narrative of that pivotal epoch, I want to step back and attempt a reflection on those events from a distance of 41 years.

First, I must admit it is somewhat disturbing that to the extent we are known to a wider world, it is because of events that played out when we were still achingly young. Though most of my life has occurred after our trip to La Chorrera, the years since then have been haunted by its shadow, and I believe the same was true for Terence while he was alive. We went on to pursue careers and raise families, to write books and conduct research, to travel and teach in our efforts to make our mark in the world. We kept plugging away at the Mystery, though without the energy or recklessness that fueled our original quest. Nevertheless, the unsettling fact is that what we'll be remembered for, if we're remembered at all, is an episode of aberrant behavior that others might have tried to expunge from their life stories.

Whatever our separate accomplishments, they are modest indeed compared to what we hoped to accomplish at La Chorrera, which was nothing less than to trigger an end to history, to throw open the gates of a paradise out of time and invite humanity to walk in. You can't get more ambitious than that. But what was it that led us to form that wild ambition in the first place? Megalomaniacal obsessions rarely rise to such a level, and they're generally diagnosed as pathology when they do, to be treated with medication and even physical restraint. Whether by cleverness or luck, we got to act on our obsessions to an appalling degree. And yet, looking back on that interlude, I have to wonder: Was there more to it than mere pathological delusion? Were any of the apparent paranormal phenomena "real"—that is, objectively verifiable? Who was the Teacher and why were its lessons such a strain on credulity and yet so insistent? Subsequent analysis has shown many of our ideas to be outlandish and implausible, but not all of them—a few appear to have been gems of actual insight. For example, research has shown that tryptamines and beta-carbolines, among other compounds, can intercalate into DNA, at least in the test tube. And while no one has proven that DNA and other macromolecules might behave like superconductors under certain conditions, the concept has not been disproven, let alone entirely dismissed. Both issues have been taken seriously in the years since La Chorrera, though neither was even suspected before then. (For example, on DNA as a superconductor, see Lakhno and Sultanov 2011 and Kasumov et al. 2001.)

As for Terence's timewave, it may not be an accurate map of time, much less a tool for predicting some final event, but it does embody genuine insights, including his discovery of an ancient calendrical function to the *I Ching* that modern scholars had apparently not detected. Like the *Book of Changes*, the timewave may be a useful divinatory tool in itself if one is willing to see divination as basically the discernment of correspondences between inner and outer states. In that sense the timewave works, much as astrology and other such methods work—just don't expect scientific proof or quantifiable verification.

When I reflect on what led us to undertake our quixotic journey, I'm led back to the years in Berkeley and Boulder when we first encountered and puzzled over DMT. As I've suggested, this substance wasn't just the most astonishing drug we'd ever encountered, it was the most astonishing thing— and as such it was surely worthy of investigation. Given our intellectual path until that point, it wasn't in us to say, "Oh, that's interesting" and then move on. A major reason for our fascination could be attributed to our lifelong immersion in science fiction, aliens, other dimensions, and related topics. As Terence eloquently put it, the DMT experience is "an audience with the alien nuncio." Taken under the right circumstances—high doses, darkness, and paying close attention—DMT and psilocybin seem to emerge straight from a mash-up of Arthur C. Clarke and Philip K. Dick. One sees cartoon-like, multicolored, 3-D visions, urgently presented by elfish or clownish beings who may seem amusing but who, it is clear, desperately want the "viewer" to understand what is being presented. Whether one is seeing architectures, or landscapes, or machines, or organisms is not entirely clear. The visions partake of the quality of all of these and more, but what they are exactly remains inexplicable. What is clear is that they are fascinating to contemplate, and their contemplation evokes ecstasy. Terence and I were convinced that DMT had some connection to aliens long before we ever considered going to La Chorrera. We thought that DMT bore a message of some kind, either from another dimension or another civilization elsewhere in our universe.

Is it possible that we were right? I still believe it might be so. Most "sober" discussions about the search for extraterrestrial intelligence, or SETI, presume that contact with aliens will first occur via radio signals we'll eventually detect if we build ever-better radio telescopes and search many bandwidths in all parts of the sky. Any other interpretation or scenario is immediately dismissed. For instance, what about the notion that crop circles are messages from alien intelligences? This isn't seriously discussed, yet crop circles remain a real mystery, a phenomenon that certainly appears to be the handiwork of intelligence even if we have no other clue as to what they actually mean. And I'm sorry, but to explain away crop circles as hoaxes perpetrated by midnight revelers after the pubs close doesn't stand up to scrutiny. That may be true of the crudest and smallest examples, but the gigantic, geometrically complex circles that appear overnight are not the work of drunken hooligans stumbling about in the dark.

So in crop circles we have solid physical evidence of a phenomenon that indubitably exists, that is completely beyond human understanding and abilities, and that almost certainly originates from a nonhuman intelligence. And yet the response of the "respectable" SETI community is a big ho-hum; crop circles do not sit well with their assumptions that extraterrestrial contact, when and if it comes, will arrive in the form of an electromagnetic signal visible to our detectors. This notion seems almost laughably absurd. A galaxy-spanning civilization tens of thousands or even millions of years ahead of our own is not going to use a crude, 19th-century invention like a radio transmitter to contact us. Such pedestrian thinking is the reason why conventional approaches to SETI are doomed to fail; they are preprogrammed to focus on a single technology that most technological civilizations will have only utilized for a tiny fraction of their history if at all. Signs of alien intelligence that fall outside this model are ignored.

Any civilization that wants to communicate with us (or wants us to be aware of its existence) is apt to proceed cautiously and use unanticipated means to make contact. Considered in this light, the notion that DMT, psilocybin, and the other psychoactive tryptamines are the calling cards of an advanced civilization is not so far-fetched. This explanation certainly seems to be the message that many people take away from their experiences with high doses of DMT or mushrooms. It was the message that was downloaded to us at La Chorrera in 1971 and regularly reaffirmed in subsequent encounters.

One important difference between then and now is that many more people have taken mushrooms and, to a lesser extent, DMT. What's more, growing numbers have shared the sense of alien contact, the sci-fi tinged ideations, the quasi-techno quality of the bizarre machine-like objects that we first experienced at La Chorrera (and many times since). The consensus suggests that these visions are intrinsic to the experience rather than to the personalities of two nerdy brothers. People who have never heard of us, and who aren't science-fiction enthusiasts, nevertheless commonly report experiences permeated with a sense of the alien "other." Such reports have even entered into the scientific literature, as in the experiences documented by Rick Strassman, MD, in his FDA-approved study using high doses of pure injected DMT. Many of the experiences reported by his subjects bore an uncanny resemblance to classic descriptions of UFO close encounters, even to the extent of being enclosed in a dome-like space, surrounded by seen or sensed alien entities, and undergoing a medical examination of some kind. As Strassman recounts in his 2001 book *DMT: The Spirit Molecule*, those stories were impossible to stuff into any kind of explanatory framework acceptable to conventional science. "I chose to disregard reports I had heard about contact with beings on DMT and was unprepared for dealing with their frequency in our work," he writes. That and other factors, including the inadequacies of the biomedical model upon which he'd been required to conduct his study, eventually led him to discontinue it and return his clinical-grade DMT to the granting agency.

So here we have a phenomenon: There exists in nature a family of related metabolites widespread in plants, fungi, even in animals, including ourselves, that are close chemical relatives of the oldest known neurotransmitter, serotonin, and that are two or three trivial biosynthetic steps away from tryptophan, an amino acid found in all earthly organisms. When these metabolites are consumed by a certain class of omnivorous primates with complex nervous systems and hypertrophied cerebral cortices, the substances regularly, though not always, reveal the existence of what appear to be other dimensions, or other places, objects, and images like nothing seen in ordinary waking consciousness. The substances, once ingested, are often associated with a sense of the presence of other entities or forms of consciousness, which commonly seem to be proffering a message or lesson of some kind, or at least suggesting that the aforementioned big-brained primate pay attention and "get it." Moreover, there is often a good deal of congruency between what is seen and experienced by different individuals; though the experiences are difficult to articulate, there is enough similarity that those who have had such experiences can share information and make sense to each other, though not necessarily to those who have not had them. The experiences have a quality of consensual reality that is at least as clear and communicable as most experiences of ordinary reality. So what is going on?

Possibility number one is that there actually are other dimensions, parallel realities that these substances render accessible by temporarily altering our neurochemistry and perceptual apparatus. According to this model, there really are entities that want to communicate with us, or at least don't spurn communication, when we poke our heads into their dimension. This is very close to the understanding of reality that prevails in most shamanic worldviews.

Possibility number two is the more parsimonious explanation, but it is almost as bizarre. For some reason, our brains have evolved the innate capability to generate three-dimensional visions of indescribable complexity and beauty that in psilocybin or other tryptamine states are presented to our inner perception accompanied by a sense of great emotional and intellectual import and often seem to be narrated by a helpful entity, or entities, that are perceived as distinct from the self.

Whether the first or second postulate is true, the conclusions from either are rather earth-shattering. If the first is true, then we are forced to reject, or at least radically revise, everything we think we know about reality. It makes our current models hopelessly obsolete and incomplete. All of human knowledge, all of our science and religion, must be reexamined in the light of the understanding that our cosmic neighborhood just "over there" is of a completely different ontological order and, moreover, an order that is inhabited by entities as intelligent as we are or many times more intelligent, but that share with us the quality of consciousness, of mindedness. And they are entities that want to share their reality with us, their wisdom and knowledge, perhaps even form a symbiotic partnership or some sort of diplomatic relationship. Whatever "they" are, they do not seem to be hostile, and they appear to take a compassionate interest in our species, much as an adult might want to love and nurture a child.

On the other hand, if the second case is true, then the question stares us in the face: Why? Why, in the course of neural evolutionary history, has the brain developed the neural architecture and systems to sustain such experiences? What is the point of it all? Perhaps it is a side effect of the evolutionary events that resulted in cognition, language, and our ability to discern meaning in abstractions and symbols. Those familiar with psychedelic states will be aware that psychedelics, especially mushrooms and other tryptamines, often trigger synesthesia, the translation of one sensory modality into another. Anyone familiar with the psychedelic experience will probably have experienced synesthesia at some point; it is the "hearing" of colors or the "seeing" of sounds though these are only the most trivial examples. Some people have a genetic propensity for synesthesia and experience the phenomenon routinely. Other people only experience it under the influence of psychedelics, and even then it can be rare. There are many kinds of synesthesia, and often they are associated with the perception of numbers, letters, or words. For example, in grapheme-color synesthesia, individual numbers or letters are tinged with colors. In sound-color synesthesia, music or other sounds can induce firework-like displays or can change the color, scintillation, or directional movement of a perceived color. Even more bizarre forms of synesthesia are known, including "ordinal linguistic personification," in which ordered sequences of numbers, words, or letters seem to have personalities, or the rarer lexical-gustatory synesthesia in which words or phonemes evoke gustatory sensations.

Synesthesia is a fascinating but real phenomenon that has only recently reattracted the attention of modern neuroscience. The connection between genetic or inherent synesthesia and psychedelic synesthesia has either been largely overlooked or deliberately ignored. I suspect the latter is true, but I'm puzzled by science's failure to understand that psychedelics could be important research tools in our efforts to understand synesthesia and by extension cognition and consciousness itself.

For years I've argued in lectures and writings that psychedelics, probably mushrooms accidentally or deliberately ingested by early primates, triggered synesthetic experiences that formed the critical foundations of human language and cognition, the association of inherently meaningless sounds or images with inherently meaningful symbols and ideas. Spoken or written language is a synesthetic activity that takes place effortlessly and automatically in the process of understanding a language. In speaking, the vocal apparatus produces "small mouth noises," small puffs or explosions of air that are inherently meaningless. But because we have learned the language, we all participate in the consensus that certain meaningless noises are associated with inner, visualized images or symbols that, as cognitive constructs, are imbued with meaning. These images and symbols, seen by the mind's eye and associated with symbolic import, supply the "meaning" to various vocal expressions. In reading, the process is similar, except that a written symbol or word evokes an inner perception of the sound that is associated with the written word or symbol, and this, in turn, evokes an inner visualization of the meaningful symbol or word associated with that sound. Is this not also synesthesia?

What I'm suggesting, in effect, is that early on in the evolution of the human neural apparatus, the ingestion of psychedelics triggered the invention of language. I am not arguing here that psychedelics somehow affected our genes, at least not directly; rather, that they are teaching tools. Creating and using language is an acquired skill, dependent on an ability to discern meaning—significance—in images, sounds, and symbols. Psychedelics taught us how to do that and they are still teaching us! Once a small group of primates had acquired that skill, it could be easily taught to others, especially with the aid of the psychedelic teaching tools.

Language—and by this I mean complex language that depends on the comprehension of abstractions—is the critical skill that separates humans from all other species. The widespread emergence of language is the most important event in the evolution of human culture. Language allowed humans to transition from a species that existed in a state akin to that of other primates, with seemingly limited cognitive activity, to a species that is immersed in a world of abstractions and symbols—in short, in an ocean of ideas—as real to our perceptions as the physical world. Without language and an ability to comprehend it, we could not have made the transition from biological to cultural evolution. Language provides a means to codify and store information and transmit it across time and space, down through generations and across geographical boundaries, without depending on the genome.

While language is an extragenomic technology for storing and sharing accumulated knowledge, an enormously large proportion of the human neural architecture is devoted to speaking and comprehending it. At some point in our evolution, there must have been a feedback between the acquisition and practice of language that resulted in a relatively rapid change in primate brain structures over a few hundred thousand years—perhaps an epigenetic effect transmitted through the maternal line (Wright and Gynn 2008). The consequences are seen in the rapid emergence and spread of civilizations and technologies that started about 100,000 years ago and have been accelerating ever since. Having now literally wrapped the globe in our externalized nervous systems, we are nearing a moment when we'll find ourselves constantly embedded in an ever-expanding totality of human knowledge.

To a large extent, this has already occurred. Nature—the biosphere—is now encased within the cybersphere, and though the current instantiation is somewhat crude, made of machines and fiber optic networks and satellites and electromagnetic signals, I think that will probably change very soon. As new biotechnologies and nanotechnologies emerge, we will reintegrate our externalized neural networks and they will again disappear back into our bodies, the boundaries between "bio" and "techno" will dissolve, and we will become a new type of human, individual nodes in a globe-spanning mycelial network. We will still be humans, but not the same humans that first chipped stone axes on the Serengeti plains and gazed up at the stars and wondered. At that point, just as our ancestors did, we will again stand at a threshold in our evolutionary odyssey, ready to emerge from our earthly chrysalis and begin our diaspora to the stars.

If humanity is to have a destiny beyond the current dreary prospect of proliferating population and the increasingly rapid strangulation of our planetary life support systems, this must surely be it. It is a mythos built into the human imagination; it is what psychedelics have been telling us is our destiny ever since the first mushroom was tasted by the first curious primate. To embrace this destiny may be the only way we can traverse the cultural, environmental, and economic narrow passage that we are now confronting. This passage is the birth canal leading to a new age, beyond history, beyond death, beyond time.

In Stanley Kubrick's *2001: A Space Odyssey*, he and cowriter Arthur C. Clarke articulate a vision for humanity's future that is not unlike the destiny we imagine for ourselves. In the film, the monolith—a mysterious alien artifact that is never explained—appears at critical junctures in our evolutionary and cultural history, just when it is needed to nudge our species along to the next evolutionary jump. I would suggest that the psychedelic experience was what Kubrick had in mind when he introduced the concept of the monolith, or the film's famous light show, as I've noted earlier. Indeed, I'll go further and venture that psychedelics have played a role in human neural and cognitive evolution similar to that of Kubrick's monolith.

Psychedelics, particularly psilocybin and DMT, may in fact be alien artifacts seeded into the biosphere millions of years ago by a biotechnological supercivilization that has mastered the art and science of planetary biospheric engineering. Our planet, our biosphere, and our species could be the result of a kind of science experiment lasting hundreds of millions or even billions of years, an experiment initiated by a superior technological civilization partly out of curiosity (the real motivation behind all good science) and partly, I would suggest, out of loneliness. This hypothetical civilization may have wanted someone to talk to and thus created an intelligent species that could talk back.

It would be a trivial matter for a biotechnologically sophisticated supercivilization to "seed" the early terrestrial biosphere with genes coding for the biosynthesis of tryptophan and the simple tryptamines arising from it, including the oldest neurotransmitter in evolutionary terms, serotonin (5-hydroxytryptamine), and the simple indolealkylamines, which include the psychedelic tryptamines DMT and its relatives, psilocin, psilocybin, and others. In evolutionary terms, the light receptors are among the oldest receptors, and serotonin receptors are closely homologous to them; they are nearly a billion years old in the phylogenetic history of life. Serotonin has always played a critical function in signal transduction, and there is evidence that the evolutionary diversification of the main subtypes of biogenic amine receptors occurred first in the Precambrian, before the separation of arthropods from vertebrates, followed by a second occurrence about 400 million years ago that may have signaled the cephalization of vertebrates (Vernier et al. 1993). In other words, serotonin and the other tryptamines played a key role in the evolutionary emergence of complex nervous systems. Serotonin is of special importance to fetal brain development, particularly the wiring of the forebrain. Recent research has shown that the placenta, rather than the mother, is the source of this hormone in the critical developmental stages (Bonnin et al. 2011). The developing fetal mammalian brain is subject to other maternal and placental influences, including those due to plant secondary products in the diet of the mother.

This may seem like a pretty wild speculation—and it is—but given serotonin's critical evolutionary role, the long process leading to the human brain could have been influenced or even controlled by a civilization that deliberately intervened in the history of life on earth, bioengineering the evolution of intelligent species by seeding the biosphere with the gene complexes needed to foster, over the course of hundreds of millions of years, the appearance of complex nervous systems. Once the process was set in motion, our benevolent superscientists had only to sit back and let nature take its course. Eventually a big-brained species would emerge that could respond to the "message" encoded into psilocybin and DMT molecules— molecules specifically bioengineered to interact with those serotonin receptors that were able to receive the message. The supercivilization would have finally realized its desire to transmit a message by creating a species that could understand it.

I am not the only one to speculate that evidence of alien civilizations—or at least the possibility of such—will be found not in radio signals from a distant star but within our own genomes. This idea is reflected, for example, in a 2010 paper by computational neuroscientist Jean-Pierre Rospars in *Acta Astronautica*, the journal of the International Academy of Astronautics.

Rospars argues that the evolution of intelligence in the universe, far from being a rare and contingent event, is structurally built into the constraints of physics, chemistry, and biology. The fact that living creatures exhibit predictable limits on body size, among many other functions, suggest there are universal "laws" that order evolution, including the evolution of intelligence. Human cultural evolution is an emergent and inevitable consequence of this process. According to this theory, there could well be more complex intelligent species than ours endowed with far more complex brains. Furthermore, we could be separated from these civilizations not so much by spatial distances but by temporal and cognitive distances. Such alien intelligences may be vastly older than our species, and so much more advanced in their cognitive evolution that not only are we incapable of communicating with them, we are incapable of recognizing them.

Randall D. Shortridge, a molecular biologist at the State University of New York at Buffalo, is likewise trying to elaborate a fuller picture of life and consciousness in what he calls BioSeTI, his "tongue-in-cheek" name for "identifying patterns . . . in the molecular-world of what might be loosely called 'terrestrial space.'" As he notes on the project's website, his approach is "a form of Complexity Theory applied to analysis of the human genome." He acknowledges that mainstream science has assembled a pretty good view of the human genome and the information it contains for coding the biological processes that constitute life. His hunch, however, is that there's a lot more going on in the genome, where "many higher levels of complexity exist beyond what is normally viewed as concrete and measurable." He then adds, "The basic hypothesis of BioSeTI is that the human genome may contain identifiable sequence patterns beyond what it is essential for growth and maintenance of the biological organism." He makes a point of distancing himself from both sides in the creation debate, though he acknowledges that some of his ideas "might be shared with those espousing intelligent design."

> Preliminary evidence shows a surprisingly high correlation between ancient cultural and mystical traditions with contemporary discoveries in molecular biology. These visible correlations suggest that there might be other patterns yet undiscovered. More specifically, sequence and number patterns in DNA appear to correlate well to ancient cosmological traditions (e.g. Chinese *I Ching*) as well as contemporary technology (including computing technology; binary mathematics) and, possibly, modern cultural traditions. Such correlations may not be entirely coincidental. Possible correlations of DNA to language even raises the incredible possibility that genomes might ultimately be decoded into symbols and cosmological ideas that are lacking in the current scientific perspective.

Where have we heard these ideas expressed before? In some respects, these words read like the gnosis downloaded directly from the Teacher at La Chorrera—the notion, for example, that DNA functions in a way akin to the legendary akashic records, that it contains information at higher levels of organization that extend far beyond its function in coding for protein synthesis. It may contain cosmological, metaphysical, linguistic, possibly calendrical and mathematical information that is not readily apparent from a reductionist view of DNA that is narrowly focused on its function as a blueprint for gene expression. The reference to the analogies between DNA and the *I Ching* is particularly telling and, as Shortridge notes, he isn't the first to point this out. Nor was Terence. The analogy is indisputably there, which begs the question, just what "message" was the Teacher trying to convey to us at La Chorrera? And, along with that, are the "mushroom" and the Teacher one and the same?

Terence encapsulated his view in a "myth" that first appeared in our how-to manual, *Psilocybin: Magic Mushroom Grower's Guide*, published in 1976. Here's an excerpt:

The mushroom speaks, and our opinions rest upon what it tells eloquently of itself in the cool night of the mind:

"I am old, older than thought in your species, which is itself fifty times older than your history. Though I have been on earth for ages, I am from the stars. My home is no one planet, for many worlds scattered through the shining disk of the galaxy have conditions which allow my spores an opportunity for life. The mushroom which you see is the part of my body given to sex thrills and sun bathing. My true body is a fine network of fibers growing through the soil. These networks may cover acres and may have more connections than the number in a human brain. My mycelial network is nearly immortal—only the sudden toxification of a planet or the explosion of its parent star can wipe me out. By means impossible to explain because of certain misconceptions in your model of reality, all my mycelial networks in the galaxy are in hyperlight communication across space and time. The mycelial body is as fragile as a spider's web, but the collective hyper mind and memory is a huge historical archive of the career of evolving intelligence on many worlds in our spiral star swarm. Space, you see, is a vast ocean to those hardy life forms that have the ability to reproduce from spores, for spores are covered with the hardest organic substance known. Across the aeons of time and space drift many spore-forming life-forms, in suspended animation for millions of years until contact is made with a suitable environment. Few such species are minded, only myself and my recently evolved near relatives have achieved the hypercommunication mode and memory capacity that makes us leading members in the community of galactic intelligence. How the hypercommunication mode operates is a secret that will not be lightly given to man. But the means should be obvious: It is the occurrence of psilocybin and psilocin in the biosynthetic pathways of my living body that opens for me and my symbionts the vision screens to many worlds. You as an individual and humanity as a species are on the brink of the formation of a symbiotic relationship with my genetic material that will eventually carry humanity and earth into the galactic mainstream of the higher civilizations." (*Psilocybin: Magic Mushroom Grower's Guide*, pp. 8–9)

Could any of that be true? Is the human species really being led toward a cosmic destiny by establishing a symbiotic alliance with an intelligent mushroom from the stars? I have no idea. I would like that to be true. As wild as that scenario sounds, it is at least as plausible as any other cosmological vision we may choose to believe in, and it is much more plausible than most of the myths posited by the world's great religions, or even the scientific myths that are served up as alternatives. On one hand, we have the Abrahamic creation stories that arose from the oral traditions of various Middle Eastern tribal cultures. There is not a shred of evidence that any of them are true. In fact, the close parallels between those traditions only reveal how culturally bound they are, thus undermining any claims they each might make to being the one and only truth. But science also fails to portray a myth worthy of human destiny. The best that science can offer is that we are the accidental product of random events, a chaotic mix of particles aimlessly tumbling through space and time in a cold, dead universe devoid of mind or beauty or love or any of the qualities that we experience and value. Really? This creation myth seems to my mind at least as unlikely than those posited by various religions.

Science, to its credit, abjures faith and demands that any scientific model of reality be backed by evidence. Science does an excellent job of studying phenomena in isolation and in great detail, but it does a poor job of fitting all those small, dissected pieces of reality together into a unified whole that hangs together and seems to fit our holistic experience of being. The reductionist scientific models are impoverished and unsatisfying. They leave more unexplained than they explain, and they too seem unable to account for the improbable situation in which we find ourselves.

And highly improbable it is indeed. Think about it: We are a conscious, minded species that somehow arose on a minor planet circling a G star in some backwater of the Milky Way. We have invented language and, proceeding from that, science, technology, religion, art, war, and all the other accoutrements of civilization. We have no idea whether we are unique in the universe, but there's no reason to think so. In line with the ideas of Jean-Pierre Rospars and many others, life evolves in accordance with certain "rules" of evolution—wherever the conditions are favorable, life will arise, and once it has arisen, it's likely that it will achieve intelligence. There's no reason to think it has not happened dozens, hundreds, or millions of times in the history of the universe. But we have no proof that it has. It's only a reasonable assumption at this point, a working hypothesis if you will.

And then "the mushroom" or whatever/whoever the mushroom represents comes along and matter-of-factly tells us how the boar ate the cabbage—how things really are. We are an immature species involved in a symbiosis with a much older and wiser mentor species. This species is trying to get us to wise up so that we can join the galactic community of minds, and do so before we manage to blow up the planet and ourselves. It's probably a scenario that has been repeated many times in the history of the galaxy. It is a comforting myth, at least, and we can choose to believe it or not. Is there evidence for it? The closest thing to that so far is a shared interpretation of what the mushroom seems to be telling us, as reported by a growing number of people who have experienced psilocybin firsthand.

That is not "hard" evidence, but it is evidence of a sort. And it does not require faith, unlike religious myths, which do. No one is asking you to abdicate your critical faculties. The mushroom, or whatever that term stands for, demands the exact opposite; it demands that we reject faith. All we need is the courage to experience the phenomenon and judge it for ourselves. Those who take this empirical, scientific view are apt to be presented with a model that is plausible, or is at least not impossible, a model that suggests there just may be such a thing as human destiny—and that our existence, as individuals and as a species, may have meaning after all.

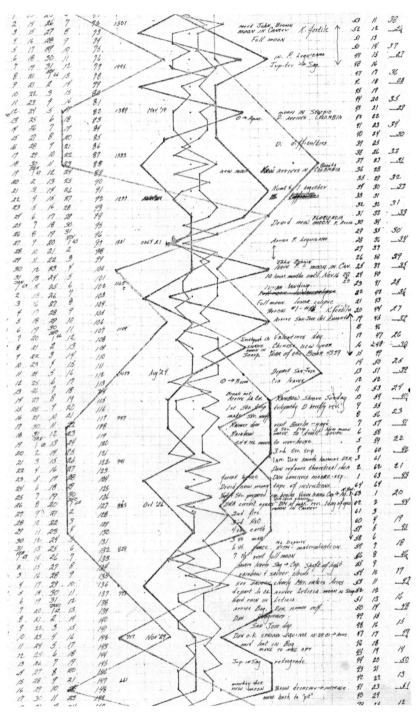

An early graph of the timewave from Terence's notebook, 1971.

Part Three: Invisible Landscapes

The book jacket photo of Dennis and Terence from the first edition
of *The Invisible Landscape*, 1975.

35
Invisible Landscapes

By early summer 1971, I was living in a tiny room in Boulder and trying to reinvent the poor student I'd been before I left. I busied myself in summer school and found a job as a dishwasher and server in a rest home. It wasn't the most edifying work, but I took pleasure in the normality of it. I was still dealing with the memories of our experiences in the jungle, but I had no one to talk to about them, least of all the pure-minded, fair-haired Peggy, my longed-for, if mostly imaginary, flame. In a brief encounter with her, I tried to explain a bit about what had happened to me, but it was useless. Her reaction was one of alarm, and no wonder with me raving like a wild-eyed prophet back from his 40 days in the wilderness. She didn't know what to make of my account beyond not wanting to hear any more of it. She gently broke it to me that she had a new boyfriend, but I hardly took notice, being so caught up in my own drama.

Terence, meanwhile, had spent the previous months in Berkeley, utterly absorbed in adapting his idea for a model of time to the inner machinery of the *I Ching*. As I noted earlier, the *I Ching* consists of 64 hexagrams, each corresponding to a different phase in a cyclical, Taoist model of time. Based on that, Terence had, by then, assigned the numbers 6 and 64 a special significance in his calculations. In *True Hallucinations*, he writes that he realized his relationship with Ev began 64 days after our mother's death. Counting forward from our mother's death by 6 such units, or 384 days, he discovered a 13-month lunar year that would end on his upcoming birthday, November 16, 1971. These were the initial correspondences that got Terence thinking about applying the *I Ching* to his timewave theory. Indeed, his birthday became the first of his projected end dates for the so-called concrescence— the final event the timewave seemed to predict.

Then as before, Terence's obsessive writing and charting seemed to be part of a reintegration he'd begun after the bizarre events in March. Early on, the numerical constructs he'd apparently downloaded from the Teacher had been keyed to our personal and familial history. He'd continue to refine the timewave concept for years, pushing it beyond its narrow confines toward something wider and more intricate, even elegant, in its peculiar, numerological way. He came to believe that the cycles within cycles he detected on a personal level were active on a historical, geological, and cosmological scale. Terence would later use the term "fractal time" to characterize these nested cycles, though when he first began his investigation the term *fractal* had yet to be coined.

There is also the curious relationship between the *I Ching* and the structure of DNA—that is, the "language" that DNA utilizes to code for the proteins that exist in all living things. I've alluded to this earlier. Indeed, talk of this coincidence was in the air at the time. Since the mid-1950s, there had been a growing popular interest in the ancient Chinese classic and in the double-helix structure of the DNA molecule as well. The number of hexagrams in the *I Ching* can be written as 2^6, or the number of six-line hexagrams that can be made from lines that can appear in either "broken" or "unbroken" form. In DNA, the number of three-letter codons that can be generated from four nucleotides can be written as 4^3. The product in both cases: 64. That seemed to resonate with our belief at La Chorrera that we'd somehow hacked into the central store of knowledge that life had acquired and carried over time on a molecular level.

Among the first to note the resonance between DNA and the *I Ching* was one Gunther Stent, a German-born professor of molecular biology at the University of California in Berkeley. Stent explored the idea in his book *The Coming of the Golden Age*, which appeared in 1969. Terence actually visited Stent on campus, eager to share the insights from La Chorrera. Terence's account of the put-down that followed is one of the more comical and painful moments in *True Hallucinations*. The encounter was not unlike mine with Peggy in a sense. Each of us had tried to express the ineffable to someone we hoped would understand, only to confront a reflection of ourselves raving like lunatics. I was lucky in that mine occurred with a friend on the street. For Terence, the rebuff from one of the era's leading biologists revealed something of his ambivalence about science. He loved scientific concepts and language, both of which he was known to borrow for his own playful and metaphoric purposes. He knew the lessons of La Chorrera involved an intuitive leap over an abyss that science in its current state was unable to bridge. And yet he may have wanted the scientist to acknowledge an insight that couldn't be verified in scientific terms. He had asked one of

the leading scientists of his day to endorse what was, in essence, a deconstruction of science, even a rejection of it, with humiliating results.

That's not to say his only doubters at the time were mainstream academics. During that spring and early summer, Terence's efforts continued
to baffle most of his friends; despite his inborn persuasiveness, he had yet
to win them over. In addition, rumor had it that the FBI had gotten wind
of his illegal return to the country, arousing his fear that the net cast after
the 1969 hash bust might be closing. Both factors played into a decision by
Terence and Ev to embark on what struck me, at least, as unthinkable: a
return to La Chorrera.

Overall, the rationale for that second trip seemed less than entirely
rational. One unspoken motivation, I think, was nostalgia—a yearning
for paradise that motivates humans to envision, and seek, magical realms
beyond space and time, an impulse that may go back to when our womb-
born species first began seeing itself as a creature fallen from an original
state of grace. La Chorrera might have made for an unlikely Shangri-La,
but there was no doubt that in our imagination it had taken on this numinous aspect.

While Terence felt compelled to go back, I had excellent reasons not to,
as I made clear in our talks. He thought we should try to repeat the experiment, even as he paradoxically insisted that, according to the Teacher, we'd
already succeeded and now just had to wait for the concrescence to manifest. Our only task was to identify, if possible, when and where the concrescence would occur. For my part, I had no stomach for another expedition.
I was happy to be back in ordinary reality and not eager to put my ass and
sanity back on the line. Moreover, I argued, what we'd experienced was an
irreproducible event. It was the classic Heraclitean conundrum: we couldn't
travel the same river twice. What happened, I argued, shouldn't be called
an experiment for several reasons, but most notably because it couldn't be
repeated. We could call it the singularity, the occurrence, or the events at La
Chorrera, but whatever it came to be known as, an experiment it was not.

I had thrown myself into my studies, by then redirected toward science, which I believed (and the Teacher agreed) would give me the tools to
understand our experiences. I belonged in school. According to Terence, his
friends were troubled enough by his singular focus to encourage his return
to the field, literally—back to the mist-enshrouded pasture from which his
obsessions had sprung. He needed to get away. What's more, unlike me, he
and Ev had the means to do so, having bought a quantity of emeralds just

before departing Colombia. Back in the States, they'd sold them for enough to travel and live modestly in South America for the foreseeable future.

By mid-July they found themselves downriver from Puerto Leguizamo, pressing ever deeper into the jungles of the lower Putamayo. Over the weeks ahead, they renavigated the maze of rivers, drawn by the siren song of the fungal fruiting bodies that grew near an isolated mission on the Río Igara Paraná. They arrived in late August. Aside from the rare letters they entrusted to the police captains at various towns along their route, I'd hear nothing from them for nine months.

After my summer classes ended, I moved into a communal house a couple of blocks down Pine Street from where I'd lived the year before. My housemates were a familiar assortment of counterculture types, with one exception: Beverly, a fellow student from Boston whom I immediately liked. Intelligent, studious, Jewish, and cute, she had an infectious laugh and liked my jokes. I have no idea what she saw in me, but before long we'd gotten together. Beverly was no hippie chick. I took delight in corrupting her, but I didn't get very far. Both of us disliked living in a house with four other people, and by Thanksgiving we'd found our own place—a tiny upstairs apartment a bit closer to the foothills.

By then, Terence and Ev were on their way out. Their second visit had been less productive in terms of mushrooms, which were less abundant than before. What trips they took seemed less charged with the immanence of the Other—there were no UFO sightings, and the weather during the dry season yielded fewer mysterious anomalies. Terence did a lot of writing and thinking, however, much of which he chronicled in his journal. He continued to refine his speculations on the hidden patterns of time despite a frustrating lack of reference materials. His first predicted date for the concrescence—his 25th birthday in November—came and went without incident, a disappointing test for the timewave in its prototypal form.

Word had reached him via our father that a plea deal for his prior smuggling activities might be in the offing. The time seemed right for heading home. The trip was full of delays, weeks spent in mosquito-infested, riverine outposts that wore them down. They finally reached a city we'd passed through earlier, Florencia, the capital of the Department of Caquetá in southeast Colombia. In a chance encounter in a *tienda*, they met a guy who was home for Christmas from Europe. The son of a local journalist, Luis Eduardo Luna was about a year younger than Terence. Terence was trying to buy a few items using his broken Spanish. Luis Eduardo, overhearing him, offered in perfect English to help. Luis Eduardo had been studying philosophy and literature at the Universidad Complutense in Madrid. After hearing an account of what had led the weary travelers to Florencia, he invited them to stay in a small house his family owned a few miles out of town. Thus began a friendship that was to last until Terence's death.

Their stay at Villa Gloria, as the place was called, was an idyllic time for Terence and Ev, a chance to rest, eat good food, and enjoy the pleasant company. Terence had a quiet place to work on his writings, which by then were coalescing into a book. He also had a receptive audience for his outlandish and captivating raps. I wasn't there, of course, but I picture something like what I'd seen in Berkeley where similar scenes played out many times. As for Luis Eduardo, he'd never been exposed to such ideas, let alone to the Santa Marta gold that Terence had brought with him. A former seminary student, Luis Eduardo was leaning more toward Marxism and atheism at the time, but those long talks at Villa Gloria may have encouraged him to revisit an earlier fascination with the mysteries of existence. By the time he returned to Europe, his academic priorities had shifted to physics, chemistry, botany, and neuroscience. He later earned a PhD from the Institute of Comparative Religion at Stockholm University, where his thesis focused on the study of *vegetalismo*—the use of ayahuasca in shamanic practices among the Mestizo populations of Peru (Luna 1986). Luis Eduardo is now considered the world's authority on the ethnography of ayahuasca. I didn't meet him until 1981, but since then he has been one of my closest colleagues and friends. Following his fieldwork in the Peruvian Amazon in 1982, we collaborated, with Neil Towers, on a review of the botany and chemistry of ayahuasca admixture plants that was published in 1986 in the journal *America Indigena* (McKenna, Luna, and Towers 1986) and later reprinted in a collection edited by R. E. Schultes entitled *Ethnobotany: Evolution of a Discipline* (1995).

Terence and Ev eventually made their way back via Bogotá and Mexico City, Terence's false passport again serving him well, and landed at my door at the end of January. Or rather "our" door: Beverly and I had been living together for a few weeks. Though she joined me in welcoming them, she might not have been sure what to make of these two gypsy seekers blown up on a southerly wind. I, of course, was delighted to see them. The core of the brotherhood was together again.

Terence's dubious legal status made it necessary for him to keep a low profile. He and Ev found menial jobs cutting roses at one of the flower businesses near Longmont. They got up early to catch the bus to work and spent all day at their easy task; each night the dope came out and the conversation flowed as we reflected on the previous year and tried to sort out what it all meant. It was a time of bonding and camaraderie for us, but not for Beverly, who felt left out. I must admit I didn't help matters, partly because of my ambivalence toward our relationship, which I attribute to the sense of emotional unavailability I felt—and may have cultivated in my attachment to a series of likewise unavailable love interests. The simple fact was that, instead of getting their own place, Terence and Ev had moved into an apartment that was too small for four people.

Ev, who wasn't apt to be friendly toward any woman who got near Terence at the time, turned alpha female and made it uncomfortable for Beverly to stick around. After a number of painful episodes, Beverly decided to move out. I behaved quite badly during this time in not sticking up for her, and yet our friendship somehow survived. Though she certainly had her doubts about Terence, she might have seen something worthy of emulation in his intrepid character. I thought of her as a girl who was afraid of things like bugs, who had no truck for camping or roughing it in any way. But after graduation she went on to work for various relief organizations in some of the most challenging places on earth: Haiti, Nicaragua, and the Congo, among other countries. You never know what reserves of strength may reside in a person, especially in that untested phase of life.

Over those weeks, Terence and I began collaborating on the manuscript he'd begun, then entitled *Shamanic Investigations*. We even had a few copies bound at a local bindery that specialized in university theses. It was satisfying to see the large volume with its many hand-drawn charts and graphs fixed between hard covers. At least something had resulted from our adventures beyond madness and bizarre ideas. We had no prospects for publication and were not really looking for them.

After a few months clipping roses, Terence and Ev began talking about a return to Berkeley. Before then, however, Terence had to deal with his legal issues. I'm not sure what inquiries were made or how the matter proceeded to be so easily resolved; I do remember that Terence and our father went to the Federal Building in Denver accompanied by a lawyer. As Terence later told it, he announced at the courthouse that he was there to turn himself in, but nobody seemed to know what he was talking about. After a search, someone found the paperwork and had him fill out a few forms and schedule a court appearance. It was all politely bureaucratic—hardly the reception an international fugitive might have expected after eluding capture for nearly three years.

Once the case was settled, I believe he got three years unsupervised probation in return for telling them "everything he knew" about his hashish suppliers. Terence's response was a long, rambling account with references to an auto body shop in a back alley in Bombay, as I recall.

When I read the statement months later, I assumed he'd made it all up, but it apparently satisfied the authorities. To the best of my knowledge, the whole mess ended there; he never heard another word about it.

Terence and Ev moved to Berkeley early in the summer of 1972. They found a small home only a block or so from the Telegraph House where Terence had lived before his travels began in October 1967. His life soon fell into a familiar routine. He reconnected with some of his butterfly contacts, including a wealthy Japanese broker who had subsidized Terence's collecting efforts in Indonesia while he was on the run. Before long, new specimens to mount began arriving in batches via the mail, creating a great job he could do stoned, at home, and in the presence of company. After I moved to Berkeley a year later, I spent many an hour in the upstairs loft where Terence worked. Various characters from our eclectic and peculiar circle would stop by for a smoke and a bit of raving. By then Terence had filled a formerly neglected garden out back with various psychoactive species, including a riot of morning glories dotted with a few datura bushes along the fence. He was back in his element.

Terence's departure for California marked a new stage in the slow bifurcation of our lives. Another familial shift during the summer of 1972 was our father's remarriage. Lois, a woman from Delta he'd met through his golfing friends, looked a bit like our mother, though the similarities ended there. Dad had been lonely after Mom's death and was slowly sinking into alcoholism and despair. I was happy when he found a nice person to live with, and on balance I'd say his second marriage benefited him. But the union wasn't an entirely happy one. Nobody could have replaced our mother in our father's eyes, though I think he unfairly expected that of Lois. She may have resented him for putting that on her, and rightly so; he may have resented her for not being the love of his life. They remained together 25 years until my father's death.

The undergraduate degree I completed in the spring of 1973 was in a thing called "distributed studies," meaning my coursework had been "distributed" over several areas rather than concentrated in one or two majors. My primary emphasis was in biology with secondary specialties in anthropology and philosophy, particularly the philosophy of science. It was a degree that qualified me for almost nothing except graduate school—and certainly not a job.

Nevertheless, my education post–La Chorrera was far from a waste. I valued it for helping me make sense of our experiences there and for directing me toward my later studies. I've mentioned how my trip to South America left me eager to learn more about science and scientific thinking, if only so I could more honestly reject the scientific worldview. I threw myself into biological studies for the remainder of my undergraduate years, thanks largely to a gifted mentor, Charles Norris, a biology professor who encouraged my interest in the philosophy of science. Under his guidance, I designed my own curriculum and independent-study courses. Instead of rejecting science, I found myself transfixed by the latest thinking in theoretical biology. The works that influenced me included *The Phenomenon of Life* (1966) by the philosopher Han Jonas; *General Systems Theory* (1968) by the biologist Ludwig von Bertalanffy; *Hierarchical Structures* (1969), edited by Scottish thinker Lancelot Law Whyte; the chemist Ilya Prigogine's ideas about non-equilibrium thermodynamics, dissipative structures, and self-organizing systems; and the neurosurgeon Karl Pribram's holographic model of certain brain processes. Terence was conducting his own inquiry into these and other works. In sharing our insights, we were amazed to discover a conceptual framework in which some of the "crazy" ideas that emerged at La Chorrera seemed not so crazy after all.

Of all these new influences, the work of Alfred North Whitehead had the greatest impact on us. Whitehead's "organismic" philosophy provided a logically rigorous metaphysics that seemed not only consistent with the current scientific understanding of reality but also fit many of our own speculations. Whitehead's notions about "process" and the "ingress," or entrance, of novel events into reality greatly appealed to us. By then, the timewave was on its way to becoming a complex metaphysical system in itself; Whitehead's concepts seemed a way to describe and even quantify its principles. Though Whitehead had been one of England's leading mathematicians earlier in his career, his later philosophical works incorporate certain aspects of Eastern thought and animism. We realized we had no need to seek a rationale for our beliefs in exotic and alien religions or philosophies; Whitehead's metaphysics, though ensconced in the Western tradition, had what we were looking for, namely, the perspective that in some sense everything is alive and changing over time. In Whitehead's view, everything from atoms to galaxies are "organisms" with their own processes and rules of self-organization. Another key idea is that consciousness pervades the continuum; it is as fundamental to the structure of reality as the electron or the quark. Truth and beauty, even love, are intrinsic to existence, not qualities pasted onto a dead universe by deluded souls longing to find a meaning that isn't there.

Thus, for us, Whitehead's philosophy seemed to demolish existentialist despair. Far from being a lifeless, terrifying place, the universe teemed with life; indeed the universe *itself* was alive. All this meshed with what the Teacher had imparted at La Chorrera and what our own evolving views had insisted upon. Whitehead's insights were good news for a couple of Catholic kids who had long since rejected the comforting fairy tales offered up by their tradition. His philosophy didn't demand faith. Rather it allowed us to look at the universe through the lens of a metaphysics that was open to scientific insight. My studies might not have made me a scientist per se, but they did give me an understanding of science that went beyond that of many practitioners who hadn't stopped to think about what science really was and how it operated. The events at La Chorrera had shoved our faces hard up against those questions, and Whitehead's ideas in particular provided some answers. Decades later that's still true, and to the extent that I have a spiritual belief, it is a secular system based largely on Whitehead's philosophy.

By the time of my graduation, however, my knowledge of theoretical biology and the holographic brain still had me in the dark when it came to the patterns of my love life. Beverly had finished school and returned to Boston. Peggy was still in Boulder but the fact she was seeing someone else left little chance we'd get together. I had more cause to think that Deborah and I might have reunited now that she'd finished school. Instead, the girl with whom I'd shared some of the happiest times I'd ever known was moving in with a fundamentalist surfer dude on a boat. I should have made that the last heartbreak tied to my unhealthy attachment to her but, well, I didn't. Looking back on my romantic misadventures from that era, I marvel at how miserable they made me and how much time I wasted because of that misery. When my mother left me off in Boulder for the start of college in 1969, I had no idea the years ahead were destined to be so emotionally difficult and lonely at times. Do others become as obsessed over romantic loss as I did then? I suppose they do. According to the familiar adage, it's better to have loved and lost than never to have loved at all. I'm not so sure.

With no prospects for a good job in Boulder or Denver, I figured I might as well relocate and take a menial job in the Bay Area. By late summer 1973, I was working as a porter at a fancy restaurant in Kensington, near Berkeley. My job was to arrive early in the morning and open the place—collect the dirty laundry, mop the floors, chop up a big tub of salad greens, and generally get things ready for the chefs when they arrived midafternoon. It was a good gig that fit my temperament. I'd get there at 6:30, fix myself a huge breakfast and a pot of coffee and read the *San Francisco Chronicle* before lifting a finger. Nobody cared what I did as long as I finished my chores on time. In the afternoon, I'd stop by Terence's, get loaded, and join that day's activities at the perpetual salon. By the summer and fall of 1973, Nixon's Watergate scandal had begun to preoccupy the country. Over the months until the president's forced resignation on August 9, 1974, we followed the television coverage obsessively and gleefully as Tricky Dick became ever more mired in troubles of his own making. Every day, it seemed, there'd be a new outrage reported on the evening news, and we could hardly wait to tune in.

By the spring of 1974, the manuscript Terence and I had worked on in Boulder, and again over the previous summer, had gotten the attention of Justus George Lawler, an editor at Seabury Press. I don't recall how Lawler, a respected Catholic scholar and author, became aware of our book, but he asked us to submit a copy for examination, which we did. Lawler said he loved the book and wanted to publish it.

Seabury, a small publishing house in New York originally established in the early 1950s by the Episcopal church, seemed an unlikely venue for us. Its backlist included many religious and theological books, and the closest they'd come to a radical work like ours was *The Thought of Teilhard de Chardin* by Michael H. Murray (1966). Lawler, however, may have been pushing the company beyond its usual repertoire. Around that time, Seabury also published the Polish sci-fi author Stanislaw Lem's weird surrealist drug novel, *The Futurological Congress*. Lawler's support was great news, but he insisted on a title other than *Shamanic Investigations*. I took a walk in Tilden Park in the hills behind Berkeley, and after a little assist from Sister Mary, I came up with *The Invisible Landscape*, which both Terence and Ev liked. We got a modest advance ($1,200 split between us, as I remember) and a deadline: Seabury needed the final manuscript before the end of the year to release our book the following spring.

We had a lot of work to do. Certain parts of our exposition had to be supported, if possible, with scientific evidence, and our wildest assertions needed to be toned down. Most important, the mathematical basis of the timewave had to be developed and a computer program devised to generate the numbers. This task was beyond us, but luckily one of Terence's friends had access to the university computers and wrote some code. (Other programmers would later contribute to the timewave as well.) Terence and I had a lot of fun working together over the next few months. We knew we were on a creative roll, and the revisions forced us to reexamine our assumptions as we tried to render them comprehensible to the outside world. By mid-September we'd finished a version and submitted it to the publisher.

36 The Timewave

Before resuming my account, I want to give my take on Terence's Timewave Zero theory, which figured centrally in *The Invisible Landscape*. Briefly stated, what Terence first conceptualized (or channeled) at La Chorrera is a mathematical model that supposedly reveals the structure of time. As a means for mapping the past and future, the timewave can be used, in Terence's view, to chart the advent of "novelty" and its impact on later events. The "wave" aspect refers to the belief that novelty levels predictably ebb and flow, and that periods of intense novelty coincide with disruptions in the patterns of culture, evolution, and even physics. As for "zero," that marks the point of "maximized" novelty, which as I write purportedly lies just months ahead. Anyone familiar with Terence's timewave knows that he settled on the winter solstice in December 2012 as its end point, which is also the generally accepted date for the "end" of the Maya calendar. At different times he cited both December 21 and 22 as the actual day.

Though I wrote certain sections of *The Invisible Landscape* that dealt with my own experiences at La Chorrera, I'm actually one of the harsher critics of the timewave theory. In fact, I don't believe it is a true theory in scientific terms. There are gaps and loopholes in Terence's construct that, under scrutiny, are hard to defend. As the brother of the person who arguably has done more than anyone to turn the winter solstice of 2012 into a global meme, some might accuse me of being at best unsporting on this issue and at worst an annoying curmudgeon. I plead guilty on both counts.

Terence and I became fascinated with the idea of novelty, as Whitehead understood it. His concept of novelty can be loosely characterized as the belief that there really *are* new things under the sun and the "ingression" of these unexpected events can affect the ongoing process we think of as reality. Based on his metaphysics, I'm willing to grant that there is such a thing as novelty and that its appearance can trigger massive change. But Terence and I disagreed over how this actually happened. Indeed, some of our more animated discussions over the years were about defining novelty. What qualifies as a truly novel event? How does it enter the continuum, and how do you know when it has? More specifically, how can the timewave map and predict the arrival of novelty if you're not precisely sure what novelty is?

Terence favored what might be called the "punctate" theory of novelty. Novelty arrives in the form of dramatic events with global impact, like the atomic bomb blast over Hiroshima in 1945, the Kennedy assassination, the crucifixion of Christ, or the terrorist attacks on September 11, 2001. In his view, events of that magnitude have enormous impact on history and the subsequent unfolding of human affairs. As truly novel occurrences, he saw it as possible to "fit" the timewave to such moments in human history, or even to events like the impact of the Chicxulub asteroid that is thought to have killed off the dinosaurs some 65 million years ago. Once calibrated to past events, the timewave could then be extended out beyond the realm of what has already undergone "the formality of actually occurring," in Whitehead's irresistible phrase, to predict, among other things, the future moment of its own end.

In contrast, I argued in favor of the "gradualist" theory of novelty. Major historical or geological events may appear to erupt into time, but that's an illusion, one that ignores the chain of cause and effect that must precede them. Which event is truly novel—the nuclear explosion over Hiroshima, or that of the test device in the New Mexican desert a few weeks earlier? Or was it when Enrico Fermi first engineered a sustained nuclear reaction at the University of Chicago in 1942? The mathematical basis for the bomb can be traced to 1905, when Einstein stated that mass was a measure of energy, and vice versa, a brilliant insight he boiled down to a famous equation, $E=mc^2$. And surely Democritus contributed by intuiting that the world is made of atoms back in the fourth century BCE. My point is that novelty does not "erupt" so much as "ooze" into history, thus making the identification of a truly novel event that much more problematic. The wave is hard to fit against the historical, geological, or evolutionary record because there are few points at which one can reliably align the map. And there is no way to quantify these events; Terence defined no criteria for measuring whether one event is more novel than another.

This is to my mind a major flaw in his novelty theory. Science works on measurement and quantification; to qualify as a scientific theory, it must be validated using measurable, quantifiable, and ideally mathematical criteria. A true theory must also state what new data or discovery can invalidate it. (Here it is worth noting that a theory can be disproved, but never definitely proved; there is always the possibility that new data will overturn it.) The timewave does none of this. Thus it is not really a theory. It is a speculation, an interesting idea, a hallucination, a fantasy—but not a theory. Terence never provided a quantifiable definition of novelty. I don't think he knew how, and I'm not sure anyone does. But the result is that novelty in his "novelty theory," as it is also known, was defined as whatever Terence postulated it to be.

So, interesting as it is, Timewave Zero is utterly useless as a map of time, a predictor of events, or a mathematical theory that describes something fundamental about the world.

The timewave's other major influence was the *I Ching*, in particular an ancient arrangement of its 64 hexagrams known as the King Wen sequence. In devising the timewave, Terence appears to have explained how that sequence may have been used in neolithic China as a calendar. It's too bad he didn't leave it at that. If so, he would have received kudos from a small coterie of Chinese scholars and very little notice beyond those circles. Instead he asserted that he'd discovered a map, not only of history, or limited to earth, but of time itself.

Here we have to remind ourselves again that at some deep level Terence never really escaped the legacy of his Western, Christian past, the existential horror of being trapped in history, trapped in time. As he noted of the timewave in *The Evolutionary Mind* (1998), a collection of his conversations with Rupert Sheldrake and Ralph Abraham, "This idea is basically Catholicism with the chrome stripped off. It restates Teilhard de Chardin's idea of the Omega Point, the Telos attracting and drawing history into itself."

In the course of doing so, he introduced another crucial flaw—he took an ancient cyclical Chinese calendar and made it linear. He did this by declaring time "fractal"—which means, on close inspection, short spans of time are revealed to be "microversions of the larger patterns in which they are embedded." What's more, his model of time became an ever-tightening spiral that had to have a beginning and an end. Built into its structure was the notion that novelty would eventually reach a critical point where the wave collapses, presumably at the instant of an Ultimate Novel Event, whatever that might be. Some call this moment the "singularity" but this is a vague and perhaps misleading term. The concept implies that at some point we'll cross a threshold where all of our assumptions—about causality, time, space, and virtually everything else—will no longer apply. The singularity could be just about anything, so the term is not that helpful in predicting what it might entail.

There was no reason why Terence's timewave had to end. I see this as simply an expression of his acute longing for an escape from history, an escape from death. But once it had an end, the question became where the end should be. Much of the controversy over the timewave dealt with how to fit it to events in the past, which in effect would lock it to an end date in the future. That guessing game posed a dilemma: the end had to occur in our lifetimes so we could witness it. If not, what was the point? But it couldn't be too soon, because the postulated grand finale might come and go, compromising the predictive value of the timewave (which happened several times over the years). What's more, the event should ideally be linked to some other widely anticipated historical or cosmic transition, and few were better than a date near the solstice in December 2012, the so-called end of the Maya calendar.

As I understand it, such an event would be either a mass disaster or a more hopeful awakening of some sort—but always on a global scale. Examples range from benevolent aliens showing up in their mile-wide ships to help us get our act together (as in *Childhood's End*), or a wrathful Jesus arriving by golden chariot to smite the wicked and beam up the righteous for an eternity of harp playing and bingo. Perhaps the embryonic artificial intelligence lurking in the Internet will suddenly cross the threshold into self-awareness and realize, in three nanoseconds, that we're the creatures screwing things up, a problem solved easily enough by causing the world's nuclear reactors to melt down while launching the world's entire nuclear arsenal. All these events would certainly be dramatic and novel enough to validate the timewave if they occurred anywhere near the postulated end date. But no event of that magnitude is likely to happen.

Terence's selection of the timewave's end date did not hinge on serious mathematical analysis. His theory and the Maya calendar have nothing to do with each other, the delusions of the current zeitgeist notwithstanding. While most credible Mayanists agree that the Maya did have a calendar that ends, so to speak, on the winter solstice in 2012, there's little evidence the day was imbued with great significance. The end of that cycle—known as the Long Count—may simply have marked the start of a new one. According to various scholars, efforts to associate that date with a doomsday event are baseless and self-serving.

The ancient Maya actually tracked several calendrical cycles. One was a 365-day calendar called the *haab'.* Another was the *tzolk'in*, a 260-day sacred calendar based on a series of 13 periods, each 20 days long. Those systems aligned on a specific date once every 52 years, thus delineating a third unit of time called the Calendar Round. To chronicle longer periods, the Maya and other Mesoamerican cultures relied on the Long Count mentioned above. According to Western calendars, the Long Count began on a late summer day in 3114 BCE, marking the start of the human epoch. Certain Maya texts suggest there were earlier prehuman "worlds" of long duration before the gods got it right. And there would be other worlds afterward. For whatever reason, the Maya designed these epochs, including the Long Count, to consist of thirteen *b'ak'tuns*, each 144,000 days in length. According to the math, we are as I write somewhere very near the end of that 5,125-year period, and thus very near the start of the next.

In other words, just as Terence based the origin of the timewave on an ancient cyclical Chinese calendar, so he tied its end to an ancient cyclical Maya calendar. It appears the timewave tells us much more about him, in some sense, than it does about time. His deep-seated longing to escape time and history is one he shared with millions. Every life has a beginning and an end; we are pushed along inexorably by time from the moment we are born to the moment the plug is pulled and the sheet is drawn up. Nobody has ever escaped from time, though all of the world's religions are scams predicated on the notion that we can. We all confront our own singularity at the end of time, the end of our own personal history. This is the only eschaton we can realistically look forward to. No one can say definitively what happens to consciousness beyond that threshold, whether it is extinguished forever or translates into some sort of virtual reality, whatever that means when we're talking about life after death. Someday, we may understand this. Someday, technology may advance to a point where it's possible to consider uploading one's consciousness or "soul" (whatever that is) into some kind of virtual environment maintained by supercomputer networks that are vastly more powerful than anything we have today. If that day ever arrives, it will mark the collapse of all of the world's religions, an unintended consequence that I for one would relish.

Until that day, here we are, trapped in our own personal history, which in turn is nested in human history, and that in turn is embedded in biological, evolutionary, geological, and cosmological history. Beyond the personal level, history won't end today or tomorrow or on a date in late December 2012. The timewave's point of "maximal" novelty is destined to come and go—as for many readers, surely, it already has—reduced to one of those quirky wrap-up pieces delivered on the nightly news. There will be no celestial chariots or mile-wide ships, no massive asteroid impact or volcanic eruption, no gamma-ray burst from a distant supernova that wipes out 99 percent of earthly life. Such events could happen, I suppose, but I don't believe they can be predicted. With the rare exceptions of global natural catastrophes that occur every few million years, novelty works more locally and slowly than these scenarios would have us believe.

Whatever the predicted end date, we'll wake up the next day facing the same intractable woes we faced the day before. Rather than confront those challenges, however, many of us will choose to focus our hope and dread on a new zero point ahead, longing for some resolution to our dilemma, some final outcome no matter how catastrophic. Strange, perhaps, but we are a species so adept at denial that even a vision of the apocalypse is a welcome distraction from the thought of devoting ourselves to making the time we are afforded the best it can possibly be.

I've been hard here on Terence's concept from a scientific perspective, partly because he spoke of it in scientific terms, imagined it could be calibrated with scientific precision, and invited scientific minds to critique it. That said, I'm keenly aware that the timewave has a value and beauty that lies outside the grasp of science. Does it describe the structure of time itself, as Terence postulated? I doubt it. But in the tantalizing way of astrological correspondences and the *I Ching* itself, the timewave does seem to describe *something* about the world, something significant and yet impossible to define. The element of subjectivity is so intrinsic to interpreting these constructs that one can read into them whatever one wants to find. Somehow, paradoxically, that suggests both their fatal flaw and their mysterious power as mirrors of the hidden self.

There's yet another way of looking at the timewave, I realize—one in which its predicted end time is already upon us. The rate of change in global events, environmental decline, and technological advance gives every sign of speeding up. Even as things seem to be falling apart faster than ever, there are developments that could lead the era through the historical bottleneck that appears to loom just ahead. It is a race between the forces of entropy and chaos and those of order, evolution, and progress.

Come to think of it, maybe that has always been so. Perhaps our age is not as unique as we might like to believe. It's very hard to discern the nature of the present, let alone to envision the future. Terence's gift may not have been the ability to predict what events would undergo the formality of actually occurring but to understand before most of us which ones already had.

37
To See the Great Man

Once Terence and I had finished the manuscript for *The Invisible Landscape* in the early fall of 1974, we drifted apart again. After a year in the Bay Area, I was tired of my restaurant job and craving an adventure, away from Terence and his influence. On some level I think he was still concerned about my stability, not yet fully trusting me not to spin off again into madness or delusion. He was playing dual roles as elder brother and in some respects as father. His concerns were sincere, but I had to push back. I was also beginning to think about what I should do with my life. Eager to get out of Berkeley, I hatched a plan.

In those days, Greyhound offered a bus ticket for $60, I believe, that let you travel for 60 days anywhere along their routes in the United States and Canada. It was a great way to see the country, provided you could stand that much bus riding. Having saved some money from my restaurant work, I took that and some of my book advance and headed out.

My ultimate intention was "to see the great man" as the *I Ching* would have it—that is, to approach a figure with the wisdom and authority to change my life. In seeking out the master, the student isn't waiting for novelty to make its entrance but inviting and even taunting it to do so. The benefits can be tremendous, but there is always an implicit danger as well. I hadn't forgotten my brother's encounter with Gunther Stent.

In my case, the great man was Richard Evans Schultes, the famous ethnobotanist at Harvard, director of its botanical museum and the world's expert on hallucinogenic plants. As I mentioned, it was his leaflet on "*Virola* as an Orally Administered Hallucinogen" that had lured us to La Chorrera, looking for the obscure Witoto hallucinogen *oo-koo-hé*.

La Chorrera was the ancestral home of the Witotos, and Schultes had made important collections there. In addition to meeting Schultes, I wanted to ask him if there might be a chance I could pursue graduate studies under him.

My roundabout route began with a detour for visionary purposes. In the three and a half years since my return from La Chorrera, I'd almost entirely avoided psychedelics. I had one experience with peyote that went well and revealed no signs of a lurking proclivity to psychosis. I felt it was time to reconnect with the mushroom mind. By then it was known that *Psilocybe cubensis* was not only abundant in South America but also fairly common throughout the southern United States, found just about anywhere there were cattle and pastures. As it happened, some former acquaintances in Boulder had recently moved to Hammond, Louisiana, and opened a hippie leather and crafts shop. They had rented a little house outside of town near a pasture that should have been prime mushroom habitat. Assured there would be mushrooms and a place to stay, I headed to Hammond. That fall had been dry and the crop was sparse, but I found enough to ingest several times, and that proved a good reintroduction to my fungal friends. The shrooms there were much weaker than those at La Chorrera, which was a lucky accident; the gentle trips were a good way to ease back into that dimension.

After a week or so in Hammond, I rode on to Richmond, Virginia, where I visited a linguist who at the time was perhaps the only nonnative speaker of Yanomaman, the language spoken by the Yanomami peoples of the Amazon along the Venuezelan–Brazilian border. In our correspondence, he told me he had several samples of *epená*, the DMT-containing *Virola* snuff used by the Yanomami. I was more interested in the drug than the people, unfortunately, but my host generously shared his collections. Years later I was able to include them in the analytical work on *Virola* that I carried out as part of my doctoral thesis work.

From there I headed for Boston and my meeting with Schultes. I arrived in Cambridge on a sweltering afternoon and went immediately to Harvard Square and the botanical museum. I cleared the receptionist in the lobby and was ushered upstairs to the office of the great man himself.

The door was ajar, the shades within closed against the afternoon glare. Peering into the gloom I couldn't see anyone at first. Then my eyes adjusted and I caught sight of him toward the back of the room. Clad in a white lab coat, he was literally hugging an air-conditioner in one of the windows! It was most incongruous to see this swashbuckling legendary figure, now portly and middle-aged, snuggled up to his air-conditioner. The afternoon was terribly hot in the way that only late Indian summer days can be, and I hardly blamed him. I was charmed, in fact, to see this display of vulnerability. Apparently even the great jungle botanist enjoyed his creature comforts when he had them.

Noticing me, he came forward and introduced himself. We had corresponded so my visit was more or less expected, but we hadn't set a time. Schultes was everything I had hoped he would be. He was completely charming and kind, every bit the fatherly mentor. How many other bearded, bedraggled hippies had made this pilgrimage? I was surely one in a long line. For anyone with my level of interest in hallucinogenic plants, Schultes was a luminary and meeting him was an unparalleled honor. I was disheveled and sweaty from my walk from the bus station. I had been on the bus for days and probably smelled like it, but if that bothered him he didn't let on. Having greeted me as a colleague and equal, he shut up his office and took me to dinner at the Harvard Faculty Club.

Along with his pioneering collections in the Amazon, Schultes was known for the diverse and talented cadre of students he attracted. One of them was Wade Davis, today a well-known ethnobotanist, writer, and "explorer-in-residence" at the National Geographic Society. While I was chatting with the professor in his office, Davis was traveling in South America with Tim Plowman, another Schultes protégé, researching coca, the plant from which cocaine is derived. Davis would later write about their long journey in *One River: Explorations and Discoveries in the Amazon Rain Forest* (1996), a book that features affectionate portraits of Plowman, a brilliant ethnobotanist destined to die young, and the mentor they shared in Schultes. As Davis notes of the latter, "At any one time he had students flung all across Latin America seeking new fruits from the forest, obscure oil palms from the swamps of the Orinoco, rare tuber crops from the high Andes." Schultes had a remarkable influence on the young people who in his later years became his eyes and legs in the field.

As Davis observes of Schultes's letters, "It was impossible to read them without hearing his resonant voice, without feeling a surge of confidence and purpose, often strangely at odds with the esoteric character of the immediate assignments."

I felt something like that in his presence at Harvard. We spent the afternoon discussing our mutual interests and my ambition to study under him and perhaps further investigate *Virola*. My spotty academic record came up. I had taken some basic botany courses, plant morphology, and taxonomy of the angiosperms, but practically no chemistry. He advised me I needed to get organic chemistry under my belt, and maybe more taxonomy, in order to qualify for admission to graduate school. If I could do that, he said, he thought I could probably be accepted, and he assured me he'd try to facilitate my application. I left the meeting fired with ambition, utterly stoked and ready to do whatever it took to work with him.

My friend Beverly and I spent time together over the next few days touring the city's museums and art galleries. It was a great reunion, a renewal of our friendship after its rocky chapter in Boulder. I got back on the bus and stopped in Ann Arbor for a day to rest and check out some bookstores, then headed for Vancouver. Though bus travel could be grueling, I had a secret that made it not only tolerable but pleasant: a stash of hashish–tobacco cigarettes I'd prerolled and disguised to look like ordinary cigarettes. The buses were never crowded, so it was easy to stake out a couple of seats toward the back. I'd bide my time until well after midnight when most of the passengers were asleep and then discreetly light up. The ventilation system wafted away the smoke, which smelled mostly like tobacco in any case. Or so I told myself, enjoying my thoughts and my visions of a new future as the bus cruised through the velvet darkness after midnight.

I arrived in Vancouver just in time for a Grateful Dead concert, stayed with friends for a few days, and then made it to Berkeley in time for Thanksgiving. But that was just another stop along the way. Schultes had helped me define a mission. I was bound for Colorado and determined to get back in school.

My plan was to live in Boulder but I ended up at Colorado State University in Fort Collins, where a friend had a job tending the horticulture greenhouse. I found an apartment in the building where he lived and registered for the next semester. I took two classes—one in "grass systematics," a taxonomy course that had me struggling a bit with the arcane keys used to identify various species, the other in introductory organic chemistry, which I loved. The professor of the second, Frank Stermitz, turned out to be a natural products chemist specializing in alkaloids and a gifted teacher. I remember him illustrating a lecture with a look at LSD, comparing synthetic production to the biosynthetic route in the ergot fungus. Needless to say, I was rapt.

38 Fun with Fungi: 1975

PSILOCYBIN
Magic Mushroom Grower's Guide

O.T. Oss & O.N. Oeric

Cover of the *Grower's Guide*, first edition, 1976.

The move back to Fort Collins was a first step in the new direction I had embarked on after my pilgrimage to see Schultes. I had separated, again, from a life near Terence and begun charting a new career. But my brother and I still had an important bit of business inspired by the Teacher we'd yet to finish—figuring out how to cultivate the mushrooms.

We wanted to have a steady supply so we could easily revisit those dimensions; more important, we wanted others to have their own experiences as a way of testing ours. At La Chorrera, we had collected spore prints from the mushrooms. Later, in Boulder, we made efforts to germinate the spores and grow mycelia on petri plates. We didn't know what we were doing and had little success, but we hadn't given up.

By the spring of 1975, we weren't the only ones who were interested in developing this piece of psychedelic technology. A fellow student I'll call Mark had access to the agronomy department's tissue culture lab and he became an enthusiastic collaborator. We managed to get some spores germinated and were growing mycelial cultures on potato dextrose agar in the lab; that was the easy part. We still hadn't gotten them to fruit—that is, to form mushrooms. Then I stumbled on a paper in the journal *Mycologia* that described a simple method for growing fruiting bodies of the common edible mushroom *Agaricus bisporus* in canning jars on a substrate of sterilized rye grain (San Antonio 1971). Though not a practical method for large-scale cultivation, it was presented as a way to grow a few fruiting bodies for use in genetic studies. We could have cared less about that, but it looked like it just might work for *Psilocybe cubensis*.

We lost no time in sterilizing a batch of canning jars. The mycelium grew rapidly and permeated the substrate within a few days. After that, we removed the lids and "cased" the jars with a layer of sterilized peat moss and vermiculite. I then took the jars back home so I could spray them every day and look after them. Ten days passed. Nothing happened. The mycelium appeared to be growing through the casing soil and spreading on the top of it. Not good. I added more soil and kept watching. Five more days—nothing. I was disappointed to say the least. One night I came home and took a look at the jars as I had been doing every day, and still saw nothing.

It was my friend in the building who noticed first: along the side of the jar, squashed between the mycelial block and the glass, was a little penis-shaped structure, an elongated white stem topped with a rounded, dark brown tip. A mushroom primordium! Excitedly, we checked the other jars and they all had them. Over the next few days, they broke through the surface and expanded into beautiful, golden-capped mushrooms.

They were also quite adequately strong, as we soon learned. By this time, even the uncased mycelial blocks that Mark had kept in the lab were producing fruits as I discovered the next day when I found him there bent over in uncontrollable laughter. There was every reason to be happy, even without the assistance of psilocybin. This changed everything.

Those familiar with Terence's talents as a raconteur won't be shocked to learn he could be an unreliable narrator at times. And with respect to his account of how we perfected our mushroom-growing method, as noted in *True Hallucinations* among other places, I have some debunking to do. According to Terence, he'd been conducting his trials in the shed at the lower end of his garden in Berkeley. He'd tried growing the mycelium on beds of sterilized rye and manure–compost mixes without success. Finally in frustration he closed up the shed and went away for a couple of weeks. Upon his return, he threw open the shed door and found the beds were covered with large, beautiful clusters of mushrooms. Great story, but our discovery occurred as I've explained it above.

Here's the abstract: Working in the tissue culture lab over several weeks, Mark and I succeeded in establishing mycelial cultures. Then we stumbled across the paper from *Mycologia*. We applied the method described there and it worked.

I immediately shared the method with Terence, who also had success. The technique was tricky at first, but once we knew its quirks, growing mushrooms in mason jars on blocks of sterilized rye grain was quite easy. In *Psilocybin: Magic Mushroom Grower's Guide*, we described our method as about as complex as a seventh-grade science fair project. It would be almost another year before we tried growing mushrooms on composted beds in a manner akin to what Terence described, but even then we had little luck, as I'll relate.

Nevertheless, the jar method was a major breakthrough. We considered it further validation of the gnosis that had been given to us at La Chorrera, now that we were in full symbiotic allegiance with the mushroom. The Teacher had intimated that we'd be given the knowledge of a technology that violated no physical laws but which we'd understand to have verified its teachings. Clearly, this simple methodology was what the Teacher meant. And we used our book to convey that knowledge to thousands of others around the globe. After *Psilocybin* was published, anyone could produce a pure, natural, potent psychedelic using materials largely available at the grocery store. Any college student with a spare closet could now produce magic mushrooms in modest quantities and give them to friends. It really was another psychedelic revolution, of a quieter kind.

We published *Psilocybin* under pseudonyms. Only years later was it widely known that O. T. Oss and O. N. Oeric were Terence and Dennis

McKenna, respectively. In many respects I regard that book as our most significant accomplishment. It continues to have a positive cultural impact, that is, if you believe the mushrooms and their influence are good, as I do. More than our wild ideas and theories, which may well be flawed and destined to be forgotten, we can claim a modest credit for the role we played in implementing a global symbiosis with the mushrooms. Even in the years after Wasson's article in *Life* on the mushroom cults of Mexico, the experience remained the secret knowledge of a few. Now millions have experienced the mushrooms and the dimensions they open to exploration.

Shortly after we developed our new method, I finished my courses at CSU and moved temporarily to a small house in the Big Thompson River canyon just outside Loveland, Colorado. I had a great day job at a wheat genetics lab a few miles away and plenty of spare time at home to set up and experiment with some jars. Back at CSU, I'd had a work-study job as an assistant to an art professor. During that time, many of the art students became my good friends. I remember the lovely experience we had when some of them visited Loveland and we all got quite loaded in a sunny glade in the aspen forest a few miles up the canyon.

My Loveland interlude was short lived, perhaps luckily so. I stayed in the house on the Big Thompson through the end of July. A year later, on July 31, 1976, torrential summer rains swept down the canyon and engulfed my former quarters during what proved to be one of the worst flood disasters in Colorado history. Among the 143 fatalities were my landlord (who lived up the road) and my next-door neighbor and her adult mentally disabled son.

Earlier in my Loveland summer, I had gotten the final word on my application to study under Schultes at Harvard. Though I'd taken his advice on how to improve my chances by studying chemistry and taxonomy, I hadn't been accepted. Fortunately, the refusal did not end my friendship with him, and I had opportunities to spend time with him in later years, and to earn his respect for my eventual achievements. To be honest, I wasn't terribly disappointed by the rejection. With the new technology we now had at our disposal, I was actually leaning toward mycology and getting less interested in the taxonomy of higher plants.

After my Loveland interlude, I returned to California. I bought an old car for $100 and set out for the West Coast. I put my best mycelial cultures onto slants and stuffed them into a styrofoam box, which sat on the front seat beside me. My car wasn't up to the freeways, so I mostly stayed on US

Route 50, billed as the "Loneliest Highway in the World." The road lived up to its reputation, but at least I had the company of my fungal symbionts, quiet though they were.

I arrived in the Bay Area to a scene that had radically changed. Ev and Terence had broken up, spectacularly, after she'd started sleeping with a friend of Terence's who had helped him with the timewave software. Terence had already moved to Oakland and had started a relationship with Kat, the woman he later married. Kat had grown up in the town of Avalon on Santa Catalina Island off the coast southwest of Los Angeles. Like Terence, she had traveled widely in the late 1960s; the two had apparently first met in Jerusalem and reconnected years later. Kat was smart, pretty, and fun to be around; she and my brother made a good match. Only half in jest, I tried to warn her that Terence could be difficult. For his part, he'd turned up the charm and ripped the knob off.

Our first project was to complete *Psilocybin*, which had been accepted by a small local publisher, And/Or Press. We finished the entire manuscript in under a month and saw it published early in 1976. I wrote the technical parts and Terence provided the foreword, including the well-known set piece I excerpted earlier, "The Mushroom Speaks."

Over those weeks, Kat and Terence had been planning a move to Hawaii, which they did in October. I first traveled to Hawaii in December 1975 to spend the holidays with them on the Big Island. Their rented house was small, but the land behind it looked ideal for a little experiment in outdoor mushroom cultivation. I arrived only a few days after they'd had a brush with the dark side of the mushroom experience, as described by Terence in *True Hallucinations*. Mushrooms are not always about giddiness and giggles. They can hint at, even starkly reveal, certain alien dimensions otherwise closed to the mind. Terence and Kat had been sobered by their encounter with that darker aspect and were in no hurry to repeat it.

Meanwhile, a journey was in the works. We had all been impressed by a book called *Wizard of the Upper Amazon* by F. Bruce Lamb, an account of the life of an *ayahuasquero* named Manuel Córdova-Rios. Rumor had it that Córdova-Rios was still alive and living in Iquitos, Peru. Enticed by his story, Terence and Kat had begun planning a trip to Iquitos to find him and to investigate ayahuasca. I decided to stay in their place while Terence and Kat took off in search of legendary shamans and magic decoctions.

By late winter 1976, I had moved to Hawaii and Terence was headed for Peru. There was something slapdash about their adventure, though as one who shared their wanderlust, especially for South America, I understood the allure. As it turned out, their travels would later help me in ways I could not have foreseen. Terence and Kat did contact Córdova-Rios, who, as Terence writes in *The Archaic Revival*, was by then in his early 90s, his eyes clouded by cataracts. He said the *ayahuasqueros* around Iquitos were mostly charlatans and suggested that Terence and Kat move their search to Pucallpa instead. Taking his advice, they met a practitioner there who would later assist me at the start of my professional life in 1981.

I'd applied to the graduate program in the botany department at the University of Hawaii at Manoa, on the island of Oahu, and had been accepted for the fall term in 1976. The idea of living on the Big Island for a few months seemed like an attractive prospect. I ended up enjoying the solitude, even if our dabbling in outdoor fungiculture never panned out. I left that place and flew to Honolulu in early June, loaded what little stuff I had in a rented beater, and raced around for a couple of days looking for a place to live. I finally found a studio apartment just a few blocks from the University of Hawaii campus and moved in, along with my All-American canning pressure cooker, an essential tool for sterilizing cultures. My next-door neighbor introduced me to friends of his who lived in a communal student house nearby. They were nice hippies, fellow psychedelic enthusiasts who shared my appreciation for the abundance of the autumn harvest. Before long, I began to think of Hawaii as my home.

39
A Lab in Paradise

Shortly before classes started, I got a letter, forwarded from Colorado, from my former girlfriend Deborah. After years of living with the surfer in Florida, she'd married him, given birth to a daughter, and moved back to California. Fool that I was, the letter gave me a flicker of hope.

She clearly wasn't very happy; maybe we could see each other again. But I was too busy with the start of graduate school even to dwell on past love. I had been offered a research assistantship by the botany department funded through the US Forest Service. This was a break—it meant I could focus on research and did not have to work as a teaching assistant. My grantors didn't care what I worked on, they said, as long as it was Hawaiian and as long as it was a tree!

I knew nothing about Hawaiian flora at the time except that *Acacia koa* and some of its close relatives were important trees on the islands. I knew that some of the African and Australian *Acacia* species had high levels of DMT and other tryptamines, also beta-carbolines, in the bark and leaves. It was perfect! I thought I could study the tryptamine chemistry of the indigenous Hawaiian *Acacia* species. I'd compare the alkaloid profiles among them and see if those compounds could be used as chemotaxonomic markers. The possibility that they might also yield significant quantities of DMT would be another, if unstated, research goal. The only problem, I soon discovered, was that the Hawaiian *Acacia* species are all notable for their lack of alkaloids. Like many indigenous island plants, they had long since lost the need to produce protective secondary products like alkaloids, having few predators. Instead, I focused on the nonprotein amino acids and phenolics, which were abundant in the Hawaiian *Acacias*. I ended up comparing these profiles among different island populations and also with some of the closely related Australian *Acacia* species (which did contain tryptamines).

It didn't really matter. It was a good, challenging project that enabled me to learn hands-on plant chemistry and how to conduct myself in the lab. Eventually I got a master's degree out of that work, though none of my findings were published in a journal, much to the disappointment of my original supervisor, who had secured the forestry grant that funded my research assistantship.

As it happened, I ended up working more closely with another professor, Sanford Siegel, PhD, who eventually became my research supervisor, mentor, and friend. Siegel was one of the most remarkable people I have ever known. He was truly a Renaissance man and a brilliant and creative scientist. I had seen in the literature that arrived with my acceptance notice that among the faculty was one Sanford Siegel, whose research interests, among many things, included exobiology, the study of extraterrestrial life. What? How could anyone study that since there was none available to study, mushrooms notwithstanding? I had to meet this guy. A couple of weeks before the semester began, I visited the department just to nose around and see who was there. That was the mid-1970s, the era of the "energy crisis," and the corridor lights were dimmed. I approached an odd-looking, rumpled character in the gloom and asked if he knew where I could find Dr. Siegel. He peered at me myopically through thick glasses and quietly replied that he was Dr. Siegel. He looked like a gnome, short and quite round.

He invited me into his office and we chatted. It quickly became clear that we were on the same wavelength. For one thing, we both loved science fiction. For another, we shared this interest in extraterrestrial life, chemistry, and pharmacology. He had never had experience with psychedelics, but when I mentioned them he didn't freak out like so many in his generation might have done. I queried him about his research and it turned out that he was, among many things, an environmental toxicologist who studied "stress physiology" in plants (and animals) and extreme environments.

That was the exobiology angle; he had grants from NASA to study the effect of simulated extraterrestrial conditions on earth organisms to determine the environmental parameters under which they could survive. He also studied mercury cycling in the environment, which explained what he was doing in Hawaii. The volcanoes spew forth megatons of mercury in numerous chemical forms, and many organisms—such as those that inhabit volcanic steam vents—have adapted to its presence and can tolerate extremely high levels of the metal. He was using satellite vegetation mapping technology to chart the distribution of mercury-tolerant species and thereby locate volcanic vents, which are potential sources of geothermal energy.

In his NASA-funded work, he was extremely creative in his thinking about stress physiology and extreme environments. For example, he wondered what would happen if he tried to grow a cactus underwater. Turns out it grows fine as long as you bubble oxygen and carbon dioxide through the water. How well does a tarantula survive under a radiation flux similar to that at the Martian surface? It survives just fine—for months. Can you germinate onion seedlings in liquid ammonia as a substitute for water? Yes, ammonia can substitute for water in many biological processes. He had a genius for thinking up these incredibly creative, exciting, simple experiments. And yet they all had a rationale and a reason behind them. He was an out-of-the-box thinker.

Sandy was like a father to me, my scientific father. I loved the guy. And he loved me, too. Really, he loved all of his students. Whenever an interesting professor came to town, Siegel would invite all the grad students up to his house in Manoa for pizza and beer, and we'd spend the evening having the most fascinating conversations. His wife, Bobbie, was also a scientist and a brilliant microbiologist; they had one of those science-based marriages like Pierre and Marie Curie. Those of us who were part of Sandy's circle called ourselves "Siegel-Lab." One of the marks of truly great minds in my opinion is they tend to love teaching, and Sandy did.

Through Sandy I met a number of gifted students who became my close friends. Maggie, for instance, eventually became a well-funded, highly published professor. Her work had something to do with the regulation of the cell cycle, most of it so complicated I couldn't understand it and still can't. She played in a bluegrass band that performed every weekend at a roadhouse in Ewa Beach, which for many of us became the focus of our grad-school social lives. Another new friend, Lani, was a winsome island girl with long blonde hair. She was an excellent taxonomist, knew all of the Hawaiian plants, and was clearly on track to carry on the legacy of Harold St. John, the former botany professor after whom the plant sciences building had been named. Lani died of lymphoma in the late 1990s. I was saddened to lose a friend and respected colleague when she was still so young.

I discovered Lani's remarkable knowledge of local plants, and my lack thereof, shortly after the semester started. I was thrilled to have a bench in Siegel's lab with the tools of basic phytochemistry at my fingertips: a thin-layer chromatography apparatus, extraction vessels, and rotary evaporators. What I lacked was expertise. One afternoon I took a break to walk down the hill to the bank a few blocks away. When I stepped out of the bank I was struck by a strong, almost overpowering smell of DMT! As I walked back up the hill the odor became stronger. Finally I came to its source: a small tree in full flower on the main mall of the campus. Excitedly, I collected an armload of flowers, leaves, and twigs, indifferent to the fact that I was vandalizing one of the university's ornamental trees. Back in the lab, I started grinding up the various plant parts, putting them into alcohol, bound for the shaker to extract. I was sure I had found the DMT mother lode until a moment later when Lani walked in, picked up a flowering branch, and said something like, "Oh, I see you've found *Sterculia foetida*! Really stinks, doesn't it?"

Well, at least I had a name, but I still thought it might be DMT. Subsequent analysis proved otherwise. As it turns out, *Sterculia foetida* does have interesting chemistry, namely a group of unusual cyclopropene-containing lipids that have marked anti-inflammatory activity. These would be volatile and highly aromatic but not hallucinogenic.

A few weeks into the semester, I moved out of my tiny apartment near the campus to a bigger place in Nu'uanu Valley, where I stayed less than a year. One notable thing about that time was that it coincided with, if not the end, at least the beginning of the end of the two romantic attachments that had defined my early adulthood. The first was with Peggy, who was still living in Boulder. Having enrolled in a nursing program, she was going through her own set of personal and academic challenges. Her boyfriend from a few years back was long gone. She was lonely and I was still in love with her, having come to accept both my feelings and their futility as a chronic condition. Without really expecting anything, I offered to send her a ticket to come visit. I was surprised—overjoyed, actually—when she accepted. Maybe after all that pain and heartache, love longed for and lost, we'd actually get together.

Peggy flew out, and we went to the Big Island for a few days. We stayed in the cabins at Mauna Kea State Park, on the flanks of the volcano that is Hawaii's highest point, and took some mushrooms up there. Our trip together was excellent, our lovemaking less so. It just didn't seem to have the passion that I had long imagined it would. It was not her fault, or mine, really. There was just no spark. She was beautiful and I lusted for her, but afterward I had to admit we just couldn't be comfortable together. It was not the end of our friendship, but more important it wasn't the beginning of the relationship I had desired for so long. Peggy went back to the mainland with a cloud of ambivalence and uncertainty hanging over us, and I slipped into a funk. I had interesting work and a circle of nice friends but no one to love.

Terence and Kat had returned from their trip to Peru earlier that year and settled in California. I traveled there in November for their Thanksgiving weekend wedding. I had another agenda, one I could trace back partly to my disappointing visit with Peggy, but more to that forwarded letter I'd gotten months earlier from Deborah. Married and a mother though she was, I decided to visit her. It was an utterly stupid thing to do. I didn't know what was going to happen, but I knew what I wanted to happen. I wanted Deborah to leave the surfer and come live with me in Hawaii—an unrealistic hope and a selfish one to boot. I knew from our correspondence that she wanted to see me and so I went.

When I arrived, I found her husband to be remarkably cordial, considering the situation. Then again I was supposedly visiting there as a friend. He was barely out of the driveway on his way to his night job before Deborah and I were locked in passionate embrace.

There was a big scene when he got home. Deborah told him she no longer wanted to be married and no longer loved him; she wanted to be with me. The poor guy had been blindsided. Our mushroom grower's guide had just been published and I'd brought a copy for Deborah. Her husband saw it and threatened to call the cops. I fled in horror and anger, leaving a wrecked if formerly unhappy marriage behind me. It was a shameful, rotten thing to do. There was no excuse for it. Deborah was foolish and selfish but I was no less so. Many times I have regretted my role in their breakup.

Within a year, Deborah was divorced and struggling financially. We believed we were in love again and would be together soon. This long-distance relationship, rekindled by a betrayal and sustained by a delusion, went on for nearly a year. During that time, Deborah got involved with another man, a guy who ironically was growing mushrooms using our newly published method. Deborah wasn't a person who had much self-reliance or who could be centered within herself. I should not have been surprised that she couldn't remain "true" to me, whatever that meant in such circumstances. I tried to be sanguine about this new turn of affairs, still convinced that if we could be together for a while we'd rediscover the love we'd shared before.

Finally, she planned a visit in August 1977. She and her ex-husband shared custody of their young daughter, and he amicably agreed to look after the child for the two weeks Deborah planned to spend with me. Reflecting on this, I'd say he was either a saint or a fool or possibly both.

He certainly reacted to the situation with a lot of maturity. I was beside myself with hope and desire as I counted down the days until her arrival.

Early on the morning Deborah was supposed to arrive, she called to say that she wouldn't be coming after all. She'd thought it over, she said, and a relationship between us just couldn't happen. She needed to live where her daughter could be close to her father. I was devastated. We had words and in my anger I said hurtful things. She responded in kind. It was the last conversation we ever had.

It took me a long time to get over that call. At first I became profoundly depressed. I seriously contemplated suicide. Life had no meaning for me. I dated many women, almost in rebellion for what had happened, but I was in no shape to start a meaningful relationship. Perhaps a trace of such anguish lingers, of course, but I do not blame Deborah for any of it now. She did the right thing. Her daughter needed a father as well as a mother, and though I was ready to accept her daughter as part of a family of our own, that would not have been the same.

I first came to realize that nearly two years later. I had taken a very high dose of mushrooms, by myself and for no particular reason. It was the best thing I could have done. I understood, with their help, that Deborah really had no choice but to do what she had done. She hadn't wanted to hurt me, but I'd backed her into a corner and something had to give. Grasping that, finally, I could hardly blame her for what had happened. Not that she needed forgiveness, but I did forgive her, and I forgave myself. It was one of the most therapeutic psychedelic experiences I've ever had. After that, the clouds lifted on my gloomy mood and I became much more the cheerful person I was and still am. When I think of Deborah now, it isn't with anger but with love.

The voice of the mushroom is not always so healing, let alone reliable, as an episode shortly after my breakup with Deborah revealed. In the worst of my grief, I thought it might be good to do exactly what I later did so usefully—spend some time alone and take some mushrooms. I put a few things in a pack and flew into Hilo on the Big Island and rented a car. I spent a night at the park at Laupahoehoe on the windward side, but it poured the entire time. I checked out the park at Mauna Kea, but it was rainy and chilly there, too, so I drove down the island's leeward, drier side to Spencer Beach, a favorite tourist spot near Kawaihae.

That's where I met Brad and Kris. Blackjack dealers at a big casino in Las Vegas, they were camping their way around the Big Island over an off-season break. They seemed friendly and normal enough, and after talking for a while they asked me if I knew where to get some acid. No, I said, but I did have some shrooms. Before long we were talking about finding a spot to take them. As it happened, I had the perfect place in mind. Earlier that year, Terence and Kat had briefly visited the island and acquired a parcel of land on the Kona side. There were as yet no structures on the property, which could only be reached by four-wheel drive up a dreadful road. No one lived nearby so we wouldn't be disturbed, and the couple's rental vehicle could handle the track.

By dusk, we'd pitched our tents on the empty land and were ready for the mushroom soup that had been simmering on the fire. Kris called it "blue soup" because of the blue color imparted by oxidation of the psilocin in it. I'd put all the mushrooms I'd brought into the soup, and we split it three ways. It didn't take long before the effects began to manifest, and they seemed incredibly strong. I hadn't eaten anything since breakfast, and I figured that was the reason. We smoked a little weed to mellow things out. Kris began telling me about her misadventures in Las Vegas, the time she'd dropped acid on the strip and ended up naked and raving in the local police station. She did have a bit of the volatile raver in her, and I could see how she might have attracted attention had we been in public.

As darkness fell, the psychedelic effects deepened. We lit a lantern, and Brad and Kris invited me to come sit in their larger tent. They weren't exactly into an orgiastic scene, but we got into some touchy-feely stuff—Kris inviting me to feel her up a little, the three of us snuggling, that kind of thing. The effects of the mushroom were coming in waves, as they often do. Periods of relative lucidity alternated with long internal reveries; we would surface and exchange a few words, fumble a toke on the last of our joint, and then submerge again in our own personal hallucinatory ocean. Quite honestly, we were much too stoned to engage in any hanky-panky even if we'd wanted to. It was all we could do to hang on.

As the evening progressed, the visions faded a bit. Our eyes were more often open but we weren't talking much. The faces of the odd couple looked grotesque in the yellow lantern light. I suddenly went cold with a sense of overwhelming dread. There was something sinister about them. I revisited their story—happy casino dealers off to Hawaii to spend some of their easily earned dough. It didn't ring true.

Suddenly it hit me: they were serial murderers, sex killers, cannibals! I had fallen into their trap. All traces of their grisly feast would be buried up there in that empty place and they'd be on a plane before the sun rose, leaving my gnawed bones to molder in a shallow grave.

My only hope, I decided, was not to fall asleep. I looked at them in the lamplight—nothing unusual, just a pair of young people like me. I wasn't fooled. I muttered something about turning in and went back to my tent, where I grabbed my flashlight and machete. Pulling my sleeping bag partly over me, I sat upright in the darkness, ready to lash out if they made a move. The night was dark and moonless. It would be a long wait until dawn. I was completely down by then. No residual effects of the mushrooms remained except the scenario I'd concocted, which still seemed totally plausible. I'm not sure how long I stayed awake, but I surely didn't make it to the light of day.

The next morning, everything was fine. We brewed up some coffee, packed up, and headed down the dirt road. They asked for, and I gave them, my address. They'd be passing through Honolulu in a few days and promised to look me up if they had time. They proved as good as their word. We spent a delightful evening together eating Chinese food and getting loaded on my best Hawaiian bud.

The incident says more about the ambivalent nature of the mushroom experience than it does about the Big Island odd couple. In deep mushroom states, one can be seized by outlandish conceits that are very hard to shake. The mushrooms can be tricksters at times, and they have a way of presenting delusions as self-evident truths. Many of the events and insights at La Chorrera are good examples. Like certain Irish bards I could mention, the mushrooms can, at times, be the best of bullshitters. They usually have an interesting story to tell, but it's not necessarily the straight story. It's important to keep one's critical faculties tuned to the highest level of sensitivity in order to filter what you've learned, or think you've learned, from mushrooms.

By the start of the new semester in the fall of 1977, I'd accepted an offer from Siegel to move into a small apartment at his home in Manoa. This new living situation gave me a chance to befriend the two Siegel kids still living at home. His daughter, pale and soft-spoken, lived there with her boyfriend and their baby boy. The guy was a motorcyclist, a bit of a rebel but an intelligent fellow, a physics, astronomy, and philosophy buff, and we hung out regularly and had many good discussions. Siegel's son was interesting and quite eccentric in his own right. Enamored of all things British, he too was blond and fair, but he had his father's barrel chest. He put it to good use by becoming an accomplished bagpipe player, recognized all over Oahu for this talent. The Siegels were anything but a typical American family, and it could not have been otherwise given such brilliant, driven parents and their inevitable influence on their children. Though I lived among them, I never pried into the family dynamic. I didn't want to know the details, really. Siegel was a mentor and a role model to me and I preferred not to have any of my bubbles burst.

Siegel's grad students used to worry about his health. After all, we loved him as much as he loved us. He got no exercise and viewed his body as a vehicle to carry around his amazing brain, which may have been his undoing. On any given day I'd arrive at the lab and ask Lani or Maggie or someone else, "Well, how bad is he today?" We all expected him to keel over at any moment. We judged the state of his ill health by his pallor. Some days he looked pretty good; others, he was gray and clearly having problems.

Siegel eventually became the department chairman years after I'd left. He performed those duties well, but he really belonged in the lab where his creativity could flower. In 1992, I was working as a research pharmacologist at Shaman Pharmaceuticals in San Carlos, California, when I got the news that Sandy had collapsed and died at his desk the day before. I think I cried more on hearing that than I did when my own father died. His death was a terrible loss, to science and to those who loved him, and there were many. He was as fine a human being as I have ever met.

After living at Siegel's place for just under a year, I moved to another apartment. I was tired of the cramped quarters and I wanted a place of my own where I could bring someone after a date. The breakup with Deborah still haunted me, but I was determined to move on.

The next big phase in my life began unexpectedly at one of those beer-and-pizza gatherings that Siegel liked to throw for visiting colleagues. The guest of honor that night was Siegel's friend Neil Towers, a professor of botany at the University of British Columbia in Vancouver. In the course of a lively conversation, Neil mentioned that he had a master's student who was working on characterizing an enzyme in the biosynthetic pathway to psilocybin (which he pronounced "si-LO-cybeen"). His student, he said, had started the project but then had dropped it to work on something else. Towers mused that he thought it was an interesting problem; what a pity there was no one to pick it up where she'd left off. I practically fell off my chair! Trying not to spew my beer, I set it down and stammered something like, "Well, Dr. Towers, that's very interesting. I've had some interest in these mushroom metabolites as well, for some time." Trying not to betray my excitement, I added, "I don't suppose you'd have a place for a new graduate student to work on this problem?" In fact he did, as I quickly learned. We started corresponding, and he made sure my application to UBC was accepted, and with a four-year fellowship in the bargain. It was one of those shifts in the time stream that sets you off in an entirely new direction and leaves you wondering who's writing the script.

A year after that pivotal event, I found myself in a taxi on a drive to the Honolulu airport. I'd finished my master's in the spring of 1979 and was getting ready to start my doctoral work in Vancouver. I was leaving Hawaii behind, heading to a new country and a new phase of my life.

Though I've returned many times to Hawaii and have maintained my connections there, I've never again had the pleasure of calling it home. Most people are never confronted with a choice to leave a paradise like Hawaii, and doing so carries with it the potential for major regret. I could have gotten my PhD there. Siegel would have been happy to have me, there was stipend money, and I might have ended up sticking around like those I knew who came to Hawaii to study and never left. Driven by ambition, the prospect of a career, and new adventures, I gave up that bucolic life, which seemed the right thing to do at the time. Now I'm not so sure. I do know that once you leave Hawaii, it's hard to get back.

Perhaps if current cosmological theories are true, we live in a world in which all time lines exist, every possibility is actualized; somewhere on one of those alternate tracks the doppelgänger of Dennis McKenna never left Hawaii. It's fun to speculate about such things, and useless, destined as I am to live out the consequences of the decisions that have led me to this particular nexus of space and time.

While I was busy pursuing my graduate studies in Hawaii, Terence and Kat were making their own choices as they built their life together. Shortly after their marriage in 1976, they moved from Kensington to a more rural setting not far from Santa Rosa. Within a year they'd bought their property on the Big Island. As shareholders in a "hui," a collective land ownership association, they'd tied their futures to the paradise I'd later depart. Their first child, Finn, was born on April 7, 1978.

By then, Terence's career was beginning to take shape. Our first book, *The Invisible Landscape*, hadn't made the bestseller lists, but it got some attention in esoteric circles, and Terence had attracted notice as well. Shortly after his wedding, just before Christmas in 1976, I was listening to the radio when suddenly I heard my brother's voice—unmistakable then and now. He was going on about extraterrestrial intelligence and how it would be hard to recognize even if we did encounter it. It might present itself in some surprising form, he said, perhaps as a mushroom. It was a 30-second snippet on an obscure station, but that was the first time I'd heard him air those peculiar notions to a wide audience. For me, that was the beginning of his public career. It was also the seed of a self-replicating meme that would propagate like a virus through the cultural body for decades and indeed is still doing so.

Terence had left the family and Colorado at 16 while I stayed behind. Nevertheless, our lives remained entwined, linked not so much by physical proximity as by our shared interests and obsessions. That bond culminated at La Chorrera, where events brought us about as close as two siblings could get. There at the peak of our folie à deux, the metamorphosis we attempted with light and sound and mushrooms was an operation on a single entity, or so we imagined. That's how we understood it then, and that's actually how it was.

Everything after that critical moment would be an expression of two lives drifting apart. Like two boats formerly lashed together, we rode the same current, at times closer and farther apart but always within hailing distance. That ended 12 years ago when Terence was swept into the vortex of his own personal singularity, the same one we'll all face someday. How long before my journey ends, I cannot know. Whatever distant shore Terence has come to rest on, may it be a lovely tropical island and not a frozen reef. My feeble signals to him vanish in the night like the wan glow of a semaphore in a howling gale. So far there has not been, nor do I expect there will ever be, a responding light.

40 In the Trenches

Before leaving Hawaii, I shipped my books and a few other things worth keeping to a friend in Seattle. Upon arriving there in the summer of 1979, I borrowed her car and drove to Vancouver, found a scuzzy apartment, unloaded my stuff, and headed back to the States for a month with friends and family in Colorado. In Paonia, I paid $400 at a local garage for a 1973 Mercury Monterey, a huge thing that had literally been driven to the post office and back by a little old lady. With the cruise control set and the AM/FM radio cranked up, I floated to Vancouver in what turned out to be great wheels, a perfect road machine I'd drive for the next five years.

By late summer, I was eager to start the new semester and begin my research. Like most foreign graduate students at the University of British Columbia, I had a two-year fellowship that would be renewed for another two years if I kept up my grades. I'd already completed a lot of my work in Hawaii—in plant physiology, biometrics, calculus, and plant biochemistry. My first two courses at UBC were in fungal genetics and advanced organic chemistry. Both were a challenge, and I was under a lot of pressure to excel. Among the many good incentives to keep my fellowship was that it relieved me of any teaching duties, giving me more time to focus on my research.

My research supervisor, Neil Towers, ran his lab as an incubator for a succession of eccentric but brilliant students. For Neil, our work was as much a social activity as a scientific one, but his standards were high. By then, we had agreed that my project was to characterize the enzymes involved in psilocybin and psilocin biosynthesis. For this, of course, I was well prepared. I knew all about growing mushrooms as a result of my extracurricular hobbies. Health Canada, the country's public health department, had helpfully provided the synthetic psilocybin and psilocin I needed for my analytical work. My first task was to develop methods for detecting and quantifying these two metabolites in fungal cultures and fruiting bodies. I requisitioned a growth chamber in the basement of the biology building, and for most of that fall and spring I had it stuffed with prolifically fruiting jars.

My first-year goals were to devise techniques for extracting psilocybin and psilocin from the mushrooms and then develop ways of using high-performance liquid chromatography and thin-layer chromatography to analyze and quantify those extracts. Once these methods had been perfected, the reasoning went, we'd extract the biosynthetic enzymes from the fruiting bodies or the mycelium and incubate radioactively tagged precursors with them, and then quantify the resulting products: psilocybin, psilocin, and their intermediates. In a later phase, we planned to look at the genetic regulation of biosynthesis in the mushrooms. To do so, we'd first use mutagenic agents to make mutant strains, select these, and then examine the variations in the biosynthetic products associated with them. I never got to that point, as I'll explain, but I did manage to develop some reliable analytical methods.

I didn't know any of the other graduate students when I first arrived at UBC. I was an outsider, an American, and a loner, but as in Hawaii, I soon met other kindred spirits. One was Terry, a "moss man" from Ontario working on bryophytes under a prominent taxonomist in the field, the late Wilf Scofield. Terry was never into mushrooms or psychedelics, but he was peculiar enough in the best of ways without them. Another wonderfully odd new friend was Paul, who wasn't actually a student but a renowned amateur mycologist whose interest in the "neurotropic" species led him to discover and name several British Columbian *Psilocybe* species over the years. When I started hanging out with these folks, we'd retire every Friday to the graduate student center on campus and drink beer—strong Canadian beer—and I'd get smashed. It wasn't really my thing, but the camaraderie was a pleasure.

During my first semester, in the fall of 1979, I had moved into another dreary basement suite in West Point Grey. I then bought a used bike so I could commute to school along the bike trail that wound through the Endowment Lands, a kind of green belt between my neighborhood and the campus. A construction crew had been working along a road that ran parallel to the trail. One day the construction crew dug a trench 8 feet deep and 20 feet long right in the middle of the bike path, as I unluckily discovered that night. I left the lab late. It was rainy, dark, and dreary, and I thought I was coming down with a cold. I climbed on the bike to start home, and my bike light was pathetically weak on the wet pavement. The crew had placed a small sawhorse mounted with a flashing light at the lip of the trench—not six or eight feet in front of it, but right at the edge. By the time I got there, the warning light had either died or was barely working. In the darkness and the rain, I plowed through it and went head over heels into the trench with the bike landing on top of me. I briefly lost consciousness. When I came to, I assessed the situation.

The top of the trench was a couple feet above my head, and I had broken something. It was very painful to stand. I couldn't put all my weight on my left leg. I realized I had pushed the only barrier to the trench out of the way, meaning another cyclist was very likely to plunge in on top of me. I started to shout as loud as I could and shined my bike light out of the trench. In fact, what I had feared was narrowly averted—another botany graduate student was a few minutes behind me on the trail. He heard my screams and helped me get out of the trench. Another rider soon headed off to call an ambulance.

I had a hairline pelvic fracture, a concussion, and compressed vertebrae. I spent the next two weeks in Vancouver General Hospital, my first introduction to the Canadian healthcare system. The final bill for the excellent treatment I got there totaled $7.50. In today's acrimonious political climate, American conservatives love to bash the Canadian healthcare system, but it has provided high-quality universal coverage for all Canadians (and American students) since 1962. I find it sickening that our country has yet to enact something as effective and probably never will.

My injuries called for bed rest followed by physical therapy. Seeing as how I was in the process of failing organic chemistry, my hospital stay provided a graceful exit from that dilemma. When I got out, I remained on crutches for eight weeks and had daily physical therapy. I also resumed practicing yoga, as I had been doing in Hawaii, and that may have accelerated my recovery. I was still in a lot of pain and couldn't easily get around on my crutches, so I tended to hole up in my cold and damp apartment, covered in blankets. Occasionally, I'd get the energy to drive to campus and check my mail. I'm sure I cut a pathetic figure as I hobbled into the botany department mailroom. At least one person seemed to think so, a cute graduate student named Sheila with beautiful long red hair. I was struck by her and tried not to show it, but we exchanged friendly greetings.

As the winter and spring wore on, I gradually recovered. I continued to stay home a lot studying for my comprehensive exams, which I passed without incident in May. In July the department hosted Botany 80, a large conference that brought in more than a thousand botanists from around the world, including some of my colleagues and friends from Hawaii. As students in the host department, we were enlisted to help with logistics. My job was to greet arriving dignitaries at the Vancouver airport, and I was surprised and delighted to find that Sheila had been assigned to the same group. Typically, I broke the ice by bumming a cigarette. With little to do except hang at the airport waiting for various flights to arrive, we had time to get to know each other. She was currently in a master's program studying algae under Dr. Bob DeWreede, who had studied under Maxwell Doty, a notoriously tyrannical phycologist at the University of Hawaii.

At the same time that Botany 80 was in full swing, so was the Vancouver Folk Festival, one of the biggest such events in North America. On a slow night at the conference I decided to check out the festival. I remembered Sheila mentioning she liked folk music, and I was hoping I might run into her there, though that seemed unlikely in a crowd of 10,000. As it happened, I'd only been there half an hour when I literally stumbled over her sitting on a blanket in front of the main stage. And she was alone. I knew she'd recently been going out with a fellow botany student, but his tastes apparently ran more to classical music rather than folk, so there she was, a lovely and unaccompanied redhead. I pretended to be nonchalant about it but my wish had come true.

We soon moved to the edge of the crowd and fell into conversation, sharing our life stories. Sheila had grown up in the interior of British Columbia, the daughter of a rancher outside of Kamloops. She had three siblings—a sister about 14 years older, a brother about 9 years older, and another sister 2 years younger. Many of her experiences growing up were not unlike mine in Paonia, although she'd lived on a ranch and I was what she called a "townie." She was a bookworm like me and had a quick mind and strong opinions. She loved to argue, I quickly learned, and was a good match in conversational give-and-take. We both were children of the 1960s who had done our time in hippie houses and been influenced by the counterculture. We talked to the end of the concert and then reluctantly parted.

It was clear there was a deep resonance between us. I at least was intrigued and wanted to see her again as soon as possible, all the more so when I learned that she and her boyfriend were breaking up. By mid-August I'd moved again, to a different part of Point Grey. I invited Sheila over to hang out, and she ended up spending the night. That was the start of something, but I wasn't sure what. I had no idea she'd become my wife or that one day we'd be the proud parents of a daughter. I only knew that she seemed to enjoy my company as much as I enjoyed hers.

My work with the *Psilocybes* continued into the fall of 1980, but I was having trouble keeping my interest up. I had begun to doubt whether fulfillment lay in the direction of fungal genetics and enzymology. One day in mid-October Neil called me into his office. "I've got a little extra money in the grant this year," he said. "Would you be interested in going to Peru?" He handed me a flyer from an outfit called the Institute of Ecotechnics.

From what I gathered, the institute owned a research vessel, the RV *Heraclitus*, and they were soliciting scientists to join their Amazon expedition the following spring. For a relatively modest cost, they would provide a berth on the boat, meals, and access to some of the remotest collection areas in the Peruvian Amazon. It sounded too good to be true and as we found out later, it was.

But with my supervisor waving dollars and the chance of an Amazonian adventure in front of me, how could I turn him down? For one thing, I immediately recognized it as a chance to redeem myself. I wanted to prove that I could return to the Amazon and do real science this time—and not go crazy. January 1981 would be the 10th anniversary of my first and only trip to the Amazon, the journey that took us to La Chorrera and beyond. This was an opportunity I couldn't pass up.

So I dropped my psilocybin thesis project and rewrote my entire program. Instead of working on the enzymes and genetics of *Psilocybe*, I would direct my efforts toward a comparative investigation of the botany, ethnobotany, chemistry, and pharmacology of two important Amazonian hallucinogens: ayahuasca and *oo-koo-hé*, the orally active preparation made from *Virola* species that had first lured us to La Chorrera. It was an interesting project. Both substances were orally active hallucinogens with DMT as the apparent active compound. In the case of ayahuasca, the monoamine oxidase (MAO) inhibiting beta-carboline alkaloids in the stems and bark of a liana, *Banisteriopsis caapi*, apparently allowed the DMT in the leaves of the admixture plants to be orally activated. In theory, the MAO inhibitors in the brew blocked the gut enzymes that normally degraded DMT. As a result, the DMT entered the circulation unchanged and from there readily crossed the blood–brain barrier. The hypothesis seemed reasonable but no one had actually proven it. *Oo-koo-hé* was even more poorly understood. The substance involved no admixture plants, or none that were known. The sap of various *Virola* species that were high in DMT, 5-MeO-DMT, and related compounds was cooked down to a thick paste, mixed with ashes, and ingested in the form of little pastilles or pills.

All this posed a fascinating riddle. Here were two Amazonian hallucinogens derived from entirely separate botanical sources, both ingested orally, both having tryptamines—namely, DMT—as their active hallucinogenic components. In the case of ayahuasca, the mechanism seemed to involve the blockade of MAO by the beta-carbolines. But for *oo-koo-hé*, the mode of action was much less clear—the active hallucinogens were tryptamines, but did the *Virola* sap also contain its own MAO blockers? It seemed like a reasonable explanation—in fact, I knew that tryptamines and beta-carbolines were closely related compounds that occasionally were found in the same plants. But no one had yet determined if *Virola* sap contained beta-carbolines or not.

The two hallucinogens occupied different ethnographic niches as well. Ayahuasca was used in the Amazon by many Indigenous groups and had been adopted into Mestizo folk medicine. Many admixture plants were associated with it, and there were almost as many different blends as there were individual *ayahuasqueros*. In contrast, *oo-koo-hé* had a highly restricted cultural distribution. It appeared to be used only among the Witoto and the closely related Bora and Muinane tribes. The alkaloid chemistry of some *Virola* species had been studied to a certain degree, but *oo-koo-hé* itself had not been. If the paste contained admixture plants, they were unknown.

It seemed like the ideal thesis project, just waiting for me to get my arms around it. My first objective was to collect as many samples of each preparation as possible, along with specimens of their plant ingredients. From an ethnomedical perspective, I wanted to document how the substances were prepared and applied. Back in the lab, I'd develop methods for determining if those constituents contained tryptamines and beta-carbolines and if so how much. Finally, I'd devise assays to measure MAO inhibition and then evaluate sample extracts for this activity.

With my course now redirected, I pursued my work with renewed enthusiasm. Meanwhile, as winter neared, my relationship with Sheila deepened. We were spending a lot of time together and I was definitely smitten. I discovered she was an excellent cook with a special flair for Indonesian food and a gift for accomplishing culinary marvels on a single hotplate. Even better! It's sometimes said that the way to a man's heart is through his stomach, and in Sheila's case there was some truth to that. Without quite realizing it, I was falling in love again.

41

An Encounter with Ayahuasca

I continue to be astonished by how readily the mind confabulates, creating its own story to fill in the holes in memory, to the point where I can imagine looking back at the end of life and wondering if any of it really happened. This point was driven home recently when I ran across a daily journal I'd kept on my expedition to Peru. My prolific notes now provide me with a record of many events I'd largely forgotten. This is a blessing, of course, but also a curse in that it poses an obligation to reconcile what I remember with what I wrote at the time.

Don Fidel Mosombite, the *ayahuasquero*, and his family.

Among the recovered details are those that suggest my state of mind in late 1980 as my departure neared. I had mixed feelings about leaving Vancouver for six months, because, having just turned 30, I realized I'd found in Sheila the love I had been longing for. Even as I was admitting that to myself, I had a strong sense that a major epoch in my life had ended and that a better chapter was about to begin. That explained my reluctance to leave her for so long. But once again the siren call of the quest was strong. My destiny seemed to be taking me back to the Amazon.

I'd be traveling to Peru with a fellow graduate student named Don, a soft-spoken guy from Victoria, British Columbia. Don intended to focus his collecting on the *Euphorbiaceae* family, which is notorious for its many toxic members. The plants often contain what are called "phorbol esters," after the family name, a class of diterpenes that are known to affect cellular processes in many ways; some are considered carcinogens, cocarcinogens, and protein kinase inhibitors. Phorbol esters were important tools for investigating such processes, and newly found ones were always valued. While a few "euphorbs" were used in Amazonian ethnomedicine, a far greater number were recognized as simply toxic. Don's project was to collect specimens of ethnomedical interest, characterize their chemistry, and devise methods to investigate their activity and mechanisms of action.

While Don and I had been getting ready to depart, Terence and Kat, then living in northern California, had been awaiting the arrival of their second child, Klea, born in December 1980. I was pleasantly surprised when Terence told me he was hoping to join us at some point during the six months we planned to be in Peru. I wasn't sure how practical his decision was, but he was clearly determined to go.

Don and I left Vancouver in mid-January and drove to California, where I left my car with Terence and Kat. We then took a bus to the Los Angeles area, staying briefly with a professor friend of Neil's. We were there just along enough to watch the televised spectacle of Ronald Reagan's first inauguration and the simultaneous release of the Iranian hostages after 15 months of captivity in the American embassy in Tehran. The next day, January 21, we caught our flight to Lima.

The Amazon and Orinoco watersheds, with their teeming diversity of life, had been drawing Western scientists for more than two centuries. Among the earliest were Prussian naturalist Alexander von Humboldt and the French botanist Aimé Bonpland, who arrived around 1800. One could argue the modern era began in the 1840s with the Amazon journeys of the British evolutionary theorist Alfred Russel Wallace and Richard Spruce, perhaps the greatest botanist of his day. A century later, a young Schultes modeled his career after Spruce's and then went on to inspire a new generation of plant hunters, to which I belonged.

No sooner had I signed on for my voyage than I began encountering some of my illustrious contemporaries. The first was Timothy Plowman, Schultes's protégé, who was working at the Field Museum of Natural History in Chicago, home to an impressive collection of Peruvian plants. Our consultations with Plowman primed us on what to expect in Peru. Tim had spent a lot of time in South America and was happy to share his experience with us. By then the world's leading expert on the coca plant, he was widely regarded as the heir apparent to Schultes. Many ethnobotanists, myself included, were saddened when Tim died of AIDS in 1989. The field had lost a talented scientist and a good man.

In Lima, we visited the herbarium at the Museo de Historia Natural and the government offices that issued collection permits (which were easy to get back then). A few days later, we flew on to Pucallpa, a rough tough Amazonian frontier town on the Río Ucayali. The place was a pit—literally. A mud-caked bulldozer, half sunk into the mire of the unpaved main street, looked like it had been there for months. We checked into a nearby flophouse. If it were possible to give a hotel a negative five-star rating, this place qualified. Our room had no air-conditioning, no hot water, and a single fluorescent light in the ceiling. There were two filthy mattresses without sheets, and it looked like someone had bled to death on one of them. From what we could see, the favorite forms of recreation were drinking, fighting, and playing loud music until three A.M., all of which we could watch through a grimy window above the street.

Breakfast in the dining room at another hotel on the corner consisted of an egg sandwich and Inka Kola, the fluorescent, greenish-yellow soft drink loved by many, apparently, but which tasted to me as ghastly as it looked. As usual in Peru, coffee was a syrupy concentrate made from Nescafe that one diluted to taste with hot water. We'd encounter this preparation everywhere and grew to loathe it. While the country appeared slow to embrace the concept of freshly brewed coffee, despite growing some of the best in the world, Pucallpa at least was ahead of its time when it came to the drive-through window. Some of the locals enjoyed bursting through the swinging, saloon-style doors on their motorcycles to order breakfast. It was all very entertaining and a bit shocking for two mild-mannered Canadian graduate students.

Our first field trip took us out to Puerto Callao, a town on Lago Yarina-cocha, an oxbow lake cut off from the Ucayali. There were a few Indigenous communities nearby, including a Shipibo village called San Francisco, but we were bound for another enclave, the Peruvian headquarters of a global operation known as the Summer Institute of Linguistics. Established in the 1930s, the SIL ostensibly sought to promote literacy among Indigenous peoples and to translate the Bible into Indigenous languages. By then, the SIL had established a far-flung network of outposts as well as ties to many top linguists and anthropologists. Now known as SIL International, the non-profit organization drew support from evangelical churches, which helped to pay for the planes and boats that gave them access to remote cultures. Though the group denied being a missionary organization, rumor had it otherwise. Later, the journalists Gerard Colby and Charlotte Dennett would argue that the SIL had been entangled with American oil interests and even the CIA, with dire consequences for both the Amazon region's native peoples and their land (Colby and Dennett 1995).

We were somewhat aware and leery of the group's reputation, but we had bumped into one of their linguists on the plane to Pucallpa, who told us we'd find a colleague of ours there known to us only by reputation: Nicole Maxwell. Given the name of another SIL linguist who could help us find her, we headed to the compound to track her down. What we found at the SIL base was a surreal piece of small-town America lifted up from Iowa or Nebraska and plunked down in the Amazon, complete with modest bungalows, white picket fences, sidewalks, and neatly trimmed lawns—not to mention a white church with a steeple. It was like an evangelical theme park designed to make its inhabitants feel at home, or at least feel anywhere but where they were. Even the residents seemed to be playing roles in one of those tourist re-creations of an authentic village, Valley Forge or Old Richmond, where the employees wear period dress and pretend to be blacksmiths or chandlers. In this case, the village was a re-creation of a 1950s, Mayberry-style town. I got the feeling the people were politely "nice" to us in a way that let us know they really viewed us as degenerate hippie scum. Our inquiries eventually led us to Nicole having Sunday dinner with one of the local families.

Nicole, when she came to the door, was a refreshing dose of reality. Tall, rail thin, and ancient, she was already a legend in the small world of ethnobotany, partly because of her book *Witch Doctor's Apprentice*, first published in 1961 (and reprinted in 1990 by Citadel Press with an introduction by Terence). The book is her account, most likely embellished, of her quest to find medicinal plants in the Amazon beginning in the late 1940s. Having grown up a wealthy San Francisco debutante, Nicole became a well-known, free-spirited figure in Paris during the 1920s, occasionally dancing with the Paris Opera and modeling nude. After the end of her 12-year marriage to an air force officer, she moved to South America in 1945 and became a correspondent for the *Lima Times*, according to her obituary in the *New York Times*. Her fascination with jungle medicine began on a trip into the rainforest. After she'd been badly cut by a machete, her Indian guide treated the gash with a folk remedy known as *sangre de grado*, or "dragon's blood," derived from a reddish sap. We now know the source of this wound-closing seal-ant was the latex from *Croton lechleri*, a "euphorb" like those my colleague Don was studying. The gash quickly healed without becoming infected or leaving a scar. Thanks to that experience, Nicole discovered the mission that was to define the rest of her life—ferreting out jungle remedies and trying to interest big drug companies in developing them. Like many other ethnobot-anists, she didn't have much success, but her story was compellingly told, and by the time I met her she'd become a legend. We became fast friends and I remained in touch with her until she died, impoverished and largely abandoned, in a Florida nursing home in 1998.

When we first met on the porch of the bungalow, she still cut a dashing figure even for a frail lady of 75. The white-bread surroundings made her earthiness stand out all the more. Her profanity would have put a long-shoreman to shame. She insisted she owed her long life and good health to smoking at least a pack of unfiltered Peruvian cigarettes a day, washed down with a quart of *aguardiente*, a popular liquor distilled from sugarcane.

We had a lively conversation when she dropped by our hotel the next afternoon. Nicole had a habit of jumping from topic to topic, rarely focusing on anything for more than a moment, but we did get her to pass on some contacts in the Iquitos area that proved useful in our search for *oo-koo-hé*. We promptly abandoned the muddy center of Pucallpa for a place called El Pescador, a cheaper, quieter hotel in Puerto Callao, after Nicole said she'd find us a place to store our supplies. In return, we helped her move out of an apartment in Callao and into a house on the SIL base. Over the next few days we spent a lot of time with Nicole and her circle. Most of them were affiliated with the SIL but weren't missionaries. Despite my earlier skepti-cism, they proved genuinely friendly and quite helpful.

Our next task was to locate Don Fidel Mosombite, the *ayahuasquero* that Terence and Kat had met in 1976 when they'd traveled to Peru in search of the brew. We had no address, only his name and vague assurances that a cer-tain woman herbalist at the market could put us in touch. When we finally connected with her, she arranged for one of her sons to take us to see him.

The man who opened the gate was a stocky, barrel-chested man who could have been anywhere from 45 to 60. He lived with his young wife, the baby girl she was nursing, and two boys who looked to be about five and six. Neither Don nor I spoke much Spanish, but I haltingly introduced myself and mentioned Terence and Kat. I said as best I could that we too wanted to learn about ayahuasca, the plants it contained, and his methods of preparing it. Don Fidel projected considerable gravitas; it was clear he was an intellectual or rather a sage, a man who knew many things, though not a scholar as most would think of it. Whether he was actually literate or not, he was a genuinely wise and generous man who was willing to share what he knew.

In conversations we had over the following days, he conveyed some of his knowledge about the plants and their properties and about his understanding of cosmology and the way the sacred world was organized. The world is divided into three realms, he said—the earthly realm, the upper realm of God, and the lower realm of the devil and demons. When one takes ayahuasca, he said, one sees enchanted cities in the upper realm and lost cities in the diabolical realm. Everything he knew about the healing properties of plants and how to prepare such medicines had been taught to him by ayahuasca in the trance. Surprisingly, he said that he sometimes used mushrooms, but he regarded ayahuasca as very different and much stronger. Except for his comment about mushroom use, the rest of his statements were consistent with what other ethnographers had said about practitioners of *vegetalismo*, which is the syncretic Mestizo tradition in which Don Fidel was firmly embedded. After a few conversations, I realized Don Fidel, then 56, was a genuine shaman, a practitioner of long experience and in every respect the real deal. He was as good as any *ayahuasquero* I've ever drunk with and better than most.

A few days later, I had my first real encounter with ayahuasca. While living in Hawaii, I'd tried a sample that Terence had brought back, but I'd felt no effect other than the expected purging. Here was a chance to drink the real thing in a traditional setting, freshly made and presumably strong. When we showed up at 7:30 on a beautiful moonlit night, Don Fidel was already seated at a crude table at one end of the one-room hut. He had a plastic bottle filled with an orangey-brown liquid and had removed the wooden cork and was softly whistling into it. He informed us the *"la purga"* was *"muy fuerte"* and *"bien bueno'"* (very strong and very good). Don and I sat for a while in the gathering dusk as others drifted in: three men, one of whom was apparently Don Fidel's apprentice; two women, one of whom was pregnant and another with swollen legs whom Don Fidel had been treating at the house that afternoon; and Don Fidel's wife.

We all sat on narrow and uncomfortable wooden benches arrayed along the inner walls of the hut. Another plant substance that figured in the setting was *mapacho*, a South American tobacco variety known for its strength. We

Dennis and helpers preparing voucher
specimens, 1981.

smoked and chatted quietly in the gathering gloom until Don Fidel brought
down a small cup fashioned from a gourd. He uncapped the bottle, blew a
little more *mapacho* smoke over it, whistled, and then filled the cup to the
brim and handed it to me. It was bitter and acrid but I was prepared for
much worse. I tasted it and then knocked it back in a single gulp. Those who
are familiar with ayahuasca will say that the first taste is always the best. It
only gets worse after that. Having taken it now several hundred times over
the last 30 years, I can attest to the truth of this. And yet somehow I always
get it down.

I retired to my place on the bench while Don went forward to receive
his portion and then sat back down beside me. One by one, all of the men
received their allotment, taking less than we did; Don Fidel took about a cup
and a half. The women did not drink. We settled in to wait. Conversation
ceased. Presently there was only the gentle creaking of Don Fidel's wife
rocking in the hammock, the ever-present trill of insects, and the distant
barking of dogs. After a little while Don Fidel reached up and extinguished
the single candle on the shelf above my head, then began to sing his beautiful *icaros*. Some of his songs were in Spanish, others in a language I didn't
recognize then but I now know was Quechua. His apprentice, Don Miguel,
softly joined in.

After each song Don Fidel would invoke a brief benediction in Spanish that always ended with the same refrain: "In the name of the father, son, and holy spirit." He then blew sharply on his pipe several times. We sat quietly in the darkness and waited for something to happen. I could feel the ayahuasca in my gut but beyond that only the extreme discomfort in my posterior from sitting on the hard bench. There were occasional hints of images when I closed my eyes, and the glow from a lit cigarette left a persistent trail in the darkness. Otherwise, nothing.

While I was waiting, hoping for an effect, others in the group were retching loudly over the sideboard of the house. It would have been unspeakably rude under any other circumstances, but here it was just part of the scene. During the singing, I had fleeting suggestions of imagery in muted, earthy tones, but nothing as overt or clear-cut as I'd had on mushrooms. Most of the effect was somatic. I felt paralyzed and dissociated from my body, but I think this was more from the discomfort of prolonged sitting than the ayahuasca. It was clear that I had taken a sub-threshold dose; next time, I thought, I'd need a bit more. After a while Don Fidel asked me, in Spanish, if I was feeling *borracho* (drunk) and I replied, "*Un poco,*" a little. He offered me more, but I declined, saying this was fine for the first time, then complimented him on the beauty of his *icaros*.

A curing session followed. One by one, the men approached the table and sat on a stool while Don Fidel blew *mapacho* smoke into their eyes, ears, noses, and faces in short, staccato breaths. Each then returned to his spot as another stood up. The pregnant woman and the woman with leg trouble did not approach the table but got their treatment lying down. Don Miguel, the apprentice, was loudly sucking on their affected areas making a smacking, popping sound while Don Fidel sang. I knew this process was supposed to remove the *virotes*, or magical darts, that were believed to be cause of many illnesses. These darts, projected through a curse, were the work of unscrupulous shamans or *brujos* who were willing to use their powers to harm a victim, often for pay. In the darkness, the sucking noises were startling and unsettling.

Another young man came forward, someone who had apparently entered the hut at some point without me realizing it. His treatment involved smoking a pipe of *mapacho*. He took several huge inhalations and coughed and retched violently but did not purge.

After the last treatment, Don Fidel lit a candle and we sat around talking for another half-hour before people started shuffling out into the night. I asked Don Fidel if I could take a small sample of *la purga* and he obliged, filling a small plastic bottle I'd brought. I gave him a 1,000-*soles* note, worth about a dollar at the time, and we departed. It felt so good to stand up! The moon had set by then, and the night sky was star-studded and crystal clear. There was a cool breeze, and the phrase "enchanted evening" popped into my head. That it was. We reached our room at about three.

In the next two or three sessions at Don Fidel's, I experienced the same sub-threshold effects. It couldn't have been poor quality brew; others in the group, including Don, were clearly affected. It was something wrong with me. For some reason, I wasn't "getting" it. Reflecting on those first experiences, I think that ayahuasca is in ways a learned experience. If you don't know what to expect, nothing may happen. Also, my uptight hypervigilance may have prevented me from relaxing enough to allow the experience to manifest. I was a stranger in a strange land. Though there was nothing overtly threatening, and certainly nothing threatening about Don Fidel, I was too invested in maintaining control to let it flow. This may have been partly due to the fact that this was the first time I was back in South America and taking a psychedelic since my misadventures in Colombia 10 years earlier. I was highly invested in making sure that that didn't happen again—I didn't want to trigger any kind of psychotic break. I had taken psychedelics quite a few times over the previous 10 years, but not in South America. I was keeping myself on a tight leash.

During our stay in Pucallpa, Don Fidel and his uncle, Don José, were very kind. They understood the science of what we were there for. They obligingly prepared several batches of ayahuasca, pointing out the differences between the varieties they knew, offering me specimens of all the plants in each preparation and samples of the final products. I carefully preserved them in small plastic bottles of methanol I'd brought with me for this purpose. Later these collections served as the basis for my lab work at the university. Over the next few months, I collected a number of additional samples from different practitioners in other parts of Peru. Eventually, back in Vancouver, I compared their alkaloid profiles. Based on my analyses, the samples provided by Don Fidel and Don José were the gold standard, as strong or stronger than any other samples I collected. This was further proof that my failure to respond was not due to deficiency in the brews. It was a deficiency in the apprentice.

42

The River of Poisons

Wade Davis and Dennis en route to Pebas, March 1981.

While we were visiting the realms of ayahuasca with Don Fidel, the various players in our river trip were converging on Iquitos 500 kilometers to the north. The RV *Heraclitus*, on its Amazon cruise, was wending toward Iquitos, and we planned to be on hand when the boat arrived. Terence was due there as well, having set aside a few weeks to spend with us. Don and I were still not sure of the details. We decided to split up. Don wanted to stay in Pucallpa and collect plants with the help of Don Fidel and a few others we'd met through Nicole. Meanwhile, I'd fly to Iquitos and get the lay of the land. Our plan was to meet up again in Pucallpa and then head off to greet our mystery ship together.

I enjoyed being on my own in Iquitos, exploring the streets of a town I was destined to visit many times. I was keenly aware of its importance among modern botanists as a gateway to the upper Amazon. My first chore in Iquitos was to figure out when our foray would begin. Unknown to Don, I'd also be looking into the feasibility of returning to La Chorrera. According to our plan, our search for *oo-koo-hé* would lead us to Brillo Nuevo, a village on the Río Yaguasyacu. Rumor had it that trails led north from there to the town of Arica on the Río Putumayo. A modest boat ride upriver from Arica would take us to El Encanto, the starting point for the four-day hike to La Chorrera. I had serious doubts about this scenario. For one thing, there wasn't enough time. For another, the area we'd have to traverse was now beset by drug traffickers and best avoided. Or so I learned. The idea had been Terence's, not mine. He wanted me to investigate whether such a side trip might be possible—which I did, and it was not.

I had thought I'd spend three days in Iquitos. The usual travel delays extended that to a week, but my stay was productive. Both Tim Plowman and Nicole had suggested I look up a woman named Adriana who had worked for years in the local botanical trade. Her assistance proved crucial. Adriana was part Witoto and her grandfather was the headman at Puco Urquillo, a Witoto village on the Yaguasyacu just downstream from Brillo Nuevo. That would be our first stop in our quest for *oo-koo-hé*. The Witotos were relative newcomers to that area. The rubber boom and its depredations in the early 1900s had left the Witoto, Bora, and Muinane peoples decimated by slavery and disease. Most of the survivors were forced from their ancestral home near La Chorrera to lands south of the Putumayo, along the Yaguasyacu near its confluence with the Río Ampiyacu. Our hope was that the Witotos there had not lost their ancestral knowledge of the fabled hallucinogen and how to prepare it. If anyone could help us find out, it would be Adriana's grandfather, Don Alfredo.

As for the whereabouts of the RV *Heraclitus*, the news was good, or so it seemed. The boat had left Leticia and was due to dock in Iquitos any day. I got the report from Franklin Ayala Flores, the director of the Herbarium Amazonense at the Universidad Nacional de la Amazonía Peruana, or UNAP. We'd been in touch with Dr. Ayala, as I called him, before leaving Canada, so he was expecting us.

I found him in his office at the herbarium, which back then was housed in a ramshackle wooden building, a firetrap, not to mention a habitat for the myriad insects that were slowly munching the collections into pulp. There was a room in the back with some gas-fired driers where the pressed specimens were dried prior to mounting; the place looked like it could go up in flames at any time. Ayala greeted me warmly. He had met my supervisor, Neil Towers, in 1977 when both were onboard the RV *Alpha Helix*, the well-appointed research vessel operated at the time by the Scripps Institution of Oceanography and funded by the National Science Foundation. Schultes had been part of that cruise as well. Neil's presence on that expedition had helped me in Iquitos and would do so again later in my career.

Ayala introduced me to his assistant, Juan Ruiz, who was then studying forestry at UNAP. Ayala appointed Juan to act as our field assistant, which in reality meant he'd be the field leader. His job was to accompany us on local collecting forays and, once the *Heraclitus* arrived, travel with us down the Amazon to Pebas and then up the Ampiyacu. I can imagine Ayala privately telling Juan to make sure the foolish gringos didn't get themselves killed.

Juan didn't warm to us immediately, and our lack of Spanish didn't help. Nonetheless, our meeting that day was the start of what has been a 30-year friendship and scientific collaboration. Juan is an amazing botanist and ethnobotanist. He is extremely knowledgeable about the plants of the Peruvian Amazon, most of which he can recognize and name on sight. I owe him greatly for all his help; I would not have had my career without him. Dr. Ayala, his mentor, has retired but still lives in Iquitos and continues to work on his massive catalogue of the region's flora. Juan is now the curator of the herbarium, which has moved to a three-story concrete building built largely with funds from the Missouri Botanical Garden. It is a real herbarium with about 100,000 specimens, many of them only known to science from its collections, an important resource for researchers around the world. Dozens of research groups have passed through over the years, each required to deposit duplicates of their collections. Needless to say, this has created a backlog of unmounted, uncatalogued specimens. Kat and I collaborated in launching an effort to scan and digitize the specimens, the first step toward creating a digital herbarium that researchers could access over the Web. Juan, Kat, and others are carrying on the work as a project of Kat's nonprofit, Botanical Dimensions, whose origins I discuss in a later chapter.

The day after meeting Juan, I returned to the herbarium and examined a few *Myristicaceae* specimens from the Puco Uquillo area, prepping for our visit. That family includes the *Virola* species used for *oo-koo-hé*, but a better-known member is nutmeg. While at the herbarium, I ran into Al Gentry, a legendary botanist then working in the field for the Missouri Botanical Garden. Gentry frequently collected out of Iquitos. Following his death at age 48 in a plane crash near Guayaquil, Ecuador, in 1993, the salon of the herbarium was named in his honor. The crash, during a "tree-top survey" near the coast, killed five, including two other scientists, American ornithologist Theodore Parker and Ecuadorian ecologist Eduardo Aspiazu. All were key figures in neotropical conservation biology. Like Juan, Gentry was a plant fanatic who could identify specimens by genus if not by species on sight. Fully half of all the collections at the UNAP herbarium are Gentry's, and a greater number are catalogued at the Missouri Botanical Garden and available through its massive database, Tropicos (www.tropicos.org).

The next day, I accompanied Gentry and a couple of grad students on a short outing near Iquitos. For him, it was hardly more than an afternoon stroll, but I learned a lot—about both Gentry's field skills and the incredible biodiversity of the Amazonian ecosystem. Even on that brief trip, he collected several specimens that were unknown to science at the time. I got a crash course in field collecting, Gentry-style. He went at it like a crazy man, grabbing specimens and stuffing them into large plastic bags. Occasionally his team would deploy a set of extendable clippers on a long pole to reach flowering branches or epiphytes growing in the tree crotches. He made no effort to separate the specimens or even to treat them carefully. He just stuffed everything into a bag as fast as he could, as if it were a race. He told me the specimens would be sorted out later at the herbarium, which was near enough to eliminate the need to preserve the specimens more carefully. It's no wonder he collected nearly a million specimens over his tragically shortened career.

Back at the herbarium, Ayala informed us that the *Heraclitus* had arrived the previous night. We all piled into the street and went down to the dock to see it. The boat wasn't the gleaming white, graceful craft I had envisioned but a black vessel with a ferro-cement hull and the silhouette of a Chinese junk. It was also a lot smaller than I had imagined. It was definitely not the RV *Alpha Helix* with its white-coated waiters, crystal champagne glasses, multiple labs, and luxury berths. Still, if our party could fit onboard (and that looked doubtful) we'd make it work.

I met Robert Hahn, the director of the expedition, and some of the crew, who preferred to be addressed by nicknames, among them Moving, Moondance, Nada, and Bamboo. This was the first of many peculiarities that would surface about this group over the next few days. What I learned from Robert was disappointing. He didn't see his vessel going anywhere before April 1, then six weeks away. That wasn't going to work for us. Terence was due to arrive in two weeks, at the end of February. We had to find a way to get out of Iquitos and reach the collection areas or all our efforts would have been fruitless. Robert suggested that we might be able to take one of his small speedboats and go on ahead with two crewmembers. The *Heraclitus* would meet us later at Pebas. This wasn't what we'd been promised, but I thought it might work.

I returned to Pucallpa with my report on February 17. Robert had heard that Nicole was in Pucallpa and invited her to visit the boat and possibly join the expedition. Don and I were delighted when she agreed to fly back with us. We were a frazzled trio by the time we arrived and found modest lodgings just off the Prospero, the bustling main street of Iquitos's commercial sector.

The next few days were filled with logistical preparations for our trip downriver. Terence's scheduled arrival was on February 28, which seemed to pose another delay, but that turned out to be the least of our problems. I soon saw firsthand why successful military campaigns require a commander at the top functioning as a dictator. Our plan of heading downriver to Pebas and then north from there, up a network of Amazonian tributaries, required a simple coordination of machines, supplies, resources, and personnel. But what should have been relatively easy became almost impossible given the consensual style of decision-making insisted on by our new shipmates. Despite their hype and bravado, the Heraclitistas, as we dubbed them, appeared to be if anything even more clueless than we were about how to stage this event.

Meanwhile, in my absence, the *Heraclitus* had come out the loser in a tangle with a barge while tied up at the port and now had a 15-inch hole in its cement hull. The vessel wasn't going anywhere for the foreseeable future except dry dock; the materials for repair had to be shipped in from Lima. Even the absurd departure date of April 1 now seemed like an optimistic fantasy. We had no choice but to go with Robert's speedboat plan. The welcome news that Nada and Moondancer would be joining us was tempered by the realization that there wasn't room for everyone on the boat, let alone our gear and supplies.

A rumor had surfaced that Wade Davis, then a student of Schultes, was on his way to Iquitos from Ecuador and might join the expedition. Luckily, this proved to be true. He had been asked—and had tentatively accepted—to be the voyage's chief science officer and soon arrived to check things out. None of us knew Wade well at the time. A native of British Columbia, he'd briefly been a forestry student at UBC and had taken some courses under Neil Towers before I joined the program. He'd left for Harvard when the chance arose to work with Schultes. A skilled outdoorsman, he already knew his way around South America, and I welcomed his arrival. With our inexperienced crew, we needed somebody with a strong personality to come in and take charge.

Meanwhile, it had become quite clear that the Heraclitistas were not only disorganized and dysfunctional but rather weird. They had a humorlessness about them that seemed out of place in easygoing Peru. There were intimations of a hidden agenda, or at least things about themselves they hadn't fully explained. We knew that the Institute of Ecotechnics, which owned and operated the *Heraclitus*, was loosely affiliated with a theater troupe called the Theater of All Possibilities and several other peculiar enterprises. Only years after our encounter with this odd group did we piece together the convoluted and fascinating details of their story.

It turned out that the institute, the theater troupe, and even the *Heraclitus* itself could all be traced to a remarkable and enigmatic man named John P. Allen. A metallurgist turned Harvard MBA turned systems ecologist, Allen, now in his 80s, may or may not have been a meglomaniac in his heyday, as his critics claimed, but he was certainly the producer, director, and star of his own legend. In 1969, Allen and a few others had started an "ecovillage" in Santa Fe, New Mexico, called Synergia Ranch. It was there that the Institute for Ecotechnics and the theater troupe got their start. First envisioned by Allen as a vessel big enough for a crew of 14, with both a science lab and a theater, the RV *Heraclitus* was communally built in Oakland and launched in 1975. It has been plying the world's waters ever since, often under sail, though the craft was relying on its engine for its long trip up the Amazon. According to the boat's website, its Amazon cruise in 1980 had been inspired by Schultes, who spoke at a conference on jungles sponsored by the Institute for Ecotechnics in Penang, Malaysia, in 1979. On that occasion, Schultes challenged them to carry on the river mission he'd begun aboard the *Alpha Helix*. As to how that may have influenced Wade's decision to join us aboard the black junk, I do not know.

In the mid-1980s, Allen and several colleagues founded Space Biospheres Ventures, an organization that became known for founding, managing, and eventually mismanaging Biosphere 2, a three-acre ecological research facility under glass located in the Arizona desert in Oracle, near Tucson. The project's major financier was the billionaire Ed Bass, one of the well-known Bass Brothers from Fort Worth, whose family wealth was derived mainly from oil and gas revenues. Of the four, Ed was considered the most offbeat. In the early 1970s, he spent time at the Synergia Ranch, where he met others who shared his dual interests in drama and environmental causes.

Biosphere 2 was originally conceived as a massive, closed-system laboratory (full of plants) that simulated, in miniature, the planetary biosphere—which the founders called Biosphere 1. One goal was to study the human impact on natural ecosystems; another was to create a self-sustaining artificial ecosystem that generated its own food and recycled all its waste. Some viewed it as a prototype for an eventual colony on Mars, or even a kind of panic room after an ecological disaster on earth. The *Heraclitus* apparently cost $90,000 to build; Biosphere 2 cost $150 million, with millions more spent annually to maintain and operate it.

As proof of concept, Biosphere 2 conducted two "closure" missions during which a small group of "biospherians" hoped to remain sealed inside the enormous, greenhouse-like dome without any outside resources. All food was to be grown in the dome, and ecological dynamics would be used to keep carbon dioxide levels low and oxygen levels within acceptable limits. The first such mission, which began in 1991, lasted two years. The second, in 1994, ended in acrimony after six months. By then the entire venture had foundered amid accusations of scientific fraud and financial mismanagement. Though the project had many laudable goals, the management team's internal conflicts and lack of scientific expertise, among other factors, eventually turned what could have been a pioneering research project into a farce. The facility has passed through other hands over the years and is now overseen by the University of Arizona. The story of Biosphere 2 and the colorful personalities that originally built and operated it is a lesson in the unanticipated outcomes born of the collision between scientific goals, human hubris, vast wads of cash, and competing personal agendas. Despite all the psychodrama, the project did produce some credible science, along with plenty of dubious science and scandalous gossip, a history recounted by Rebecca Reider in her excellent 2009 book *Dreaming the Biosphere: The Theater of All Possibilities*.

All that lay in the future on March 1, 1981, when we found ourselves gathered on the deck of the *Heraclitus*. Our departure was still a week away, but with all the players by then in town, Robert had invited us to join the crew for dinner and a group discussion of the ever-changing plans. Terence had shown up the night before, and Wade and his girlfriend Etta had surfaced earlier in the day. Don was onboard, of course, along with Al Gentry, who we'd invited to join us for the evening. Rounding out the guest list was

Nicole, who was up for the party but not the expedition, having stumbled on a bit of uneven pavement and skinned her knee. The scrape would be fine, thanks to *sangre de grado*, but she'd been unnerved enough to reconsider being trapped with our motley bunch up a jungle river.

The Heraclitistas included the captain and several others whose names I don't recall. I do remember Terence describing one of them as looking like he'd been sleeping in an open grave. It all started out normally enough. We sat on the deck conversing, smoking, and waiting for dinner, its delicious aroma wafting from the hold below. Then the Heraclitistas started howling, an ululating keening that went on for several minutes and then ceased as abruptly as it had begun. The rest of us looked at each other quizzically, expecting some explanation, but none came. Conversation resumed as though nothing had happened. Then dinner was served, and we dug in. There was silence for a bit as we ate hungrily, and then we started chatting and joking again, as one would normally do over such a feast, until we realized we were the only ones talking. Our chatter faded, and we finished eating as the crew maintained a stony silence.

After dinner, we sat in a circle as they took turns delivering short monologues. I expected them to address the upcoming trip or its research objectives, but they did not. Their comments were mostly unrelated to what we'd been discussing, and a few made no sense at all. The crewmembers seemed to be engaging in a free-association exercise during which everyone expressed whatever happened to be on their minds. No one interrupted these monologues or ventured a response.

That made for an uneasy and somewhat bizarre evening. Absent any explanation, we felt a bit like ethnographers invited to participate in the customs of an unfamiliar tribe. We concluded their rituals stemmed from their theatrical roots. In other words, they behaved as they did in part because everything was a performance for them. This explanation actually helped us to understand their eccentricities. Life on the RV *Heraclitus* was a work of performance art. And maybe the same could be said of the events that unfolded 20 years later inside Biosphere 2.

Wednesday, March 4, marked the 10th anniversary of the Experiment at La Chorrera. It was not a good day for me. Since my departure from Vancouver in January, my communications with Sheila had been sporadic, as often happened on trips to remote locales in those pre-Internet days. I was pleased to find an aerogramme from her waiting for me when I showed up at the herbarium that morning. I wasn't pleased by its contents, which amounted to a Dear John letter. She had grown lonely, she said, during the weeks of my absence and had started dating another student in the department. One thing had led to another, and now they were getting seriously involved. She had written to let me know that our relationship, on which I had placed such hopes for the future, was over. I was stunned and angry. I couldn't believe that her feelings for me had turned out to be so short-lived. Just weeks before I'd left, I had come to believe, or had let myself believe, that Sheila was "the one" and that our destinies were intertwined. I'd now discovered otherwise, just as I was heading into the jungle for what we guessed would be seven weeks. This news plunged me into a depression that hung over me for the rest of my time in Peru.

We spent the next few days in a frenzy of preparations, getting our gear packed and organized for the trip. I was swept with doubts about the wisdom of striking off into the jungle, all tied somehow to thoughts of Sheila and the temporal echoes of La Chorrera. On the rainy eve of our departure, I slipped on the slick stairs as I headed below decks and landed hard but on my feet, badly shaken but unhurt. In my journal entry that night, I wondered if I was being softened up for later as one by one the stops that kept

Don Marcos preparing *ku-ru-ku* hallucinogenic paste in Puco Urquillo, 1981.

me oriented in reality were kicked away. Was I about to plunge again into a madness from which this time I wouldn't return? No. I resolved that wasn't going to happen.

Finally, on March 7, we managed to disengage from the increasingly tense scene in Iquitos and departed downriver for Pebas. The *Heraclitus* stayed behind. We'd cover the first leg by river launch and then proceed from there in stages, by speedboat. As Iquitos disappeared from view, I was brooding. In my darkened mood, I had begun to wonder why Terence had even come to Iquitos. I was there to conduct ethnobotanical fieldwork, to collect the specimens I needed to complete my investigations back in the lab. I took my mission seriously. I had no interest in returning to La Chorrera or repeating our "experiment" or anything related to that craziness. Fortunately, as I've noted, we'd already determined that reaching the Putumayo from the south—the first step to La Chorrera—was impossible. Nevertheless, I felt Terence might have had something in mind other than mere botanizing. I knew he'd be looking for *Virola* and other tryptamine-containing plants: samples for analysis as well as living specimens. To that extent, we were on the same page. But in his egging-on way, he wanted to push the envelope. That didn't mean he'd push his *own* envelope. He wanted somebody else to plunge over the abyss while he watched—and, if necessary, gave a little push. I wasn't buying it. I made it clear that I intended to carry out my research and successfully conduct my fieldwork. I was not in Peru to take mushrooms. If we stumbled on mushrooms during our travels, fine, I'd consider taking them, but I was not interested in re-creating what had happened at La Chorrera. The message must have gotten through to him because he didn't lean on me. Instead, he seemed to be trying to undermine the interpersonal dynamics of our group, which were already shaky enough. First he cast aspersions on Don, suggesting to me that my traveling partner was in a state of advanced culture shock and was ready at any moment to go off the deep end. Indeed, Don had grown more quiet and withdrawn, but he was a quiet man to begin with. In view of all the craziness—of being in Peru and hanging out with so many odd and complex people—I wasn't surprised that he was keeping his own counsel. He not only had to deal with the nutty Heraclitistas but with my nutty brother. Don must have wondered what he'd gotten himself into, but I had no doubts about his sanity.

Terence then voiced doubts about Wade. It's true that Wade and his girlfriend appeared to be having issues, but I saw this as a personal matter between them with no bearing on his abilities as an explorer. Nevertheless, Terence seized on what he saw as Wade's macho swagger. I for one was a bit in awe of Wade and was glad he'd agreed to join our party. He had every reason to give it a pass, and I viewed his acquiescence as an act of kindness. Here was a guy who had crossed the Darién Gap on foot. He was clearly among the most experienced member of our ragtag group, *and* he spoke perfect Spanish. But Terence in his provocative way loved to stir things up, if only with a few snarky asides. But what was he doing? I didn't know. Justified or not, my suspicions festered as we neared our port.

Pebas sits at the confluence of the Amazon and the Ampiyacu, which flows in from the north. Ampiyacu means "river of poisons," after *ampi*, a virulent arrow poison used by the Witoto. The area along the Ampiyacu and its tributary, the Yaguasyacu, would be the site of our search for the orally active *Virola* preparations.

The Río Yaguasyacu, or "river of the Yaguas," bears the name of the people who have traditionally lived nearby. They now shared their ancestral home with the Witotos and the closely related Boras who, as noted earlier, had been driven from their territory north of the Putumayo. The Witotos and Boras living in the Pebas region were a culturally traumatized people whose plant knowledge had largely degenerated or been lost. Nevertheless, we still viewed them as our best bet for obtaining samples of *oo-koo-hé*—or *ku-ru-ku*, as the Bora called it. We intended to start collecting around Puco Urquillo, a short distance up the Ampiyacu, then move to Brillo Nuevo, a more remote Witoto village on the Yaguasyacu.

It took us a couple of runs to haul the entire party and our supplies upriver to Puco Urquillo. We arrived with a recorded message in Witoto for Don Alfredo, made by his grand-daughter, Adriana, back in Iquitos. The impressive introduction worked. After hearing the tape, he invited us to string our hammocks in the main *maloca*, the large, oval-shaped, thatched structure that served as the village's community center. We were in! Beyond the *maloca*, the village men apparently had their own place

Don Alfredo and his first sample of *oo-koo-hé.*

where they gathered after dark to chew coca, tell stories, and sing. On our first night, we heard their mournful voices wafting across the clearing. The words were in Witoto, but the melody was eerily familiar. Then it hit us—the tune was "The House of the Rising Sun," adapted to their evening chant. The effect was incongruous and strange.

Our collecting efforts around the village were incredibly productive. Don Alfredo and his son, Vicente, took us out to collect *cumalas*—a generic name for various *Virola* species—and we found about a dozen types. They promised to provide us with *oo-koo-hé* in a day or so. The next day we repeated the exercise with a Bora man, Don Marcos, who likewise showed us a number of *cumalas* and noted those he viewed as *fuerte*—that is, suitable for making the *ku-ru-ku*. Finally, we found a medium-sized tree he said would do, chopped it down, stripped off about 60 kilograms of bark, and hauled the material back to his hut. This took about five hours.

Don Marcos separated the inner cambial layers from the outer bark, tearing them into long strips that he placed in a metal pot with a few liters of water. This was allowed to simmer over a low fire for about three hours. The inner bark was blood red and had a strong, spicy aroma. Finally, he removed the bark strips from the pot and cooked down the resulting decoction until the result looked like reddish-brown chocolate sauce. This he mixed with some powdered ashes made from the rind of an unknown fruit and macerated the whole mess together. It had a doughy consistency and looked basically like excrement. It looked even more like that when he finally scraped it from the pot, deposited it on a banana leaf, and kneaded it into a turd-like shape. This was the finished product. When I asked him how much to take, he showed me the tip of his thumb.

A day or so later, Don Alfredo showed up with his first sample, which looked similar: a reddish-brown, turd-shaped object wrapped in a banana leaf. Altogether we ended up with seven samples—four from Don Alfredo, one from Don Marcos, one from another Bora, Don Jorge, and, back in the lab in Vancouver, a sample of *oo-koo-hé* that Terence had collected at La Chorrera on his second trip. When I finally ran the analyses back in Vancouver, our informants proved as good as their word, with one exception. All of Don Alfredo's samples contained high levels of tryptamines, including DMT, 5-MeO-DMT, and related compounds. Don Marcos's samples were high in 5-MeO-DMT with smaller amounts of 5-MeO-N- methyltryptamine. Don Jorge's samples had no alkaloids, and the voucher specimen revealed it was made from *Virola pavonis*, a species known to lack alkaloids.

Our "large animal biosassays" yielded definite but not spectacular effects. Terence tried the first of Don Alfredo's preparations and said it was definitely active. I tried Don Marcos's sample shortly after we had moved upriver to the village of Brillo Nuevo. Here's what I wrote in my notes the next day:

16 March

I took the *ku-ru-ku* prepared by Don Marcos last night; about a gram to a gram and a half. Within 10 minutes, a strong effect was apparent. This first appeared as a strong burning sensation in my mouth, lips, and tongue, quickly developing into a general numbness of mouth parts, extending into the throat and causing a tightening of the throat, as though it was sore. It was difficult to swallow... my breath was labored. The numbness that began in the mouth gradually spread over the rest of my body and limbs... the extremities of my limbs tingled. I was somewhat alarmed at the rapidity of onset, and found myself reflecting on the use of *Virola* as an arrow poison—I can see how it could be an effective one. If I had to do any physical exertion in this state, I can imagine that it would have put my body under greater stress, possibly even lethal. All I could do was lie in my hammock and concentrate on continuing to breathe. My body felt very heavy, numb, and dissociated from my mind.

There were never any frank hallucinations—only brief flashes and the feeling that they were almost ready to effluorish [sic] out. I was in this semi-narcotized state for perhaps one half hour to 45 minutes. My body also felt cold… a pronounced and abrupt lowering of body temperature that accompanied the general slowing of autonomic functions. This effect persisted the longest—in fact, I was chilly all night. After about 45 minutes … breathing eased slightly, and I fell off into a drowsy reverie somewhere between sleeping and waking … no visual hallucinations ever became the overwhelming feature of the experience. Judging from the effects, I would say the 5-MeO-DMT is the principle component of this resin. Most of the "pressor amine" properties were present, but almost no "psychedelic" feeling. It seems to be more effective as a general anesthetic than as a hallucinogen.

Thus Terence and I became the first non-Indigenous people to bioassay the legendary orally active *Virola* "narcotic" resin, or at least the first to report on its effects. My speculation that it was mainly 5-MeO-DMT proved accurate. Back in the lab, this sample analyzed out to contain a high level of 5-MeO-DMT and a small trace of 5-MeO-N-methyltryptamine. There was no DMT at all in the sample. It was interesting, but the heavy body load was a bit scary. I had no particular desire to repeat it. Compared to mushrooms, as a psychedelic this was nothing to write home about.

I was totally stoked over the results of the last few days of collecting. Our efforts had turned out to be everything I had hoped for. I managed to collect an extensive series of *cumalas*, complete with voucher specimens, pickled samples, and notes from our local informants. In addition, we had collected six fresh samples of the orally active pastes and photographs of Don Marcos preparing one of the batches. Our fieldwork was a total success and gave me plenty of material to sort out later in the lab.

Brillo Nuevo, on the Yaguasyacu, lived up to its name: New Shine. As we moved upriver, we found our new base to be more picturesque than Puco Urquillo. We moved into a nice guesthouse by the river, which compared to the communal *maloca* afforded us a modicum of privacy. A short stroll down a path through the forest took us to a lovely pasture where a number of zebu cattle grazed contentedly—an ideal habitat for mushrooms. Here's what I wrote in my notebook that afternoon:

19 March

We have broken through into some kind of paradisiacal place—Brillo Nuevo is certainly paradisiacal compared to Puco Urquillo. Certainly a strange experience to walk up to those pastures after settling in here yesterday afternoon. A heavy feeling of déjà vu. After 10 years, we return to the same place (essentially) but this time, we see it clearly and understand how much we understand. But do we really know anything?

Gentle rains fell a couple of days after our arrival, ensuring that mushrooms would magically manifest in the pasture within a day or two. We were not disappointed. The morning of March 21 dawned sunny and warm, and the pasture, still steaming from the showers the night before, was dotted with big clusters of carpophores. We lost no time in collecting a healthy haul of the biggest and best and planned to take them together that very evening, or at least some of us did. Terence and I had been busy trying our *oo-koo-hé* and *ku-ru-ku* samples over the previous days, but we figured there had been sufficient time to clear the residual tryptamines from our systems.

That night Nada, Moondancer, Terence, and I all took mushrooms in our guesthouse. Wade, Etta, and Don took a pass, as did Juan, our faithful but taciturn and ever-enigmatic guide. It was a quiet but strong trip. The next day, Terence, feeling peaceful and renewed, pronounced it "the trip I came here to have." This bugged me. I wasn't so sure it was the trip *I* had come to have. It started out typically enough with the usual efflorescence of

The village of Brillo Nuevo.

hallucinations, but then I was plunged into a dark and depressing place. I felt my many long-standing grudges against Terence bubbling up and was surprised by my anger and resentment. The events of the last weeks, the rejection letter from Sheila, the weird interpersonal dynamics of the Hera-clitistas, Terence's provocative behavior, my old childhood jealousies—all of this coagulated into a toxic knot of resentment in my gut. It was not a pleasant experience or a particularly useful one.

Days later, as we slowly made our way back upriver to Iquitos, I reflected on this:

23 March

My trip . . . became very introspective and depressing. I found myself wondering what in God's earth had motivated me to come here, why I had sacrificed the woman I love to come to this hell hole in search of . . . what? I had the feeling that the work I am trying to do . . . is of no possible significance to anyone, not even myself. Particularly myself in view of what I have lost in order to do this thing. . . . I found myself feeling great resentment toward Terry in this regard. . . . He is already talking about my thesis and how great it is going to be, as though he had written it. In his mind, he regards it as already done. Easy for him—he is not looking at two to three more years of continued poverty and loneliness in order to make it a reality—a reality from which he will undoubtedly benefit as much or more than I. These feelings are not quite as strong now, in the light of two days away from the trip that precipitated them. Still, there is food for thought here and some points that would bear discussion . . . perhaps if we get a chance to travel alone we can talk about them.

If I was feeling conflicted, I was not alone. Since we'd achieved the goals of our expedition ahead of time, thanks to our lucky break in collecting *cum-ala* specimens and the paste preparations, we decided to head back to Iquitos earlier than planned. For most urbanized outsiders, being in the jungle for any length of time is uncomfortable no matter how favorable the weather or the circumstances, and the environment was beginning to take its toll on us. Terence aptly observed that we were like infectious microbes injected into the circulation. As soon as the barrier is breached, the invader is attacked by swarms of macrophages that start to nibble away, slowly tearing it apart piece by piece. And we'd only been in the field for a couple of weeks. Ours was an unlikely group to have been thrown together. Far more wearing than the physical discomforts were the tensions that seemed to be infecting our little band. Those we'd brought with us and, in close quarters and under stress, they'd festered. Why is it usually the psychodynamics that tend to undermine these efforts and turn them into misadventures? Maybe that's what the Heraclitistas and the Biospherians were really studying. In the end, human beings are ornery, recalcitrant, and screwed up. Whether or not one takes psychedelics has little influence on that.

Writing in my notebook as we made our way back to Iquitos, I could feel the tensions of our strange interlude lifting somewhat. It was clear to me that another two or three weeks in that hostile environment would have broken us in health and spirit. Looking around, I could see I wasn't the only one with private worries and pressures. Wade had been under stress, concerned about the course of his scientific career, the choices before him, dealing with his girlfriend. He'd certainly had enough of us.

Nada and Moondancer were caught up in the peculiar life-structure of the community aboard the *Heraclitus*; they were with our party but not of it. Terence, thorny as usual, always the trickster, had his own idiosyncratic understanding of what we'd accomplished. Don seemed in better spirits, and who could blame him?

As I concluded in my journal entry that day, Iquitos and civilization would never look so good as it would when we arrived there in the morning.

* * *

Terence standing beside a *cumala* tree near Puco Urquillo.

Back in Iquitos, we spent the next few days recuperating, drying and processing specimens, and sorting out the voucher samples we'd give to various institutions. I had contracted a serious chigger infection at Brillo Nuevo and my legs were a mass of sores; I went on a regimen of tetracycline and hydrogen peroxide washes to control it. We had brought back fresh *Virola* seeds and live cuttings and planted them temporarily at Adriana's place until they could be dug up and prepared for transport. We reconnected with Nicole and spent a few pleasant evenings with her at Don Giovanni's Italian Restaurant (those who are familiar with Iquitos today will know it as the site of the Yellow Rose of Texas, the current gringo watering hole in town). Nada and Moondancer returned to their berths and their shipmates on the *Heraclitus*. Wade was completely done, in every sense, with the Heraclitistas and with us, and he and Etta decided to move on to Lima. Don had separated himself from our group, pleading a desire to move into a cheaper hotel. It was as good an excuse as any.

Terence and I still had one mission to accomplish before he departed for California. By this time, we'd collected many tryptamine-containing specimens, but one important plant had eluded us: *chagropanga*, also called *oco-yagé*, the jaguar *yagé*, or spotted *yagé*. In ayahuasca, this plant was sometimes used in lieu of the common DMT admixture, *Psychotria viridis*. In fact, *oco-yagé* was a liana in the same family as *Banisteriopsis*, the other key component in the brew, and at one time had been considered a *Banisteriopsis* species. Now properly known as *Diplopterys cabrerana*, this vine differs from *B. caapi* in that it doesn't contain the MAO-inhibiting beta-carboline alkaloids that render DMT orally active. Rather, its leaves were apparently a source of DMT itself, and in staggering amounts—perhaps two or three times the levels found in *Psychotria*. In Ecuador, and in Colombia north of the Putumayo, *oco-yagé* was the admixture of choice, but most practitioners around Iquitos shunned it. In 1976, when Terence asked Don Fidel about this plant, he said he knew of it but dismissed it as "*muy bizarro*." Yes, very bizarre—in other words, just what we were looking for.

Inquiries among our informants had come up dry. Terence and I wanted to get our hands on it so he could take cuttings back. We had one lead left—Tim Plowman had collected it in Tarapoto in the mid-1970s. He had given us a collection number and a specific location so we resolved to track it down.

The morning of April 7 found us 450 kilometers south of Iquitos, having just landed at the airport in Tarapoto. We checked into a hotel just off the

Plaza de Armas, kicked back, smoked a little hash, and went off to explore the place. Tarapoto sat about 350 meters above sea level, and the higher altitude made it cooler than Iquitos. It seemed like a lovely little town, and I remarked in my notebook how much it reminded me of Kauai. We went immediately to the site where Tim had collected his *chagropanga* sample, Plowman 6041, nearly a decade earlier—a spot on the edge of town near the Río Shilcayo, a small stream running through a shallow valley dotted here and there with modest houses and gardens. Unfortunately, the collection site had been bulldozed years before and was now the site of a fancy tourist hotel.

What to do? In similar situations, we'd found that if we went to the market and talked to the herb ladies, we'd quickly meet someone who knew about ayahuasca, or who knew someone else who knew. That's how we'd met Don Fidel in Pucallpa. So we figured we'd give that a shot. The next morning we found every conceivable thing for sale at the crowded market except herbs. There were no herb ladies or herb stalls to be seen. Someone suggested we look up the owner of a bar where the *vegetalistas* hung out sometimes, and off we went.

Terence packing seeds to take back to California, April 1981.

Thus began a rambling search that lasted seven days. One inquiry led to another. Every person sort of knew about what we wanted but knew others who would certainly know. Sometimes valuable discoveries occur while you're looking for something else. In this case, it was the acquaintance of one Francisco Montes Shuña, the proprietor of a photo studio upstairs from a restaurant. A tall thin man, Francisco was originally from Pucallpa. He said he knew Don Fidel. He suggested I look up his cousin when I returned to Pucallpa, a guy named Pablo Amaringo Shuña, an English teacher, painter, and musician.

Our eventual encounter with Pablo Amaringo would lead to a series of friendships and events that would play out over many years. Then unknown to the world, Pablo would later gain fame as a brilliant, self-taught painter of ayahuasca visions, thanks in part to my efforts and those of Luis Eduardo Luna. We "discovered" him and brought his work to the attention of a wider audience, a story I'll save for another chapter. Francisco, Pablo's cousin, turned out to be an excellent ethnobotanist and *ayahuasquero*, and I ended up working with him on my second trip to Peru in 1985. During the 1990s, Kat helped him establish an ethnobotanical garden outside Iquitos called the Jardín Etnobotánico Sachamama.

Back in Tarapoto in April 1981, however, we were focused on getting our hands on *chagropanga*. We learned it was known locally as *"pucahuasca"* and not much about it beyond that. Though we never did find it, our quest brought us in contact with many interesting people and a variety of plants and plant knowledge. We also got serious cases of dysentery after a grueling hike with some local informants. For the next two days we lay wracked with diarrhea and abdominal cramps in our hotel room. It was all we could do to crawl to the toilet and back to the bed. We could barely muster up the energy to smoke hash, and that was all we wanted to do. Terence had thought to include a small bottle of laudanum (tincture of opium) in his medicine kit, so we alternated between smoking hashish and taking periodic droppers of opium. There is nothing better than opium for diarrhea, and I believe we would have been much worse off without it. The symptoms gradually faded, and we flew to Iquitos.

By then, Terence's return to California was quickly approaching. Our recent confinement had only heightened the irritation I'd felt toward him since our time on the River of Poisons. Terence's brusque way of dealing with the people we met in our search had begun to disturb me. I rankled at what I perceived to be his lack of respect as he seemed to verge on saying, "Just shut up and cough up the plant, already." While I surely had some cause to be annoyed, I could sense my reaction was overblown. Why couldn't I just shrug it off? As I knew even then, the psychological dynamics at play were far more interesting than my gripes. Once again, I turned to my notebook in an effort to make sense of the peculiar virulence of my reactions.

For both of us, the mushroom trip at Nuevo Brillo seemed to have awakened what I called "the 'brother' business" at La Chorrera. At issue was our conceit about being parts of a single mind. In a long passage, I found myself exploring this idea, wondering if something in our ancestry or genetic makeup might have accounted for the close connection between us. That led me to wonder what effects, if any, embryogenesis might leave on the mother, a biochemical imprint of some sort that might later influence the development of a subsequent child. My thoughts were mostly a form of escape or play—a chance to speculate about the mysterious complexity of life. I sensed a glimmer of insight hidden in those musings, one that would never be articulated until Terence and I had "explored the potentially traumatic and hair-raising psychological back-alleys of what it means for us to be brothers." A few words later, my thought broke off, never to be resumed.

Reading that passage 30 years later, I found it puzzling and yet somehow important. If nothing else, I could see that even 10 years after La Chorrera, I was still struggling to come to terms with what had happened there.

Easter Sunday in Iquitos dawned wet and dreary. We spent it as we had the days before, preparing for Terence's departure, organizing our specimens, securing the necessary permits to export live plants, and packing them for shipment. The drizzle continued the next morning as our taxi threaded its way through the rain-slick streets of Iquitos to the airport.

As I watched his plane disappear into the lowering overcast, I was overcome with a feeling of sadness and loss. I somehow knew we'd never again be in South America together. I could sense that his departure marked the close of a chapter in our relationship, a chapter that had opened 10 years previously, at another airport in another country, when my plane touched down in Bogotá prior to our trip to La Chorrera. That event was many twists back in the helical spiral that bound our lives. I had no idea what the next turn of the spiral would bring. The confusion and conflict that I had felt toward my brother during our most recent adventure had brought little clarity or resolution. All I knew for certain was that the currents of fate and destiny that had brought us together were now, inevitably, causing us to drift apart. We were still in touch, but we would never be as close as we had been during the decade just past. At least not until the end, an end that neither of us imagined or wanted and that was still nearly 20 years in the future.

Don had already departed by the time we returned to Iquitos. He'd left a message saying that he was heading to the Sierra for more collecting and probably would not meet me in Lima for the flight out in a week or so. This was probably the last time he was going to be in Peru for a long time, his message said, maybe ever. He wanted to stay a few weeks longer and use the time to see what the highlands had to offer. I'm sure part of his motivation was to escape us and our peculiar preoccupations.

I was ready to leave. My funds were running low, and I felt that I had accomplished what I had come for. I missed North American food, and I wanted a bit of old-fashioned, first-world comfort. First, however, I decided to stop in Pucallpa. I wanted to see Don Fidel again and have another ceremony with him, and if possible collect some additional samples of ayahuasca and *chacruna*, the *Psychotria* admixture. I also wanted to track down samples of *chicorro*, a purportedly hallucinogenic sedge that was important in Shipibo medicine. I also thought I might be able to secure a few more *Psilocybe* spore prints to augment those I had collected at Brillo Nuevo. My journal entry for April 30 reflects my less than sanguine mood:

> Another rainy day in Pucallpa. The place is beginning to pall on me, the filth, the mud and squalor seem depressing and almost too much to tolerate. I have had enough of Peru for a while, and find my thoughts increasingly turning over the mechanics of how to engineer a satisfactory exit out of here.

It took me another four days to catch a flight out to Lima. Once again, the delay proved fortunate. I decided to use the extra time to look for Pablo Amaringo Shuña, the cousin of Francisco Montes, the man I'd met in Tarapoto. The address Francisco gave me for Pablo led me to the same village where Don Fidel lived. At Pablo's house, an old woman said he was out but due back later. I decided to stop in at a local cantina and return in an hour or so.

I was nursing my second beer through a drowsy afternoon when a small, sharp-faced man approached me at the bar. Introducing himself in Spanish

Pablo Amaringo (on guitar) and friends.

as Pablo Amaringo, he said his mother had mentioned I'd been looking for
him. I explained what I'd been doing in Peru and how that led me to meet
his cousin. We had a nice conversation in Spanish and English over a couple
of beers. It turned out he taught English in the local high school in addition
to his amateur work as a painter and a musician. After we returned to his
house, he introduced me to his mother, who turned out to be the woman
I'd met earlier, and showed me his battered guitar.

Opening a dresser in his bedroom, he pulled out a bunch of paintings
on what appeared to be fiberboard. They were representations of various
jungle scenes—pretty, I thought, but unremarkable. When I told him that
I was due to leave Pucallpa for Lima the next evening, he insisted that I
come back out to the village the next afternoon so he and his friends could
perform a concert for me. I was not particularly into it, but I wanted to be
polite and so I accepted, promising to bring some beer.

When I got there the next day, he and three or four of his companions,
each playing a different instrument, regaled me with a performance that was
memorable more for its exuberance than its polish. We had a wonderful time. I
eventually left in a taxi for the hotel and collected my luggage for the flight out
later that evening. I departed Pucallpa with music still echoing in my memory,
pleasantly buzzed, and suffused with the warm glow of new friendship. My
gloom had dissipated; it was the right way to leave Peru. Whatever its faults,
the warmth and kindness of its people more than make up for them. I still

cherish many of the friendships I made on that first trip, and many others I've made there since then. Pablo would become one of my closest Peruvian friends, our fates intertwined in ways we could not have imagined.

Midnight on May 10 found me on a direct flight from Lima to Vancouver. As the jet taxied out before takeoff, my thoughts were heavy with reflection. I had gotten a letter from Sheila a couple of days earlier, and it had stirred up much of the confusion and resentment I'd been struggling to suppress. She'd broken up with her new boyfriend, who was headed to Ontario to continue his studies. Her note was not an apology or a plea to get back together, but it hinted, perhaps, at a modicum of regret that our relationship had ended as it had. Which only made me angry. For God's sake, I thought, can't these things ever just be over? Why did we have to stir all this up again? Why drag it out? I'd done too much of that already in my life. It seemed just better to be done with it, to make a clean break. Here's what I wrote:

12:00 A.M. 10 May—aboard CP Air 423

Waiting aboard the 747 warming up to scream me out of here, I find much opportunity for reflection on the trip and the return—what awaits me (or does not await me) in North America. In many ways I am sad to leave Peru—the experiences we have had, the people we have encountered, the sights we have seen will be with me always. It is definitely a country I must return to someday; it is far too complex to be understood in one visit ... funny that I have come to feel more at home in Peru than in Vancouver. All the different scenes, good and bad, that await me there leave me with mixed feelings. Much of this revolves around Sheila. Her most recent letter has stirred everything up again. The thing that I have to realize is that the affair is over; no matter what is said, nothing can restore it. But I suppose at this stage to rant and rave will have little effect; it is probably better just to say as little, and see her as little, as possible. There are many other things to keep me busy, and to take my mind off it; it is these that I must concentrate on. Only time will tell what other possibilities exist on the social/emotional horizon. But one thing is certain: there is nothing to further misguided efforts to resurrect a relationship that is dead. It's dead, and that's it.

In a few minutes now I will be torn from Peruvian soil, perhaps never to return ... very strange to think about, how fast these past four months have gone, when one thinks about it. What new discoveries and adventures lie ahead? This is the thing to think of; the future is alive with undreamed of possibilities.

And later:

Dawn . . . somewhere over North America . . . beautiful, bright and clear day here in the stratosphere . . . I would guess we are somewhere over the Southwest. A few hours sleep, comfortable cozy sleep here in the tender cares of CP Air, and Peru becomes like a dream . . . did it ever happen? Or was it merely a brief flash during a momentary snooze? Yet the physical evidence, the metal airplane, my bags and bottles and beads, &c., is testimony that indeed I was in Peru, traveled and worked there, saw its sights and met its people. Odd then how thoroughly obviated the experience becomes by the simple act of leaving. Not even arrived in Vancouver yet and already it seems a fading memory.

At Canadian customs in the early morning light, I figured the one sleepy-eyed officer would thoroughly inspect everything. I had a shitload of specimen bottles, pressed herbarium specimens, dried barks, baskets, woven chambira bags, Shipibo textiles, blowguns, bark paintings, and live plants—in short, all the things one might accumulate over four months of collecting in the jungle. I also had my plant import permits and phytosanitary certificates at the ready, as well as Neil Towers's phone number in case things got sticky. I was prepared for a shakedown lasting two or three hours. The customs agent looked at me and then at my stuff spread out on the table. Looking back at me with a shake of her head, she said, "You're the person my supervisor warned me about. Get out of here."

And I did! I was home.

Inspired by my good luck in the field, I lost no time in plunging back into my work. I found another skanky basement apartment and settled in. I had plenty to do. I first saw Sheila a few weeks after returning. Our encounter wasn't at all what I'd expected. These things never are. I was prepared to denounce her and move on. Instead we fell into each other's arms. All the hurtful things I was prepared to say, I could not say. All the bitterness and anger I had nursed for months just melted away. She was sorry for what had happened. She wanted to be with me again, and I wanted to be with her. What had happened in my absence was forgiven and forgotten as a bad misunderstanding.

Over that summer, we realized we were meant to be together. By the time the fall semester started, we were sharing an apartment. My heart was full. I felt I'd finally moved beyond emotional upheavals of my 20s. I had exciting work ahead of me, and a good woman, a woman I loved, at my side. Life was good.

43 Adulthood and Its Victims

Dennis working in the lab in Vancouver.

The three years between my return from Peru and the completion of my graduate degree in 1984 was a time of work and study. While I continued my lab investigations, Sheila pursued a degree in nursing. Shortly before we'd moved in together, she'd decided that estuarine seaweed ecology, the focus of her master's project, was not really her passion. She was more interested in the health sciences, and nursing in particular. She had worked as a nurse's aide in Kelowna in previous summers, so she had some knowledge of what that life involved. Her decision was also a practical one. Nursing is a portable profession that allows one to get a job almost anywhere, unlike algal ecology—or ethnopharmacology, for that matter. Her employability would benefit both of us over my years ahead as an itinerant scientist.

In 1981, we spent our first Christmas together in Kamloops with Sheila's parents and siblings. Though her family members were quite different from me—and from Sheila, really—they were kind and genuine people who accepted me, however strange I must have seemed to them. I would have seemed even stranger, I'm afraid, had I really been myself. Sheila knew I was putting on a bit of an act and she played along, though even she was perhaps not yet fully aware of my peculiar interests—or at least that's what I felt. For the time being, that I could pretend to be normal would apparently be good enough.

That December in Vancouver, I first met Luis Eduardo Luna, the Colombian scholar whom Terence had befriended a decade earlier in Florencia, after his second visit to La Chorrera. Luis Eduardo struck me as extremely reticent and polite. I knew who he was, of course, and the story of how his time with Terence and Ev in 1971 had affected the course of his life. Their chance encounter was all the more unlikely in that Luis Eduardo was something of a stranger in his hometown, having been away for much of his youth. His early schooling had largely taken place in Bogotá. At 17, he'd moved to Spain and begun his studies in Madrid. It was Terence who first told him about the use of *yagé* among the Amazon tribes much closer to Florencia. Luis Eduardo's father had known, however, and reminded him of an Ingano shaman named Apolinar Yacanamijoy who occasionally visited the town. In early 1972, Luis Eduardo tracked him down and asked him if he'd be willing to teach him about *yagé*. Don Apolinar told Eduardo he'd have to spend an extended time with him mastering the lore and following the apprentice's special diet.

Eduardo then returned to school in Europe. His immersion in shamanism would have to wait. After finishing his studies in Madrid, he moved to Norway, where he lectured about Spanish and Latin American literature at Oslo University while taking courses in the natural sciences and linguistics. In 1979, he got a teaching job at the Swedish School of Economics in Helsinki, which gave him the security he needed to begin his ethnographic research on *yagé* in the company of the Ingano shaman he'd approached seven years earlier.

On a visit with Don Apolinar in 1980, the old man agreed to work with Luis Eduardo over the summer of 1981, if he lived that long, he said. In May 1981, shortly before Luis Eduardo's scheduled return from Europe, word reached him that Don Apolinar had died.

Unsure how to proceed with his research, he sought advice from Terence, who suggested he redirect his efforts to the area around Iquitos. There, in 1981, Luis Eduardo met a number of old-school Mestizo *ayahuasqueros*—there wasn't yet a new school—including Don Emilio Andrade Gómez. Don Emilio became Luis Eduardo's primary mentor and informant for nearly 20 years, until his death in 1997. The use of *yagé*, or ayahuasca, among the region's tribal peoples had already been documented by Western scholars. Much less was known about its role among Mestizo practitioners. Luis Eduardo spent the next several years researching that question. His PhD thesis, "*Vegetalismo*: Shamanism Among the Mestizo Population of the Peruvian Amazon" (1986), became the definitive ethnographic work in this field, and he gained a well-deserved reputation as the world's authority on *vegetalismo*. His 1982 documentary about Don Emilio entitled *Don Emilio and His Little Doctors* has since been recognized as a classic of ethnographic filmmaking.

Sheila and I didn't do much traveling over those years, tied down as we were by our studies. In the fall of 1981 we took a vacation to Hawaii on some of the funds from the settlement over my bike accident. A more memorable trip occurred two years later, when we drove to California for a brief stay with Terence and his family. That was Sheila's first chance to spend time with them—and to learn the scope of the peculiar ideas my brother and I had entertained over the years. After a few days, Terence must have realized I hadn't shared all of my checkered past with my new love. At one point he turned to her and said, "He hasn't told you yet, has he?"

And in truth I had not. I didn't want to frighten her away. She knew I liked mushrooms and was a bit of a freak; she, too, had been immersed in the counterculture so that didn't alarm her. My fear was she had no idea how "counter" the counterculture could be. Terence handed her a copy of *The Invisible Landscape* and told her she needed to read it, which she proceeded to do. When afterward she didn't run away screaming, I took that as a very good sign.

By then, Terence had begun getting a lot of attention for his "rap," as he called it. His personality and ideas began to attract a wider audience. He'd been doing some radio, notably *Something's Happening*, the program created in 1977 by Roy Tuckman, alias Roy of Hollywood, on the Los Angeles station KPFK. If I recall, Terence had another work in progress at the time, an audiocassette version of *True Hallucinations*, released in 1984, almost a decade before that story appeared in book form. In May 1983, Terence had appeared at a landmark conference on psychedelics at the University of California, Santa Barbara, alongside luminaries like Albert Hofmann, Sasha Shulgin, Andrew Weil, and Ralph Metzner. His edgy talk was titled

"Hallucinogens: Monkeys Discover Hyperspace, aka Return to the Logos." It was quite unlike anything else presented there and marked an important moment in the emergence of his public persona. People loved hearing his wild ideas, and Terence's mesmeric voice and articulate presentation made him the perfect spokesman.

In one sense, it might not have mattered what he said. His audiences tended to be uncritical, or at least they seldom challenged him. People usually listened in slack-jawed fascination. I used to kid Terence that he could stand up and read the phone book and listeners would hang on every word, because it wasn't what he said, it was that he said it so darn well. His rap was not science. It was not exactly philosophy either. It was poetry, and Terence was inventing himself as the Irish bard of the psychedelic zeitgeist. The things he said resonated with people. Terence became popular precisely because he could say what he said so much better than anyone else, but obviously many had been primed for his message by their psychedelic experiences. His talks were works of art; they were beautiful, and people heard in that beauty a confirmation of their own psychedelically illuminated insights. Through him, many listeners learned to trust their intuitions rather than simply accepting the assumptions of science and secularism, dreary existentialism, and religion. Terence told stories that post-scientific rationalists could believe, and in doing so he reinfused the universe with magic and wonder. He became the wizard-shaman of a resacralized cosmos scintillating with psychedelically charged portent and permeated with life and intelligence and love. Having discovered the "machine elves" that seemed to exist in the hyperspace of the tryptamine state, he became their ringmaster, jumping them through their hoops for an enthralled new generation of psychedelic acolytes.

This was Terence's strength and talent, and I give him his due for being able to articulate that message to so many and for so long. Indeed, his talks seem as fresh and stimulating today as they were back in the 1980s and '90s. Twelve years after his death, they remain remarkably contemporary and timely. He has achieved a weird kind of immortality. He has become a kind of ghost, haunting the back roads of cyberspace, and the vast body of his talks and raps will live forever on the Net. I think Terence would have appreciated that.

I am contacted by many young people who were in diapers or not even born when Terence was at the height of his career, who tell me they first started thinking and wondering about the Big Questions, questions about the meaning of life for us as individuals and as a species, as a result of listening to Terence's speeches and raps. Many tell me that his work has brought hope and meaning, curiosity and wonder, into their lives. Some of them have become my students and friends over the years, and I owe Terence for that. It's really Terence they want, not me. I'm much more down to earth, more scientifically oriented, and people appreciate that, too. But if it weren't for Terence and his cultural impact, no one would care very much about what I might think or have to say. So for that, and for giving me platforms like this book to tell my story and share my ideas, I'm grateful to him.

While Terence had begun forging his public persona, I'd been in the lab in Vancouver, slowly working toward my degree. When he wasn't teaching in Finland, Luis Eduardo had been making his film and furthering his research with Don Emilio in Peru. Like many others who at some point had belonged to our circle going back to the Berkeley days, we'd more or less managed to integrate the heady ideals of earlier times into our adult lives.

Not everyone had been so fortunate. My last encounter with John Parker occurred in 1983, on our way back to Vancouver after our visit with Terence and Kat. John, an important early mentor, had disappeared from my world; we hadn't spoken for years. In the interim, I'd heard he'd become increasingly dysfunctional. Erik and Lisa, Terence's good friends, had by then moved to Ukiah, California, to join a Buddhist community known as the City of Ten Thousand Buddhas, founded by Lisa's longtime teacher, Hsuan Hua. (Lisa, my first real girlfriend, had been following her Buddhist practice since before the two of us were briefly together in 1969.) John, meanwhile, had moved to the nearby town of Willits. Erik and Lisa weren't in touch with him but they knew the woman he was living with, a poet. Through her they set up a time when Sheila and I could say hello to John at a local coffee shop when we passed through. He had no job; he lived off a California welfare program that gave aid to the totally disabled, which sadly he'd become. He could no more have supported himself with a job than the sun could rise in the west. It was not within the realm of possibility.

The sight of him shocked me. As odd and eccentric as John had always been, he was also brilliant and I had learned much from him in those early days, especially during our hash-fueled, late-night conversations in Boulder. I had loved him and looked up to him. The staring creature across the table from me in the coffeehouse, shrunken into a shabby woolen coat, was a shadow of the friend I had known. He had lived a hard life and it had taken its toll. Bouts of homelessness, serious abuse of alcohol and meth—all had left their mark. His sallow skin was grizzled and pockmarked, his meth-rotten teeth stained with tobacco, his eyes rheumy. He was the very picture of a man caught in a long spiral toward dissolution and death.

Our conversation was disjointed and rambling. His attention wandered, and he did not seem able to follow the thread. Only once did he brighten momentarily, the old twinkle returning to his eyes when he described his encounter with a fairy back in the woods near where he was living in a kind of cave. His spirit and passion had burned so brightly—his quick mind and amazing ideas, his kindness and humor, his freely shared knowledge of the esoteric and arcane—all of it had meant so much to me as a curious young man with an affinity for the peculiar. Now all of that was gone. The wizard's wand had lost its charge long ago. He was now a pathetic derelict, poisoned by drugs, tormented by delusions and hallucinations, his head filled with voices and visions of fairies. It made me want to cry.

It was the last time we spoke. He was Terence's age at the time, about 36, though he looked 70. We fell out of touch again for decades, and I assumed he had died at some point. I was surprised when Erik contacted me in 2005 to say that John had shown up unexpectedly at the office where he worked and that since then the two of them had occasionally gotten together for lunch. Erik, John's only link to his former friends, gave me his P.O. box number. Lisa had made it quite clear that she wanted no contact with him, and he had honored her wish.

I sent John a long letter in 2006, a rambling recap full of reminiscences, but we never communicated after that. He died a few years later outside the rotting welfare motel in Willits where he'd been living alone. Someone found him naked in the motel parking lot, draped over the hood of a car. It may have been an overdose, or poor John's abused body may have just given up. There will never be another John Parker. It was a dismal end for a singular soul.

44
The Plant Teachers: 1985

Despite all its literary associations, the year 1984 turned out to be nothing like the dystopian future we might have feared, even if we were in the darkest days of the Reagan administration. Compared to what we've witnessed since, that was an age of enlightenment and reason. In Canada, we were insulated to some degree from the idiocies of American politics, but that was about to change as we both reached the end of school. Sheila graduated with her nursing degree, and I managed to complete my PhD. Once I had completed my doctorate, the kind government of Canada, which had supported and paid for my education, let me know that my student visa was about to expire and that I needed to clear out or become an illegal immigrant. Their message, back then at least, was, "Now that you have your education, go home and help your Third World country, the United States."

So I left for California in May that year to seek my fortune. I wanted to leave British Columbia; I didn't want to leave Sheila. She was open to the idea of joining me in the States once I'd found a gig. I didn't know whether I was looking for a job or a postdoctoral fellowship. I was now an expert on the chemistry and pharmacology of two Amazonian hallucinogens, ayahuasca and *oo-koo-hé*. I had a newly minted thesis and several papers "submitted" to prove it. It wasn't a lot to parlay into an entry-level position in the Silicon Valley biotech industry.

Then I heard about a possible semi-legitimate job as an MDMA chemist. At the time, MDMA or "ecstasy," among other names, was not yet scheduled as a controlled substance—that is, it was still legal. When I arrived in California, Terence told me about a gentleman in Mendocino, an entrepreneur from Texas who was planning to establish a large-scale MDMA production operation and needed a chemist. I, with my newly minted PhD, was an ideal candidate, though I am not really a chemist. This information came indirectly through another friend and mentor, Alexander (Sasha) Shulgin, who is renowned in the psychedelic world as the brilliant inventor of numerous synthetic psychedelics. His important contributions to psychedelic pharmacology grew out of his chosen specialty: investigation of the structure/activity relationships of molecules related to mescaline. Over his career, he created and published on over 300 such derivatives. Sasha had kindly agreed to act as the outside examiner on my thesis, so we were in frequent contact. Though Sasha did not invent MDMA, he had learned of it through his students. After synthesizing and testing it on himself in 1976, he quickly recognized its potential therapeutic uses. By 1984 the drug had attracted the attention of underground therapists, who believed it could be used to facilitate psychotherapy. Though it was eventually scheduled, it is now being evaluated in several clinical studies for the treatment of post-traumatic stress disorder, or PTSD.

Terence and others encouraged me to pay this Texas fellow a visit, which I did. He was a smooth talker with big plans, but the cultlike atmosphere of the operation put me off. It seemed to be a kind of commune where MDMA was consumed more or less constantly. There was something a little strange about the whole thing. Although MDMA was not yet scheduled, there were already rumblings that it soon would be. Outside a secret plan for world dominion, I wasn't sure that producing several kilos of MDMA every week in semiautomated laboratories was such a good idea. For one thing, it was bound to attract the attention of the authorities sooner or later and I wanted to make my living legally. But after enduring relative poverty for years, I was certainly tempted. About that time, in May 1984, I was invited to a conference on psychedelics at Esalen on the topic of "Technologies of the Sacred," along with Terence, Sasha, Stan Grof, and other psychedelic celebrities. It was a marvelous, stimulating event. Having just completed my work on ayahuasca and *oo-koo-hé*, I had something to contribute to this community, but I wasn't sure how to turn my knowledge into a legitimate career.

The situation temporarily resolved itself when I got a call from Dr. Charles Thomas, director of Helicon, a small private nonprofit foundation in San Diego dedicated to investigating the relationship between nutrition and cancer. Somehow, Thomas had gotten one of the many resumes I'd mailed out before leaving Canada. He had funding for a project to investigate the relationship between dietary selenium and cancer. There was epidemiological and demographic evidence that a diet rich in selenium could prevent cancer, and he had a theory that selenium prevented mutations. He was investigating this by using mutation-prone strains of yeast and needed a postdoc quickly, and invited me down for an interview. My qualifications were nil except that I knew sterile inoculation techniques from all my previous work on mushrooms, so I figured I could do as well with yeast. It was a gig, and a way to get back to the States, so I accepted his offer.

I returned to Vancouver, packed up the Merc, and drove the battleship south for the last time. I barely made it to San Diego and traded in the car as soon as I did. I quickly found a small house fronting a back alley in a San Diego neighborhood known as Normal Heights. (We used to joke: is it a place or a state of mind?) Sheila had stayed on in Vancouver to work over the summer and joined me in the fall.

I settled in at Helicon Foundation, which was located in a large warehouse in an industrial district of San Diego. Thomas was an eminent Harvard-trained molecular biologist and virologist. His father had been chairman of the board at Monsanto, so he had some family wealth. Helicon was Charlie's plaything. He didn't need the money or any outside funding; the foundation was a platform for him to conduct any research that caught his fancy. Some of the work was quite solid, and some of it was less so. Thomas belonged to a small coterie of scientists who believed that the virus known as HIV was not the cause of AIDS. In this, he's had some pretty good company, including Berkeley cell biologist Peter Duesberg and Nobel Prize winner Kary Mullis, a key developer of the polymerase chain reaction (PCR) methods that revolutionized molecular biology. I'm not qualified to say whether there is any validity to such ideas. Most mainstream scientists consider AIDS "denialism" to be a crackpot conspiracy theory. Then again, when it comes to questioning accepted dogma, mainstream science can be as hidebound and close-minded as the most fundamentalist religion, as anyone who has worked in the field of psychedelics will know. The fact that Charlie was among this group of heretics tells you a lot about the guy. He was a pain in the butt of orthodoxy. We liked each other on that basis alone. That may have surprised us both, considering how much he offended my liberal sensitivities and how I surely must have rankled the conservative in him. We maintained a productive, if edgy, relationship. He was not without a sense of humor, and I think he was at least a competent scientist even if he did have funny ideas about AIDS.

Soon after, Sheila joined me in San Diego. The time had arrived for us to formalize our relationship and get married, in part so she could apply for a green card and find a job. Both Sheila and I were recovering Catholics who wanted nothing to do with Roman Catholicism. Instead, we made plans to get married in a local Gnostic church with a laid-back, sandal-wearing

A proud father and his two sons on Dennis's wedding day, 1984.

pastor. It was a perfect fit for us. The Gnostic faith seemed more genuine and less revisionist to us than our childhood religion. The Gnostics, after all, were the real deal, and perhaps even mushroom cultists in the distant past. This little church specialized in weddings; that's how they supported themselves. They'd perform the simple ceremony and sign the certificate, no muss, no fuss, and they wouldn't be coming after us to attend services or otherwise take part in their community.

We had a very sweet, and very small, wedding in October. Dad and his wife Lois were there, along with Terence, Kat, and their kids, our friends Mike and Ellen from our UBC graduate student days, and Iris Pugh, who together with her late husband Truman had taken Terence in for his senior year in high school in Lancaster. We had the reception in our backyard. We stayed overnight at a local bed-and-breakfast—our honeymoon—and the next day the entire family went to the San Diego Zoo in Balboa Park. It was about as low-key (and cheap) a wedding as one could hope for.

And with that our lives resumed. Sheila found a job in a long-term care facility, which wasn't the most desirable position, but there were no jobs available in acute-care hospitals. As for me, the Helicon gig was just that, a gig. I had no particular interest in the work. I was an ethnobotanist, after all, and saw my career path as lying more in that direction. I started plotting my next move almost as soon as I got to San Diego.

It was only after we had moved to San Diego that I started to benefit, indirectly, from Terence's growing fame. When Roy Tuckman learned that I lived in San Diego, he invited me on *Something's Happening* a couple of times, so that afforded me my first modest entry into the public arena. Later, in 1986, with the help of Terence and one of his Hollywood friends, we organized a conference in Santa Monica called "Hallucinogens in Ethnomedicine." Terence was a featured guest, along with Luis Eduardo Luna and Douglas Sharon, the director of the San Diego Museum of Man. Sharon had become a minor figure in the psychedelic pantheon thanks to his book *Wizard of the Four Winds: A Shaman's Story*, published in 1978. That turned out be a nice little gathering, though far less influential than the earlier Santa Barbara event.

In 1985, Luis Eduardo Luna invited me to present a paper on my work on ayahuasca at the 45th International Congress of the Americanists, to be held at the University of the Andes in Bogotá, Colombia, that July. He had organized a satellite symposium on ayahuasca and invited me along with a number of established anthropologists, including Michael Taussig from Columbia University. I was the only botanist or phytochemist to be invited. Luis Eduardo had been conducting ethnographic fieldwork in Peru every summer with his mentor, Don Emilio, and teaching during the winters in Helsinki. Together we presented a paper combining the ethnographic data we'd collected, mainly from Don Emilio but also from other informants, on the "plant teachers," or *plantas que enseñan*, with the phytochemical and pharmacological data I had collected, mainly through extensive literature reviews.

In the *vegetalismo* tradition, ayahuasca is at the center of a vast pharmacopoeia of medicinal plants that are used either as admixtures to the brew or by themselves. Like ayahuasca and its most commonly used DMT-containing admixtures, all these plants are regarded as intelligent, and the apprentice shaman must learn their properties by keeping a strict diet and consuming the plants, either alone or as part of ayahuasca. In this way, the plants will "teach" the apprentice their properties and uses in curing. Some of the plants in this traditional pharmacopoeia are among the most toxic and biologically active plants known from the Amazon, so it is not surprising that they possess a complex chemistry and pharmacology, even apart from their spiritual qualities.

Eduardo and I had collaborated on this paper before I left UBC, and we presented it at the conference. We submitted it for publication in the symposium proceedings, and it was published in Spanish in the prestigious journal *America Indigena*. Later, an English version was published in a book coedited by Schultes entitled *Ethnobotany: Evolution of a Discipline* (1995).

I also presented another paper on my chemical and pharmacological investigations of ayahuasca and some of my work on *oo-koo-hé*. Both of my papers had been recently published in the *Journal of Ethnopharmacology*, and I was quite proud of the recognition my work had gotten. My pride quickly withered, however, when Michael Taussig launched into a 30-minute polemic, in Spanish, that was basically a criticism of reductionist science and the absurdity of my presumption that studying the chemistry or pharmacology of these plants could ever explain anything of significance about them or their true role in ethnomedicine, that all this work was bullshit and I was a fool and charlatan (not to mention a pawn of the pharmaceutical industry) for having the temerity even to show up at this symposium, and that I should be publicly flogged, if not executed, on the spot for being the contemptible piece of shit that I was. Or something like that. I understood very little Spanish at the time and could not really defend myself against this tirade, which was probably merciful or I would have been even more mortified. It was a useful lesson in the viciousness of academic discourse, and probably in my need for humility. Many years later, one of Taussig's students was in an ethnobotany course I taught in Ecuador, and he suggested that I should not have felt singled out for persecution. Taussig treated pretty much everyone that way, he said; it was just his style of discourse.

It didn't really matter. I had come back to South America for bigger things than simply going to the conference. I had managed to raise enough funds to support six weeks of collecting in Peru following the conference. Eduardo had invited me to visit his ancestral home in Florencia, and I spent some time there after the conference. I then headed south to Iquitos, where I met up with two Iranian guys who had seen my talks in San Diego and were interested in learning about ayahuasca and mushrooms. They had agreed to pay part of my travel expenses if I'd act as their guide for a couple of weeks and show them the ropes. This went quite smoothly. By then Nicole was living in Iquitos, in a small casita inside a walled pension owned by the Schapers, an old Iquitos family, and we were able to stay there as well. Mushrooms were easy enough to find in the pastures out along the highway, and we connected with a good *ayahuasquero* for several satisfying trips. The Iranians left happy.

Eduardo and I had arranged to meet in Pucallpa after I finished in Iquitos, and I flew there and checked into the beloved El Pescador out near Lago Yarinacocha. If corporate had sent down a memo to upgrade the place, it had gotten lost in the mail. The hotel was as basic and shabby as it had been on my visit four years earlier. They'd added another porcelain toilet, which was perpetually clogged, and a small cantina with *cervezas* that were more or less chilled, so I guess that qualified as improvement.

The purpose of my trip was to reconnect with Francisco Montes Shuña, the cousin of Pablo Amaringo whom Terence and I had originally met during our search for the elusive *chagropanga* in Tarapoto. Francisco had moved back to Pucallpa and over the intervening years had collected live specimens of many medicinal plants, including a good selection of the "teacher plants" that Eduardo had been documenting. I planned to purchase these specimens from him and import them to the States, clear them through the USDA facility in Los Angeles, and then ship them on to Hawaii. The plan was for Luis Eduardo to join me in San Diego at the conclusion of our trip, pick up the collections in L.A., and transport them on to Hawaii. All of this involved a lot less red tape than it would today. Terence and Kat were temporarily living in the house they'd recently built on the Big Island and were eager to receive the specimens.

A secondary goal of our work in Pucallpa was to introduce Luis Eduardo to Don Fidel, the *ayahuasquero* with whom both Terence and I had met earlier. Luis Eduardo had been spending time with Don Emilio and other *ayahuasqueros* in his fieldwork around Iquitos but had yet to visit Pucallpa. The visit was a chance to renew contact with Don Fidel and benefit from his remarkable insights and skills.

The most significant event of our stay in Pucallpa was unanticipated. I had taken Luis Eduardo to meet Francisco and his family and look at the plants he had for us, ready to ship. Afterward, I suggested we stop by Pablo Amaringo's house and we were lucky enough to catch him. Thanks to Luis Eduardo, I learned a number of things about Pablo I hadn't gathered during our previous conversations. The big surprise was that Pablo had been a powerful *ayahuasquero* years earlier but had given up that practice after getting into fights with other shamans, *brujos*, on the astral plane.

Those familiar with the traditions of *vegetalismo* know that it has a serious dark side. Much of the practice involves witchcraft and battles between shamans. The causes of illness and misfortune (which are viewed as aspects of the same thing) are attributed not to physical causes but to magical ones. *Brujos* and *brujas* are unscrupulous sorcerers or witches who harm their victims by introducing the magical darts called *virotes* into their bodies. As I noted earlier, *virotes* are akin to pathogens or infectious agents, but they act on the psychic plane. They are psychic darts that the shaman produces and keeps in his phlegm. But, like pathogens, they can cause physical and mental illnesses as well as accidents and other misfortunes. A jealous lover, for example, might pay a *brujo* to project a *virote* into a rival for the affections of a husband or boyfriend, to harm them or make them regret their actions in some way. There is a strong element of jealousy and rivalry in Mestizo society in Peru. If someone gains an advantage over another, for example, or is simply perceived to possess more wealth or social status, it's widely understood that they achieved it through skullduggery of some kind, not through hard work or good fortune. That person then becomes a target for *brujeria*.

Most *vegetalistas* are neither all good or all bad. They are "guns for hire," and if one wants to put a spell on another, there are other *vegetalistas* that one can pay to neutralize the spell, to grab the *virote* and send it back to the person who intended the harm. It's very much about power play, a shamanic arms race. A shaman's power is measured by how many teacher plants he or she has mastered, how long he or she has kept the diet, and various other criteria. If you suspect you have been hexed by an evil *brujo* or *bruja*, then you have to pay a stronger, tougher shaman to protect you and deflect the energy back.

All of this emerged in our conversation with Pablo. He had been a powerful *ayahuasquero*, he said, but had gotten into a battle with a *bruja*, a witch. It became clear to him that if he stayed in the game he faced a choice— he had to either kill her or be killed. Instead he elected to step away. He stopped practicing. He no longer took ayahuasca or used the power plants.

Pablo also described to us how he had gotten involved in *vegetalismo* in the first place, which was another fascinating story. In his early 20s, he said, he had been diagnosed with an intractable heart defect. The physicians told him there was nothing they could do. He had a congenital illness that would likely shorten his life by several decades. He consulted an *ayahuasquero* as a last resort. After a series of powerful sessions, he was visited during one ceremony by a number of white-coated figures he described as "American doctors." In his trance, he seemed to be lying on a table in a domed operating room, surrounded by high-tech equipment and these spirit healers. Disembodied, he watched as they sliced open his chest and removed his heart. They held it up above his chest and did things to it, making various incisions at strategic points, then they reimplanted it and closed up his chest. After that, he claimed, his heart condition was cured and his human doctors could detect no heart murmur or other indications of a defective heart.

Pablo's tale resembled other stories in the Mestizo ayahuasca tradition of "spirit doctors" performing magical surgeries. Given the remarkable reports of physical and spiritual healing that have been attributed to this medicine, perhaps there is something to it. It seems certain that we do not yet fully understand the dynamics of shamanic healing.

During our chat, Pablo brought out some of his paintings to show to us. Eduardo asked him if he'd ever tried to paint his ayahuasca visions. It was almost as if a light came on in his head. No, he said, that had never really occurred to him but he was willing to give it a try. When we came to his house the next morning, he showed us two visionary ayahuasca paintings that he'd done overnight. They were somewhat primitive and crude but affecting in their simplicity. It was indicative of Pablo's innocence and complete lack of any commercial motive that he had not even signed the paintings. A day later, he had created two more. He gave two to me and two to Eduardo, and the paintings that Pablo gifted to me have been proudly displayed in a place of honor in every home I have lived in since then.

Those four paintings marked the beginning of an extraordinary career. Pablo went on to create hundreds of visionary paintings over the years until his death in 2009. Luis Eduardo forged an alliance with Pablo and took on the role of his agent. He found markets for his work and arranged exhibitions in Finland, Los Angeles, and Japan. Together, Pablo and Eduardo collaborated on one of the most unique books ever created in the ethnographic literature, entitled *Ayahuasca Visions: The Religious Iconography of a Peruvian Shaman* (1991). The book consists of full-color reproductions of 49 painted "visions" depicting various aspects of the *ayahuasquero*'s apprenticeship and practice of *vegitalismo*. On each facing page, Luis Eduardo, writing in English, explains the various elements of the painting and their significance. These elements are not random, he notes. Every depicted plant, animal, and spirit has a symbolic significance and archetypal status in the Mestizo belief system. The result is a remarkable window into the cosmology of contemporary Mestizo shamanism and ayahuasca's place in it. By studying the paintings and their interpretation, one could learn a great deal about what it takes to become an accomplished *vegetalista*. Of course, the practice cannot be learned from a book alone, since two essential elements would be missing: the master who teaches the apprentice and the teacher plants themselves, particularly the plants used in making ayahuasca.

In 1988, Pablo and Luis Eduardo cofounded the Usko-Ayar Amazonian School of Painting, an art academy that in its early phases operated out of

Pablo's home outside Pucallpa. Admission was free to all the children of the village, and at one time some 300 students were enrolled to study painting under Pablo's tutelage. The art of the students was not visionary but rather focused on remarkable depictions of the plants and animals of the rainforest, astonishing in their detail and accuracy. This ability seems innate among young people who grow up surrounded by the natural environment and whose perceptions are not "clouded" by literacy. Pablo, too, produced some hyperrealistic paintings, but his stock-in-trade continued to be his visionary work. The school appeared to be a wonderful success. It gave many students a skill and a livelihood derived from depicting the rainforest rather than exploiting it. When tourists and outside markets began to take notice, some students found they could make relatively good money from the sale of their paintings. They (and their parents) began to appreciate the virtues of protecting the environment. A number of students went on to become recognized artists. Meanwhile, the "Amaringo style" of painting would have its own lasting impact. Today, in galleries in Iquitos and Pucallpa, one can find the work of many who try to emulate that style. But few truly succeed.

Like many feel-good stories, this one ended sadly, at least for Luis Eduardo, as he explained in a recent e-mail. Beginning in 1988, he worked tirelessly to promote the school. He helped obtain a grant from the Finnish government to support the school and organized exhibitions and found buyers for the paintings. He bought high-quality art supplies for the students, photographed the paintings for promotional purposes and archiving, and wrote articles about the school in various periodicals. He finally resigned in 1995, exhausted by internal squabbles and by the apparent misuse of the money he had raised by an individual who was close to Pablo. He'd also grown concerned about Pablo's use of the school as a platform to espouse his religious beliefs as he became more involved with the Jehovah's Witnesses. The final blows were the baseless accusations leveled at him, Luis Eduardo wrote. The more money he brought to the school, the more others suspected that he was putting money into his own pocket. He'd had enough.

"The project was at the end for me completely unsustainable," he explained. "It was totally pro bono. I did work as Pablo's agent, but I never took any commission from selling the art from the school, which was my way of doing something for the Amazon. My idea was the creation of a series of art schools and botanical gardens associated with them along the

Ucayali and Amazon rivers, but it was impossible." Everywhere he went in the country in pursuit of his dream, he encountered people who sought to take advantage, even as they accused him personally of stealing.

In 1995 he stopped selling Pablo's work. The two briefly reconnected in 1998, though Luis Eduardo made it clear he wanted nothing more to do with the school. He had organized an exhibition for Pablo in London and was supposed to attend another show for him in Japan. Instead, Pablo went there with someone else representing him, with unfortunate results. As Luis Eduardo put it, "he did not sell a single painting, as his work is practically unintelligible without the cultural context I was providing."

The two men never did business again.

Pablo received world recognition for the founding of Usko-Ayar and for its contributions to environmental awareness. At the Earth Summit in Rio de Janeiro in 1992, he was awarded a place on the United Nations Environmental Program Global 500 Roll of Honor. Luis Eduardo was never acknowledged for his contributions. Over the years, we've worked together and shared numerous adventures. I regard Luis Eduardo as almost like a second brother to me, and one of the most upright and ethical people I know. Once he stopped working to promote the school, others tried to do so, but the school eventually closed after Pablo's death.

Long before those tensions, in 1985, Luis Eduardo and I had a remarkable experience with Pablo, Don Fidel, and Francisco Montes. For me, the story perfectly captures the Mestizo worldview, in which the most mundane occurrences are freighted with significance and the boundary separating ordinary and nonordinary reality is thin indeed.

We had gone to Don Fidel's simple dwelling a few times and undergone the ayahuasca ceremony with him. His uncle, Don Jose, also an accomplished *ayahuasquero*, had been present at one of those sessions and invited Eduardo and me, along with Don Fidel, to come to his home the next evening and take ayahuasca again. We accepted the invitation and walked a considerable distance outside of town to Don Jose's house, a modest structure even humbler than Don Fidel's, made of earthen bricks plastered over with adobe. There was also a small walled garden. It was a cloudless night, and the moon was full.

We gathered inside the one-room hut and drank the brew at about nine or a little later. It was a peaceful, meditative session. I didn't have strong visions. After the effects had more or less passed, or so I thought, I went outside to have a cigarette and get some fresh air. The night was bright; the swollen moon had not yet set and its light, falling through a small *Brugmansia* tree, cast shadows of the branches on the hut's adobe wall. I gazed at the wall while I smoked my cigarette. Then I did a double take. The shadows cast by the moonlight bore a striking resemblance to a human face! It looked like the face of a young girl, wearing a veil over her long hair and with her hands folded in prayer. I looked away and looked again. It was definitely there. The resemblance was unmistakable. I couldn't quite believe what I was seeing and I thought I was hallucinating, though the effects had faded hours before. Finally I got up, went back into the hut, and called Eduardo outside to have a look. He agreed that it was remarkable. We both saw the same thing. We tucked that away and didn't think much about it for the rest of the evening. Later, we started our long walk back to the El Pescador, saying good night to Don Fidel, who sauntered toward home in the other direction.

The next morning, after breakfast we went over to visit Pablo, who had some bad news. Francisco's daughter, about five years old, had come down with severe diarrhea the day before and had died about three A.M. The parents had searched for Don Fidel to get some treatment for her, but he was with us at Don Jose's. They took the girl to the hospital, but the staff there was unable to provide any of the oral rehydration solution they needed to save her. It was very sad news but not uncommon in the area. Many young children die from intractable diarrhea and dehydration. The condition isn't difficult to treat, but one must have access to the remedy. In this case, circumstances had prevented Francisco from finding help for the girl. There would be a wake, a ceremony to bless the little girl, at Francisco's home that evening.

When we arrived at the house to pay our respects, everyone was dressed in their finest church clothes. We walked into the room where the little girl was laid out in a kind of crib or small bed. She was dressed in a white dress, her head was covered with a white veil, and her hands were folded in prayer over her chest. Her eyes were closed and there was a peaceful expression on her face. The image of her there before me was an exact match to what I had seen in the shadow cast by the moon on the wall the night before. Both Eduardo and I were struck by the resemblance. The little girl had died about three or four in the morning, which corresponded closely to the hour I was sitting in the garden gazing at the image. It was just that and no more. The memory has stayed with me all these years.

Nothing evokes the dreamlike nature of the magical reality that, for these people, is reality as much as this incident.

Toward the middle of August, we completed our business in Pucallpa and prepared all the live plants we had collected for export. At the time, this was quite easy to do if you had the proper permits. You needed phytosanitary certificates from the Peruvian government and USDA plant import permits, all of which we had. Peruvian permits are not so easy to obtain these days due to concerns about biopiracy. On the Hawaiian side, importing alien species is now almost impossible, and rightly so given that every nonnative species has the potential to become invasive.

Even then, the specimens for export had to be prepared for suboptimal conditions during transport and the horrible things that were done to them on the receiving end by the USDA plant import authorities. Our method was to buy a large woven basket at the market, about three feet tall with a lid that could be lashed on. We cleaned and washed all the cuttings, wrapped them in damp muslin, and put those in the basket along with packets of seeds that needed to remain moist. After lashing up the basket, I treated it as part of my luggage. In Lima, nobody even looked at it except for a young policeman with an AK-47, who took one desultory glance inside and waved me through.

In Los Angeles, it was a different story. I dropped off the collections along with our documents at the USDA import facility, where the staff unwrapped all the collections and fumigated them. I had presented phytosanitary certificates and requested that the collections not be fumigated, but the staff didn't listen. I really believe that the USDA does its best to kill all live plant imports; that's their job as they see it. Once the cuttings had been unwrapped and fumigated, they were dumped back into the basket (no one bothered to wrap them again) and left to sit for about a week until we were notified that they were ready for pickup. Luis Eduardo then flew with them to Hawaii, but by the time they arrived, nearly all the cuttings had lost their leaves and looked like dead sticks for the most part. With careful tending from Terence and Kat, about half of the plants survived.

By then, in 1985, Terence and Kat had turned nine acres of the land they'd acquired on the Big Island into an ethnobotanical reserve. They also founded Botanical Dimensions, a nonprofit organization based in California whose mission was "to collect, protect, propagate and understand ethnomedically significant plants and their lore" as noted on its website

(Botanicaldimensions.org). As its president and project director, Kat ran the nonprofit from the start, managing the Hawaii site and applying for grants. That remains true today. Over the years, the organization has used grants and contributions to complete projects ranging from watershed restoration to ethnobotanical research in the Amazon.

Back in 1985, Botanical Dimensions provided me with the cachet and destination I needed to import the plants I had collected in Peru. Since the days when Kat and Terence first began their gene bank in the Hawaiian rainforest, many of its earliest arrivals have reached maturity, and there are now many species of rare Peruvian medicinal plants in the garden, along with specimens from elsewhere on the planet. The site has played an important role in the ethnobotany courses Kat teaches, including "Plants in Human Affairs," which we have taught together since 2002.

45 The Perpetual Postdoc

I began making plans to leave the Helicon Foundation soon after I returned to San Diego. By then, the papers I'd written on the results of my thesis work had stirred quite a bit of interest. I'd gotten numerous reprint requests, including one from Dr. Juan Saavedra, a section chief in the Laboratory of Clinical Pharmacology at the National Institute of Mental Health, or NIMH.

Saavedra's name seemed familiar to me, then I remembered—he'd been a colleague of Julius Axelrod, the Nobel Prize–winning neuroscientist who had done pioneering work elucidating the molecular basis of neurotransmission. Axelrod was one of the giants of neuroscience. He and Saavedra had published an early paper on the endogenous synthesis of DMT, characterizing the enzymes in rat brains, human brains, and other tissues that used tryptamine and serotonin to make DMT, 5-MeO-DMT, melatonin, and other neurohormones (Saavedra and Axelrod 1972). Saavedra had requested a reprint of my paper on ayahuasca from the *Journal of Ethnopharmacology*. If he's crazy enough to ask for that, I figured, maybe he's crazy enough to take me on as a postdoc. I wanted to redirect my efforts toward psychedelic research, toward something that ideally would combine pharmacology, which I wanted to learn, and ethnobotany, which I had credibly done.

I sent him the reprint along with a polite letter mentioning my supervisor, Neil Towers, and my mentor, Schultes, and inquired if there might be an opportunity to work in his lab at NIMH on some aspects of ayahuasca pharmacology. At the time, I was unaware that Saavedra had been one of the scientists from the National Institutes of Health (NIH) who had joined the RV *Alpha Helix* expedition to the Amazon in 1977. Schultes had been chief science officer on the expedition, and Neil had been selected to go along with the NIH chemist John W. Daly, who achieved fame for his pioneering work on frog venom alkaloids. Saavedra had been selected because of his work on endogenous tryptamines and also because of his South American (Argentinian) heritage.

In response to my note, Saavedra sent back a letter encouraging me to apply to a program at NIH, the Pharmacology Research Associate Traineeship, or PRAT, a fellowship for young investigators who were outside the field of pharmacology but wanted to acquire skills in that discipline. I applied in the fall of 1985. The application process involved selecting three potential supervisors in order of preference and then visiting the NIH campus in Bethesda, Maryland, for interviews. Naturally, I selected Saavedra as my first choice, followed by Axelrod and John Daly. I had an interesting interview with Axelrod, in which we discussed the function of endogenous DMT. In other words, why was DMT naturally present in the human brain? He said that he thought it had no function, it was basically metabolic "noise," which surprised me.

It was clear from the start that my supervisor would be Saavedra. He had encouraged me to apply, he had the connection to Schultes and Towers, and he had an interest in ayahuasca. It wasn't clear what we would work on together, but there were many possibilities. It seemed likely our project would somehow involve the endogenous synthesis of tryptamines and beta-carbolines.

I returned from my visit quite stoked. I had a dawning belief that with a little luck and hard work, my career might actually go somewhere. In mid-February 1986, I learned I'd been accepted into the program. Sheila took a week off from her job and went out to Washington, DC, and Bethesda to find a position in one of the hospitals there. Going out on her own was a good experience for her. The United States was still a foreign and slightly threatening country to her at the time, but surviving her "expedition to America" was a tremendous confidence builder. She interviewed at four or five hospitals in the Washington area and was offered positions at all of them. She elected to work at one of the area's biggest inner-city hospitals. She thought the diversity of both the patient population and the staff would be more interesting, and she was right.

The hospital's clientele included many of the most disenfranchised of the urban poor. The health effects of violence, crack addiction, and AIDS were destined to become familiar sights in the course of her work.

Our transition to Bethesda became our American pilgrimage, a chance to discover the country together and to discover each other more in the process. During our two years in San Diego, we'd gone through one beater after another, so at the start of our journey we bought our first new car, a 1986 Honda Accord. We felt very much like upwardly mobile young marrieds, which we were. We took off in mid-May for three weeks of travel before we were due at our respective jobs.

We stopped to see the 200-inch Hale telescope at Palomar, a mecca for the kid astronomer in me still enthralled with outer space. Sheila had never seen Esalen, so we headed up Highway 1 along the coast to Big Sur and pulled in there for a look at that observatory of inner space as well. In Santa Cruz, we dropped in on my Aunt Tress, then drove through San Francisco and across the Golden Gate Bridge, pulling in for a few days with Terence and Kat. Moving on, we reached Vancouver eager to see Expo 86 and our old friends, by then grad-school survivors and more or less gainfully employed. We spent a couple of nights with Sheila's parents in their place outside Kamloops, and then dropped in on her sister in Slocan, a village in the pretty Kootenay region of southeastern British Columbia.

Another long leg took us through Idaho to Utah, where we gave ourselves a day to gawk at the Mormon Temple and Salt Lake, then moved on, clearing our heads in Goblin Valley State Park, a lonely, weird place with lots of mushroom-shaped rock formations carved by the wind. The opening scene of the cheesy psychedelic movie *Altered States* was shot there, the only thing good about the film. I'm sure it would be most interesting to chomp down five grams or so in the Goblin Valley around dusk, but we had miles ahead of us and shoved on. Moab, Spanish Fork, Monticello, Dove Creek, Cortez—this was familiar territory to me, evoking memories of the weekend trips our family had taken to Arches National Monument or Mesa Verde, flitting in and out like celestial beings on the shining wings of Dad's little plane, insulated from the mundane concerns of the folks who lived in that beautiful but harsh and arid land.

Sheila and I visited some of the earliest attempts at building a life there: the Anasazi ruins at Mesa Verde and Hovenweep. We then turned north and stayed a few days with my Aunt Mayme in Paonia, my first chance to introduce Sheila to my extended family. With our time growing short, we surmounted the Rockies and dashed to St. Louis, and then on from there, finally reaching greater Washington, DC, in sweltering rush-hour traffic like neither of us had ever seen before.

Within a few days, we'd found a funky place on a nice dead-end, leafy street lined with older townhouse-style quadriplexes, about half a block from the Bethesda Metro. The NIH was one stop north. Bethesda is a nice place to live, especially if you like good food. Our two-year stint there was destined to be one of the best times of our lives.

* * *

When I applied for the fellowship at NIMH, Saavedra and I had discussed doing some research related to tryptamines and beta-carbolines and building on the research he'd done years earlier on the endogenous synthesis of DMT. He was interested in ayahuasca. We thought that endogenous ayahuasca analogs involving both tryptamines and beta-carbolines might be produced in the brain under some circumstances, and this seemed like a promising avenue for investigation. As it turned out, I ended up working on an entirely different problem, unrelated to ayahuasca or natural products, but it was still a useful experience.

At the time, there was a lot of interest in neuroscience in characterizing neurotransmitter receptor subtypes using subtype-selective drugs. For example, a compound that selectively bound to a particular subtype of a receptor for the neurotransmitter serotonin, or 5HT, could be labeled with radioactive isotopes like tritium or iodine 125. Equipped with these radioactive labels, a researcher could use receptor-binding assays to do some interesting things. One could characterize the molecular properties of receptors in brain tissue, for instance, or compare the affinity of an unlabeled drug for a particular receptor type by determining how much of it was needed to displace a labeled drug from the binding site. The technique had

Sheila and Dennis, about 1993.

been developed by Solomon Snyder and his student Candace Pert, whose landmark work on opiate receptors led to the isolation of the brain's own morphine—the endogenous opiate peptides known as enkephalins and endorphins. Snyder and Pert had developed this methodology in the early 1970s at Johns Hopkins, and it had since revolutionized neuroscience.

During my time at NIMH, and later at Stanford, many investigators were busy using these radioactively "hot" molecular probes to fish for new receptor subtypes of the major known neurotransmitters. Serotonin receptors were getting a lot of attention because of their known or suspected role in brain disorders such as depression and schizophrenia. Serotonin receptors also appeared to play a role in the psychedelic response. Research dating back to the 1950s had demonstrated that drugs like LSD acted on serotonin receptors, but no one knew exactly which receptor subtypes LSD and other psychedelics targeted, let alone how these subtypes were affected. The "hallucinogen receptor" became the object of a quest. Various subtypes were proposed as the likely culprits. By the time I arrived at NIMH, in 1986, a consensus was emerging that the hallucinogens acted as "agonists" at one particular serotonin subtype, the so-called $5HT_{2A}$ receptors. (In pharmacology, an agonist is a drug that binds to a receptor and initiates an effect, often acting in a way that is similar to the native neurotransmitter. The opposite type, antagonists, block the binding of the native neurotransmitter but do not have any effect themselves.)

As luck had it, some of the so-called psychedelic amphetamines developed by my colleague and mentor, Sasha Shulgin, happened to display extraordinary selectivity for the $5HT_{2A}$ receptor subtypes. Shulgin's compounds were called amphetamines because they relied on a basic amphetamine structure, but they did not act as stimulants. They were really mescaline analogs, and some were almost pure $5HT_{2A}$ receptor agonists. Conveniently, one of the most effective in this regard was an "iodinated" analog of the mega-hallucinogen known to pharmacologists as DOM and more widely as STP after its notorious appearance on the street in the late 1960s. Its iodinated derivative was known as DOI. Because DOI included an iodine atom, highly radioactive forms of the compound could be synthesized using isotopes like iodine 125. This "hot" tag or label would allow us to track where this compound bound in neural tissue.

Until then, these receptor-binding assays were usually carried out in homogenous tissue, that is, in tissue that had been blended like a smoothie into a liquid. After tagging, the labeled receptor fragments were filtered out, and the amount of bound drug could be determined by measuring the radioactivity levels. By the time I joined Saavedra's lab, he was just starting to use a technique known as autoradiography, which added a new dimension to how receptors could be characterized: researchers could now map receptor distribution in slices of brain tissue.

In autoradiography, the tissue, for example a rat's brain, is frozen in liquid nitrogen and then sliced into extremely thin sections using a special cutting tool called a microtome. The slices are mounted on glass slides and incubated in buffer containing the radioactive drug, which binds to the receptors. Following incubation, each slide is exposed to radiation-sensitive film in a special cassette that holds the adjacent slide and film in place. Exposure can take a while. The film, once developed, bears a perfect a black-and-gray photographic negative of the brain slice. This image can be scanned with a densitometer, and the concentration of bound drug in a given region can be calculated based on the darkness of the image. Iodine 125 and other radioactive gamma-ray emitters are perfect for autoradiography because they expose the X-ray film in a matter of days instead of weeks or months as is required for drugs labeled with less radioactive tags such as tritium.

Most of my postdoc colleagues were working with these techniques on atrial natriuretic peptide, a potent vasodilator important in the regulation of cardiac, renal, and vascular functions. I got to work on hallucinogen receptors, which I thought were much sexier. The compound we intended to use, DOI, occurs in two configurations, each a mirror image of the other. The R(-) enantiomer readily binds to $5HT_{2A}$ receptors, while its mirror image, the S(+) enantiomer, doesn't bind or binds only at high concentrations. This correlates with their known effects in humans: R(-) DOI is strongly psychoactive at less than one milligram, while S(+) DOI is essentially inactive.

Thanks to our connections to the Lawrence Berkeley National Lab, notably Shulgin, we were able to get hold of both enantiomers in hot and cold forms. With these molecules in hand, I could answer some interesting questions about the distribution and function of $5HT_{2A}$ receptors, at least in rat brains. I won't go into the details. The curious can read the papers I published with Saavedra and others, which are listed in the bibliography. Our key finding was that cold R(-)DOI would displace its hot form from specific sites in the rat brain slices, but when hot LSD was used to label the binding sites instead, then cold DOI would displace it from a subset of receptors in certain brain regions, although not from all of them. Conversely, cold LSD would displace all of the DOI binding sites, and more besides. These extra sites were not $5HT_{2A}$ binding sites, and LSD is not $5HT_{2A}$-selective compared to DOI.

In retrospect, these findings seem almost trivial, and perhaps they are. But they were important at the time because they demonstrated that two hallucinogens, having very different molecular structures, nonetheless occupied the same receptor sites, and their localization in different brain regions matched closely. It was a solid contribution to the field, if not exactly the sort of finding that would get one "the call" from Stockholm.

At NIMH, I was reminded that when people work closely together, it's the psychodynamics that are most problematic. As a graduate student, I'd been lucky to have amazing mentors in the persons of Sandy Siegel and Neil Towers, but I never enjoyed anything close to that rapport with my various postdoc supervisors. Saavedra and I had a number of clashes during my tenure there. Most involved my insistence on listing those at Lawrence Berkeley who had synthesized the labeled compounds we relied on in our research as coauthors on the papers that Saavedra and I published. From my perspective, they'd done us a big favor in providing us with a set of crucial molecular tools, but my supervisor saw it otherwise. Our disagreement suggested a philosophical difference to some degree. I viewed science as inherently a team effort that relied on collaboration to get things done. Others adhered to a more competitive model. Despite our disagreements, we published a number of interesting papers over what I believe was a productive relationship for the two years I spent there.

Most of the postdocs in the lab were foreigners, Japanese or Finnish or Argentinian, working under guest visas. Being transplants from elsewhere, we banded together and became excellent friends. Sheila invited the postdocs and their families to our tiny apartment for a traditional Canadian-American style Thanksgiving dinner the first year we were there. We loved introducing them to what might well have been as exotic a meal as they'd ever been served.

That first year, I ran an incubation experiment over the holidays that required me to come to the lab at about 11 and shut it down for the night. On Christmas Eve, Building 10, the enormous Clinical Research Center where I worked, was mostly dark, but there was a light coming out of our lab. Sitting at the bench beside mine was Kazuto, an older Japanese postdoc, a cool guy but quite reserved and a very hard worker. He had a wife and children living with him in Bethesda, but it seemed he rarely saw them. On a normal morning, I'd get to my bench about eight. Kazuto would already be at his bench and had been for hours. I'd leave for the evening around six and he'd still be there. That night, at 11 on Christmas Eve, there was Kazuto hunched over his work.

"For God's sake," I said, "why don't you go home to your family? After all, it's Christmas Eve." To which he replied, "Well, I am Japanese. It doesn't mean so much to me. I would rather be here." I could hardly keep from cracking up; it was so matter-of-fact and true to his own character. In fact, all of us were workaholics who had more or less renounced the concept of "after work." But as an American, my situation was somewhat different. Most of my cohorts were foreigners working under guest visas who, as a result, were under even more pressure than I was. Their visa status depended on the goodwill of their supervisors, so it was in their interests to keep their heads down and toe the line. I had to wonder how this power dynamic affected the research. During my years after graduate school, I'd have many such glimpses into the nature of science conducted in corporate and institutional settings.

So, despite some rocky episodes, my postdoc at the NIMH would be a productive and solid start along a career path I actually wanted to pursue. By the end, I was able to parley that experience into yet another postdoc in the Department of Neurology at Stanford University under Dr. Stephen Peroutka, a well-known researcher in the serotonin field. At least I had answered the question I'd occasionally heard at NIMH: What's a botanist doing in the Laboratory of Clinical Neuropharmacology? The answer: surviving, and trying to do reasonably competent work. I managed to do both.

Sometime during our second August in Bethesda, "we" became pregnant. Rather, Sheila became pregnant with my help. We had both been enjoying our status as well-employed young marrieds with no kids and two cats. We could go out every weekend if we felt in the mood, and we often were, dining out at some of Bethesda's tremendous restaurants. But there was something missing. I thought that we should try to have a baby but Sheila was not so sure, perhaps having a woman's keener sense of who did most of the work during—and after—pregnancy.

Nevertheless, one night we did try, and we chose our moment well. Forty-two weeks later, on May 6, 1988, our daughter Caitlin was born. I was in the birthing room with Sheila and cut the umbilical cord. I have never been higher in my life, never experienced a sense of ecstasy that even came close to what I felt at that moment. I'm still high from it, and I hope I always will be. Caitlin is the best thing that ever happened to me, and to us.

It was clear from the start that Caitlin was special. Maybe in some other dimension there's an Oort cloud of drifting souls awaiting their chance to be incarnated. Every once in a while, with the appearance of suitable parents, one of those souls will split off from the crowd and plunge into the inner solar system, so to speak, and take up residence in the mother's womb. I'd like to think that's how it happened with Cait. She is an "old soul," clear-eyed and intelligent from the start, and our purpose in life, to the degree that we had one, has been to provide this amazing being with a chance to enter and flourish in this world under our love and care. Twenty-four years later, our efforts have paid off. She is kind and intelligent, compassionate and beautiful—everything a father could want in a daughter—and we are blessed to have her. She is now an adult, as much a friend and mentor as our child, and one of the most interesting people I know.

As I recall it, when Caitlin first began to talk, she didn't start out calling us "Mama" or "Dada," but rather "Dennis" and "Sheila." She eventually settled on "Mom" and "Dad" like any other kid would, but I've always interpreted that earlier phase as evidence for the old-soul hypothesis. It was like she was checking us out at first, seeing if we were suitable vessels for her incarnation. Then I guess she decided that we'd do and settled into being our kid. I give thanks every day to whatever merciful beings there are in this universe that she decided to stick around.

Cait's hospital birth wasn't typical. Or perhaps it was, making it a sad commentary on the way a normal, natural process is routinely overmedical-ized. When she was about two weeks overdue, Sheila's obstetrician advised us that it was time to induce labor. We knew the result of that might be rough. Sheila made it clear that she wanted to breastfeed, and to have a natural, drug-free birth if possible. The nurses were not supportive. At the height of Sheila's labor, when she was in the most pain and ready to throw in the towel, the nurses kept urging her to have an epidural, a rather new pain-control method at the time. I was there with her, and so was Kat, who had come out to help us. We both urged Sheila to hang in and refuse the meds, but the nurses undermined her resolve at the height of her vulner-ability. Thankfully, the birth proceeded without complications. Cait was born about six in the evening. Afterward, when all of us were gathered in Sheila's hospital room, I was swept by the feeling of being in the presence of a new life. If you've never experienced that for yourself, there is no way to convey it. I remember a sense of warmth and heightened colors along with a pervading mood of calm, peace, and love. It was a lot like being on a low dose of MDMA only much, much better. I suspect there are hormonal and pheromonal reactions in the mother and father and others present that create this ambiance. Kat was the perfect companion at this pivotal, life-defining event; she knew just what to do and how to support us at every turn. I had a very real sense of the power of the feminine in that room. I was humbly reminded that there is no event more evocative of the sacred mystery of life than giving birth, a miracle that only women can fully know.

Sheila initiated breastfeeding right away. She had been reading up and taking classes, so she knew what to do, and it seemed to be going well. We had been very clear that we were going with breast milk only; no formula or other liquids were to be administered. By the time Kat and I left the hospital late that night, Sheila was tired and Cait was sleeping after a good feed. I too was exhausted and desperate for sleep, but when I left the hospital I felt like I was walking two feet above the ground.

About one A.M. we got a call from Sheila. She was hysterical and crying. She had developed a low fever, which is common after an epidural and rarely anything to be concerned about. The nurses had interpreted this as a likely infection and had used that as an excuse to seize Caitlin and spirit her off to the nursery, to "protect" her, they said, from being infected. Once in the nursery, they immediately fed her formula, against our explicit instructions.

Sheila was upset and furious. Not only had her baby been ripped from her arms for no reason; she was then dispatched to the nursery and fed toxic formula against our wishes. In the emotionally volatile state that Sheila was in already, I could see how upsetting this was for her. But there was nothing we could do. We couldn't go back to the hospital that night, so we managed to calm Sheila and get the obstetrician to allow her to go home in the morning. Indeed, we packed up and left just over 12 hours after Sheila had given birth.

Once at home, the breastfeeding went great and the bonding continued. It was a magical weekend and it changed both of us forever. Being parents will do that. One consequence was that Sheila became impassioned about breastfeeding. In the years when Cait was young and still breastfeeding, Sheila got involved in La Leche League and went on to lead breastfeeding groups wherever we've lived since then. Sheila eventually used her experience with breastfeeding, her botanical training, and her knowledge of herbal medicine to write a book about herbs and their use as aids in breastfeeding. The result, *The Nursing Mother's Herbal,* received a prestigious award as the best new publication in consumer health in 2004 from the American Nurses Association (Humphrey 2003).

Now Sheila has combined her personal knowledge and her professional qualifications as an RN and IBCLC (International Board Certified Lactation Consultant) into a career as a lactation consultant at a hospital near our home in Minnesota. This work has become a kind of crusade for her. She is as passionate about breastfeeding as I ever was about psychedelics. There are certain similarities in how these subjects are viewed by the biomedical establishment. Both have the potential to benefit physical and mental health. Both also exist in the shadows of biomedicine and have been viewed as highly suspect by "conventional" medicine. I am told the situation is getting better for breastfeeding in light of the overwhelming clinical evidence for its benefits. And yet most physicians know far too little about the subject. Something similar could be said of what most medical professionals know about psychedelics, and many are so misinformed as to be unqualified to say anything about them at all.

Two weeks after Caitlin's birth I left for the Bay Area to find us a place to live and get ready to start my new postdoc at Stanford. Sheila stayed in Bethesda. On my drive in the Honda, I stopped in West Lafayette, Indiana, to visit Dave Nichols at his lab at Purdue University. Nichols was a medicinal chemist who, like Shulgin, had focused his research on structure–activity investigations of psychedelics. Unlike Shulgin, however, he had far better tools at his disposal in his well-funded lab at Purdue, so he was able to carry his work much further than Shulgin was able to do. I'd met him at the psychedelics conference at Esalen four years earlier, and even discussed the idea of doing a postdoc at his lab at one time before circumstances led me elsewhere.

What I found at Purdue was certainly an interesting scene. This was the place to be if you had a serious interest in psychedelics. He and his graduate students were actively involved in pursuing studies on the molecular characterization of the $5HT_{2A}$ receptors, developing animal behavioral protocols to assess the activity of new compounds and studying the structure–activity relationships of psychedelics in all classes. They had it all: medicinal chemistry, pharmacology, animal models—not to mention an ever-changing pool of students who loved Dave and were happy to put in long hours in the lab. He was passionate about his work and it was infectious. Dave's group was on the cutting edge of neuropharmacology and many of his graduate students went on to make their mark on the field. It was a stimulating research environment, and I left a little jealous. But I had my own career track to pursue at Stanford, and I was eager to get started.

Once I got to the Bay Area, I quickly found a house to rent in Redwood City, and Sheila and Cait flew out to join me. Sheila and I had agreed that she would be a stay-at-home mom for as long as we could afford it. Not having two incomes caused some economic hardship, but we have never regretted the choice of giving our daughter the benefit of a mother's presence for the first 12 years of her life.

I saved a little money by taking the bus to work as far as I could, and then walking the last leg to the lab. My new supervisor, Stephen Peroutka, was a few years younger than I was and yet already an up-and-comer in the serotonin field. We'd met at the annual Society for Neuroscience meeting in New Orleans six months earlier and hit it off. He was also interested in serotonin receptor subtypes and wanted to further characterize the $5HT_{2A}$ receptors with the new "hot" iodinated DOI. Like many other investigators, he was also getting very interested in MDMA.

New evidence was emerging that MDMA, by then illegal, was selectively neurotoxic to certain serotonin neurons, at least in rats and primates. Meanwhile, MDMA was becoming increasingly popular as a "club drug," and law enforcement authorities had begun to voice concern about having another drug abuse "epidemic" on their hands. That, plus the indications of neurotoxicity, meant there was lots of funding through the National Institute on Drug Abuse (NIDA) and other agencies to investigate the neurotoxic effects of MDMA.

Steve's lab was all over this. We cowrote a definitive review of the current understanding of MDMA neurotoxicity, and that became my first publication from his lab and the first paper to be published in *Journal of Neurochemistry* in January 1989. Later in my postdoc, with Shulgin's help, I published a paper on the structure–activity relationships of a series of MDMA analogs, correlating their effect on the release of tritiated dopamine and serotonin from rat brain synaptosomes, with differential neurotoxicity in rats. To put that simply, I was looking at whether these ecstasy-like compounds damaged rat brain nerve cells. It turned out to be a nice piece of work. Peroutka didn't sign on as a coauthor, but he let me publish it together with Shulgin and another postdoc.

I don't recall why he chose not to join in the publication. I do know that by then MDMA was a political football in science. Any findings that suggested a lack of neurotoxicity, let alone that—gasp—the substance might even have therapeutic benefits, were heresy. According to our results, many of the analogs we tested had little or no neurotoxicity—findings that were not in synch with conventional wisdom or the expectations of the funding agencies. In a letter that appeared in the *New England Journal of Medicine* in late 1987, Peroutka noted that a survey of 369 Stanford undergraduates found that 39 percent of them had tried ecstasy at least once. I suspect he took some heat for that.

For me, the MDMA work was interesting but not really my main focus. I was still interested in characterizing the $5HT_{2A}$ receptor subtypes and learning more about the applications of the receptor-binding techniques. Steve's lab was the perfect place to do that. There were four or five other postdocs as well as undergrads working in the lab. The place was a paper mill; if we didn't submit a paper at least once a week, we weren't working hard enough. I don't mean that I had to submit a paper, but collectively the lab had to keep pace.

In this competitive environment, with its emphasis on the quantity of scientific publications, quality may have been compromised at times. At the time, all kinds of novel subtypes for various neurotransmitters were being described in the literature, and the serotonin field was particularly active in this regard. Steve was very interested in discovering new 5HT receptor subtypes, and indeed had already done so. He really wanted to find a new hallucinogen-specific $5HT_2$ subtype, and that was the task we diligently, if not obsessively, pursued. The consensus among most neuroscientists involved in this work was that the $5HT_{2A}$ selective agonists like DOI bound to a high affinity conformation of the receptor, not to a distinct receptor for such compounds. This was the current understanding of the molecular pharmacology of the $5HT_{2A}$ receptors at the time, and it made sense. But Steve insisted that what the radio-labeled agonists had indicated was a distinct subtype—that is, the "real" hallucinogen receptor. After I learned more about the high-affinity agonist binding characteristics of the $5HT_{2A}$ receptor, it was clear that we had embarked on a wild goose chase in search of this mythical receptor. Other papers we turned out were better, including one in which we screened a series of tryptamine analogs against

$5HT_{2A}$ and $5HT_{1A}$ receptors (McKenna et al. 1990). This one received kudos from Dave Nichols at Purdue, which made me very happy.

After our return to California, we lived for about a year in Redwood City and then rented a house in Menlo Park near East Palo Alto, which for a while back then was known as the country's "murder capital." Despite its location, the house was wonderful, a Spanish Colonial Revival place built in the mid-1920s with a big unkempt backyard, an old chicken shed and other outbuildings, room for a big garden, and even its own well. The place had been a part of an intentional community formed by a group of freethinkers who supported biodynamic gardening and communal living. Our dwelling had been one of several small household farms in a loose-knit cooperative whose families shared their skills and resources to support each other while selling produce in San Francisco. Our house, which we called "Housie" at Cait's insistence, was the rare spread that was still more or less intact. It was a great place for Caitlin and our two cats, and we loved it.

When we first came to the Bay Area, we hardly knew anyone other than Terence and Kat. They lived up north in Sonoma County and we saw them infrequently. Our limited social life suited us, but we looked forward to the occasional Friday night dinners organized by Sasha Shulgin and his wife, Anne, for the crème de la crème of Bay Area psychedelic society. These pot-luck affairs usually took place at a beautiful home in the hills above Marin that belonged to Anne's ex-husband. It was only through the kindness of Sasha and Anne that we were invited. We knew we had found a compatible bunch of friends when they not only encouraged us to bring Caitlin to these events but made a big deal over her when we showed up. She would crawl around underneath the tables and chairs and through a forest of adult legs. Nobody ever stepped on her as far as I know and everyone would find a chance to pick her up and engage with her. Sasha and Anne, the quintessence of an earth mother, were especially fond of her. Sasha, with his twinkling eyes, halo of wild white hair, and beard, may as well have been Santa Claus as far as Cait was concerned. Cait never had much of a chance to be close to her grandparents on either side of our family, so Sasha and Anne were the ideal surrogates.

46
Climbing the Vine: 1991

Preparing *hoasca* at the UDV temple in Manaus, Brazil.

My seemingly perpetual status as a postdoc came to an end sometime in the spring of 1990. Peroutka was about to leave Stanford for a plum position as the director of neuroscience at Genentech, the first of several positions he'd go on to hold in the world of corporate biomedicine. He told me that I should start making plans to find a real job, if such was to be had. I had been applying for various academic positions, but none of the recruiting committees seemed to know quite how to respond to my peculiar academic pedigree as a botanist/neuroscientist with a passionate interest in psychedelics. I was ready to move on from Stanford, because I wanted to find a way to merge my newly acquired skills in neuroscience and central nervous system (CNS) pharmacology with my long-standing interests in ethnobotany and natural products. But the way forward wasn't clear, and I was worried about finding the next gig.

Then, a lucky break: I was contacted by Mark Plotkin, a Yale ethnobotanist and protégé of Schultes who would soon achieve national fame for his 1993 book *Tales of a Shaman's Apprentice: An Ethnobotanist Searches for New Medicines in the Amazon Rainforest*. We had met briefly when I attended a presentation he made at NIH. There was a new startup company being formed in the Bay Area called Shaman Pharmaceuticals, he said, and its mission was focused on ethnobotanically driven drug discovery, especially drugs from the Amazon basin. They already had one antiviral candidate in the pipeline, and were planning to create a CNS drug discovery program. They needed young, smart, ambitious people like me.

Shaman Pharmaceuticals was the visionary brainchild of Lisa Conte, an ambitious young entrepreneur who had been a vice president at a venture capital firm with offices in the area. She had managed to garner about $4 million in venture capital funding as well as personal funds and had founded Shaman after observing local healers using plant medicines during travels in Asia. Schultes, and later the famous pharmacognosist Norman Farnsworth, were persuaded to join their advisory board. At the time, Conte needed people to join the core team, Mark told me, and they were hiring. I should go talk to her, which I did.

For me, it was like a dream come true. Ever since San Diego, I had made efforts to found a company that would do exactly what Shaman Pharma intended to do. I had good ideas for drug discovery but no business experience or expertise whatever. Now here was a new company run by those with the business skills to realize what I had only dreamed of doing. Moreover, I had something to offer in the form of the skills I had developed during my postdocs at NIMH and Stanford. Although their primary therapeutic target was antivirals, they also were interested in novel analgesics and needed people to work in both areas.

My stint at Shaman would be my introduction to corporate science. I stayed with the company until the end of 1992 and enjoyed my work there. The other scientists, with some exceptions, were a good bunch to work with, and we believed in our mission. I felt like I had a contribution to make.

For most of my tenure at Shaman I was a lab rat, working in the receptor lab on the lower floor of their facility in San Carlos. Other Shamanites got to travel the world in search of exotic plants, a role I might have envied had I not been so happy to stay at home with my wife and young daughter. In

1991, I did escape temporarily, thanks to an invitation I got to describe my work on ayahuasca at a conference in São Paulo, Brazil. The conference had been organized by the medical studies section of the União do Vegetal, or UDV, one of the syncretic churches in Brazil that uses ayahuasca as a sacrament. (Ayahuasca in Portuguese is called *hoasca*, and UDV followers often refer to it as *vegetal*.) The conference was a multidisciplinary event that included chemists, neuroscientists, pharmacologists, anthropologists, and psychiatrists. My friend Luis Eduardo was there along with other knowledgeable figures.

For the UDV, it was an important event given its political subtext. At the time, CONFEN, the Brazilian drug agency, was debating whether ayahuasca was a dangerous substance liable to abuse and whether its use in religious practices should be banned. The UDV wanted to show that *hoasca* was inherently safe, not subject to abuse, and that its ritual use should be allowed. By inviting a distinguished roster of international experts, they hoped to present an impressive conference that would favorably influence the CONFEN authorities. It seemed strange to me that I was regarded as one such "distinguished" expert on ayahuasca, but I suppose I was.

During our travels in Peru in 1985, Eduardo and I had both mused about the possibility of conducting a biomedical study of ayahuasca. Many of the *ayahuasqueros* we dealt with seemed remarkably healthy in mind and body and many, though quite elderly, were still quite strong.

We asked a naive question: was there something about long-term, regular ingestion of ayahuasca that enhanced their health and vigor? We speculated about ways that we might approach that question, and I even started drafting a grant application to NIDA after we returned home. I quickly realized that, in Peru, we'd have trouble conducting a study that involved asking for blood and urine samples—that wouldn't be appropriate in light of cultural attitudes about witchcraft. And even if we got the samples, they'd be difficult to preserve. Beyond the logistical problems loomed the simple fact that NIDA would never fund such a study. So we shelved the idea at the time.

But it turned out that the organizers of the UDV conference had exactly that kind of a project in mind. That was their real agenda—they wanted to enlist the help of recognized foreign scientists to carry out a biomedical study among UDV members that, they hoped, would support their petition to CONFEN to allow the sacramental use of the *hoasca* tea. In this case, the logistics were more realistic. Many of the UDV members were themselves physicians, there was no cultural baggage involving witchcraft to contend with, and there were many UDV members who were eager to submit themselves to poking and prodding. So with the encouragement from top UDV *mestres*, I returned to the States and dusted off my old proposal. I revised and submitted it to them for their approval, which they gave. I started soliciting funds through Botanical Dimensions, and over the course of the next couple of years we were able to raise about $75,000 to conduct the study.

But that lay ahead. Back at the conference, after three days of Power Points and roundtables at a UDV temple on the outskirts of São Paulo, the event culminated in an ayahuasca ceremony with the foreign dignitaries as the guests of honor. About 500 people took part in that ceremony. I had a profound visionary revelation, in which I experienced photosynthesis from a molecule's eye view and understood the importance of this everyday miracle for the sustenance of life on the planet. It was a cathartic and moving experience, one of my most profound ayahuasca journeys. The following account of my "lesson from the Teacher" has been adapted from an earlier version that appeared in *Ayahuasca Reader: Encounters with the Sacred Vine* (Luna and White 2000).

On the night in question, the weather was humid and balmy. In the gathering dusk, we all walked the short distance from the dormitories where we had been staying to the temple, nestled in a small valley about a quarter-mile away. In the center of the amphitheater-like space, a long table was arranged, with chairs arrayed around it and a picture of Mestre Gabriel, the UDV founder and prophet, hung beneath an arch-shaped structure decorated with the sun, moon, and stars at one end. Several gallons of *hoasca* tea, a brownish liquid the color of café latte, was in a plastic juice dispenser placed on the table beneath the picture of Mestre Gabriel. Beside it was a stack of paper picnic cups.

A special set of chairs had been reserved for the visiting dignitaries along one of the terrace-like elevations close to the center of the amphitheater. We threaded our way among the members already seated and took our places in the reserved spot.

After everyone had gotten settled, the *mestre* in charge rose to start dispensing the brew, helped by a couple of acolytes. The members formed an orderly line, and one by one we filed down to stand before the *mestre* and be handed a paper cup containing our allotted draft. The size of the servings varied from person to person and seemed to be measured according to body weight and the *mestre*'s assessing gaze. One got the feeling that he was taking the measure of the soul and spirit of the supplicant standing before him. Each person took their cup and returned to stand in front of their chair. Once everyone had been served, the *mestre* gave a signal and all raised the cups to their lips and drained the bitter, foul-tasting beverage in two or three gulps. One of the Brazilian scientists standing beside me slipped me a small piece of dried ginger to chew to kill the aftertaste. I was grateful for the kind gesture.

Having drained their cups, everyone sat back in their comfortable webbed chairs. I kept hoping someone would turn off the glaring, buzzing fluorescent lights overhead that were altogether too bright and quite annoying. They were to stay on during the entire evening, however. For about 45 minutes everyone sat, absorbed in their own thoughts. The crowded hall was absolutely silent. After this period, a few people began to get up and totter toward the bathrooms as the nausea, a frequent side effect in the early stages, began to take hold. About the same time, the *mestre* began singing a beautiful song, called a *shamada*, and though I could not understand the Portuguese words, the melody was quite moving. The sound of the heartfelt *shamada* mingling with the wretching, gasping noises of people throwing up violently in the background made me smile at the incongruity, but no one else seemed to notice.

My own experience was not developing as I'd hoped. My stomach was queasy but not enough to send me to the bathroom, and I felt restless and uncomfortable. I felt very little effect except for some brief flashes of hypnagogia behind my closed eyes. I was disappointed; I had been hoping for more than a sub-threshold experience. When the *mestre* signaled that he was ready to give a second glass to anyone who wanted it, I was among the group of about a dozen gringos that queued up in front of the table. Apparently I was not the only one who was having a difficult time connecting with the spirit of the tea.

I took my second drink and settled back into my chair. It tasted, if possible, even worse than the first one had. Within a few minutes it became clear that this time it was going to work. I began to feel the force of the *hoasca* course through my body, a feeling of energy passing from the base of my spine to the top of my head. It was like being borne upward in a high-speed elevator. I welcomed the sensation as confirmation that the train was pulling out of the station.

The energized feeling and the sensation of rapid acceleration continued. It was much like mushrooms but seemed to be much stronger. I had the sense that this was one elevator it would be hard to exit before reaching the top floor, wherever that might be. Random snippets of topics we had been discussing at the seminars in the previous days began to float into my consciousness. I remembered one seminar that had addressed the UDV's concept that the power of *hoasca* tea is a combination of "force" and "light." The force was supplied by the MAO-inhibiting *Banisteriopsis* vine, known as *mariri* in the local vernacular, while the light—the visionary, hypnagogic component—was derived from *chacruna*, the DMT-containing *Psychotria* admixture plant. I thought to myself what an apt characterization this was; *hoasca* was definitely a combination of force and light, and at that moment I was well within the grip of the force and hoped that I was about to break out into the light.

At the instant I had that thought, I heard a voice seeming to come from behind my left shoulder. It said something like, "You wanna see force? I'll show you force!" The question was clearly rhetorical, and I understood that I was about to experience something whether I wanted to or not. The next instant, I found myself changed into a disembodied point of view, suspended in space, thousands of miles over the Amazon basin. I could see the curvature of the earth, the stars beyond shone steadily against an inky backdrop, and far below I could see swirls and eddies of clouds over the basin, and the nerve-like tracery of vast river systems. From the center of the basin arose the world tree in the form of an enormous *Banisteriopsis* vine. It was twisted into a helical form and its flowering tops were just below my disembodied viewpoint. Its base was anchored to the earth far below, lost to vision in the depths of mist and clouds and distance that stretched beneath me.

As I gazed, awestruck, at this vision, the voice explained that the Amazon was the omphalos of the planet, and that the twisted, ropelike Yggdrasil-*mariri* world tree was the lynchpin that tied the three realms—the underworld, the earth, and the sky—together. Somehow I understood—though no words were involved—that the *Banisteriopsis* vine was the embodiment of the plant intelligence that embraced and covered the earth, that together the community of the plant species that existed on the earth provided the nurturing energy that made life on earth possible. I "understood" that photosynthesis—that neat trick, known only to green plants, of making complex organic compounds from sunlight, carbon dioxide, and water, was the "force" the UDV was talking about and indeed was the force on which all life depends; I was reminded of a line from Dylan Thomas, that photosynthesis is "the force that through the green fuse drives the flower."

In the next moment, I found myself instantly transported from my bodiless perch in space to the lightless depths beneath the surface of the earth. I had somehow become a sentient water molecule, percolating randomly through the soil, lost amid the tangle of the enormous root fibers of the *Banisteriopsis* world tree. I could feel the coolness, the dank dampness of the soil surrounding me, I felt suspended in an enormous underground cistern, a single drop among billions of drops. This sensation lasted only a moment, then I felt a definite sense of movement as, squeezed by the implacable force of irresistible osmotic pressures, I was rapidly translocated into the roots of the *Banisteriopsis* tree; the sense of the rising, speeding elevator returned, except this time I was being lifted rapidly through the vast pipes and tubes of the plant's vascular system. I was a single molecule of water tumbling through the myriad branches and forks of the vertical maze, which grew progressively narrower the higher I went.

Finally, the sense of accelerating vertical movement eased off. I was now floating freely in a horizontal direction. No longer feeling pushed, I was suspended in the middle of a stream flowing through an enormous, vaulted tunnel. More than that, there was light at the end of the tunnel, a green light. With a start I realized that I had just passed through the petiole of a sun-drenched leaf and was being shunted into progressively narrowing arteries as I was carried through the articulating veins toward some unknown destination. It helped that the voice—or my own narrative self, I'm not sure which—was providing occasional commentary on the stages of the journey as it unfolded.

Desperately I tried to remember my old lessons in plant physiology and anatomy. By this time I had been given the wordless understanding that I was about to witness, indeed, participate in, the central mystery of life on earth: a water molecule's view of the process of photosynthesis. Suddenly, I was no longer suspended in the arterial stream of the leaf vein. I had somehow been transported into an enormous enclosed space, suffused with greenish light. Above me I could see the domed, vaulted roof of the structure I was inside of and I understood that I was inside a chloroplast. The roof was translucent and beams of sunlight streamed through it like a bedroom window on a bright morning. In front of me were flat, layered structures looking like folded sheets stacked closely together, covered with antenna-shaped structures, all facing in the same direction and all opened eagerly to receive the incoming light. I realized that these had to be the thylakoid membranes, the organelles within the chloroplast where the so-called light reaction takes place. The antenna-like structures covering them literally glowed and hummed with photonic energy, and I could see that somehow this energy was being translocated through the membranes of the thylakoids they were mounted on. I recognized, or understood, that these antenna-like arrays were molecules of chlorophyll and the "anchors" that tied them to their membrane substrates were long tails of phytic acid that functioned as energy transducers, funneling the light energy collected by the flower-shaped receptors through the membrane and into the layers beneath it.

Next thing I knew, I was beneath that membrane; I was being carried along as though borne on a conveyor belt. I could see the phytic acid chains dangling above, and beyond them, through the semitransparent "roof " of the membrane, the flowerlike porphyrin groups that formed the chlorophyll's light-gathering apparatus loomed like the dishes of a radio telescope array. In the center of the space was what looked like a mottled flat surface, periodically being smited by enormous bolts of energy that emanated, lightning-like, from the phytic acid tails suspended above it. On that altar water molecules were being smashed to smithereens by the energy bolts. Consciousness exploded and died in a spasm of electron ecstasy as I was smited by the bolt of energy emitted by the phytic acid transducers and my poor water-molecule soul was split asunder.

As the light energy was used to ionize the water, the oxygen liberated in the process rose with a shriek to escape from the chamber of horrors, while the electrons, liberated from their matrix, were shunted into the electron-transport rollercoaster, sliding down the chain of cytochromes like a dancer being passed from partner to partner, into the waiting arms of "photosystem I," only to be blasted again by yet another photonic charge, bounced into the close but fleeting embrace of ferredoxin, the primary electron acceptor, ultimately captured by $NADP^+$ to be used as bait to capture two elusive protons, as a flame draws a moth. Suddenly I was outside the flattened thylakoid structures, which from my perspective looked like highrise, circular apartment buildings. I recognized that I was suspended in the stroma, the region outside the thylakoid membranes, where the mysterious "dark reaction" takes place, the alchemical wedding that joins carbon dioxide to ribulose diphosphate, a shotgun marriage presided over by ribulose diphosphate carboxylase, the first enzyme in the so-called pentose phosphate shunt. All was quiet and for a moment. I was floating free in darkness. Then miraculously—miracles were by this time mundane—I realized that my disembodied point of view had been reincarnated again and was now embedded in the matrix of the newly reduced ribulose diphosphate / carbon dioxide complex; this unstable intermediate was rapidly falling apart into two molecules of phosphoglycerate, which were grabbed and loaded on the merry-go-round by the first enzymes of the Calvin cycle. Dimly, I struggled to remember my early botany lessons and put names to what I was seeing.

I recognized that I had entered the first phases of the pentose phosphate shunt, the biochemical pathway that builds the initial products of photosynthesis into complex sugars and sends them spinning from thence into the myriad pathways of biosynthesis that ultimately generate the molecular stuff of life.

I felt humbled, shaken, exhausted, and exalted all at the same time. Suddenly I was ripped out of my molecular rollercoaster ride, and my disembodied eye was again suspended high over the Amazon basin. This time there was no world tree arising from its center; it looked much like it must look from a spacecraft in orbit. The day was sunny and the vista stretching to the curved horizon was blue and green and bluish-green. The vegetation below, threaded with shining rivers, looked like green mold covering an overgrown petri plate. Suddenly I was wracked with a sense of overwhelming sadness, sadness mixed with fear for the delicate balance of life on this planet, the fragile processes that drive and sustain life, sadness for the fate of our planet and its precious cargo.

"What will happen if we destroy the Amazon?" I thought to myself. "What will become of us, what will become of life itself, if we allow this destruction to continue? We cannot let this happen. It must be stopped, at any cost." I was weeping. I felt miserable, I felt anger and rage toward my own rapacious, destructive species, scarcely aware of its own devastating power, a species that cares little about the swath of destruction it leaves in its wake as it thoughtlessly decimates ecosystems and burns thousands of acres of rainforest. I was filled with loathing and shame.

Suddenly, again from behind my left shoulder, came a quiet voice. "You monkeys only think you're running things," it said. "You don't think we would really allow this to happen, do you?" And somehow I knew that the "we" in that statement was the entire community of species that constitute the planetary biosphere. I knew that I had been given an inestimable gift, a piece of gnosis and wisdom straight from the heart-mind of planetary intelligence, conveyed in visions and thought by an infinitely wise, incredibly ancient, and enormously compassionate "ambassador" to the human community. A sense of relief, tempered with hope, washed over me. The vision faded, and I opened my eyes to see my newfound friends and hosts all eagerly gathered around me. The ceremony had officially ended a few minutes earlier, but I had been utterly oblivious to whatever was going on in the world beyond my closed eyelids. "How was it," they wanted to know, "did you feel the *buhachara,* the strange force?" I smiled to myself, feeling overjoyed at the prospect of sharing the experience and knowing that I had indeed been allowed to experience the ultimate "force," the vastly alien, incredibly complex molecular machine that is "the force that through the green fuse drives the flower."

47 New in Town

I eventually became disillusioned with aspects of my job at Shaman Pharmaceuticals, or perhaps my doubts were really about my potential for success as a corporate scientist. I'd grown to like my colleagues and enjoy the work, but I decided to look for other opportunities. Andrew Weil contacted me to suggest that I meet his friend Horst Rechelbacher, the founder of Aveda, a Minnesota-based cosmetics company that reflected his environmentally conscious views. Aveda was committed to using sustainable, organic ingredients from around the world, and Horst was looking for an ethnobotanist to help the company develop products from botanical ingredients. The word was that impending changes in regulatory policy would look favorably on herbal medicines, and the industry would explode as a result. Aveda was weighing whether to enter the market for nutraceuticals and dietary supplements and would need help in that area if they did.

Thanks to Weil, I got a chance to chat with Rechelbacher at a Seeds of Change conference in Santa Fe in the fall of 1992. (The event has since been renamed the Bioneers Conference and is held each year in San Rafael.) Our meeting went well. I knew the Austrian-born Horst by reputation as a visionary and an entrepreneurial genius. A self-made multimillionaire who had worked in the salon trade since his early teens, he'd built the Aveda Corporation from scratch. I wasn't sure what I could do for him, I said; after all, I was a CNS pharmacologist and ethnobotanist. I did view myself as a natural products chemist to some extent, but what did I know about cosmetics or cosmetic formulations? Horst assured me that didn't matter. In effect, what he said was that if I came to work for him he'd pay me twice as much as I'd been making at Shaman, and I could do whatever I wanted. An offer like that was hard to pass up.

He invited me to visit their headquarters outside Minneapolis, and shortly after the conference I flew out to meet with him and some of his executives. I stayed at the Aveda Spa in the St. Croix Valley nearby his palatial home in Osceola, Wisconsin, and they treated me like royalty. Even though it was November and well into a gray autumn, the St. Croix Valley was beautiful, and the rural setting appealed to me. A move there would be a welcome escape from the urban density of the Bay Area. There was no way we could ever afford a house in California, but in Minnesota we just might pull it off. We were also drawn to the prospect of finding a nice school for Caitlin. All things considered, it made sense to pick up stakes and move. I returned to Menlo Park and gave notice at Shaman.

We left Menlo Park on New Year's Eve 1992, angling the Honda south to avoid a blizzard that had blocked the passes along I-80 on the route through Tahoe. After a stop to visit Aunt Mayme in Paonia, we ran east over the plains, trying to outrace another storm that had swept in over the coast behind us. The snows finally caught up to us in Iowa, forcing us into a Holiday Inn outside Des Moines. When we finally reached Minneapolis and stepped out of the car, it was into near-zero temps and an icy, biting wind. As lightly clad California refugees in an unlikely promised land, we suddenly had our doubts about what we'd gotten into.

Day by day, however, we settled in. One lesson I'd learned at Shaman the hard way was that a verbal agreement wasn't worth much in the corporate world, at least when it came to a starting salary. Horst, however, was as good as his word. I had a new position at more than twice what I'd been making, with an impressive title: Senior Research Pharmacognosist. I was delighted, of course, and launched into my new work with great hopes. Horst was open to finding and incorporating natural ingredients from all over the globe and, if possible, sourcing them from Indigenous communities. The new regulations wouldn't become law for more than a year—the Dietary Supplement Health and Education Act of 1994, or DSHEA—but there were already plans afoot to position the company for the impending herbal gold rush. If predictions held, the new law would open new markets for natural medicines and create lots of opportunities for "pharmacognosists" like me. (The term is derived from the Greek *pharmakon*, for drugs, and *gnôsis*, knowledge; it refers to a specialist in the scientific study of drugs of natural origin.) Despite my title, I wasn't formally a pharmacognosist, but I was charged with taking the lead on product innovation in that arena.

We had a good meeting about the new mission shortly after I started my job. Weil, who had done so much to help me, was there, and we talked about the new direction we were charting. Shortly after that, Horst took off to

India for six months and left me to the tender ministrations of the director of R&D and the chief financial officer. I began making plans for a trip to Brazil in the spring. Aveda already had a part-time field consultant in Manaus, a city in the heart of the Amazon, and had considered setting up a lab there. I wanted to connect with her and begin collecting around Manaus, looking for plants that could potentially be used as cosmetic ingredients, dietary supplements, or even food sources. As I settled into my new job, Sheila started scanning the papers, searching for a house. We considered some neighborhoods in the Twin Cities but we really wanted to live somewhere along the St. Croix River. Over the course of our Sunday drives, we became utterly charmed by Marine on St. Croix, a quiet hamlet of 604 souls about 10 miles north of Stillwater. We decided our new home had to be there. There wasn't much on the market, but finally we made an offer on a very small house in Marine, a classic case of the ugliest house on the best street in town. Twenty years later, we're still here. After a modest renovation and expansion, it has been the perfect home for us ever since.

Marine proved to be the ideal community it appeared to be. It has all the good things that small towns can offer and, yes, some of the warts and blemishes as well. Garrison Keillor's Lake Wobegon, his mythical Minnesota town, is often regarded as being loosely based on Marine. Keillor lived in Marine a few years before we arrived, and many of the skits and vignettes on his radio show, *A Prairie Home Companion*, were apparently inspired by the local array of eccentric characters and places. Ralph's Pretty Good Grocery, the Chatterbox Café, and the Sidetrack Tap certainly seem like parodies of local businesses well known to any Marine resident.

Our choice to settle in Marine was fortuitous. It had a tiny elementary school, only about 170 students in total, recognized as one of the best K–6 schools in the state. All the children really were above average! We quickly made friends. There was another California refugee family from San Jose, a software developer and his wife who had arrived the year before with their two daughters, one of whom was Cait's age. We met others in the community the same way, and we soon were part of a close-knit circle of friends based around our kids, not to mention similar liberal political persuasions. The kids are all grown now, but our little circle remains close. One could not wish for a finer bunch of friends and neighbors.

That first year in Marine was a rewarding time for me—at home, at work, and in the wider scientific circles whose respect I valued. I met good people at Aveda and enjoyed my modest prosperity. As I prepared for my trip to Brazil, I also followed up on a plan that emerged from the União do Vegetal conference in São Paulo in 1991. After that conference, I had drafted a proposal to carry out a biomedical investigation of ayahuasca that had since been approved by the UDV's medical committee. We had also raised enough funds through Botanical Dimensions to carry out the study. I'd be in Brazil for almost eight weeks, most of them in Manaus, so we made plans to conduct the field phase of our study there in June. Our work took place over about five weeks at one of the oldest UDV temples in Manaus, Nucleo Caupari.

The Hoasca Study, as it came to be known, turned out to be a milestone event in the scientific investigation of the long-term use of ayahuasca. My colleagues and friends fulfilled important roles: Charles Grob, MD, now a professor of psychiatry and pediatrics at UCLA, was the principle investigator, and Jace Callaway, an American biochemist at the University of Kuopio in Finland, carried out most of the analytical and pharmacokinetic work. Many others also contributed. One key figure who went unacknowledged in the published findings was our friend Annelise Schinzinger, a long-time UDV member who worked closely with us as a Portuguese translator. The project could not have been accomplished without her help, and her recognition is long past due. Our study triggered a small surge in ayahuasca research, resulting in at least six peer-reviewed papers, several review papers, and major advances in our understanding of ayahuasca pharmacology. There were only 14 citations on ayahuasca in PubMed between 1960 and 1994; since then, there have been 82 publications.

In 1993, I also helped establish the Heffter Research Institute, a nonprofit organization committed to investigating "the appropriate and safe use of classical hallucinogens in a medical context." The institute was the brainchild of David Nichols, the Purdue professor of pharmacology and medicinal chemistry I mentioned earlier, a world expert on the study of psychedelic compounds. The institute was named after Arthur Heffter, an obscure but admired figure in the history of psychedelic research. A German chemist, pharmacologist, and Renaissance man, Heffter was the first to systematically investigate the alkaloids of peyote cactus and demonstrate, in careful self-experiments, that mescaline was the major hallucinogenic compound in the plant. Beloved and admired by his students, Heffter didn't fit the usual stereotype of the 19th-century German "Herr Professor." We chose the name because he exemplified both the spirit of bold scientific exploration and the high ethical standards we wanted our institute to represent.

In addition to Nichols, Grob, and myself, the original Heffter board included Mark Geyer, a psychopharmacologist from the University of California, San Diego; George Greer, MD, a psychiatrist and MDMA researcher from Santa Fe; and Philip Wolfson, MD, a Bay Area psychotherapist. Our first meeting took place at the Mount Baldy Zen Center in the Angeles National Forest east of L.A., a rustic spot perfect for planning and "envisioning." While the board has changed over the years, it continues to include many leading researchers in the field, and the Heffter remains the premier sponsor of basic and clinical research on psychedelics (www.heffter.org). I've always been proud to be affiliated with the institute, though I've sometimes felt a bit out of place, lacking a high-level research position, lab, or other such resource. But someone had to represent the interests of ethnopharmacology, and I was fortunate to have that role fall to me.

After my trip to Brazil, I continued my efforts to expand my employer's presence there, as part of the company strategy we'd drawn up when I started the job. Indeed, I spent much of my time writing and presenting budgets and work plans to the "steering committee," a group that ran the operation in the absence of the visionary who had created it. I was learning the ropes of corporate life, or so I thought. It took almost the entire year to get the OK on my budgets, but the results looked good. The committee approved nearly $600,000 to set up a lab in Manaus and start collecting and evaluating plants for possible use in cosmetics and medicine or as food sources. There was even a line item to buy a small boat for expeditions up

José Cabral and Dennis preparing voucher specimens, UDV study, 1993.

the more remote tributaries. I'd come a long way from my days with the Heraclitistas on the River of Poisons.

Or had I? I soon discovered there was something just as problematic about steering by committee north of the equator. I figured that getting the go-ahead was a mere formality. Instead, at a meeting early in 1994 I was informed that getting a budget approved didn't mean I could actually spend it. Which surprised me. It turned out there was a reality parallel to the one I'd been living in, and that's where the spending decisions were actually made. To put it simply, there would be no new lab in the Amazon, no botanical explorations, and no boat.

I'd be at Aveda another year and a half, but from that moment on I realized I'd never accomplish the goals we'd defined at the outset. The clues were there before, of course, even if I'd chosen not to articulate them. There was a difference between Horst's vision, which was environmentally oriented and forward-looking, and what really went on from day to day. He wanted to save the planet; the middle managers running the place basically viewed their mission as getting shampoo out the door. Anything that didn't directly support that rather mundane goal became an impediment.

I finally gave notice in 1995. Most people who left Aveda didn't do so by choice. Perhaps because I did, Horst and I parted amicably and remained friends. I respect him very much, and I'd like to believe the feeling is mutual. After he sold his company to Estée Lauder in 1997 for a reported $300 million, I think it's fair to say he became more relaxed and playful. And who wouldn't? Having that kind of money in your account will do wonders for stress, especially if having the money means you're able to spend it.

By then, the herbal boom triggered by DSHEA had fully begun. After leaving Aveda, I took a job as the R&D director for Nutraceutix, a company based in Redmond, a position that let me work from home for three weeks each month and spend a week at its plant in Washington. The company made probiotic supplements for livestock feed but wanted to capitalize on the burgeoning demand for dietary supplements for humans. After developing some formulations for Odwalla, the organic juice company in Santa Cruz, California, we started a project to grow ginseng using "hairy root" propagation, a cool technology for generating large amounts of root biomass in vats without actually growing entire plants. In theory, that made the hairy-root technique an efficient method for producing high-value metabolites that are hard to synthesize. Our goal was to produce "super ginseng" with enhanced levels of active metabolites. I reconnected with my mentor Neil Towers and the lab at UBC to help us carry out a pilot study. We discovered the high-tech methods cost too much compared to just growing ginseng the old-fashioned way, and the project was dropped. I left the company in 1998 when it decided the real money lay in sports supplements. Since those were made up almost entirely of synthetic ingredients, there wasn't much reason for a plant guy to stick around.

I made a good living for the next couple of years as an independent consultant. More important than the money, I learned, was having control over my time. Business was good. Kava kava, the Polynesian anxiolytic beverage, was becoming quite popular, and there was keen interest in creating drinks that incorporated a dose of kava for relaxation and as a social lubricant. Many Hawaii farmers saw kava as the next big cash crop, reviving a local economy that had been sluggish since the sugarcane market had collapsed decades earlier. I consulted for a company that was starting work on what is known as a supercritical extraction plant on the Big Island for kava and other organic biomaterials. Meanwhile, another client had ties to a large ranch on the island of Molokai that had begun committing many acres to kava cultivation. That led to a modest grant through the Heffter Research Institute to characterize the "chemotypes" of the recognized varieties of Hawaiian kava, or "awa" as it is called there. The study was somewhat outside the Heffter's mission scope, but we undertook it, given that the research concerned the ethnobotany of a culturally important psychoactive plant. The result, published in 1999, was the first detailed investigation of the chemistry and morphological diversity of "awa" in Hawaii (Lebot et al. 1999).

Back on the mainland, I worked with a startup company, Pharmanex, whose founders were developing a line of high-quality supplements to be sold through pharmacies. My job was to produce scientific write-ups on each product as part of an effort to educate pharmacists about herbal supplements, a big project I finished with the help of two colleagues, medical writer Kenneth Jones and ethnobotanist Kerry Hughes. Pharmanex published the work as a desktop reference, but by then the firm had been acquired by Nu Skin Enterprises, a larger company whose direct-sales strategy had no role for pharmacists, much less a book to inform them. Our orphaned text eventually caught the attention of Haworth Herbal Press, which published an updated edition as *Botanical Medicines: The Desk Reference for Major Herbal Supplements* in 2002. I went on to serve as editor in chief of Haworth Herbal Press until the imprint was discontinued after the sale of its parent, Haworth Press, to Taylor and Francis in 2007.

So that's a sketch of my career through the 1990s. Looking back, I'd say my experiences at Aveda, and earlier at Shaman, were quite valuable and have colored my perspective ever since. I realized I didn't work well in a corporate structure, subject to someone else's idea of how best to use my time. I did better work as a consultant, and most of my subsequent forays into the corporate world would be in that capacity. Since 2001, I've served as an adjunct assistant professor at the Center for Spirituality and Healing at the University of Minnesota in Minneapolis. In recent years, I've also taught summer field courses for pharmacy students in Ecuador and Peru. I've mentioned how lucky I was to encounter talented mentors and teachers whose love of plants was a gift they were driven to share with their students. I'm grateful now for the chance I have to impart my love of the natural world in turn.

48 The Bard in Light and Shadow

It's been more than 30 years since that rainy Monday in April 1981 when Terence packed up seeds and gear and said good-bye to me at the airport in Iquitos. While our farewells were temporary, my sadness at the time said otherwise. On some level, I knew the occasion marked a pivotal transition for us, and I think he felt the same. Over the decades ahead, we'd be caught up in the same relentless flow of time that carries every being toward its separate fate. There would always be something akin to quantum entanglement between us, at least binding our minds. Though we saw each other frequently and remained in close touch over the ensuing decades, the vicissitudes of life largely kept us focused on our own separate tracks.

While I'd been finishing my thesis in Vancouver and working through various postdocs, building a scientific career and raising a daughter in a new hometown, Terence had been striking off in new directions of his own. He had abandoned plans for an academic career and, publicly at least, had rejected science or any other sort of conventional professional identity. Always a maverick, he eschewed anything like a "real job." Fortunately, he was clever and talented enough not to need one. Like Marshall McLuhan, another contemporary maverick that we both admired, Terence was able to carve out a unique place at the table in the ongoing cultural conversation.

During the 1980s, interest grew in the philosophical ideas and peculiar notions that Terence espoused. The books we had coauthored, *The Invisible Landscape* and *Psilocybin: Magic Mushroom Grower's Guide*, were important early texts in that regard. The former exposed readers to a mind-stretching plethora of odd but appealing ideas, and the latter gave them a do-it-your-self method for visiting the realms we postulated if they wanted to try it at home.

Over time, Terence used his talents as a charismatic lecturer and racon-teur to develop a devoted following. He became closely identified with mushrooms and the peculiar ideas associated with them, and discussed them openly in his ever-more-frequent radio interviews and public appear-ances. Even though mushrooms themselves were illegal, there was no law against talking about them, and Terence's open advocacy of the psychedelic experience was reminiscent of Leary's, another Irish gadfly who in his prime had used psychedelics to poke a stick in the eye of an uptight establishment. During the Reagan era and the "just say no" phase of the war on drugs, Ter-ence's message got under the skin of many of the more humorless arbiters of morality and cultural correctness. He always had a gift for the provoc-ative statement, and for him to put himself out there as the chief advocate of psychedelic gnosis when no one else was doing so took some courage.

Psychedelics are not suppressed because they are dangerous to users; they're suppressed because they provoke unconventional thought, which threatens any number of elites and institutions that would rather do our thinking for us. Historically, those in power have always sought to sup-press free thought, whether bluntly or subtly, because it poses an inherent challenge to their rule. That's no less true today, in an age when corporate, political, and religious interests form a global bloc whose interests threaten all earthly life, including human life. Mushrooms have a way of inoculating the mind against the kind of thought control the prevailing order in any age needs to sustain itself. I'm not naively suggesting that the work of building a better world stops with the psychedelic experience. But it could be where it begins, or is renewed—in the moment of freedom when one glimpses the transient nature of reality and its ever-present potential for change.

Terence, by example, gave people permission to explore consciousness, to think, and to entertain new ideas. He reminded his listeners that it's fun to exercise the imagination; astonishment and wonder awaken our desires to look inwardly at who we are and outwardly at the marvelous universe we inhabit. No matter how much we come to understand, there will always be infinitely more to be understood. One of Terence's favorite quotes was from the English geneticist J. B. S. Haldane: "My own suspicion is that the universe is not only queerer than we suppose, but queerer than we *can* suppose." Terence reveled in that insight. The fact is that "funny ideas," no matter how strange, play a crucial role in enticing us beyond the perimeters of the imaginable. As a leading late-20th-century advocate of funny ideas, Terence deserves credit for leaving the scope of what we can suppose just a bit wider than he found it.

One challenge for him was finding a way to turn his gift of gab into tangible products that would help him pay the bills. He began working with others to capture and market his raps on tape. One early example was the original version of *True Hallucinations*, an audiobook account of our trip to La Chorerra that he read aloud, released by a company called Sound Photosynthesis in 1984. That and other early recordings helped him garner renown and some royalties, which Sound Photosynthesis, for one, eventually stopped paying. Terence's talks and lectures are now widely available for free on the Internet, which is great in one sense and heartbreaking in another. Unlike the ephemeral "works" of other legendary conversationalists, Terence's talks will live on as long as people care to listen. On the other hand, once such creations are available to all in digital form, they cease to belong to their creators or their families, making it that much harder for an unaffiliated free thinker like Terence to achieve the kind of stability needed to make ends meet, let alone to step back and assess one's work, or push it in new directions.

By 1990, Terence had fully assumed his role as the bardic, shaman-trickster figure that became his beloved (and occasionally ridiculed) public persona. In addition to his role as spokesman for the new psychedelic culture, he'd achieved some notoriety for his timewave theory and its predicted end of history. He had found his "shtick," as he sometimes lightly called it, and that kept him on the public stage before a growing legion of fans. There was no real competition for his niche; Leary was still around, but by then he was old and boring. If the original 1960s psychedelic message was about peace, free love, Eastern wisdom, and getting back to nature, Terence's take, while deeply informed by all that, had its own distinct edge. His audiences were mostly younger inhabitants of the Global Village foreseen by McLuhan and by the early 1990s becoming a reality. They were far from Luddite back-to-the-landers; these were world-spanning techno-nomads of an emerging global tribalism, the enthusiastic vanguard of a new post-historical archaic revival. Two decades ago, the hyperconnected informational environment and global neural network that most of us inhabit today was still nascent. Terence was the perfect avatar to give voice and vision to that emerging shift. Cool, articulate, eclectically educated, funny, steeped in psychedelics and sci-fi, Terence channeled the logos of the age. Silver-tongued and a riveting speaker, he articulated the concepts that his fans groped for but could not express, and he did so in a witty, disarming way. He was the gnomic trickster and bard, an elfin comedian delivering the cosmic punch line, even as he assured us we were all in on the joke. You just had to love him, and many people did, and still do.

Another important step for Terence was his association with the Esalen Institute in Big Sur. In the late 1980s into the early '90s, he spent time as a "scholar in residence" at Esalen during the summers. During those years, he also began to attract notice from publishers. *The Archaic Revival: Speculations on Psychedelic Mushrooms, the Amazon, Virtual Reality, UFOs, Evolution, Shamanism, the Rebirth of the Goddess, and the End of History* appeared in 1992. Terence was never one for the short, catchy title. *Food of the Gods: The Search for the Original Tree of Knowledge and a Radical History of Plants, Drugs, and Human Evolution* was also published in 1992, as was *Trialogues at the Edge of the West: Chaos, Creativity and the Resacralization of the West*, the first of three published conversations with the mathematician Ralph Abraham and the theoretical biologist Rupert Sheldrake. *True Hallucinations* first appeared in book form in 1993. Of all Terence's writings during this prolific period, that work stands out for me as his most accessible and personal. Most of our contemporaries never embarked on such an adventure, but many could understand why we did; Terence's account of it is a quest narrative at heart, imbued with the dreams and illusions of our time and of youth in general. The story's broad appeal and his skillful telling of it resulted in what is arguably a classic of the era's literature.

I always thought Terence was at his best when he spoke on topics that were not directly related to the timewave or psychedelics. He was extremely well-read on a variety of interesting and obscure topics, partly because of his experience in the Tussman program at Berkeley but mostly through the books he lovingly accumulated over years of creating his amazing library, which eventually numbered more than 3,000 volumes. He told me he'd read most of them and I believe him. He was an astute observer of contemporary culture and often prescient about many of the social, historical, and technological forces that have created our post-millennial world. That may explain why so many of Terence's lectures survive on the Internet, and why people are still listening to them. Even though they date back to the 1980s and '90s, they sound as fresh and timely as if they were uttered yesterday. As I've noted, Terence's genius was that he could see the future that was immanent in current events, and then articulate that insight for the rest of us. He may have gotten the details wrong in places, and been hobbled by the assumptions of the metaphysics he constructed, but one only has to look around to realize that basically he got it remarkably right. If Terence returned tomorrow, he would be unsurprised by most of what has transpired since his death. He would no doubt have incisive thoughts to share about the world at present, and the future impending within it, invisible to all but the few with his gift of perceiving it.

Terence put his ideas out there, but he was never wedded to them or inclined to present them as scripture. He was antidogmatic by nature. He always maintained a sense of humor and a bemused perspective about his theories, and that was part of his appeal. He insisted that people should think for themselves and make their own judgments about his "crazy" notions. His ability to keep those notions at arm's length, so to speak, was an affirmation of his inherent stability. He was able to say, "Hey, here's a whole set of really wild ideas that are fun to think about; maybe some are even true. What do you think?"

It was an irreverent stance for a guru, which he never wanted to be. He had no desire to tell people what they *should* think; he just wanted them to think, period. I believe he viewed himself as a teacher, perhaps in some respects an entertainer, but never a guru. Many younger people have told me that what they've learned from Terence was more relevant to them than any other part of their educations, which is an enormous compliment to him and his talents.

And yet for every charismatic figure there is a legion of people who are eager to follow, and a certain contingent of Terence's audience viewed him in that way. He liked being recognized and admired, of course, but he never took himself that seriously and had no desire to lead a flock. Most of the world's religions are empowered by the human readiness to worship charismatic figures and seek solace in mass identification. Religious and political demagogues use these impulses to lure believers into relinquishing self-responsibility and the capacity for critical thought. Sociopathic or psychopathic personalities who achieve fame are usually quite happy to exploit their status, unburdened as they are by conscience, self-insight, or doubt.

Terence wanted no part of that sick dynamic. He was keenly aware of the difference between how some chose to see him and who he really was. One of his thoroughly sane admirers told me a story that revealed Terence's healthy perspective on his celebrity. The moment occurred at an appearance he made with the spiritual leader Ram Dass, who had his own issues with guru worship and cult followers. It happened during the 1990s, at a time when Terence was dealing with his share of personal setbacks. In their dialogue, Ram Dass said, "Your life is your message," a typical guru-esque pronouncement; Terence replied, "My life is a mess. My *message* is my message."

So that was Terence, as I saw him, at the zenith of his creative powers and career. I daresay those years, especially later on, were not his happiest. By the time my family and I moved from Bethesda back to the Bay Area in 1988, Terence's marriage was already under strain. By the time we left for Minnesota in late 1992, he and Kat had decided to get a divorce. The end of their marriage would affect my ties to both of them in profound and lasting ways. Terence visited us in Minnesota in late 1993, and we thoroughly enjoyed his company. With my new job and comfortable home life, it was a good time for me. After his recent publishing successes, Terence had much to be proud of as well. I may have thought we were adjusting to the fact of his pending divorce, which would be finalized in the year ahead, but I was underestimating its impact on both of us.

Though he sometimes railed against monogamy in his lectures, Terence was basically a serial monogamist at heart. Multiple partners and free love didn't work for him. He may have had a few short affairs in the period of emotional turbulence after his separation, but what he was looking for was someone to share the next phase of his life. Eventually he found her, or so he felt. Terence met Jill at a conference near Palenque, the famous Maya ruins in southern Mexico. Known as the Entheobotany Seminars, the event, hosted annually by the Botanical Preservation Corps, had become the place to see and be seen by everybody who was anybody in the psychedelic world. Terence had actually met Jill's mother, a Jungian psychologist, years earlier when she invited him to give a workshop she was organizing in Los Angeles. Jill had been busy raising her own young daughter at the time and had not attended. Terence and Jill dated for several months and then moved in together on the Big Island in mid-1994. They parted in late 1997.

In retrospect, I realize that by 1994 Terence was dealing with one of the most difficult periods in his life. His separation and eventual divorce had left him depressed. He was regularly suffering migraines, a malady that had plagued him off and on since adolescence. He was also feeling the pressures of maintaining a public persona, the constant travel it required, and the effort it took to meet the expectations of his audience. Jill was one of the few people he could turn to for emotional support, and their relationship became a refuge from the demands of his work.

My sense is that Terence felt a growing ambivalence about his career. One event that may have contributed to that feeling occurred at the Palenque seminars in early 1996. Prior to the conference, Terence had been corresponding with a young mathematician named Matthew Watkins, who wanted to discuss what he believed to be flaws in the calculations underlying the timewave. The two agreed to meet in Palenque and talk it out.

Watkins later said he didn't set out to "debunk" the timewave. In fact, over the conference, the two men had several friendly conversations about what Terence later dubbed "the Watkins Objection." During their chats, Watkins more or less deconstructed the timewave theory, to the point where Terence conceded that his challenger had identified some critical flaws. The sessions amounted to a cordial but serious exchange between two serious thinkers discussing the merits of a fairly arcane and abstract set of concepts.

Nevertheless, I believe the encounter deeply affected Terence. Watkins's critique was perhaps the first time anyone with mathematical expertise had questioned the tenets of his theory; as such, it carried more weight than previous criticisms, including my own. To make things worse, Terence had been suffering such severe migraines that he was barely able to leave his room much of the time. Once back home in Hawaii, he posted a response to Watkins on his website Hyperborea (www.levity.com/eschaton/hyperborea.html) but took it down when Watkins declared it unsatisfactory. He then allowed Watkins to furnish his own response, which Terence linked to under a title he'd given it: "Autopsy for a Mathematical Hallucination?" The statement remains posted to this day (www.fourmilab.ch/rpkp/autopsy.html).

There was a brief flurry of revisionism by certain timewave supporters, which according to Watkins, in a 2010 recap, failed to produce a better version. Much of this history is recounted from a different perspective on Peter Meyer's website (www.fractal-timewave.com). Meyer is the computer programmer who worked with Terence during the mid-1980s to develop the Timewave Zero software program that he still sells on CD-ROM. Back in 1996, the Watkins Objection remained front and center for a while on the Novelty List, an e-mail forum devoted to timewave-related topics, devolving at certain moments into objections aimed at Watkins himself. While eventually the contributors moved on, the impact lingered for Terence. I believe the affair shook his confidence in the validity of the timewave, a project that constituted a major part of his life's work.

At the time, I was living in Minnesota, tending to my own career and family. It was a difficult period in my relationship with Terence. Whether my perceptions were accurate or not, I wasn't happy with the way he'd been dealing with the fallout from his divorce. I also challenged him for not "walking his talk." He was active on the lecture circuit promoting psychedelics but taking them only rarely, just at a point when I thought he should have been taking them to facilitate insight and self-reflection. He disagreed and resented my efforts to engage him on it. For me, the emotions tied to these events stirred up a lot of turmoil and memories dating back to our earliest childhood. We didn't overtly argue, but tensions between us were definitely high.

Looking back on that period from a distance of 15 years or so, I can see now that I failed to appreciate how depressed Terence was at the time, and how badly he felt about the failure of his marriage and the challenges of his career. I should have had more compassion for him. I am chagrined and a little ashamed to admit that I was not there for Terence at a moment when a brother should have been.

Terence was 50 when our father died in 1997, and I was 46. Dad had long since retired to Mesa, Arizona, and lived there with Lois, his second wife. The rheumatic fever he'd had as a child had caused a heart valve defect that deteriorated over time. "Leaky valves" in old age are a common long-term outcome of this childhood disease, and the accepted treatment is a pig valve transplant. Our father had this procedure in the early 1980s, and it fixed the problem for more than a decade. He wasn't climbing mountains or hang gliding, but he played golf and swam regularly and had few problems until the mid-1990s.

After that, the valve became less efficient, but a second transplant wasn't indicated because of his age; what awaited him was advancing congestive heart failure. During this period we happened to be on a family vacation in Colorado at the same time Dad and Lois were. We were all staying at the Redstone Inn on the Crystal River, our old childhood family haunt. Dad became so short of breath sitting in the dining room I thought he was going to faint. He could barely make it upstairs to his room and appeared on the verge of a heart attack. Fortunately, the episode passed (it was probably triggered by high altitude) but he was definitely on the decline. He made a remark that day that has stuck with me: "You're just living your life and everything is going along fine," he said, "and the next thing you know, you look in the mirror and you see an old man looking back at you. You suddenly realize that you're old. How did that happen?" He seemed genuinely puzzled. By then he could do little but sit in a chair. He was very uncomfortable and usually short of breath. It was wrenching to see this old man, my old man, suffering so much. It almost seemed as if death would be merciful even though he was "only" 80 at the time. His doctors came up with the brilliant idea of implanting a defibrillator in his chest. Neither Terence nor I were consulted or even informed about this until the deed had been done. When I found out, I was furious. Dad did not have arrhythmia or irregular heartbeat; he had congestive heart failure. Though some would argue the devices reduce the risk of "sudden death," a defibrillator struck me as an inappropriate treatment for a man of his age and condition. For me, convincing him to undergo the procedure amounted to malpractice. But Medicare would pay for it and reward his physicians well for doing so—another regrettable illustration of high-tech medicine out of control.

We had no idea just how regrettable until our father's death—or rather, his many deaths. His ordeal began on April 27, 1997, a day when I had flown to Boston for a meeting with a company I was consulting for. Terence, as it happened, was also on the East Coast, giving a workshop in North Carolina. There was a message from Sheila awaiting me when I checked into the hotel. Lois had called to tell her my father had fallen in the shower after suffering an apparent heart attack or stroke. He'd been taken, unconscious, to the emergency room and died shortly thereafter. I went to my room and called Lois. After talking to her a few minutes, I hung up and sat there gathering my thoughts. The news wasn't a surprise. We'd been expecting something like it for some time.

Then Lois called back with an odd and disturbing follow-up: it seemed that Dad had not died after all. He had not recovered consciousness, but his heart had started beating again due to the defibrillator, which kept kicking in when his heart stopped. The thing would literally resurrect him every time. Lois gave me the number at the hospital, and I called and talked to a nurse, explained the situation to him, and asked if they could just turn off the defibrillator. Clearly, Dad was not going to recover and yet was being denied a peaceful death.

The nurse's answer shocked me. Actually, no, he said, they could not turn off the device because it belonged to the corporation, and only a company technician could access the software codes that deactivated it. The request to do so had to be authorized by my father's physician.

"Well, get the goddamn physician on the line and have him authorize it!" I demanded, by now screaming into the phone. But the physician was on a golf junket in Florida and couldn't be reached, and no one was aware of a plan B. The nurse, who shared my distress, said the only way to resolve the matter was for me to get there as soon as I could and get in someone's face.

I hung up and called Terence at the conference center, and we both started making plans to get to Mesa. I left around 10 P.M. and finally made it to Phoenix 3 stops and 12 hours later. Terence had been going through the same nightmare and reached the hospital an hour before me. Overnight, the staff had finally gotten someone to turn off the device, but Dad had lingered on until Terence arrived and then stopped breathing 20 minutes later. I arrived shortly after that, but by then Terence, having no idea when I'd get there, had left, hoping to catch his connection for Hawaii out of L.A.

Being in the presence of someone who has just expired is a strange experience. The room was still crackling with the energy of our father's departing spirit; I had a definite, eerie sense that it was still hanging around, as if reluctant to leave until I showed up. The sight of him was enough to tell me his death had not been peaceful. The device in his chest would not permit that. The signature of his suffering, his agony and exhaustion, was etched into his face, and I will never forget it.

Both of our parents' deaths were fraught with drama. Our mother's had been disrupted by our concern over Terence, at the time a fugitive, trying to sneak into the country to spend some final moments with her. That did not happen, and Mom died never getting the chance to forgive or speak with her eldest and favorite son. At least Dad got to see Terence before he died, though I don't know if Dad was conscious when Terence was with him. I felt like the one who lost out; Dad had expired by the time I got there. Over the years, reflecting on these events, I've often berated myself for not taking legal action against the physicians who implanted the device. The death of a loved one is often a moment of great vulnerability. Lawyers and lawsuits are the last things a survivor wants to think about, and I didn't, though I feel now I should have. It wouldn't be the last time that a paralysis born of grief would cloud my judgment and keep me from making the right decision. I had no idea how to go about filing a suit, and I had doubts about whether we'd have the resources to sustain such a long and costly action if we did file. Life was pressing in and I made the decision to move on.

I've often regretted it. Dad was a good and ethical man. He was a good husband to our mother and a good father to Terry and me despite the grief we caused him. He fought bravely in the war and paid a price for it. He enjoyed his friends, his fishing and hunting, his golf, his flying. He was an admirable person in many ways, someone to look up to and emulate. He was certainly not "an average guy"even though that's how he wanted to think of himself. He was a good, practicing, believing Catholic to the very end. I hope he went to that heaven, if that's the one he wanted, because he deserved to.

In January 1998, I took part in a 12-day ayahuasca workshop in Iquitos, Peru, at Francisco Montes's retreat, Jardín Etnobotánico Sachamama, an hour outside Iquitos. Luis Eduardo Luna showed up, as did Francisco's cousin, the painter Pablo Amaringo. The workshop had been touted as a splendid retreat in a beautiful setting, and that proved to be true. Luis Eduardo, Pablo, and I were there to provide entertainment in the form of our lectures. The group would be taking ayahuasca with Francisco, who had begun practicing *vegetalismo*, and with some other local practitioners. Luis Eduardo and Pablo had not been on good terms since their falling out over the art school in Pucallpa a few years earlier, but they both agreed to show up. We were hoping the reunion would bring some healing and reconciliation, which it did, although the truce was an uneasy one.

Among the interesting people there was a gentleman with some serious mental issues. For one, he believed he was the reincarnation of Jesus Christ and had come back to earth to overcome a coven of witches and warlocks who were bent on destroying the world. This evil cabal turned out to be us— the workshop participants. He became convinced we had lured him there to kill him. Muttering darkly under his breath, he let us now know he was on to us and, come nightfall, "the tables would turn." He was quite serious about it and at one point tore off into the forest in a paranoid mania. Another group member, Bill, probably the sanest among us, found him hours later in a farmer's yard, sitting in the lotus position and wearing only a towel, with a machete stuck into the ground beside him. After 30 or 40 minutes of conversation, during which the guy didn't open his eyes, Bill convinced him to find a hotel room in town and get some rest. The guy's girlfriend, who had brought him to the workshop, later confided that he'd suffered these paranoid delusions for years and that she'd hoped the ayahuasca could help him.

Earlier, in a lucid moment, he told a fascinating story about how he had cured his severe dyslexia in adolescence using high doses of LSD. He'd always had difficulty reading, he said, because the letters just seemed to float off the page. Apparently, he'd taken LSD to play football in high school, believing that it improved his game. He was a good player, and his skill helped him gain social acceptance despite his learning disabilities; maybe LSD could help him tackle those as well. He described to me how, in a series of high-dose sessions, he was able to visualize the "wiring" in his brain, as he put it, and the "damaged filing cabinets" where his linguistic functions resided. In a shamanic act of psychic neurosurgery, he then identified a set of "alternate" cabinets and transferred his linguistic functions into them. After that, he never had any problems with dyslexia, he said. He read easily and enjoyed it.

I have no reason to doubt his story, though it obviously warrants skepticism in light of his mental health issues. It did lead me to speculate about the use of LSD as a potential treatment for dyslexia. We have a limited understanding of neuroplasticity, to say nothing of how psychedelics might affect it. That man's anecdote hints at the curious link between psychedelics and language, as do the more prevalent accounts of synesthesia I've discussed earlier. Psychedelics have some fundamental relationship to the way our brains create meaning and understanding out of sounds and images. I'm convinced that further investigations into this phenomenon would yield new insights.

Another participant was Jill, Terence's ex-girlfriend. The two had very recently split up, and one reason she attended the workshop was to look for some understanding and peace of mind. I'd gotten to know her somewhat on my visits to Hawaii while she and Terence were together. Back then I'd mistaken her quiet self-possession and reserve for shyness. I knew their parting had hurt her, though I believe it had been her choice. I was still feeling a lot of turmoil over my own relationship with Terence and, fairly or otherwise, Jill's experience may have heightened those emotions, which started surfacing for me in the ayahuasca sessions. They were difficult sessions, very dark and disturbing. I kept seeing images of Terence with a black shadow in the center of his chest, a black, hard knot located over his heart. Given my feelings at the time, I interpreted this as an expression of his coldness and lack of compassion. Only later did I understand what the aya-huasca was really showing me. It was a foreshadowing, literally, of a black tumor, the seeds of which even then were forming, though in my anger I had misplaced its location. I can't vouch for the validity of this perception, of course. It was an ayahuasca vision, after all. But in reflection, I have come to believe this is what I'd been shown—a premonition of the nightmare to come, still more than a year in the future.

Indeed, the rest of 1998 passed quietly. Terence went to the Palenque entheobotany event as usual, and in May he visited us briefly in Minnesota when he came out to speak at the Whole Life Expo in St. Paul. He informed me that he had a new girlfriend, Christy, whom he'd met in Palenque, a young woman from Ohio. I wouldn't actually meet her for another year, but her age alone, 25, had me privately conjuring up all sorts of presumptions about what she had to be like. Surely as impatient with me as I was with him, Terence wasn't in the mood to care what I thought, so we really didn't discuss it.

49 A Desperate Situation

Aunt Amelia, Terence, Christy, and Dennis, 1999.

By the spring of 1999, Terence was living with Christy in his recently completed house on the Big Island. He was busy dealing with various investors and others involved in organizing an event to be held on the island in September, the AllChemical Arts Conference. Billed as an exploration of the relationship between hallucinogens and the creative process, the event would feature Terence as the keynote speaker, followed by other well-known figures in the psychedelic and visionary arts community, including Alex Grey, Robert Venosa, Annie Sprinkle, Tom Robbins, Mark Pesce, Bruce Damer, and others. It was going to be quite an event.

I wasn't invited, which was OK with me; I was more on the science side of things and would not have had much to contribute. Terence and I hadn't fully resolved the tensions that had developed between us over the last few years, but we were at least getting along. In the meantime, I was busy producing the herbal supplement desk reference and lining up other consulting gigs. I wasn't focused on developments in Hawaii.

I got the news on May 23, when I picked up a voice mail left the previous day on my office phone. It was from Dan Levy, Terence's friend and former editor. Terence had suffered some kind of seizure, Dan said, and was currently in the Queen's Medical Center in Honolulu, where he had been airlifted by helicopter.

I immediately called Dan to get the full story. He wasn't sure exactly what had happened, he said, but he'd gotten an urgent message from Christy. Terence had recently returned from a long, exhausting tour on the East Coast, she said, and had been feeling poorly for several days. He'd been suffering flu-like symptoms and had taken to his bed. That alone was not unusual. Terence was often exhausted after a tour and would sometimes be sick for a few days afterward. But this time was different; he hadn't bounced back. As Christy told Dan, Terence had gotten up at one point and suffered a massive seizure. They both knew this was serious and that he had to get to the hospital. Somehow, Christy managed to get Terence into their jeep and started careening down the hill on the rugged road as Terence faded in and out of consciousness. She had called 9-1-1 from the Internet phone connection—they had no cell phones. While they waited at the bottom of the hill for the ambulance, Terence had another seizure, lost consciousness, and appeared near death.

Christy flagged down two passing motorcyclists for help. As it turned out, one of them had EMT training and was able to resuscitate Terence, almost certainly saving his life. The ambulance finally arrived, and the paramedics administered antiseizure medication and took him to Kona Community Hospital. At the hospital, a CT scan revealed no signs of an aneurism, but it did detect what was called a "shadow" in the right anterior part of Terence's brain. That was all Dan knew, but the word *tumor* hovered unspoken in the air.

I hung up the phone and collected my thoughts. I made arrangements to leave immediately for Honolulu.

When the taxi left me off at the medical center after an overnight flight, Christy was already there, as was Terence's son, Finn, who had been staying near him on the Big Island. It was the first time I'd met Christy, who was blonde, blue-eyed, and petite. Her feat of getting Terence down to the road seemed that much more remarkable when I saw how small she was. We would get to know each other well over the following months. Terence's daughter, Klea, was in Europe when she got the news; she soon arrived as well.

Terence had gotten an MRI by then, and the higher-resolution technology confirmed our worst fears. There was a dark mass, a tumor, about the size of a walnut, buried deep in his right forebrain. It would take a biopsy to determine the type of cancer, but we all feared the worst: glioblastoma multiforme, the most common and aggressive form of brain cancer. Fewer than 2 percent of glioblastoma sufferers survive more than a year after their tumors are detected. It's a rare cancer (about 20,000 cases in the United States each year) and all but incurable: surgery and radiation might prolong life at most a few months. Terence's neurooncologist was a compassionate man and an excellent doctor. He also struck me as one of the more depressed physicians I'd ever met, possibly because, as a specialist in this lethal disease, he'd never saved a single patient. His advice to Terence was blunt—he advised him to put his affairs in order. Terence might have a year to live, probably less, and no more than 18 months. The chances that the tumor was benign were slim to none, the doctor said, and the biopsy soon verified that.

By the time we had this conversation at Terence's bedside, he was feeling pretty good. He'd been given massive doses of antiseizure medicine and steroids to reduce swelling. The combined effects, bizarrely, made him slightly euphoric and pumped. He was sitting up in bed, fully conscious, no pain, cracking jokes, while the rest of us were looking glum. The hospital had a nice inner courtyard and garden, and Finn and Terence and I sat there for a while under an enormous banyan tree in the late afternoon sun and tried to sort things out. I was agitated, overwhelmed with feelings of fear, apprehension, helplessness, and desperation. Any residual anger with Terence over our petty differences had evaporated. My job was to be there for my brother as fully as I could.

My conversation with him in the garden was intense and strange. It was almost as if we were back at La Chorrera, 28 years earlier and thousands of miles away. This was the next twist of the helix, I told him; what we had started at La Chorrera was not finished. Our experiment was still in progress and only now nearing its resolution. We were about to encounter each other again, moving backward and forward in time as we had been then and ever since. But now it was my turn to be the anchor, the one who stayed behind. Terence would be the hyperspatial explorer, the one taking the shamanic hero's journey to the edge of the universe, perhaps never to return.

I don't know where my inspiration came from, whether I was channeling the Teacher, which is what it felt like, or whether I was slipping again into some kind of manic state. Perhaps I was just trying to frame the conversation in terms that were familiar and that would give Terence (and all of us) some hope. But I had a clear vision of the task in front of us. I told him our theory at La Chorrera had been right: beta-carbolines and tryptamines did intercalate into DNA, as other investigators since then had confirmed. The brain tumor, like any tumor, was a mass of rapidly dividing cells. We had to carry out what amounted to shamanic surgery, by administering massive doses of ayahuasca and/or psilocybin and directing sound energy—the "hypercarbolation buzz"—at the tumor. The buzz would trigger the intercalation of the compounds and would block replication of DNA in the rapidly growing cells. The net effect would be to arrest the growth of the tumor and cause it to shrink.

That was the best outcome. But if it didn't work, I said, our shamanic surgery would build Terence's resurrection body; we'd reconstruct him as the starship, the hyperdimensional object, the philosopher's stone, all the images of a super-technological fusion of mind and matter we'd invoked at La Chorrera. In other words, the treatment would either save Terence or transform him into a hyperdimensional vehicle that, at the moment of transition, would allow him to seize the controls and sail off, painlessly, joyfully, and triumphantly, into the sunset of eternity. We'd almost done that in La Chorrera. This was our second chance.

I really don't know why I was saying these things. I was babbling, grasping at straws, reaching for any metaphor, any scenario, that might cast a hopeful light on this terrible situation. I don't know that I really believed it, but I was saying it.

Over the previous summer, I'd been doing ayahuasca workshops with Luis Eduardo. I knew he'd been planning to visit Hawaii in July, which suddenly seemed providential. Luis Eduardo, one of our closest friends, had become an excellent *ayahuasquero*. I've told the story of how Terence had met him after his second trip to La Chorrera, and how later Luis Eduardo and I worked and traveled together over the years, sharing many adventures. We'd invite him to take part in this shamanic work with us, I said. I don't know if my raving convinced Terence, but he reluctantly agreed at least to give it a try.

Back in the world of allopathic medicine, Terence was facing very limited options. His biopsy had confirmed that the tumor was indeed glioblastoma multiforme. Moreover, the tumor was inoperable. Conventional chemotherapy drugs tended to be ineffective, the oncologist said, because they didn't readily cross the blood–brain barrier and thus had trouble penetrating the tumor. With surgery ruled out, his doctor recommended a procedure called "gamma knife," which targeted the tumor with a beam of focused, high-energy gamma radiation. The beam could potentially "stun" the tumor and slow its growth, or even force it into remission in rare cases. That procedure would be followed by six weeks of focused soft-radiation therapy to catch any surviving cancer cells. Such tumors often recurred; the follow-up therapy improved the chances of remission after the initial gamma-knife procedure. According to the doctor, the diffuse border of such a tumor sends articulations into the normal surrounding tissue. He compared these to "mycelia," as opposed to the "fruiting body" of the main tumor mass.

What were the long-term consequences if the treatments actually worked? Most likely dementia, we were told: possibly moderate, possibly severe. To think of my brother's beautiful, scintillating mind being eaten away by a malignancy, or burned away by radiation, left me shaken. There were no good options. The gamma knife, crude as it was, seemed better than nothing. We agreed that the best course would be to have the procedure and then see what happened. After a brief time to recover, Terence would then begin the follow-up radiation treatments, which were intended to buy time and quality of life during that time. The treatments were never referred to as a cure.

Word of Terence's situation soon got out. Jill, his former girlfriend, showed up unexpectedly, having flown over from the Big Island as soon as she got the news. I was surprised and impressed by her compassion for Terence. To his credit, Terence received her warmly, and Christy did as well. Christy certainly hadn't bargained for anything like this when she and Terence had hooked up. Now, as the person closest to Terence on a day-to-day basis, she'd been cast into the stressful role of primary caregiver, and she proved herself more than equal to the task.

Dan Levy, Terence's agent, flew out from New York to see him. Thanks to the steroids and the antiseizure meds, Terence felt quite well, and there was no reason for him to stay in the hospital after he recovered from the biopsy procedure. Friends who had places on Oahu offered us accommodations while Terence awaited the gamma-knife procedure. The situation was almost surreal. We were going out for expensive meals every night and acting like a bunch of good friends on holiday. Terence seemed more cheerful and upbeat than I had seen him in some time.

A few days after the biopsy, the gamma-knife "cybersurgery" went off without a hitch, as far as anyone could tell. This high-tech procedure was akin to magic in that it harnessed invisible energies whose effectiveness we accepted on faith. Our faith was in science and technology, of course, but afterward there was no outward sign that anything had changed. Terence looked the same and felt the same, except for a little fatigue. But the docs assured us they had zapped the tumor good—there was nothing to do but wait. Their plan was to monitor the effects for a few weeks and then begin the six weeks of radiation therapy. Terence and Christy went home to the Big Island. I returned to Minnesota to handle some business matters and clear the decks as much as possible. We agreed that I would come back out later in the summer with Luis Eduardo after Terence had completed his radiation therapy in Honolulu.

As May turned into June and the weeks rolled on, word of Terence's dire situation reached his fans. Many responded with an incredible outpouring of good wishes, love energy, and lots of suggestions for alternative therapies. It was touching, and humbling, to realize that Terence was loved by so many. He had an enormous extended family, and everyone was pulling for him. It became impossible for him to respond to the hundreds of e-mails he got every day. Fortunately, Dan Levy, who maintained the levity.com servers where Terence's website was housed, set up a page where we could post periodic updates, which are still there (www.levity .com/eschaton/index.html).

This excerpt from a post by Terence gives some hint of what he was thinking at the time.

June 25, 1999

Dear Novelty Folks:

I am not properly set up, mentally or technologically to receive or respond to email while I am in Honolulu getting my cancer treatments, but my goal is to come home to my secret rebel base on the Big Island every two weekends or so. And once again I am there. Just a bit of an update on my situation: it is now more than three weeks since I had the gamma knife surgery. The further it recedes into the past the better I feel. However I am having focused radiation treatments five days a week and the docs assure me that in a while, a couple of weeks or more I will begin to feel less well under the impact of that treatment. So this time is being presented by the allopathic guys (and gals) as a window of good feeling sure to fade. Naturally I go through all sorts of changes about my situation, and the drugs I take, seizure suppressing carbamazepine and the steroid decadron combine in different ways at different times and move me around from a kind of "whatever" euphoria to very emotional and thought provoking states.

I have had all sorts of advice and well meaning suggestions . . . but here is my sort of general position on my personal fight with brain cancer. I think that it was wise to have the gamma knife surgery, though it was radical and high tech and somewhat experimental it was important to reduce the size of the tumor. The follow-on soft focus radiation is more controversial in my own mind but as an old mushroom cultivator I know how very important it is to work clean and to not assume that a little contamination is a containable thing. I have so far refused chemotherapy . . . these therapies may have to be tried if things get worse further downstream. But my intuition is that the people who survive unusually long times are those who follow the surgery and radiation with extreme attention to cleaning up their diets and then supplement their diet very wisely. It is a wake up call to be very attentive to what goes into my body. You would think that an old psychonaut would have learned that long ago but what can I say? In other words attention to the details of food and nutrition will significantly prolong my life. How long? Who can say? People who are taken hostage for long periods inevitably develop accommodating relationships with their oppressors. Cancer seems to be a bit like that, at least to me now. If it insidiously undermines me I may change my tune but for the moment I accept no diagnosis, though I have deep respect for my doctors and I simply wish to believe that those who wish to live and who inform themselves concerning the details of human nutrition and metabolism have the best luck with these sorts of situations.

Generally my spirits are high and my life is certainly very interesting and more emotionally rich than before. I am being taught many things and I welcome this. And I welcome the love and support of friends, this is a mad and wild adventure at the fractal edge of life and death and space and time. Just where we love to be, right, shipmates? I will send more news as I can. . . .

And the band played on.

Love,

T

By then I was back home in Minnesota. Terence and Christy were spending five days a week at St. Francis Medical Center in Honolulu and weekends on the Big Island, as much as they were able. The optimistic tone of my own posts on the site mentioned above belied my true state of mind. I was anguished. There seemed to be no escape from this, all the evidence pointed to this disease being a death sentence. It was only a matter of time. But we were furiously searching for a solution.

We had plenty of help. The daughter of my friend Sid had a different kind of brain tumor, astrocytoma, and had been able to survive far beyond projected expectations using a number of different complementary and conventional treatments. Sid and his daughter and her physician were compassionate and generous about sharing information, and we were grateful for their advice. Sadly, considering how rare glioblastoma was supposed to be (I'm not sure I believe the statistics), our former neighbor from NIH days in Bethesda, Woody, came down with the same type of cancer at about the same time, so we were sharing information and support with his wife Cathy. Woody also succumbed to the disease, as most did, and still do.

Because Sheila and I were the only ones in our group with any background in science or biomedicine, it fell to us to scour the medical literature to try to identify some treatments that might offer a solution. We spent several hours a day on PubMed trying to learn more about the disease, and we started searching the NIH-sponsored site for new therapies undergoing clinical trials (www.clinicaltrials.gov) to see if there might be any new trials that could help Terence. It's a daunting and thankless task. Every clinical protocol has strict exclusion criteria, and if a candidate has had certain prior treatments, they may be disqualified for an experimental therapy even though it may seem promising. One becomes trapped in a vast decision-tree matrix; a decision to go with one clinical protocol often slams the door on others due to the exclusion criteria. Every decision becomes life-or-death, and there is no way to determine which is which. It's impossible to know if you are making the right decision or not. Or that's how it feels. This was the dilemma we were in. In the end, given the outcome that we now know, none of the decisions that we made were the correct ones. The outcome would in all probability have been the same for Terence no matter what course we chose.

Sometime during this period, while Terence was shuttling back and forth to Honolulu for his treatments, I met some friends in California for a weekend. They had rented a beautiful condo and had what they said was a new LSD analog they wanted to share, which in retrospect I think was really just LSD. I was up for it. I was quite distressed about the situation with Terence, and I thought the experience might help me get some perspective on it.

The material we took was in a crystal form, in a tiny vial. We had no scale and had to "eyeball" the doses as best we could. However much I took, it was much more LSD than I had ever taken in my life, there was no doubt of that. It was one hell of a ride. The effects came on within minutes, and within minutes I was so out of it I was oblivious to everything except what was going on inside my head. And that was all about Terence and our shared dilemma. I saw the tumor as an evil black spider extending its lethal web through Terence's brain. He was an insect futilely struggling in that web, desperately seeking an escape. A voice kept insisting, "The only way out is to go in." I took that to mean there really was no escape, that death was the only escape. I confronted that idea with all the grief, anxiety, and fear that I'd been keeping bottled inside. I thought about Terence's death and what that would mean, and the aftermath, and the sadness and grieving that would inevitably follow. It was as if I had been granted an opportunity to experience all of that grief in advance, go through it then and there, and get past it, in order to cleanse my system of all that negative energy and be ready for the ordeal that lay ahead.

There was nothing fun about the trip, but it was healing and therapeutic in the slap-you-upside-the-head way that psychedelics can be sometimes. It was a hard lesson, shoved into my face. "Deal with it," was the message. "You can't escape from this ordeal. The only way out is to go in."

Terence finished his radiation treatments in early August and settled in at home, waiting to see what would unfold. Klea and Finn spent a great deal of time with their father that summer, and indeed over the hard months after it, a crucial part of the story they alone can tell, as the most important people in Terence's life. Various friends traveled to Hawaii to see him. Caitlin and I spent time with him, as did our Aunt Amelia. Terence grumbled about having "that old battle-ax" around, but there was no stopping her. Amelia could be as gruff and abrasive as Terence when she wanted to be. In the end I think he appreciated her effort. It could not have been easy for an 86-year-old woman, but she insisted, as if to say: I'm here, I love you, and you're just going to have to deal with it. Shortly after Caitlin returned to the mainland, Luis Eduardo showed up. We were preparing to initiate the program of shamanic surgery I'd discussed with Terence in the hospital garden. Terence didn't seem very enthusiastic about the idea. "What's this all about?" he asked me. "What do you think is going to happen?" I told him I didn't really know. At best, I said, we'd cure his cancer and he'd be OK. If not, I hoped he'd have an epiphany of some kind that would help him come to terms with the fact of his illness and the possibility of death. He was skeptical.

"Let's just try it," I said. "We don't know what will happen. Eduardo, your best friend, has come all this way to help you, I'm here for you, we all love you. I think you should at least try." Reluctantly, he agreed.

But in the end it didn't work. Terence was not spared, nor did our actions really lead him to a moment of insight. I had secured some strong ayahuasca brew, but there was debate about whether Terence could safely take it. The thought was that pure psilocybin would be much easier on him.

Over the next couple of weeks, the *ayahuasqueros* at least had occasion to take plenty of these medicines. We sang *icaros*, we blew *mapacho*, we sucked *virotes*, we massaged Terence's head; we danced around and made the hypercarbolation scream. We told Amelia what we were doing and she totally got it. In our sessions, we sat around a small fire in front of Terence's deck, and when we weren't shamanizing, we talked. Terence only took a small amount of psilocybin, and for him the effects were light and recreational. He was obviously enjoying himself, but our conversations had no depth. Terence described them as a mile wide and an inch deep. I didn't know how to steer us in a more productive direction. Our recent tensions had not been entirely forgotten. My brother obviously distrusted me and held himself back.

My consoling thought was that no one could decide for another how to confront death. Terence had to choose his own way, which he bravely did. We tried to help him, tried to ease the pain for him, and for others around him, but like his other treatments, shamanic surgery had failed.

August faded into September. Luis Eduardo returned to Finland, and I went home to Minnesota. Terence, who was still feeling pretty good, remained on the Big Island with Christy. The AllChemical Arts Conference took place in mid-September and by all accounts was a great success. His wider community was aware that the event was quite possibly his last major public appearance, and that put the focus even more on him. He gave some of his best talks and interviews during the conference, which I think marked the start of a gradual process of letting go, both for him and for his fans.

By late September matters were becoming urgent. The effects of Terence's treatments with the gamma knife and the subsequent radiation therapy were beginning to wear off. The tumor's growth had slowed for a short while, but now it had resumed. I continued to search the literature for a clinical trial that might prove to be the escape hatch we all were hoping for. Finally, after evaluating many clinical trials and consulting with Terence's physicians and other experts, we found a clinical trial that seemed to hold promise. It was one of the early experiments in gene therapy, an industry-sponsored Phase I clinical study being conducted at the University of California, San Francisco Medical Center, home to one of the best neuro-oncology departments in the world. We were initially concerned because Terence's oncologist in Honolulu had assessed his tumor as inoperable. But his surgeon in San Francisco was confident the tumor could be removed as the first step prior to the gene-therapy stage. It seemed like the closest thing to a magic bullet that we had found. It was our best and last hope.

Both phases of the operation went well. Here's part of the update I posted afterward:

October 12, 1999

Terence successfully completed the second phase of his treatment at UCSF today. He had a craniotomy, followed by additional gene therapy. The surgery was a success by all measures. According to the surgeon . . . all visible traces of the tumor have been removed. It will take some more time to assess whether the gene therapy has been effective, but even if it was not, Terence has benefitted from the surgery. He is now recovering on the Neuro ICU unit at the hospital.

As far as anyone can tell, he is the same old Terence: sense of humor fully intact, bemused perspective fully functional, and no obvious impairments of speech, cognition or movement. So, for now, it seems that an important phase of Terence's treatment has been completed. With a bit of luck, the gene therapy will prove effective and may actually amount to a cure, although that is a word we do not use lightly around here. What is important, for now, is that these procedures have bought more time—possibly much more time—while not diminishing quality of life.

Following the operation, Terence and Christy remained in San Francisco, living in an apartment, kindly offered by a friend, close to the UCSF Medical Center. This made it easier to check in for the close follow-up that the procedure required. So far everything looked good. Terence seemed to be rallying a bit. The operation had gone as well as expected, and that alone gave us some hope. Now it was a matter of waiting to see if the gene therapy worked, which would be indicated if the tumor had stopped growing and was beginning to shrink. The next major checkup for Terence was scheduled for late January. He and Christy returned to the Big Island in late October.

During November and December, we permitted ourselves to think that this high-tech approach just might have worked. The message of my LSD experience six months earlier came back to remind me that the only way out was to go in. Well, Terence's doctors had gone in and excised the malignant spider that had taken up residence there. Now it only remained to see if, in fact, this procedure had created a way out.

After recovering from surgery, Terence felt better than he had in a while, but that respite didn't last long. Soon after returning to Hawaii, he developed a great deal of pain in his left leg. His doctors thought that both his pain and loss of strength might have been related to his steroid medications, which can break down muscle tissue. Terence had been taking steroids since his initial diagnosis, and his doses had gone up following the operation. The doctors suggested that he gradually taper off the steroids, and by late December he had. But after a brief period when his symptoms seem to improve slightly, they got worse.

It was a dreary Christmas for all of us. Terence and Christy remained in seclusion on the Big Island, the situation becoming ever more dire. I was in Minnesota with my family, trying to pretend that we were celebrating a normal Christmas, but we all knew better. Minnesota was in the grip of its usual icy winter, and I became obsessed with keeping the fire going in the new woodstove we'd installed a few months earlier as our single hedge against Y2K. At least it was something I could do—keep my family warm in the face of winter and impending global disaster.

In a bizarre prefiguration of the events predicted for 2012, much of the world seemed on the verge of Y2K hysteria. The computer wonks were predicting the imminent collapse of civilization due to the so-called Millennium Bug—computer systems the world over would abruptly malfunction as their clocks switched over from 1999 to 2000. By convention, computerized calendrical systems used the last two digits of the year to program dates instead of all four digits. The fear was that these systems would mistake 2000 for 1900 and the entire global Internet would crash, triggering a new dark age as our short-lived digital age ended in chaos.

As it turned out, nothing much happened. Whether the worldwide preventive measures actually worked or the danger had been exaggerated was never clear. (I suspect the latter.) Whatever the case, Y2K turned out to be a giant nonevent. Back on the home front, we were so preoccupied we barely noticed.

Terence and Christy returned to the Bay Area for his checkup in January. I was there as well, having put my work and other activities aside. They were planning to continue on from there to the Entheobotany Conference in Palenque in mid-February, but that was looking unlikely. Terence's problems had worsened. An MRI during his checkup revealed that the tumor had metastasized. This was unexpected and disturbing; it is extremely rare for glioblastomas to spread beyond the site of initial growth. There was no way to determine if this was an unintended consequence of the gene therapy, but it may have been.

In any case, the doctors more or less threw up their hands. There was nothing more they could do, they said. They thanked Terence for making his contribution to science and sent him home. The tumor was now proliferating in critical areas close to the autonomic centers that regulate cardiac and respiratory functions. If he was "lucky"—the term sounded pretty hollow at this point—he would live six months. In all likelihood, his time on earth would be much shorter, closer to three or four months. After that news, Palenque was out of the question. Terence had no energy and no longer any will to fight the thing. What he wanted was to go home to the Big Island, but even that simple wish could not be granted to him. Christy could not be expected to take care of him alone in a remote place with no easy access to emergency care. She was willing to try, but Terence's friends Jack and Ricci joined me in saying that wouldn't work.

Jack and Ricci had a place in Marin, a nice suburban house they rented in San Rafael overlooking an inlet of San Rafael Bay. They invited Terence and Christy to stay with them. It was there that Terence passed his final days. I respect Jack and Ricci for taking on a task that turned them into caregivers, guardians, and gatekeepers. They arranged for Terence to have access to hospice care if needed and they engaged a pain specialist to manage his pain medications as his condition worsened. They created and maintained a firewall to protect Terence from the many fans who, out of misguided love, were desperate to connect with him—and from several old girlfriends who wanted to reconnect. Betsy, another member of their circle, offered me the use of a studio with a spare bedroom in her house if I should need it—the first of many kindnesses she has extended to my family since then.

Terence was rapidly declining. Within the space of a week he had lost the ability to walk with a cane and was confined to a wheelchair. About this time, Jack and Ricci arranged to have a farewell party for Terence. Some of his oldest and best friends were there, including Vanessa, who had played the role of the "responsible adult" at La Chorrera. Others from the early Berkeley days showed up and Terence was clearly moved, as were we all. Everyone knew they were saying good-bye.

Throughout February and March, Terence continued to lose strength and energy. Klea, who had started her freshman year in the fall at UCLA, had transferred to UC Santa Cruz to be closer to her father. I returned to the Bay Area with my family in mid-March. Ralph Metzner had organized a conference entitled "Ayahuasca, Shamanism, and Spirituality," sponsored by the California Institute of Integral Studies and held at the Cathedral Hill Hotel in San Francisco. Metzner had just published and edited a collection of essays and scientific articles on ayahuasca, and the conference was in part a platform to promote the book (Metzner 1999). I spoke at the event, along with others in the ayahuasca field, including my colleagues from the UDV study, Charlie Grob and Jace Callaway. Luis Eduardo was also there, as were Jeremy Narby and attorney Roy Haber, who was working to secure recognition for the Santo Daime under the Religious Freedom Restoration Act. It was an excellent conference, one of the first on the topic in the Bay Area. Sheila had not seen Terence since before he'd been diagnosed, and Caitlin had not seen him since the previous summer in Hawaii.

We planned to go to Marin to see him after the conference, not exactly a joyful reunion but an important one. The first day of the conference, March 17, was warm and sunny, and we were all standing around by the pool after breakfast, waiting for the program to start. Sheila, Cait, and I were talking to Luis Eduardo and Roy. I looked away for a minute and when I looked back, Sheila had disappeared. Next thing I knew, she was emerging from the swimming pool, fully clothed and dripping wet, clutching a child to her chest. While the rest of us were standing around distracted in conversation, Cait had spotted a small child motionless at the bottom of the pool and had alerted Sheila. Sheila's EMT training kicked in: she dove into the pool and rescued the little girl, laid her by the side of the pool, and administered mouth-to-mouth resuscitation. Luis Eduardo stepped in to help and found that she had a pulse, so Sheila could continue with her mouth-to-mouth. The rest of us stood by watching, stunned. After a few minutes, the girl coughed up some water, took a deep breath, and let out a lusty cry. Sheila had saved her life! It turned out it was Roy's daughter, at the time about five years old. Roy and his wife were deeply shaken, of course, and extremely grateful to Sheila. The paramedics took her to the hospital where she fully recovered. By the next day, she was back at the conference, dancing around. That frightening moment created a bond between Sheila and Roy that has continued to this day.

Following the conference Sheila, Cait, and I went with Luis Eduardo to Marin to see Terence. He was confined to his bed, and the encounter was difficult for all of us. What words can one find to speak to a dying man? Cait, 11 at the time, became upset as it dawned on her that she'd probably never see her uncle alive again. We all eventually confront the proof of life's brevity in the face of someone dear to us. That was the lesson Cait was learning as her beloved uncle tried to wipe her tears and reassure her.

After spending a night or two in Marin at Betsy's place, we flew back to Minnesota. A few days later, I returned to be with Terence. Time was growing short. When I got back to Marin on March 28, it was clear that things had taken a dramatic turn for the worse. There had been a traumatic event of some kind; it appeared to me that he'd suffered a stroke that had rendered him largely paralyzed and aphasic.

In my absence other events had occurred, the consequences of which I would not fully grasp until later. It seemed there had been conversations with Terence, if that's what you'd call such exchanges when the key person cannot speak, about changing his will. The changes involved the distribution of some of his properties, particularly his cherished library. At some point, one of Terence's friends had visited his house on the Big Island and returned with a photographic inventory of some of Terence's possessions—mostly art objects like his Tibetan thangkas. Apparently at Terence's request, another friend had called in lawyers over the weekend to rewrite Terence's will. I didn't learn what the changes were until after Terence had died. I was suspicious and wondered why I had been excluded from these conversations. Just prior to my return to Minnesota, I had asked Terence to name me the executor of his will. He granted my request, but it turned out to be a burdensome responsibility, as I later found out.

During this period, I was staying at Betsy's and spending every day with

Terence, a vigil I shared with Klea and Finn. It's not easy to be with someone who is dying, especially when they are unable to speak. The time passed slowly. My cousin Judy and her husband Laddie, in the area visiting their daughter, came by to pay their respects. In a moment I described earlier in the book, our Aunt Tress, whom Terence had been on the outs with since high school, phoned to offer some words of comfort. I spent long hours by Terence's bedside, sometimes reading, sometimes sharing passages aloud, often just sitting in silence. I talked to Terence, trying to overcome my anguish, to say something meaningful. It was surprising how hard it was to get these simple words out: I love you. I forgive you. I ask that you forgive me. That was what I needed to say. There wasn't much point in trying to say anything more than that. I'm pretty sure that he heard me, though he couldn't respond.

I was not at Terence's bedside when the end came. It happened at 2:15 A.M. on the third of April. His children and I had been with him the previous evening. Around 10 or 11 we said goodnight, and Finn and I went to our lodgings at Betsy's. Terence didn't respond to our farewells, because he couldn't. Christy was the only one with him at the end. Suddenly he came fully awake, lifted himself up from the mattress, and tried to say something. His face was transfixed in an expression of ecstasy. Then he settled back, let out a long sigh, and was gone. Christy walked to the window and looked out across the bay. The sky was cloudless and clear. It was the darkest hour. As she stood and watched, a shooting star flared and faded in the night. At least, she said this happened and I believe her, because I want to believe her. I know it was Terry in his crystal ship, kicking it into warp drive, accelerating smoothly into hyperspace. Just like we always said it would be.

The news arrived the next morning when Christy came over to tell us. I actually heard it from Finn as I was descending the stairs from Betsy's studio. When he told me, I let out an involuntary wail, an anguished cry like a wounded animal. I have never made a sound like that before or since. I couldn't have prevented it even if I had wanted to. Something reached into me at that moment and tore out a piece of my soul. After that, I was just stunned. We went back to the house together. It was like being in a dream; there was a strange, muffled quality to external sounds, almost like my head was wrapped in gauze. We walked in and there was Terence, on his bed in his room. His face expressed ecstasy and peace. My beautiful brother, my mentor and tormentor, was gone.

50 Into the Fire

In keeping with Tibetan Buddhist practice, the body of a departed spirit should be left undisturbed for a few days. The soul is at a critical point of transition, and this final link to the world of the living should be maintained, to let the soul take its leave in peace and in its own time. Though we were not practicing Buddhists, similar practices are found in many shamanic traditions, and it seemed to make sense. So Terence stayed with us in his bed at Jack and Ricci's place while I arranged for a cremation at the Mount Tamalpais Mortuary.

The ceremony on April 6 was simple and small. Finn and Klea did not attend, having chosen to honor their father in their own way. Only Christy and I, and Terence's old friends Lisa and Erik, loyal to the end, were present. Terence looked good. He was lying in a cardboard casket, dressed in his favorite tweed jacket, with amulets and necklaces from his close friends encircling his neck. He looked at peace. We closed up the casket, which was elevated on a bed of rollers. The attendants slid it into the oven and closed the door. We retired to the chapel to wait. It took just over an hour for the cremation to be finished. There were no sermons, nothing formal. We sat around and reminisced about the days in Berkeley and even earlier, the days in Menlo Park and Lancaster when Terence was just Terry and we were just happy hippies, unknown and obscure, full of hope and idealism, dreams and delusions. How young and innocent and guileless we were back then.

A year or so after the cremation, I had an ayahuasca experience in which I relived the cremation from Terence's point of view. In my vision, it was just a flash of searing flames and heat, and it seems right somehow that it should be that way. At least that was the vision of cremation that I was granted by ayahuasca. I have no idea if it matches reality or not, but I was grateful to share the experience vicariously with Terence. After all, we had shared so much in life, to the point where at times I had felt we were like one person. It seemed fitting somehow to be able to share this final moment of alchemical transmutation.

Even in the face of death, life, ever impatient, hastens us along to the next act. We are not permitted the luxury of indulging the impulse to pause and reflect. That's how it seemed after Terence's death. Even before Terence's body was consigned to the flames, I was summoned to a meeting at the lawyer's office for a reading of the new will, the one that had been crafted in secret and in my absence. Terence's former will was a simple, two-page document that basically stated his intent to bequeath all of his possessions to his children. The new will was a 10-page, densely worded document with an 11-page appendix specifying gifts of specific personal property. It had been drafted and signed on March 24, a day during the period when I had been absent. Nothing about it sat well with me. I wondered how Terence, in the terminal stages of brain cancer, unable to speak and perhaps not fully capable of clarity of thought, could have participated in the drafting of such a document when his only way to respond would have been to raise a finger or nod. It seemed to me that his children had gotten short shrift. In particular, the new will specified that Terence's beloved library was to be placed in a trust under the curatorship of a wealthy couple, friends of Terence's and benefactors of the Esalen Institute. Terence had promised the library to Finn and Klea in earlier conversations in the summer of 1999, one of which I witnessed. The revised will nullified his intent as he had expressed it prior to his apparent change of heart. According to the new will, the library was to be donated to the Esalen Institute after probate had been settled.

I was named as the executor of Terence's will, as I had requested of him. I had no previous experience with legal matters of this kind, and I wanted to carry out my duties within the letter of the law. I was also still grieving—the will was read two days after Terence's death, and I don't think I was thinking clearly. Looking back on it, had I been thinking more clearly, and had I better understood my prerogatives and rights as the executor and next of kin, I would have contested the will on the spot, on the grounds that Terence had not been of sound mind when it was drafted. But I did not take such action at the time, and the opportunity was lost.

The probate process turned into a can of worms that dragged on for years. It caused me a great deal of stress as I tried to balance my fiduciary duties with my wish to heal some wounds and find closure. Other than his art and his books, Terence had no real assets, so in order to pay off his medical bills and other expenses I was forced to put the house in Hawaii up for sale. This was difficult because the property was part of a collective ownership agreement and had no free title and no insurance. It took years, but I eventually found a person who was willing to buy Terence's "shares" in the hui. Though far from perfect, it was the best resolution of the matter that I could manage under the circumstances.

Fulfilling Terence's directive to bequeath the library to Esalen was the most contentious and stressful challenge I faced. Its resolution turned out to be tragic. The executor of a will has a great deal of power; but that power must be exercised within constraints. The executor's duty is to carry out the wishes of the deceased as expressed in the will, even if you disagree with those wishes. I felt this tension acutely. I was torn between wanting to do what I felt was right and carrying out the directives of the will that, as the executor, I was bound to do.

I knew there would be problems within a couple of weeks after Terence's death, when I received a strident and dictatorial document from a lawyer representing the curators Terence had named. The point was to tell me what I was going to do with the library and how the matter would be handled. I thought this was unnecessarily adversarial, as I had every intention of carrying out the directives even though I didn't agree with them. At the time, the library was under my protection as the executor, along with all assets of the estate. This is standard procedure in probated wills, because if there are liens against the estate, assets may have to be sold to settle the debts. None of the assets of the estate, even those bequeathed to other purposes, are shielded until the obligations are settled. In the case of Terence's estate, there were liens, primarily because of medical bills, and the possibility existed that some of the more valuable titles in the library would have to be sold off. I had engaged the services of a lawyer by this time, and had instructed her to notify the curators that the library would be released to their curatorship only after probate had been settled. Until then, any and all decisions regarding the assets of the estate were mine to make.

Fate has a way of intervening in unexpected ways, and it did in the case of Terence's library. As the probate process ground on, I managed to work out an agreement with the curators about when and how to transfer the library to Esalen. The books sat in the house on the Big Island for far too long, but after a time they were packed up and transferred to a storage facility in Kona. The curators and the estate reached an agreement to ship them to the mainland, where they were stored in a space overseen by Esalen in an old building in downtown Monterey. As I've noted earlier, the plan had been to store the books there until a new building would be constructed where Terence's collection, among other works, could be suitably housed.

On the evening of February 7, 2007, a fire broke out in a sub shop on the street level of the building where Terence's books and personal papers were stored. The flames spread quickly, and Terence's entire collection was soon lost. I didn't learn of this tragedy until the next morning when I picked up a voice mail from David Price, who was the son of Esalen's cofounder Dick Price and who Terence knew well from his long association with Esalen. Both David and Gordon Wheeler, Esalen's CEO, were distraught and upset by this disaster, but I assured them that I didn't consider it their fault. The books were not insured separately from Esalen's property insurance, so there was no possibility that the family would receive some modest compensation for the loss. The books were stored at the facility on shelves, so technically they were accessible as per the conditions of the bequest. But Terence's wish, that they be accessible at a site on the Esalen campus in Big Sur, had not been fulfilled.

Although the administrators at Esalen expressed heartfelt regret over this tragedy, I never heard from the curators, a fact that speaks for itself. That Terence lost not one but two irreplaceable and unique libraries to fire—the first in Berkeley in 1970, and the second in 2007—is now part of his life story. It's a double tragedy. Terence's friend Erik Davis later posted a moving essay about the loss on his website, Techgnosis. So much of Terence's soul and being was bound up in his library it was almost like a living part of himself. After this fire took that away, irrevocably and forever, I began to feel that he had truly departed this world.

The conflicts that arose over Terence's will, and the turmoil that created, dragged on for years and caused me great distress. Over the years, and with Betsy's help, I have achieved a kind of closure with most of those involved. I don't see any point in nursing old grudges, as they poison mainly the person that holds them, and there is already enough pain associated with Terence's life, and death, to last the rest of mine. In the end (so I tell myself) we each lived through these difficult times together, and each tried to do the right thing. We differed in our understanding of what that was, but I give those with whom I differed the benefit of the doubt. We may never be close friends, but I will always be grateful for what they did for Terence in his time of need. That makes up for a lot.

* * *

Time, in its way, just keeps flowing, no matter how much we might wish it would stop for a moment and let us catch our breath and gaze back along the distance we have traveled. In my story, at least, I have arrived at such a point, and I think I'm going to leave it here. Terence's departure from the realm of the living on that early April morning of the year 2000 was not really the end of his story, or the end of mine, or the end of our intertwined destinies. A tale such as ours never really ends any more than it ever really begins; it is a frozen snapshot of an infinitesimal slice of time, pressed between the pages of an expired past and indeterminate future like a dried flower in a weighty tome. We behold it for an instant highlighted by the strobe flash of scrutiny, reflection, and recollection and then the light moves on, leaving only a fading afterimage in the mind. Finally, even that vanishes into darkness and is gone.

A lot has happened since Terence took his leave just over 12 years ago. During that period, our collective experience of historical time has accelerated in a cascade of staggering events: the hijacked elections of 2000, the attacks on 9/11, wars in the Middle East, earthquakes, tsunamis, oil spills, global financial meltdown, looming environmental collapse, exploding technological change. Terence didn't live to witness these events, but they would not have surprised him, as a prophet of his times. We are gripped by the intuition that we are heading toward some sort of unimaginable historical singularity; Terence articulated this intuition for us. He envisioned the future in all its terror and promise and made that vision real for the rest of us. He made us reflect on our existential, cosmic, and historical dilemma; he made us think, he made us laugh, and, most important, he gave us hope. It's for that reason, I believe, that he speaks to us from the past in a voice that rings so true and timely today.

An important part of me died with Terence. Nevertheless I soldier on, diminished and damaged but still standing, for how much longer I do not know. At times, my intuition tells me it won't be that long. At other moments, I feel I could live for decades. If I've learned anything from being granted a relatively long life, it's that the whole point of the exercise is to live and cherish each day as if it were our last. As trite as that sounds, it is a profound truth that requires a lifetime to realize. As a milestone marking a finished leg in life's journey, the completion of this book is an important one for me. Whether other works will follow I cannot say. But this story is one I have wanted and needed to tell for some time. I know it will be reviled and praised, criticized and mocked, loved and condemned. Trust me—no one is more acutely aware than I am of its serious imperfections. Yet it's the best I can manage. It's a tale told as well as I am able to tell it. Make of it what you will. It's the tale I set out to tell, and now it is done.

Epilogue

Following Terence's cremation, his ashes were divided among the important people in his life. Christy and I each got some, and a portion went to Terence's children. Over the years, those ashes have been scattered in many places, including the Big Island, the Black Canyon, and in Sonoma near where Terence had lived with his wife and children. I had the mortuary send my portion to Aunt Mayme in Paonia for safekeeping until we could have a memorial there for Terence. That finally took place in the summer of 2001. In a family gathering, we buried most of those ashes alongside our mother and father in Cedar Hill Cemetery, overlooking the valley. I kept a few ounces back, and after the memorial a few of us went camping in Lead King Basin near the headwaters of the Crystal River. I took the mason jar that held the ashes and walked alone along the trail beside the stream a short distance above our camp. I knelt beside the stream in a spot where the current flowed swiftly. I meditated for a few minutes, then removed the lid and poured the ashes into the rushing water.

"Goodbye, Terry," I said. "Now you are free."

I liked the thought of Terence's ashes, the last remnants of his mortal substance, mixing with the water and soil and trees of the place where we had spent our childhood. His molecules and atoms will diffuse out into the world from there. Eventually, they might mingle with parts of himself deposited in different places. Eventually, he will be everywhere.

Afterword

The Rearview Mirror

Twenty-two years ago, in the early morning hours of April 3, 2000, my dear brother Terence gave up his months-long battle with glioblastoma and took leave of corporeal existence. His passing left a scar on my heart and those of the many who loved him. There will never be another Terence McKenna. He will never be forgotten either; the Internet will see to that. Whether or not he transitioned into some sort of metaphysical afterlife, as posited by most of the world's religions, there is no doubt that his digital ghost—in the form of his words and images scattered across cyberspace—survived and continues to survive. It is a legacy he left to the world, and his thoughts and "raps," as he called them, are as timely and thought-provoking today as they were 22 years ago. They are timeless and, because they were forward looking, Terence is still very much a participant in the cultural conversation. Largely as a result of the events we lived through together at La Chorrera in 1971 and his lifelong preoccupation with time, whose conceptual seeds took root in those events and found expression as the Time Wave, most of Terence's life unfolded as an anticipation of the future. His gaze was ever set on the 21st century, and yet ironically he did not live to cross that millennial threshold, 2000 being the last year of the 20th century.

From my perch in the present—early 2022—that year seems impossibly remote. It seems about as relevant to what is happening now as the late 12th century. Even 2012 and the 10 years since this book was published fade as a distant memory. Terence was diagnosed with glioblastoma in May 1999, and the waning months of that year were horrific for Terence and all those who shared his vigil, as he spiraled ever closer to that personal singularity, that black hole whose threshold every one of us will cross someday. The world was collectively holding its breath as we lived in dread of what might be called the last apocalypse of the 20th century, Y2K, the event that was projected to trigger the collapse of the global Internet. As the clocks ticked over into the first minute of the New Year—so we were told—computer systems everywhere would collapse into digital chaos as their calendrical systems, improperly programmed and unable to distinguish 00:00.2000 from 00:00.1900, brought cyber disaster upon the anxious world. The event would have wide-ranging consequences as air traffic control systems jammed, power grids went dark, ships ran aground, and airplanes fell out of the sky even as, in the darkest scenarios, scrambled missile defense software—no longer constrained by automated fail-safe programs—unleashed a lethal rain of ICBMs from both sides of the pond, the world perishing in a bizarre Strangelovian farce. This is the way the world ends...

Of course none of this happened. Y2K turned out to be one of the greatest nonevents in human history. Whether this was because the frantic efforts of IT administrators to correct the problem on a global scale actually worked or whether the systems proved to be more robust than anticipated and there was never much to worry about has never actually been totally understood. More than anything, Y2K turned out to be a sardonic commentary on our culture's preoccupation with end-time catastrophes, which if anything has become even more intense in the ensuing decades.

At the time all this went down, we hardly paid attention. We were focused on more personal events closer to home. At the end of 1999, after spending months shuttling back and forth to California, I had returned to Minnesota to be with my family over the holidays. It was a very sad time for us all. Our sole gesture toward Y2K had been to install a soapstone-clad wood-burning stove in our home a few months earlier. We figured that with that, plenty of wood available, and a freshwater stream just down the street, we could probably survive the end of the world at least for a while.

Terence was staying in Hawaii with his companion Christy, in a rapidly deteriorating condition that would soon force him to forever leave his beloved Hawaiian home—his "secret rebel base," as he fondly called it—to return to California where his team of oncologists at UCSF would puzzle over the experimental treatment that was heading seriously in the wrong direction. He had been enrolled in an FDA-approved clinical trial a few months earlier that was one of the earliest attempts at gene therapy. Although we all had high hopes at the start of the treatment, by the end of 1999 it was apparent that, if anything, it was making Terence's condition even worse. I returned to California in early January to be with Terence shortly after he arrived back in San Francisco. He had reached that sobering juncture where the doctors said, "We're sorry. There's nothing more we can do." Hearing that is even worse than "Get your affairs in order," which is what his oncologist in Honolulu had said to him when he received his initial diagnosis back in May. Terence and Christy had hoped that by this point he would be on the road to recovery and perhaps even feel well enough to attend the upcoming Entheobotany conference organized by the Botanical Preservation Corps in Palenque, Mexico, every spring. Alas, this was not to be. Most of those close to Terence at the time knew that this was never realistic. Still, it hurt to see the disappointment and despair in his eyes. It really marked the end of all hope for him.

Shortly after his hospital stay, he relocated to San Rafael, where his friends Jack and Ricci opened their home and provided the most supportive and compassionate hospice environment that anyone could ask. The long weeks that followed were a dismal vigil, one that I shared with Klea and Finn, Terence's children. Fortunately for us, my friend Betsy owned a home not far from Jack and Ricci's that had an extra studio, and it became a refuge for us when we were not sitting with Terence, which was most of the time.

Terence never left their home until he passed away on April 3, 2000.

The two decades that have passed since then weigh on me acutely. The world that has emerged in the last decades, and that we live in now, has been shaped and molded in ways that almost no one anticipated back in 2000. In 2000, Bill Clinton was still president, only to be succeeded by George W. Bush in November—the first hijacked election in US history. The dot-com bubble reached its peak in March and began a precipitous fall as the stock market collapsed 78 percent over the remaining months. The first long-term inhabitants of the International Space Station (ISS) took up residence in November.

The al-Qaeda attack on the World Trade Center took place on September 11, 2001, and the United States invaded Afghanistan and toppled the Taliban regime, initiating the longest war in US history, which ended only last year in a hasty and chaotic exodus. That invasion was followed three years later by the invasion of Iraq, the toppling of Saddam Hussein, and the start of an eight-year war. These two events largely defined global geopolitics for the next 22 years.

So many developments in politics, society, the Internet, technology, climate change, and media over the last decades have transformed our world into a science fiction dystopia/utopia that is scarcely recognizable. In 2000, we could only see the dim outlines of this emerging future. Now it is the world we live in, and it promises to become ever more bizarre, ever more grim, and yet at the same time ever more astonishing and wonderful. That's the "history" that we're now living in—we are creating that future history even as we are living it.

We are still too embedded in the history of the last two decades to bring any kind of meaningful perspective to it. Trying to select and identify truly novel or significant historical events is an enormous guessing game, perhaps a fool's game at that, and ultimately, the choices are subjective. I am reminded of the conversations Terence and I used to have over many a bowl of fine Afghani hash: What constitutes Novelty? Which events are truly significant? Who gets to decide and on what criteria? Terence obsessed about these matters for much of his life. Sometimes a seemingly significant event may turn out to be not so significant after all, and an overlooked or seemingly insignificant event may end up having an impact on human affairs that no one could have imagined.

A good example of this is something that did take place in the waning hours of 1999. While the world was preoccupied with the anticipation of Y2K, something else did happen that night that was hardly noticed or remarked upon at the time: Validimir Putin assumed the role of acting president of the Russian Federation, precipitated by the abrupt resignation of Boris Yeltsin. This was quickly followed by an election on March 26, 2000, in which Putin received 53 percent of the vote. He was inaugurated president on April 7, 2000, just four days after Terence's death on April 3. This event may turn out to have profound consequences for the survival of civilization in the 21st century.

Twenty-two years later, a shocked and horrified world is waking up to what a terrible turn of events this was. Putin is a monster, a soulless autocrat who envisions himself to be either the reincarnation of Peter the Great or perhaps Joseph Stalin. His unprovoked invasion of Ukraine on February 24, 2022, no matter its eventual outcome, is surely an inflection point that will mark the trajectory of history for at least the next 50 years. Putin may like to believe that he is destined to re-create the Russian Empire, but he lacks the intelligence of either Peter the Great or Stalin—though he seems to aspire to Stalinesque levels of brutality.

No one can say at this point how all this is going to play out. Putin may come to his senses, realize the egregiousness of his error, and seek a face-saving way out. Or he may double down. He may amp up the brutality of his genocidal campaign and pour even more troops and military machinery into Ukraine. He may even (and this is what everyone fears most) resort to the use of chemical, biological, or even nuclear weapons. If this happens, no one can predict or control the consequences. Not since the Cold War has global civilization been in such peril.

The events that began on February 24, 2022, were certainly an eruption of

Novelty into the continuum but perfectly illustrate the principle that I have always espoused: Rarely does Novelty erupt dramatically. Rather, there are disruptive events that may seem surprising when they occur, but the seeds of that novelty can be found in the much less noticed, quieter events that lead to them. The appointment of Putin as interim president on December 31, 1999, was the truly triggering novel event. Only the most astute observers of geopolitics would have predicted that the present state of affairs would be the consequence.

The explosion of the COVID pandemic in the early spring of 2020 was a marker signifying the end of the world as we knew it. The Russian invasion of Ukraine is yet another sign that the world we thought we knew has ended. Looking back, I think it's useful to reflect on what seem to me to be the most significant events of the last 22 years. They are, after all, the foundational precursors to the present moment and the future history being woven out of it. While they can be grouped into several broad categories, it's important to remember that in the actual unfolding of events all of these trends are interactive and inseparable. With this in mind, I think we can still gain some insights by focusing our gaze on each of these broad spheres.

Geopolitics. Geopolitical events certainly set the tone for the early years of the dawning 21st century, beginning with the 9/11 attacks on the World Trade Center and other high-profile targets. 9/11 ushered in an era dominated by terrorism and asymmetrical conflict, and the United States' totally inappropriate responses to that event (the invasions of Iraq and Afghanistan under false pretenses—neither nation was actually involved in triggering the attacks) have defined and hobbled foreign policy ever since. The United States reacted like a wounded animal, becoming increasingly paranoid and inept while terrorism has proliferated worldwide and led to the further destablization of nations, particularly in the Middle East. Democratic ideals and principles, once thought to be the bedrock on which the United States was founded, have been increasingly abandoned in favor of a gradual inching toward authoritarianism, in which human rights, international conventions, and common decency are ignored in the exigencies of the moment. In more recent events, Putin's unprovoked invasion of Ukraine owes its genesis in part to a gradually growing distrust of the United States by its global partners and a resultant weakening of those alliances. Putin took this as an opportunity to make his long-sought move toward the resurrection of the former Soviet Empire. But it is increasingly clear that Putin has badly miscalculated and that those alliances, so badly eroded in the Trump era, may be stronger than he thought. Now, in the face of Putin's hegemonic ambitions, those alliances are reasserting themselves and the world seems to be returning to an uneasy standoff between democratic or quasi-democratic nations and authoritarian, militarily aggressive states, all balanced on the knife-edge threat of mutual nuclear annihilation. Hardly an improvement in international geopolitics. Won't we ever learn?

Climate change and natural disasters. Bad enough in itself, global political instability comes at a most inconvenient time. It distracts the international community from paying attention to the most serious existential threats facing our species and the planet: the collapse of ecosystems due to climate change, most of it human-caused. At a time when we should be coming together to slow down our planetary death spiral, uniting in a common cause to ensure that the planet remains hospitable to human life, we are too caught up in our monkey-squabbles to even pay attention. We do so at our peril. We do not have the luxury of putting off the response to climate change for the next 10 years or even 5 years. We are rapidly approaching the point where the homeostatic feedback mechanisms that keep the planet within the relatively narrow parameters tolerable by life are being stretched to the limit. The biosphere is incredibly resilient in its ability to maintain and restore balance, but it does have a breaking point. Once crossed, balance cannot be restored, or at least not on any time scale that is meaningful to humans. Climate change is a kind of "slow apocalypse." While the rate of change is accelerating and we are experiencing alarming trends in all the critical environmental parameters, it is happening on a longer time scale than the more customary rate of change in human affairs in the societal and political spheres. This results in the comforting delusion that "there is still time," that the real crunch is still some decades out. This is not the case. The Earth has become a "fire in a madhouse." The inmates have escaped from the asylum and have seized the wheelhouse, steering us toward the brink even as Spaceship Earth is on fire, and sinking at the same time.

Social unrest and transformation. 9/11 marked the crossing of a threshold that threw into question many of our previous assumptions about the stability of societies, governments, and ideologies. This loss of ideological moorings has been reflected by increasing social turbulence. This will inevitably be exacerbated by climate-related disruptions such as climate-driven mass migrations, famine, drought, and the collapse of the agricultural and marine food chains. The emergence of social media, never anticipated in 2000, has created a situation in which we can't even agree on basic facts. Now there are only "facts" and "alternative facts" and people are free to barricade themselves in whatever delusionary silos they find most comfortable. The algorithms built into social media platforms reinforce this collective cognitive dysfunction, while providing the means for propagating disinformation and misinformation at the speed of light. As a result, it's become nearly impossible to develop a social and political consensus about the challenges we are confronting and how to respond to them. If we can no longer even have a rational conversation about these matters, how are we going to come up with workable solutions?

Scientific discoveries. On a more positive note, the first two decades of the 21st century have been an era of unprecedented scientific discovery. Humans are curious animals, and science is a prime example of a curiosity-driven activity, something that we do well and for the purest of motives: to understand ourselves and our place in nature. Within the last decades, scientists have developed tools that serve this curiosity and enable us to extend our senses to the furthest reaches of the cosmos, while on the microcosmic scale, we are probing the most foundational elements of reality. Our space probes and space-based telescopes have provided a more complete picture of the near solar system and our "neighbors" in that realm, even as some probes, launched in the mid-1970s, are still gamely transmitting data back to Earth after more than 50 years, as they cross the threshold into trackless interstellar realms beyond the solar system. We have achieved a better understanding of ourselves, of our evolution, and of the workings of living systems. Genetics and paleontology have filled in a more complete picture of our evolutionary origins and of ancient civilizations that were far more sophisticated and advanced than we ever imagined. Genetics and molecular biology have also provided tools to explore—and in many cases to manipulate—living things in ways that were inconceivable even 10 years ago. Like many inventions of science, these capabilities are two-edged swords and will demand great wisdom in how they will be utilized—wisdom that we have not yet developed but hopefully are acquiring. Advances in neuroscience and psychopharmacology are also providing the tools to explore "the universe within," and with their help, we are learning a great deal about the nature of consciousness and its biological and molecular underpinnings. If you are a scientist, or simply a curious person, the past two decades and the present moment have been a wonderful time to be alive.

Technological innovations. Technological innovations mainly arise as spin-offs from scientific discoveries and are much more problematic than pure science because they cross the line from observation to manipulation, affording new ways to interact with the world. Like scientific discovery itself, technological innovation seems to have accelerated almost exponentially since the end of the last century. We have witnessed and participated in this process mainly through the explosion of the Internet and the info-sphere that it opens, smartphones, and social media. But other innovations, particularly in medicine, have also profoundly impacted how we live and die. What distinguishes technological innovations from pure discovery is that they carry an inherent moral imperative: to use them wisely or, in some cases, not at all. The dilemma is that our cleverness very often exceeds our wisdom. While there may be technological innovations that can make us smarter, there is, as yet, no invention that can make us wiser (except perhaps psychedelics). And wisdom is desperately needed as we face choices in how to deploy technologies such as artificial intelligence, genetic engineering, surveillance technology, nanotechnology, and other innovations that could potentially threaten life on earth or lure us into a techno-dystopia as easily as its opposite. I believe the moral and ethical determinants of the path we choose lie within the human heart and will not be found in any technical innovation. Psychedelics, carefully and thoughtfully used, may help us to discover that heart-centered wisdom.

The Moving Moment

No list of the tumultuous events of the last two decades can ever adequately summarize this recent and transformative history. Too much has happened too quickly; each day we live in the aftershock of this history even as the shock wave of the future roars down upon us. If we have been searching for Novelty, the universe has certainly obliged us.

Climate change is a good illustration of the conversations Terence and I used to have about Novelty. Does Novelty *erupt* into the continuum, or does it *leak* into the continuum? Terence argued in favor of dramatic, catastrophic events being novel. I argued in favor of the leakage theory of Novelty—a tornado or tsunami are certainly dramatic, but are they really novel?

The truly novel conditions that lead to catastrophic events develop slowly, almost without being noticed, until they finally trigger some dramatic event. This is one reason why it's so difficult to have rational discussions about climate change. We have gotten used to it. Climate change has become the new normal. It's the classic "frog in the pot of boiling water" conundrum— by the time the frog notices that the water is heating up, it's too late to react. Every summer is the hottest on record; every hurricane season produces the largest and most destructive hurricanes ever seen; every wildfire season starts earlier, destroys more hectares, and ends later than the last season. The planetary climatic changes that are the root causes—carbon emissions that trigger droughts and wildfires in the West and floods in the East, causing mega-hurricanes and tornadoes—take place gradually (though they are accelerating) and it becomes tempting to retreat into denial: "Oh, it's always been like this." Or, "There have always been heat waves, hurricanes, floods, deep winter freezes; this is just weather, not climate change." No, it hasn't always been this way. We are seeing more frequent, more destructive, larger climate disasters than ever before. Once-in-a-millennium droughts, once-in-a-century hurricanes now happen every year. There are things that can be done. But it takes collective will—it requires that we acknowledge that there is a problem and take steps on a global, international level to implement solutions. I am concerned that will never happen because our societies are so factionalized, not only in the United States but also globally. Neither does it help that willful ignorance, science denial, and collective delusion have clouded our judgment and ability to reason. At the historical moment when we most need reason, intelligence, and wisdom, we are getting ignorance, stupidity, and denial. We are killing the planet. We are the murderers, and we cannot look ourselves in the mirror.

Climate change is the whispered conversation that overshadows everything else. It is the major existential threat to the survival of our species. And from that perspective everything else—any collective conversations that are *not* about climate change: war, geopolitical crises, politics, media, technology, societal destabilization, all of it—seem basically irrelevant. What does any of it matter if the planet will be inhospitable to life within a few decades?

And yet, one cannot ignore these other things. The world is a complex system, and everything is related. And climate change itself is about much more than pollution or greenhouse gas emissions. These may be the physical causes driving climate change, but the roots of climate change are to be found in our cultural mindset. At least in the West, it has been poisoned by the Judeo-Christian worldview that devalues nature, telling us it exists to be dominated, exploited, and degraded. Nature is responding to this unambiguously, forcefully reminding us who is running this show.

When I reflect on the events of the last two decades, several emerging trends appear to set a trajectory for the future. No set of global changes can be considered in isolation from any other; the world is much too complex to allow for that. What we can say is that these trends are accelerating, converging, and reinforcing each other. There has been a marked proliferation in international and domestic terrorism; this in turn has triggered a rise in authoritarianism, accompanied by the erosion of democratic institutions and the collapse of global alliances such as NATO and the European Union. Climate change and more recently the global COVID-19 pandemic have combined with geopolitical forces to generate immigration and refugee crises, genocidal conflicts, and a rising threat of famine in some areas. COVID-19 is the first truly global pandemic since the influenza pandemic of 1918, which killed 50 to 100 million people, making it the first modern global pandemic. It will not be the last. And here's a further comforting thought: the next one may be engineered in some lab by bioterrorists. The sudden appearance of COVID-19, its rapid spread, and its serious impact on societal functions have come as a shock that highlights the fragility of modern civilization. It really didn't take much, or very long, for COVID to effectively throw global civilization into some kind of weird quasi-functional limbo. Should we be horrified by these developments, or perhaps take heart in how the world continued limping along?

Social media is another example of a technological/societal change that no one saw coming at the start of the 21st century. When the early social media platforms, such as Facebook, debuted in 2004, they were hailed as a new way for people to connect, share information, and learn together. Eighteen years on, social media of all kinds—Facebook, Twitter, Instagram, and all the rest—are now becoming recognized as perhaps the most destructive force in society originating from technological innovation. Social media is very good at propagating information and memes instantaneously and globally; it is not so good at filtering the quality of the information, nor are people very good at bringing healthy skepticism and critical thinking to the constant barrage of information. As a result, the social media ecosystem has become saturated with lies and misinformation, delusions and conspiracies. This has created a situation that almost no one foresaw: Reality itself has fragmented. There is no longer collective consensus on what is true.

Of course, historically there have always been various perspectives on truth. What is different now is that the corrective mechanisms that used to operate and, through a kind of Darwinian selection, favor the emergence of collective consensus, have been disabled, while the power to propagate misinformation has increased exponentially. Rather than enhancing connectivity, social media has imprisoned us in various cognitive, political, and cultural silos. Now even the most batshit-crazy notions will find, on the Internet, at least a few thousand uncritical followers, and sometimes millions.

The technologies that facilitate this, always closely coupled to the social media platforms, must also be called out. Inventions such as the iPhone are classic examples of the double-edged sword nature of technology.

Smartphones can connect almost anyone in the world to anyone else, instantly. They can afford access to vast repositories of shared knowledge. This has to be a good thing. And yet, the price we pay for this is that we have become tethered to these machines. The iPhone was released in early 2007 and by April 2022, it and other smart phones had found their way into nearly every pocket and purse on the planet. Prior to 2007, a walk in the park or a ride on the subway was a very different experience than it is now. People looked around—sometimes they even looked at each other and saw a fellow human looking back. Now in the same public spaces, probably three out of four people are staring at their screens, never looking up to see who may be right next to them. We each exist in an impervious electronic bubble, oblivious to those around us, "connected" to everyone, and lonelier than ever.

Considered altogether, the outlook for the unfolding decades seems grim indeed. There is plenty of cause for gloom and doom. Is there anything good on the horizon? I believe there is. One source of hope is the cultural shift in societal attitudes toward psychedelics that has taken place over the last 20 years. It's a perfect example of novelty leaking into the continuum, rather than erupting. Psychedelics are nothing new. They have been integral to Indigenous medical and spiritual practices for millennia, quite possibly for millions of years. Indeed, the so-called Stoned Ape Theory, which Terence postulated in his 1993 book *Food of the Gods*, suggests that they had a catalytic role in the emergence of consciousness in our earliest hominid ancestors. There are strong arguments in favor of this notion, and even stronger arguments have emerged since the book was written, as we have come to understand more about psychedelics and their long-term effects on cognition and neural organization. Psychedelics have a revered and ancient

Indigenous history, even as they have been feared and vilified in so-called civilized societies. In the 20th century, psychedelics came to the attention of a few psychologists, pharmacologists, philosophers, and anthropologists, beginning with mescaline, first isolated from the peyote cactus by Arthur Heffter in 1897 and later synthesized by Ernest Späth in 1918. The synthesis of LSD by Albert Hofmann in 1938 and his subsequent "accidental" discovery of its remarkable properties in 1943 led to renewed interest in psychedelics among psychologists as well as certain philosophers and students of consciousness. Indeed, its discovery was an important influence in the genesis of modern neuroscience, as its resemblance to and effects on the neurotransmitter serotonin began to be understood.

But LSD cannot be credited with introducing psychedelics into mass awareness. That distinction belongs to psilocybin, specifically to "magic mushrooms," which were brought to the attention of Mr. and Mrs. Everyone by the publication of R. Gordon Wasson's article "Seeking the Magic Mushroom" in *Life* magazine in May 1957. Six days later, his wife Valentina's first-person account of their expedition to Mexico was featured on the cover of *This Week* magazine, which was inserted into the Sunday edition of 37 newspapers and reached nearly 12 million readers.

These publications really mark the moment when psychedelics became part of the cultural conversation. Of course, mushrooms were relegated to the background in the decade that followed, while LSD took center stage— thanks largely to its promotion by Timothy Leary, who was a natural showman and had serious messianic tendencies. It quickly became a cultural flash point, while remarkable and promising research was being conducted in a few laboratories (e.g., for the treatment of alcoholism by Humphrey Osmond, who coined the term "psychedelic," at Weyburn Mental Hospital in Saskatchewan, which was largely overlooked).

Meanwhile the flames of mass hysteria were fanned by craven politicians and self-styled media arbiters of cultural correctness. Soon LSD and other psychedelics were denounced, vilified, and ultimately banned. Research was prohibited and the door to the investigation of these promising substances was forced closed for the next 20 years. But prohibition did not cause psychedelics to go away. Attempts at prohibition never work and, in fact, only spark greater interest among the curious. So in the dark decades following the global prohibition of psychedelics, first in the States and then globally through the UN Convention on Psychotropic Substances, small but significant numbers of people in the underground continued to work with psychedelics. Research, although not human research, continued in a few university labs but was rarely encouraged or funded.

Then, in the mid-1970s, a landmark event took place that signaled yet another shift in the cultural landscape around psychedelics. This was triggered, in large part, by the publication of a small book—really almost a pamphlet—titled *Psilocybin: Magic Mushroom Grower's Guide* by And/Or press, a small Berkeley publishing house. Terence and I were the authors, writing under the pseudonyms of O. T. Oss and O. N. Oeric. It described a simple method for growing *Psilocybe cubensis* on substrates of sterilized rye grain. It was based on work that I had carried out while living in Fort Collins, Colorado, from 1975 to 1976, while taking additional courses at Colorado State. This has all been described in the chapter of this book titled "Fun with Fungi: 1975." Though I worked out the simple techniques and wrote the technical descriptions, Terence helped write the book and penned the amazing foreword that has become a classic in psychedelic literature. His girlfriend at the time and future wife, Kat Harrison, contributed the beautiful black and white drawings. Our friend Jeremy Bigwood (listed as Irameus the Obscure in the book) produced the photographs that accompanied the technical descriptions of the method described in my text. The technical pictures were small and grainy, but they had the information needed. I used to chide Jeremy about whether his pseudonym was a reference to his photographic technique! But that was rather unkind, and now I feel badly about it. To Jeremy's credit, the color inserts in the book—stunning photos of robust carpophores sprouting out of mason jars—really got people's attention and were a big reason the book sold so well.

At the time we were working on this, there were certainly other people also trying to figure out how to grow these mushrooms, and some succeeded. I think what made the difference was that we were the first to publish a simple method for growing small amounts of potent mushrooms that could be easily mastered by an intelligent 10th grader using materials that could be purchased in any grocery store. Unlike LSD, which required a high degree of chemical expertise, relatively well-equipped laboratories, and a global distribution infrastructure controlled by criminal cartels to produce, homegrown mushrooms could be quietly produced by anyone with a bit of patience and time on their hands and a spare bedroom or closet. And many people did! Including Terence and me for several years, enthusiastically, until concerns about possible legal repercussions led us to seek more legitimate—or at least less prosecutable—careers.

Within a few years, psilocybin mushrooms became the most widespread and easily accessed psychedelic in the underground. There were lots of home hobbyists around college campuses and other neighborhoods, and it was easy enough to score "shrooms" in these areas. And the mushrooms were friendlier than LSD for lots of people, nontoxic, and, best of all, kick-ass visionary psychedelics that, in Terence's words, "opened the vision screens to many worlds." They did indeed. And for that reason, they kept the conversation about psychedelics alive during those dark decades of the 1980s and '90s when psychedelics were still very much "forbidden knowledge" and yet widely discussed. Terence deserves much of the credit for this as his reputation as the bard of psychedelics grew and he began to develop the memes and raps that outlasted him and that today are still a very active corner of the YouTube ecosystem.

The rediscovery of psychedelics by the scientific community, following more than 20 years of neglect following their prohibition at the end of the 1960s, did not begin with psilocybin but instead with its close chemical cousin, DMT. DMT—N,N-dimethyltryptamine—is a natural compound that occurs in many plants and animals, and even in the human brain. It is not orally active but when smoked or injected produces a rapid, extremely intense psychedelic experience that is highly visionary and can be quite overwhelming. Fortunately the trip lasts only about 20 minutes, so by the time people might start to become alarmed, it is already diminishing. Terence was as fascinated by DMT as mushrooms, and there are lots of YouTube clips of him talking about it.

The door to the revival of academic psychedelic research was forced partially open by a friend of Terence's and mine, Dr. Rick Strassman, an MD and psychiatrist who was on the faculty of the School of Medicine at the University of New Mexico in the early 1990s. Dr. Strassman had been working on melatonin, one of the important hormones in the pineal gland that is involved in the regulation of diurnal cycles. It is closely related, structurally, to DMT. (Melatonin is 5-methoxy-N-acetyl tryptamine.) There was reason to believe that the pineal gland also contained DMT, while previous work in the 1970s had shown that it occurred endogenously in the lungs and elsewhere in the body. Dr. Strassman applied for and received funding from the National Institute on Drug Abuse to conduct a clinical study of DMT in healthy human subjects. This marked the first time in over 20 years that the government had funded any human research with psychedelics. Dr. Strassman conducted a dose-escalation study by administering DMT intravenously to over 60 subjects across a range of doses. He measured various physiological parameters and recorded their subjective reactions using specialized questionnaires and post-session interviews. Their reports were outlandish, bizarre, and very hard for Dr. Strassman—who was basically a fairly buttoned-up clinician—to get his head around. Eventually this led him to discontinue the study, thinking that any honest recounting of these experiences in his reports to NIDA would probably spell the end of his career. Later he wrote a popular book on his work entitled *DMT: The Spirit Molecule* that has become a classic of psychedelic literature. I highly recommend it to anyone with an interest in psychedelics, and also in the challenges faced by a brilliant scientist who had the courage to work on the outermost frontiers of neuroscience.

In the context of this narrative, Strassman's work was pivotal because it marked the resumption of human clinical studies with psychedelics. Following the publications of his papers starting in 1994, not much happened for about another decade. Then in 2006, Roland Griffiths and his group at Johns Hopkins published the first of many studies using psilocybin and reported on its remarkable ability to induce "mystical type" experiences (a finding that will come as no surprise to people who have taken mushrooms in appropriate settings, but for "mystical experiences" to be studied and reported in medical journals is rather significant). It was the first of many studies to follow, and Griffiths and his colleagues have been the pioneers in this new renaissance of psychedelic research. His lab published at least 44 peer-reviewed papers on psilocybin in the ensuing 16 years. Their work has been rigorous, well conducted, and well received, demonstrating the therapeutic utility of psilocybin to treat a variety of mental disorders, including major depressive disorder, anxiety and depression at the end of life, PTSD, addiction, smoking cessation, and others.

Griffiths's group led the parade, but many other researchers at respected institutions such as NYU, UCLA, Harvard, Yale, UCSF as well as universities in the United Kingdom and Europe have joined in. Not surprisingly, this has attracted the attention of the investment community—never known to overlook an opportunity to make a profit—and there is now a plethora of new psychedelic start-up companies looking to cash in but also to develop new therapeutic modalities that just may improve mental health care, which is sorely in need of improvement. Psilocybin sits firmly at the center of the aspirations of most of these companies. Other psychedelics are also now being investigated, of course, but it was psilocybin that really got things started. This is rather amazing when one thinks about it. Psychedelics have gone from being banned and condemned in the latter half of the 20th century to now being hailed as the Holy Grail in the field of mental health care. What is going on?

Whatever is going on as psychedelics are becoming accepted into medicine, these developments have been paralleled—since the early 1990s—with a growing interest in the healing modalities of psychedelics outside of conventional medicine. Many of the high-profile figures in this movement, such as myself, are "old hippies" who have been involved with them since the 1960s. Now there is a younger generation of spiritually adventurous people who have become attracted to the Indigenous traditions, particularly around ayahuasca, the now-legendary Amazonian brew. They have been influenced by many cultural forces, including of course many of Terence's raps and talks. Two books were particularly influential for me in this regard as well. One is *The Teachings of Don Juan* by Carlos Casteneda, which came out while I was still a "young hippie." In fact, Terence gave me a copy of the first edition for my 18th birthday in 1968. It was my first insight into the ethnographic, Indigenous side of psychedelics. Psychedelics wasn't just about Timothy Leary anymore. The book made clear that psychedelics were an ancient and revered part of Aboriginal societies for thousands of years. Many of my generation were similarly enthralled by Castaneda's book and the many that followed it. Since the first one, which I believe was based on at least a modicum of fieldwork, critics have questioned the veracity of much of Castaneda's writings. But that didn't really matter to me. I didn't question it at the time, and importantly, it showed me this crucial facet of psychedelics.

At about the same time, another book, the *Ethnopharmacologic Search for Psychoactive Drugs,* the published proceedings of a symposium sponsored by the National Institute of Mental Health in San Francisco in 1967, came onto my radar. I'm not even sure how I got my hands on it, but these two books were seminal for me. Castaneda's book, even though largely fiction, presented the ethnographic side, and ESPD presented the nuts and bolts—botany, chemistry, pharmacology, and anthropology—and made me see that there was real science underlying this field. It is what led me down the career path I have followed, ethnopharmacology. In fact, so inspired was I by the first ESPD conference that I organized a 50th anniversary follow-up symposium, ESPD50, in 2017. In May 2022, I helped to organize another follow-up conference, ESPD55, a five-year follow-up to the 2017 conference and a 55-year follow-up to the original 1967 conference. It was a great success and will also yield an additional symposium volume.

The book that, in my opinion, really sparked widespread interest in ayahuasca was published by my friend Dr. Luis Eduardo Luna, in partnership with the visionary Peruvian artist Pablo Amaringo. Amaringo was a gifted artist who painted eidetic memories of his ayahuasca experiences. I first met him during my fieldwork in 1981 and introduced him to Eduardo when we were together in Pucallpa, Peru, in 1985. The story of how this encounter took place, and what followed, is recounted in this book. Luna and Amaringo ended up forming a collaboration and in 1993 published *Ayahuasca Visions: The Religious Iconography of a Peruvian Shaman*. The book was in classic coffee-table style and consisted of 49 high-resolution color reproductions of Pablo's visionary paintings. On the facing pages were Eduardo's explanations, in English, of the significance of the figures, plants, animals, and spirits in the paintings, all arranged under appropriate categories pertaining to the different aspects of the practice of *vegetalismo*, the Mestizo ayahuasca tradition. *Ayahuasca Visions*, with its stunning, luminous paintings, provided a window into the cosmology and belief systems of the ayahuasca tradition never before seen. I believe that it was as influential in making ayahuasca known to a wider world as the Wassons' 1957 magazine articles were in putting magic mushrooms on the cultural radar of the day. Like those articles, which inspired droves of countercultural enthusiasts to travel to Oaxaca in the 1960s to seek magic mushrooms, *Ayahuasca Visions* inspired many adventurous people to travel to Peru to seek their own *ayahuasqueros* to guide their own visionary experiences.

Thus the phenomenon of ayahuasca tourism can trace its roots to this book. It continues to this day. Iquitos, Peru, where Eduardo first conducted his fieldwork with his respected teacher, informant, and friend, Don Emilio Andrade, soon became the epicenter of ayahuasca tourism. Since the early 1990s, literally hundreds of ayahuasca retreat centers have opened up in the environs of Iquitos and now in other parts of Peru, such as Pucallpa (where Amaringo came from), Tarapoto, and the Sacred Valley in the Andes, near Cusco. By now, thousands of people have made this pilgrimage. I have played my own small role in this, having organized and participated in ayahuasca retreats and conferences near Iquitos and in the Sacred Valley since about 2012. Since COVID, many of these activities have been put on hold, but now are slowly beginning to revive again.

I have had mixed feelings about this and about my own role in the genesis of this phenomenon. There is no doubt that ayahuasca tourism has changed traditional practices, as practitioners scrambled to package their "product" to appeal to globe-trotting tourists, who bring their own expectations with them. This has been a mixed blessing. Sometimes the economic disparities this has created in local communities have led to jealousy and resentment; a small number of *ayahuasqueros* have been elevated to near rock-star status, while the economic benefits of the influx of tourist dollars rarely diffuse into the wider community. In other cases, more equitable sharing of benefits result from the opening of retreat centers, where the ethics of the owners and founders (who are almost always gringos) include building community relations and helping the community as a whole. Another adverse impact has been the pressure tourism has put on the supplies of the plants used to prepare ayahuasca, *Banisteriopsis caapi* (the vine) and the DMT admixture, chacruna (*Psychotria viridis*). Prior to ayahuasca tourism, there was plenty to go around, but now overharvesting has resulted in both of these plants becoming endangered, particularly the large, ancient "mother" vines of ayahuasca, found only in the deep forest. There is a clear need to create cultivation infrastructures for both of these plants to ensure a sustainable supply. This problem is being recognized and projects are being undertaken by NGOs such as the International Center for Ethnobotanical Education, Research and Service (ICEERS), as well as in local communities. There are solutions, but like many well-intended efforts, these projects tend to be underfunded.

On the positive side, I think ayahuasca tourism reflects a global shift in consciousness and a radical reframing of our relationship with nature that is essential if this planet is to survive. Most ayahuasca tourists are not looking for thrills; they are by and large serious spiritual seekers who have been drawn to the medicine because they are spiritually bereft—they no longer find meaning in the major institutional religions. Indeed, institutional religions have often been bludgeons to keep people in line and discourage asking too many pesky questions. They have also historically devalued nature and treated it as a commodity to be dominated, monetized, desecrated, criminalized, and ultimately destroyed. We have only to look at the current devastations due to climate change to see the consequences of this rape of nature over the last 2,000 years. Institutional religions have become hollowed-out shells; empty ritual and dogma have replaced any actual spiritual depth or moral authority, and this is becoming ever more widely understood.

I think there are profound historical, societal, and even coevolutionary forces at work here. Indigenous people have been the keepers of this knowledge; they have maintained stewardship of the plants and their habitats, which also happen to be their own habitats. Now all of these are threatened—they always have been but now even more so—under the pressures of globalization, expansion, climate change, and economic "development."

Yet at the same time, increasing numbers of people are having psychedelic experiences, whether they travel to exotic locales or find them closer to home. Very often, the take-home lesson from these experiences is that we have to wake up before it is too late, to recognize how out of balance we have become in our relationship to nature. But waking up is not enough. We then have to "wise up": that is, we have to respond to our awakening by "becoming wise." We have to carefully think about what choices we must make in order to shift our relationship to nature from dominance and exploitation to harmony and symbiotic partnership. There are ways to do this—solutions do exist, and despair is not one of them. But the challenge is that this shift in global consciousness must be widespread, and it has to happen quickly! Are psychedelics the answer? Clearly, all by themselves they are not. They are catalysts, effective tools to nudge our species toward this necessary shift in global consciousness. They have always been our symbiotic partners, in some respect our teachers, possibly as ancient as consciousness itself. But over vast spans of historical and evolutionary time, their lessons have been lost to all but a few marginalized societies. It's time for us, as a species, to remember.

Ayahuasca is not the only, or even the most important, psychedelic catalyst. On a global scale, mushrooms are far more accessible to more people than ayahuasca, and people are discovering in them much the same message: that we have become estranged from nature and we have to realign with it. Ayahuasca, in fact, may not be that ancient. The magic combination of plants that give ayahuasca its consciousness-altering properties may have been a relatively recent discovery, even among Indigenous people. It exemplifies a rather sophisticated folk technology that may only have been discovered a few hundred years ago, probably no more than a couple of thousand years at most. Mushrooms, on the other hand, do not require any technology in their preparation—just the curiosity to pluck them from a cow pie and consume them. There are all sorts of good reasons for thinking that they have been symbiotic partners with our species for possibly millions of years, and may have been a critical catalyst fostering the emergence of consciousness. So it makes sense that on the global scale, mushrooms are at the heart of the psychedelic renaissance. They are easily cultivated in massive quantities, so there is really no supply issue, and they have been used in multiple shamanic traditions worldwide, so there is less cultural appropriation associated with them. They are the common heritage of our species, more ancient than any of the others. And they are the perfect psychedelic! Visionary, profound, nontoxic, compatible with human physiology, and yet transformational. Mushrooms are the perfect coevolutionary symbiotic partner for humanity, nature's secret elixir with the potential to heal the soul of our species and the planet we have so severely wounded.

Our species has rediscovered the natural psychedelics, which have always been there. It is our new recognition and appreciation of these most profound gifts of nature that give me hope. Properly integrated into global society, psychedelics have the potential to take us to the next level in human evolution, to make us kinder, wiser, more compassionate, and more aware than we have ever been. They have always been nudging us in this direction, but we have not been listening. Now perhaps we will begin to wake up. It is not too late.

There is another element of the ever-changing present as it morphs into the future that gives me cause for hope: as we are beginning to understand that we are just one among a plethora of species that constitute the biosphere, we are finally opening our eyes to the cosmos again. There is renewed interest in space exploration, a new curiosity about the near solar system and the vast expanses that lie beyond. I believe this encourages us to be humble, at the same time inviting us to dream of a possible future that only our great-great-grandchildren will see, if our species survives long enough. Far from assured, yet it is an antidote to despair. Just as psychedelics remind us of how little we know, the marvelous machines that open a window to the very edge of the Universe remind us of how small we are. Our species has been self-centered and arrogant for far too long, and this has led to the mess we're in now. There should be no place for either of these in our collective worldview.

The completion and successful deployment of the James Webb Space Telescope (JWST) in December 2021 was one of the most hopeful, inspiring events in space science since the ISS was occupied at the turn of the century. The JWST is perhaps the most complex technological artifact ever created by humankind. And it is beautiful in so many ways. Not only is it a technological marvel, but it was created in the service of curiosity and scientific discovery. As over budget and past deadline as it is, it does not matter. This machine will extend our vision and open our eyes, as well as our minds, to the marvelous universe we inhabit in ways they have never been opened before.

It was Socrates who said, "wisdom begins in wonder." I am encouraged that we are rediscovering wonder as we extend our gaze ever farther into the cosmos. It is a necessary complement to looking inward, as we now do with psychedelics. In fact, as psychedelics and humanity's mystical traditions have taught for thousands of years, there is really no difference between ourselves and the cosmos: We are all one. What is not here, is nowhere, as the Hermetic philosophers have told us for centuries.

Over 50 years ago now, 53 years to be exact at the date of this writing, we finally landed humans on the Moon. It was more a political stunt than anything else, a trumpeting of our technological superiority over the "Russkies." Its scientific value was dubious. That first Moon landing was followed by several others over the following decade, and then the interest began to fade. We were overcome by timidity and a sense of "What now?" We momentarily stuck a figurative toe in the waters and then recoiled as the realization that any step beyond the paltry baby step to the Moon was likely to remain well beyond human capabilities for decades, perhaps for centuries. Perhaps forever, especially given that the rapid deterioration of everything on Earth, from political institutions to the environment, has forced us to focus on the more immediate challenges here on Earth. Not that we have been very effective in solving them so far.

In the 1960s there was great excitement about psychedelics and their promise for healing, but the exploration of the universe within that they revealed retreated into the background as they became caught in the culture wars of the day. It took another 50 years for science to rediscover them, and the fact that we have speaks to a certain necessary maturation of our society. Much the same has happened with space exploration. Just as psychedelics never really went away, space exploration continued at the margins. In the waning months of the last year of the 20th century, the first long-term inhabitants of the ISS took up residence.

In the first edition of this book, I railed against the shortsightedness of the space program of the 1960s and its goal of putting a man (of course it had to be a man!) on the moon by the end of the decade. We achieved that goal, but it did not lead to establishing any sort of long-term presence in space. In the earlier edition, I said that instead of putting a man on the moon and bringing him back, our goal should have been to establish permanent residence in near Earth orbit, and then build on that platform as a spring-board to the moon and other planets. I discussed this in the chapter titled "The Big Picture," but it bears repeating here:

> I have often wondered how different the 21st century might have been if Kennedy had given careful thought to the real goals of space exploration. What if he had called for a permanent manned space station instead of a lunar program whose consequences were pretty much limited to proving that, yes, 'Merica could do it? If Kennedy had made such an orbital base the country's goal, we now might be mining asteroids for the bulk of our water and minerals, generating all of the world's energy from solar-power satellites, and maintaining bases on the Moon, possibly on Mars, and even in orbit around the outer planets. Instead he chose machismo over substance, threw down a technological gauntlet to the Russians, and pushed the Cold War to further heights of hostility.

It was a critical strategic error that has held us back technologically and has contributed to many of the problems that we are facing due to overexploitation of Earth-based resources and diminished capacity to develop a space-based civilization. Had we done so, we would find ourselves inhabiting an environment with access to nearly unlimited resources, including energy, minerals, even water. As it is now, all of these critical resources place serious constraints on growth, and even growth itself is seen as a threat to survival because we are imprisoned on a finite planet. Had we had the foresight to envision such a future and commit ourselves to it in the 1960s, the world today would be much more like we imagined it would be in 1968, when the movie *2001: A Space Odyssey* was released. That movie was a vision of where we thought we would be by the turn of the century. It did not happen. We have lost critical decades. Have we also lost the will?

The next decade will answer this question. I am encouraged that there is renewed interest in the commercialization of space, and a gradual process of handing over the challenge of space exploration to the private sector seems to be taking place. This is a necessary phase if we are to establish a more permanent human presence in space. Of course much of it is driven by greed, fueled by the prospect of vast profits to be made by corporations through the development of off-planet resources. Undoubtedly, many mistakes will be made and it is not all going to be pretty. But there is one thing about capitalism that we have to acknowledge: it's a way to get things done, often in situations where government institutions cannot because they are too tied up in bureaucracy and politics. Much the same criticism could be leveled at the current rush to cash in on the "psychedelic renaissance." In the last few years, new start-up companies dedicated to the development of psychedelic therapeutics have sprung up like a flush of mushrooms in a pasture after a warm rain. All of these companies are hoping to make a profit. Many are also motivated by good intentions, hoping to revolutionize mental health care with psychedelics. The potential for doing this has never been better. Not all have pure motives; the prospect of vast fortunes to be made has a way of strangling the small, still voice of ethics. But it is all part of the process. Our economy is profit-driven and psychedelics will not find a place in medicine unless there are profits to be made. How this is handled will depend largely on the ethical and moral compasses of the people creating these companies. In the case of psychedelics, we may hope that the entrepreneurs remember to taste their medicine on occasion and perhaps derive some guidance and wisdom from those experiences.

In the case of space exploration it is much the same. The establishment of a permanent threshold in the Near Earth solar system is going to cost trillions, and it will be spearheaded by mega-entrepreneurs like Jeff Bezos, Richard Branson, and Elon Musk. Modesty is not their strong suit. These people have egos as big as the known universe, but it's going to take people like that, with the resources to match, to make this happen. So while I think publicity stunts consisting of getting other billionaires to pay for a half-hour suborbital flight are distasteful, it's also something that has to be done to get people's attention. It's not unlike what happened during the emergence of commercial aviation in the early 20th century. The people who did that were showmen as much as anything. They craved attention, and their exploits got people excited. But in the end, in a more mature phase, it led to the development of the aviation industry and we have all benefited from that.

I am concerned that as the space industry develops, we will make the same mistake we did back in the 1960s and succumb to the seduction of establishing colonies on the moon or on Mars. Both of these places are inimical to life and neither is likely to become a desirable place to live in the foreseeable future. It's possible that with extensive terraforming, these worlds could be transformed, but that would be a project spanning centuries and requiring technologies far beyond our current capabilities. I think we should abandon the rather impractical idea of colonizing Mars. Why spend all that money and effort to again trap ourselves at the bottom of a gravity well on a planet that will kill an unprotected person in minutes? In fact, cis-lunar space, the region between the Earth and Moon, is much better suited to human colonization. Gerard K. O'Neill wrote of space colonies in the 1970s, and his book *The High Frontier: Human Colonies in Space* fired up the imaginations of many young space enthusiasts. I should know—I was one of them. But O'Neill's vision, as wild as it might have seemed at the time, was actually a practical envisioning of how humanity could begin to expand the reach of civilization beyond the confines of the planetary surface. It pointed toward a radical redirection for the space effort following the Apollo program. It was roundly criticized, denounced, and ultimately ignored.

Now it's time to revisit this concept. The success of the ISS has demonstrated, at least on a small scale, that it's possible to build human habitats in space. The ISS is in fact a small space colony, a prototype that is a proof of concept. There have been technological advances in materials science, heavy lift capabilities, and sustainable life support systems that make space colonization not such a crazy idea after all. It is possible, or it will soon be possible, to build a permanently inhabited space station that is ten or a hundred or even a thousand times larger than the ISS. Fifty years from now, if we manage not to destroy the planet or blow ourselves up, some of our descendants may one day be born, live, and die in these orbital space cities.

The colonies will probably not look much like the cylindrical, barrel-shaped colonies envisioned by O'Neill. Recent work by visionary aerospace scientist and exobiologist Dr. Bruce Damer with the SHEPHERD project has described approaches to the capture of small asteroids in extremely large mylar envelopes, gently moving them to desired orbital positions, and then extracting resources such as metals and gases, applying materials technology and biotechnology to create artificial biospheres. These would essentially be terraformed "mini-earths" that could sustainably house thousands to hundreds of thousands, along with the animals, plants, and other biotic resources needed to sustain the ecosystem. There is nothing impractical or impossible about this vision. It is nearly within present technological capabilities, and if there was a sufficient will to muster the resources, the first prototype asteroid-based artificial biosphere could be constructed within 10 years. It is a much more achievable and practical goal than a Mars or moon colony.

Space colonization is not only a practical solution, it is also a transformational one in terms of how it will affect the way we think of our species. This step, after all, is a necessary threshold that we must cross if we are to propagate biospheric DNA beyond Earth, at first into the local solar system but eventually to the stars beyond. Instead of thinking of ourselves as members of tribes or nationalities, it will change our perspective on who we are. We are humans, we are earthlings, we are participants in the planetary symbiotic superorganism, and as such, expansion into this new frontier will go far toward dissolving and rendering irrelevant the petty, earthbound divisions that have poisoned humanity for far too long.The question, as always, is whether we will have the will to match our vision. Given that this is perhaps the only way to save our planet in the long term, one may hope so.

The Road Ahead

So now we find ourselves in the present moment, the moment that we inhabit in perpetuity because the future does not exist and the past is but memory. From this perch, we can gaze back on what has been and look ahead to what may be on the horizon. Here I will indulge in speculations about where we may be headed and some of the events that may emerge out of that murky horizon, which we can see but never reach, because it ever recedes ahead of us.

The world as we know it ended more or less on schedule in 2020. The COVID pandemic disrupted global civilization in ways that only a very few anticipated, and now we are still living in the traumatic aftershock of that event, even though it is still with us and may be with us for some time to come. As world-ending events go, COVID was rather kind—the next one may not be so gentle. But for now, society has adjusted. We have learned to live with the pandemic. We understand the commonsense measures that would enable us to cope, to minimize its impact. It's not the pandemic that has disrupted society so much as the societal and ideological divisions that it has brought into sharp focus and exacerbated. Our encounters with COVID have provided us with valuable lessons and a disturbing new understanding of the basic fragility of our civilization. One thing COVID has taught us: in a society riven by ideological differences and algorithm-driven conspiracy theories that propagate through the social meme-osphere at the speed of light, we have a difficult time adopting a "we are all in this together" mindset. It is more like an "everyone for themselves, and you are my enemy" mindset, and it will be this—and not the virus—that brings civilization down. It is for this reason that we must recognize the threat posed by social media. It is also a technology that can achieve much good if properly deployed. We need to come to some consensus about how it can be regulated to curb its destructive potential without taking away our freedoms. It's a tall order and we may not be able to do this given the immaturity of our species.

As we look toward that far horizon, a decade or two in the future, one would have to be deluded not to recognize some pretty grim prospects. Of course, many have chosen delusion over an honest assessment of our existential situation, and that's much of the problem. Delusion is certainly no solution. Salvation will not be found in either denial or despair, and we're getting very good at both. Instead, what is needed is a realistic acknowledgment of the mess we're in, clear thinking, and a certain cautious optimism, because solutions exist—if only we can develop the collective determination to pursue them.

Barring some unforeseen cosmic disaster such as a massive asteroid impact, it's possible to imagine a number of lesser but still catastrophic events that may occur in the next 20 years. Thanks to the success of our asteroid surveillance programs, we can be reasonably confident that we won't have to worry about a planet-killing asteroid for at least the next 200 years. By then, if one does show up, there will either be no one left around to worry about it or we'll have technologies in place to deflect or destroy it, providing our surveillance is thorough.

We are living in a time of increasing geopolitical instability, with democracy under siege in the United States and in many other countries. Tensions are high. Even as I write these words, Russia has invaded Ukraine, China is making noises about the annexation of Taiwan, and North Korea is boasting about their new ICBMs. China, Russia, and the United States are sitting on top of massive stockpiles of nuclear weapons. The Cold War never really went away, and it's not hard to imagine many global scenarios that could trigger a nuclear exchange. Such an event, depending on scale, may not totally destroy civilization, but it could. It would, in any case, be highly inconvenient. How likely it is depends on how unhinged our leaders are. There is much reason for concern on that score; crazy seems to be going around, and there is a lot of it. It is only a guess, as all of these are, but conservatively I would place the chances of a global nuclear exchange in the next two decades at around 10 percent. If we get through this bottleneck, we can hope that by then our civilization will have matured enough that we have abandoned nuclear weapons entirely. Just this January (2022), the five permanent members of the United Nations signed a joint declaration that "a nuclear war can never be won and must never be fought." Declarations are all well and good, but when are we going to act on them?

Climate change is the biggest global catastrophe of them all, but there are solutions. We've reached the point where we have to start thinking about geoengineering. It's a scary thought. Geoengineering is deliberate manipulation of planetary dynamics on a global scale to arrest, or drastically slow, the rise in atmospheric greenhouse gases that cause global warming; the melting of the polar ice caps; the rising sea levels; and the mega-hurricanes, floods, and droughts that devastate our environment every year in an ever-worsening spiral. Geoengineering is scary because we're talking about interfering in processes that have maintained climatic stability for millions of years, and we don't fully understand the consequences. Yet we have little choice. It's important to remember that we are already engaged in unintentional and undirected geoengineering, and have been since the dawn of the Anthropocene era. What is different now is that we actually have a better understanding of planetary dynamics and are in a position to implement intelligent geoengineering, if we choose to do so. Given the divisions that separate societies and governments, it may be difficult to get consensus on a geoengineering project. If it is done at all, it may have to be initiated by the private sector.

Other environmental disasters, not directly related to climate change except that they also originate in the abuse and misuse of petroleum products, are plastic pollution and pharmaceutical pollution. Both of these have been well underway for decades and are almost impossible to reverse. Neither is getting the attention they deserve in current discussions of the most serious threats to the biosphere. Plastic pollution may be the most insidious. It is not the islands of plastic waste the size of small countries that now exist in every ocean that are the most concerning; it is the microplastic (MP) and nanoplastic (NP) particles that now permeate every ecosystem on the planet, and can be detected in nearly every organism including humans. These are neuroendocrine disruptors, among their other adverse effects, and are dramatically affecting fertility rates in humans and many other species. There is no way that this can be reversed. Similarly, megatons of pharmaceutical pollutants, originating from pharmaceutical manufacturing plants, medical waste streams, and even the graves and toilets of ordinary citizens, are being released in water systems everywhere. These also have disruptive and unpredictable effects on organisms in every ecosystem. Pharmaceutical and plastic pollution happens relatively slowly, and there is little to trigger alarm until it has accumulated to critical levels. We have already reached and passed that point. These pollutants—more than global warming, rising sea levels, or collapse of ecosystem food chains, even global nuclear catastrophe—may be the most serious threat facing all life on this planet. I have been aware of these concerns for some time, but Stephen Harrod Buhner's *Earth Grief* has recently brought home to me just how serious this problem is.

Invasion by a vastly more advanced alien civilization is another such possibility. This is possible, but it is impossible to calculate the probabilities. My guess is that it's very unlikely, because I've come around to the view that advanced, technologically capable civilizations are extremely rare. They may be so rare, in fact, that ours may be the only one in the galaxy. I think that life in the galaxy is fairly common, but in most instances, it never gets beyond the microbe stage, because the very special circumstances that can lead to the emergence of consciousness and technological capabilities are quite rare. Life has existed on earth for at least 3.8 billion years—possibly as long as 4.4 billion years—but multicellular life, let alone complex life-forms, did not show up until relatively recently: "only" about 550 million years ago! There is reason to believe that the unique qualities of the Earth–Moon system constituted an ideal incubator for the emergence of complex life forms.

Of course, it may also be the case that technological civilizations arise fairly frequently, but with an inherently short life span. As a result those other civilizations are temporally isolated from ours. We have our own as the only example. We have had technologies that broadcast our presence to the universe at large since Marconi's invention of radio in the 1890s, so the lifetime—so far—of our technologically capable civilization is a little less than 140 years. The galaxy may be littered with the ruins of alien civilizations that reached a similar stage, then blew themselves up or poisoned their planets, as we are now in the process of doing. We can also turn this dismal view of alien contact on its head and imagine a more optimistic possibility. Perhaps an alien civilization that is advanced enough to invent interstellar travel is morally advanced as well, so instead of ravening beasts coming to destroy and conquer us, the aliens—when they do show up—will be kind and wise, ready to welcome us into the galacterian community. This is the hopeful vision of many science fiction novels and, I venture to say, many uplifting and transcendent psychedelic experiences (although the terrifying alien contact movies seem to sell better at the box office).

New technologies including artificial intelligence (AI), nanotechnology, and genetic engineering also show great promise and many potentially beneficial applications. However, if misused, deliberately or accidentally, any of them could bring civilization down and even threaten all terrestrial life. This goes to the heart of something that I've taken to haranguing people about in my lectures, which is the disjunction between cleverness and wisdom. Our species is extremely clever, and we have invented technologies that have the potential to save the world or destroy it, depending on how (or whether) they are used. Technology itself has no inherent moral qualities. It can be used for good or ill. The moral dimension comes from within the human heart. We are clever, but we are not yet wise. To evolve greater wisdom is the challenge that we must address in this century, so that we become aware of the double-edged nature of so many technologies and develop the moral clarity to use them for the benefit of our species and all species on this planet (or in some cases to make decisions—guided by moral principles—not to use them at all).

We can now wield technologies that, in the most extreme cases, are capable of completely eradicating all terrestrial life. But this is highly unlikely. The fossil record of life on earth shows that the planet has endured more than one extinction-level event, such as the Ordvician-Salurian event, 450 million years ago; the Permian–Triassic extinction event, 250 million years ago; and the asteroid impact that knocked out the dinosaurs, 65 million years ago (Paleogene–Cretaceous extinction). For instance, in the most severe case, the Permian–Triassic extinction (also known as the Great Dying), up to 82 percent of all genera, 81 percent of marine species, and 70 percent of terrestrial vertebrate species were driven into extinction. And yet, life persisted. In fact, in the aftermath of most of these events, the ecological niches that were opened resulted in a profound proliferation of biodiversity in the succeeding epochs. But the time frames for the recovery from these global cataclysms are measured in tens of millions of years. So I don't worry too much that we will wipe out all life on earth. As I sometimes say in my lectures to make the point: "Gaia is one tough bitch." Terrestrial life is incredibly resilient, and the record shows that it will recover from the most dire catastrophic events, given enough time. Our species, on the other hand, is not so tough, and we may well create a situation where the planet is no longer hospitable to human life. Within the next 30 to 50 years, we will reach a point where we will know whether this is going to happen. Not that we will be extinct—but we will know by then whether the processes that we have set in motion can be arrested or reversed.

Above I've considered various apocalyptic scenarios that may take down civilization sometime in the next hundred years. Things seem to be closing in, and probably every civilization in history has lived in the expectation of its imminent demise. But is there any reason for optimism? What might mitigate these dark outcomes? I believe there are several emerging technologies that could be game changers, provided we can muster the collective will to develop them and then deploy them. One of the most promising is sustainable fusion. It has been sought for decades and remains elusive, but we are closer than ever to achieving commercially viable sustainable fusion. It is truly "clean energy" that can be generated from abundantly available materials and releases neither radioactive waste nor greenhouse gases into the environment. Several private companies now claim to have developed sustainable fusion technologies that could be widely deployed in under a decade. This single technological breakthrough could make all the difference. It would not solve the problem of global warming overnight—nothing will do that—but fusion could provide the means to start to turn the situation around. Fusion, together with carefully and intelligently applied geoengineering, could be the key technology that will make it possible to slow, and then reverse, catastrophic global warming and begin to restore the planetary feedback loops that keep the global climate within the narrow parameters that are hospitable to life.

Airships are another technology that are well within our current capabilities and could be massively deployed in under a decade. Airships have been known since the early 20th century, but in the aftermath of the Hindenburg disaster in 1937 the technology was largely abandoned. A number of companies are now developing a new generation of airships that use nonflammable helium instead of hydrogen. Helium airships will not, in themselves, stop global warming but they can have a significant impact. They can be constructed with ultrastrong, lightweight carbon composite polymers and coated with flexible photovoltaic fabrics that can generate sufficient solar energy that will render them not simply carbon neutral but carbon negative. With unlimited solar power, they can remain aloft for prolonged periods, only coming to earth to load or offload freight and passengers—or, by coupling them with massive cargo drones to effect the transfers, they can remain in the upper atmosphere indefinitely. Airships of all sizes, ranging from that of a small boat to that of an ocean liner, can be constructed. Airship transport could revolutionize the global freight and passenger industry. Currently, the global freight transport system relies on container ships, which burn fossil fuels and carry a significant risk of pollution due to fuel spills, all in order to transport cargo containers to trucks and trains that also run on fossil fuels. These systems are also vulnerable to numerous hazards associated with surface transport, such as hurricanes and other extreme weather events. Airships, coupled with cargo drones, could provide a carbon-negative solution that would also obviate the need to clog the highways with massive, polluting freight trucks, while lessening their impact on highway infrastructure. If such airship technology were available, it's also likely that new forms of recreational air travel would emerge. Much in the manner that luxury ocean liners were popular for leisure travel in the 20th century, passenger airships would spawn a new leisure travel industry for those travelers who want to take their time and view the world from a new perspective. For those in a hurry, supersonic jet travel would still be available, but many fewer jets would be needed. And one may hope that the new generation of supersonic passenger jets would also run on solar-powered electric engines. All of these are under development. Earlier in this chapter I also discussed the game-changing possibility of establishing permanent space colonies in the Earth–Moon space environment (cislunar space).

Another technological development that is currently much less likely—but not out of the question considering the ingenuity of the human spirit—would be the invention of practical faster-than-light (FTL), or space warp, technologies. This is not yet possible considering what we think we understand about the laws of physics. Einstein's theory of relativity postulates that FTL is not possible, and so far empirical evidence has validated the theory despite numerous attempts to disprove it. Nonetheless, this has not prevented many very clever people from thinking about how to overcome the speed-of-light barrier. This must happen if we are ever to expand human presence beyond the solar system. FTL, should it ever be invented, will throw open the gates of the cosmos to our species. Even if it is possible, it is likely to be centuries in the future, but the key discoveries that lead to it may well be made in the next hundred years. This is another very good reason not to destroy ourselves. If we're going to take that interstellar leap someday, we need to ensure that there is someone around to take it.

* * *

The End of the Road?

In the previous section I've speculated on some possible futures that may manifest over the next 50 to 100 years. Some of the scenarios I've outlined are dystopian and quite terrifying. Others are less so. While the world is beset with challenges, it is still possible to envision a better world, one more akin to that future cislunar civilization portrayed in Kubrick's movie *2001: A Space Odyssey*. The choices we make in the next 30 years will determine which of these paths our species will travel. The situation is not hopeless. Extinction is far from inevitable, if we can only come together as a species, realize that we are all in this boat together, stop fighting, and start working to save ourselves and our beautiful, wounded planet.

I am basically an optimist, and I know that history is full of surprises. That is the fundamental premise of the notion of Novelty, which was not an invention of Terence's but is in fact an element of the process philosophy of Alfred North Whitehead, whose writings influenced both Terence's and my thinking about these matters. Process theory is complex, but if it can be condensed to a nutshell, it comes down to the notion that there are new things under the sun. Events occur every day that have never before happened in the history of the universe. This fact means that being receptive to those surprises may be the main justification for what we might call cautious optimism. No one knows for certain what is going to happen tomorrow. The world we imagined we lived in has ended, not just once but several times in recent years. Most of those world-shattering events seem to foreshadow doom, but we would do well to remember that some more positive world-transforming event may be just around the corner. As we look back on the arc of history, we can take comfort in the knowledge that such changes have in fact taken place. Nature and the planet, life on the planet, are resilient; humanity, as craven and willfully ignorant as it is, is also strong, intelligent, and loving. As hopeless as these times may seem, these traits may yet save us and the planet. My father often used to tell me, "While there's life, there's hope." More profound words have never been spoken. Let us nurture and cherish this life, and this hope, because if anything is certain, it is that despair will not save us.

In the previous section I used the word "we" a lot, meant to represent our species as a whole. In this final section I want to pull in my elbows a bit and revert to a personal perspective. What does it all mean for me, Dennis McKenna, just one human soul among billions? The only honest answer of course is that I don't know. What I do know is that I hope to be able to stick around long enough to see some of these changes happen, whether dystopian or full of possibility. At the end of this year I will turn 72. While that is an age that only a few years ago was well beyond what a white male could expect to live, now—with access to medical care and a reasonably healthy lifestyle—it's not unrealistic to expect to live well into my 80s or even beyond. Knowing my own genetics and family history, and having learned in the past couple of years some sobering things about my cardiac health, I hope to complete my 80th decade but probably won't live much longer than that. My brother was 53 when he died; my mother, 57. Both died of cancer. So far I have been spared. My father died of heart failure at the age of 82. It's likely that I will die of cardiac problems at around the same age, unless something intervenes. On the other hand, one cannot know. My mother's sister, Aunt Mayme, lived to 97; her sister, Aunt Tress, lived a healthy active life to age 90 and then abruptly passed on; my father's younger brother, Uncle Aut, died in the spring of 2019 at 97. So my family lineage has both the cancer genes and the longevity genes. I am grateful for the time I have lived, for the people I have known and loved, the adventures I've had, for whatever tiny slice of the Big Picture I've been able to grasp, and for whatever future I may yet live to see.

I have noticed that at this age, at a point where most of my life is now past, no matter how many more years I may live, I increasingly feel the weight of those decades. As a youth, I didn't have much empathy for old people who spend so much time thinking about the past. Now I understand why they do that. It's because most of their lives have already passed: the memories are there to cherish and share, and they enrich their stories in advancing age. However much of the road may be left to travel, it is surely a short journey compared to the road already traveled. I am blessed to still have good friends, a good woman who has traveled much of it with me, and a wonderful daughter who will discover her own destiny in the evolving future, however it may turn out. I hope that I am lucky enough to keep those memories. In the end, they are all one has.

Acknowledgments

The writing of this memoir has consumed more than a year of my life, and it has been an intensely personal, at times emotionally taxing experience. I will always remain grateful for the confluence of circumstances and support from the broad community of friends, family, and fellow travelers who gave me the opportunity to manifest this work in the real world. To borrow a phrase from one of our favorite philosophers, Alfred North Whitehead, the book has now undergone "the formality of actually occurring." Now that the formality is past, it's clear that the book never would have happened were it not for a good deal of luck and the assistance and encouragement of many who participated in the birthing process. It may be my story, but telling that story to the wider world has been a team effort.

First of all, I want to thank those who are closest to my heart, and who have the not always pleasant task of putting up with me from day to day: my wife, Sheila, and my daughter, Caitlin. Their support in this endeavor has been unflagging, and their tolerance of my moods and preoccupations has been more than I have any right to expect. I thank them for generously giving me the space, and time, that writing this book has demanded, and for asking for so little in return. Beyond that, both have contributed to the outcome by reading the manuscript as it has taken form with careful and critical eyes, always making astute suggestions for edits and improvements. Likewise, I want to acknowledge Terence's family: his ex-wife Kat Harrison, son Finn, and daughter Klea. Their honest feedback and suggestions have made this a better book than it would have been without their valued input. Other members of my family have also been generous in sharing their time, memories, and family treasures, especially old photographs and documents. Memory is such an ephemeral and fragile thing, as I have learned, and their help has been invaluable in my attempts to reconstruct the specifics of names and places, dates and events, of a misty past that is now a bit less so, thanks to them.

In particular, I want to thank my beloved Aunt Tress, my mother's youngest sister, for those wonderful interviews at her kitchen table in the summer of 2011. I learned so much that I had never known, and it gave me a chance to renew bonds with a favorite aunt that I will always cherish. My other favorite, my dear Aunt Mayme, Mom's other younger sister, passed away at age 97 while this book was in progress. I will always love her and remember all that she did for Mom and "the boys" during our long and problematic childhood. I'm so sorry that she did not live to see the outcome of this work, but she has been an inspiration for it nonetheless, and I am grateful to her. I also want to thank her daughters, Judy and Jody, and Judy's husband, Laddie, for the rich conversations we had in the course of my research, and for the photos and documents that helped me reconstruct the backstory to my account. I thank them also for their hospitality and for always extending a warm welcome to this wayward traveler on my rare visits back to the old hometown. They are the ones who have made this story real, by providing me with a window to the past and a connection to the family clan that is very much a part of the present and future as well as the past. They remind me that I do have a family on my mother's side, quite an extensive one, and I am proud to be a part of it.

On my father's side of the family, I want to thank and acknowledge my Uncle Aut (Austin), or "Mack" as he's now known, and his wife, Fran. They are my living connection to our father's family, and all the more beloved and cherished because of that. Aut freely shared his time, recollections, documents, and photos and helped me to reconstruct our father's childhood, the life that he shared with his brothers and sister and our paternal grandparents. He also painted a vivid picture of our parents' lives before and after World War II, a reminder that they were all young once, too, and led rich, full lives long before "Terry and Denny" were anywhere to be seen. Of course, I must acknowledge our parents, Joe and "Hadie" (Hazelle) McKenna, to whom this book is dedicated. They have both been gone for many years now, but I cherish their memory and thank them for providing Terence and me with a loving home and an environment that allowed us to flourish. We gave them fits, more than any parent should have to tolerate, and yet they loved us through it all. It took many years before I fully came to appreciate what extraordinary people they were.

I also want to acknowledge those old friends who knew Terence and me back in the day, and who were kind enough to share their reminiscences. Some are mentioned under pseudonyms in the book, a small gesture to preserve their privacy, but you know who you are. You were there from the early days, and we lived through some crazy times together. Thank you for sharing your stories and more. I am especially grateful to Sara Hartley for kindly allowing the use of her photographs. Thanks also to

Terence's good friend William Patrick Watson for permission to reprint his "shamanic talismanic" poem "Pursuing to Peru the G'nostic Guru" as an appendix to this book. It was the perfect incantation for our quixotic quest then, and it remains so to this day. Thanks also to Jill Wagner for sharing her recollections.

Wade Davis was generous with his valuable time in providing an interview for my Kickstarter project, and also shared his wisdom and experience in the publishing realm with me. I owe him thanks for much, but most importantly for his friendship through the years.

My friend George Douvris also deserves a sincere thanks for providing an interview for the site, and for his enthusiastic support in getting word of the project out to the community of fellow travelers.

I want to give special acknowledgment to those who engineered the "nuts and bolts" of this book. My editor, Jeremiah Creedon, long-suffering, gifted, insightful, brilliant, deserves far more credit than me for sculpting my unwieldy prose into something we're ready to show to the world. I had no idea when I started out how important it would be to have a good editor covering for me; Jerry has been there for me every step of the way. I want to give a special thanks to Mark Odegard, my best friend in Minnesota. He introduced me to Jerry, and he has applied his considerable skills to designing the layout, the cover, and jacket for this book. Thanks to Mark, this book is a thing of beauty from its cover to the final page. I also owe Mark for urging me to undertake this project in the first place; he pressed me for years, and I finally gave in, and he was always there with an encouraging word. Another close friend, Mac Graham, has given freely of his time and skills as a copy editor and proofreader; many thanks to him for his generous contribution to the process. Thanks are also due to Tom Healy and Mary Ricci for their copyediting and proofing as the final layout took form. Tom and Mary brought their sharp minds and eyes to the task at just the right moment.

I am entirely responsible for any errors in this account, and any inaccuracies in my recollections of people and events, and I'm sure there are a few and perhaps more than a few. I humbly accept any blame that is due and apologize to my readers.

I want to thank Dan Levy, Terence's former editor, for his suggestion that I try using Kickstarter to secure the funds and time to create this book. It seemed like a crazy idea when we discussed it in December 2010, but it worked better than either of us could have imagined. It was a brilliant idea. I want to thank Seal Dwyer and her team at North Star Press of St. Cloud for handling the production and printing of this book as well as providing invaluable guidance in creating the e-book versions. With their help, and Kickstarter's, we've created a new model for self-publishing that I hope will be an inspiration to others. We also want to extend a special thanks to our friend Keith Cleaversly, an enthusiastic supporter of this project who didn't hesitate to step into the breach at a most critical juncture. For all that you do and are, Keith, many thanks. The project could not have succeeded without you.

Finally, I want to thank my loyal and patient Kickstarter supporters. Thanks to you, this book exists. I don't know how it could have happened otherwise. Thanks to you, I discovered that Terence and I are both loved by a vast community of fine, compassionate people who identified with our story, and who stepped in to make it possible to tell it to the wider world. As I promised, the names of those who contributed at the "patron" level are listed below. To all who contributed, I offer my profound gratitude. I humbly offer all of you the fruit of our labors and hope that you will find it worthy.

—Dennis McKenna
Marine on St. Croix, Minnesota
October 1, 2012

Patrons

Many people helped make this book possible.
Those who contributed at the "patron" level are listed below.

Doug Aanes	Jeff Bustard
Paul Altese	Frank Caligiuri
Garth Anderson	Andrew Carroll
Maria Andrade	Sharee Carton
Christine Andrews	Paul Cheever
Cat Asche	Eric Cifani
David Atkinson	Matt Clough
Jaron Azaria	Mark Colburn
Robert Barnhart	Jarrett Cole
Mark Barry	Rick Connolly
Chris Bava	Patrick Couch
Ciaran Beahan	Jonathan Crocker
Jaime Beauchamp	Geo Crosby
Greg Bell	Lynne Dablow
Laila Benkrima	Greg Daggett
Zachariah Bobby	Mitch Dame
Michael Bock	Bruce Damer
Galen Bodenhausen	Shad Damron
Bryan Bogatz	Yaroslaw Darmos
Richard Boire	Earl Davis
Bob Bowman	David De Candia
Josh Bownes	Jeffery DeCelles
Ollie Boyd	Elke Dehner
Paula Brown	Bavid Dirney
Ethan S Bruce	Richard Doyle
George Bruder	Wendy Drake
Phillip Bryant	Robb Duncan
Robert Bulterman	Keith Edley
Rodney Burge	Omar El-Kassaby
Sam Burgett	Robert Emerson

Stefan Engström
EnTheoSelf
Erowid Center
Juan Escobar
Mathew Evans
Richard Faasen
Mack Faith
Matthew Fauver
Christopher Foley
Michael Fortwengler
Tom Fox
Gordon Freeman
David Gaian
Barbara Ganschow
Nigel Gericke
Indradeep Ghosh
Adam Giangregorio
Damian Glover
Adam Golding
Andrew Gonzalez
Linda Gooding
Art Goodtimes
Elizabeth Gordon
Christopher Gose
Shane Gough
Bill Grable
Zach Grant
Grant Green
George Greer
Nicholas Grenier
Roland Griffiths
Robert Griffitts
Janda Grove
Lorenzo Hagerty
Jason Hall
Colby Ham
Randall Hankins
Jon Hanna

Goni Harlap
John Harrison
Even Hauen
Dereck Hawco
Thomas Healy
Philip Heath
Kody Hedger
Nathaniel Heidler
Kieran Hennelly
Mike Henning
Klas Henriksson
Mark Herbert
Georgina Herman
Dwayne Hickman
Brian Holcomb
Cosmic Hooker
Tim Howe
Jeff Hutner
Sarah Hutt
Adam Jeal
Leonard Jenkins
Matthew Johnson
Phillip Johnson
W. Joling
Phillip Jones
Todd Jones
Theresa Jump
Sid Kalcheim
David Kalugerovich
Matthew Kamp
Darius Karrasavidis
Falco Karrasavidis
Aran Kate
Justin Kirkland
Greg Knight
Thomas Knowlden
John Kokko
Joshua Kostka

Chris Langberg
Colleen Lawson
Hal Lee
Brice Lemke
Dan Levy
Chris Lewis
James Lewis
Robert Lint
William Linton
Judy Livingston
Doug Long
Wiley Long
Noah Lowenstein
Patrick Lundborg
Oliver Lurway
Cynthia Luzius
Coral Mack
Scott Mader
Timus Martinus
Victor Matekole
Chris Mays
Matt Mazur
Alan McCoughtry
Jason McGann
Zac McGehee
John Medeski
Richard Meech
Jeff Merkel
Christopher Mielke
Chris Mighton
Ryan Mills
Spider Miranda
Zevic Mishor
Dariusz Misiuna
Kim Moody
Donna Moon
Stephan Moore
Scott Mossman

Reid Mukai
Eric N
Joe Naab
Ron Nadeau
Laurne Neeff
David Nichols
Grant Nicholson
Joy Nielsen
Odd Nilsen
Shane Noland
Terrence O'Brien
R. J. O'Driscoll
Sean O'Neill
Mark & Elizabeth Odegard
Miklos Oravetz
Garrett Outland
Darrell Pacini
Bridget Palu
Amy Phillips
Tom Pinkson
Daniel Potter
Richard Racette
William Ratterman
Frederick Rawski
Ron Rice
Jeff Ritzmann
Mark Robertson
Richard Rockman
Jakob Roelofs
Benjamin Running
Ethan Russo
Nicolas Sampson
Tommy Sandöy-Blom
Randy Sarbacher
Bill Scheel
Alex Schiller
Simeon Schnapper
Connie Schultz

Sebastians Ghost
Martin Seger
Susanne Seiler
Gregory Sergi
Sa'ad Shah
Remey Shand
Murray Sheret
James Shields
Ellen Shouler-Faith
Stephen Siebert
Diana Slattery
Dariusz Slepczuk
Mike Smethurst
Steve Smith
James Spencer
Christos Stathopoulos
Ian Stehlik
Chris Steinmetz
Robert Stek
Vladimir Stepan
Andy Strieby
Jesse Stroess
Lee Svec
Connie Swan
Jeremy Sylvester
Zsolt Szende
Masayasu Takayama
Alexandre Tannous
Cameron Taylor
Michael Tempesta

Chris Thomson
Rainer Tiedemann
Gareth Tucker
Kenneth Tupper
Fox Ultrafeel
Jon Upton
Robin Vernau
Noah Vickstein
Paul-Alexandru Vida
Julian Vitcetz-Kondas
Joseph Voelbel
Jill Wagner
Rob Waldman
Alex Warren
Andy Warren
Kelvin Weesner
Jonathon Weisberger
Aja West
Jami Whiting
Michael Wiberg
Thomas Wilkenson
Kath Williamson
Jim Wilson
Julie Wissinger
Matthew Wolfson
Bruce Woodside
Warren Wright
Richard Yensen
Jen Zariat
Michael Zehnder

Bibliography

I. Key References

Alfvén, Hannes. 1966. *Worlds-Antiworlds: Antimatter in Cosmology*. Translated by Rudy Feichtner. New York: W. H. Freeman & Co.

Amaringo, Pablo, and Luis Eduardo Luna. 1993. *Ayahuasca Visions: The Religious Iconography of a Peruvian Shaman*. Berkeley, CA: North Atlantic Press.

Bonnin, A., et al. 2011. "A transient placental source of serotonin for the fetal forebrain." *Nature* 472: 347–50.

Burroughs, William S., and A. Ginsberg. 1963. *The Yage Letters*. San Francisco: City Lights Books.

Campbell, Joseph, ed. 1957. *Papers from the Eranos Yearbooks*. Vol. 3. *Man and Time*. Bollingen Series 30. Princeton University Press.

Castaneda, Carlos. 1968. *The Teachings of Don Juan: A Yaqui Way of Knowledge*. Oakland, CA: University of California Press.

Clarke, Arthur C. 1953. *Against the Fall of Night*. New York: Gnome Press. First published in 1948 in *Startling Stories* November 1948.

——. 1953. *Childhood's End*. New York: Ballantine Books.

——. 1956. *The City and the Stars*. New York: Harcourt, Brace, and World.

——. 1968. *2001: A Space Odyssey*. New York: New American Library.

Colby, Gerard, and C. Dennett. 1995. *Thy Will Be Done: The Conquest of the Amazon: Nelson Rockefeller and Evangelism in the Age of Oil*. New York: Harper Collins.

Davis, Erik. 2007. "Terence McKenna's Ex-Library." from the website Techgnosis. https://techgnosis.com/terence-mckennas-ex-library/

Davis, Wade. 1996. *One River: Explorations and Discoveries in the Amazon Rain Forest*. New York: Simon & Schuster.

Dick, Philip K. 1965. *The Three Stigmata of Palmer Eldritch*. New York: Doubleday.

——. 1981. *VALIS*. New York: Bantam.

——. 1981. *The Divine Invasion*. New York: Simon and Schuster.

——. 1982. *The Transmigration of Timothy Archer*. New York: Pocket.

——. 1991. *In Pursuit of Valis: Selections from the Exegesis*. Edited by Lawrence Sutin. Nevada City, CA: Underwood Books. Terence McKenna's afterword in this edition can be accessed at: http://www.sirbacon.org/dick.htm.

Eccles, John. 1973. *The Understanding of the Brain*. New York: McGraw-Hill.

Eliade, Mircea. 1959. *Cosmos and History: The Myth of the Eternal Return*. Translated by W. R. Trask. Paperback edition. New York: Harper Torchbooks.

——. 1959. *The Sacred and the Profane: The Nature of Religion*. Translated by W. R. Trask. San Diego: Harcourt.

——. 1970. *Yoga: Immortality and Freedom*. Translated by W. R. Trask. 2nd ed. Bollingen Series in World Mythology. Princeton University Press.

——. 1972. *Shamanism: Archaic Techniques of Ecstasy*. 2nd ed. Bollingen Series. Princeton University Press.

Flores, Franklin Ayala. 2003. *Taxonomía Vegetal: Gymnospermae y Angiospermae de la Amazonía Peruana*. Iquitos, Peru: Centro de Estudio Teológicos de la Amazonia.

Gamow, George. 1961. *One Two Three . . . Infinity: Facts and Speculations of Science*. New York: Viking Press.

——. 1964. *A Star Called the Sun*. New York: Viking Press.

Gardner, Martin. 1964. *The Ambidextrous Universe*. London: Penguin Books.

Graves, Robert. 1948. *The White Goddess*. Van Nuys, CA: Creative Age Press.

Haldane, J. B. S. 1927. *Possible Worlds*. London: Chatto & Windus.

Hardenburg, Walter E. 1912. *The Putumayo: The Devil's Paradise*. London: T. Fisher Unwin.

Heim, Roger, and R. Gordon Wasson. 1968. *Les Champignons Hallucinogénes du Mexique*. Paris: Editions du Muséum National d'Histoire Naturelle.

Hoyle, Fred. 1957. *Frontiers of Astronomy: A Revolutionary New View of the Universe*. Paperback ed. New York: New American Library.

Humphrey, Sheila. 2003. *The Nursing Mother's Herbal*. Minneapolis: Fairview Press.

Husserl, Edmund. 1960. *Cartesian Meditations: An Introduction to Phenomenology*. The Hague: Martinus Nijhoff.

——. 1962. *Ideas: General Introduction to Pure Phenomenology*. 3rd ed. Springfield, OH: Collier Books.

Huxley, Aldous. 1963. *The Doors of Perception and Heaven and Hell*. New York: HarperCollins.

Jantsch, Erich. 1980. *The Self-Organizing Universe*. New York: Pergamon Press.

Jaynes, Julian. 1977. *The Origin of Consciousness in the Breakdown of the Bicameral Mind*. Boston: Houghton Mifflin.

Jonas, Hans. 1966. *The Phenomenon of Life*. New York: Dell Publishing Co.

Jung, Carl G. 1953–1967. *The Collected Works of C. G. Jung*. Bollingen Series XX. Princeton University Press.

——. Vol. 9i. *The Archetypes and the Collective Unconscious*. 1959.

——. Vol. 9ii. *Aion: Researches into the Phenomenology of the Self*. 1959.

——. Vol. 10. *Civilization in Transition*. 1964.

——. Vol. 12. *Psychology and Alchemy*. 1953.

——. Vol. 14. *Mysterium Coniunctionis: An Inquiry Into the Separation and Synthesis of Psychic Opposites in Alchemy*. 1963.

——. Vol. 16. *The Practice of Psychotherapy*. 1954.

——. Foreword to *I Ching or Book of Changes*. 1950. Translated by Richard Wilhelm (German) and Cary F. Baynes (English). Bollingen Series XIX. Princeton University Press.

——. 1978. *Flying Saucers: A Modern Myth of Things Seen in the Skies*. Extracted from Vol. 10. Princeton University Press.

——. 2009. *The Red Book (Liber Novus)*. Edited by Sonu Shamdasani. New York: Philemon Series and W. W. Norton & Co.

Kasumov, A. Y., M. Kociak, S. Guéron et al. 2001. "Proximity-induced superconductivity in DNA." *Science* 291: 280–282.

Keim, Brandon. 2009. "Biosphere 2: Not Such a Bust." Wired.com. April 20, 2009. http://www.wired.com/wiredscience/2009/04/biospheresci

Keyes, Daniel. 1967. *Flowers for Algernon*. New York: Bantam Books.

Lakhno, V. D., V. B. Sultanov. 2011. "On the possibility of bipolaronic states in DNA." *Biofizika* 56: 230–34.

Leary, Timothy, Ralph Metzner, and Richard Alpert. 1965. *The Psychedelic Experience: A Manual Based on the Tibetan Book of the Dead.* New York: University Books.

Letcher, Andy. 2007. *Shroom: A Cultural History of the Magic Mushroom.* New York: Harper Collins.

Levine, Stephen, and Ondrea Levine. 1989. *Who Dies? An Investigation of Conscious Living and Conscious Dying.* New York: Anchor Press.

Little, W. A. 1965. "Superconductivity at room temperature." *Scientific American.* February 1965.

Lovecraft, H. P. 2011. *H. P. Lovecraft: The Complete Fiction.* New York: Barnes & Noble.

Luna, Luis Eduardo. 1986. *Vegetalismo: Shamanism Among the Mestizo Population of the Peruvian Amazon.* Stockholm: Almqvist & Wiksell International.

Maxwell, Nicole. 1990. *Witch Doctor's Apprentice: Hunting for Medicinal Plants in the Amazon.* Introduction by Terence McKenna. 3rd ed. New York: Citadel Press.

McLuhan, Marshall. 1962. *Gutenberg Galaxy: The Making of Typographic Man.* University of Toronto Press.

——. 1964. *Understanding Media: The Extensions of Man.* New York: McGraw-Hill.

Merleau-Ponty, Maurice. 2002. *Phenomenology of Perception.* Routledge Classics. 2d ed. Oxfordshire, UK: Routledge.

Metzner, Ralph, ed. 1999. *Ayahuasca: Human Consciousness and the Spirits of Nature.* Philadelphia: Running Press.

Munn, Henry. 1973. "The Mushrooms of Language." From Michael J. Harner, ed. *Hallucinogens and Shamanism.* Oxford University Press.

Plotkin, Mark J. 1993. *Tales of a Shaman's Apprentice: An Ethnobotanist Searches for New Medicines in the Amazon Rainforest.* 3rd ed. New York: Viking Adult.

Prigogine, Ilya. 1980. *From Being to Becoming.* San Francisco: Freeman.

Prigogine, Ilya, and Gregoire Nicolis. 1977. *Self-Organization in Nonequilibrium Systems.* New York: Wiley-Interscience.

Reider, Rebecca. 2009. *Dreaming the Biosphere: The Theatre of All Possibilities.* University of New Mexico Press.

Rinpoche, Sogyal. 1992. *The Tibetan Book of Living and Dying.* Harper San Francisco.

Rospars, Jean-Pierre. 2010. "Terrestrial biological evolution and its implications for SETI." *Acta Astronautica* 67: 361–65.

Saavedra, J. M., and J. Axelrod. 1972. "Psychotomimetic N-methylated tryptamines: formation in brain in vivo and in vitro." *Science* 175: 1365–66.

San Antonio, JP. 1971. "A laboratory method to obtain fruit from cased grain spawn of the cultivated mushoom, Agaricus bisporus." *Mycologia* Jan–Feb; 63(1): 16–21.

Schrödinger, Erwin. 1944. *What Is Life?* Cambridge University Press.

Schultes, Richard E. 1969. "*Virola* as an orally administered hallucinogen" in

Botanical Museum Leaflets. Harvard University Vol. 22, No. 6. June 25, 1969.

Schultes, Richard E., and Albert Hofmann. 1973. *The Botany and Chemistry of Hallucinogens*. Springfield, IL: Charles C. Thomas Publishers.

Sharon, Douglas. 1978. *Wizard of the Four Winds: A Shaman's Story*. New York: Free Press.

Silverman, J. 1967. "Shamans and acute schizophrenia." *American Anthropologist* 69: 21–31.

Smythies, J. R. 1969. "A possible role for ribonucleic acid in neuronal membrane." *Communications in Behavioral Biology* 3: 263–78.

——. 1970. "The chemical nature of the receptor site." *International Journal of Neurobiology* 13: 181–222.

Smythies, J. R., and F. Antun. 1969. "Binding of tryptamine and allied compounds to nucleic acid." *Nature* 223: 1061–63.

Snyder, S. H., S. P. Banerjee, H. I. Yamamura, and D. Greenberg. 1974. "Drugs, neurotransmitters, and schizophrenia." *Science* 184: 1243–53.

Stewart, Omer C. 1987. *Peyote Religion: A History*. Civilization of the American Indian Series. University of Oklahoma Press.

Strassman, Rick. 2001. *DMT: The Spirit Molecule: A Doctor's Revolutionary Research into the Biology of Near-Death and Mystical Experiences*. Rochester, VT: Park Street Press.

Szent-Gyorgyi, Albert. 1960. *Introduction to a Submolecular Biology*. New York: Academic Press.

Tryon, E. 1973. "Is the universe a vacuum fluctuation?" *Nature* 246: 396–97.

Udenfriend S., B. Witkop, B. Redfield, and H. Weissbach. 1958. "Studies with reversible inhibitors of monoamine oxidase: harmaline and related compounds." *Biochemical Pharmacology* 1: 160–65.

Vernier P., H. Philippe, P. Samama, and J. Mallet. 1993. "Bioamine receptors: evolutionary and functional variations of a structural leitmotiv." *EXS* 63: 297–337.

Von Bertalanffy, Ludwig. 1968. *General Systems Theory: Foundations, Development, Applications*. New York: George Braziller.

Wiener, H. 1966–1968. *External Chemical Messengers. New York State Journal of Medicine*.

——. 1966. *Part I: Emission and Reception in Man*. Vol. 66: p. 153.

——. 1967. *Part II: Natural History of Schizophrenia*. Vol. 67: p. 1144.

——. 1967. *Part III: Mind and Body in Schizophrenia*. Vol. 67: p. 1287.

——. 1968. *Part IV: Pineal Gland*. Vol. 68: p. 912.

——. 1968. *Part V: More Functions of the Pineal Gland*. Vol. 68: p. 1019.

Wells, H. G. 1895. *The Time Machine*. New York: Henry Holt.

Whitehead, Alfred North. 1958. *The Function of Reason*. Boston: Beacon Press.

——. 1967. *Science and the Modern World*. New York: The Free Press.

——. 1968. *Modes of Thought*. New York: The Free Press.

——. 1969. *Process and Reality*. New York: The Free Press.

Whyte, Lancelot Law. 1965. *Internal Factors in Evolution*. New York: George Braziller.

——. 1969. *Hierarchical Structures*. Edited by A. G. Wilson and D. Wilson. Amsterdam: Elsevier.

Wright, Tony, and Graham Gynn. 2008. *Left in the Dark: The Biological Origins of the Fall from Grace*. Kaleidos.

II. Books by Terence McKenna

McKenna, Terence K. 1993. *True Hallucinations: Being an Account of the Author's Extraordinary Adventures in the Devil's Paradise*. HarperSanFrancisco.
——. 1992. *The Archaic Revival: Speculations on Psychedelic Mushrooms, the Amazon, Virtual Reality, UFOs, Evolution, Shamanism, the Rebirth of the Goddess, and the End of History*. New York: HarperCollins.
——. 1992. *Food of the Gods: The Search for the Original Tree of Knowledge: A Radical History of Plants, Drugs, and Human Evolution*. New York: Bantam Books.
——. 1984. *True Hallucinations*. Talking book version. Mill Valley, CA: Sound Photosynthesis.

III. Books Coauthored by Terence McKenna

Abraham, Ralph H., Terence K. McKenna, Rupert Sheldrake, and Dennis J. McKenna. 2005. *The Evolutionary Mind: Trialogues on Science, Spirit & Psychedelics*. Revised edition. Rhinebeck, NY: Monkfish Book Publishing. Includes a new preface by Dennis McKenna and new chapters on the evolution of the human mind and skepticism.
——. 2001. *Chaos, Creativity, and Cosmic Consciousness*. Rochester, VT: Park Street Press. Revised edition of *Trialogues at the Edge of the West*. 1992. Bear and Company.
——. 1998. *The Evolutionary Mind: Trialogues at the Edge of the Unthinkable*. Santa Cruz, CA: Trialogue Press.
——. 1992. *Trialogues at the Edge of the West: Chaos, Creativity, and the Resacralization of the World*. Santa Fe, NM: Bear & Company Publishing. First edition.
Ely, Timothy C., and Terence K. McKenna. 1992. *Synesthesia*. New York: Granary Books.
McKenna, Terence K., and Dennis J. McKenna. 1993. *The Invisible Landscape: Mind, Hallucinogens, and the I Ching*. Revised and updated edition. New York: HarperCollins Publishers.
——. 1975. *The Invisible Landscape: Mind, Hallucinogens, and the I Ching*. New York: Seabury Press.
Oss, O. T. [Terence McKenna], and O. N. Oeric [Dennis McKenna]. 1976. *Psilocybin, Magic Mushroom Grower's Guide: A Handbook for Psilocybin Enthusiasts*. Berkeley: And/Or Press. A revised second edition was published in 1986 by Lux Natura, followed by a 1991 printing from Quick American Publishing.
Venosa, Robert, Ernst Fuchs, H. R. Giger, Mati Klarwein, Terence K. McKenna. 1999. *Robert Venosa: Illuminatus*. Sydney, Australia: Craftsman House.

IV. Books and Papers by Dennis McKenna (and Coauthors)
BOOKS

McKenna, Dennis J., Kerry Hughes, and Kenneth Jones. Coauthors and editors. 2000. *Natural Dietary Supplements Pocket Reference: Pocket Reference Guide to Botanical and Dietary Supplements*. Institute for Natural Products Research (INPR).

——. 2002. *Botanical Medicines: The Desk Reference for Major Herbal Supplements.* Binghamton, NY: Haworth Herbal Press.

BOOK REVIEWS AND POPULAR ARTICLES

McKenna, Dennis J. 1989. "It's a Jungle Out There: Biochemical Conflict and Co-operation in the Ecosphere." *Whole Earth Review* 64: 40–47.

——. 1989. "Plant Wisdom Resources." *Whole Earth Review* 64: 48–49.

——. 1990–1991. Review of *The Sacred Mushroom Seeker: Essays for R. Gordon Wasson*, edited by Thomas J. Reidlinger. *Shaman's Drum*, Winter 1990–91 and *Whole Earth Review*, Spring 1991.

——. 1991. Review of *The Healing Forest: Medicinal and Toxic Plants of the Northwest Amazonia*, by R. E. Schultes and R. F. Raffauf, *Shaman's Drum*, Spring 1991 and *Planta Medica* 57: 509.

——. 1992. "DMT: Nature's Ubiquitous Hallucinogen." *Interdependences*, Fall 1992.

——. 1992. "Tryptamine Hallucinogens of the New World: An Ethnopharmacological Survey." *Interdependences*, Fall 1992.

——. 1992. Review of *Ayahuasca Visions: The Religious Iconography of a Peruvian Shaman*, by Luis Eduardo Luna and Pablo Amaringo. *Shaman's Drum*, Spring 1992.

——. 1992. Review of *PIHKAL: A Chemical Love Story*, by Alexander T. Shulgin and Ann Shulgin. *Gnosis*, Spring 1992.

——. 1995. "Bitter Brews and Other Abominations: The Uses and Abuses of Some Little-Known Hallucinogenic Plants." *Integration Journal of Mind-Moving Plants and Culture* 5: 99–104.

——. 1999. "Ayahuasca: An Ethnopharmacologic History," in *Ayahuasca: Hallucinogens, Consciousness, and the Spirit of Nature*, edited by Ralph Metzner. New York: Thunder's Mouth.

——. 2000. "An Unusual Experience with Hoasca: A Lesson from the Teacher," in *Ayahuasca Reader: Encounters with the Amazon's Sacred Vine*, edited by S. F. White and Luis Eduardo Luna. Santa Fe: Synergetic Press.

——. 2006. "Mescaline: A Molecular History," *Fate Magazine*, January 2006.

PEER-REVIEWED SCIENTIFIC ARTICLES AND REVIEWS

Anderson, B. T., B. C. Labate, M. Meyer, K. W. Tupper, C. R. Barbosa Paulo, C. S. Grob, A. Dawson, and D. McKenna. 2012. Editorial: "Statement on Ayahuasca." *International Journal of Drug Policy* 23: 173–175.

Mishor, Z., D. J. McKenna, and J. C. Callaway. 2011. "DMT and Human Consciousness." *Altering Consciousness: Multidisciplinary Perspectives Vol. 2: Biological and Psychological Perspectives.* Edited by E. Cardeña and M. Winkelman. Westport, CT: Praeger Publishers.

McKenna, D. J., J. M. Ruiz, T. R. Hoye, B. R. Roth, and A. P. Shoemaker. 2011. "Receptor screening technologies in the evaluation of Amazonian ethnomedicines with potential applications to cognitive deficits." *Journal of Ethnopharmacology* 134: 475–92.

McKenna, D. J. 2007. "The healing vine: ayahuasca as medicine in the 21st century." *Psychedelic Medicine: New Evidence for Hallucinogenic Substances as Treatments*, edited by M. J. Winkleman and T. B. Roberts. Westport, CT: Praeger Publishers.

Donelson, R., G. Ostroff, D. McKenna, and J. Slaton. 2006. "Quantitative determination of beta-glucan constituents in Trametes versicolor (L.:Fries) Pilát." Poster presented at the 47th Annual Meeting of the American Society of Pharmacognosy, Crystal City, Virginia. August 5–9, 2006.

Callaway, J. C., C. S. Grob, D. E. Nichols, A. Shulgin, and D. J. McKenna. 2006. "A demand for clarity regarding a case report on the ingestion of 5-methoxy-N,N-dimethyltryptamine (5MeO-DMT) in an ayahuasca preparation." Letter to the editor. *Journal of Analytical Toxicology* 30: 406–7.

McKenna, D. J., R. Kingston, and I. Harris. 2006. "Introduction to botanical medicines." Peer reviewed online learning module offered by the Association of American Medical Colleges (AAMC). http://www.csh.umn.edu/modules/index.html.

McKenna, D. J. 2005. "Ayahuasca and human destiny." *Journal of Psychoactive Drugs* 37: 231–34. Special issue of JPD devoted to ayahuasca use in cross-cultural perspective.

McKenna, D. J. 2004. "Clinical investigations of the therapeutic potential of ayahuasca: rationale and regulatory challenges." *Pharmacology and Therapeutics* 102: 111–29.

Hughes, K., K. Jones, D. J. McKenna, and L. Mischley. 2004. "Co-enzyme Q10 and cardiovascular health." *Alternative Therapies in Health and Medicine* 10: 22–30.

McKenna, D. J. 2003. "Kava in the treatment of anxiety." *Natural Pharmacy* 7: 16–17.

McKenna, D. J., K. Hughes, and K. Jones. 2002. "Astragalus." *Alternative Therapies in Health and Medicine* 8: 34–40.

McKenna, D. J., K. Hughes, and K. Jones. 2002. "Co-enzyme Q-10: efficacy, safety, and use." *Alternative Therapies in Health and Medicine* 8: 42–55.

McKenna, D. J., K. Hughes, and K. Jones. 2001. "Efficacy, safety, and use of Ginkgo biloba in clinical and pre-clinical applications." *Alternative Therapies in Health and Medicine* 7: 70–86, 88–90.

McKenna, D. J., K. Hughes, S. Humphrey, and K. Jones. 2001. "Black Cohosh: Efficacy, safety, and use in clinical and preclinical applications." *Alternative Therapies in Health and Medicine* 7: 93–100.

McKenna, D. J., K. Hughes, and K. Jones. 2000. "Green tea monograph." *Alternative Therapies in Health and Medicine* 6: 61–84.

Lebot, V., E. Johnston, Q. Y. Zheng, D. McKern, and D. J. McKenna. 1999. "Morphological, phytochemical, and genetic variation in Hawaiian cultivars of 'awa (kava, Piper methysticum Piperaceae)." *Economic Botany* 53: 407–18.

Callaway, J. C., D. J. McKenna, C. S. Grob, G. S. Brito, L. P. Raymon, R. E. Poland, E. N. Andrade, E. O. Andrade, and D. C. Mash. 1999. "Pharmacokinetics of hoasca alkaloids in healthy humans." *Journal of Ethnopharmacology* 65: 243–56.

McKenna, D. J., J. C. Callaway, and C. S. Grob. 1999. "The scientific investigation of ayahuasca: a review of past and current research." *Heffter Review of Psychedelic Research* 1: 65–76.

Callaway, J. C., and D. J. McKenna. 1998. "Neurochemistry of psychedelic drugs." Chapter 6.6 in *Drug Abuse Handbook*, edited by Stephen B. Karch. Boca Raton, FL: CRC Press.

Callaway, J. C., L. P. Raymon, W. L. Hearn, D. J. McKenna, C. S. Grob, G. S. Brito, and D. C. Mash. 1996. "Quantitation of N,N-dimethyltryptamine and harmala alkaloids in human plasma after oral dosing with ayahuasca." *Journal of Analytical Toxicology* 20: 492–97.

McKenna, D. J. 1996. "Plant hallucinogens: Springboards for psychotherapeutic drug discovery." *Behavioural Brain Research* 73: 109–16.

Grob, C. S., D. J. McKenna, J. C. Callaway, G. S. Brito, E. S. Neves, G. Oberlender, O. L. Saide, E. Labigalini, C. Tacla, T. Miranda, R. J. Strassman, K. B. Boone. 1996. "Human pharmacology of hoasca, a plant hallucinogen used in ritual context in Brazil." *Journal of Nervous & Mental Disease* 184: 86–94.

Callaway, J. C., M. M. Airaksinen, D. J. McKenna, G. S. Brito, C. S. Grob. 1994. "Platelet serotonin uptake sites increased in drinkers of ayahuasca." *Psychopharmacology* 116: 385–87.

McKenna, D. J., L. E. Luna, and G. H. N. Towers. 1995. "Biodynamic constituents in ayahuasca admixture plants: an uninvestigated folk pharmacopoeia," in *Ethnobotany: Evolution of a Discipline,* edited by S. von Reis and R. E. Schultes. Portland: Dioscorides Press.

Torres, C. M., D. B. Repke, K. Chan, D. J. Mckenna, A. Llagostera, and R. E. Schultes. 1992. "Botanical, chemical, and contextual analysis of archaeological snuff powders from San Pedro de Atacama, Northern Chile." *Current Anthropology* 32: 640–49.

Mathis, C. A., J. M. Gerdes, J. D. Enas, J. M. Whitney, S. E. Taylor, Y. Zhang, D. J. McKenna, S. Havlik, and S. J. Peroutka. 1992. "Binding potency of paroxetine analogues for the serotonin uptake complex." *Journal of Pharmacy and Pharmacology* 44: 801–5.

McKenna, D. J., X. M. Guan, and A. T. Shulgin. 1991. "3,4-methy3lenedioxyamphetamine (MDA) analogues exhibit differential effects on synaptosomal release of H-dopamine and H-5-hydroxytryptamine." *Pharmacology, Biochemistry, and Behavior* 38: 505–12.

Nichols. D. E., R. Oberlender, and D. J. McKenna. 1991. "Stereochemical aspects of hallucinogenesis." Chapter 1, pp. 1–39 in *Biochemistry and Physiology of Substance Abuse,* Vol. III, edited by R. R. Watson. Boca Raton, FL: CRC Press.

McKenna, D. J., and S. J. Peroutka. 1990. "Serotonin neurotoxins: Focus on MDMA (3,4-methylenedioxymethamphetamine, "ecstasy")" in *Serotonin Receptor Subtypes: Basic and Clinical Aspects,* edited by S. J. Peroutka. New York: Alan R. Liss Publishers.

McKenna, D. J., D. B. Repke, L. Lo, and S. J. Peroutka. 1990. "Differential interactions of indolealkylamines with 5-hydroxytryptamine receptor subtypes." *Neuropharmacology* 29: 193–98.

McKenna, D. J., and S. J. Peroutka. 1990. "The neurochemistry and neurotoxicity of 3,4-methylenedioxymethamphetamine (MDMA, "ecstasy")." *Journal of Neurochemistry* 54: 14–22.

Hekmatpanah, C. R., D. J. McKenna, and S. J. Peroutka. 1989. "Reserpine does not prevent 3,4-methylenedioxymethamphetamine-induced neurotoxicity." *Neuroscience Letters* 104: 178–82.

McKenna, D. J., D. B. Repke, and S. J. Peroutka. 1989. "Hallucinogenic indolealkylamines are selective for 5HT2A binding sites." *Neuroscience Abstracts* 15: 485.

McKenna, D. J., and S. J. Peroutka. 1989. "Differentiation of 5-hydroxytryptamine$_2$

receptor subtypes using I-R-(-)-2,5,-dimethoxyphenylisopropylamine (125I-R-(-)-DOI) and H-ketanserin." *Journal of Neuroscience* 9: 3482–90.

McKenna, D. J., A. J. Nazarali, A. J. Hoffman, D. E. Nichols, C. A. Mathis, and J. M. Saavedra. 1989. "Common receptors for hallucinogens in rat brain: a comparative autoradiographic study using 125I-LSD and 125I-DOI, a new psychotomimetic radioligand." *Brain Research* 476: 45–56.

McKenna, D. J., A. J. Nazarali, A. Himeno, and J. M. Saavedra. 1989. "Chronic treatment with (±)DOI, a psychotomimetic 5HT$_2$ agonist, downregulates 5HT$_2$ receptors in rat brain." *Neuropsychopharmacology* 2: 81–87.

Nazarali, A. J., D. J. McKenna, and J. M. Saavedra. 1989. "Autoradiographic localization of 5HT$_2$ receptors in rat brain using 125 I-DOI, a selective psychotomimetic radioligand." *Progress in Neuropsychopharmacology and Biological Psychiatry* 13: 573–81.

McKenna, D. J., C. A. Mathis, and S. J. Peroutka. 1988. "Characterization of 125I-DOI binding sites in rat brain." *Neuroscience Abstracts* 14: 247.12.

Himeno, A., D. J. McKenna, A. J. Nazarali, and J. M. Saavedra. 1988. "(±)DOI, a hallucinogenic phenylalkylamine, downregulates 5HT$_2$ receptors in rat brain." *Neuroscience Abstracts* 14: 229.2.

McKenna, D. J., and J. M. Saavedra. 1987. "Autoradiography of LSD and 2,5-dimethoxyphenylisopropylamine psychotomimetics demonstrates regional, specific cross-displacement in the rat brain." *European Journal of Pharmacology* 142: 313–15.

McKenna, D. J., C. A. Mathis, A. T. Shulgin, and J. M. Saavedra. 1987. "Hallucinogens bind to common receptors in the rat forebrain: a comparative study using 125I- LSD and 125I-DOI, a new psychotomimetic radioligand." *Neuroscience Abstracts* 13: 311.14.

McKenna, D. J., C. A. Mathis, A. T. Shulgin, Sargent, Thornton III, and J. M. Saavedra. 1987. "Autoradiographic localization of binding sites for 125 I-(-)DOI, a new psychotomimetic radioligand, in the rat brain." *European Journal of Pharmacology* 137: 289–90.

McKenna, D. J., L. E. Luna, and G. H. N Towers. 1986. "Ingredientes biodinamicos en las plantas que se meszclan al ayahuasca. Una farmacopea tradicional no investigada." *America Indigena* 46: 73–101. (Spanish with English abstract.)

McKenna, D. J., and G. H. N Towers. 1985. "On the comparative ethnopharmacology of the malpighiaceous and myristicaceous hallucinogens." *Journal of Psychoactive Drugs* 17: 35–39.

McKenna, D. J., and G. H. N Towers. 1984. "Biochemistry and pharmacology of tryptamine and ß-carboline derivatives: A mini review." *Journal of Psychoactive Drugs* 16: 347–58.

McKenna, D. J., G. H. N Towers, and F. S. Abbott. 1984. "Monoamine oxidase inhibitors in South American hallucinogenic plants: tryptamine and ß-carboline constituents of Ayahuasca." *Journal of Ethnopharmacology* 10: 195–223.

McKenna, D. J., G. H. N. Towers, and F. S. Abbott. 1984. "Monoamine oxidase inhibitors in South American hallucinogenic plants, part II: constituents of orally active myristicaceous hallucinogens." *Journal of Ethnopharmacology* 12: 179–211.

McKenna, D. J., and G. H. N Towers. 1981. "Ultraviolet-mediated cytotoxic activity of ß-carboline alkaloids." *Phytochemistry* 20: 1001–4.

Appendix

This poem was written by William Patrick Watson, one of Terence's oldest and best friends from his high school years in Los Altos and later in Berkeley. The date of its composition is not completely clear even in the recollection of the author. What we do know is that it was written at least a year before our departure for La Chorrera, sometime in late 1969 or early 1970. In our discussions of a possible South American adventure at the time, we assumed we would be headed to Peru. Later, we changed our plans in favor of traveling to La Chorrera to seek the fabled *oo-koo-hé*. The poem has not been previously published.

—Dennis McKenna

Pursuing to Peru the G'nostic Guru: A Poetic Talisman
For T. McKenna, Irish Shaman
By W. Watson, Unauthorized Bard

Pursuing to Peru
The g'nostic guru
Who doesn't come to you
Out of sunyatic blue.

Questing the star shaman
Hidden in the bindu
Of hyperstellar semen
Whose lore you thought you knew.

In vine-shrouded jungle
Do not your mantras bungle
Lest a god-plant eat you
And into void excrete you.

On peaks both bleak and eerie
Of two-faced gods be leery

Especially if they're hairy
Of them be most be-wary.

Beware the Incan tangle
And saucer siren jangle
Which may your body dangle
From ridge-pole all amangle.

And dye your beard an umber
Or better, put it under
A green hindu bandana,
Lest a wild head hunter
Make of it a banner
For his jungle manor.
(I know that wouldn't please you
So please of these hints heed you.)

By shores of Titicaca
Smoke the silver hookah
Erect your star antenna
Broadcast the name McKenna
In acrostics Kabbalistic
And pun it in Mandaean
Then surely crypto-mystic

Will come the alchemic lion.
The demons are of many kinds
Some made of ions, some of mind
The ones of DMT you'll find
Stutter often and are blind.

While swimming toward galactic isles
Watch out for stellar crocodiles;
They have the most enticing smiles
But nonetheless are full of wiles.
If you be transmogrified

To tiny monads side by side (of a millimeter wide)
by spiderweb together tied,
Recite th' Tibetan mantra phat
Which instantly will make you fat;
Tho sitting on Benares ghat,
At least you'll know the place you're at.
(You might in transit lose your hat
But mantras can't account for that.)

If you encounter scorpions
While making transgalactic runs,
Remember they're immune to puns
But shrivel if near onions.
(By all means you should carry one
Unless you have a garlic gun.
The latter is of effective use
In dealing with the gnostic goose
Who often aeons let run loose
To snatch the shaman seeking nous.)

If you meet a tree toad
At a forking of the road,
Inquire of him yage's abode
But if he doesn't speak your mode,
Do not goad the tree toad,
Lest he should explode
Each ganglionic node
Of what you thought you knowed.
Of the moonherb Soma
That puts you into coma
And alters every chromosome
(Disguising you for journey home)
Just say the mantra OM AH
And instantly you'll start to foam

With elixer of Chandra
Churned from the lunar chakra
(Watch for the evil raksha!)
And thru the star clouds freely roam,
But if you should begin to come
(to hide the seed we are agreed)
Then say the quelling mantra HUM;
(this may attract the cosmic bees
Who drone with Proustian reveries,
Drowning you with memories;
To counteract, it's best to sneeze).
Of sodomic witch doctors
Who hang heads on their doors
Beware their brew of spores
They'll rub into your pores.

But witches resembling Kali
Who offer you an ally
Are oftentimes quite lovely,
On them you'd best rely.

If you find at landing ramp
The lake resembles summer camp
With every kind of psychic vamp
Sunning beneath a solar lamp,
And gaudy-dressed and rosy queers
Who greet you with their shouts and cheers,
Embracing you with smiles and tears
While whispering mantras in your ears;
By no means should you be perplexed
Or any wise outraged or vexed
To find yourself transformed of sex,
(such happenstance you must expect.)

If in dire need you should be
Send an express wire to me
Via telepathic telegraphy
And I'll cable spells to set you free.

Or if you need a helping hand
Swallow thirteen grains of sand
Raise aloft your crystal wand
And send coordinates whereon to land.

I'll quickly zip into my ship
And unto Titicaca trip
And track you down by radar blip
And from the hands of demons rip
You, ere they can you much molest,
And I'll take you to an isle of rest
(Your body and your mind distressed
if you should falter in your quest).

But let me say your journey's blest
And if you follow these words behest
Then surely in a star you'll nest
Or be made of DMT at best.

About the Author

DENNIS MCKENNA is an ethnopharmacologist who has studied plant hallucinogens for over 40 years. He is the author of many scientific papers and coauthor, with his brother Terence McKenna, of *The Invisible Landscape: Mind, Hallucinogens, and the I Ching* and *Psilocybin: Magic Mushroom Grower's Guide*. He holds a doctorate from the University of British Columbia, where his research focused on ayahuasca and *oo-koo-hé*, two hallucinogens used by Indigenous peoples in the Northwest Amazon. He received postdoctoral research fellowships in the Laboratory of Clinical Pharmacology at the National Institute of Mental Health, and in the Department of Neurology, Stanford University School of Medicine. In 1990, he joined Shaman Pharmaceuticals as Director of Ethnopharmacology, and in 1993 became the Aveda Corporation's Senior Research Pharmacognosist. Dennis has been an adjunct assistant professor at the Center for Spirituality and Healing at the University of Minnesota since 2001, where he teaches courses in ethnopharmacology and botanical medicine. He has taught summer field courses in Peru and Ecuador and has conducted fieldwork throughout the upper Amazon. He is a founding board member of the Heffter Research Institute, a nonprofit organization focused on investigation of the potential therapeutic uses of psychedelic medicines.